Kodály in the Kindergarten Classroom

Kodály Today Handbook Series

Micheál Houlahan and Philip Tacka

Kodály Today: A Cognitive Approach to Elementary Music Education, second edition

Kodály in the Kindergarten Classroom: Developing the Creative Brain in the 21st Century

Kodály in the First Grade Classroom: Developing the Creative Brain in the 21st Century

Kodály in the Second Grade Classroom: Developing the Creative Brain in the 21st Century

Kodály in the Third Grade Classroom: Developing the Creative Brain in the 21st Century

Kodály in the Fourth Grade Classroom: Developing the Creative Brain in the 21st Century

Kodály in the Fifth Grade Classroom: Developing the Creative Brain in the 21st Century

Kodály in the Kindergarten Classroom

Developing the Creative
Brain in the 21st Century

Micheál Houlahan
Philip Tacka

OXFORD
UNIVERSITY PRESS

OXFORD
UNIVERSITY PRESS

Oxford University Press is a department of the University
of Oxford. It furthers the University's objective of excellence in research,
scholarship, and education by publishing worldwide.

Oxford   New York
Auckland   Cape Town   Dar es Salaam   Hong Kong   Karachi
Kuala Lumpur   Madrid   Melbourne   Mexico City   Nairobi
New Delhi   Shanghai   Taipei   Toronto

With offices in
Argentina   Austria   Brazil   Chile   Czech Republic   France   Greece
Guatemala   Hungary   Italy   Japan   Poland   Portugal   Singapore
South Korea   Switzerland   Thailand   Turkey   Ukraine   Vietnam

Oxford is a registered trademark of Oxford University Press
in the UK and certain other countries.

Published in the United States of America by
Oxford University Press
198 Madison Avenue, New York, NY 10016

Library of Congress Cataloging-in-Publication Data
Houlahan, Micheál.
Kodály in the kindergarten classroom: developing the creative brain in the 21st century/Micheál
Houlahan, Philip Tacka.
pages cm. — (Kodaly today handbook series)
Includes bibliographical references and index.
ISBN 978-0-19-939649-8 (paperback) — ISBN 978-0-19-935587-7 (online file) — ISBN 978-0-19-935588-4
(online content)   1.   Preschool music—Instruction and study.   2.   Kodály, Zoltán, 1882-1967.
3. Kindergarten—Curricula   I. Tacka, Philip.   II. Title.
MT1.H837 2014
372.87—dc23
2013038241

9 8 7 6 5 4 3
Printed in the United States of America
on acid-free paper

This book is dedicated to the
memory of Katalin Forrai, who inspired
us to think inside and outside the box!

———————————————————————

Contents

Acknowledgments

A debt of gratitude is due to the many individuals who inspired, encouraged and helped us with our research for this publication. We were both fortunate enough to study at the Franz Liszt Academy/Kodály Pedagogical Institute in Hungary and at the Kodály Center of America with world-renowned Kodály experts, many of whom were his pupils and colleagues, who shared their knowledge with us over many years. Among them were Erzsébet Hegyi, Ildiko Herboly-Kocsár, Lilla Gabor, Katalin Komlos, Katalin Forrai, Mihály Ittzés, Klára Kokas, Klára Nemes, Eva Vendrai, Helga Szabo, Laszlo Eösze, Peter Erdei, and Katalin Kiss. We are especially indebted to Katalin Forrai for her support and encouragement for the research contained in this publication. We were both honored to have studied with Professor Forrai in Hungary as well as in the United States. Our research is grounded in her many valuable insights and work related to teaching music in the early childhood classroom. Special thanks are due Betsy Moll, friend and collaborator of Professor Forrai and Rachel Whitcomb, professor and program director of the Early Childhood Music Initiation at the Mary Pappert School of Music at Duquesne University. Their willingness to help with critical comments and careful reading have served to make this book a more valuable and accurate reflection of the inspiration we received from all our teachers. We are indebted to Lauren Bain, elementary music specialist in the Northeast School District of San Antonio, Texas for her willingness to pilot the kindergarten lesson plans and document her teaching through videos. This was a tremendous labor of love.

Special thanks are due to the following individuals for critically reading portions of the manuscript and for their insightful suggestions regarding this approach to instruction and learning: Georgia Katsourides, music specialist in the Lancaster City School District, Pennsylvania; Vivian Ferchill, retired music specialist from Round Rock, Texas; JoAnn Gerbig, and music specialist in the Austin Independent School District, Austin, Texas. We would also like to thank Holly Kofod and Lisa Roebuck for their comments, which helped us bring this book to completion. Special thanks are due Nick Holland, lower school music teacher at St. Paul's School in Baltimore Maryland; for his contributions to the final versions of the lesson plans and for providing videos that incorporate the use of Smart board technology.

We are grateful to Patty Moreno, Instructional Coordinator of Fine Arts for the Austin Independent School District, Texas and director of the Kodály Certification Program at Texas State University, San Marcos, Texas for her support and continued encouragement of this project. For more than a decade she has facilitated our research and field-testing with teachers in the Austin Independent School District as well as the Houston Independent School District and the Sicorro Independent School District in El Paso, Texas.

Many of our students in Kodály Certification Programs at Texas State University, Belmont University in Nashville, Tennessee, and the Eastman School of Music in Rochester,

New York, have helped us shape the approach to instruction and learning that is presented herein. Our many years of work with our students have not only contributed to the information we present but also served as a continuing source of inspiration with the pedagogical processes we have shaped.

We would like to thank our students at Millersville University of Pennsylvania for helping with technical and practical matters related to the manuscript. Special thanks are due Emma Noble, Andrea Kurnat, Demetrius Archer, and Chelsea Snow for their hands-on assistance. A special debt of gratitude is due Lillian Noble and Honorah Harvey for their assistance with bibliographic details, and Jamie Duca for her practical viewpoints and editorial help.

This book would not be as complete as it is in terms of pedagogy and educational content were it not for the readings and comments from Blaithín Burns, math teacher and Kodály instructor at the Blue Coat School in England. She provided invaluable assistance in the initial design of the book and field-tested many teaching strategies. Richard Schellhas deserves thanks for his personal patience and understanding as well as words of encouragement and advice throughout the writing of this manuscript.

Research for this publication was supported by a grant from Millersville University, the State System for Higher Education in Pennsylvania. The university's library assistance; technical, administrative, and financial support; and overall encouragement for this project have allowed us to bring this volume to completion. We would like to express our gratitude to Gabriella Montoya-Stier and Faith Knowles for their permission to include songs from their collections *El Patio de Mi Casa: Traditional Rhymes, Games and Folk Songs from Mexico* and *Vamos a Cantar*.

We are especially grateful to Katalin Forrai's children, András Vikár, Tamás Vikár and Katalin van Vooren Vikár, for permission to use materials and ideas from their mother's book *Music in Preschool* (edited and translated by Jean Sinor, Budapest, Hungary: Kultura, 1995; original publication 1988).

We wish to thank Suzanne Ryan, editor-in-chief of humanities and executive editor of music at Oxford University Press, for her encouragement and critical guidance. We thank Jessen O'Brien, assistant editor at Oxford University Press, and Erica Woods Tucker, senior production editor, Lisbeth Redfield, assistant editor, and Molly Morrison project manager with Newgen, for their support in the production of this manuscript. A very special thanks is due our editor, Thomas Finnegan, for his impeccable scrutiny and thoughtful editorial assistance with our manuscript.

Introduction: Developing the Creative Brain of the Young Learner Through Music and Literature

Purpose of Book

The primary purpose of this book is to give music teachers a realistic guide to providing a musical education for young children based on the Kodály concept of music education, which is cognitively and developmentally appropriate. The lessons and activities are aligned to National Music Content Standards as well as Core Curriculum Content that will enhance creativity, reinforce aural skills, and promote visual literacy as well as numeracy skills in children. This is a practical guide to teaching Kindergarten music classes (predominantly ages five and six), grounded in research from the fields of music perception and cognition, that is aligned with information contained in *Kodály Today*[1] and national standards in music that will promote twenty-first-century music learning. The foundational aspects of this book yield a detailed guide for teaching children to sing, move, and play instruments; for developing music literacy skills; for enhancing music listening; and for promoting creativity skills. The hallmark of this teaching pedagogy is that it integrates the development of problem solving, critical thinking skills, and collaboration skills into the teaching and learning of music. The importance of this approach is identified in the National Research Council's July 2012 report, wherein the authors cite these skills as "21st century skills" or "deeper learning."[2] It is our goal that every teacher will absorb the process of teaching outlined in this publication, and blend it with his or her own creativity, which will ultimately result in a lively and musical experience for children.

Focus discussions and surveys with music teachers reveal their concern regarding the lack of specificity relating to teaching Early Childhood music.[3] Teachers have reported that their preparation for teaching Early Childhood music was not dealt with adequately in their teaching preparation. Although many teachers have acquired a number of techniques for teaching music activities, many are concerned about the development of a more holistic approach to teaching music in the Early Childhood classroom. Teachers are looking for more direction on how to develop an organic curriculum for these classrooms and are looking for more guidance on how to:

- Select music materials for the early childhood classroom
- Develop appropriate singing and movement skills that are cognitively and developmentally appropriate
- Develop the foundations of music literacy skills
- Develop creativity skills
- Develop improvisation skills

- Connect the work of the Early Childhood music classroom with that of the elementary music classroom
- Reinforce literacy as well as numeracy skills in the music classroom
- Develop evaluation and assessment tools

This text addresses these concerns. The ideas reflected in the proposed text have been field-tested and shaped over a period of ten years with Early Childhood music teachers. The innovative approach to the development of this book and the collaboration of music teachers with a group of researchers to design the contents of this publication is truly pioneering. This alone makes this publication different from other Kodály-related Early Childhood texts on the market. Furthermore, the methodology developed in this text has also been given a stamp of approval by leading national and international Kodály master teachers as well as researchers working in the fields of music perception and cognition. This work began many years ago while we were studying and working with Katalin Forrai, the past president of the International Society for Music Education and an architect of the early childhood curriculum in Hungary. We are grateful for her support and encouragement.

Childhood is a period of development and change, but how children grow differs significantly according to social group, community, and culture. Therefore, it is difficult to write a book that addresses the needs of Early Childhood music teachers. No two music classrooms are identical. But the approach to teaching music that we suggest in this book offers the advantage of developing a multitude of additional skills in the early childhood classroom.

- Singing and listening to music builds aesthetic awareness and helps the child recognize that music evokes different moods.
- Teaching children to sing cultivates greater clarity of speech, and an increased vocabulary.
- According to the *Oxford Handbook of Music Education*, "It is suggested that developing musical abilities at an early age will enhance children's abilities in processing the musical elements in speech, which is crucial for languages acquisition."[4]
- Fostering a child's response to music helps develop his or her emotional security and confidence as well as a more sophisticated emotional and imaginative palette.
- Teaching music literacy skills through a cognitive orientation enhances literacy skills, problem-solving skills, memory skills, and reasoning skills.
- Learning how to translate sounds into symbols develops the child's ability to develop abstract thought.
- Developing movement skills and playing games promotes effective communication among peers and therefore expands social skills and encourages imagination. Taking turns and choosing partners in games and movement activities develops discipline skills and social skills.
- Acquiring an understanding of rhythm and an awareness of dynamics improves fluency of speech.
- Developing breath control and support and participating in rhythmic activities helps to improve motor and coordination skills.
- Developing improvisation skills enhances creativity.

We hope that this book will offer music specialists, kindergarten teachers, and music education students a possible point of entry to engage children in meaningful musical and educational activities. In spelling out the teaching procedures in detail, we recognize that there is a danger of being taken too literally. The suggestions given should be used as a starting guide that is expanded through the teacher's own creativity. The lessons are presented as a framework that will ensure thorough and clear presentation of each concept. Sometimes, younger educators feel they need to "follow the directions" or else risk doing things incorrectly. However, it is important, particularly in today's classrooms, for teachers to respond thoughtfully to the needs of their unique children. There is also a tendency on the part of teachers (both trained and untrained in the Kodály concept) to be too prescriptive with ideas from Kodály. Indeed, there are those in the teaching profession who see the word "Kodály" and automatically associate it with strict rules. It is expected that teachers will apply the teaching procedures and suggestions we present in a way that is responsive to the specific needs, backgrounds, and interests of their children. We also recognize that teachers must develop their own philosophy for teaching music and that they must consider such factors as the frequency of music instruction, class size, the length of the class, and the current musical abilities of the children. But the most important goal for the music teacher is to

Teach music and singing at school in such a way that it is not a torture but a joy for the pupil; instill a thirst for finer music in him, a thirst which will last for a lifetime. Music must not be approached from its intellectual, rational side, nor should it be conveyed to the child as a system of algebraic symbols, or as the secret writing of a language with which he has no connection. . . . Often a single experience will open the young soul to music for a whole lifetime. This experience cannot be left to chance; it is the duty of the school to provide it."[5]

How Is This Book Different from Other Related Texts?

During the last several years music educators and researches having been calling for the development of alternative music pedagogies that are more relevant for students. Barrett (2007) states that music curricula "have limited what is learned and taught by narrowly defining musical engagement and musical knowledge."[6] Sometimes we forget how important musical play is in engaging children: "Given that every child is born with musical sensibilities, how are the intricacies of musical art to be taught? What must the path of instruction be like that keeps alive the spontaneous sensibilities and proud creativity while bringing forth new ways of using the voice or hands within particular traditions? Clearly the child is not a tabula rasa or passive receiver of cultural wisdom. . . . The solution would seem to harness the youthful enthusiasm in a development or cultivation of cooperative musical work that is also play."[7]

The advice is clear: children will be encouraged to participate in the music lesson if it is playful and enjoyable. We have strived to develop a new pedagogy for teaching Early Childhood music that blends traditional and innovative teaching techniques. Throughout this text we delineate the process for presenting musical concepts and developing music skills using a cognitive model of teaching music that will develop "deeper learning skills." We have developed this process with music teachers who teach in suburban, urban, and

Title 1 school settings. Our approach to teaching is also based on research findings from the fields of music perception and cognition, as well as working in the field with Early Childhood teachers and music specialists. The intent of this book is to present a music curriculum that is shaped by research and to update instructional techniques in the Early Childhood music classroom.

Although several texts describe musical techniques and activities for teaching music to Early Childhood children, few articulate the teaching procedures for presenting musical concepts in detail. Even further, this text stands apart in that it communicates the development of musical skills in a cognitive manner that is aligned to a theory of learning. In this book we present a model of learning and teaching that is appealing to both children and teachers. In teaching music we believe that we have to incorporate both traditional and innovative pedagogies. There are many ways this can be achieved and will depend on the musical expertise of the teacher. The teaching orientation in this book is based on "sound to symbol" pedagogy; simply stated, children experience concepts through singing and playing and movement before they learn the formal names or symbols for these concepts. Creativity is at the heart of this pedagogy. For example, when we ask children to improvise a greeting or a new melody to a familiar text we might require them to use a certain number of beats so as to maintain the connection to the song, but other times it is important that they improvise using any number of beats they need so as to express their own individuality. Likewise we might teach children a traditional singing game with accompanying movements and later ask them either individually or in a group to improvise their own movements for this game. In this manner we keep building bridges between tradition and innovation. Our goal is to encourage children to be critical thinkers and creative individuals while as teachers we are formally teaching information and maintaining a pedagogical tradition. We have created an Early Childhood curriculum that presents a cohesive picture of the teaching and learning processes. We encourage every teacher to consider our process of teaching and add his or her own creativity so the result is a lively and purposeful musical lesson. Additionally, within each chapter of this book there are sections that discuss how to link music and reading literacy. Music teaching and the teaching of reading share common methods and procedures that are mutually enhancing and complementary. We are convinced that the overall goal of Kindergarten education is more one of nurturing the process of development of musical skills than of expecting a certain level of achievement.

Outline

Each chapter in this book begins with an introduction and sets a context for the issues discussed in it. At the end of each chapter are discussion questions that allow the reader to practice and reflect on the suggestions offered in the text. All chapters also include a bibliography. There are nine chapters in the book.

Chapter One

Developing a Music Repertoire of Songs and Books for the Kindergarten Music Classroom. This chapter lays out a rationale for the selection and analysis of music repertoire and Early Childhood books for teaching Early Childhood music during the first few weeks of music classes as well as throughout the year. Sample lesson plan, song repertoire, and books are provided. There is an accompanying website link for this chapter that includes recordings of songs used. The appendix for this chapter (Appendix 1) features a pedagogical analysis and musicological analysis for songs and rhymes as well as a book list that can be used for teaching in the early childhood music class.

Chapter Two

Building the Framework of a Kindergarten Music Curriculum. This chapter offers teachers an overview of a sample Early Childhood music curriculum that also includes the teaching of emergent literacy and music skills.

Chapter Three

Developing Creative Expression Through Singing, Movement, and Playing Instruments. This chapter concentrates on developing the various components of teaching performance skills in an Early Childhood classroom such as singing, part work, movement, and playing music instruments.

Chapter Four

A Model of Learning and Instruction for Teaching Music Concepts and Skills. This chapter discusses a model of learning for developing music knowledge and skills in the Early Childhood classroom. The hallmark of this teaching and learning model is that it integrates the development of problem solving, critical thinking, and collaboration skills into the teaching and learning of music. There is also a discussion of how this model promotes deeper learning in young children.

Chapter Five

Teaching Music Concepts in Kindergarten. This chapter presents teaching strategies for core readiness concepts in the Early Childhood classroom based on the model of learning presented in Chapter Four. Teaching strategies include how to teach the concepts of loud and soft, beat, high and low related chants and melodies, fast and slow, and rhythm.

Chapter Six

Cultivating Music Skills and Creativity. This goal of this chapter is to furnish teachers with ideas to practice concepts in combination with music skills such as reading, writing, form, listening, and improvisation in the Early Childhood setting that will promote creativity in the classroom. The accompanying website contains examples of music teachers teaching music using this model of learning.

Chapter Seven

Sequencing and Lesson Planning. This chapter describes several types of lesson plan structures and how the teaching strategies described in the chapter are transformed into lesson plans. It includes thirty-five music lesson plans that serve as a model for teaching concepts.

Chapter Eight

Assessment and Evaluation in Kindergarten. This chapter describes how to assess and evaluate learning as well as to evaluate a successful lesson plan. Sample rubrics are supplied for each concept.

Chapter Nine

Organizing Your Teaching Resources for the Kindergarten Classroom. This chapter presents some general considerations and resources for teaching music in the early childhood. There is also a discussion on developing a teaching portfolio for organizing materials in the early music classroom.

The accompanying video for the introduction presents an overview of the book and is posted on at the companion website (Web 0.B Overview).

Who Should Read This Book?

This book will appeal to methods instructors, pre-service music teachers, beginning music teachers, and practicing/veteran music teachers for a number of reasons. It is a book with a robust methodological foundation that focuses on creatively enhancing the learning environment of young children. Therefore, it appeals to methods instructors who will use the book over the course of a semester to show the necessary elements of a comprehensive Early Childhood music education. Effective methods instruction includes what to teach, how to teach, and why to teach, and this book addresses all of these areas. Second, pre-service music teachers will gravitate toward the sequencing and lesson planning included here, as well as the specific resources (songs, books), when practice-teaching during methods courses, field experiences, and student teaching. Third, beginning teachers are often most concerned with long-term planning for each grade level. The unit and lesson plans within *The Kodály Method for the Twenty-First Century Early Childhood Classroom* will appeal to these teachers. Finally, this book will be of value to practicing/veteran music teachers because it can be used to refresh knowledge of teaching music in the Early Childhood classroom while presenting it in ways that can advocate for music education (e.g., connections to literacy).

Discussion Questions
1. Identify research that supports the inclusion of music in the Early Childhood classroom.
2. Explain the value of a music education and the place of music in the Early Childhood school curriculum.
3. Collect three research articles that document the effects of music on cognitive development of children. Discuss your findings with your peers.
4. What are the multiple dimensions of musicianship training?
5. Check websites for three school districts. Locate their philosophy statement and write a summary statement for each district.
6. What are some ways in which teaching music supports literacy and creative skills?

Ongoing Assignment

Write a statement of your personal philosophy of music education for the Early Childhood classroom.

Helpful Websites

http://ies.ed.gov/ncee/wwc/—What Works Clearinghouse: provides information on which instructional techniques and curricula are effective.

http://www.aft.org./earlychildhood/—American Federation of Teachers Early Childhood Educators Page: has links to information and resources of use to Early Childhood educators and child care providers.

http://www.colorincolorado.org/—Colorín Colorado: an online service furnishing information, activities, advice, and resources for educators and families of Spanish-speaking English language learners.

http://www.naeyc.org/—National Association for the Education of Young Children: features journal, magazine, and position statements related to Early Childhood education.

http://www.reading.org/—International Reading Association: Offers magazines, journals, and links related to language and literacy.

References

Adachi, Mayumi, and Sandra Trehub. "Musical Lives of Infants." In Gary E. McPherson and Graham F. Welch (ed.), *The Oxford Handbook of Music Education*, vol. 1, pp. 229–247. New York: Oxford University Press, 2012.

Altenmuller, E., W. Gruhn, D. Parlitz, and G. Liebert. "The Impact of Music Education on Brain Networks: Evidence from EEG-studies." *International Journal of Music Education,* 2000, *35*: 47–53.

Altenmuller, E., M. Wiesendanger, and J. Kesselring. *Music, Motor Control, and the Brain.* Oxford: Oxford University Press, 2006; and Movement Center, 1989, 1992, and 1996.

Andress, B. *Music Play Unlimited: Understanding Musical Approaches for Children Ages 2–5.* Brown Mills, NJ: World of Peripole, 1983.

Andress, B., and Walker, L. M. (eds.). *Readings in Early Childhood Education*, pp. 43–50. Reston, VA: Music Educators National Conference. 1992 (Reprinted from Music in Early Childhood, 1973, Reston, VA: Music Educators National Conference.)

Barrett, J. R. "Currents of Change in the Music Curriculum." In L. Bresler (ed.), *International Handbook of Research in Arts Education* (pp. 147–162). Dordrecht, The Netherlands: Springer, 2007.

Barrett, M. S. "Sounding Lives in and Through Music: A 'Narrative Inquiry' of the 'Everyday' Musical Engagement of a Young Child." *Journal of Early Childhood Research*, 2009, *7*(2), 115–143.

Barrett, Margaret. "Commentary: Music Learning and Teaching in Infancy and Early Childhood." In Gary E. McPherson and Graham F. Welch (eds.), *The Oxford Handbook of Music Education*, vol. 1 (pp. 227–228). New York: Oxford University Press, 2012.

Bilhartz, T. D., R. A. Bruhn, and J. E. Olson. "The Effect of Early Music Training on Child Cognitive Development." *Journal of Applied Developmental Psychology*, 1999, *20* (4), 615–636.

Borthwick, S. J., and J. W. Davidson. "Developing a Child's Identity as a Musician: A Family 'Script' Perspective." In R. A. R. MacDonald, D. J. Hargreaves, and D. E. Miell (eds.), *Musical Identities* (pp. 60–78). New York: Oxford University Press, 2002.

Boynton, S., and R. Hoh (eds.). *Musical Childhoods & the Cultures of Youth* (pp. 105–120). Middletown, CT: Wesleyan University Press, 2006.

Burton, S. L., and C. C. Taggart. *Learning from Young Children: Research in Early Childhood Music Education.* Lanham, MD: Rowman & Littlefield Education, 2011.

Canadian Music Educator, 30/2 (1989): 51–59. See also "The Effects of Music Education Based on Kodaly's Directives in Nursery School Children: From a Psychologist's Point of View." *Psychology of Music* [ISME IX Research Seminar], 1982, p. 63–68.

Chen-Hafteck, Lily, and Esther Mang. "Music and Language in Early Childhood Development and Learning." In Gary E. McPherson and Graham F. Welch (ed.), *The Oxford Handbook of Music Education*, vol. 1 (chap. 2.4, p. 261–278). New York: Oxford University Press, 2012.

Costa-Giomi, E. "Music Instruction and Children's Intellectual Development: The Educational Context of Music Participation." In R. A. R. MacDonald, G. Kreutz, and L. Mitchell (eds.), *Music, Health, and Wellbeing* (pp. 339–356). Oxford: Oxford University Press, 2012.

Custodero, L., and L. C. Hafteck. "Harmonizing Research, Practice, and Policy in Early Childhood Music: A Chorus of International Voices." Special Issues, *Arts Education Policy Review*, 2007/2008, *109*(2–3).

DeNora, T. *Music in Everyday Life*. Cambridge: Cambridge University Press, 2000.

"Education for Life and Work Developing Transferable Knowledge and Skills in the 21st Century." Report Brief. July 12, 2012. National Research Council.

Flohr, J., and C. Trevarthen. "Music Learning in Childhood: Early Developments of a Musical Brain and Body." In W. Gruhn and F. Rauscher (eds.) *Neurosciences in Music Pedagogy* (pp. 53–100). New York: Nova Biomedical Books, 2008.

Gardner, Howard. *Frames of Mind: The Theory of Multiple Intelligences*. New York: Basic Books, 1983.

Green, L. *Music, Informal Learning and the School*. Hampshire, UK: Ashgate, 2008.

Guilmartin, K. K. and Lili M. Levinowitz *Music and Your Child: A Guide for Parents and Caregivers*. 3rd ed. Princeton, NJ: Music and Movement Center of Princeton, 1996.

Houlahan, Micheál, and Philip Tacka. *Kodály Today: A Cognitive Approach to Music Education*. New York: Oxford University Press, 2008.

Jordan-Decarbo, Joyce, and Jo Ann Nelson. "Music and Early Childhood Education." In Richard Colwell and Carol Richardson (ed.), *The New Handbook of Research on Music Teaching and Learning* (pp. 210–242). Oxford: Oxford University Press 2002.

Kodály, Zoltán. "Children's Choirs." 1929. *The Selected Writings of Zoltán Kodály*. London: Boosey & Hawkes, 1974, p. 120.

Lancy, D. F. *The Anthropology of Childhood: Cherubs, Chattel, Changelings*. Cambridge: Cambridge University Press, 2008.

Lum, Chee-Hoo, and Kathryn Marsh. "Multiple Worlds of Childhood: Culture and the Classroom." In Gary E. McPherson and Graham F. Welch (ed.), *The Oxford Handbook of Music Education*, vol. 1. (pp. 381–398). New York: Oxford University Press, 2012.

Marsh, Kathryn. "Commentary: Music Learning and Teaching During Childhood: Ages 5–12." In Gary E. McPherson and Graham F. Welch (ed.), *The Oxford Handbook of Music Education*, vol. 1. (pp. 317–321). New York: Oxford University Press, 2012.

Mithen, S. *The Singing Neanderthals: The Origins of Music, Language, Mind and Body.* London: Weidenfeld & Nicholson, 2005.

Mithen, S. "The Music Instinct: The Evolutionary Basis of Musicality." *Annals of the New York Academy of Sciences*, 2009, *1169*, 3–12.

Moog, H. and Clarke C. *The Musical Experience of the Preschool Child.* London: Schott Music, 1976.

Pantev, C. "Musical Training and Induced Cortical Plasticity." *Annals of the New York Academy of Sciences*, 2009, *1169*, 131–132.

Papousek, H. "Musicality in Infancy Research: Biological and Cultural Origins of Early Musicality." In I. Deliège and J. Sloboda (eds.), *Musical Beginnings: Origins and Development of Musical Competence* (pp. 37–55). Oxford: Oxford University Press, 1996.

Peery, J. C., I. Peery, and T. Draper. *Music and Child Development.* New York: Springer-Verlag, 1987.

Pink, D. H. *A Whole New World: Why Right Brainers Will Rule the Future.* New York: Berkley Publishing Group, 2005.

Pistone, N., and D. Brzoska. "Preschool Children." [Special supplement, XIIth International Research Seminar in Music Education], 2002, published in German, 1968.

Qvortrup, J., W. Corsaro, and M. S. Honig (eds.). *The Palgrave Handbook of Childhood Studies.* Basingstoke, UK: Palgrave Macmillan, 2009.

Rauscher, F. H., Shaw, L. J. Levine, E. L. Wright, W. R. Dennis, and R. L. Newcomb. "Music Training Causes Long-term Enhancement or Preschool Children's Spatial-temporal Reasoning." *Neurological Research* (February 1997), *19*.

Rogoff, B. *The Cultural Nature of Human Development.* Oxford: Oxford University Press, 2003.

Schellenberg, E. G. "Examining the Association Between Music Lessons and Intelligence." *British Journal of Psychology*, Feb 2011. Advance online publication. Doi: 10.1111/J.2044-8295

Seidel, S., S. Tishman, E. Winner, L. Hetland, and P. Palmer, *The Qualities of Quality: Understanding Excellence in Arts Education.* Cambridge, MA: Harvard Graduate School of Education, 2009.

Sloboda, J. A., and J. W. Davidson. "The Young Performing Musician." In I. Deliège and J. Slodoba (eds.), *Musical Beginnings: Origins and Development of Musical Competence* (pp. 171–190). New York: Oxford University Press, 1996.

Smithrim, K., and R. Upitis. (eds.). *Listen to Their Voices: Research and Practice in Early Childhood Music*, vol 3. Research to Practice: A Biennial Series. Lee Bartle (ed.). Canadian Music Educators Association, 2007.

Standley, J. M., and C. K. Madsen. "Comparison of Infant Preferences and Responses to Auditory Stimuli: Music, Mother, and Other Female Voice." *Journal of Music Therapy*, 1990, Volume 27 Issue 2 pages 54–97.

Trehub, S. E., L. A. Thorpe, and L. J. Trainor. "Infants' Perception of Good and Bad Melodies." *Psychomusicology*, 1990, *9*(1): 5–19.

Trevarthen, Colwyn, and Stephen Malloch. "Musicality and Musical Culture: Sharing Narratives of Sound from Early Childhood." In Gary E. McPherson and Graham

F. Welch (ed.), *The Oxford Handbook of Music Education*, vol. 1 (chap. 2.3, p. 254) New York: Oxford University Press, 2012.

Tudge, J. (2008). *The Everyday Lives of Young Children: Culture, Class, and Child Rearing in Diverse Societies.* Cambridge: Cambridge University Press. meNet: Music Education Network, 2008. http://menet.mdw.ac.at?menesite/engligh/index.html [accessed October 27, 2010].

Weikart, P. S. *Round the Circle: Key Experiences in Movement for Children Ages 3 to 5.* Ypsilanti, MI: High/Scope Press, 1987.

Welch, G. F. "The Musical Development and Education of Young Children." In B. Spode and O. Saracho (eds.), *Handbook of Research on the Education of Young Children* (pp. 251–267). Mahwah, NJ: Erlbaum Associates, 2006.

Welch, G. F. "Addressing the Multifaceted Nature of Music Education: An Activity Theory Research Perspective." *Research Studies in Music Education*, 2007, *28*: 23–37.

Young, S. "Digital Technologies, Young Children, and Music Education Practice." In K. Smithrim and R. Upitis (eds.), *Listen to Their Voices: Research and Practice in Early Childhood Music* (pp. 330–343). Waterloo, ON: Canadian Music Educators Association, 2007.

Zentner, M., and J. Kagan. "Perception of Music by Infants." *Nature*, 1996, *383* No 29, p. 29.

About the Companion Website

www.oup.com/us/kodalyinkindergarten

Username: Music5
Password: Book1745

There are web resources to accompany this book. Their primary purpose is to provide music teachers with realistic demonstrations of how to impart a musical education for kindergarten students based on the Kodály concept of music education that is cognitively and developmentally appropriate. The videos and activities are aligned to National Music Content Standards as well as Core Curriculum Content that will enhance creativity, reinforce aural skills and visual literacy, and expand numeracy skills in children.

Each chapter for the book contains samples of kindergarten teachers teaching concepts and skills using the teaching processes outlined in the book. In addition, each chapter includes a "teacher's perspective" on its content. All teaching video activities are aligned with information contained in *Kodály in the Kindergarten* and *Kodaly Today*.[1] The foundational aspects of these videos offer a detailed guide for teaching children to sing, move, play instruments, and develop music literacy skills, to enhance music listening and promote creativity skills. The hallmark of this teaching pedagogy is one that integrates the development of problem solving, critical thinking skills, and collaboration skills into the teaching and learning of music.

All of the videos for this website have been videotaped by teachers in their own classrooms. Videos have not been edited. This provides kindergarten teachers with an opportunity to get a glimpse into real kindergarten music classrooms and see the challenges that a music kindergarten teacher faces.

References to materials on the Companion Website are found throughout the text and will be signaled by the symbol shown at right.

Kodály in the Kindergarten Classroom

Chapter **1**

Developing a Music Repertoire of Songs and Books for the Kindergarten Music Classroom

This chapter provides a rationale for the selection and analysis of music repertoire for teaching kindergarten music. The videos accompanying this section of the book contain samples of the songs and rhymes used in music lessons (Web 1. Repertoire B). There are posts of kindergarten music teachers talking about developing a repertoire of musical songs and books on (Web 1. Repertoire C).

A child's music education should begin with the folk music and rhymes of her own culture. According to David Elliot:

> It is through the indigenous music of their cultures that children receive the stories of their people, those that ancestors pass down from generation to generation and others that are contemporary and reflect new customs. Folk music is the treasure trove of children's values, beliefs, cultures, knowledge, games and stories. The music of children's own cultures must be given respect and status in the classroom, indirectly giving children a sense of their own values and status. Receptivity toward the music of other cultures can be developed from this point of reference, thereby fostering cultural awareness, tolerance and respect.[1]

We use folk music because it belongs to the oral tradition and it "draws on the power of repetition and the human urge to generate and create."[2] In the best folk songs there is a unity between the rhythm and melody; word and musical accents fall together logically. According to to Lily Chen-Hafteck and Esther Mang, "The Kodály approach uses games songs that are highly repetitive and melodically simple to help build 'inner hearing' (aural) skills and accurate singing (oral) skills. Those music activities could be valuable to the development of social skills and self–confidence in children, including those children with special needs, whereby language experience, aural sensitivity and discrimination, and motor skills are cultivated in enjoyable and purposeful music game settings."[3]

Kodály himself observed:

> Children's singing games allow a more profound insight than anything else into the primeval age of folk music. Singing connected with movement and action is a much more ancient and more complex phenomenon than a simple song.[4]
>
> Each nation has a rich variety of folk songs, very suitable for teaching purposes. Selected gradually, they furnish the best material to introduce musical elements and make the children conscious of them. Singing first by ear, then writing, combines methods to yield surprisingly quick results. It is essential that the materials used should be musically attractive.[5]

As Bruno Nettl notes, "But it is important to acknowledge that . . . children are not simply musical embryos waiting to become musical adults but have a musical culture of their own, with its own musical and social rules, and with functions such as integration of person and expression of ethnicity."[6]

Folk music provides a first-rate repertoire that is developmentally appropriate for children. Through singing and through the movement games associated with the songs, children experience the joy of music making. Through singing they also experience the artistry of music making.

The final purpose of all this must be to introduce pupils to the understanding and love of great classics of past, present and future.[7] As Kodály writes: "Once the connections to folk music are established, children may be guided to understand the association between folk music and classical music. For instance, Haydn, the best to begin with, has manifest connection with folk song, but even in many works of Mozart it is easy to recognize the sublimated Austrian folk song. Beethoven's many themes are also folk-songlike. And all the national schools originated already in the nineteenth century have as a foundation their own folk music."[8]

A responsibility of the music specialist is to explore and research to find the most authentic folk musics for the music curriculum. This will sometimes include a variety of music from different music traditions. According to Elliot: "By building the multi-cultural musical experiences of the young, we are nurturing the familiar cultures of the children and facilitating their musical development within and across cultures. The musical experiences the children have now are those from which they create the music of their future."[9]

The songs that are referenced in this book have been primarily selected from the following publications.

Peter Erdei and Katalin Komlós. *150 American Folk Songs to Sing, Read and Play.*
   Ed. Peter Erdei and the staff of the Kodály Musical Training Institute. Collected
   principally by Katalin Komlós. New York: Boosey & Hawkes, 1985, p. 120.
Eleanor G. Locke. *Sail Away: 155 American Folk Songs to Sing, Read and Play.*
   New York: Boosey & Hawkes, 1981, p. 164.

Ida Erdei, Faith Knowles, and Denise Bacon. *My Singing Bird, vol. II of 150 American Folk Songs from the Anglo-American, African-American, English, Scottish and Irish Traditions.* Wellesley, MA: Kodály Center of America, 2002, p. 164.

Faith Knowles, ed. *Vamos a Cantar: 230 Folk Songs of Spanish-Speaking People to Sing, Read, and Play.* Columbus, OH: Kodály Institute at Capital University, 2006.

Gabriella Montoya-Stier. *El Patio de Mi Casa: 42 Traditional Rhymes, Chants, and Folk Songs from Mexico.* Chicago: GIA, 2009.

It is important to listen to authentic recordings of songs before teaching them to children. Song transcriptions do not always capture the "soul" of this music. Learning to sing this repertoire from memory will aid the teacher in "owning" this music repertoire and it will be a pleasant surprise to see how easily children engage in the singing process if this material is sung with enjoyment and artistry. Sometimes teachers find it hard to believe that they can keep the imagination of a young child engaged by singing simple unaccompanied folksongs. It can be achieved if the teacher sings this material in an aesthetic pleasing manner and can capture the imagination of the young child.

The repertoire selected for classroom use should be of high quality and include not only songs that incorporate musical concepts for teaching, but also songs to advance the pure joy of singing, seasonal songs and multicultural songs. Sometimes music teachers choose song material to help children remember classroom rules, or it can be used as an aid in developing literacy skills or numeracy skills. Although these songs are useful for developing children's social skills, they should not be the primary singing material of the Early Childhood music program. We need to find ways to connect what we are doing in the classroom with the community at large. We need to find opportunities to acknowledge children's own music interests; as Jeanneret and Degraffenreid write, "When children's preferences and tastes in music are acknowledged and incorporated into the music curriculum, they can be helped to understand a wider range of music through active involvement in listening."[10] Asking children to perform a song or a movement they have developed or piece of music they have learned from the web, television, or their parents is important. Finding ways to connect this repertoire to music activities in the classroom can be powerful. Inviting musicians into the classroom to perform live music for children is also a great way to make a musical connection with the community. In this way we come to understand "music as an activity to be engaged in and made between people, rather than as a 'thing' to be learned, or set of uniform skills to be imparted, and, moreover, to see how music and musical practices are ever-changing."[11] Quality materials allow the development of a child's imagination and creativity. The recordings of Ella Jenkins listed here contain a variety of song material that can supplement your own song choices and will hold great appeal to children in the Early Childhood music classroom. Though these materials are excellent, consider teaching them using a higher key than the original recording. Many of Jenkins's recording are available from Smithsonian Folkways (SWF).

Call and Response: Rhythmic Group Singing (SFW 45030)
Adventures in Rhythm (SFW 45007)
African American Folk Rhythms (SFW 45003)
Rhythms of Childhood (45008)
Songs and Rhythms from Near and Far (SFW 45003)
Rhythm and Games for the Little Ones (SFW 45027)

Counting Games for the Little One (SFW 45029)
You'll Sing a Song and I'll Sing a Song (SFW 45010)
Play Your Instruments and Make a Pretty Sound (SFW 45018)
Seasons for Singing (SFW 45031)
And One and Two (SFW 45016)
My Street Begins at My House (SFW 45005)
This a Way, That a Way (SFW 45002)
Jambo and Other Call and Response Songs (SFW 45017)
Nursery Rhymes: Rhyming and Remembering (SFW 45019)
Growing Up With Ella Jenkins: Rhythms, Rhymes and Songs (SFW 45032)
Songs Rhythms and Chants for the Dance (SFW 45004)
Travellin' with Ella Jenkins: A Bilingual Journey (SFW 45009)
Early, Early Childhood Songs (SFW 45015)
Little Johnny Brown (SFW45026)
Come Dance by the Ocean (SFW 45014)
Looking Back and Looking Forward (SFW)
Hopping Around from Place to Place, volumes 1 and 2 (SFW)
I Know the Colors of the Rainbow (SFW)
Sharing Cultures (SFW 45058)

Getting Started: Repertoire to Teach During the First Weeks of Music Lessons

The curriculum content of an Early Childhood music program includes teaching children singing games; music play; exploring sounds through using their own voices and bodies, as well as music instruments; learning basic information about duration and melody; reading books that encourage the development of music improvisation skills; and developing the skill of listening.[12]

Spend the first weeks of the school year building a repertoire of songs. Singing to small groups of children, or even singing a song using props or a picture book to help illustrate the text of the song, helps capture a child's attention. Below is a list of songs you can teach your children during the first few weeks of class. Please consider the lesson plans in Chapter 7, Unit 1, written for the first few weeks of class, to get some ideas as to how these songs may be performed. You might also want to check some YouTube sites to see if you can find a video that might illustrate the text for your children while you are singing the song. Remember that some of these recordings may not be suitable for young children; if they are harmonized, they can distract children from paying attention to the words, melody, and rhythm of a song. We're convinced it's better for a young child to concentrate on the text and the melody performed by one person without accompaniment.

The following rhymes and songs can be taught during the first few weeks of class. We've included some teaching suggestions.

The Rhyme "Bee, Bee, Bumblebee"

1. Introduce a picture of bee or a puppet. One we find particularly successful is a bee in a flowerpot. There is a stick attached to the bee through the bottom of the flowerpot.
2. "Look over at the bee puppet sitting in the flower pot. Did you know that this bee did some very bad things earlier today? He stung a man on his knee, and then

he stung a pig on his snout. What do you think a snout could be? [Point to one child] He promised me he wouldn't sting anyone anymore because he doesn't want to go sit in time out or get his clip turned. He did want me to show you how to do the bee dance, though."

3. Show the bee dance with the poem. (Create your own motions to go with the rhyme.)
4. "I bet you could do these motions with me. Repeat after me, phrase by phrase."
5. Everyone stands and does the bee dance, repeating after the teacher.
6. "I bet you can all say the whole rhyme; let's try it!"

The Song "Johnny Works with One Hammer"
1. There are several versions of this song on YouTube, but the original melody has been altered. Simply turn down the volume but use the visual to teach the song.
2. Sing: "Copy my motions, please." Sing the song and do the motions while children copy.

The Rhyme "Bate, Bate Chocolate"
This is excellent for performing the beat.

The Song "Cobbler, Cobbler," also Listed as "Hunt the Slipper"
1. "While you were walking around, a hole appeared on the sole of your shoe! Take your foot and pretend to hammer it while I sing about someone who fixes shoes."
2. The teacher uses a hammer to keep the beat while singing the song.

The Song "Snail, Snail"
1. Introduce Mr. Snail (a puppet is helpful).
2. Have children learn how to do the snail wave (antennas on head and wave forward and back).
3. Snail sings his song for the children. "Wave goodbye to the snail!"

The Song "Teddy Bear"
1. Teacher sings "Teddy Bear" to a picture of a Teddy Bear (or a bear puppet or stuffed animal).
2. The teacher and children sing and do motions.
3. Repeat, choosing a new child each time to come up and hold the Teddy Bear.

Developing a Musical and Sequential Early Childhood Lessons for the First Weeks of Music Classes

We have developed several specific lesson plan structures for music lessons and for music literature lessons. Lessons plans are sequenced to reinforce repertoire and skills so children develop confidence when participating in activities. This scaffolding approach relies heavily on constant informal assessment of children's progress. New skills are introduced once children have mastered preceding skills. The skill sequence we suggest is based on our research and collaboration with Early Childhood specialists and research in the fields of education, cognition and perception, and psychology.

Although designed to be thirty-minute music lessons, the sections of the music and music-literature lessons can be used on their own by the classroom teacher. Understanding the elements of these lesson plans and their relationships to one another will aid you as a classroom teacher in using music in your classroom activities. Keep in mind that songs and rhymes need to be repeated many times in each section of the lesson.

Most Early Childhood music instructors and Early Childhood classroom instructors will gradually increase the amount of time spent in teaching music until they are able to work through an entire thirty-minute music lesson. This will be especially true in a class comprising younger children (three- and four-year-olds). Just as each complete lesson builds on the successes of those that came before it, the entire lesson plan structure can be broken down into distinct levels that, implemented over time, will gradually strengthen children's abilities and interests to enable them to participate in a full thirty-minute lesson. In addition to building the children's skills, this approach also gives you an opportunity to become comfortable planning and leading the several sections of the lesson plan until you are comfortable with planning an entire lesson.

In order to feel comfortable creating a complete music lesson, we propose the following four steps.

Step 1: Teach a New Song

At first, you will introduce new songs; eventually, you will spend more time singing songs the children already know and are comfortable singing. Regardless, it is imperative to be consistent in how you invite the children to sing with you, and how you set up the songs. Ask yourself the following questions:

- What song will I be singing?
- How fast will I be singing the song?
- What pitch will I begin singing the song on?
- What visuals will I be using to help children learn the text?

Any seasoned Early Childhood instructor will tell you that consistency is incredibly important. If you are consistent in how you set up songs when you sing casually in the classroom, you will prepare your children for greater success when singing during structured lessons later in the year; you should also discover greater participation among your children. These songs will form the foundation for your instruction, in developing children's musical skills. By this we simply mean that one song can be used to teach a variety of skills. Keep in mind that repetition is often comforting to children, and clear articulation is essential on the part of the teacher.

When you want to invite children to sing with you, it is important to let them know what song you will be singing, and what pitch you will begin singing on.

There are a number of things you can do when setting up a song (or chant) to clearly establish the beat. The first occurs naturally when you sing/speak in a steady rhythm to invite the children to sing/chant with you, using a phrase like "Rain, rain, sing with me" or "Bee, bee, here we go." Clapping or tapping motions or using an instrument such as a drum to accent the beat as you speak this phrase yields an additional reinforcement of the beat. Clapping, patting, or musically striking the drum with a large, deliberate motion also reinforces the beat visually.

The tempo, or speed, of a song is measured in beats per minute (bpm). For example, one beat at a tempo of 60 bpm is equal to one second. Just as a watch is used to tell time in units of seconds, minutes, and hours, a metronome is used to keep a steady beat at various tempos. On a piece of music, you may see this tempo expressed as MM = 60. MM stands for metronome marking.

The tempo at which children can successfully demonstrate a steady beat through movement increases with age as their motor skills develop. Although the type of movement used to demonstrate beat affects the speed at which a child can successfully keep a steady beat, here is a general guideline:

Three or four years   MM = 66–80

Four or five years   MM = 80–92

Over five years   MM = 92–108

Developing a student's ability to keep a steady beat is an essential component of each lesson.

If a child in your class seems to have trouble finding and keeping a steady beat, the first step is to think about how the child is trying to demonstrate the beat. Is the movement too challenging for the child? If it is, offer him or her another way to demonstrate the beat by modeling it.

If physical coordination isn't the problem, try giving the child a tactile experience to reinforce the beat. Use your hands (or a puppet, or otherwise) to tap the beat on the child's palms, shoulders, feet, etc., until she or he begins to keep the beat with you. You may need to repeat this over many singing sessions until the child can maintain the beat without this reinforcement and repeated guidance.

Even if "the heartbeat" is not the focus of your lesson or activity, you can reinforce your children's sense of steady beat any time you sing or listen to music with them; simply model keeping the steady beat on your own body, or supply them with an audio reinforcement of the beat, such as the beat of a drum. Some children may imitate you, and others may just watch; but over time (with considerable repetition) the children will internalize this concept.

Before children sing a song, it is important to give them the name of the song, the starting pitch, the tempo, and the character of the song. Consider practicing singing songs in front of a mirror so that you can develop appropriate facial expressions and motions to accompany your singing. Sing the song with the correct tempo and dynamics. Depending on the song, you may decide to slow the tempo to emphasize the text.

Children need this information before the song begins so that all of you can sing the song together as a class. However, children's eagerness to sing, or a mistaken understanding of the setup cues, can result in some children launching into the song during your setup. Two things may help with this. First, try to avoid using words in your setup that are the same as those at the beginning of the song. Though it is very natural to use the opening lyrics of a song in your setup (such as "Twinkle, twinkle, sing with me" or "Bee, bee, here we go," some children may be confused by this, think you have already begun to sing the song, and thus join you too early. To avoid this at the beginning, instead of "Bee, bee, here we go" you might say, "Here comes the bee, now here we go." Remember not to spend too much time talking about the song. Just sing it many times for the children.

Table 1.1 Lesson Plan for Step 1

UNIT *ONE* LESSON *ONE*	
Outcome	• Learn song repertoire • Develop beat skills • Develop listening skills
INTRODUCTORY ACTIVITIES	
Introduction	• Use a favorite song to lead C (children) into the room and into a seating chart. You might want to sing the song and then make up words to the melody that remind C of the classroom rules. It starts the class musically, establishes the behavior expectations, and focuses their minds on the task at hand. This song is only for you to sing to your C; later during the year they can join you. • Using a song such as "Here We Go 'Round the Mulberry Bush" so that C know how to follow you into the music room, and eventually lead them into a circle formation. For example this text may be sung to "Here we go 'Round the Mulberry Bush": Follow me into music class, music class, music class Follow me into music class and we'll all sing and play Make a circle in music class, music class, music class Make a circle in music class and we'll all sing and play
CORE ACTIVITIES	
Teach a new song	"Bee, Bee, Bumblebee" (bee puppet in a flower pot) • T: "Look over at the bee puppet sitting in the flower pot. Did you know that this bee did some very bad things earlier today? He stung a man on his knee, and then he stung a pig on his snout. What do you think a snout could be? (Point to one child.) He promised me he wouldn't sting anyone anymore because he doesn't want to go sit in time out. He did want me to show you how to do the bee dance, though." • T shows the bee movements with the poem. • T chants and C do bee dance (several repetitions). • T: "Bee is looking for his hammer . . . do you see it hiding somewhere?"
Teach a new song	"Johnny Works with One Hammer" (hammer toy) • T sings, C copy motions.
SUMMARY ACTIVITIES	
Review the new songs Folk song/folk song tales sung by teacher	Review one or two of the new songs with C.

Step 2: Initiate a Greeting;
Review a Known Song or Teach a New Song

Use a greeting with the children before singing a few songs. This begins to establish a sense of "music time," the early form of the dedicated music and develops tuneful singing. Signal the beginning of the special time with a standardized greeting children will come to recognize as the signal that it is time to sing. For example, you might sing to children, "Come and sit in a circle with me." This may be said as a rhythm or you can sing it. Review a known song or teach a new song.

Table 1.2   Lesson Plan for Step 2

UNIT ONE LESSON ONE	
Outcome	• Develop tuneful singing through a greeting • Develop beat skills • Review song literature • Learn song repertoire • Develop listening skills
INTRODUCTORY ACTIVITIES	
Introduction	• Use a favorite song to lead C into the room and into a seating chart. You might want to sing the song and then make up words to the melody that remind C of the classroom rules. It starts the class musically, establishes the behavior expectations, and focuses their minds on the task at hand. • Use a song such as "Here We Go 'Round the Mulberry Bush" so that children know how to follow you into the music room, and eventually lead them into a circle formation. For example, this text may be sung to "Here we go 'Round the Mulberry Bush": Follow me into music class, music class, music class Follow me into music class and we'll all sing and play Make a circle in music class, music class, music class Make a circle in music class and we'll all sing and play
Develop tuneful singing	T sings greeting using the pitches of the first phrase of "Snail, Snail." C reply with the same pattern.

(*Continued*)

Table 1.2   (continued)

CORE ACTIVITIES	
Teach a new song	"Bee, Bee, Bumblebee" (bee puppet in a flower pot)
	• T: "Look over at the bee puppet sitting in the flower pot. Did you know that this bee did some very bad things earlier today? He stung a man on his knee, and then he stung a pig on his snout. What do you think a snout could be? (Point to one child.) He promised me he wouldn't sting anyone anymore because he doesn't want to go sit in time out. He did want me to show you how to do the bee dance, though." • T shows the bee dance with the poem. • T chants and C do bee dance. • T: "Bee is looking for his hammer . . . do you see it hiding somewhere?"
SUMMARY ACTIVITIES	
Review the new songs	Review one or two of the new songs with C.
Folk song/folk song tales sung by teacher	"Over in the Meadow" You might use some simple pictures or visuals. Do not show the book to C at this time, as you want them to listen to the song and watch the vocal model.

Step 3: Initiate a Greeting; Review a Known Song; Teach a New Song; Play a Known Game or Movement Activity

Children should now be seated in a circle. Begin with your greeting, sing a song (or a few songs), and then play a game. Review a known song from a previous lesson. Teach a new song to children. In addition to singing songs, play a music game or introduce a listening activity. Watch the children for cues regarding their attention span, and take the opportunity to sing the song several times.

Table 1.3   Lesson Plan for Step 3

UNIT *ONE* LESSON *ONE*	
Outcome	• Develop tuneful singing • Develop beat skills • Learn and review song repertoire • Develop listening skills • Develop movement skills

(Continued)

Table 1.3   (continued)

INTRODUCTORY ACTIVITIES	
Introduction	• Use a favorite song to lead C into the room and into a seating chart. You might want to sing the song and then make up words to the melody that remind C of the rules. It starts the class musically, establishes the behavior expectations, and focuses their minds on the task at hand. • Using a song such as "Here We Go 'Round the Mulberry Bush" so that C know how to follow you into the music room, and eventually lead them into a circle formation. For example, this text may be sung to "Here We go 'Round the Mulberry Bush."
Develop tuneful singing	T sings greeting using the pitches of the first phrase of "Snail, Snail." C reply with the same pattern. • T sings song on "loo" C recognize • C sing the song and play the game • T uses the pitches of the first phrase of "Snail, Snail" and substitutes an alternative text.
CORE ACTIVITIES	
Teach a new song	"Bee, Bee, Bumblebee" (bee puppet in a flower pot) • T: "Look over at the bee puppet sitting in the flower pot. Who remembers the bad things he did? He stung a man on his knee, and then he stung a pig on his snout. What do you think a snout could be? (Point to one child.) He promised me he wouldn't sting anyone anymore because he doesn't want to go sit in time out. Let's see if we remember the bee dance." • T shows the bee dance with the poem. • T chants and C do bee dance.
Teach a new song	"Johnny Works with One Hammer" (hammer toy) T sings; C copy motions.
Singing game/ creative movement	Play any piece of music with a strong beat and a moderate tempo. C mirror the T's movements. • T performs the beat. • T taps the beat on different parts of her body. • T walks to the beat.

(*Continued*)

11

Table 1.3 (continued)

Teach a new song	"Cobbler Cobbler"
	• T: "While you were walking around, you wore out your shoes and holes started to appear. Take your shoe and pretend to hammer it while I sing about someone who fixes shoes." T initially sings the song without tapping, to focus attention to the text.
	• T uses hammer and taps to the beat while singing the song.
SUMMARY ACTIVITIES	
Review the new songs	Review one or two of the new songs with C.
Folk song/folk song tales sung by teacher	"Over in the Meadow" You might use some pictures or visuals. Do not show the book to Cat this time, as you want them to listen to the song.

Step 4: Initiate a Greeting; Review a Known Song; Vocal Technique Exercise; Teach a New Song; Play a Known Game; Review a Known Song; Do a Closing Activity

Children should now be seated in a circle. Initiate a greeting, teach a vocal technique activity, review a known song, teach a new song, play a known game, and end with a closing activity. Begin with a musical greeting to the children. Review a known song. Develop their singing voices through a simple but playful technical exercise. For example, have children imagine they smell different kinds of flowers, to develop breath control. Teach them a song (or a few songs); then play a game. Watch the children for cues regarding their attention span. Note that the activities within the lesson are sequenced to promote success: begin by singing a known greeting, reviewing a known song, followed by a vocal technical exercise, followed by teaching them a new song. Playing a familiar game that reinforces their confidence and enjoyment of the lesson follows this. Sing another known song. Work on practicing musical concepts such as beat, fast-slow, loud-soft, or high-low. During the closing section of the lesson, children are seated once again and asked to be attentive while you sing a song for them. This constitutes a listening activity for the children.

Table 1.4 Lesson Plan for Step 4

UNIT *ONE* LESSON *ONE*	
Outcome	• Develop tuneful singing through vocal exercises
	• Develop beat skills
	• Learn and review song repertoire
	• Develop listening skills
	• Develop movement skills
INTRODUCTORY ACTIVITIES	
Introduction	"That's a Mighty Pretty Motion"
	• T sings "That's a Might Pretty Motion" with motions for C.
	• T sings "That's a Might Pretty Motion" with motions; C copy motions.
	• T sings and C improvise beat motions for the whole song.

(Continued)

Table 1.4 (continued)

Develop tuneful singing	• T sings greeting using the pitches of the first phrase of "Snail, Snail." C reply with the same pattern. Repeat activity, but this time C must sing, clapping the way the words go. • C pretend to be a bird, or in a plane, etc., and fly with their voices on a journey through the music room. • C pretend to be animals by making the sounds of particular ones.
Review known songs and concepts	"Cobbler Cobbler" • T sings uses hammer to tap the beat on a shoe while singing the song. • T sings with motions and C copy. • T sings with other beat and C copy.
CORE ACTIVITIES	
Teach a new song	"On a Mountain" • T sings with beat motions; C copy.
Review old song	"Johnny Works with One Hammer" • T sings with beat (hammer) motions and C copy. • T and C sing. • T sings with other motions and C sing and copy. • C sing and improvise their own motions.
Singing game/ creative movement	• Play any piece of music with a strong beat and a moderate tempo. C mirror the T's movements. • T claps to the beat. • T taps the beat on different parts of her body. • T walks to the beat. • C form a circle holding hands and swaying to the beat.
Teach a new song	"Good Night Sleep Tight" • T sings and asks C to rock the baby to sleep to the beat. • Teach C the first phrase and T sings the second phrase.
SUMMARY ACTIVITIES	
Review the new songs	Review one or two of the new songs with the children.
Folk song/folk song tales sung by teacher	"Bandy Rowe"

Repertoire for Singing, Movement, and Playing on Instruments

Song repertoire is critical to the success of a music curriculum. Both the instructor and the children should enjoy the songs, games and activities. Selected repertoire should include:

- Songs for singing, movement, and playing on instruments
- Songs for listening
- Songs that can be used for teaching music concepts and skills

13

The Early Childhood music curriculum may also include songs with no specific pedagogical purpose other than the enjoyment of singing. Such songs are often an opportunity for solo singing as well as improvisation. In some songs, the children will be able to sing all verses, while in others it might be appropriate for them to sing selected verses. When considering song materials for primary grades, instructors may also select repertoire that is appropriate for listening, as well as songs that can be performed on instruments.

Music teachers in the United States may include a selection of Anglo-American, African American, Hispanic, Asian American, and Hebrew materials. It is possible to include music of England, Ireland, Scotland, Wales, France, and Germany because of the close connection with Anglo-American folk music. When working with a predominantly Hispanic population, music of Latin America and Spain may form the basis of their curriculum.

Songs for classroom use, meaning songs that will be taught to children or sung to them, may include the following:

Songs for Singing

- Children's games:

  Nursery rhymes and songs
  Jump-rope games
  Counting out rhymes
  Lullabies
  Acting out games
  Wind-up games
  Circle games
  Choosing games
  Partner games
  Double circle
  Line games
  Double line games

- Folk music:

  Folk songs
  Play parties

- Composed music:

  Kodály believed that composers should dedicate a portion of their creative efforts to composing music for children. He writes, "Original works are to be written, compositions starting from the child's soul, from the child's voice in text, tune and color alike."[13]

Songs for Listening

Songs selected for listening activities function as an important part of the music curriculum. Folksongs as well as folksong tales (songs that tell a story) should be included. Later, these songs may be reintroduced in the upper elementary grades for teaching musical concepts. Although intended for listening, it may be appropriate to accompany some of these songs. The goal of singing to children is to allow them to discover the joy of listening attentively to a live performance of songs sung or played on an instrument.

Live musical performances are meaningful to children. Songs will often have more meaning to them if the songs are connected to learning centers in the class or connected to books used for language arts. They do a great deal to develop children's emotional sensibilities. YouTube videos of musical performances may also be used in the classroom, although we are convinced that nothing will bring as much meaning to the children as the teacher singing to the class.

Repertoire for Teaching Musical Concepts and Skills

These songs are included in the curriculum as beautiful examples of music as well as significant aids to teaching rhythmic or melodic concepts. For example, we can sing a song to develop beautiful singing, the understanding of beat, loud-soft, fast-slow beats, high-low tones, or rhythm.

Guidelines for Selecting Repertoire Material for the Early Childhood Classroom

Table 1.5 is a simple illustration of age-appropriate guidelines for selecting musical material.

Table 1.5

	Three Year Olds	Four Year Olds	Five or Six Year Olds
Songs/ rhymes	Twenty-five	Thirty	Thirty-five
Text	Should include songs that have repetitive text or phrase	Songs chosen should be related to curriculum themes and learning centers	Songs chosen should be related to curriculum themes and learning centers as well as the child's environment
Songs and tone sets	Songs should include pentatonic motives, pentatonic songs, and pentachord songs	Songs should include pentatonic, pentachord, and hexachord songs	Songs should include pentatonic, pentachord, and hexachord songs and diatonic songs
Rhythm	Songs include simple and compound rhythm patterns	Songs include simple and compound rhythm patterns	Songs include simple and compound rhythm patterns and rests
Range	Range of songs should be limited to a range of a sixth from D to B	Range of songs should be limited to a sixth from D to B	Range of songs should be about a sixth from D to B and moving to a range of songs about an octave, D–D
Tempo	MM: 65–80	MM: 80–90	MM: 90–100

Traditional children's songs, rhymes, and play songs are particularly appropriate for classroom use, as is composed music that is developmentally appropriate. You will undoubtedly notice a similarity between many songs we're suggesting for classroom use, in tone set, range, and rhythm. We take the same approach to teaching music as classroom teachers use when teaching reading. Just like teaching reading to young children, it is important to select repertoire that is different yet similar so that young children will become familiar with melodic and rhythmic patterns and ultimately memorize the repertoire.

In addition to songs, rhymes from the children's own cultures as well as other cultures are appropriate for the early learner. In performance, a rhyme should be said with precise articulation and a regular beat. There are usually two ways of saying the same rhyme:

1. With a regular accent on every quarter note (pulse or beat) with movements or motions following the beat
2. With the vocal accent following the movement

Songs, games, and rhymes from the children's own cultures and other cultures, as well as suitably composed songs and games, form the foundation of the Early Childhood curriculum. The basic repertoire taught to young children should initially have the vocal range of a sixth, from middle D to B. Initially, it is best to use songs with a narrower range; once intonation is secure, and the instructor may gradually expand the vocal range.

Songs suitable for the Early Childhood classroom tend to use melodies that include pentatonic motifs and melodies. These motifs often repeat or can appear in a sequence. Here are examples of songs with tone sets used in the Early Childhood classroom:

Melodies built on the notes of a child's chants (*so-mi-la* abbreviated to *s-m-l*)

"Little Sally Water"

"Pajarito"

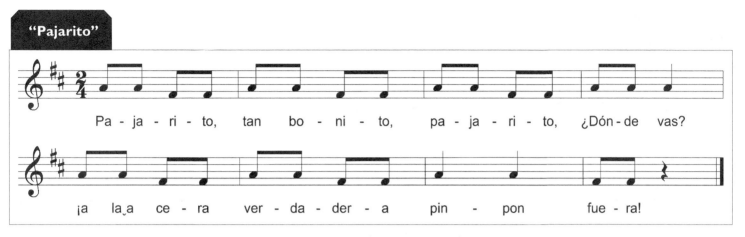

Pa - ja - ri - to, tan bo - ni - to, pa - ja - ri - to, ¿Dón - de vas?

¡a la͜a ce - ra ver - da - der - a pin - pon fue - ra!

Translation: Beautiful bird beautiful bird, where are you going? To the green forest away!

"See Saw"

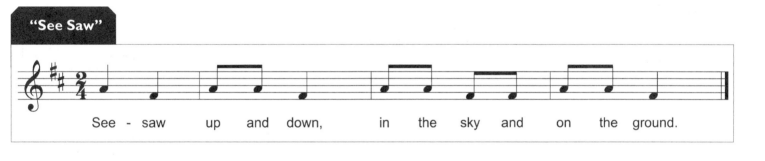

See - saw up and down, in the sky and on the ground.

"Sol Solecito"

Sol, so - le - ci - to, ca - lién - ta - me͜un po - qui - to

hoy y ma - ña - na y to - da la se - ma - na.

Translation: Sunshine, warm me up a little bit today and tomorrow and throughout the week.

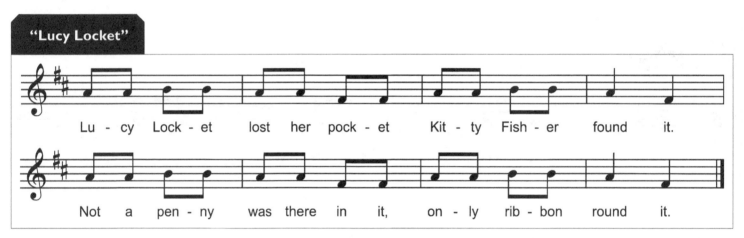

Literal translation: Round and round, the hot north wind swirls,
in the garden of Palan, the plums will fall.

"Chini, Mini"

Translation: Eenie, meenie minie, mo!

Melodies built on the first three notes of a scale, *me-re-do* motifs (m-r-d)

"Hot Cross Buns

"Hop, Old Squirrel"

"Miss Spider (Doña Araña)"

Do - ña A - ra - ña se fue a pa - sear,

Hi - zo un hi - lo y se pu - so a tre - par:

Verses:
Vi-no el vien-to,
la hi-zo bai-lar,
vi-no la tor-men-ta,
la hi-zo ba-jar.

Literal translation:
Miss spider went for a stroll,
She spun a thread and tried to climb up,
Along came a wind that caused her to dance,
Along came a rain storm that made her come down.

Melodies built on the first three notes of a scale (*m-r-d* motifs) and a child's chant *(l-s-m)*

"Bluebird"

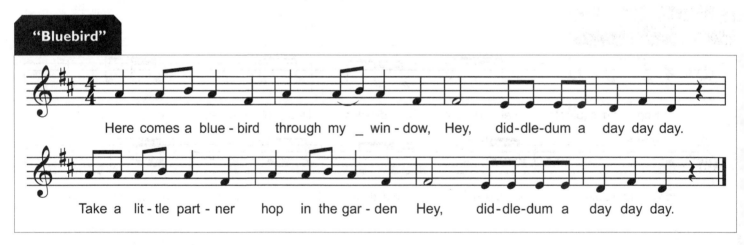

Here comes a blue - bird through my _ win - dow, Hey, did-dle-dum a day day day.

Take a lit - tle part - ner hop in the gar - den Hey, did-dle-dum a day day day.

"Bow, Wow, Wow"

Bow, wow, wow, whose dog art thou? Lit-tle Tom-my Tuck-er's dog bow, wow, wow.

Pentatonic and Nonpentatonic songs, especially those with *so-fa-mi-re-do* (*s-f-m-r-d*) ending melodies, may be included as well. For example:

"Caracol Col Col"

Literal translation:
Little Snail, snail snail, dry your feelers in the sun.
They have just withdrawn by the shore of the sea.

21

"Duerme Pronto (El Canto de Madre; "Go to Sleep Now—Mother's Song")

Literal translation:
Go to sleep soon dear little child,
Sleep now without crying,
You're in the arms of your mother.

"Este Niño Lindo (The Beautiful Boy)"

Es - te ni - ño lin - do, que na - cio de no - che, quie - re que lo lle - ven a pa - sar en co - che.

Es - te ni - ño lin - do, que na - ció de di - a, quie - re que lo lle - ven a co - mer san - di - a.

Literal translation: This beautiful boy, that was born during the night, wants us to take him for a ride in the car. This beautiful boy, that was born during the day, wants us to take him to eat watermelon.

"Con mi martillo (With My Hammer)"

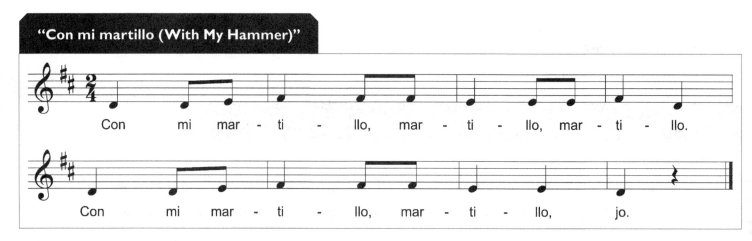

Con mi mar - ti - llo, mar - ti - llo, mar - ti - llo.

Con mi mar - ti - llo, mar - ti - llo, jo.

Literal translation: With my hammer, jo.

"Brinca la tablita (Jump over the Board)"

Brin - ca la tab - li - ta, ya yo la brin - que,

brin - ca la tua ho - ra qué yo me - can - se.

Literal translation: Jump over the board, I jumped it, Jump it again, I am already tired.

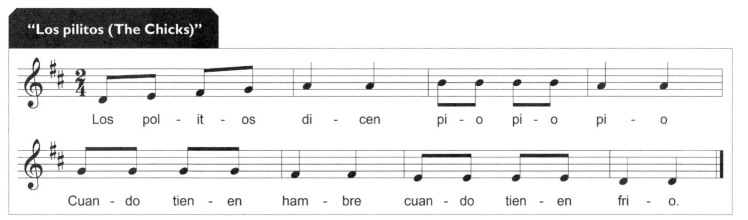

"Los pilitos (The Chicks)"

Los pol - it - os di - cen pi - o pi - o pi - o

Cuan - do tien - en ham - bre cuan - do tien - en fri - o.

Literal translation: The chicks say pio, pio, pio,
when they're hungry, when they're cold.

Building Blocks of Children's Songs and Games

Here is a list of songs containing examples of the important building blocks in children's songs and games. Knowing the common rhythmic and melodic patterns will help teachers recognize the musical connection between songs. For example, echo clapping of typical rhythmic patterns can be practiced more thoroughly once the teacher understands what patterns repeat in song repertoire. Knowledge of the melodic building patterns enables teachers to develop children's vocal singing, create greetings built from known repertoire, and use melodic patterns for improvisation activities. We suggest avoiding song materials with an anacrusis initially.

The list of songs is arranged according to like rhythmic and melodic patterns. Grouping the songs or arranging them by rhythmic and melodic patterns enables the teacher to better sequence teaching activities such as echo singing, echo clapping, singing greetings, and improvisation games. (*Asterisks denote which phrase of the song contains the pattern.)

Heartbeat Simple Meter
"Bee, Bee, Bumble Bee"
"Bounce High Bounce Low"
"Cobbler Cobbler"
"Engine Engine #9"
"Snail, Snail"

Heartbeat Compound Meter
"Here We Go Round the Mulberry Bush"
"No Robbers out Today"

Quarter and Eighth Notes

"Bounce High Bounce Low"
"Button *2"

"Good Night"
"Snail, Snail"
"Star Light, Star Bright"
Two Four Six Eight

"Bee, Bee, Bumble Bee"
"Bee, Bee, Bumble Bee"
"Queen Queen Caroline"
"Rain, Rain"
"See Saw"

"All Around the Buttercup"

"Bee, Bee, Bumble Bee, Bee, Bee, Bumble Bee" *2, 3, 4
"Bobby Shaftoe"
"Bow Wow Wow" *3
"Cobbler Cobbler"
"Doggie Doggie"
"Engine Engine #9"
"Good Night" *2
"I Climbed up the Apple Tree"
"Johnny's It"
"In and Out" *2
"Nanny Goat"
"Rain, Rain" *2
"See Saw" *2
"Snail, Snail" *2
"Star Light, Star Bright" *4
"We Are Dancing in the Forest" *2, 4

"Bobby Shaftoe" *4
"Bounce High Bounce Low" *2
"Button"
"Clap Your Hands Together"
"Frog in the Meadow" *3
"Here Comes a Bluebird"
"Little Sally Water"
"Lucy Locket" *2, 4
"Ring Around the Rosie"
"Shovel Little Shovel" (Pala Palita)

"Bye Baby Bunting"
"Down Came a Lady"
"Frog in the Meadow"
"Here Comes a Bluebird"

s–m
s m s m
"Good Night"
"A Nip and a Peck" (Pica Perica)
"Pipis y Ganas"
"Snail, Snail"
"Who Are These People?" (Quien es esa Gente?)

s m ss m
"Rain, Rain"
"See Saw"
"Lemonade"

ss mm ss m
"Doggie Doggie"
"Good Night"
"See Saw" *2

sm s sm s
"In and Out"
"This Old Man"

Rest

"All Around the Buttercup" *2, 4
"Bow Wow Wow" *4
"Down Came a Lady" *2
"Hot Cross Buns"
"Pease Porridge Hot" *4

"Frog in the Meadow"
"Pease Porridge Hot"

"Clap Your Hands Together" (* second and fourth motifs)
"Naughty Kitty Cat"
"Who Are These People?" (Quien es esa Gente?)
l (the overarching melodic element is the syllable *l*)
slsm (there is one syllable per beat)
s mlsm (the second beat has two sounds)
"Little Rooster" (Pipirigallo)

s l s m
"Bounce High Bounce Low"
"Star Light, Star Bright"

ss ll s m
"Bobby Shaftoe"
"Bounce High Bounce Low" *2
"Lucy Locket" * 2, 4
"Round and Round" (A la Ronda Ronda)

ss ll ss m
"Bobby Shaftoe"
"Chini, Mini"
"Snail, Snail" * 2
"Star Light, Star Bright" *4
"We Are Dancing in the Forest" *2, 4

ss ll ss mm
"Lucy Locket"
"We Are Dancing in the Forest"

s sl s m
"Bye Baby Bunting"
"Here Comes a Bluebird"

ss sl s m
"A Tisket a Tasket"

"Bye Baby Bunting"
"Doggie Doggie"
"Fudge Fudge"
"Here Comes a Bluebird" *3
"Hush Baby Hush"
"It's Raining It's Pouring"
"Johnny's It"
"Little Sally Water"
"Nanny Goat"
"No Robbers out Today"
"Rain, Rain"
"Ring Around the Rosie"

Two-Beat Meter
"Bounce High Bounce Low"
"Button"
"Nanny Goat"
"See Saw"
"Star Light, Star Bright"
"This Old Man"

Compound Meter
"Jack and Jill"
"No Robbers out Today"

25

Rhythm patterns in children's songs tend to be simple, and they are normally in simple duple and compound meter, whereas the more difficult rhythms appear in songs sung by adults to children. Music notation is only a guide as to how the actual song should sound or be performed. In order to get a feeling for the song and teach it correctly, the teacher should sing the song many times. That being said, the notation found in this book should be thought of as only a basic representation of the song. Remember that while many of the songs in this book look as if they are composed of just one or two even sounds on the beat, we have to consider that if the songs were transcribed from the original performer, there might be some variation in performance. It is important for children to learn the songs artistically and with a significant awareness of the beat. Later, some of these songs may be used to teach rhythms or melodic patterns; then the children will be able to sing the songs in a very metrical manner to figure out the number of sounds on individual beats and which beats have high and low pitches.

Guidelines for Selecting Repertoire for Classroom Use

The aforementioned considerations should be guiding principles concerning the types of musical materials we select for classroom use.

- Songs must be of the highest musical quality and should be tuneful.
- Songs must have a musical appeal.

- Songs must use an appropriate range for the young learner.
- The text of the song and the music should complement each other; the rhythmic accent and melodic inflection should match the structure of the language.
- If you say the words of a song out loud in an exaggerated manner, you can almost hear the melodic line that will be used in a song.
- Songs should be developmentally appropriate; songs should be relevant for specific age groups.
- Selected songs should reflect the cultural backgrounds of children in your classroom.

In summary, teachers need to look for repertoire that is of "good quality" and that fits into the organic model of teaching we are proposing in this book. It is important to use folksongs in the music curriculum as this repertoire should be considered the foundation of the curriculum, and they will allow for the development of children's own musicianship and creativity. We support Harwook and March in their recommendations: "For teachers it means finding repertoire within your school's and cultures' context that is participatory by nature and including such experiences as part of the curriculum. Examples could include drum circles, children's playground songs and games from their own and other cultures, line and other dancing and associated singing, rapping and popular and vernacular adult musics as appropriate." We need to develop children's ability to discern what is great music, regardless of style.[15]

Creating an Alphabetized Song Repertoire List

On the basis of the criteria given above, we can compile a list of suitable and appropriate repertoire. Arrange the songs in alphabetical order and include a rationale for selection of the song. For example, we might choose a particular song not just because children will enjoy singing it but because it can also be used to reinforce a particular melodic or rhythmic concept or element. Include the source for the song and the type of game or movement activity associated with the song. This information may be organized in chart form, as in Table 1.6.

Table 1.6

Song (Alphabetical Listing)	Date Taught	Tone Set	Game/Movement	Source

The repertoire list should include songs that:

- Reflect the cultural diversity of a community
- Are appropriate for developing beautiful and tuneful singing
- Develop music literacy skills
- Develop listening skills
- Are suitable for creative activities such as improvisation and composition
- Are appropriate for holidays and special events

The appendix of songs includes a suggested repertoire of songs and games for the Early Childhood and kindergarten classroom.

Analyzing Song Repertoire

It is important for teachers to be able to analyze song repertoire to understand the rhythmic and melodic building blocks of the material they are teaching their children. Analysis (the examination of a song's phrase structure, rhythmic and melodic content, etc.) helps determine how a song may be used in a curriculum. Analysis enables us to see pedagogical implications within a body of song repertoire. (See also our *Kodály Today: A Cognitive Approach to Music Education*, pp. 41–59.)[14]

Here is a sample of a simplified analysis sheet that may be used for analyzing songs. After analyzing your repertoire, you may construct a database or retrieval system using the information from the analysis of your songs to help you plan. You are encouraged to view the database of folk songs made available by the Kodály Program at Holy Names University in Oakland, California (http://kodaly.hnu.edu/).

Who's That Tapping at the Window?

Origin: MM: 110   Comfortable Starting Pitch: F

Stick notation:

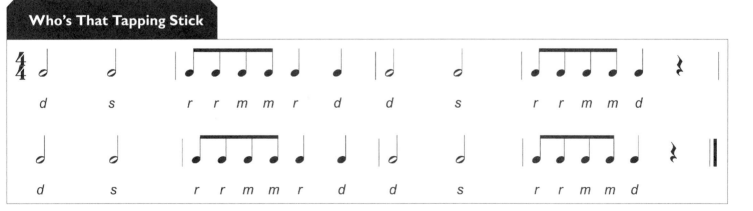

Table 1.7

Analysis	Pedagogical Use
Tone set: *d r m s*	Rationale: Keeping the beat Antiphonal singing
Rhythm: ♪, ♩, 𝄾♩	
Form: A A	Connections to books
Game: Guessing	
Other:	Other: Listening activity for C. Sing the song for C.

Source: Erdei, Peter, and Katalin Komlós. *150 American Folk Songs to Sing, Read and Play.* New York: Boosey & Hawkes, 1985 p. 7.

Game

Have the children sit in a circle. One child is selected to sit in the middle such that he or she cannot see who will be singing. Everyone sings the first verse. One child will answer back with, "I am tapping at the window. I am knocking at the door." The child in the middle now needs to guess who was singing.

Analysis Definitions

Name of song. Write the title of your song for inclusion in your database. It is usually best not to include beginning articles such as "The" or "A" when you are entering this into your alphabetical listing or retrieval system.

> *Origin.* This category is for listing the ethnic origin of the song, geographic location, or any historical connections; for example, "Hispanic folk song," "Jamaican folk song," "Civil War Era," etc.
>
> *CSP (comfortable starting pitch).* Some song collections are written so that all songs in the collection end on G. Ethnomusicologists adopt this approach to notating songs so that it is easier to compare variations of the same song. In this case, it is necessary to indicate the CSP to pitch the song in the best singing range for your children. If the song is written in a comfortable range for them, you do not need to indicate the CSP.
>
> *Staff notation.* Write the song in staff notation. In most cases, it is preferable to write the song phrase by phrase as this allows you to see the structural similarities.
>
> *Stick notation.* Write the song in stick notation (traditional rhythmic notation without note heads). For analysis purposes, it is sometimes easier to analyze songs written in stick notation. It especially helps clearly define motifs in solfège. Again, it is preferable to write the stick notation phrase by phrase.
>
> *MM (metronome marking).* Indicate an appropriate metronome marking for performing the piece of music.

Analysis and Pedagogical Use

You will notice that at the end of the analysis sheet for each song there are two sections: Analysis and Pedagogical Use. These categories appear on the analysis side:

Tone set. This is sometimes referred to as pitch class set or scale. We use relative solfège syllables to indicate the notes of the tone set. Tone sets are written in ascending order. Write solfège syllables in lower case and italicized. When identifying notes below d use a subscript mark ($d,$) and mark notes above t with a superscript (d'). Underline or circle the final note to indicate the tonic of the song.

Rhythm. This section is for listing the specific note values and rests (such as quarter notes, half notes, etc.) from the smallest to largest note value. You may also include the meter of the song as well as whether the song has upbeats. Rhythmic motifs used for echo clapping (usually found in four beat patterns) may also be included in this category.

Melodic form. Indicate the form of phrases using capital letters. When a phrase is four beats in length, use capital letters. For phrases or motifs that are less than four beats, use lowercase letters. Variants of phrases may be indicated with a subscript "v," for example, A, Av. Melodic patterns that can be used for greetings or improvisation activities can also be included here.

Game. Describe the type of game (circle, double circle, partner, double line, follow the leader, etc.). You might also describe the category of song such as a holiday song or work song.

Other. This will allow you to note anything interesting about the song. For example, does the song have a sequence or repeated phrase where a repeat sign might be used? You might have to explain a word or term, such as "petticoat."

Pedagogical Analysis

Rationale. This is where we indicate the pedagogical purpose for using the song. A song can be used for many reasons, including singing, teaching a game, performing on an instrument, as the basis of an improvisation exercise, for noting a specific form, listening, or teaching a rhythmic or melodic element.

Other. Indicate whether the song is appropriate for movement or improvisation, form, etc. Sometimes you might want to list a listening example that could be connected to this folk song. You may wish to note any melodic and rhythmic difficulties children could encounter in learning the song.

Source. Source refers to the resource where the song was found. Generally speaking, it is important to list whether the source is primary or secondary. It is also useful to include references to other variations of the folk song.

Connections to books. This category is useful for indicating connections between the song and a related book. As we introduce a musical pedagogy that links the teaching of music literacy and reading literacy, it becomes clear that the disciplines of music and reading share techniques that are mutually enhancing and complementary. One way we can connect the teaching of music literacy to reading literacy is to choose reading books that can be used for reinforcing music concepts and skills.

We also make a number of recommendations for choosing reading books to use in the music classroom. Select books:

- That follow a call-and-response structure
- That have repeated phrases
- Where the text can be accompanied by a beat
- Where children can clap the rhythm of the text easily
- Where children can say part of a repeated refrain
- Where the melodic patterns from other songs may be used to sing a text
- That illustrate a song
- That have clear pictures useful for text or song improvisation
- That have characters and animals for use with known song materials
- That are good for developing a sequence of events

In summary, teachers should look for children's books that can be incorporated into the music lesson. Reading specialists understand that the selection of quality literature allows children to develop their own literacy and creativity skills. For the music teacher, it is also important to identify reading books that are participatory by nature and encourage children to develop their music literacy and creativity skills. The music specialist should look for opportunities to skillfully reinforce music literacy skills with reading skills. Likewise, the reading specialist should be attuned to the possibilities of engaging children in reading books using some of the techniques employed by music teachers. Following the recommendations above allows for this interdisciplinary approach to teaching both literacy and music literacy skills.

What Are the Connections Between Music Literacy and Reading Literacy?

We believe that the approach to music literacy presented in this book is closely aligned to current methodologies for teaching literacy and can promote both music literacy and reading literacy skills in children. Music processing often uses "overlapping regions in the brain and shares processing components with language."[16] "Cognitive psychologists have found that music and language stem from common origins and are dominated by common processing tendencies."[17] There are now numerous research studies that support the connection between music literacy and reading literacy. Both Armstrong[18] and Strickland's[19] research identify several studies that call attention to the link between developing aural skills in music and developing word recognition.

Focus group discussions with experienced Early Childhood music teachers reveal that they believe there is a significant connection between teaching music literacy and reading literacy. More often than not, a child who has mastered some basic music skills, such as keeping a beat, pointing to icons, singing with correct phrasing, and breathing and understanding how to inflect one's voice, is also a good reader. This is to say that music can help the learning process in the classroom; the success a child has in a music curriculum with a clear literacy component is also often an indicator of how a child is performing in a reading class. Patricia Wolfe writes:

Contrary to the popular misconception that music is the property of the right hemisphere, new imaging techniques have shown that music is distributed across specialized regions in both hemispheres. In fact, many musical experiences can activate the cognitive, visual, auditory, affective, and motor systems, depending on whether you are reading music, playing an instrument, composing a song, beating a rhythm, or just listening to a melody. The mental mechanisms that process music are deeply entwined with the brain's other basic functions, including emotion, memory, and even language.[20]

Connections Between Singing and the Development of Literacy

The definition of *literacy* is an evolving phenomenon. Our use of the term in the title of previous methodology texts[21] we've written distinguishes our approach to music teaching as one that is based on education principles that cross many subject areas and disciplines (specifically, reading). Therefore for us "literacy" includes the ability to understand and use particular symbol systems. Because our primary focus is teaching the art of music, the understanding of music notation and its meaning is of significant interest. Literacy has no finite end point. There is no real end to the development of literacy because being literate includes the ability to understand the spoken word as well as decode the numerous symbol systems involved in reading as applied to any science or art in any community. Literacy is essential to critical thinking, communication, and ultimately collaboration and creativity. Here we cite several connections between singing and the development of literacy as points central to our convictions about the importance of literacy in a musical education.

Singing Helps Us Use Our Voices Expressively

Using the voice expressively is essential for successful reading. When children are taught how to sing correctly, they learn how to use their voices, as well as how to use dynamics to add expression and mood to their singing.

Singing Helps Us Make an Emotional Connection to a Book

When children sing about a character, they make emotional connections with the character in the song. When we link a singing activity to a character or object in a book, children make a greater emotional connection with the book and will want to listen and look at the book more often. For example, the teacher could sing a lullaby while showing the children the cover of book *Goodnight Moon*. Choose a song that helps children identify with the emotional content of a book, or help them connect with a character in a book. Here are some ideas as to how to make a connection between singing and reading.

> *Brown Bear, Brown Bear,* by Bill Martin and Eric Carle. In order for children to make a connection to the book *Brown Bear* we could ask them to sing the song "Here Comes a Bluebird" and play the accompanying game but substitute the words "Blue Bird" with "Brown Bear" to help them make a connection with the book. We could sing the song "We Are Dancing in the Forest" and change the word *wolf* to *bear.*
> "We Are Dancing in the Forest." Ask children to sing a song that captures how they feel about a book. For example, if they are happy about a book they could sing a happy song such as "Bounce High Bounce Low" or "See Saw."

We are Dancing in the Forest

32

Jump Frog Jump, by Byron Barton. The songs "Frog in the Meadow" and "Frog Went A-Courting" connect to the characters in *Jump, Frog Jump* by Byron Barton. We could change the words "Blue Bird" to "Blue Frog" to make a connection with a book and singing.

"Here Comes a Bluebird"

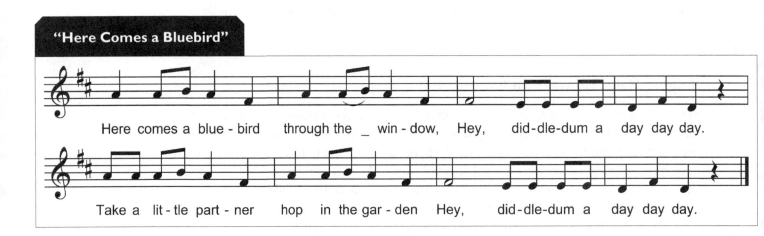

Going on a Bear Hunt, by Helen Oxenbury. Sing "Teddy Bear" and "Bear Went over the Mountain" to make a connection to the book. Sing "Let Us Chase the Squirrel" to "Let Us Chase the Bear" to make a connection with "Going on a Bear Hunt."

Let Us Chase the Squirrel

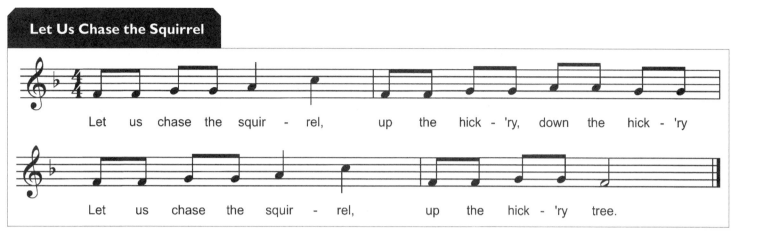

The Mitten, by Jan Brett. The children could sing "A Tisket, a Tasket" and change the words "I wrote a letter to my love" to "I knit a mitten for my love and on the way I dropped it."

33

A Tisket A Tasket

Singing Songs Helps Us Develop Coordination

Singing songs while playing games that use large motions helps children develop the necessary coordination required for reading.

Some children who have difficulty reading also have trouble physically crossing the midline of the body fluently. For example, some have a difficult time training their eyes to read from left to right. In music class, the music teacher teaches songs and motions that enable children to develop this skill. As they are playing games and using motions to represent beats, the instructor may simultaneously work on developing their fine motor skills.

With younger children, the teacher works on large motor skills to represent the beat kinesthetically. As children develop these skills, the teacher can begin to work on fine motor skills such as clapping the rhythm of the words with two fingers of the right hand on the left palm.

The movements or lyrics of a song may be adapted for any animal or character in a story. For example, in "Just from the Kitchen," we could substitute the words "hop over yonder" for a rabbit, or "trot over yonder" for a horse. We could ask how different characters could move. We could ask children to "leap over yonder" for the book *Jump, Frog, Jump!* by Byron Barton (ISBN 0874997887).

Singing Songs Develops Literacy Skills

Singing songs helps with alphabet awareness, concepts concerning print, vocabulary development, phonics, and decoding and encoding. Use a picture and write a letter or word underneath to help children memorize a song. For example, with "Down Came a Lady," children sing the song while the teacher shows a picture of Daniel's wife in a blue dress with the letter B or word *blue* written underneath. For each new song learned by the children, the teacher has a picture to represent the song with the name of the song printed underneath it.

Singing Songs with Correct Phrasing and Breathing Has an Impact on Reading

Children who can sing and phrase music correctly will have acquired an understanding of how to control their breathing. The melodic contour of songs mirrors the inflection of speech, especially in folk music. All of these skills are necessary for reading.

Singing Songs While Keeping a Beat Improves Reading

Children who have learned how to keep a steady beat in music are generally much better at reading as they are able to feel the beat in the text. Strengthening a child's ability to keep a beat facilitates emergent literacy skills. As the teacher reads "Crocodile Beat" by Gail Jorgensen, the children will be able to keep the beat as the text is being read. This helps them develop fluency with reading.

Singing a Song While Clapping a Rhythm for Four or More Beats Improves Reading

Children who have learned how to clap the rhythm of a chant or melody in music are generally much better at reading as they are able to feel the beat and the rhythm of the text. Therefore, strengthening a child's ability to clap rhythms facilitates emergent literacy skills, especially syllabic awareness. In music, it is important to move beyond clapping just one word to figure out the sounds. During the music lesson, children should clap the rhythm of four- and eight-beat phrases. The instructor may ask them to point to icons as they sing the phrase. This aids in their being able to identify the number of syllables in a word.[22]

The rhyme "Engine Engine #9" can be used to transition into "Quack and Count," by Keith Baker, as it uses the same rhythm as a narrative in the book.

Singing Develops Phonological Awareness

The authors of *Learning to Read and Write* say, "Phonological awareness refers to the whole spectrum, from primitive awareness of speech sounds and rhythms to rhyme awareness and sound similarities, and at the highest level, awareness of syllables of phonemes."[23] This, according to the authors of *Put Reading First*, is the "ability to hear, identify, and manipulate individual sounds-phonemes-in spoken words."[24] Through singing we can explore a variety of activities to help children become aware of different sounds:

- *Using vowel sounds such as "oo" for pitch exploration.* Learning to chant and singing songs enables children to become aware of word sounds.
- *Saying chants that rhyme.* Changing the consonant of a song, such as singing "Bingo" but changing the first consonant of each time the song is sung, for example, *Fingo* or *Dingo*.
- *Asking questions about a song.* This can help develop sound and syllable awareness. For example:

  Let's sing the song "Bounce High Bounce Low" and point to the icons on the board.
  What is the first word of this song?
  What is the first sound in this word?
  Are there other words in the song that begin with this sound?
  What word do we have when we remove the sound "b" from *ball*?
  What happens when I add an "s" to *ball*?

Singing Develops Auditory Analysis

We can ask children questions about the characters or events in a song. There are a variety of approaches to asking questions about the song. The easiest questions focus on the ability of children to simply find the answer to the question in the song. Eventually, the teacher might challenge the children to determine answers to questions using their own imagination and evidence from the song, as for example with "Lucy Locket."

- Who lost the pocket?
- Who found the pocket?
- What was in the pocket?
- What was around the pocket?
- Where do you think Lucy lost her pocket?
- Are Lucy and Kitty friends?

Using Music Symbolic Notation Helps Develop Associations Between Letters and What They Represent

Children can easily learn to associate pictures with words. The words *high* and *low* can be represented by a baby's voice and a grandfather's voice; and *fast* and *slow* can be represented by a train straining to go up the mountain and going quickly down the mountain.

The use of symbols helps young children understand that these pictures represent a way to perform something, just as we use letters to represent sounds.

Creating a Songbook Helps Develop Reading Skills

Select some of the children's favorite songs with illustrations for key words and put them in the classroom book center. You may also create an audio CD that they can listen to and sing as they follow the pictures illustrating a song. It could also be helpful to have a CD of an instrument playing the melody. For example:

Teddy Bear

Create a picture book for Teddy Bear. Each page should capture the Teddy Bear performing different motions:

Turning around
Touching the ground
Shining shoes
Touching toes

Write the text of the song under each picture. In this way children are encouraged to read the song book and point to the words and either say or sing them.

"Bought Me a Cat"

When singing the song show illustrations of each animal in the book with the name of the animal printed underneath each picture. These activities help with recognizing print, characters, plots, story comprehension, and sequencing.

Pointing to Beat Icons Develops Left-to-Right Coordination

Children in the Early Childhood class are always singing and keeping the beat. Sometimes we ask children to point to beat icons on a board while we sing a song. This helps children develop left-to-right hand-eye coordination, as they have to point to icons that represent four to eight beats in a musical phrase.

Developing Sequencing Skills in Song Repertoire Develops Reading Skills

Allow children to figure out the correct sequence of events in a song. For example, when playing "The Farmer in the Dell," show a picture with a letter or word underneath. Mix them up and ask children to identify the order of the characters and animals in the song.

Developing Improvisation Skills Helps Develop Reading Skills

We can use a simple known melody that uses two or three pitches, such as "Snail, Snail," and improvise a new text that is based on a book. The teacher may record this text for the children. For example instead of "Snail, Snail" we can substitute other words such as *moon, hare, bear,* etc.

Making Connections Between Songs and Books

There are several ways to make a connection between a song and book. Throughout this book we will be giving you the titles of books as well as songs connected to these books that can be used for developing performance and music skills. Here are some ideas as to how we can use children's songs to connect to books.

Book Cover

Sometimes the cover of a book makes a connection to song repertoire. For example, if there is a picture of a moon or stars on the cover children can sing "Star Light, Star Bright."

Storyline or Plot

An event in a book might be used to connect to song material. When events take place in a forest or on a farm or in a town, they can be linked to the storyline or plot in a book.

Movement Activity

A movement activity in a song may connect to a movement in a book. For instance, if the text is about bees, children can flap their wings and chant "Bee, Bee, Bumble Bee." Or the words of "Here Comes a Bluebird" may be changed to accommodate characters in a book and the children can create a motion to go with the new text.

Word or Sound Associations

Children can create sound or word associations for different characters. For example, the children can create a "ssss" sound for a snake and you can sing the song "Black Snake" and read a children's book featuring a snake.

Emotional Connection

You can guide children to sing songs to characters in a book. If a character is sleepy, children can sing a lullaby. In Chapter 3 we list book suggestions useful for developing singing skills.

Form of a Book

Sometimes a book is written in a call-and-response style. You may chant the call and the children chant the response. Or you may also improvise a melody to accompany the call and the chant. In Chapter 6 we provide a list of books connected to the teaching of form.

Soundscapes

Children may be guided to create their own soundscapes to accompany the reading of a book. For example, the appearance of various characters can be accompanied by different percussion instruments.

Using Music Concepts to Make Connections

Throughout this book we will be showing you how to teach a variety of music concepts to children. These concepts include loud-soft, beat, high-low, fast-slow, and rhythm. Although children might understand these words outside a musical context, these words take on another meaning in the music class. For example, children will understand the concepts of loud and soft only if they can:

- Sing a song in a loud or soft voice and keep the beat
- Identify a teacher or another child who is singing with a loud or soft voice
- Represent loud or soft by creating a picture
- Sing and point to beat bars using a loud or soft voice

We can return many times to a book to either prepare or reinforce a concept. Children might like to sing greetings to characters in a book using their daytime or nighttime voice. Later in the year, after children have been introduced to the words *loud* and *soft*, you can return to a familiar book and ask them to sing greetings using their loud or soft voice. In Chapter 5 we present a list of books connected to the musical readiness concepts to be taught in the Early Childhood classroom.

Improvisation

The teacher and children can use a picture in a book to create improvisations based on the text. The teacher might ask the children what they see, and they must answer by singing whatever they see. Likewise they could create a melody for the entire book based on known melodic patterns used in the greeting part of the lessons. In Chapter 6 we list books and songs suitable for encouraging and developing this type of musical improvisation.

Connections to Literature

We suggest the following books to Early Childhood instructors. The texts and themes presented in these books all focus on topics presented in this chapter.

Song Incorporated into a Book

Adams, Pam. *This Old Man*. New York: Child's Play International, 1989.
Bryan, Ashley. *All Night, All Day: A Child's First Book of African-American Spirituals*. New York: Aladdin Paperbacks, 1991.
Campbell, Ross. *The ABRSM Song Book*. Kettering, UK: ABRSM, 2008.
Christelow, Eileen. *Five Little Monkeys Jumping on the Bed*. London: Sandpiper, 2006.
Frazee, Marla. *Hush Little Baby*. San Francisco: Chronicle Books, 1997.
Hoberman, Mary Ann. *Miss Mary Mack*. New York: Little, Brown, 1998.
Saport, Linda. *All the Pretty Little Horses*. New York: Clarion Books, 1999.

Trapani, Iza. *The Bear Went over the Mountain*. New York: Sky Pony Press, 2012.

Trapani, Iza. *Row, Row, Row Your Boat*. Watertown, MA: Charlesbridge, 1999.

Song Related to a Character or a Plot in a Book

Adams, Pam. *This Old Man*. New York: Child's Play International, 1989.

Brett, Jan. *Honey . . . Honey . . . Lion!* New York: Penguin Putnam, 2005.

Brown, Margaret Wise. *The Train to Timbuctoo*. Racine, WI: Golden Books, 1979.

Cannon, Janell. *Stellaluna*. New York: Scholastic, 1993.

Carle, Eric. *The Very Busy Spider*. New York: Philomel Books, 1984.

Carle, Eric. *The Very Lonely Firefly*. New York: Philomel Books, 1995.

Carle, Eric. *Mister Seahorse*. New York: Philomel Books, 2004.

Child, Lauren. *I Am Too Absolutely Small for School*. Somerville, MA: Candlewick Press, 2003.

Feierabend, John M. *The Frog and the Mouse*. Chicago: GIA, 2011.

Galdone, Paul. *Over in the Meadow*. New York: Aladdin Paperbacks, 1986.

Hoberman, Mary Ann. *Miss Mary Mack*. New York: Little, Brown, 1998.

Langstaff, John. *Frog Went A-Courtin'*. San Diego, CA: Voyager Books, 1972.

Langstaff, John. *Oh, A-Hunting We Will Go*. New York: Aladdin Paperbacks, 1974.

Lester, Helen. *Tacky the Penguin*. London: Sandpiper, 2006.

Locker, Thomas. *Cloud Dance*. San Diego, CA: Voyager Books, 2000.

McBratney, Sam. *Guess How Much I Love You*. New York: Walker Children's Hardbacks, 2009.

Miranda, Anne. *To Market, To Market*. New York: Harcourt Brace, 1997.

Raffi, and Sylvie Wickstrom. *The Wheels on the Bus*. St. Louis: Turtleback Books, 1990.

Taback, Simms. *There Was an Old Lady*. Swindon, UK: Childs Play International, 2007.

Westcott, Nadine Bernard. *The Lady with the Alligator Purse*. New York: Little, Brown, 1998.

Zelinsky, Paul. *The Wheels on the Bus*. New York: Dutton Juvenile, 1990.

Improvisation

The text of the suggested books can be set to an original melody (for example, a child's chant).

Carle, Eric. *From Head to Toe*. New York: HarperFestival, 1997.

Frazee, Marla. *Hush Little Baby*. San Francisco: Chronicle Books, 1997.

Martin, Bill, Jr. *The Maestro Plays*. San Diego, CA: Voyager Books, 1996.

Martin, Bill, Jr. *Chicka Chicka Boom Boom*. San Diego, CA: Beach Lane Books, 2009.

Setting a refrain in a text to music (refrain can be set to an original melody, for example, a child's chant).

Adams, Pam. *This Old Man*. New York: Child's Play International, 1989.

Calmenson, Stephanie. *Engine, Engine, Number Nine*. New York: Scholastic, 1996.

Carle, Eric. *The Very Busy Spider*. New York: Philomel Books, 1984.

Carle, Eric. *From Head to Toe*. New York: Harper Festival, 1997.

Dr. Seuss. *Mr. Brown Can Moo! Can You?* New York: Random House Books for Young Readers, 1996.

39

Gollub, Matthew. *Gobble, Quack, Moon* (1st ed.). Santa Rosa, CA: Tortuga Press, 2002.
Kalan, Robert. *Jump, Frog, Jump!* Logan, IA: Perfection Learning, 2010.
Litwin, Eric. *Pete the Cat Rocking in My School Shoes.* New York: HarperCollins, 2011.
McDonald, Megan. *Is This a House for Hermit Crab?* London: Orchard Books, 1993.
Piper, Watty. *The Little Engine That Could.* New York: Philomel Books, 2005.

Improvisation

Brown, Ruth. *Snail Trail.* New York: Crown, 2000.
Carle, Eric. *From Head to Toe.* New York: HarperFestival, 1997.
Child, Lauren. *I Am Too Absolutely Small for School.* Somerville, MA: Candlewick Press, 2003.
Crews, Donald. *Parade.* New York: Greenwillow Books, 1986.
Dr. Seuss. *Mr. Brown Can Moo! Can You?* New York: Random House Books for Young Readers, 1996.
Eric, Carle. *Today Is Monday.* London: Puffin, 1993.
Fleming, Denise. *Beetle Bop.* New York: Harcourt, 2007.
Martin, Bill, Jr. *Brown Bear, Brown Bear, What Do You See?* New York: Holt, 2004.
Rollings, Susan. *New Shoes, Red Shoes.* New York: Orchard Books, 2000.
Williams, Linda. *The Little Old Lady Who Was Not Afraid of Anything.* New York: HarperCollins, 1986.

Lullabies

Brown, Margaret Wise. *Goodnight Moon.* New York: Scholastic, 1947.
Cannon, Janell. *Stellaluna.* New York: Scholastic, 1993.
Frazee, Marla. *Hush Little Baby.* San Francisco: Chronicle Books, 1997.
Saport, Linda. *All the Pretty Little Horses.* New York: Clarion Books, 1999.

Books Related to American Folk Songs

Campbell, Ross. *The ABRSM Song Book.* Kettering, UK: ABRSM, 2008.
Longstaff, John. *Frog Went A-Courtin'.* San Diego, CA: Voyager Books, 1972.
Owen, Ann. *She'll Be Coming Around the Mountain.* New York: Greenwillow Books, 2003.
Frazee, Marla. *Hush Little Baby.* San Francisco: Chronicle Books, 1997.

Developing a Lesson Plan Framework Based on Quality Musical Repertoire

Considering the information presented in this chapter, we find these points worth reflecting on for inclusion in our lesson plan.

- The selection of song materials that are age-appropriate for singing
- The selection of song materials that can be used for music literacy development
- The selection of movement and game activities that are age-appropriate
- The selection of appropriate song materials for listening

We have provided a selection of appropriate song materials in the appendix to this chapter.

Using a Generic Lesson Plan Format to Design a Music Lesson

Lesson Planning

At the end of each chapter of this book, we supply information for developing specific lesson plans for teaching Early Childhood music. In this chapter, our goal is to present a generic lesson plan format. Throughout, we will modify this basic design to incorporate and reflect knowledge acquired from each chapter. What follows is an explanation of a generic lesson plan for preparing and practicing a musical concept. This is the modified version of the lesson plans provided earlier in the chapter.

Table 1.8

Outcome	
INTRODUCTORY ACTIVITIES	
Sing known songs	In this portion of the lesson, we develop beautiful singing through singing known songs, as well as performing warm-up exercises and breathing exercises.
Develop tuneful singing	One of the goals of the introduction of the lesson is for C to sing a known song, and then move to tuneful singing activities that develop their singing voices. This can be accomplished by singing simple greetings that you improvise.
CORE ACTIVITIES	
Teach a new song	Instructors present new repertoire to C for a variety of reasons. Some songs are taught to develop singing ability; sometimes a song may be taught because we need to provide a musical context for teaching future musical concepts. A new song may be linked by using the same key, rhythmic or melodic motives, same meter, same character, or simply the same tempo.
Preparation of new concept	The goal in this section of the lesson is for C to sing and move in a way that will illustrate the new concept. For instance, if we are teaching the concept of fast and slow, C sing familiar songs or rhymes with a fast tempo or slow tempo.
Singing game/ creative movement	In this section of the lesson, you develop C's movement skills on the basis of game activities associated with song material. A sequence for age-appropriate movement skill development is provided in Chapter 3.
Practice of known concept	This is the section of the lesson that reinforces knowledge of musical concepts and focuses on a particular music skill such as reading, writing, or improvisation/composition.
SUMMARY ACTIVITIES	
Review the new song Review lesson outcomes Folk song tales sung by T	Here you review the new song, review the goals of the lesson with the C through a song activity, and perform a song as a listening activity for the children.

41

Explanation of a Generic Lesson Plan
Format to Design a Music Literature Lesson

Table 1.9 is a sample lesson plan that may be used for a music literature lesson. The primary goal of the lesson is to use singing to reinforce reading. Where possible, focus on the music elements, and try to emphasize the sequencing story events as well as recalling story events, characters, and plots in the book.

Table 1.9

Outcomes	
INTRODUCTORY ACTIVITIES	
Sing a greeting	In this portion of the lesson, we develop beautiful singing through singing known songs as well as warm-up exercises and breathing exercises. Begin the class by singing a greeting based on a motif from a known song. At the beginning of the school year, the notes of a child's chant (when C sing the phrase "You can't catch me," they use the notes of a child's chant) should be used in the greeting. Later, you may extend the range of notes to include melodic turns from songs used in the class. You may sing the greeting to the children; they may answer your greeting pretending to be one of the characters in a book.
Sing known songs	Have C sing to the characters of the book. Point to the character in the book and pretend they are the character; sing a greeting to C. You may use different voices.
CORE ACTIVITIES	
Read the book	Read a book to C. Sometimes you can choose books based on songs that children have learned. The goal is for you to read and, if appropriate, C can keep the beat as you read.
Singing game/ creative movement	In this section of the lesson, you develop C's movement skills on the basis of game activities associated with the book.
Connect the book to known repertoire and/or concepts	This is the section of the lesson that reinforces knowledge of the book and the practice of musical concepts and skill areas. Connect the book with music familiar to the C by choosing songs that link to characters, events, or places in the book. Depending on C's knowledge of music concepts, try to reinforce music concepts while making connections to the book.
CLOSING ACTIVITIES	
Sing good-bye to characters in the book Folk song, sung by T, connected to the book	Here you sing a goodbye song to the C. To develop a child's imagination, you could pretend to be one of the characters of the book. As you close the book the C can sing a good-bye to characters in the book. The lesson ends with your singing a folksong tale to the children that is tied to the theme, character, or plot of the book.

Discussion Questions

1. How is an alphabetized repertoire list useful for teaching?
2. What kinds of repertoire should be included in an alphabetized repertoire list?
3. What criteria do we use for selecting repertoire for the Early Childhood classroom?
4. Talk to reading specialists or Early Childhood teachers and ask them to explain how they select books to read to their children. Make a list of all of their suggestions and draw a parallel between selecting books for use in the classroom and selecting musical repertoire.
5. How important is it to think about the quality of the song material you use when teaching?
6. Are there appropriate songs from your own heritage or culture that might enhance the music-learning environment?
7. What opportunities are available to you as a teacher to include more diverse styles of music in the classroom?
8. How can you as a music teacher create partnerships with the school community and community at large?

Ongoing Assignments

1. Talk to reading specialists or Early Childhood or preschool teachers and ask them to share with you some of their favorite books. Make a list of all of their suggestions and try to draw a parallel between selecting books for use in the classroom and repertoire.
2. What kind of activities can you do in the music class that will reinforce emergent literacy skills?
3. Songs and games should be selected because they are fun. Discuss.
4. There are many commercial recordings of children's songs available for use in the Early Childhood classroom. Children enjoy listening to these songs and moving to them. Discuss.
5. Teaching emergent literacy skills should not be part of the job description of the music teacher. Discuss.
6. What criteria would you use for selecting books for inclusion in a class?
7. Go to one of your own family members and see if there's any song from your own heritage that might be used in the classroom.
8. How can we be more thoughtful about the kinds of repertoire and activities we use while working in multicultural contexts?
9. Should we use popular culture content in the music classroom?
10. Your principal has just announced that the music program for the Early Childhood class might be cut next year. You are invited to appear before the school board to make a case for its continued inclusion in the curriculum.

11. Identify several books that you might use in the Early Childhood classroom.
12. Review the repertoire list and find some songs that you could sing to children while using the pictures in the book.

Bibliography

Note: some of these references are out of print; we are including them because of their significance.

Anderson, William M., and Patricia Shehan Campbell, eds. *Multicultural Perspectives in Music Education.* Reston, VA: Music Educators National Conference, 1996.

Anvari, S. H., L. J. Trainor, J. Woodside, and B. A. Levy. "Relations Among Musical Skills, Phonological Processing, and Early Reading Ability in Preschool Children." *Journal of Experimental Child Psychology,* 2002, 83(3), 111–130.

Armbruster, Bonnie B., Fran Lehr, and Jean Osborn. *Put Reading First: The Research Building Blocks for Teaching Children to Read.* Jessup, MD: National Institute for Literacy, 2003.

Armstrong, Thomas. *The Multiple Intelligences of Reading and Writing: Making the Words Come Alive.* Alexandria, VA: Association for Supervision and Curriculum Development, 2003.

Barrett, Margaret S. "Commentary: Music Learning and Teaching in Infancy and Early Childhood." In *The Oxford Handbook of Music Education*, vol. 1, ed. Gary E. McPherson and Graham F. Welch (chap. 2.1). New York: Oxford University Press, 2012.

Barrett, Margaret, and Johannella Tafuri. Creative Meaning-Making in Infants and Young Children's Musical Cultures. In *The Oxford Handbook of Music Education*, vol. 1, ed. Gary E. McPherson and Graham F. Welch (pp. 296–313). New York: Oxford University Press, 2012.

Bishop, J. C., and Curtis, M. *Play Today on the Primary School Playground: Life, Learning and Creativity.* Buckingham: Open University Press, 2001.

Bonis, F. (ed.). *The Selected Writings of Zoltán Kodály.* Trans. L. Halapy and F. Macnicol. London: Boosey & Hawkes, 1974.

Bredekamp, S. *Developmentally Appropriate Practice in Early Childhood Programs Serving Children Birth to Age 8* (expanded ed.). Washington, DC: National Association for the Education of Young Children, 1987.

Campbell, P. S. "The Child-song Genre: A Comparison of Songs by and for Children." *International Journal of Music Education,* 1991, 17(1), 14–23.

Campbell, P. S. *Lessons from the World: A Cross-cultural Guide to Music Teaching and Learning.* New York: Schirmer, 1991.

Campbell, P. S. *Teaching Music Globally: Experiencing Music, Expressing Culture.* Oxford: Oxford University Press, 2004. http://www.smithsonianglobalsound.org.

Campbell, P. S., J. Drummond, P. Dunbar-Hall, K. Howard, H. Schippers, and T. Wiggins (eds.). *Cultural Diversity in Music Education: Directions and Challenges for the 21st century.* Brisbane: Australian Academic Press, 2005.

Campbell, Patricia Shehan, and Trevor Wiggins (eds.). *The Oxford Handbook of Children's Musical Cultures.* New York: Oxford University Press, 2013.

Campbell, Patricia Shehan, Sue Williamson, and Pierre Perron. *Traditional Songs of Singing Cultures: A World Sampler.* Miami: Warner Bros. Publications, 1996.

Chen-Hafteck, L. "Music and Language Development in Early Childhood: Integrating Past Research in the Two Domains." *Early Child Development and Care,* 1997, 130, 85–97.

Chen-Hafteck, Lily, and Esther Mang. "Music and Language in Early Childhood Development and Learning." In *The Oxford Handbook of Music Education*, vol. 1, ed. Gary E. McPherson and Graham F. Welch (chap. 2.4). New York: Oxford University Press, 2012.

Choksy, Lois, and David Brummitt. *120 Singing Games and Dances for Elementary Schools.* Englewood Cliffs, NJ: Prentice-Hall, 1987.

Douglas, S., and P. Willatts. The relationship between musical ability and literacy skills. *Journal of Research in Reading,* 1994, 17(2), 99–107.

Dowling, W. J. "Tonal Structure and Children's Early Learning of Music." In *Generative Processes in Music*, ed. K. Sloboda (pp. 113–128). Oxford: Oxford University Press, 1998.

Elliott, David J. *Praxial Music Education: Reflections and Dialogues.* New York: Oxford University Press, 2005.

Gaunt, K. D. *The Games Black Girls Play: Learning the Ropes from Double-dutch to Hip-hop.* New York: New York University Press, 2006.

Hargreaves, D. J., C. North, and M. Tarrant. "Musical Preference and Taste in Childhood and Adolescence." In *The Child as Musician: Musical Development from Conception to Adolescence*, ed. G. E. McPherson (pp. 135–154). Oxford: Oxford University Press, 2006.

Harwook, Eve, and Kathryn Marsh. "Children's Ways of Learning Inside and Outside the Classroom." In *The Oxford Handbook of Music Education*, vol. 1, ed. Gary E. McPherson and Graham F. Welch (chap. 3.2). New York: Oxford University Press, 2012.

Houlahan, Micheál, and Philip Tacka. *Kodály Today: A Cognitive Approach to Elementary Music Education.* New York: Oxford University Press, 2008.

Houlahan, Micheál, and Philip Tacka. *Sound Thinking: Developing Musical Literacy*, vols. 1 and 2. New York: Boosey & Hawkes, 1995.

Jeanneret, Neryl, and George M. Degraffenreid. "Music Education in the Generalist Classroom." In *The Oxford Handbook of Music Education*, vol. 1, ed. Gary E. McPherson and Graham F. Welch (chap. 3.6). New York: Oxford University Press, 2012.

Jentschke, S., S. Koelsch, and A. D. Friederici. "Investigating the Relationship of Music and Language in Children: Influences of Musical Training and Language Impairment." *Annals of the New York Academy of Sciences,* 2005, 1060, 231–242.

Jones, P. M. "Music Education for Society's Sake: Music Education in an Era of Global Neo-imperial/neo-medieval Market-driven Paradigms and Structures." *Action, Criticism, and Theory for Music Education,* 2007, 6(1), 2–28.

Kodály, Zoltán. *Bulletin of the International Kodály Society,* 1985, no. 2, 18.

Kodály, Zoltán. "Children's Choirs." In *The Selected Writings of Zoltán Kodály*, ed. F. Bonis, trans. L. Halapy and F. Macnicol. London: Boosey & Hawkes, 1974.

Kodály, Zoltán. "Children's Games." In *The Selected Writings of Zoltán Kodály*, ed. F. Bonis, trans. L. Halapy and F. Macnicol, pp. 46–47. London: Boosey & Hawkes, 1974.

Kodály, Zoltán. "The Role of Authentic Folksongs in Music Education." *Bulletin of the International Kodály Society,* 1985, no. 1, 18.

Lamont, A., D. J. Hargreaves, N. A. Marshall, and M. Tarrant. "Young People's Music in and out of School." *British Journal of Music Education,* 2003, 20(3), 229–241.

Marsh, K. *The Musical Playground: Global Tradition and Change in Children's Songs and Games.* New York: Oxford University Press, 2008.

McLucas, A. Dhu. *The Musical Ear: Oral Tradition in the USA*. Farnham, Durrey, UK: Ashgate, 2010.

McPherson, Gary E., and Graham F. Welch (eds.). *The Oxford Handbook of Music Education*. New York: Oxford University Press, 2012.

Nettl, Bruno. *Folk and Traditional Music of the Western Continents* (2nd ed.). Englewood Cliffs, NJ: Prentice Hall, 1991.

Nettl, Bruno. "Foreword." In Patricia Shehan Campbell, *Songs in Their Heads: Music and Its Meaning in Children's Lives*. New York: Oxford University Press, 1998.

Nettl, Bruno, Charles Capwell, Philip V. Bohlman, Isabel K. F. Wong, and Thomas Turino. *Excursions in World Music* (3rd ed.). Englewood Cliffs, NJ: Prentice Hall, 2000.

Neuman, Susan B., Carol Copple, and Sue Bredekamp. *Learning to Read and Write: Developmentally Appropriate Practices for Young Children*. Washington, DC: National Association for the Education of Young Children, 2000.

Parsons, M. "Art and Integrated Curriculum." In *Handbook of Research and Policy in Art Education*, ed. E. W. Eisner and M. D. Day (pp. 775–794). Mahwah, NJ: National Art Education Association, 2004.

Rice, T. "Traditional and Modern Methods of Learning and Teaching Music in Bulgaria." *Research Studies in Music Education*, 1996, 7(1), 1–12.

Riddell, C. *Traditional Singing Games of Elementary School Children in Los Angeles*. Unpublished doctoral dissertation, University of California, Los Angeles, 1990.

Roberts, D., and P. Christenson. "Popular Music in Childhood and Adolescence." In *Handbook of Children and Media*, ed. D. Singer and J. Singer (pp. 395–413). Thousand Oaks, CA: Sage Publications, 2001.

Schippers, H. *Facing the Music: Shaping Music Education from a Global Perspective*. New York: Oxford University Press, 2010.

Schön, D., M. Boyer, S. Moreno, M. Besson, I. Penetz, and R. Kolinsky. "Songs as an Aid for Language Acquisition." *Cognition,* 2008, 106(2), 975–983.

Seeger, A. "Catching up with the Rest of the World: Music Education and Musical Experience." In *World Musics and Music Education: Facing the Issues*, ed. B. Reimer (pp. 103–116). Reston, VA: MENC, 2002.

Seeman, E. "*Implementation of Music Activities to Increase Language Skills in the At-risk Early Childhood Population*. Unpublished M.A. thesis, Saint Xavier University, Chicago, 2008.

Strickland, Susan and K. G. Burriss. "Review and Research: Music and the Brain in Childhood Development." *Childhood Education: Infancy Through Early Adolescence,* 2001–02, 78(2), 100–103.

Trehub, S. E., and L. J. Trainor. "Singing to Infants: Lullabies and Play Songs." *Advances in Infancy Research* 1998, 12, 43–77.

Trehub, S. E., L. J. Trainor, and A. M. Unyk. "Music and Speech Processing in the First Year of Life." *Advances in Child Development and Behavior,* 1993, 24, 1–35.

Trevarthen, Colwyn, and Stephen Malloch. "Musicality and Musical Culture: Sharing Narratives of Sound from Early Childhood." In *The Oxford Handbook of Music Education*, vol. 1, ed. Gary E. McPherson and Graham F. Welch (pp. 248–260). New York: Oxford University Press, 2012.

Tsang, C., and N. J. Conrad. "Does the Message Matter? The Effect of Song Type on Infants' Pitch Preference for Lullabies and Playsongs." *Infant Behavior and Development*, 2010, 33, 96–100.

Turner, M. E. "A Child Centered Music Room." *Early Childhood Connections*, vol. 6, 2000, no. 2, 30–34.

Wolfe, Patricia. *Brain Matters: Translating Research into Classroom Practice.* Alexandria, VA: Association for Supervision and Curriculum Development, 2001.

Wong, P.C.M., E. Skoe, N. M. Russo, T. Dees, and N. Kraus. "Musical Experience Shapes Human Brainstem Encoding of Linguistic Pitch Patterns." *Natural Neuroscience*, 2007, 10, 420–422.

Young, Susan, and Beatriz Ilari. "Musical Participation from Birth to Three: Toward a Global Perspective." In *The Oxford Handbook of Music Education*, vol. 1, ed. Gary E. McPherson and Graham F. Welch (chap. 2.5). New York: Oxford University Press, 2012.

Catalogues for Music Repertoire

The Whole Folkways Catalog (a catalog of historic folkways recordings). Smithsonian/ Folkways, Center for Folk Life Programs and Cultural Studies, 955 L'Enfant Plaza, Suite 2600, Smithsonian Institution, Washington, DC 20560; phone (202) 287–3262.

World Music Press (a catalog of world music resources). West Music, 1208 Fifth Street, P.O. Box 5521, Coralville, IA 52241.

Internet resource: http://kodaly.hnu.edu/; see the American Folk Song Collection.

Selected Folk Music Bibliography

Abrahams, Roger, Almda Riddle, and George Foss. *A Singer and Her Songs: Almeda Riddle's Book of Ballads.* Baton Rouge: Louisiana State University Press, 1970.

Ames, L. D. "Missouri Play Party." *Journal of American Folklore*, 1911, vol. 24 No 93, p. 295–318.

Armitage, Theresa. *Our First Music.* Boston: C. Birchard and Co., 1941.

Arnold, Byron. *Folksongs of Alabama.* Birmingham: University of Alabama Press, 1950.

Asch, Moses. *104 Folk Songs.* New York: Robbins Music, 1964.

Baez, Joan and Elie Siegmeister. *The Joan Baez Songbook.* New York: Ryerson Music, 1964.

Beckwith, Martha W. *Folk Songs of Jamaica.* Poughkeepsie, NY: Folklore Publications, Vassar College, 1922.

Bierhorst, John. *A Cry from the Earth: Music of the North American Indians.* New York: Four Winds Press, 1979.

Bierhorst. John. *Songs of the Chippewa.* New York: Farrar, Strauss & Giroux, 1974.

Botkin, Benjamin A. *The American Play Party.* New York: Frederick Ungar, 1963. 1st ed. University of Nebraska Press, 1937.

Botsford, Florence H. *Songs of the Americas.* New York: G. Schirmer, 1930.

Boyer, Walter E., et al. *Songs along the Mahatongo*: Pennsylvania Dutch Folk-Songs. Hatbow: Pennsylvania Folklore Associates, 1951.

Broadwood, Lucy E. *English County Songs.* London: Boosey and Company, 1893.

Bronson, B. H. *The Singing Tradition of Child's Popular Ballads.* Princeton, NJ: Princeton University Press, 1976.

Brown, Florence W., Neva L. Boyd, and G. Shoemaker. *Old English and American Games for School and Playground.* Chicago: Saul Brothers, 1915.

Brown, Frank C. *Collection of North American Folklore.* Durham, NC: Duke University Press, 1962.

Brown, Frank C. The Frank C. Brown Collection of *North Carolina Folklore.* Duke University Press: Durham, 1952.

Burlin, Natalie C. *Negro Folk-Songs.* New York: G. Schirmer, 1918.

Burton, Thomas G., Ambrose N. Manning, and Annette Wolford. *East Tennessee State University Collection of Folklore: Folksongs.* Institute of Regional Studies, monograph no. 4. Johnson: East Tennessee State University Press, 1967.

Chappell, Louis W. *Folk-Songs of Roanoke and the Albernarle*. Morgantown, WV: Ballad Press, 1939.

Chase, Richard, and Joshua Tolford. *American Folk Tales and Songs*, and Other Examples of English-American Tradition as Preserved in The Appalachian Mountains and Elsewhere in The United States. New York; Dover, 1971.

Choksy, Lois, and Zoltán Kodály. *The Kodály Context*: Creating an Environment of Musical Learning. Englewood Cliffs, NJ: Prentice Hall, 1981.

Choksy, Lois, and David Brummitt. *120 Singing Games and Dances for Elementary Schools*. Englewood Cliffs, NJ: Prentice Hall, 1987.

Colcord, Joanna. *Roll and Go: Songs of American Sailormen*. Indianapolis: Bobbs-Merrill, 1924.

Colcord, Joanna and Lincoln Colcord. *Songs of American Sailormen*. New York: Oak Publications, 1964.

Coleman, Satis N. *Songs of American Folks*. New York: John Day Co., 1942.

Courlander, Harold. *Negro Folk Music U.S.A.* New York: Columbia University Press, 1963.

Courlander, Harold. *Negro Songs from Alabama*. New York: Oak Publications, 1963.

Cox, John Harrington. *Traditional Ballads, Mainly from West Virginia*. New York: National Service Bureau, 1939.

Creighton, Helen. *Songs and Ballads from Nova Scotia*. New York: Dover, 1972.

Dallin, Leon, and Lynn Dallin. *Heritage Songster: 320 Folk and Familiar Songs*. Dubuque, IA: W. C. Brown, 1966.

Dykema, Peter. *Twice 55 Games with Music: The Red Book*. Boston: Birchard & Company, 1924.

Eddy, Mary O. *Ballads and Songs from Ohio*. Hatboro, PA: Folklore Associates, 1964.

Elder, J. D. *Song Games from Trinidad and Tobago*. [n.p.] Publication of the American Folklore Society, 1965.

Erdei, Peter, and Katalin Komlos. *150 American Folk Songs to Sing, Read, and Play*. New York: Boosey & Hawkes, 1974.

Farnsworth, Charles J., and Cecil F. Sharp. *Folk-Songs, Chanteys and Singing Games*. New York: H. W. Gray, 1909.

Fenner, T. P. *Religious Folk Songs of the Negro*. Hampton, VA: Hampton Institute Press, 1909.

Fife, Austin E., and S. Alta. *Cowboy and Western Songs*. New York: Clarkson N. Potter, 1969.

Fife, Austin E., and S. Alta *The Songs of the Cowboys*. (Thorp Collection). New York: Clarkson N. Potter, 1966.

Fowke, Edith. *Sally Go Round the Sun: Three Hundred Children's Songs, Rhymes and Games*. Garden City, NY: Doubleday, 1969.

Fowke, Edith, and Norman Cazden. *Lumbering Songs from the Northern Woods*. Austin: University of Texas Press, for American Folklore Society, 1970.

Fulton, Eleanor, and Pat Smith. *Let's Slice the Ice: Black Children's Ring Games and Chants*. St. Louis: John S. Swift, 1978.

Gillington, Alice E. *Old Surrey Singing Games and Skipping-Rope Rhymes*. London: J. Curwen & Sons, 1909.

Glass, Paul and Herman B. Vestal. *Songs and Stories of the North American Indians*. New York: Grosset and Dunlap, 1968.

Gomme, Alice B., and Winifred Smith. *Children's Singing Games*. London: Novello and Co., 1912.

Gomme, Alice B. *Traditional Games of England, Scotland, and Ireland*, 2 vols. New York: Dover, 1964. 1st ed. 1894–1898.

Gordon, Dorothy. *Sing It Yourself: Folk Songs of All Nations*. New York: Dutton, 1928.

Greenleaf, Elisabeth B., and Grace Yarrow Mansfield. *Ballads and Songs of Newfoundland*. Cambridge, MA: Harvard University Press, 1933.

Greig, Duncan. *The Greig-Duncan Folk Song Collection I.* Aberdeen, Scotland: Aberdeen University Press, 1981.

Hall, Doreen, and Arnold Walter. *Orff Schulwerk, Vol. I Pentatonic*. Mainz and London: B Schott Sohne, 1956.

Harlow, Frederick Pease. *Chanteying Aboard American Ships*. Barre, MA: Barre Gazette, 1962.

Hein, Mary Alice, and Lois Choksy. *The Singing Book: Second Level*. Cotati, CA: Renna/White Associates, 1983.

Henry, Millinger E. "Still More Ballads and Folk-Songs from the Southern Highlands." *Journal of American Folklore*, 1932, vol. 45.

High Road of Song: Then and Now, Music for Young Americans. Chicago: Scott Foresman, 1971.

Hofman, Charles. *American Indians Sing*. New York: John B. Day, 1967.

Hopekirk, Helen. *Seventy Scottish Folk Songs*. Boston: Oliver Ditson, 1905.

Hudson, Florence. *Songs of the Americas*. New York: G. Schirmer, 1922.

Hugill, Stan. *Shanties and Sailor's Songs*. New York: Praeger, 1969.

Ives, Burl. *The Burl Ives Song Book*. New York: Ballantine Books, 1953.

Jackson, Bruce. *Wake up, Dead Man: Afro-American Worksongs from Texas Prisons*. Cambridge, MA: Harvard University Press, 1972.

Jackson, George Pullen. *Spiritual Folksongs of Early America*. New York: Augustin, 1937.

Johnson, Guy B. *Folk Culture on St. Helena Island, South Carolina*. Hatboro, PA: Folklore Associates, 1968.

Johnson, James Weldon, and J. Rosamund. *The Books of Negro Spirituals*. New York: Viking Compass, 1969. 1st ed. Viking Press, 1925.

Jones, Bessie, and Bess Lomax Hawes. *Step it Down: Games, Plays, Songs, and Stories from the Afro-American Heritage*. New York: Harper and Row, 1972.

Karpeles, M. *Folk Songs from Newfoundland*. London: Faber and Faber, 1971.

Katz, Bernard. *The Social Implications of Early Negro Music in the US*. New York: Arno Press, 1963.

Kennedy, Robert E. *Black Cameos*. New York: Albert & C. Boni, 1924.

Kenney, Maureen. *Circle Round the Zero Play Chants and Singing Games of City Children*. St. Louis: Magnamusic-Baton, 1974.

Kersey, Robert E. *Just Five—A Collection of Pentatonic Songs*. Capitol Heights, MD: Westminster Press, 1970.

Kolb, Sylvia, and John Kolb. *A Treasury of Folk Songs*. New York: Bantam Books, 1948.

Korson, George. *Pennsylvania Songs and Legends*. Philadelphia: University of Pennsylvania Press, 1949.

Kwami, Robert Mawuena. *African Songs for School and Community: A Selection Form Ghana*. New York: Schott, 1998.

Landeck, Beatrice. *Songs to Grow On: A Collection of American Folk Songs for Children*. New York: Edward B. Marks Music, 1950.

Langstaff, John. *Hi-Ho the Rattlin' Bog, and Other Folk Songs for Group Singing*. New York: Harcourt, Brace and World, 1969.

49

Langstaff, John, P. Swanson, and G. Emlen. *Celebrate the Spring: Spring & Mayday Celebrations for Schools and Communities*. Watertown, MA: Revels, 1998.

Larkin, Margaret. *The Singing Cowboy*. New York: Knopf, 1931.

Leisy, James. *The Folk Song Abecedary*. New York: Bonanza, 1966.

Locke, Eleanor G. *Sail Away: 155 American Folk Songs to Sing, Read and Play*. New York: Boosey & Hawkes, 2004.

Linscott, Eloise Hubbard. *Folk Songs of Old New England*. Hamden, CT: Archon Books, 1962.

Lloyd, A. L., et al. *Folk Songs of the Americas*. New York: Oak Publications (for UNESCO), 1966.

Lomax, Alan. *The Folk Songs of North America*. New York: Doubleday, 1960.

Lomax, John, and Alan Lomax, with Charles Seeger and Ruth Crawford Seeger. *Folk Song USA*: III Best American Ballads. New York: Signet New American Library, 1966.

Lomax, John, and Alan Lomax. *Our Singing Country A Second Volume of American Ballads and Folk Songs*. New York: Macmillan, 1941.

Matteson, Maurice. *American Folk-Songs for Young Singers*. New York: G. Schirmer, 1947.

McIntosh, David. *Singing Games and Dances*. New York: Association Press, 1957.

McIntosh, David S, and Dale R. Whiteside *Folk Songs and Singing Games of the Illinois Ozarks*. Carbondale and Edwardsville: Southern Illinois University Press, 1974.

Mendoza, Vicente T. *Lirica Infantil de Mexico*. Mexico D. F.: El Colegio de Mexico, 1980.

Morse, Jim, et al. *Folk Songs of the Caribbean*. New York: Bantam Books, 1958.

Moses, Irene E. P. *Rhythmic Action, Plays and Dances*. Springfield, MA: Milton Bradley, 1915.

Murray, M. *Music for Children*, vol 1. Arranged by Carl Orff and Gunild Keetman, English version adapted by Margaret Murray. London: Schott & Co., 1976.

Newell, William Wells. *Games and Songs of American Children*. New York: Dover, 1963. 1st ed. 1882.

Niles, John Jacob. *Seven Kentucky Mountain Songs*. New York: G. Schirmer, 1929.

Okun, Milton. *Something to Sing About*. New York: Macmillan, 1958.

Owens, Bess A. "Songs of the Cumberlands." *Journal of American Folklore*, 1936, vol. 49.

Owens, William A. *Swing and Turn: Texas Play and Party Games*. Dallas: Tardy, 1936.

Pietroforte, Alfred. *Songs of the Yokuts and Paiutes*. Healdsburg, CA: Naturegraph,1965.

Porter, Grace Cleveland. *Negro Folk Singing Games and Folk Games of the Habitants*. London: J. Curwin and Sons, 1914.

Randolph, Vance. *Ozark Folksongs*. Columbia: State Historical Society of Missouri, 1949.

Richardson, Ethel Park. *American Mountain Songs*. New York: Greenburg, 1927.

Ritchie, Jean. *Golden City: Scottish Children's Street Games Songs*. Edinburgh and London: Oliver A. Boyd, 1965.

Ritchie, Jean. *Singing Family of the Cumberlands*. New York: Oxford University Press, 1955.

Rosenbaum, Art. *Folk Visions and Voices, Traditional Music and Song in North Georgia*. Athens: University of Georgia Press, 1983.

Sandburg, Carl. *The American Songbag*. New York: Harcourt Brace, 1927.

Scarborough, Dorothy. *On the Trail of Negro Folksongs*. Hatboro, PA: Folklore Association, 1963.

Seeger, Pete. *American Favorite Ballads*. New York: Oak Publications, 1961.

Seeger, Ruth Crawford. *American Folk Songs for Children*. Garden City, NY: Doubleday, 1948.

Seeger, Ruth Crawford. *American Folk Songs for Christmas*. Garden City, NY: Doubleday, 1953.

Seeger. Ruth Crawford. *Animal Folk Songs for Children*. Garden City, NY: Doubleday, 1950.

Sharp, Cecil J. *Twelve Folksongs from the Appalachian Mountains.* London: Oxford University Press, 1945.

Sharp, Cecil J., and Karpeles, Maud. *English Folk Songs from the Southern Appalachianss,* vols. I and II. London: Oxford University Press, 1932.

Siegmeister, Ellie. *Work and Sing.* New York: William R. Scott, 1944.

"Sing Out." *Folk Song Magazine,* 505 Eighth Ave., New York, NY 10018.

Sturgis, Edith, and Robert Hughes. *Songs from the Hills of Vermont.* Boston: G. Schirmer, 1919.

Thomas, Jean, and Joseph A. Leeder. *The Singin' Gatherin':* Tunes From the Southern Appalachians. Upper Saddle River, NJ: Silver Burdett (Pearson Education), 1944.

Tobitt, Janet Evelyn. *A Book of Negro Songs.* Pleasantville, NY: author, 1950.

Trent-Johns, Altona. *Play Songs of the Deep South.* Washington, DC: Associated Publishers, 1945.

Trinka, Jill. *Bought Me a Cat and Other Folk Songs, Singing Games and Play Parties.* Dripping Springs, TX: Folk Music Works, 1988.

Trinka, Jill. *The Little Black Bull and Other Folk Songs, Singing Games and Play Parties.* Dripping Springs, TX: Folk Music Works, 2003.

Trinka, Jill. *My Little Rooster and Other Folk Songs, Singing Games and Play Parties.* Dripping Springs, TX: Folk Music Works, 1987.

Walter, Lavinia Edna. *Old English Singing Games.* London: A & C Black, 1926.

Warner, Anne, and Frank Warner. *Collection of Traditional American Folksongs.* New York: Syracuse University Press, 1984.

Weavers. *The Weavers Songbook.* New York: Harper & Brothers, 1960.

White, Newman Ivey. *American Negro Folk Songs.* Hatboro, PA: Folklore Associates, 1965.

White, Newman Ivey, with Jan Schinhan, music editors. *The Frank C. Brown Collection of North Carolina Folklore.* Durham, NC: Duke University Press, 1952.

Discography

1,2,3, and a Zing, Zing, Zing. Tony Schwartz, Folkways Records, FC 7003 A.

Afro-American Blues and Game Songs. Library of Congress, Recording Laboratory, AAFS L4.

American Favorite Ballads, vol. I. Pete Seeger, Folkways Records.

American Folk Songs. Sung by The Seegers, Folkways Records, FA 2005.

American Folk Songs for Children. Mike and Peggy Seeger, Rounder Records, 8001, 8002, 8003.

American Folk Songs for Children. Pete Seeger, Folkways Records, FA 701.

American Folksongs for Children. Southern Folk Heritage Series, Atlantic, SD 1350.

American Play Parties. Pete Seeger, Folkways Records, FC 7604.

American Sea Songs and Chanties. Library of Congress, Recording Laboratory, AAFS L26.

Anglo-American Songs and Ballads. Library of Congress, Recording Laboratory, AAFS L12 and AAFS L14.

Animal Folk Songs for Children. Peggy Seeger, Scholastic Records, SC 7551.

Anthology of American Folk Music. Harry Smith. Folkway Records, FA 2951, 2952, 2953.

Asch Recordings. Compiled by Moses Asch and Charles E. Smith, Folkways Records, ASCH AA 3/4.

Birds, Beasts, Bugs, and Bigger Fishes. Pete Seeger, Folkways Records.

Birds, Beasts, Bugs, and Little Fishes. Pete Seeger, Folkways Records.

Brave Boys. Sandy Paton, Recorded Anthology of American Music, NWR 239.
Children's Jamaican Songs and Games. Folkways Records, FC 7250.
Children's Songs and Games, from the Southern Mountains. Sung by Jean Ritchie. Folkways Records, FC 7059.
The Cool of the Day. The Dusma Singers (Jean Ritchie), Greehays Recordings.
Cowboy Songs, Ballads and Cattle Calls from Texas. Compiled by John Lomax, Library of Congress, Recording Laboratory. AAFS L28.
A Cry from the Earth. John Bierhorst, Folkways Records, FA 3777.
Edna Ritchie of Viper Kentucky. Folk-Legacy Records, Inc., FSA-3; Sharon, CT.
Folk Music from Wisconsin. Library of Congress, Recording Laboratory, AAFS L9.
Folk Music USA. Folkways Records, FE 4530.
Folk Song and Minstrelsy. Vanguard Recordings, RL 7624
Georgia Sea Island Songs. Alan Lomax, Recorded Anthology of American Music, NWR 278.
Instrumental Music of the Southern Appalachians. Diane Hamilton, Tradition Records, TLP 1007.
I've Got a Song. Sandy and Caroline Paton, Folk-Legacy Records, FSK 52.
Jean Ritchie Sings Children's Songs and Games. Folkways Records, FC 7054.
Latin American Children's Game Songs. Henrietta Yurchenco, Folkways Records, FC 7851.
The Negro People in America. Heirloom Records, 1964.
Negro Work Songs and Calls. Library of Congress, Recording Laboratory, AAFS L8.
Old Mother Hippletoe. Kate Rinzler, Recorded Anthology of American Music, NWR 291.
Old Times and Hard Times. Hedy West, Folk-Legacy Records, 1967, FSA 32.
Play and Dance Songs and Tunes. Library of Congress, Recording Laboratory, AAFS L55.
Ring Games. Harold Courlander and Ruby Pickens Tartt, Folkways Records, FC 7004.
Ring Games, Line Games, and Play Party Songs of Alabama. Folkways Records, FC 7004.
So Early in the Morning. Diane Hamilton, Tradition Records, TLP 1034.
Songs and Ballads of the Anthracite Miners. Library of Congress, Recording Laboratory, AAFS L16.
Songs of Love, Luck, Animals, and Magic. Charlotte Heth, Recorded Anthology of American Music, NWR 297.
Songs of the Michigan Lumberjacks. Library of Congress, Recording Laboratory, AAFS L56.
Sounds of the South. Alan Lomax, Atlantic Records, Southern Folk Heritage, 1993.
Songs Traditionally Sung in North Carolina. Folk-Legacy Records, FSA 53.
Spanish-American Children's Songs. Jenny Wells Vincent, Cantemos Records.
Spiritual with Dock Reed and Vera Hall Ward. Folkways Records, FA 2038.
Step It Down. Bessie Jones, Rounder Records, 8004.
Versions and Variants of "Barbara Allen." Library of Congress, Recording Laboratory, AAFS L54.

Chapter **2**

Building the Framework of a Kindergarten Music Curriculum

"Music is deeply rooted in human evolutionary history and belongs to our biological nature," write Chen-Hafteck and Mang.[1] And according to Margaret Barrett, "Regardless of the variation of experience and developmental pathways, for children, across the globe, music appears to be a universal feature of human experience."[2] Kodály expands these convictions, asserting, "Music is nourishment, a comforting elixir. Music multiplies all that is beautiful and of value in life."[3]

Recognizing the significance of music in education, we set as our goal in Chapters 1 and 2 to provide music teachers with a Kindergarten music curriculum that is grounded in singing quality music literature that promotes children's musical abilities. How a music teacher decides to teach music is in large part influenced by a personal philosophy of music education. We have long been convinced that a music curriculum inspired by the philosophy of Zoltán Kodály provides a solid foundation for designing a music curriculum. Kindergarten music teachers talking about the application and use of this music curriculum in public and private school settings is posted on the companion website (Web 2B Curriculum).

Through our experiences working with teachers in the field we have developed and adapted aspects of methodology commonly associated with the Kodály philosophy that are congruent with research findings from the field of music perception and cognition, national and state standards. We believe that the findings and procedures we present in this book are in keeping with the composer's philosophy and that of his students. Kodály wrote, "It is the fate of science that each successive age produces new results and usually modifies or completely refutes the results obtained by the preceding age."[4] And in his lecture *Ancient Traditions-Today's Musical Life* he stated, "But this is part and parcel of the development of science. Science keeps on changing and fluctuating."[5]

In the early 1970s Dr. Klára Kokas, a psychologist and graduate of the Franz Liszt Academy of Music in Budapest and a pupil of Kodály, began to experiment with the teaching methodology based on the philosophy of Kodály. She has long been a proponent for adaptation and modification of the methodology based on the Kodály philosophy. Dr. Kokas is another example of someone who has built her approach to teaching on the work of Kodály. She provides an insightful glimpse into her initial experiences with Hungarian music education:

> In Hungary, Kodály's principles were applied and developed within the traditional framework of centralized education. The central control exercised by the Ministry of Education, its lower representative organs, and the centralized form of assessment of teaching standards left little room for teacher initiative. Our personal visions were strongly circumscribed by the Marxist-Leninist philosophy and the aesthetics introduced by the establishment as a compulsory component at each level of education. Thus the frameworks in early childhoods—and even more so in school education— were strictly limited. In the given political set-up, Kodály's method had little scope for further refinement and development.[6]

Eszerbet Szőnyi also encourages teachers to expand the Kodály methodology for the classroom. In her well-known work *Musical Reading and Writing*, she states: "This book is not complete. Nor does it reflect the only expedient system; it merely contains the realization of a system well proven in practice. Teachers should add to it according to their choice, enriching and varying the material in order to make their work as successful as possible. . . . Sol-fa is not a closed-end system, but is constantly developing and advancing, like living music itself."[7]

Kodály's philosophy is a useful "musical compass" for developing a Kindergarten music curriculum. In a music curriculum shaped by the Kodály philosophy and taught by an artist teacher, children first are

> actively involved in a combination of music making, singing, creating rhythmic and vocal accompaniments to songs, and active listening. Second, the Kodály approach offers a rich array of tools and concepts for the development of musical literacy. Third, Kodály specialists have been at the forefront of the movement to include world folk music in the curriculum. Fourth, Kodály teaching techniques provide excellent ways of approaching what Elliott calls "musical problem solving" and "problem reduction" in music education. Fifth, children who study music in a Kodály-based program tend to develop lifelong skills and excellent musical ears."[8]

Kodály-inspired music instruction has also had a significant impact on child behavior outside the music classroom. The broad effects of this type of teaching and learning have been documented by Dr. Martin F. Gardiner of the Center for the Study of Human Development at Brown University:

> The specific methods of arts training common to these studies is Kodály Music training. The Kodály training is a methodology for building skills in individual and group singing that, along with specific musical skills, gives the children an opportunity to practice and build individual attitudes of attention, learning and sensitivity to the group, and capabilities for working together. It is possible to hypothesize that attitudes and behaviors towards learning in this arts training helped to build the more general improvements in classroom attitudes and behaviors that were documented by the teachers (Gardiner et al., 1996) and were in turn closely related to improvements in reading. Teacher reports support this viewpoint, as does recent data showing greater improvements in classroom behavior in those students receiving more extensive Kodály training).[9]

Kodály Philosophy of Music Education

Zoltán Kodály (1882–1967) was a Hungarian composer, ethnomusicologist, and music educator, who, along with Béla Bartók, is recognized for creating a new style of Hungarian art music based on the folk music heritage of Hungary. Through his efforts in music education, Kodály sought to cultivate a far-reaching, musically literate Hungarian society. His philosophical and pedagogical contributions to the field of music education have become known as the Kodály Concept or Kodály Method of music education that is now used worldwide. Here are some of Kodály's major philosophical tenets.

Justifying Music in the School Curriculum

Kodály was convinced that music should belong to everyone and not just to a musical elite: "It is the right of every citizen to be taught the basic elements of music, to be handed the key with which he can enter the locked world of music. To open the ear and heart of the millions to serious music is a great thing."[10] He further states, "With a few years' technical preparation children can achieve results measurable by the most exacting of absolute artistic standards."[11]

> Taken separately, too, the elements of music are precious instruments in education. Rhythm develops attention, concentration, determination, and the ability to condition oneself. Melody opens up the world of emotions. Dynamic variation and tone color sharpen our hearing. Singing, finally, is such a many-sided physical activity that its effect in physical education is immeasurable—if there is perhaps anyone to whom the education of the spirit does not matter. Its beneficial effect in health is well known; special books have been written on this.[12]

> With us it is scarcely every twentieth person who uses his speech and breathing organs correctly. This, too, should be learned during the singing lesson. The discipline of rhythm, the training of the throat and lungs set singing right beside gymnastics. Both of them, no less than food, are needed daily.[13]

The Importance of Excellent
Musicianship Training for Music Instructors

We believe, as did Kodály, that children must be taught music from individuals who themselves are excellent musicians. Kodaly wrote of the significance of the teacher's musicianship:

> "There is a need for better musicians, and only those will become good musicians who work at it every day. The better a musician is the easier it is for him to draw others into the happy, magic circle of music. Thus will he serve the great cause of helping music to belong to everyone."[14]

Of course, many early childhood teachers do not have the necessary training to be excellent musicians, but they do have a love of singing—and that is critical for developing children's music abilities.

The Multiple Dimensions of Musicianship

Kodály addressed the multiple dimensions of musicianship and human development. They include performance, musical literacy and critical thinking skills, creativity, and listening, as well as stewardship of musical and cultural heritage. These dimensions of musicianship are also reflected in many state and national standards for music education, as well as those states embarking on creating core curriculum standards.[15] We need to consider the different facets of what it means to be a musical human being. If we are to develop children's self-knowledge, self-awareness, and emotions, we need to educate them as performers, as stewards of their musical and cultural heritage, and as critical thinkers through the development of musical literacy skills, creativity, and listening. We summarize the multiple dimensions of musicianship as follows.

A. Children as stewards of musical and cultural heritage
B. Children as performers
C. Children as critical thinkers
D. Children as creative human beings
E. Children as informed audience members

A. *Children as Stewards of Their Cultural Heritage: Music Repertoire*

Kodály argued that both the music education of children and the education of instrumentalists and vocalists add to the quality of life within a community; if art is "presented in such a way that it was not a torture, but a joy for the pupil, it would instill in the child a thirst for finer music and affect his or her level of taste which would last for a lifetime."[16] He believed that material suited to the physical, developmental, and psychological needs of the young could be best found in folk songs. Kodály valued folksongs for their simplicity, beauty, and heritage, but he emphatically stressed the importance of using only authentic folksongs, linking them to the finest art songs and art music:

> Not even the most excellent individual creation can be a substitute for traditions. To write a folksong is as much beyond the bounds of possibility as to write a proverb.

Just as proverbs condense centuries of popular wisdom and observation, so, in traditional songs, are the emotions of centuries immortalized in a form polished to perfection. No masterpiece can replace traditions.[17]

Using folksongs and singing games provides the teacher with suitable material that is already part of the child's cultural experience. Ruth Crawford Seeger also believed that it is

one of the aims of education to induct the child into the realities of the culture in which he will live, may we not say that this traditional music and language and ideology, which has not only grown out of but has in turn influenced that culture—and is still influencing and being used by it—should occupy a familiar place in the child's daily life, even though it may not be current in the particular neighborhood in which he happens to be living.[18]

As children's skills develop, folksongs of other cultures are gradually introduced along with art music of the great composers. There are, strictly speaking, only two kinds of music: good and bad. "Bad foreign and bad native music are equally damaging, like the plague".[19] Therefore finding and teaching the best folk and composed music should be a major goal of any music instructor.

It was Kodály's belief that the communication of inferior music inhibits the growth of maximum musical understanding; therefore, he maintained that the type of material used and the manner of presentation has a lasting effect on the development of a child's musical taste:

Bad taste spreads by leaps and bounds. In art this is not so innocent a thing as in, say, clothes. Someone who dresses in bad taste does not endanger his health, but bad taste in art is a veritable sickness of the soul. It seals the soul off from contact with masterpieces and from the life-giving nourishment emanating from them, without which the soul wastes away or becomes stunted, and the whole character of the man is branded with a peculiar mark.[20]

The pure soul of the child must be considered sacred; what we implant there must stand every test, and if we plant anything bad, we poison his soul for life.[21]

The use of contrived or diluted music is not suitable for instruction:

Let us stop the teachers' superstition according to which only some diluted art-substitute is suitable for teaching purposes. A child is the most susceptible and the most enthusiastic audience for pure art; for in every great artist the child is alive—and this is something felt by youth's congenial spirit. Conversely, only art of intrinsic value is suitable for children! Everything else is harmful. After all, food is more carefully chosen for an infant than for an adult. Musical nourishment which is "rich in vitamins is essential for children."[22]

We continue to think about the need to address the current musical styles inherent in our society. We could argue about whether or not some of this type of music would be considered part of our musical or cultural heritage, and that would be quite an interesting debate. We are talking here about popular music, but we're not using the term *popular* as just pop, but also rock, country, jazz, hip-hop, etc. This type of music is not the focus of this book. However, we are concerned that teachers are separating school music and outside-of-school music more and more, and not even acknowledging the music that children are listening to at home and in other venues. This does the profession a disservice; we run the risk of being viewed in society as irrelevant. So we continue to look for ways to include outside music in the classroom and do it in a developmentally appropriate way. We need to find ways to address music that is part of the lives of children and part of the culture they're growing up in outside of school.

B. Children as Performers: Singing, Moving and Playing Instruments

Music performance is at the core of any music program. Through performance, children engage in singing, movement, and playing instruments. Therefore children must be taught in a sequential and developmentally appropriate manner how to sing, move to music, and play an instrument.

C. Children as Critical Thinkers: Music Literacy

Kodály believed that all children should become musically literate; that is, they should be able to read and write music with ease comparable to how they read and write their own language. Know repertoire should be used to teach music concepts and skills. Through teaching music in the Kindergarten music classroom, we are laying the foundations for a music literacy program that will be fostered and developed throughout elementary school.

Primary Musical Concepts to Teach in Kindergarten:
- Concept of beat in simple meter and compound meter
- Concept of loud and soft (dynamics)
- Concept of fast and slow (tempo)
- Concept of high and low (pitch)
- Concept of rhythm (duration)

Musical Skills in a Kindergarten Curriculum
- Tuneful singing
- Reading and writing
- An understanding and awareness of basic music forms
- Music improvisation
- Listening

D. Children as Creative Human Beings: Improvisation

Music improvisation, the art of composing extemporaneously, is an indispensable component of a music education. In the early childhood classroom, children learn to improvise texts, rhythms, melodies, and movements. The instructor who teaches music inspired by the Kodály concept uses improvisation to develop the child's abilities to understand the creative process in music, as well as to understand the stylistic elements of a piece of music. It stands to reason that children who are able to improvise music on the basis of the typical forms and melodic and rhythmic patterns of folk songs and art music have developed a greater feeling and understanding for music style.

E. *Children as Informed Audience Members*

Developing children's listening skills is an important component of the Kodály concept. No matter what the activity in the music classroom, children inherently learn how to listen when they perform, create, or develop their critical thinking skills. Of course, the music teacher also needs to give children specific listening activities that enable them to form connections between the song repertoire they are singing and art music.

The goal of our music curriculum is to provide Kindergarten teachers with a practical guide for teaching music. We hope that this book will enable music instructors to initiate their children into the many dimensions of musicianship that are common in both the aural/oral and written traditions.

Building the Framework of a Kindergarten Curriculum

Here is a framework we suggest for a music curriculum shaped by the Kodály philosophy of music. It is important that the curriculum provided here be only a guide as to what can be included in the early childhood music classroom. This curriculum should be used as a starting point for creating engaging music lessons. It is important to remember that we not view a curriculum as a series of activities to be mastered by children if the tasks do not stem logically from active music making. To do so runs the risk of killing the joy of music for our students. We present here a sample Kindergarten music curriculum based on the philosophy of Kodály. Remember that the specific music skills need to be modified according to the frequency of instruction.

SAMPLE KINDERGARTEN CURRICULUM

A. Repertoire: Children as Stewards of their Cultural and Musical Heritage

As the instructor, you should:
1. Expand song repertoire to add to children's knowledge of folk music, art music, and composed music.
2. Sing simple songs with a limited range and play games from diverse cultures, particularly those of the local community.
3. Learn twenty to twenty-five new songs, including some songs of various cultural origins.

B. Performance: Children as Performers

1. Singing
Children should be able to:
    a. Identify speaking voice, singing voice, loud voice, and whispering voice.
    b. Demonstrate speaking, singing, loud, whispering, and thinking voices.
    c. Differentiate between adult and children's voices.
    d. Perform all songs with good intonation, tempo, and tone quality.
    e. Perform all songs with good articulation and appropriate dynamics, phrasing, and expression.
    f. Develop individual singing.
    g. Sing, independently or in a group, simple songs with a limited range.

    h. Sing songs while keeping the beat.

    i. Sing songs while clapping the rhythm.

    j. Sing songs antiphonally.

2. Movement

Children should be able to:

    a. Perform a free movement in place (sitting).

    b. Perform a free movement in space.

    c. Move to a beat while sitting.

    d. Move to a beat while walking.

    e. Move while standing in a stationary circle.

    f. Perform small finger movements.

    g. Perform movements that are linked to changing direction.

    h. Sing and perform acting-out directions.

    i. Choose a partner before, during, and after a game.

    j. Sing and follow a leader.

    k. Perform chasing games.

    l. Perform line game movements.

    m. Perform winding movements.

    n. Move in a circle.

3. Instruments

    Children should play a variety of nonpitched and pitched musical instruments in the classroom, such as drums, cymbals, and childmade instruments, as well as resonator bells, xylophones, metallophones, and glockenspiels.

C. Literacy: Children as Critical Thinkers

1. Beat and rhythm

Children should be able to:

    a. Sing songs with a number of motions expressing the beat, using simple and compound meters.

    b. Aurally determine how many beats there are in a phrase of music.

    c. Use icons to represent the number of beats in a musical phrase.

    d. Use a music symbol such as a heart to represent the number of beats in a musical phrase.

    e. Sing songs with various motions expressing the strong and weak beats.

    f. Sing songs with numerous motions expressing the rhythm.

    g. Aurally determine if the teacher is clapping on the beat or words of song.

    h. Aurally determine the number of sounds on the beat.

    i. Describe the number of sounds on a beat with the words *long* or *short*.

    j. Use icons to represent the number of sounds on a beat in a musical phrase.

    k. Use icons to represent the rhythm of a musical phrase.

    l. Sing songs and clap the rhythm.

    m. Use simple ostinati (rhythmic accompaniments) to accompany a song (age five or six only).

    n. Sing songs using various tempi, slow and fast.

    o. Aurally determine if the teacher or another child is singing a song using a fast or slow beat.

    p. Use icons to represent a fast or slow beat.

2. Melody

Children should be able to:

    a. Chant rhymes and sing melodies using a loud or soft voice.

    b. Distinguish aurally between a "loud voice" and a "soft voice."

    c. Choose an icon that represents chanting or singing with a loud or soft voice.

    d. Choose icons or words that represent loud or soft chanting or singing.

    e. Chant rhymes using a high or low voice.

    f. Distinguish aurally between a "high voice" and a "low voice."

    g. Choose an icon that represents chanting a rhythm using a high voice or a low voice.

    h. Choose icons or words that represent high pitches or low pitches.

    i. Sing melodies composed of a minor third melody.

    j. Distinguish aurally between a "high sound" and a "low sound."

    k. Choose icons or words that represent high pitches or low pitches.

    l. Choose icons that represent singing melodies composed of minor thirds.

    m. Distinguish tone colors of instruments and voices by closing their eyes and recognizing what instrument the teacher plays or which child sings a song.

    n. Perform easy melodic echoes using known and unknown repertoire (begin with four-beat phrases and progress to eight beat phrases).

    o. Recognize familiar melodies when hummed or played.

    p. Practice dynamics using voices and instruments.

3. Reading and writing

Children should be able to:

    a. Point to visual representations of a phrase of music containing four to eight beats.

    b. Read the words "singing voice" and "speaking voice."

    c. Sing and point to beat icons, using a loud or soft voice.

    d. Select icons to represent loud or soft.

    e. Read the words *loud* and *soft*.

    f. Chant or sing with a loud or soft voice, and point to beat icons.

    g. Sing with a loud or soft voice, and point to beat icons.

    h. Sing a musical phrase, and point to heartbeats.

    i. Select icons to represent the beat.

    j. Read the word *beat*.

    k. Chant or sing and point to the heartbeat.

    l. Sing and point to beat icons using a fast or slow tempo.

    m. Select icons to represent fast or slow.

    n. Read the words *fast* and *slow*,

    o. Chant or sing with a fast or slow tempo, and point to beat icons.

    p. Sing and point to icons using high or low voice.

    q. Select icons to represent high and low voice.

    r. Read the words *high* and *low*.

    s. Chant a rhyme with a high or low voice while keeping the beat.

    t. Sing and point to icons representing pitches belonging to a child's chant.

    u. Select icons to represent pitches in a child's chant.

    v. Read the words *high pitch* and *low pitch*.

    w. Sing a melody composed of a minor third with the words *high* and *low*.

4. Inner hearing
Children should be able to:

    a. Sing phrases of songs "inside your head" with inner hearing while keeping the beat.

5. Musical Memory
Children should be able to:

    a. Learn all songs, games, and chants by rote.

    b. Perform rhythmic and melodic echoes four to eight beats in length, with and without a text.

6. Part work
Children should be able to:

    a. Sing a song and pat the beat.

    b. Participate in echo games.

    c. Do alternate or antiphonal singing.

    d. Play the beat on a percussion instrument.

    e. Sing a song and clap the rhythm.

7. Form
Children should be able to:

    a. Perform songs with correct phrasing.

    b. Perform songs and change motions for each new phrase.

    c. Do relay or antiphonal singing.

    d. Alternate between singing aloud and inside the head (inner-hearing it).

    e. Recognize same, similar, and different phrases.

D. Improvisation/Composition: Children as Creative Human Beings

1. Improvisation/composition
Children should be able to:

    a. Improvise a motion to accompany a song.

    b. Improvise new words to a familiar song, and then rewrite the text with the children.

    c. Improvise a melody to a rhyme.

    d. Improvise question and answer phrases.

2. Ear training
Children should be able to:

    a. Aurally identify loud or soft singing or chanting.

    b. Aurally identify the beat in a musical phase.

    c. Aurally identify a fast or slow tempo.

    d. Aurally identify a high or low voice in chanting a rhyme.

    e. Aurally identify music pitches an octave apart with the words *high* or *low*.

    f. Aurally identify music pitches a perfect fifth apart with the words *high* or *low*.

    g. Aurally identify music pitches a minor third apart with the words *high* and *low*.

    h. Aurally identify the long and short sounds in a musical phrase

Listening: Children as Informed Audience Members

Children should be able to:

1. Listen to a musical performance of a known or unknown song performed by the teacher or a fellow child.
2. Listen to a short musical instrumental excerpt.
3. Aurally identify changes in dynamics as "louder" or "softer" in live and recorded performances.
4. Aurally identify steady beat in live and recorded performances.
5. Aurally identify changes in tempo as "faster" or "slower" tempos in live and recorded performances.
6. Aurally identify high and low pitches in live and recorded performances.
7. Aurally identify pitched and un-pitched instruments.
8. Aurally identify some instruments of the orchestra.

F. Emergent Literacy and Music

1. Alphabet awareness
Children should be able to:
   a. Sing words from songs.
   b. Recognize the individual letters of words from songs.
   c. Recognize uppercase and lowercase letters.
   d. Use icons to represent the beat, rhythm, and melody in music.
   e. Understand that words are composed of individual letters.

2. Comprehension
Children should be able to:
   a. Sing a song with the correct sequence of movements.
   b. Retell a story through music.
   c. Make predictions about the continuation of a song story.

3. Concepts about story/song
Children should be able to:
   a. Understand the structure of stories/song.
   b. Understand the characters, beginning, middle, and end of song.

4. Emergent literacy
Children should be able to:
   a. Represent musical concepts through representation.

5. Phonological awareness
Children should be able to:
   a. Understand concepts of "same" and "different" for rhythm and pitch or melody patterns in songs.

6. Vocabulary development
Children should be able to:
   a. Acquire new words from song material.
   b. Identify and name instruments.
   c. Improvise words to songs.

G. Emergent Math Skills and Music

1. Knowledge of numbers and operations
Children should be able to:
  a. Reinforce their knowledge of numbers one to twenty in song.
  b. Demonstrate one-to-one correspondence.
  c. Create number rhymes with odd and even numbers.
  d. Classify songs according to type, for example games, lullabies.
  e. Classify songs according to how many beats make up a whole song.

2. Knowledge of patterns and algebra
Children should be able to:
  a. Begin hearing and seeing beat patterns in song material.
  b. Begin hearing and seeing rhythm patterns in song material, and classify or sort songs.
  c. Begin hearing and seeing melodic patterns in song material, and classify or sort songs.
  d. Predict what comes next in a melodic or rhythmic pattern.
  e. Recognize same and different.

3. Knowledge of geometry
Children should be able to:
  a. Learn about shapes such as circle, square, and half circle.
  b. Use words that identify where things are, such as *far* and *near*.
  c. Use positional words such as *inside* and *outside* (this activity will take place during the playing of games).

4. Measurement and estimation skills
Children should be able to:
  a. Use language to measure time.
  b. Use language such as *longer than* or *shorter than* to describe melodies.
  c. Develop their estimation skills; for example, the teacher asks children to guess how many beats are in a song or rhythm.

5. Calendar and time
Children should be able to:
  a. Use the calendar in their music class.
  b. Use the clock in the music class.

This sample curriculum will be used as a reference in the following chapters to understand how we can developing teaching techniques and lesson plans for the Kindergarten classroom.

Discussion Questions
1. Identify research that supports the inclusion of music in the Kindergarten classroom.
2. Explain the value of a music education and the place of music in the Kindergarten school curriculum.
3. As a teacher, do you really need to be guided by a philosophy of music?
4. Collect three research articles that document the effects of music on cognitive development of children. Discuss your findings with your peers.
5. What are the multiple dimensions of musicianship training?

6. Check websites for three school districts. Locate their philosophy statements, and write a summary statement for each district.
7. How does teaching music support literacy and creative skills?

Ongoing Assignment

1. Write a statement of your personal philosophy of music education for the Kindergarten classroom. How will your philosophy statement change for each grade level you teach?
2. Review the curriculum goals for Kindergarten music. Compare these curriculum goals with another music instructor. Add curriculum goals into section two of your curriculum folder.

Bibliography

Alperson, P. A. Introduction. In *What Is Music? An Introduction to the Philosophy of Music*, ed. P. A. Alperson (pp. 3–30). University Park: Pennsylvania State University Press, 1994.

Alperson, Philip. "Music as Philosophy." In *What Is Music? An Introduction to the Philosophy of Music*. University Park: Pennsylvania State University Press, 1994.

Alperson, Philip, ed. *What Is Music? An Introduction to the Philosophy of Music.* New York: Haven, 1987.

Alperson, Philip. "What Should One Expect from a Philosophy of Music Education?" *Journal of Aesthetic Education*, Fall 1991, *25*(3), 215–242.

Barrett, J. R. "Currents of Change in the Music Curriculum." In *International Handbook of Research in Arts Education*, ed. L. Bresler (pp. 147–161). Parts I and II. Dordrecht, Netherlands: Springer, 2007.

Barrett, Janet, and Kari Veblen. *"Meaningful Connections in a Comprehensive Approach to the Music Curriculum."* In *The Oxford Handbook of Music Education*, vol. 1, ed. Gary E. McPherson and Graham F. Welch (pp. 361–380). New York: Oxford University Press, 2012.

Barrett, Margaret S. "Commentary: Music Learning and Teaching in Infancy and Early Childhood." *The Oxford Handbook of Music Education*, vol. 1., ed. Gary E. McPherson and Graham F. Welch (chap. 2.1). New York: Oxford University Press, 2012.

Bass, Randall V., and J. W. Good. "Educare and Educere: Is a Balance Possible in the Educational System?" *Educational Forum*, Winter 2004, *68*, 161–168.

Bodrova, E., and D. J. Leong. *The Tools of the Mind Project: A Case Study of Implementing the Vygotskian Approach in American Early Childhood and Primary Classrooms.* Geneva: International Bureau of Education, UNESCO, 2001.

Bogard, K., and R. Takanishi. PK–3: An Aligned and Coordinated Approach to Education for Children 3 to 8 Years Old." *Social Policy Report*, 2005, *19*(3).

Bowman, W. *Philosophical Perspectives on Music.* New York: Oxford University Press, 1998.

Bowman, W. "Philosophy, Criticism, and Music Education: Some Tentative Steps Down a Less-Travelled Road." *Bulletin of the Council for Research in Music Education*, 1992, *114*, 1–19.

Bredekamp, S., and C. Copple (eds.). *Developmentally Appropriate Practice in Early Childhood Programs (Rev. ed.).* Washington, DC: National Association for the Education of Young Children, 1997.

Cadwell, L. *Bringing Reggio Emilia Home: An Innovative Approach to Early Childhood Education.* New York: Teachers College Press, 1997.

Campbell, Patricia Shehan. *Songs in Their Heads: Music and Its Meaning in Children's Lives.* New York: Oxford University Press, 1998.

Chen-Hafteck, Lily, and Esther Mang. "Music and Language in Early Childhood Development and Learning." In *The Oxford Handbook of Music Education*, vol. 1., ed. Gary E. McPherson and Graham F. Welch (chap. 2.4). New York: Oxford University Press, 2012.

Childs, G. *Truth, Beauty, and Goodness: Steiner-Waldorf Education as a Demand of Our Time: An Esoteric Study.* London: Temple Lodge, 1999.

Choksy, Lois. *The Kodály Method*, 2nd ed. Upper Saddle River, NJ: Prentice-Hall, 1999.

Dolloff, Lori-Anne. "Elementary Music Education: Building Cultures and Practices." In *Praxial Music Education: Reflections and Dialogues*, ed. David J. Elliott. New York: Oxford University Press, 2005.

Eisner, E. "Educating the Whole Person: Arts in the Curriculum." *Music Educators Journal*, 1987, *73*(8), 41–97.

El Sistema. July 1, 2010. http://www.el-sistema-film.com/ed_Sistema_The_Story.html. Accessed October 29, 2010.

Gardiner, Martin, and Alan Fox. "Letter to the Editor." *Nature*, May 23, 1996, vol. 381, 284.

Gardner, Howard. *Frames of Mind: The Theory of Multiple Intelligences.* New York: Basic Books, 1983.

Hallquist, M. "Maria Montessori: Glossary of Terms and Ideas." *Early Childhood Connections: Journal of Music and Movement-Based Learning*, 1995, *1*(3), 26–37.

Hanley, Betty, and Janet Montgomery. "Contemporary Curriculum Practices and Their Theoretical Bases." In *The New Handbook of Research on Music Teaching and Learning: A Project of the Music Educators National Conference.* New York: Oxford University Press, 2002.

Hargreaves, D. J. "Musical Education for All." *Psychologist*, 1994, *7*, 357–358.

Higgins, K. M. *The Music of our Lives.* Philadelphia: Temple University Press, 1991.

Hope, Samuel, "Why Study Music?" In *Vision 2020.* Reston, VA: Music Educators National Conference, 2000.

Horowitz, F. D., L. Darling-Hammond, J. Bransford, et al. "Educating Teachers for Developmentally Appropriate Practice." In *Preparing Teachers for a Changing World: What Teachers Should Learn and Be Able to Do*, ed. L. Darling-Hammond and J. Bransford (88–125). San Francisco: Jossey-Bass, 2005.

Houlahan, Micheál, and Philip Tacka. *Kodály Today: A Cognitive Approach to Elementary Music Education.* New York: Oxford University Press, 2008.

Humpal, M. "The Effects of an Integrated Early Childhood Music Program on Social Interaction Among Children with Handicaps and Their Typical Peers." *Journal of Music Therapy*, 1991, *28*(3), 161–177.

Hyson, M. *Enthusiastic and Engaged Learners: Approaches to Learning in the Early Childhood Classroom.* New York: Teachers College Press, 2008.

Jorgensen, E. R. "Philosophical Issues in Curriculum." In *The New Handbook of Research on Music Teaching and Learning: A Project of the Music Educators National Conference*, ed. R. Colwell and C. Richardson (pp. 48–62). New York: Oxford University Press, 2002.

Jorgensen, Estelle. *In Search of Music Education.* Urbana: University of Illinois Press, 1997.

Jorgensen, Estelle. "On Philosophical Method." In *Handbook of Research on Music Teaching and Learning: A Project of the Music Educators National Conference*, ed. Richard Colwell (91–101). New York: Schirmer, 1992.

Kamii, C., and J. K. Ewing. "Basing Teaching on Piaget's Constructivism." *Childhood Education,* 1996, *72*(5), 260–264.

Kania, A. "The Philosophy of Music." *The Stanford Encyclopedia of Philosophy.* 2007. http://plato.stanford.edu/entries/music/ Accessed June 22, 2010.

Kodály, Zoltán. "Ancient Traditions—Today's Musical Life." In *The Selected Writings of Zoltán Kodály*, ed. F. Bonis, trans. L. Halápy and F. Macnicol. London: Boosey & Hawkes, 1974.

Kodály, Zoltán. "Bartók the Folklorist." In *The Selected Writings of Zoltán Kodály*, ed. F. Bonis, trans. Halápy and Macnicol. Budapest: Zenemıkiadó Vállalat, 1964; London: Boosey & Hawkes, 1974.

Kodály, Zoltán. "Bicinia Hungarica." Preface to the Hungarian edition. In *The Selected Writings of Zoltán Kodály*, ed. F. Bonis, trans. L. Halápy and F. Macnicol. London: Boosey & Hawkes, 1974.

Kodály, Zoltán. "Children's Choirs." In *The Selected Writings of Zoltán Kodály*, ed. F. Bonis, trans. L. Halápy and F. Macnicol. London: Boosey & Hawkes, 1974.

Kodály, Zoltán. "Fifty-Five Two-Part Exercises." Cited from *The Selected Writings of Zoltán Kodály*, ed. F. Bonis, trans. L. Halápy and F. Macnicol. London: Boosey & Hawkes, 1974.

Kodály, Zoltán. "Inauguration of the New Building of the Kecskemét Music Primary School." *Bulletin of the International Kodály Society*, 1985 (1): 9.

Kodály, Zoltán. "Music in the Kindergarten." In *The Selected Writings of Zoltán Kodály*, ed. F. Bonis, trans. L. Halápy and F. Macnicol. London: Boosey & Hawkes, 1974.

Kodály, Zoltán. "On the Anniversary of Beethoven's Death." In *The Selected Writings of Zoltán Kodály.* ed. F. Bonis, trans. L. Halápy and F. Macnicol. London: Boosey & Hawkes, 1974.

Kodály, Zoltán. "The Role of the Folksong in Russian and Hungarian Music." In *The Selected Writings of Zoltán Kodály*, ed. F. Bonis, trans. L. Halápy and F. Macnicol. London: Boosey & Hawkes, 1974.

Kodály, Zoltan. *The Selected Writings of Zoltan Kodály*, ed. F. Bonis, trans. L. Halápy and F. Macnicol. London, England: Boosey & Hawkes, 1974.

Kokas, Klára. *Joy Through the Magic of Music.* Budapest, Hungary: Akkord Zenei Kiadó, 1999.

Levine, M. *A Mind at a Time.* New York: Simon and Schuster, 2002.

McCarthy, M., and J. S. Goble. "The Praxial Philosophy in Historical Perspective." In *Praxial Music Education: Reflections and Dialogues*, ed. D. J. Elliott (19–51). New York: Oxford University Press, 2009.

Mahlmann, John J. Music Educators National Conference. *What Every Young American Should Know and Be Able to Do in the Arts: National Standards for Arts Education.* Reston, VA: Music Educators National Conference, 1994.

National Research Council, B. T. Bowman, S. M. Donovan, and M. S. Burns (eds.). *Eager to Learn: Educating Our Preschoolers.* Washington, DC: National Academies Press, 2001.

Neuman, S. B., C. Copple, and S. Bredekamp, S. *Learning to Read and Write: Developmentally Appropriate Practices For Young Children.* Washington, DC: National Association for the Education of Young Children, 2000.

Regelski, T. "Curriculum Reform: Reclaiming 'Music' as Social Praxis." *Action, Criticism, and Theory for Music Education*, 2009, *8*(1), http://act.maydaygroup.org/articles/Regelski8_1.pdf. Accessed June 22, 2010.

Regelski, T. "On 'Methodolatry' and Music Teaching as Critical and Reflective Practice." *Philosophy of Music Education Review*, 2002, *10*(2), 102–133.

Reimer, B. *A Philosophy of Music Education: Advancing the Vision* (3rd ed.). Upper Saddle River, NJ: Prentice Hall, 2003.

Robinson, J., ed. *Music and Meaning*. Ithaca: Cornell University Press, 1997.

Seeger, Ruth Crawford. *American Folk Songs for Christmas*. Garden City, NY: Doubleday, 1953.

Small, Christopher. *Musicking*: The Meanings of Performing and Listening. Hanover, NH: Wesleyan University Press, 1998.

Szőnyi, Erzsébet. *Musical Reading and Writing*, vol. 1. London: Boosey & Hawkes, 1974.

Taggart, G., K. Whitby, and C. Sharp. *International Review of Curriculum and Assessment Frameworks Curriculum and Progression in the Arts: An International Study.* UK: Qualifications and Curriculum Authority (QCA) and National Foundation for Educational Research (NFER), 2004.

Trevarthen, Colwyn, and Stephen Malloch. "Musicality and Musical Culture: Sharing Narratives of Sound from Early Childhood." In *The Oxford Handbook of Music Education*, vol. 1, ed. Gary E. McPherson and Graham F. Welch (chap. 2.3). New York: Oxford University Press, 2012.

Vogt, J. "Philosophy-Music Education-Curriculum: Some Casual Remarks on Some Basic Concepts." *Action, Criticism, and Theory for Music Education*, 2003, *2*(1), http://act.maydaygroup.org/articles/Vogt2_1.pdf. Accessed June 22, 2010.

Wittgenstein, Ludwig. *Philosophical Investigations*. Oxford: Blackwell, 1953.

Zigler, E. F., D. G. Singer, and S. J. Bishop-Josef (eds.). *Children's Play: The Roots of Reading*. Washington, DC: Zero to Three, 2004.

Helpful Websites

http://ies.ed.gov/ncee/wwc/—What Works Clearinghouse: information on which instructional techniques and curricula are effective

National Institute for Early Education Research State Standards Database: lists language and literacy content standards by state

http://www.aft.org/earlychildhoo—American Federation of Teachers, Early Childhood Educators Page: links to information and resources of use to early childhood educators and child care providers

http://www.colorincolorado.org/—Colorín Colorado: an online service offering information, activities, advice and resources for educators and families of Spanish-speaking English language learners

http://www.naeyc.org/—National Association for the Education of Young Children: provides journals, magazines, and position statements related to early childhood education.

http://www.reading.org/—International Reading Association: magazines, journals, and links related to language and literacy.

Chapter 3

Developing Creative Expression Through Singing, Movement, and Playing Instruments

Introduction

Chapter 2 provided a brief survey of how to develop a philosophy of music education and how this can be used to build the basic framework for a Kindergarten music curriculum as well as a basic lesson plan. The goal of this chapter is to present ideas for developing young children's singing voices, appropriate movement activities, and instruments in the Kindergarten classroom. Additional recommendations, resources, and references are offered at the end of this chapter. The chapter also includes a section on guidelines for developing children's performance and movement abilities as well as a discussion of how teaching performance skills such as singing, movement, and playing instruments affects the planning and design of a music lesson. Comments from kindergarten music teachers talking about the application and use of the contents of this chapter are posted as videos on the companion website (Web 3B, Creative Expression).

Singing

Every child has a voice; it is the most accessible musical instrument regardless of social or cultural background, ethnicity, or musical ability. Singing has a significant impact on a child's intellectual development. It facilitates language development through beat and rhythm as well as learning to articulate the words of a song while singing; it also aids in memory and vocabulary development. A young child who is engaged in singing and movement activities is participating in an ideal learning environment for music. The repetition of songs, chants, rhymes, and activities is fundamental to learning in-tune singing in the Kindergarten classroom. Although not all children may be involved in the music lesson to the same degree, they are hearing new songs and learning the games even if they are not actively participating. It is important for the instructor to demonstrate in-tune singing in the appropriate vocal range. The basic repertoire taught to young children should have the vocal range of a sixth, from D to B above middle C. The comfortable starting pitch for all songs will be provided for you in this text.

Young children love to sing, especially if the singing is accompanied by a fun game. Encourage singing for enjoyment, while fostering correct intonation and a proper singing tone. Allow the children to hear their own voices without piano accompaniment, and to enjoy active music making. Initially, we do not want children to be distracted by the piano accompaniment; rather, we want them to be actively making music themselves. Of course, once children have mastered a song we can occasionally use the piano, an autoharp, or a guitar to accompany the song.

A cappella singing will allow children to hear their own voices and enjoy active music making. Kodály addressed the importance of *a cappella* singing.

> Most singing teachers and chorus masters believe in controlling the pitch of the voice by the piano. But singing depends on the acoustically correct "natural" intervals, and not on the tempered system. Even a perfectly tuned piano can never be a criterion of singing, not to speak of the ever "out-of-tune" pianos available at schools and rehearsal rooms. Yet how often have I found chorus masters attempting to restore the shaky intonation of their choirs with the help of a mistuned piano![1]

In the classroom, we encourage singing for enjoyment while promoting correct intonation and a proper singing tone. The instructor's vocal model can significantly improve children's singing and the development of good vocal intonation. It is interesting to note that "Infants perceive and retain more details from ecologically valid music such as expressively sung lullabies than they do from inexpressive (i.e., synthesized) instrumental music."[2]

Young voices have less volume, less endurance, and a naturally higher range than adult voices; the adult instructor should modify his or her voice to accommodate this. Male instructors should consider singing in a falsetto range with young children to help them match pitch. It is important for children to learn how to sing in their head voice. A male teacher should consider providing a model and perhaps use a good singer from the class to subsequently model for the class. The falsetto voice is fine, provided the teacher is comfortable with the quality of the model it provides.

Finding Your Head Voice and Chest Voice

The technical difference between "head voice" and "chest voice" is related to how the vocal folds vibrate when singing; the terms *head* and *chest* designate where vibrations are most strongly felt. When you sing in the head voice, the vibrations are felt behind your nose and your cheeks. When singing in the chest voice, you feel vibrations in your throat and chest. There are a number of initial vocal exercises you can do to find your head voice.

- Pretend you are talking to a baby. Notice how your speaking voice is much higher in pitch. You may also pretend to talk like Mickey Mouse. Those children who know the character are often quickly inspired to change the focus of their voice.
- Pretend to be an owl, and make a high-pitched "whoooo" sound. Repeat this several times, trying to make every "whoooo" a little higher than the last.
- Pretend you are sliding down a slide, making a "whee" sound with your voice.
- Say chants with high and low voice. Use high and low voice for the two characters in a nursery rhyme.
- Say a nursery rhyme using a high voice for one verse and a low voice for another verse.
- Toss a ball in the air and follow it with your voice.
- Draw swirls and hills on the board; follow them first by tracing the swirl with your arm, and then repeat the activity adding your voice.

It is helpful to guide young children in singing because they are still trying to make the distinction between singing and speaking. We are not saying that children should not sing at all in the chest voice. Many songs in the African American tradition sound better in the chest voice. However, as music educators, we need to make children aware of the different energies and aspects of head and chest voices. Children have a tendency to shout rather than sing in an effort to sing loudly. Model appropriate singing for your children, whether singing in head or chest voice.

Helping Children Sing in Tune

Generally speaking, the young child can perform child's chants and say nursery rhymes with vocal inflection. Young children understand the concept of the singing and speaking voice although sometimes they need help distinguishing between singing and speaking. They often sing in tune from the notes D to B above middle C, although this range could be higher or lower for some children.

Children will sing in tune if songs are short and have a limited range. Sing songs that use two or three pitches, such as "Bounce High, Bounce Low" or "Sol Solecito."

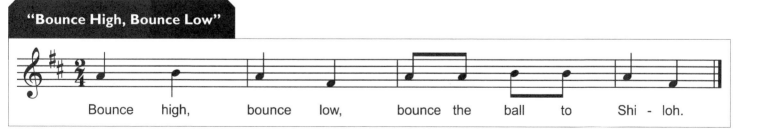

"Sol Solecito"

Sol, so - le - ci - to, ca - lién - ta - me un po - qui - to

hoy y ma - ña - na y to - da la se - ma - na.

Sing songs containing descending melodic patterns. Generally, songs that begin with a descending melodic pattern are easier for young children to hear and sing; this type of song offers a greater opportunity for the young learner to hear accurately, and subsequently a better chance to sing in tune. The songs "Doggie Doggie" and "Lemonade" have simple descending melodic patterns.

"Doggie Doggie"

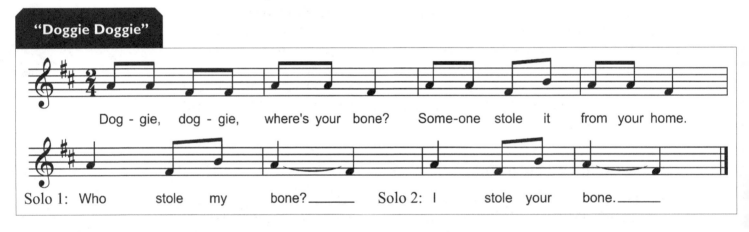

Dog - gie, dog - gie, where's your bone? Some-one stole it from your home.

Solo 1: Who stole my bone?_____ Solo 2: I stole your bone._____

"Lemonade"

Solo   Chorus   Solo

Here I come! Where from? New York.

Chorus   Solo   Chorus

What's your trade? Lem - on - ade. Give us some, don't be a - fraid.

The teacher should sing the song in tune and with the correct pronunciation and character. Remember to begin each song on a comfortable starting pitch. Young children learn the majority of songs they perform through listening and repetition.

Always indicate the starting pitch of the song. Singing the starting notes or even the entire first phrase will help set the pitch for young children. Repetition is important when teaching children to sing in tune. Sometimes encouraging children to sing with a soft voice leads to better intonation, as singing with a loud voice often leads to out-of-tune singing.

The teacher should not always sing with the class; when children sing on their own, they develop greater vocal independence because they can hear themselves more clearly. If a child has not found his singing voice, sit in front of him and let him see your mouth move as you sing. Singing into his right ear is a technique that can assist a child having pitch problems. Movement aids a child having intonation difficulties as well as helping young children perform and keep the beat.

Allow children to sing individually. It develops independence and gives the teacher an opportunity to evaluate the progress of the class. Individual singing experience encourages vocal independence. Some children can sing in tune with a group but not sing in tune when singing on their own, and vice versa.

Warm-up Activities for Singing

Here are warm-up activities well suited to developing tuneful singing.

Body Warm-up Exercises

Begin the class by allowing children to stretch and bend to relax their bodies. Eliminate tension by performing these stretching exercises with your children:

- Tip your head from side to side and roll your head back and forth.
- Rotate your shoulders in circles forward and backward.
- Drop your jaw and say "mah, mah, mah" several times.

Singing Posture

As part of the warm-up activities, help students find the correct posture for singing. The body needs to be balanced for them to project a beautiful singing tone. The next suggestions will help children find the correct posture for singing. Always demonstrate and guide the students to imitate.

- Balance the head. To accomplish this, the face should look straight ahead. Try several exercises such as moving the head up, down, and sideways to relax the head and neck muscles. Stand with your back against a wall and make sure that your head and the heels of your feet are touching the wall.
- Shoulders should be relaxed and rotated toward the back.
- Hands should be relaxed at the sides.
- Knees should be relaxed and very slightly bent.

- Feet should be firmly placed on the ground and roughly ten to twelve inches apart.
- If children are sitting when singing, they should be seated at the edge of their chairs.

Breathing Exercises

Breathing exercises teach children to inhale and exhale correctly. Controlled exhaling is a helpful exercise.

- Show children how to sip through a straw correctly, expanding their waist.
- Show children how to release air using a "sts" sound, or using the word "ha."
- Show children how to release air using the word "ha."

Exercises and Vocalizations (Pitch Exploration Activities) for Developing Resonance, Tone Production, and Tuneful Singing

We suggest these activities for use after children sing an opening song or play a singing game. Pedagogically it might be better to try transitioning from the opening game to the tuneful singing exercises. For example, if we begin the class singing "Lucy Locket" we can tell the children that Lucy is very tired and she wants to yawn or sigh. Or maybe Lucy wants to develop her singing voice and needs to do her humming exercises.

When we first begin to incorporate pitch exploration activities into our lesson, we should try to use descending sounds or pitches, as these are easier to perform than ascending ones. It is helpful to have the whole class perform an exercise and then move to a group of children before asking an individual child to perform an activity. Aim to give children an assessment that will help them develop their singing voices.

Like an athlete stretching before a run, a singer should warm up slowly and carefully before singing. Many common vocal sounds are also excellent warm-ups for the singing voice. Try these with your children:

- Yawning opens up the back of the throat and relaxes the voice.
- Sighing is a gentle way to use a higher voice than is usual for speaking. Try sighing a few times, starting each sigh a little higher than the last.
- Imitating a siren is something children delight in doing. It also engages the voice in such a way that the extremes of one's vocal range can be explored without danger of strain. When the children imitate a siren, challenge them to make soft and loud, high and low, long and short sirens, and sirens that just go up, or just come down, or do both.
- Ask one child to throw a ball or beanbag to another child. The class must follow the arc or direction of the beanbag with their voice.
- Copying animal sounds: bark like a dog, roar like a lion, and meow like a cat.
- As you move a flashlight beam projected onto the blackboard in a room, ask children to follow the contour of the moving beam of light with their voice.
- Imitate the sound of a slide whistle. Begin with descending sounds before practicing ascending ones. Then play the slide whistle, and have the children imitate the sound.

- Present children with a picture card that has a descending line drawing. Ask them to follow the line as you play the sliding whistle. Children repeat but follow the shape of the line. Once they have mastered a descending line, you can introduce a picture of an ascending line. At a later stage, you can put several cards together.
- Understand the difference between speaking voice and singing voice.
- As a music instructor, you can help children discover the difference between their speaking voice and singing voice. Young children need to become aware of the different sounds their voice can produce. Guide children to discover that they have these types of voices:

Talking voice
Whispering or soft voice
Calling voice
Singing voice
Internal voice or thinking voice

- Modulate your voice. When telling stories in class, modulate your voice to include a high, medium, and low voice registers for characters in the story, or high, low, and medium sounds for events in the story. Repeat the story and ask children to make the sounds. Select songs and rhymes that can be used to develop a child's singing voice. As young children say chants, they may be guided to speak using a "baby bird voice" (high) or a "grandfather's voice" (low). Chanting using these voice types will teach a young learner how to modulate her voice. Guide young children to perform the chant "Bee, Bee, Bumble Bee," using a high voice; then perform the chant using a low voice.
- Humming is a gentle (and quiet) way to use the singing voice. Humming a favorite song before singing it also gives children a chance to practice the song's melody without being distracted by the words.
- Encourage children to vocalize high and low sounds as well as soft and loud sounds. Songs that contain the "oo" sound are particularly effective for developing in-tune singing. Consider adding a high-pitched "toot" to the end of chant "Engine, Engine, Number Nine" while the children are marching and chanting.
- *Many ordinary vocal sounds are also excellent warm-up exercises. Sing known songs with neutral syllables such as "noo," "moo," "la," etc.*
- Sing songs that contain repeatable phrases or echo patterns. With this material, you sing a phrase and the children echo back the same phrase. For instance, sing each phrase of "Charlie over the Ocean" and have the children echo. Do the same activities with the song "No More Pie." Listen to Ella Jenkins' version found on iTunes: "Play Your Instruments and Make a Pretty Sound." Jenkins sings a phrase and echoes with an instrument so that children can sing the echo.
- Sing greetings to children. A greeting song is often sung at the beginning of music time so the children become familiar and comfortable with it. Singing this song at the very beginning of music time helps the children transtion from a previous activity to sitting attentively in the circle, ready to sing. Use a puppet to sing the greeting so that children will not be self-conscious while singing.

Initially greetings should be restricted to the notes of a child's chant, *so mi* and *la*; later the range can be expanded to further develop the voice.

- Visuals (manipulatives) such as puppets are fun in the classroom and help capture a child's attention and imagination. They are important tools to help young children understand a concept, understand a text, or develop music skills. Make sure that the visual does not detract children from the task at hand. Children need to be able to use the visual with minimal effort. Puppets may be used in teaching and subsequently be placed in a play area in the classroom, where they will inspire children to play and sing on their own. Here is a procedure we offer to help children sing a greeting using a puppet. Introduce (a stuffed animal or puppet) to the class; ask the children to sing "good morning" to him. The puppet then leads the entire class in singing the song "Good Morning Boys and Girls," in which each child is sung good morning to by name.

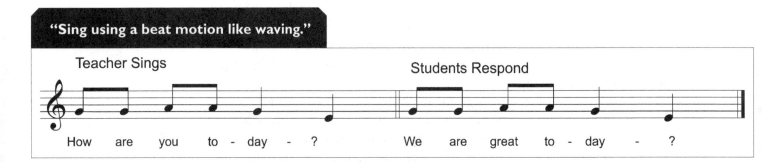

- Name songs may be sung to individual children. Instead of singing to the class, sing a greeting to an individual child using the notes of a child's chant, *so*, *mi*, and *la*. Simply sing: "Sing me your name" and the child replies, "My name is Andy." Sometimes in the Early Childhood classroom children are not comfortable singing their own name, so you might use, "Sing me his/her name" and the children will reply, "His/her name is Andy."
- It is important for the young child to begin to recognize the singing voices of other children in the class, as well as the sound of simple musical instruments. Developing the ability to identify timbre can be easily integrated using a game such as "Doggie Doggie."

"Doggie, Doggie"

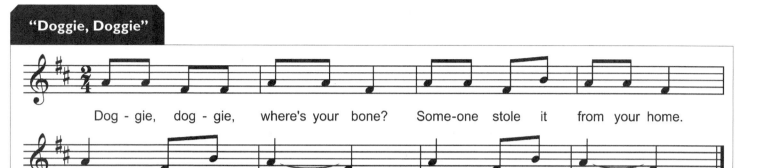

Dog - gie, dog - gie, where's your bone? Some-one stole it from your home.

Solo 1: Who stole my bone?_____ Solo 2: I stole your bone._____

In the second line of the song, the child playing the dog is hiding her eyes. One child sings the last four beats of the song: "I stole your bone." The child who is the dog in this game song must identify who sang, "I stole your bone." Once the children become adept at playing this game, a child could sing "I have the bone" and also tap out the rhythm of "I have the bone" on a percussion instrument; the child who is the dog must guess the name of the instrument as well as guess the name of the child.

77

"A La Ronda, Ronda"

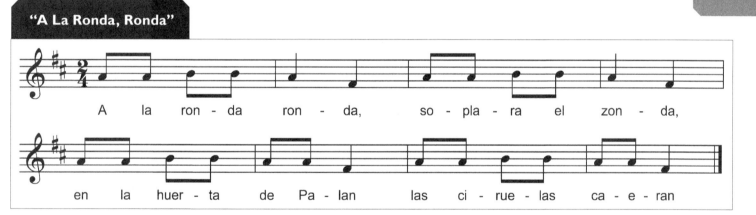

A la ron - da ron - da, so - pla - ra el zon - da,

en la huer - ta de Pa - lan las ci - rue - las ca - e - ran

Literal translation:
Round and round,
the hot north wind swirls,
In the garden of Palan,
the plums will fall.

- Once the children become adept at singing this song, a child could sing "en la huerta de Andy." The named child can select a fruit or vegetable that will fall from a tree or a bush.

Connections to Literature-Developing Singing Skills

We suggest the following books to Kindergarten instructors. The texts for these books have sections for sound and vocal exploration. Children can be guided to take the role of characters, animals, or activities in the book and create appropriate vocal sounds.

Singing (Onomatopoeia) and Songs for Vocal Exploration

Boynton, Sandra. *Moo Baa La La La*. New York: Little Simon,1982.

Brett, Jan. *Honey... Honey... Lion!* New York: Penguin Putnam, 2005.

Cronin, Doreen. *Wiggle*. New York: Atheneum Books for Young Readers, 2005.

Dr. Seuss. *Mr. Brown Can Moo! Can You?* New York: Random House Books for Young Readers, 1996.

Gershator, Phillis. *Listen, Listen*. Cambridge, MA: Barefoot Books, 2007.

Gollub, Matthew. *Gobble, Quack, Moon*. 1st ed. Santa Rosa, CA: Tortuga Press, 2002.

Greene, Rhonda Gowler. *Barnyard Song*. New York: Atheneum Books for Young Readers, 1997.

Williams, Linda. *The Little Old Lady Who Was Not Afraid of Anything*. New York: HarperCollins, 1986.

Williams, Sue. *I Went Walking*. New York: Harcourt Brace, 1989.

Teaching a New Song

All of these teaching ideas and techniques bring up the challenge of teaching a new song to the class. Remember that it may take several lessons to teach one song well enough for the children to perform it independently. The teacher serves as a model for the correct performance of the song; for this reason, music must be presented in a stylistically correct manner. It is important for the instructor to help children understand the aesthetics of the song through facial expressions. The mood for the presentation of the song may be set through a story or another well-known song. We do not use a new song to teach a new concept or music skill, as the child needs time to learn the song and become familiar with the text and melody before using the song for skill development. Nor should an instrument accompany the new song, as we want the children to focus on the melody and rhythm of the text.

General Ideas for Presenting and Teaching New Songs

- Give children a picture of the new song, with the title under the picture.
- Give them a picture or pictures illustrating a character or events from the song.
- Use the melody of the new song as part of your greeting so that the children become familiar with the melodic turn.
- Play the melody of the new song on a recorder or melody bells.

- Repeat the song appropriately, and accompany it with appropriate motions. At this level, many repetitions of a song are needed to develop security in performance. This, in turn, promotes a sense of emotional security in the classroom. Initially, it is important that the young learner simply imitate the motions used to accompany the song; once secure they can sing on their own with the motions.
- Children's intellectual abilities are developed through vocabulary from the song texts, and from memorizing songs, using the imagination (which many song texts suggest), using puppets, role playing, reasoning, discriminating, and employing logic through games involving specific forms (for example, circle and line formation games and dances).
- Teach the song with the correct phrasing. When providing an example for children, it is helpful to indicate the phrase by making an arch shaped motion for each phrase moving from (the children's) left to right. Encourage children to sing the song with this phrase motion. Have them echo-sing the individual phrases. Once children can identify the number of phrases within the song, encourage them to use the words "same" and "different" to describe the phrases; for example, "Is the first phrase the same as the second phrase?" The teacher may indicate the form by using a picture of an apple for the A phrase and a picture of a banana for the (different) B phrase.
- Table 3.1 provides ideas that may be used to teach songs.

Table 3.1

	Three Year Olds	Four Year Olds	Five Year Olds
Songs rhymes	Twenty-five	Thirty	Thirty-five
Singing	Sometimes can sing in tune with help of T	Can sing in tune as a group and individually	Can sing in tune as a group and individually
Teaching technique	T should use facial expressions and gestures with C. C love to sing games and use repetitive actions.	T should use facial expressions and gestures with C. Try to be creative as you introduce new songs and teach through a story or games. C at this age level love to play games and engage their imagination.	C at this age level love to play games but also like to demonstrate what they can do individually.

(Continued)

Table 3.1   (continued)

	Three Year Olds	Four Year Olds	Five Year Olds
Song recognition		Recognize known song from humming beginning motif or playing beginning motif on an instrument such as the recorder.	Recognize known song from humming the beginning or another motif in the melody; playing motives of the songs on an instrument such as the recorder. C can also recognize songs that have the same melody but some variation of the rhythm pattern.
Echo singing			C can sing back melodic pattern and can substitute texts. "Down came a Lady"— singing different colors in the final phrase

- **Additional suggestions for effectively teaching songs to children:**

1. Sing the song within an accessible and appropriate melodic range.
2. Be able to sing every song with the correct tempo, dynamics, and expression.
3. Learn the song from notation; listen to great recordings of the song material so you can sing each song musically. Remember that the notation is only a guide as to how to sing the song.
4. Always sing songs and say rhymes with the appropriate facial expressions and gestures.
5. Perform beat motions so that they are musical.
6. Remember what children can or cannot do in terms of movement.
7. It is important to say the rhymes and sing the repertoire from memory.
8. Give children the correct cue for beginning a song. Cue when the children are to sing a known song. The pitch and the tempo may be given by singing "Here we go" or "Ready, sing" to match the pitch of the first note of the song. It is important for the children to sing on their own, without your help.

Techniques for Teaching a Song by Rote

Teaching Songs by Asking Questions
- Ask questions relating to the text of the song. Asking questions can (1) direct children's attention, (2) help strengthen their analytical skills, and (3) aid in remembering the song.
- Use the fewest words possible. By asking specific questions, you give the children listening tasks that help them focus their attention on a particular musical element.
- Sing the song for the children after every question. The children will become familiar with the melody and text before they are asked to sing the song.

"Star Light, Star Bright" (Traditional Children's Song)

Check responses by singing the whole song to see if the children give a correct answer. Here are some techniques for asking questions:

- Ask children to complete a musical phrase by singing the last word.
- Ask children to recall what the person did in the song. For example, with "Star Light" what did the child want to make?
- Ask some open-ended questions to engage children in the song.
- Use the words *who, what, when, where,* and *why* in asking questions.
- Try to make connections to the children's own lives.

Presenting a Song Using Games and Movements

Movement activities help children learn and memorize songs quickly and easily. You and the children may create your own games and motions to accompany songs. For example, high-and-low or up-and-down motions may be used with the song "See-Saw" to convey the concept of high and low. Later, the simple motion of bending knees may be used to reflect the solfège syllables *s* and *m*. Motions that are initiated by the instructor or children may reflect the beat or recurring rhythmic patterns. Encourage children to use their imagination and create motions to accompany songs.

Performing motions or acting out a story line helps children memorize songs and rhymes (as in "Bee, Bee, Bumble Bee").

"Bee, Bee, Bumble Bee" (Traditional Children's Chant)

(Continued)

81

"Bee, Bee, Bumble Bee" (continued)

1. Phrase one: children flap their arms (wings) to the beat.
2. Phrase two: children point to their knees to the beat.
3. Phrase three: children point to their nose to the beat.
4. Phrase four: children point to other children in the circle to the beat.

"Engine, Engine, Number Nine" (Traditional Children's Chant)

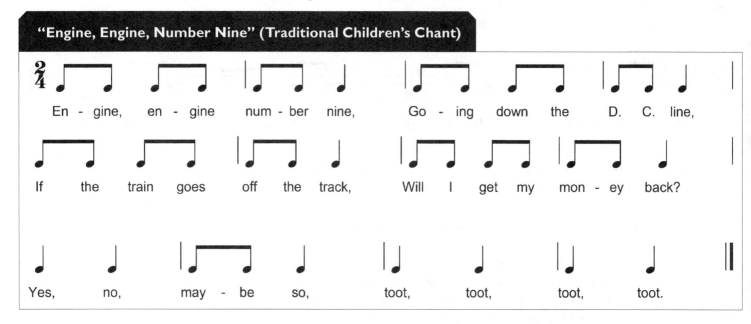

Children move their arms, imitating the motion of the wheels of the engine, and march around the classroom while chanting:

Engine, engine, number nine
Going down Chicago line (you may substitute other cities here)
If the train should jump the track
Would you want your money back
Yes, no, maybe so
Toot, toot, toot, toot!

"Hunt the Slipper" (Jamaican Folk Song)

Children can pantomime hammering their shoes to the beat of the song.

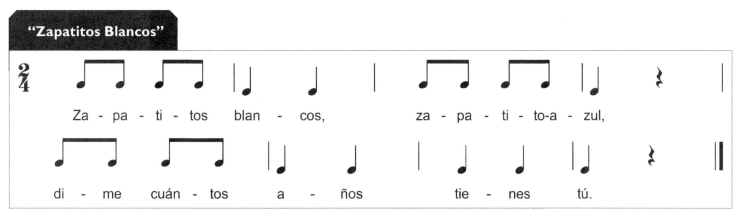

"Zapatitos Blancos"

Za - pa - ti - tos   blan - cos,   za - pa - ti - to-a - zul,

di - me   cuán - tos   a - ños   tie - nes   tú.

Literal translation: Little white shoes, Little Blue shoe,

Tell me how old you are.

When performed as a "choosing" game, the selected child may state his or her age.

Teaching Echo Songs

These are songs that have a repeated phrase. You sing the song for the class and use a puppet to sing the echo. To emphasize the "echo," use a loud or soft voice. Sing each phrase of the song and ask the class to echo-sing. Then sing each phrase and ask various children to echo-sing. This should be done only when children can sing the song together fluently. "Charlie over the Ocean" is an example of an echo song.

Teaching Call-and-Response Songs

Here is a procedure for use in teaching a call-and-response song.

1. Sing the call and response song for the children as a listening activity. Consider using two hand puppets to distinguish the call and the response. Sing the phrase and guide children to echo; use a pretend microphone to help young children understand the alternation. Later, when the song is well learned, have individual children echo the instructor.
2. Ask individual children to take the role of the instructor; they sing the call and the class can echo the response.

Examples of call-and-response songs are "Skin and Bones," "Amasee," and "Did You Feed My Cow?"

Assessing the Presentation of a Song

These questions will help you assess and evaluate your teaching of songs to your children.

- Did I introduce the song in an interesting manner?
- Have I memorized the song correctly?
- Did I determine the best method of presentation for introducing this song?
- Did I sing the song in a stylistically appropriate manner?
- Did I begin singing the song on a pitch that is appropriate for the children I'm teaching?

- Did I engage my children with eye contact and facial expressions as I performed the song?
- Did I use clear mouth movements?
- Did I stay in tune as I sang the song?
- Was the tempo appropriate for learning? Was my pronunciation clear? Could the text be easily understood?
- Did I keep a steady beat and tempo as the children were singing phrase by phrase?
- Was the teaching pace appropriate for children to understand and learn the rhyme or song?
- Did I correct children's mistakes and intonation problems by repeated modeling so they could absorb the correct way of singing?

Summary: The Many Uses of a Folk Song

The same song may be sung many times throughout the year and even revisited in different grade levels. Here are suggestions for using the same song in a variety of activities. Songs may be:

- Presented as listening activities
- Learned for their formal structure such as question and answer
- Performed with a beat or simple rhythmic pattern (rhythmic ostinato)
- Performed with a soft or loud singing voice
- Performed with a fast or slow tempo
- Performed with a high or low voice (or a higher or lower key)
- Used to make an emotional connection with plot or character in a book

Singing Games and Movement

Movement development is one of the foundations of the Kindergarten curriculum. As E. B. Church writes, in *Learning Through Play*: "Music and movement are vital to the creative educational process. We enable the whole child to grow emotionally, creatively, socially and cognitively."[3] Without movement, children will not have the necessary oxygen-rich blood needed to learn. Through movement activities children explore concepts, clarify knowledge of music, and physically respond to it. Movement can be a powerful tool for developing children's creativity. Research suggests that there is a "strong connection between physical education, movement, energizing activities and improved cognition."[4]

During the music class we teach children a core of song material that will be used to develop their emotions, singing, moving, and playing ability. It is important to realize that there is a unity within listening, singing, beat acquisition, and development of movement. Additionally we need to offer opportunities for children to develop their own creativity. By manipulating rhythmic and melodic building blocks in these songs, children can explore new ways to create compositions. As previously mentioned, we strongly believe that children should be exposed to song repertoire that is cognitively and age-appropriate. This repertoire promotes developing children's creativity. Through playing games we give young children movement sequences that become the building blocks for their own responsiveness to music. Movement exploration is a goal of teaching music in the Kindergarten classroom.

Selecting Singing Games for Kindergarten That Develop Movement Skills

There are several reasons for choosing a particular game to play with children. The primary goal is always for the children to enjoy singing and playing the game. Here are some important considerations for how and why we select musical games to play in the Kindergarten classroom:

- To help children develop their movement skills. For example, we might need to choose a game to develop children's ability to walk to the beat in a circle. We might choose a game so that we can practice keeping the beat with large motions or small ones.
- Because it contains melodic motifs that develop children's ability to sing in tune.
- Because it contains rhythm patterns that we want the children to be able to sing and perform.
- To develop a child's imagination.
- When we can link to a book that will be read to the children.

The selection of a game is based on the children's ability to perform specific motions. Keep the form of the game (circle, line, etc.), but modify the movements accordingly. Table 3.2 enhances awareness of the performance capabilities of young children.

Table 3.2

Three and Four Year Olds	Five and Six Year Olds
Free movement in place (sitting)	Free movement in place (sitting)
Free movement in space	Free movement in space
Movement to a beat while sitting	Movement to a beat while sitting
Movement to a beat while walking	Movement to a beat while walking
Movement while standing in a circle	Movement while standing in a circle
T plays with the child as a partner	Small finger movements
Partner games	Movements that are linked to changing directions
Movements starting and stopping with music	Acting out directions
	Choosing a partner
	Follow the leader
	Chasing games
	Line game movements
	Winding movements
	Moving in a circle
	Developing the ability to clap the rhythm of a rhyme or melody

Games are a significant way to develop children's imagination, social, emotional, and movement skills, as well as to reinforce musical concepts and skills. Musical games are important in part because they contain the possibility of role-play. For instance, when singing "Hunt the Slipper" children can pretend to mend shoes, or be a baker baking while singing "Hot Cross Buns." Additionally, children are involved in imaginary games where they must become a bluebird in "Here Comes a Bluebird" or a puppy in playing "Doggie, Doggie." Games for children should be age-appropriate and correspond to the children's physical development. The motions and movement activities within the games should be easy for children to follow as they sing. Playing games help develop their musical ear, singing ability, and sense of rhythm.

To effectively teach a musical game, you should be familiar with the game and able to present the motions sequentially. Address the difficult parts of the game logically in order to prepare the young learner. For variety, you may wish to present the song to the children before introducing the movements or motions. Other times, you may want the children to learn the motions prior to singing the song and playing the game. When first presenting the song and game motions together, ask children to listen as you sing and focus on the motions or movements. A singing game contains its own artistic logic. For example, every game has a beginning, a middle, and an end. Children love the energy of games and look forward to the conclusion; and they always look forward to playing multiple times.

Choosing partners and other rules for playing singing games can be tricky. Establish classroom rules that will guide children to understand appropriate behavior. Practice these things with the children:

- How to hold hands correctly
- How to walk around the circle with the correct footwork
- Keeping their heads turned to the center of the circle as they walk around it
- Matching actions to the beat

How to Develop a Child's Movement Skills Through Singing Games

Here are suggestions for teaching games in an organized manner.

Performing Beat Motions in One Position

Children remain in one position, sitting or standing, and perform a motion to go with a song. It can be related to the beat, for example, pointing to imaginary raindrops while singing "Rain, Rain, Go Away." Guide children to create their own beat movements.

Performing Beat Motions While Moving

Children move to a song while walking, hopping, or skipping. When working with these songs, make sure the children have plenty of opportunity to explore forward and backward movements as well as side-to-side movement and use of higher or lower space. When singing "Hop Old Squirrel" children can also hop, skip, march, walk etc.

"Hop Old Squirrel"

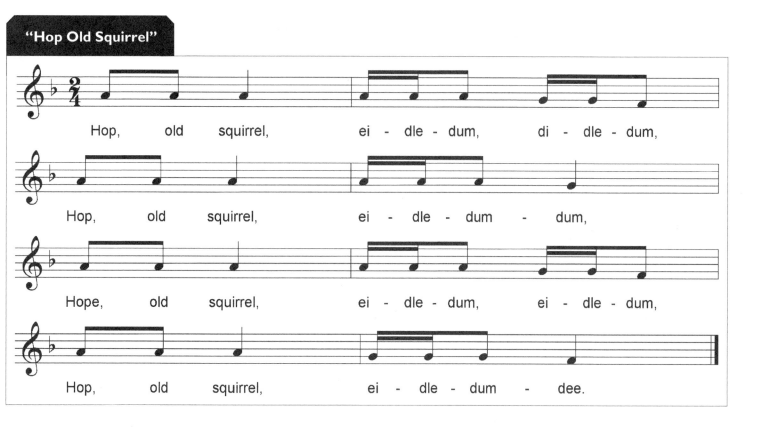

Acting Out Games from a Seated Position

Children may sing a song and act out the motions to make a cake during "Hot Cross Buns." Children can mix the batter, spoon it into the cake pan, or take out the hot buns and put them on a tray.

"Hot Cross Buns"

Acting out Games Standing in a Stationary Circle

As children sing a song in a stationary circle formation, one child walks around the inside circle and improvises a motion that the children must imitate when singing or follows the game motions of a song.

"Hey Betty Martin"

Children sing the song as one stands in the center of the circle or walks around the inside circle and improvises a motion such as jumping or skipping. Children sing the song and repeat the motion of the leader.

"Do Do Pity My Case"

Children sing the song as one stands in the center of the circle and improvises a motion. Children imitate the motion of the leader and sing the song, changing the text. For example, children sing song as a child improvises motions for hanging clothes. Then children sing the song but change the text "My clothes to wash" to "My clothes to dry."

"Button You Must Wander"

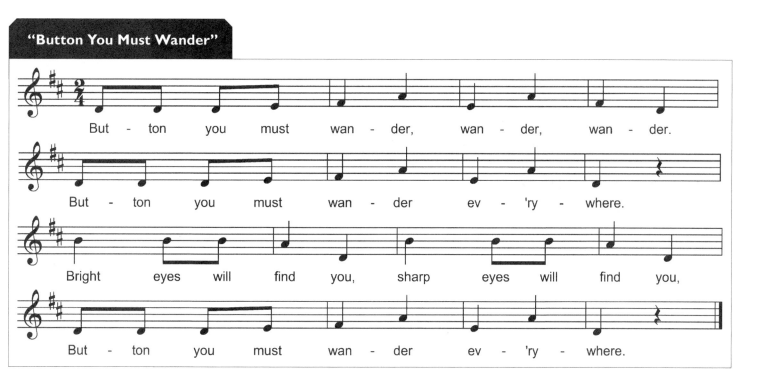

Children can stand or sit in a circle. A button is passed around the circle from child to child, but everyone pretends to be passing the button. The child in the center must figure out who has the button at the end of the song.

Choosing Games

In these games children must choose a partner.

"Here Comes a Bluebird"

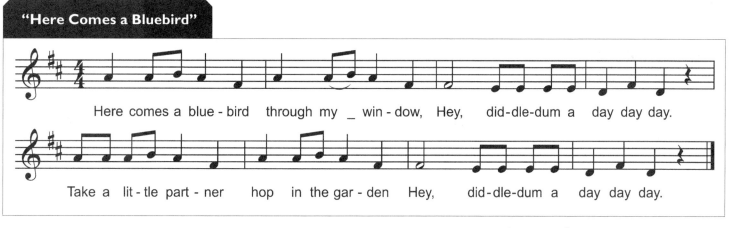

(*Continued*)

"Here Comes a Bluebird" (continued)

1. Have children stand in a circle, joining hands together, holding them up (forming windows).
2. Choose one child to walk in and under the windows.
3. On "take a little partner" this child takes a partner, and with two hands joined they face each other, gallop out through the opening where the child was taken from the ring, and back again, or dance the same around inside the circle.
4. The first child joins the circle, and the partner becomes the bluebird.

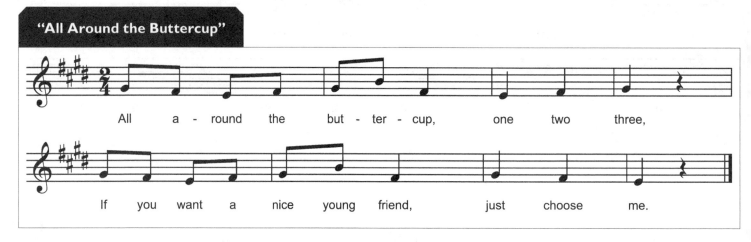

"All Around the Buttercup"

All a - round the but - ter - cup, one two three,

If you want a nice young friend, just choose me.

1. Children stand in a circle, forming windows by raising their hands upwards.
2. Choose one child to weave in and out of the windows.
3. On the last word of the song, the child taps the child in front of him or her who then becomes the leader of the line.
4. The last child left becomes the "buttercup" in the center of the new circle and the game begins again.

Chase Game with a Stationary Circle

"Charlie Over the Ocean"

Char - lie o - ver the o - cean, Char - lie o - ver the sea - - -

Char - lie caught a black - bird, Can't catch me

Variation 1

1. Have children join hands in a ring and skip to their right.
2. Choose someone to be the leader who stands outside the circle and skips in the opposite direction.

3. The leader begins the song, and the circle sings the song back to him.
4. When the leader says, "Charlie caught a blackbird," he touches someone in the ring and then begins to run around the circle.
5. The person he touched tries to catch the leader.
6. If the person touched on the shoulder cannot catch him or her before the leader reaches the empty space, then the second person is the leader.
7. If the person touched on the shoulder catches the first leader, then he or she remains on the outside of the circle and remains the leader.

"Al Ánimo"

"Al Ánimo" is played like "London Bridge."

"A Tisket a Tasket"

1. Have the children form a circle.
2. Choose a child to walk around the circle, carrying a handkerchief.
3. At the end of the song, the child will drop the handkerchief behind another child and start to run around the circle.

4. The child with the handkerchief behind him or her starts to run after the first child.
5. If the child catches the other before reaching the empty spot, the second child becomes It.
6. If the child does not catch the other child, the first child is It again.
7. We might need to be careful when singing songs with an anacrusis for children. Consider using such songs and rhymes later in the year.

Circle Game with Moving Circle

"Ring Around the Rosy"

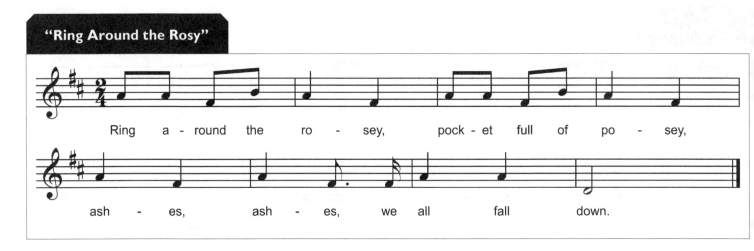

1. Children join hands in a circle and walk around singing the song.
2. At the word "down" they all squat down on their heels, then immediately get up, and the game starts again.

"Built My Lady a Fine Brick House"

1. Have pairs of children hold hands. Tell them this will represent a house.
2. Arrange pairs of children in a circle: "Now we have a neighborhood of houses!"
3. Choose a child to be It and place that child "inside a house" (standing between two children holding hands).
4. While singing the song, have the pairs raise and lower their arms to open and close their house.
5. At the third line of the song, while arms are raised, the child who is It can duck out of the house and into another house.
6. Change children, and continue the game.

"Sally Go Around the Sun"

Lit - tle Sal - ly Wa - ters, Sit - ting in a sau - cer,

Rise, Sal - ly, rise, Sal - ly, Wipe a - way your tears, Sal - ly.

Turn to the East, Sal - ly, Turn to the West Sal - ly,

Turn to the one that you love the best, Sal - ly.

1. Have the children form a circle holding hands and facing to the right, ready to walk in that direction.
2. As they are singing, they should walk to the right.
3. When they shout "BOOM!" the children should jump up in the air and then sing again.

Line Games

"Lemonade"

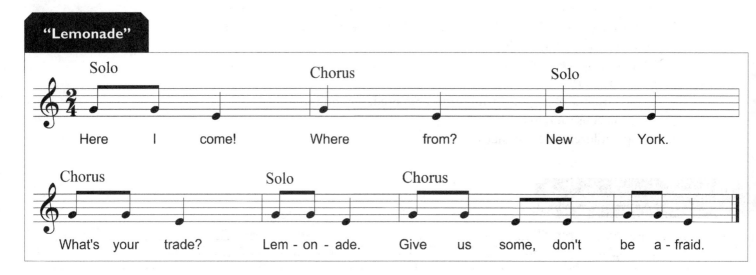

1. One player is chosen to lead off.
2. At the end of the dialogue sung in question and answer, the leader pours "pretend" lemonade into the "glasses" held by all the members of the group.

Alternative game:
1. Divide the group into two teams.
2. Alter text to "Here we come," and devise a scoring method.
3. One team is designated to act out a trade, the other to guess it.

Line Game with Arch Formation

"London Bridge"

Winding Games

1. Wind the class around the room with all holding hands, the first and last person each having one hand free.
2. Lead the children into the shell shape by winding up, turning out first.

94

3. To unwind, let go of the first child's hand, scoot over to the end of the line, and hold hands with the last child to lead them out.

"Snail, Snail"

Snail, snail, snail, snail, Go a - round round and round.

Moving Circle

There are games that involve moving around the circle with improvised motions, like "Walk Daniel" or "Jim along Josie," "Sally Go 'Round the Sun" or "We are Dancing in the Forest."

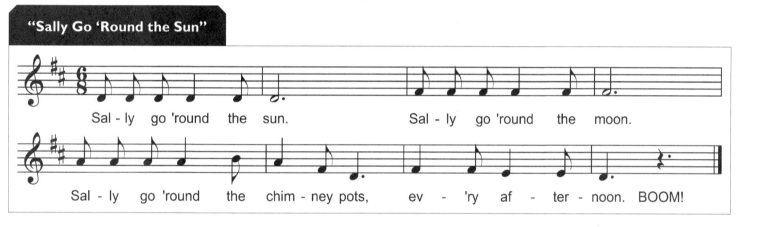

"Sally Go 'Round the Sun"

Sal - ly go 'round the sun. Sal - ly go 'round the moon.

Sal - ly go 'round the chim - ney pots, ev - 'ry af - ter - noon. BOOM!

Free-Form Chase Game

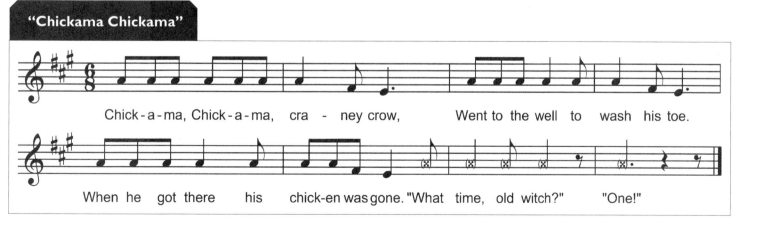

"Chickama Chickama"

Chick - a - ma, Chick - a - ma, cra - ney crow, Went to the well to wash his toe.

When he got there his chick-en was gone. "What time, old witch?" "One!"

Children stand at one end of room and the teacher or another child who is the Witch stands at the opposite end of the room. When the Witch counts "one," children run across to the Witch's side of the room, trying not to be caught by the Witch.

Free-Form Games

In this type of game, children do not move in any predetermined order. For example, when singing "Page's Train" the leader can take the children in the train on a trip all around the classroom.

"We Are Dancing in the Forest"

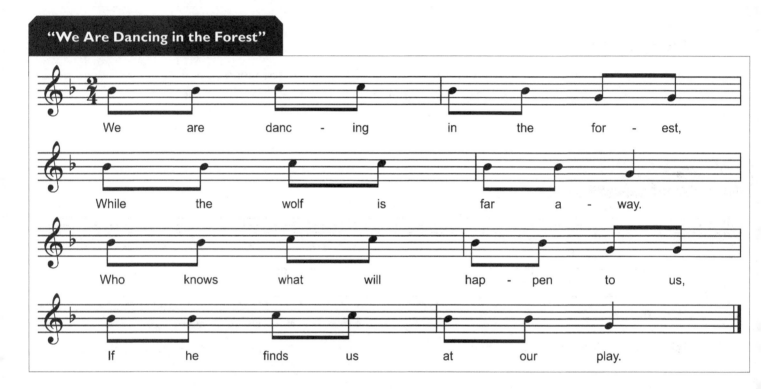

1. Children are "dancing" in a circle.
2. A child is appointed the Wolf and is hiding nearby or is in the center of the circle.
3. After singing one repetition, the circle asks, "Wolf, are you there?" to which the Wolf may answer something like, "No, I am putting on my shoes."
4. The circle continues to ask, "Wolf, are you there?" and the Wolf may improvise answers. When the Wolf answers "I'm coming to get you!" the children run, with the Wolf chasing after them.
5. When one is caught, this child becomes the Wolf and the game continues.

Alternative game:
1. One child is selected to be the Wolf, while the others are children in the forest.
2. While singing the song, the children "dance" around the room; the Wolf is in a hiding place.
3. Once the song is finished, the children freeze as the Wolf comes out to search for children.
4. If the Wolf sees any children move, he may tag them and they are out.

5. The game continues for a few rounds until several children are out; the teacher then selects a new Wolf and the game repeats.

General Guidelines for Teaching Singing Games

Before introducing children to a new singing game, it is a good idea to use the song as a listening activity, perhaps at the close of a music lesson. In this way they become familiar with the song associated with the game before the game is learned. Subsequently, teach the song as a new song in a lesson. During this section of the lesson you can teach the motions of the song. Children need time to develop the skill of moving while singing. Show them how to perform the motion that will be used in the new song or game. Once the song is well known, the game may be taught. Of course, there are many game songs that can be taught immediately to children because all they all simply follow the actions dictated by the text. Remember the sequence for teaching games; begin with stationary circles and then use games that involve moving circles.

Assessing the Teaching of a Game
Associated with a Well-Known Song

If a game is simple, teach it with the song. Sometimes you have to teach the song separately from the game. Here are questions to help you assess and evaluate teaching games to your children.

- Did I introduce the song for the game in an interesting manner?
- Did I sing the song in a stylistically appropriate manner?
- Did I begin singing the song on a pitch that is appropriate for the children I'm teaching?
- Did I engage my children with eye contact and facial expressions as I performed the song?
- Was the tempo appropriate for learning? Was my pronunciation clear? Could the text be easily understood?
- Did I demonstrate the motions for the game with one child?
- Did I demonstrate the motions for the game with a small group of children?

Connections to Literature-Developing Movement Skills

We suggest these books for Early Childhood instructors. The texts have sections or themes that center on movement activities. Children can be guided through movement activities that mimic or imitate the themes presented in the book.

Adams, Pam. *This Old Man*. New York: Child's Play International, 1989.
Brown, Margaret W. *Two Little Trains*. New York: HarperCollins, 2003.
Carle, Eric. *From Head to Toe*. New York: HarperFestival, 1997.
Cauley, Lorinda Bryan. *Clap Your Hands*. New York: Puffin Books, 1997.
Crews, Donald. *Freight Train Big Book*. New York: Greenwillow Books, 1993.
Crews, Donald. *Parade*. New York: Greenwillow Books, 1986.
Hoberman, Mary Ann. *Miss Mary Mack*. New York: Little, Brown, 1998.

Langstaff, John. *Oh, A-Hunting We Will Go*. New York: Aladdin Paperbacks, 1974.

Lester, Helen. *Tacky the Penguin*. London: Sandpiper, 2006.

Williams, Sue. *I Went Walking*. New York: Harcourt Brace, 1989.

Incorporating Improvisatory Movement into Singing Games and Listening

We develop children's movement skills when we teach them singing games. We're convinced that it is important to allow children to explore different kinds of movement activities with the repertoire they are singing and listening to. Here are some simple ideas that you can incorporate into your music lessons.

Two of our favorite and most admired movement specialists offering practical suggestions to music teachers are Phyllis Weikart[5] and Rudolf Laban (1879–1958). Weikart has written several books on movement development that are very useful for teachers.[6] Rudolf Laban provided educators with movement themes that can be incorporated and adapted into the music lesson.[7] Consider consulting more comprehensive descriptions of Laban's work if you wish, but the ideas below will furnish you with examples of the type of movement activities that can be developed in the music classroom using Laban's work as a starting point. These ideas can be explored when we are teaching beat movement activities or when we want to supply children with a repertoire of movements that can be adopted or adapted for their own movement dances and movement improvisations. You will notice that many of the motion suggestions are already incorporated into games that children play.

Laban offered four movement concept types: body, space, effort, and relationships.

Body Concepts

Body concept movements develop children's ability to become more skilled in locomotor, nonlocomotor, and manipulative skills. Some of the locomotor skills involve:

- Walking
- Running
- Hopping
- Jumping
- Skipping
- Galloping

Some of the nonlocomotor skills involve:

- Stretching
- Twisting
- Bending
- Swaying

Some of the manipulative skills involve:

- Catching
- Stroking a pet
- Mixing a cake batter

Space Concepts

Space concept movements (movement of body in space) develop children's ability to focus on where the body is moving. Children develop the ability to distinguish between personal space, different ways of moving in space, and understanding the direction of movement. Children develop skills to understand that movement can take place at various levels, such as high, middle, and low. For instance, they develop the ability to move:

- Forward
- Backward
- Sideways
- Up
- Down

Children can move on the ground or in the air using these motions:

- Straight
- Curved
- Twisted

Effort Concept Movements

Effort concept movements (how the body moves) develop children's ability to pay attention to how the body is moving in time and space. For example, can the body move in time using fast or slow movements? Can the body use a direct or an indirect route for traveling? Children can use these motions:

- Slow movement
- Fast movement
- Following a direct route to another person or object through a movement
- Following an indirect route to another person or object through a movement

Relationship Concept

Relationship aspects (how the body relates to itself or others as it moves) develop children's ability to understand how body parts work together. For example, are we using whole body movements that indicate body parts above or below, or isolated? Do body motions follow or lead, meet or mix with other children, move in unison, or move toward or away from other children?

Use Laban's concepts as a framework for incorporating movements into teaching songs. Games are also another opportunity to practice Laban's taxonomy of movements in the Early Childhood classroom music lesson. For instance, if children have played "All Around the Buttercup," the teacher might ask them to find ways a certain animal in a story or song would move as they are playing the game. Allow children to develop their own creative movement skills as an extension of what is taking place in the classroom.

By combining standard game activities with a repertoire of movement activities based on Laban's movement taxonomy, we give our children opportunities to develop their movement skills. It is important for children to be able to use their body to demonstrate

99

knowledge of music concepts. As an example, consider how we can variously show fast or slow movements and beat movements, demonstrate high or low sounds with our bodies, and show the rhythm of a chant or song.

Movement and Improvisation

Making up movements to accompany songs and changing the words to a song will encourage young children's spontaneity and creativity. Children's ideas need to be honored. Eventually they will improvise musically because they have been invited to improvise in other ways. The classroom atmosphere for such activities should be free and gamelike so children can make an error without becoming embarrassed. In a gamelike setting, children may be encouraged to have fun while putting their musical skills into practice immediately and instinctively. For those children who freeze and find they cannot spontaneously think of something, it is helpful to have a "bank of movement ideas," or even some movement icons to refer to when they first begin this process.[8] What follows are examples of movement activities that can be used in the Kindergarten classroom.

Motions That Demonstrate the Expressive Qualities of a Song

Encourage children to improvise motions and movements to a song that helps express the mood. For example, use loud or soft movements, fast or slow movements. These movements can be stationary or not. Children may chant the nursery rhyme "Eeny meeny miny mo" and decide how the tiger moves in the song. The children invent tiger motions that move to the beat.

Motions That Illustrate the Text of a Song

Children improvise motions that help with the text of a song. For example, in the game "Lucy Locket" children can act out the text while singing the song. When children sing the song "Johnny Works with One Hammer," they can act out the text of the song.

Motions to Accompany Children's Games or Songs

Children improvise motions to a singing game such as "That's a Mighty Pretty Motion," or sing the song "Good Night" and improvise motions associated with going to bed.

Motions That Illustrate the Form

Children can create motions that reflect the form of a song. For a song like "Rain, Rain, Go Away," this activity can be as simple as touching their heads for the first half of the song and waving good-bye for the second half of the song. Initially this activity will be restricted to melodies that contain two phrases that are the same or different. Children could also improvise text to a call and response song or echo-singing.

Motions That Illustrate a Concept

Initially you as teacher, and later the children, can create a movement that helps illustrate musical concepts. For example, when a child is chanting a rhyme with a bird voice he can move like a bird as he is chanting, or move like a bear or grandfather when he chants with a low voice.

Instruments

Singing should form the core of the music lesson, but instruments may be used to reinforce music skills. Children can use instruments to demonstrate such concepts as loud and soft, fast and slow, high and low, and the rhythm of a chant or melody. Once children understand the concept of high and low, we might introduce ear-training exercises where they recognize high and low pitches from pitched instruments. You should give them lots of opportunities, when learning the various key music concepts, to practice concepts in combination with music instruments. Rhythmic and melodic instruments should be used in the music classroom, for very specific purposes. They can be used to reinforce music concepts, as listening activities, developing improvisation techniques, as accompaniment to games, and developing music concepts, as well as developing the music ear to identify tone colors.

Instruments can be used in the Kindergarten classroom to enhance music lessons. The recorder is a standard instrument that all music teachers should be able to play. It sounds one octave higher than a child's voice. Sometimes the teacher can play a familiar motif or song on the recorder, and the children can recognize the song. If the teacher wants children to sing this song, she can give them the starting pitch from a tuning fork; otherwise the children will try to use the starting pitch from the recorder. The teacher may also use a guitar in the classroom, but sparingly. We should try to allow children to sing their songs unaccompanied so that they may develop the skill of listening and singing in tune without being distracted. Occasionally the teacher adds in chordal accompaniments to diatonic melodies to enhance the performance. We should not superimpose functional harmony over pentatonic motives or songs! The teacher can also use the guitar when singing as a listening experience for children at the end of a music lesson.

Simply playing one of the children's folk songs on an instrument can provide a unique listening experience for a child. If the instructor wants to sing a song as a listening activity, she may play an instrument or use an instrument to set the mood for the listening example. Occasionally it's appropriate to play an instrumental version of a game song on an instrument while the children perform the game (consider "Here Comes a Bluebird"). This is an opportunity for children to play the game, but it also develops their inner hearing as they silently sing the song while playing a game. The instructor may play a percussion instrument to reinforce the meter of a melody or perform the beat and subdivision at the same time as a rhythmic ostinato. This activity is helpful with compound meter melodies. Xylophones are wonderful to use in the music classroom, and children love to walk or march to the beat as the teacher plays familiar and unknown melodies on these instruments. A xylophone tuned to the pentatonic scale (*d, r, m, s, l*) where the tonic note is D offers a practical scale to use in the Kindergarten classroom.

Tone color or *timbre* refers to the quality of a sound or musical note. The ability to distinguish sounds of various materials, voices, and instruments should be consciously developed in the early childhood classroom. It is valuable for children to begin to recognize the timbre of the instruments found in the music classroom. Recognizing the sound of the instruments is an important part of aural discrimination. As part of developing music memory, the instructor may also use flash cards with a picture of a drum or recorder or triangle. Children can point to the card of the instrument that they hear being played. Table 3.3 is a guide to timbre activities that can be incorporated into a lesson.

Table 3.3

Timbre	Three Year Olds	Four Year Olds	Five Year Olds
	C should be able to identify three to four very different instruments or sounds.	C should be able to identify four or more instruments or sounds.	C should be able to identify different instruments, sounds, and other C's voices.

Having a "music corner" in the Kindergarten classroom, where children can play with percussion instruments, encourages their exploration of pitched and nonpitched instruments. Resonator bells, xylophones, metallophones, and glockenspiels (alto and soprano range) can enhance music lessons. Children can use them to discover high and low pitches; some children may begin to play the simpler melodies from their music repertoire. While working with music bells or xylophones, children can figure out how to play simple melodies learned in the music class. It is important to show children how to play such music instruments as the drum, triangle, cymbals, and xylophone correctly.

Children should have access to the simple percussion instruments listed in Table 3.4.

Table 3.4

Wood	Metal
Tom-tom with mallets	Cymbals
Maracas	Triangles
Sand blocks	Wrist bells
Tap-a-taps	Jingle tap
Tone block with mallet	Cluster bells
Guiro	Tambourines
Rhythm sticks	Tone bells
Snare drum	Triangles
Castanets	
Hand drums	
Tub drums	
Claves	

Instruments can be used to keep a steady beat, can create a rhythmic ostinato, or may be associated with a character from a book that the music teacher is reading to the children. With the help of the instructor, children may also construct percussion instruments that can be used to keep a steady beat. Instruments may be used to demonstrate concepts as well. For example, if children are singing with a loud or soft voice, then they can be guided to keep a beat on a percussion instrument playing a loud or soft beat, though always musically.

Additionally, instruments may be used to help with the performance of a song or chant. For example, use sand blocks to keep the beat while saying "Engine, Engine, Number Nine." Use a guiro to accompany "Frog in the Meadow." Use a woodblock to accompany the chant "Hickory, Dickory Dock." Instruments enhance performance activities in the Early Childhood music class; they can enliven music teaching in numerous ways.

Connections to Literature-Developing Instrumental Skills

The texts for these resources all have some kind of instrumental connection. Children can be guided to explore the instruments through stories or can accompany the reading of the story with simple rhythm instruments.

Percussion Instruments (Books to Which Instrumental Sounds Can Be Added)
Pinkney, Brian. *Max Found Two Sticks*. New York: Aladdin Paperbacks, 1994.
Piper, Watty. *The Little Engine That Could*. New York: Philomel Books, 2005.
Raschka, Chris. *Yo? Yes!* New York: Scholastic, 1993.
Showers, Paul. *The Listening Walk*. New York: HarperCollins, 1991.
Williams, Linda. *The Little Old Lady Who Was Not Afraid of Anything*. New York: HarperCollins, 1986.
Williams, Sue. *I Went Walking*. New York: Harcourt Brace, 1989.
Wood, Audrey. *Silly Sally*. New York: Harcourt, 1992.

Musical Instruments (Books with Instruments in Them)
Brett, Jan. *Berlioz the Bear*. New York: Penguin Young Readers Group, 1991.
Crews, Donald. *Parade*. New York: Greenwillow Books, 1986.
Friedman, Carol. *Nicky the Jazz Cat*. New York: Dominick Books, 2003.
Gollub, Matthew. *The Jazz Fly*, 1st ed. Santa Rosa, CA: Tortuga Press, 2000.
Lach, William. *Can You Hear It?* New York: Abrams Books for Young Readers, 2006.
Martin, Bill, Jr. *The Maestro Plays*. San Diego: Voyager Books, 1996.
McPhail, David. *Mole Music*. New York: Holt, 1999.
Moss, Lloyd. *Zin! Zin! Zin! A Violin*. New York: Aladdin Paperbacks, 1995.
Orleans, Ilo. *Animal Orchestra*. Racine, WI: A Little Golden Book, 1958.
Pinkney, Brian. *Max Found Two Sticks*. New York: Aladdin Paperbacks, 1994.

Discussion Questions
1. What kinds of songs should we include in our repertoire list that will promote singing in tune?
2. Discuss the various techniques that you would use with your children to help them discover their head voice.
3. Discuss how your music program can connect to physical education.
4. What kinds of instruments should you have in your music classroom?

Questions for Reflection

1. How has the information presented in this chapter contributed to your understanding of the importance of using quality song material you use when teaching in-tune singing?
2. What do we mean by the use of the word *performance* in the school curriculum?

Ongoing Assignment

1. Review the performance section and the goals and outcomes for music in the Kindergarten class.
2. Select three songs each reflecting a particular tempo and mood. Sketch out the steps you would use to teach these songs to Kindergarten children. Incorporate several techniques discussed in this chapter.

Bibliography

Adachi, M., and S. E. Trehub. "Children's Expression of Emotion in Song." *Psychology of Music*, 1998, *26*(2): 133–153.

Adachi, M., and J. C. Carlsen. "Measuring Melodic Expectancies with Children." *Bulletin of the Council for Research in Music Education*, 1995: 1–7.

Adachi, M., and S. E. Trehub. "Musical Lives of Infants." In *The Oxford Handbook of Music Education*, vol. 1, ed. Gary E. McPherson and Graham F. Welch (chap. 2.2 p. 233). New York: Oxford University Press, 2012.

Adzinyah, Abraham K., Dumisani Maraire, and Judith Cook Tucker. *Let Your Voice Be Heard! Songs from Ghana and Zimbabwe*. Danbury, CT: World Music Press, 1997

Apfelstadt, H. "Effects of Melodic Perception Instruction on Pitch Discrimination and Vocal Accuracy of Early Childhood Children." *Journal of Research in Music Education*, 1984, *86*: 10–17, Volume 32 No 1, p. 15–24.

Azzara, C. D. "An Aural Approach to Improvisation." *Music Educators Journal*, 1999, *86*(3): 21–25.

Azzara, C. D. "Audiation, Improvisation, and Music Learning Theory." *Journal of Music Teaching and Learning*, 1991, *2*(1–2): 106–109.

Bertaux, B. "Teaching Children of All Ages to Use the Singing Voice, and How to Work with Out of Tune Singers." In *Readings in Music Learning Theory*, ed. D. L. Walters and C. C. Taggart, pp. 92–104. Chicago: GIA, 1989.

Boston, L. *Sing! Play! Create!: Hands-on Learning for 3- to 7-Year-Olds*. Charlotte, VT: Williamson Books, 2006.

Brand, E. "Children's Mental Musical Organizations as Highlighted by Their Singing Errors." *Psychology of Music*, 2000, *28*(1): 62–82.

Campbell, P. S. *Songs in Their Heads: Music and Its Meaning in Children's Lives*. New York: New York University Press, 1998.

Carlton, E. "Music and Movement in HighScope Preschools." *Early Childhood Connection: Journal of Music and Movement Based Learning*. 2000, *6*(2): 16–23.

Carlton, E., and P. Weikart. *Guide to Rhythmically Moving*. Ypsilanti, MI: High Scope Press, 1997.

Cave, C. "Early Language Development: Music and Movement Make a Difference." *Early Childhood Connection: Journal of Music- and Movement-Based Learning*. 1998, *4*(3): 24–29.

Church, E. B. *Learning Through Play. Music and Movement: A Practical Guide for Teaching Young Children*. New York: Scholastic, 1992.

Collins, M., and C. Wilkinson. *Music and Circle Time: Using Music, Rhythm, Rhyme and Song.* Thousand Oaks, CA: Sage Books, 2006.

Cox, Heather, and Richard Garth. *Sing, Clap, and Play the Recorder, 1–2.* St. Louis, MO: Magnamusic-Baton, 1985.

Custodero, L. A., P. R. Britto, and J. Brooks-Gunn, "Musical Lives: A Collective Portrait of American Families." *Journal of Applied Developmental Psychology*, 2003, *24*(5): 553, 572.

Custodero, L.A. "Singing Practices in 10 Families with Young Children." *Journal of Research in Music Education*, Vol. 54.1 2006: 37–56.

Dunne-Sousa, D. "The Effect of Speech Rhythm, Melody, and Movement on Song Identification and Performance of Preschool Children." Doctoral dissertation, Ohio State University, 1988. *Dissertation Abstracts International*, 1988, *49*(8A): 2140.

Feierabend, J. M. "Music and Movement for Infants and Toddlers: Naturally Wonder-Full." *Early Childhood Connections: Journal of Music- and Movement-Based Learning*, 1996, *2*(4): 19–26.

Findlay, Elsa, *Rhythm and Movement: Applications of Dalcroze Eurhythmics.* Evanston, IL: Alfred Music, 1999.

Gallahue, D. L. *Understanding Motor Development in Children.* New York: Wiley, 1982.

Green, G. "The Effect of Vocal Modeling on Pitch-Matching Accuracy of Elementary Schoolchildren." *Journal of Research in Music Education*, 1990, *38*(3): 225–231.

Green, L. *Music, Informal Learning and the School: A New Classroom Pedagogy.* Aldershot, UK: Ashgate, 2008.

Gromko, J. E., and A. S. Poorman, "The Effect of Music Training on Preschoolers' Spatial-Temporal Task Performance." *Journal of Research in Music Education*, 1998, *46*(2): 173–181.

Hargreaves, D. J. "Musical Education for All." *Psychologist*, 1994, *7*: 357–358.

Honig, A. S. "Singing with Infants and Toddlers." *Young Children*, 1995, *50*(5): 72–78.

Jacobi-Karna, K. L. "The Effects of the Inclusion of Text on the Singing Accuracy of Preschool Children." *Dissertation Abstracts International*, 1996, *57*(11): 4682.

Jensen, E. *Teaching with the Brain in Mind.* Alexandria, VA: Association for Supervision and Curriculum Development, 2005.

Kalmar, M., and G. Balasko, "Musical Mother Tongue' and Creativity in Preschool Children's Melody Improvisations." *Bulletin of the Council for Research in Music Education*, 1987, *91*: 77–86.

Kodály, Z. *The Selected Writings of Zoltán Kodály.* Ferenc Bónis, ed. trans. Halápy and Macnicol Budapest: Zenemıkiadó Vállalat, 1964; London: Boosey & Hawkes, 1974.

Laczo, Z. "A Psychological Investigation of Improvisation Abilities in the Lower and Higher Classes of the Elementary School." *Bulletin of the Council for Research in Music Education*, 1981, 66–67: 39–45.

Langton, T. W. "Applying Laban's Movement Framework in Elementary Physical Education." *Journal of Physical Education, Recreation and Dance*, 2007, *78*(1): 17–24.

Levine, M. *A Mind at a Time.* New York: Simon and Schuster, 2002.

Levinowitz, L. M. "An Experimental Study of the Comparative Effects of Singing Songs with Words and Without Words on Children in First Grade." Doctoral dissertation, Temple University, 1987. *Dissertation Abstracts International*, 1987, *48*: 863A.

Levinowitz, L. M., P. Barnes, S. Guerrini, M. Clement, P. D'April, and M. J. Morey. "Measuring Singing Voice Development in the Elementary General Music Classroom." *Journal of Research in Music Education*, 1988, *46*(1): 35–47.

105

Montessori, M. *To Educate the Human Potential* (Clio Montessori Series). Oxford: ABC-CLIO, 1989.

Phillips-Silver, J., and L. J. Trainor, "Feeling the Beat: Movement Influences Infant Rhythm Perception." *Science*, 2005, *308*(5727): 1430.

Phillips, Kenneth H. *Teaching Kids to Sing (with Supporting Materials)*. New York: Schirmer Books, 1992.

Pica, R. *Experiences in Movement: Birth to Age Eight*. 3rd ed. Clifton Park, NY: Thomson/Delmar Learning, 2004.

Pica, R. Experiences in Movement With Music, Activities, and Theory 2nd ed., Clifton Park, NY: Thomson Delmar Learning, 1999.

Rutkowski, J. "The Effectiveness of Individual/Small-Group Singing Activities on Kindergarteners' Use of Singing Voice and Developmental Music Aptitude." *Journal of Research in Music Education*, 1996, *44*(4): 353–368.

Rutkowski, J., and Trollinger, V. L. "Singing." In J. W. Flohr, ed., *Musical Lives of Young Children*, pp. 78–97. Upper Saddle River, NJ: Prentice Hall, 2006.

Sataloff, R. T., and J. R. Spiegel. "Laryngoscope: The Young Voice." *NATS Journal*, 1989, *45*(3): 35–37.

Trehub, S. E., and Trainor, L. J. "Singing to Infants: Lullabies and Play Songs." *Advances in Infancy Research*, 1998, *12*: 43–77.

Trehub, S. E., A. M. Unyk, S. B. Kamenetsky, D. S. Hill, L. J. Trainor, J. L. Henderson, and M. Saraza. "Mothers' and Fathers' Singing to Infants." *Developmental Psychology*, 1997, *33*(3): 500–507.

Trollinger, V. L. "The Brain in Singing and Language." *General Music Today*, 2010, *23*(2): 20–23.

Upitis, R., K. Smithrim, and B. Soren, "When Teachers Become Musicians and Artists: Teacher Transformation and Professional Development." *Music Education Research*, 1999, *1*(1): 23–35.

Warner, B. *Orff-Schulwerk: Applications for the Classroom*. Englewood Cliffs, NJ: Prentice Hall, 1997.

Weikart, Phyllis S. *Movement Plus Music: Activities for Children, Ages 3–7*. Ypsilanti, MI: High/Scope Press, 1989.

Welch, G., D. C. Sergeant, and P. J. White. "The 15th ISME International Research Seminar: The Singing Competencies of Five-year-old Developing Singers." *FL, pp. 155–162*. International Society for Music Education, 1994, pp. 155–162.

Welch, G. F., E. Himonides, J. Saunders, I. Papageorgi, C. Preti, T. Rinta, M. Vraka, C. Stephens Himonides, C. Stewart, J. Lanipekun, and J. Hill. *Researching the Impact of the National Singing Programme "Sing Up" in* England: Main *Findings from the First Three Years (2007–2010). Children's Singing Development, Self-Concept and Sense of Social Inclusion*. London: Institute of Education, University of London, 2010.

Whitcomb, R. "Step by Step: Using Kodály to Build Vocal Improvisation." *Teaching Music*, 2003, *10*(5): 34–38.

Whitwell, D. *Music Learning Through Performance*. Austin: Texas Music Educators Association, 1997.

Wood, Donna. *Move, Sing, Listen, Play*. Toronto: Gordon V. Thompson, 1982.

Yang, Y. "The Effects of Solmization and Rhythmic Movement Training on the Achievement of Beginning Group Piano Students at the Elementary School Level." *Dissertation Abstracts International*, 1995, *56*(1): 132.

Zachopoulou, E., A. Tsapakidou, and V. Derri. "Research Review: The Effects of a Developmentally Appropriate Music and Movement Program on Motor Performance." *Early Childhood Research Quarterly*, 2004, *19*: 631–642.

Chapter 4

A Model of Learning and Instruction for Teaching Music Concepts and Skills

Chapter 3 describes how to develop performance skills in a Kindergarten classroom such as singing, movement, and playing music instruments. In this chapter we will show how teachers can continue to develop performance, basic music concepts, and forms of creative thinking systematically through a sound-to-symbol orientation to teaching. This model for teaching will also nourish a child's emotional development and advance a child's creative, literacy, and numeracy skills in the process. This perceptually based, systematic model of learning and instruction permits children to develop performance, music literacy, music improvisation, music listening and knowledge of music repertoire as a consequence of music instruction. Because our model of learning and instruction adopts a constructivist approach, it can be easily adapted for teaching special learners in the classroom as well as gifted and talented children. The videos accompanying this chapter include examples showing how to teach music concepts using the model of learning and instruction; all are posted on the companion website (Web 4B). Videos of Kindergarten music teachers talking about the application and use of the model are also on the website (Web 4C).

Our model of learning and instruction takes place in the context of a playful teaching environment. This is essential; as Trevarthen and Malloch write, "In formal instruction, creativity and imagination motivating actions imbued with shared cultural meanings, so much part of the young child's learning, can be replaced by a far less creative motivation to simply get complex cultural rules 'right'."[1] David Hargreaves believes that the experience and enjoyment of music is of primary importance. He contrasts this philosophy with traditional approaches to teaching music that stress the importance of "verbal description or written notation, rather than in the practical context of making the sounds themselves."[2]

The music component of our model uses constructivist and cognitive theories[3] as well as the work of Kodály scholars[4] as a foundation. Our approach to instruction and learning identifies and classifies cognitive scaffolding activities to facilitate the development of music literacy in the music classroom through a sound-to-symbol orientation to teaching.[5] Music performance and critical thinking strategies become significant teaching techniques associated with our model of learning. Children become active learners not simply learning about musical concepts but additionally learning about the process of their own learning through music performance.[6] We use Carson's Taxonomy[7] to describe the types of creative thinking that are developed and employed in the music classroom as a result of adopting this model of thinking.

Singing is one of the most important components of our model. For every concept studied, we must be mindful to consistently develop a child's singing voice. We need to work steadily on singing in the classroom, demonstrating correct intonation, phrasing, and character of the songs, furnishing a model for our children to do the same. Singing and the development of aural awareness are key elements of our model.

In Chapter 2 we outlined a music curriculum for five- and six-year-old children. Many of the concepts, loud-soft, fast-slow, high-low, are known to children from a language perspective. But these words have meaning that is much more complicated to understand from a music perspective. For example, for children to truly understand the concept of loud and soft they must be able to:

- Learn how to speak and sing with a loud or soft voice
- Sing or speak and keep a beat
- Sing or speak rhythmically and with a consistent beat while pointing to icons that represent the beat
- Aurally recognize singing or speaking that is using loud or soft voice
- Visually represent their understanding of loud and soft with an appropriate icon
- Label singing and speaking voices as being either loud or soft
- Learn to write the words *loud* and *soft*
- Improvise using a loud and soft singing and speaking voice

Each of these activities requires careful consideration and appropriate learning strategies to ensure understanding.

There are three phases of learning and instruction in our model, each with certain stages of instruction and learning: the cognitive phase-preparing concepts, the associative phase-labeling concepts, and the assimilative phase-practice of music elements. "Stage" refers to steps students go through to acquire the understanding of a concept. There are six stages or steps: kinesthetic, aural, visual, labeling sounds, presenting notation, and finally application. "Phases" group the stages. Kinesthetic, aural, and visual are grouped into the cognitive phrase because they involve thinking; labeling sounds and presenting notation are grouped into an associative or "naming" phrase; and the application of newly learned information to skills is called the assimilative phase.

Throughout the *cognitive phase*, children experience and perceive the new music concept through kinesthetic, aural, and visual activities, always within the context of performance and the enjoyment of music. In the *associative phase,* children connect their kinesthetic, aural, and visual understanding of the concept to a name, a word and/or a symbol. During the *assimilative phase,* children continue to develop their musicianship skills, incorporating the newly learned musical concept.

A Model for Music Learning and Instruction

Cognitive Phase of Instruction: Preparation

The rationale of the cognitive phase is to develop children's listening, aural, and visual awareness skills. Children experience and perceive the new concept through kinesthetic, aural, and visual activities, always conducted within the context of singing or chanting. This phase is a type of multimodal perceptual encoding that primarily strengthens aural awareness. The following illustration shows the three stages in this phase:

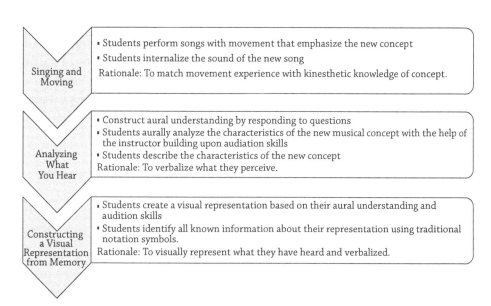

Singing and Moving
- Students perform songs with movement that emphasize the new concept
- Students internalize the sound of the new song
Rationale: To match movement experience with kinesthetic knowledge of concept.

Analyzing What You Hear
- Construct aural understanding by responding to questions
- Students aurally analyze the characteristics of the new musical concept with the help of the instructor building upon audiation skills
- Students describe the characteristics of the new concept
Rationale: To verbalize what they perceive.

Constructing a Visual Representation from Memory
- Students create a visual representation based on their aural understanding and audiation skills
- Students identify all known information about their representation using traditional notation symbols.
Rationale: To visually represent what they have heard and verbalized.

Stage 1: Singing and Moving—Developing Kinesthetic Awareness
In the kinesthetic stage children are taught a selection of core songs and rhymes by rote that will be used for teaching a music concept. The song material is taught in a stylistically correct manner and the instructor models a kinesthetic motion that helps children experience the new concept. Movement activities[8] help guide children to hear the new concept. The goal is for children to independently sing while performing a motion that illustrates the concept tangibly or perceptibly. Cutietta's research suggests that "the repeated act of performing a piece of music, without the aid of written notation or language-based instruction, can lead to substantive changes in an individual's internal representation of that melody's primary features."[10] Peretz has noted that *pitch contour* is the first aspect of melody that is stored on hearing a new melody, and *contour extraction*

is "a preliminary and indispensable step to the precise encoding of intervals."[11] This also has a positive effect on short-term musical memory.[12] Movement, rote learning, and the development of musical memory form a foundation for the promotion of musical literacy.[9] Children in the Kindergarten classroom should be able to sing repertoire fluently and independently with kinesthetic movements before moving on to the aural awareness stage.

Kinesthetic Awareness Activities

Kinesthetic demonstration of musical concepts is an unconscious activity for the young child. For example, in the case of beat it means children sing and perform a movement activity that maintains a steady fast tempo or slow tempo. During the kinesthetic stage children perform song material while exploring the beat through various movement activities. We strongly suggest that the instructor not use the words "beat," "loud-soft," "high-low," "fast-slow," or "rhythm" during the cognitive stage of instruction. We offer other ways to express these concepts that are meaningful for the children; for example, instead of saying "Let's keep the beat" we say "Let's tap the snails as we sing" or "Let's tap the raindrops on our head." We think creatively about what loud or soft might actually mean to a child. Instead of saying "sing loudly" we say "sing using your daytime voice." Instead of saying "sing softly" we suggest "sing using your nighttime voice." Before we label any concept, we want to make sure that children have the opportunity to explore and make vital music connections about the new concept with their voice and accompanying movements. This permits us to engage the children with the underlying meaning of the concept before we use the vocabulary.

Here are suggestions of kinesthetic ways to approach the teaching of selected readiness concepts.

Kinesthetic Activities for Beat

1. Children play games that are associated with the song. The children perform wheel motions to the beat with their arms as they chant.

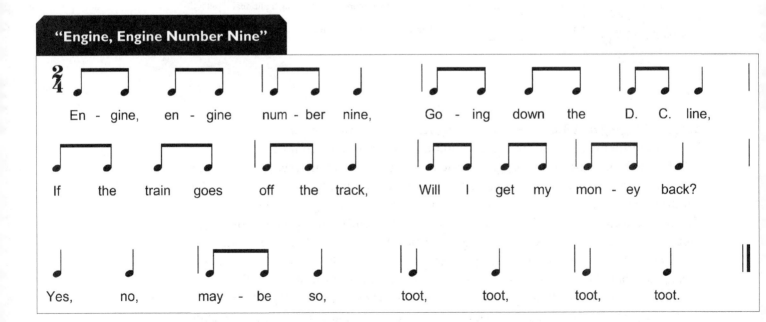

2. Children tap the beat on different parts of the body while singing a song. (For example, they may, touch their head, patch their knees, touch their shoulders, or walk, hop, or stomp to the beat.)

3. Children point to an iconic representation of the beat while singing. Although they view an iconic representation of beat in this initial phase of instruction, their task is to point to the representation created by their instructor. It is therefore not a visual task; their task is primarily kinesthetic because they're pointing as they sing. In our model of instruction and learning, we position the visual task after the development of aural awareness.

Kinesthetic Activities for Loud and Soft

As the teacher, you say the rhyme "Engine, Engine" and demonstrate the motion of the wheels turning as the train is moving during the daytime (loud voice) or during the nighttime (soft voice). Guide the children to imitate this motion. Provide the tempo by saying, "Engine Engine, here we go" in a daytime or nighttime voice. You may also ask children to point to four pictures of an engine that represent the beat; a picture of the sun or moon in front of each one indicates which voice the children must use. Later, you may put four suns or four moons to represent the beat as well as the daytime or night-time voice.

Stage 2: Tell Me What You Hear—Developing Aural Awareness

The rationale for stage 2 is to assist children in verbalizing the characteristics of the new concept and to develop children's ear training skills. Through careful questioning by the instructor, the children develop the ability to play back (inner-hear) a song or phrase to answer the teacher's question. With each question, children audiate the music phrase in order to answer the questions correctly. Many of the questions posed by the instructor can be thought of as a "scaffolding technique" and help children bridge the "zone of proximal development."[13]

Bartholomew states, "to teach the sounds before the signs is to develop musical responsiveness and thought. It is to do more than to present sounds to children. It is to help children develop the sense and the flow of music, to feel its logic, to be part of its unfolding, and to respond to the variety of relationships present in the sounds."[14] Petzold's study concludes that aural perception should precede visual perception, and that one must be able to hear music in order to develop skills in music reading.[15] Hewson's work suggests that having aural experiences prior to encountering notation facilitates the development of sight-singing skills.[16] Results of Gromko's recent research support findings that there is a "developmental link between aural perception and what the child chooses to express in writing about musical sounds. These results suggest a developmental link between the ability to discriminate between short tonal patterns and the ability to use musical symbols for pitch."[17]

We believe aural sound or awareness must precede visual representation of a musical sound. In what we define as an aural awareness stage, children gain an aural understanding of the new musical concept without any visual clues. This is critically important to developing aural awareness skills. The children are not given any visual clues during this stage of learning. This is a major difference between our model and other approaches to teaching. During the kinesthetic phase, the children are guided to physically demonstrate the new musical element. This serves as a preparation for aural awareness, where they must be able to aurally recognize the concept and identify and describe its characteristics or attributes. Problem solving and discovery learning become important teaching techniques associated with the learning process at this stage and continue in all the subsequent stages of instruction. Aural awareness teaching strategies are built on previously acquired information from the kinesthetic phase.

Children become active learners not merely by learning about music concepts, but also by learning about the process of learning. These critical thinking skills, which share many of the same skills associated with the scientific method, can also be applied to other learning environments.

Here are suggestions for aural activities to approach the teaching of selected readiness concepts.

Aural Awareness Activities for Beat

During the aural awareness stage, children are guided to answer questions about what they hear and have experienced through movement.

1. Review kinesthetic activities with the children. Children sing "Snail, Snail" and point to imaginary snails on their knees.

2. Direct the children to sing the first phrase of "Snail, Snail" while keeping the beat on a percussion instrument; have the children tap the beat on their knees and ask them, "How many snails do you hear tapping on your lap?" (Answer: four.)

Aural Awareness Activities for Loud and Soft
1. You or another child sings a song using a loud or quiet voice. The children identify if the song is sung using a daytime or nighttime voice.
2. The children may also identify whether the voice sounds as if it might be far away or close.

Stage 3: Developing Visual Awareness—Make a Picture

In the visual stage, we confront children with the problem of choosing a visual to represent a concept. Drawing on knowledge gained through the kinesthetic experience and the aural awareness stage, children choose a visual representation to show the concept (or they can create their own picture). As Perkins states, "First, to gauge a person's understanding at a given time, ask the person to do something that puts the understanding to work—explaining, solving a problem, building an argument, constructing a product.

Second, what learners do in response not only shows their level of current understanding but very likely advances it."[18]

By connecting the aural awareness stage to the visual stage, the child is allowed time to make the connection between what he or she hears and how to represent it. Bamberger argues "if the reader of the symbols (teacher/researcher or child) has failed to do the work of constructing the elements, properties, and relations inherent in the framework through which these symbols gain meaning, neither a teacher/researcher reading a child's invented symbol system nor a child reading the privileged symbol systems taught in school can make of the phenomena described by the symbols the particular sense the symbols-makers intend."[19] This approach to teaching is similar to the radical constructivism philosophy whereby knowledge and understanding "can only be constructed through a gradual process of disequilibration and accommodation brought about through reflective activity."[20]

Visual Awareness Activities

Visual awareness activities are tangible indications of how children understand new concepts. In the visual phase of instruction, children represent with symbols what they have heard and felt. For example, they might figure out how many objects should be drawn on the board to represent the sounds they hear. You might ask the children, "How will we show our nighttime voice or our daytime voice?"

Once children have chosen a visual representation for the concept, ask individual children to sing the song and point to what they have drawn. You may want to ask children about their picture: "Tell me why you chose this picture." This is also another example of how children learn to figure out how to represent the information they have captured about a concept in the kinesthetic and aural stages of learning.

Visual Awareness Activities for Beat

Children identify the known song "Rain, Rain" from the teacher's singing it using a neutral syllable. Children then sing "Rain, Rain" while pointing to imaginary raindrops on their heads.

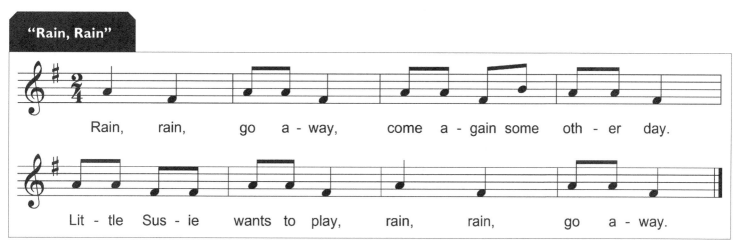

"Rain, Rain"

Rain, rain, go a-way, come a-gain some oth-er day.

Lit-tle Sus-ie wants to play, rain, rain, go a-way.

(Continued)

113

1. Children sing "Rain, Rain" and touch their heads for the raindrops.
2. Children sing the first four beats of "Rain, Rain."
3. Ask, "How many drops of rain fell on your head?"
4. Ask, "How many rain drops should we put on the board for each phrase?" "How can we represent raindrops on the board?"

Visual Awareness Activities for Loud and Soft

As the teacher, you may sing known and unknown songs; the children will then determine whether you are singing during the daytime or the nighttime, and select a picture of the moon for night or the sun for day. Of course, at a later stage, we can put four or eight moons on the board to represent how we sang as well as the number of beats in a phrase, and the children can point to the moons while singing with a soft voice.

1. Children sing "Rain, Rain" and touch their heads for the raindrops.
2. Children sing "Rain, Rain" with a daytime voice and pat the beat.
3. Ask, "How did we sing the song? Did we use our daytime or night time voice?"
4. Ask, "How can we draw a picture to show how we sang our song?"

The three stages of learning in the cognitive phase offer a valuable path to musical understanding and the development of critical thinking skills. The cognitive phase gives children the opportunity to understand the characteristics a concept from a kinesthetic, aural, and visual perspective. This phase allows them time to reenvision and reconceptualize their intuitive knowledge and provides a foundation for presenting traditional notation.[21]

We are convinced that the instructor must address the kinesthetic, the aural, and the visual awareness stages of learning in this order. A child's visual representation offers clues as to how she or he perceives the new musical element. It also provides the instructor with information for the kinds of questions and activities that could aid children who need help. Without this assessment opportunity, we lose the chance to understand the child's current perception of the new concept.

Associative Phase of Instruction: Labeling and Notating Music Concepts

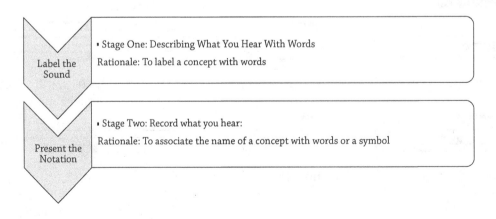

Label the Sound	• Stage One: Describing What You Hear With Words Rationale: To label a concept with words
Present the Notation	• Stage Two: Record what you hear: Rationale: To associate the name of a concept with words or a symbol

Once children can visually represent the readiness concept, we proceed to the associative phase. The associative phase has two stages.

Stage 1: Label What You Hear—Associate the Sound of the Concept with a Name

As the instructor, you guide children in describing the characteristics and reviewing the critical aural attributes of the concept. Children review the critical kinesthetic, aural, and visual attributes of the new element using familiar song material. Then make the children conscious of the new concept's name associated to the sound of music. Now you can use the words *beat, loud-soft, fast-slow, high-low*, and *rhythm* to describe concepts.

Stage 2: Record What You Hear—Associate the Name of the New Concept with Words and Symbols

Next, supply a visual representation of the new concept. Present the children with the written words for all concepts. In addition to learning how to spell the words for heartbeat, loud, soft, fast, slow, high, low or rhythm, they can also be given symbols for some of these concepts. For instance, hearts can be used to represent the pulse, and *p* and *f* for soft (*piano*) and loud (*forte*). Later we can expand the children's knowledge of music vocabulary by using such words as tempo, dynamics, pitches, skips and steps, long and short.

Assimilative Phase of Instruction: Aural and Visual Practice

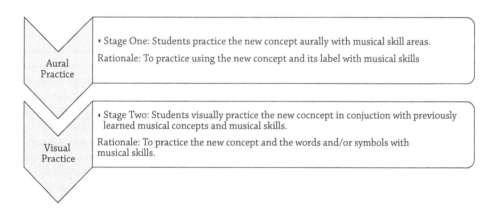

In the assimilative phase, children begin to reinforce and integrate knowledge of the new concept both aurally and visually in conjunction with musical skills. The goal is for children to use the correct terminology and symbols associated with the concept being studied.

Music skills include:

- Tuneful Singing
- Development of audiation (inner hearing)
- Writing
- Improvisation
- Development of musical memory
- Reading
- Ear training
- Part work
- Form

- Listening
- Instrumental experience
- Music theory vocabulary

Here are suggestions for aural activities to practice the teaching of readiness concepts.

Aural Activity for Beat
1. Children play a game associated with the song.
2. Teach asks students to tap the beat on parts of the body while singing the song.
3. Teacher sings songs and asks students to tap the beat.
4. Teacher sings unknown songs and ask students to tap the beat.

Aural Activity for Loud and Soft
1. Children sing the song.
2. Ask a child to sing the song with a loud or a soft voice.
3. Teacher sings a known song; children identify whether the teachers sand with a loud or soft voice.
4. Teacher sings an unknown song; students identify whether the teacher sang with a loud or a soft voice.

Visual Activity for Beat
1. Children play the game associated with the song.
2. Ask children to keep the beat while singing the song.
3. Children point to a series of heartbeats while singing the song.

Visual Activity for Loud and Soft
1. Children sing the song.
2. Ask a child to sing the song with a loud or a soft voice.
3. Place the word *loud* or *soft* in front of four heartbeats. The student must sing a song following the dynamic marking while pointing to the beat.

Summary

Our model of learning and instruction offers not just an explanation of what we are doing in the music classroom but also a structure for lesson planning and developing the various brain sets (see the section later in this chapter on the creative brain) that are integral for acquiring and expanding creativity skills. When we know what our goals and outcomes are for our children, we are able to create lessons that will develop and engage children's creative thinking. We begin with teaching a music repertoire that cultivates the development of singing, movement skills, and instrumental skills. These are then used for developing children's reading and writing skills, and they lay the foundation for developing music creativity and listening skills. Throughout the process of learning, it is essential to develop children's artistic skills *playfully*; as Alfred North Whitehead tells us, "The paradox which wrecks so many promising theories of education is that the training which produces skills is so very apt to stifle imaginative zest."[22]

We use an organic orientation to teaching. "When music teaching is approached from a holistic, contextual frame," write Wiggins and Espeland, "learners are better able to become musical thinkers and decision makers. Understanding the 'bigger picture' enables them to have a basis for making decisions and conceiving original ideas. With better understanding of what they are being asked to do in a classroom setting, learners are more apt to be willing to take risks and initiatives in their learning and more capable of taking responsibility for their own learning."[23]

Our model adopts an innovative and transformation pedagogy to learning music because "Teaching begins with student knowledge. . . . Skills, knowledge and voices develop from engagement in the activity. . . . Teaching and learning are both individual and collaborative processes. . . . Teaching and learning are transformative processes."[24] As a result, children become more engaged and motivated in the learning process, a key ingredient for deeper learning. Trevarthen and Malloch again: "As Bruner insists, and as most experienced and effective teachers learn, a factor that must be taken into consideration and respected is the learner's motivation—her curiosity and willing attention to getting the knowledge and skill, and to cooperating in shared work."[25]

How Does the Model of Learning and Instruction Promote Twenty-first Century Learning Skills and Creativity?

Our model provides specific guidance for teaching music in a manner that is relevant for twenty-first century learning skills, and for fostering important creativity skills. A hallmark of this pedagogy is that it integrates the development of problem solving, critical thinking, and collaboration skills into the teaching and learning of music. A recent report brief issued by the National Research Council in July 2012 cites these as "21st century skills" or "deeper learning skills."[26] Viewed from the prism of this report, the success of the model supports "deeper learning skills" acquired through the triptych of "Cognitive, Intrapersonal and Interpersonal Domains."

During our three phases of learning, children develop important cognitive skills that are acquired through working independently as well as with their peers. When teachers use our model to teach music concepts, they invoke thinking, reasoning, active listening, analysis, critical thinking, problem-solving skills, creativity, communication, and interpretation skills. The suggested teaching process requires teachers to be engaged in formative assessments. Unlike other models of learning, children cannot move to the next stage of learning without mastering previous stages. Teachers use "multiple and varied representations of concepts," and children are continually engaged in challenging tasks. Throughout the process of instruction, the teacher helps children develop intrapersonal skills, such as those in self-management and self- evaluation, to create music representations of a new concept that describes aurally the characteristics of new concepts or critically evaluates a performance of song, movement, or instrumental piece by themselves or another child. Group participation develops the child's sense of responsibility and self-discipline and promotes momentum toward success. Learning to create representations of new concepts and expressing and interpreting their representation to other children, as well as the reverse (interpreting other children's representations), fosters critical interpersonal skills. Creating a group movement improvisation with multiple parts that depends on teamwork and group cooperation is fundamental for developing interpersonal skills.

Developing Styles of Creative Thinking or Brain Sets

According to Shelley Carson, author of *Your Creative Brain*,[27] creative individuals are able to access a number of styles of creative thinking or brain sets to solve problems. Carson's model of brain sets is summarized with the acronym CREATES. Each letter refers to one of seven brain states: connect, reason, envision, absorb, transform, evaluate, stream. In our model of learning and instruction, we promote and develop these brain sets throughout the music lesson. Let's look at a brief description of Carson's brain sets and how they are developed in the music lesson.

The Connect Brain

In our model of learning and instruction, children are engaged in the learning process through singing and movement activities. Instructors erect the necessary cognitive scaffolding so that children can discover knowledge of the new music concept for themselves. During the cognitive phase of learning we make opportunities for developing a child's "connect brain" set. This is a style of creative thinking that allows them to make connections during music learning: "Music actively involves children in learning and helps develop important academic skills."[28]

When we teach a new song using motions that reflect the text or enhance the musical attributes of a song, children are engaged in an activity that guides their receptivity to learning. This teaching strategy allows children to generate unconscious and conscious connections about music concepts that they're exploring in the music lesson. As a result, their thinking becomes more divergent. When they sing and move like a snail or hare, or sing with their daytime or nighttime voices while using appropriate motions, they are connecting vital information about repertoire, singing, and music emotions. We are developing children's divergent thinking skills as well as their ability to create many interesting movement options.

When we teach children a variety of song material and then use the melodic and rhythmic building blocks of this material for improvising greetings or creating new songs, we open for them a pathway to developing their own spontaneous improvisatory skills as well as the connective brain set and divergent thinking skills. They will begin to understand that all music building blocks found in music materials can be used to create new improvisations.

The Reason Brain

Children learn to use their reason brain to solve problems. With the help of the music teacher, they are able to review and manipulate information to understand music concepts. When we ask them to draw a picture to capture their understanding of a concept, to figure out how to sing more tunefully, to use a movement, and to sing and point to icons with a loud voice or a soft voice, we are using the reason brain.

The Envision Brain

We use this brain set many times in teaching music. We develop it when we foster their ability to inner-hear or audiate music. Just as with good readers develop silent reading skills, music teachers develop children's inner-hearing skills. We are developing their ability to hear music internally, in their mind's ear, without the music being sung or played acoustically. "Inner hearing" or "audiation" is a skill commonly used by musicians, and development of this ability takes a considerable amount of time. In our model of learning and instruction, the aural awareness stage of learning is an opportunity to develop this skill by singing a phrase and asking sequential questions. When we ask questions in the aural stage of learning, children must audiate the phrase of music pertaining to the question before they answer. Or if we sing a melody with our daytime or nighttime voice to children and ask them to imagine a picture that represents how we sang, children connect the singing to an imagined picture of the sun or moon, thus evoking the Envision Brain.

The Absorb Brain

The absorb brain allows children to be more open to new experiences and to collect information. Verbal and nonverbal communication plays a key role in developing the absorb brain set. During the kinesthetic, aural, and visual stages of the cognitive phase of learning, we are guiding children to begin to notice certain things about the music they are singing. For example, in working on the concept of beat we engage the child's absorb brain set by linking the tempo in a song they are singing with steady and even motions that can accompany their singing. If we are singing a song with a loud voice and show a picture of the sun, or if we are singing with a soft voice and show a picture of the moon, children will absorb key information and discover for themselves the connection between singing in a soft and loud voice and the picture of a sun or moon.

The Transform Brain

The transform brain is a self-conscious and potentially dissatisfied state of mind. It is a state of mind that could lead to negative expression; in a child, this can be evidenced in undesirable behavior. If we want children to work creatively, it is important that they be in a positive mood. Sometimes when children come into a music class they may not be focused on learning because of their mood. For this reason, it is important to begin the class with a song and movement activity to transform their mood into a more positive one. Alternatively, when it is raining and children are not in a great mood, it is important to acknowledge this and begin with songs that capture their mood but slowly begin to transform it by singing songs with faster tempi and fun motions. As instructors, we may also give children a variety of music materials during the music class so that we can help them understand that music changes our mood. Understanding moods can be a good starting point for creativity as well. As an example, in reading a story to children and wanting them to develop an emotional connection with a character, we can choose songs to sing to that character that capture not just the mood of the song but the mood of the character. Knowing how to change someone's mood, or using a mood to generate a creative activity or approach to understanding, is an important skill for an instructor.

The Evaluate Brain

This is the brain set that allows children to evaluate and judge concepts, products, behaviors, and individuals. In the music classroom, the evaluate brain engages children in evaluating their performance. Performance is at the heart of any music lesson, and they should be given plenty of opportunity to perform, and in some cases have a rudimentary understanding of rubrics that assess their level of success. For example, if a child sings a song, he must eventually understand how he sang it and how he can improve his performance. When children are learning how to sing and play a game correctly they need to evaluate

119

their performance and focus on what needs to take place to improve their performance. They need to develop skills to appreciate feedback from their teacher or other children that evaluate their performance.

The Stream Brain

First proposed by Mihály Csikszentmihalyi, the stream brain results when a person is fully engaged in an activity with a clear focus and is being successful. When we set up a lesson plan design with clear goals, immediate feedback, and an appropriate level of challenge and innovation, we are fostering the correct atmosphere for the stream brain.[29] In this kind of lesson, children are totally absorbed in the learning process and engaged in the "flow of the experience." When children are fully engaged, they become more creative and the teacher can present more challenging activities. Experiencing the flow will reward children.

A Comparison of the Houlahan/Tacka Model to Others in Kodály Instruction

Most Kodály instructors adopt a model of teaching musical elements based on four steps:

1. Prepare
2. Make conscious, or presentation
3. Reinforce, or practice
4. Assessment

For the purpose of comparison, we use the Choksy model of learning associated with the Kodály concept. This is a standard model used by traditional Kodály teachers, representing the one most closely followed by Hungarian and American Kodály instructors.[30] Although we will restrict our discussion primarily to the Kindergarten classroom, it is important to observe that the model we are proposing can be adapted and used at all levels of instruction.

Organic Model of Learning That Can Be Used to Develop All Types of Activities and Lesson Plans

Teachers who have been immersed in teaching music using the Kodály philosophy of music education intuitively learn to develop lesson plans and activities that promote children's music learning. Finding ways to promote a balance among music performance, knowledge of readiness concepts, and music skills is always challenging. But many teachers want to be able to grasp the essence of the approach and be meticulous in their lesson planning and teacher. We have extended the phases of preparation, presentation, and practice into several stages of learning. Our model of learning allows teachers to plan activities in more detail for each phase and stage of learning (see the end of the chapter for a lesson plan template)

Sequential Progression from Kinesthetic to Aural to Visual

The Choksy model of learning, like the Houlahan/Tacka model, emphasizes the importance of experiencing the song material before any notation takes place during the preparation phase.

They do not, at this time, see the notation for these songs. They engage in whatever musical activities suit the nature of each song; they may sing them softer or louder and determine appropriate dynamics; they may sing them faster and slower and determine appropriate tempo; they may step the beat, clap an ostinato, perform the song rhythms that are known, and they may diagram the form. They may play the game if there is one. In other words they may engage in all the activities that require only a singing knowledge of the songs.[31]

The Choksy model give children lots of learning activities that include kinesthetic, visual, and aural activities. Although we agree with this approach to teaching, we also believe that the preparation phase of instruction requires more sequenced activities in combination with the performance of music repertoire. During our cognitive phase (preparation), we present children with a series of activities that allow them to develop their kinesthetic awareness skill, then move to aural awareness, and finally focus on developing visual awareness of the new concept, in that order. For example, when we teach children about loud and soft, they must first be able to explore this concept kinesthetically through sing-ing and movement. During this stage of learning they connect their singing to an image that represents how they are singing. Once they have gained fluency with these skills, we can move to the aural awareness stage, where they must use their memory and aural awareness skills to identify whether a melody was sung with a daytime voice or nighttime voice. No visual clues are provided at this stage of learning for the children, as the goal is to develop their aural awareness activity. This is critically important. The final stage in the cognitive phase of learning, the visual awareness stage, is where they create a picture to represent a loud of soft (singing) voice. Initially they will have the option of only using a picture of a sun or a moon, but they can find other solutions on their own. We believe children must work sequentially through these stages.

Conscious Development of Aural Awareness Skills

Children are invited to develop their aural awareness skills, especially during the aural awareness stage of learning. This stage is an opportunity for them to develop their ear training ability to describe what they hear using their inner-hearing skills. If we want a child to describe whether a song was sung with a daytime or nighttime voice, she must first begin to aurally identify what she heard and give an answer such as "it was sung with a 'daytime' [or 'nighttime'] voice." This activity is explored in phase 2, stage 1, of learning, where children are asked the same question but this time will use the correct terms *loud* and *soft*. These important steps lay the foundations of aural awareness in the Kindergarten classroom as they ask children to inner-hear a melody without any acoustical stimulus.

Developing Knowledge of Symbolic and Music Symbols

In the visual stage of learning, the teacher asks the children to draw a picture represent-ing the new concept. This time the activity is a little more complicated than in the aural awareness stage. Here is an opportunity for the teacher and the child to work collabora-tively to figure out how to represent a concept. As the instructor, you assess children's aural awareness skills by looking at their visual representations. If a child can correctly create a representation of a concept while using his auditory imagery, he will be in a better position to understand how sounds can be labeled later with music terminology. The child's aural awareness skills must be developed sequentially, without any visual aid.

This work has led us to consider the following. Pointing to an iconic representation of a concept is an effective teaching strategy for developing children's kinesthetic understanding. Later, if the child does not create his or her own visual representation of a concept derived solely from knowledge gained in the aural awareness stage, the presentation of notation can create additional complications for teaching music literacy skills. Strategy 3 (symbolic) of Bruner's instructional theory gains meaning only after children have made two important connections: successful aural analysis of the primary characteristics of the new element, and illustration of their aural understanding in a visual representation using pictures or pre-notation graphs. Eastlund-Gromko contends that this kind of activity can "prompt the classification, organization, and connections that enable the child to transform the concrete experience into one that can be represented in icons or symbols."[32] Presenting children with visuals (Bruner's strategy 2, iconic) and subsequently moving to the symbolic stage (Bruner's strategy 3) without developing children's aural awareness shortchanges their perceptual understanding and may significantly compromise the parallel development of aural imagery skills.

Developing Aural Awareness and Visual Awareness Skills

During the presentation phase of learning, Choksy suggests: "Selecting one song in which the new learning is prominent, the teacher will ask adroit questions to lead the children to discover the new element. . . . When the questions have been accurately answered the teacher names and shows notation for the new rhythm or gives the solfa and hand sign for the new note, and shows its notation on staff."[33] In other words, the symbol and the sound are presented together. Children need more time to develop their aural awareness skills before any notation is involved as this might create problems with notation of music at a later stage of learning. This is especially true when teaching concepts like high and low (pitch) and rhythm. In our model of instruction, we separate this process.

Connecting Aural and Visual Awareness to Writing and Reading in the Associative Phase of Learning (Presentation)

In the Kindergarten, we primarily introduce readiness concepts such as loud and soft, fast and slow, short and long to children, but we do not introduce rhythmic or melodic notation. We have opportunities to introduce symbolic notation to children and begin a process of teaching that will be used in later grades. Once children can aurally identify and create a representation of the new concept, we associate this concept with a name and a symbol. For example, once they have gained fluency in singing with a loud (daytime) or soft (night time) voice and can aurally identify which way a melody was sung, we show them what these words look like and introduce the symbols for *piano* and *forte*. The instructor can now apply this new knowledge in various teaching activities, and children can incorporate this new knowledge into their own performances and creative activities.

This is an important step for children in developing their reading and writing skills. The process is crucial for developing music literacy skills, especially in later grades with children. For example, we use the same process in teaching music in grade one with the introduction of rhythm patterns. When we are teaching quarter and eighth notes, children must first be able to (1) tap the beat, (2) clap the rhythm, (3) perform beat and rhythm, (4) aurally identify how many sounds occur on each beat, and (5) create a visual representation of sounds on the beat. The music instructor labels the new element with rhythm syllables without the use of any visuals. Once children aurally identify the new element in known and unknown patterns with rhythm syllables, the instructor shows how sounds can be represented using traditional notation and how children may use rhythm syllables to decode this notation. This is not difficult for young children and will ultimately allow them to make sense of what they experience musically, in instrumental lessons or as members of a choir.

Again: we do not mix up aural and visual activities during the associative stage of learning. We label the sound and provide of opportunities for children to continue to develop their aural awareness skills, before introducing music notation.

Practicing Aural skills and Visual Skills in the Assimilative Phase of Instruction

During the assimilative phase of learning, we separate the aural and visual practice of the new concept, with known and unfamiliar repertoire. All new concepts are practiced aurally and then visually through such music skills as reading, writing, and improvisation.

Developing Metacognition Skills

No matter what concept we are teaching, we always follow the same process. Children will begin to understand this process and many times figure out the next step in the learning process. Providing children with a roadmap to understanding the learning process is a critical step in their acquiring knowledge.

Assessment of Learning

Because teachers have a clear picture of all the steps in learning music, they can assess children's learning using formative and summative assessments; teachers can now assess children at all stages and phases of learning.

Summary

Taken as a whole, our model of teaching and learning offers teachers a step-by-step roadmap for developing those children's musical understanding, metacognition, and creativity skills that are relevant for twenty-first-century learning. A feature of this teaching pedagogy is that it integrates the development of problem solving, critical thinking, and collaboration skills into the teaching and learning of music. The model is a roadmap for the simultaneous development of children's performance and musical understanding that promotes deeper learning and creativity.

Developing a Lesson Plan Framework Based on the Houlahan/Tacka Model of Learning and Instruction

As a result of the information presented in this chapter, we are now able to develop two types of lesson plans, with additional specific guidance concerning the preparation, presentation, and practice of musical concepts.

123

Lesson Plan Format for a *Preparation/Practice* Lesson

We can now modify our generic lesson plan format to prepare a new concept and practice a familiar one. Table 4.1 gives an explanation of the lesson plan structure for a *preparation or practice lesson*. Remember that there should be periods of concentration and relaxation throughout the lesson.

Table 4.1

Outcome	Preparation:
	Practice:
INTRODUCTORY ACTIVITIES	
Sing known songs	In this portion of the lesson, we develop beautiful singing through singing known songs, doing movement and warm-up exercises, as well as vocal exercises to help with developing tuneful singing.
Develop tuneful singing	Introduce activities that focus on different ways of using the speaking and singing voice.
Review known songs and concepts	Review previously learned songs and concepts in a playful way.
CORE ACTIVITIES	
Teach a new song	Instructors present new repertoire to C for a variety of reasons. Sometimes they wish to teach a song to C to develop their singing ability; sometimes a song may be taught because we need to provide a musical context for teaching future musical concepts. When teaching a new song, we can link the new song to the activities in the lesson's introduction by using the same key, same rhythmic or melodic motives, the same meter, the same character, or simply the same tempo. It is important to present the whole song to C rather than teaching the song phrase by phrase.
Preparation Sing and move or describe what you hear or draw a picture	In this section, you prepares a new concept using familiar songs. Guide C through kinesthetic activities (sing and move) or aural activities (asking them to describe what they hear) or visual activities (asking them to draw a picture of the new concept). Activities for this section of the lesson are described in detail in the earlier portion of this chapter, the Cognitive Phase of Instruction.

(Continued)

124

Table 4.1   (continued)

Singing game/ creative movement	This transitioning portion of the lesson provides a break in concentration for the C. The T guides children in playing singing games and developing movement skills that are associated with specific songs outlined in the music curriculum under the title "Children as Performers." In this section of the lesson, the T develops C's movement skills on the basis of game activities associated with song material.
Practice aural or visual	In this section of the lesson, the C practice known concepts in conjunction with skills areas, aurally or visually. Reading, writing, and improvisation are specified as the three primary skill areas to address. All of these skill areas can be linked to other skills. It is important to note that by reading we mean pointing to icons. By writing we mean that C can identify words and symbols that represent concepts. Of course with older C they will learn how to physically write these words. This is the Assimilative Phase of Instruction of the Houlahan/Tacka model of learning and instruction.
SUMMARY ACTIVITIES	
Review the new song

Review lesson outcomes

Folk song tales sung by teacher | The end of the lesson is an opportunity for the T to review the new songs, and review the primary outcomes of the lesson. T can also perform a song as a listening example for the C. |

Lesson Plan Format for the *Presentation* Lesson

Once children have experienced a music concept through the three stages of learning in the cognitive phase, the teacher can present the label and the word or symbol for the new concept in a presentation lesson. The information presented in this chapter enables us to develop a *presentation lesson* plan with more specific guidance concerning the presentation of concepts. Teachers may elect to do this over one or two lessons. In this book we present the name and the label in one lesson.

What follows is a brief explanation of the generic lesson plan structure shown above.

Table 4.2

Outcome	Presentation lesson: label the sound or concept and present the symbol, the notation, and the word for the concept.
INTRODUCTORY ACTIVITIES	
Sing known songs	Same as the preparation/practice lesson plan
Develop tuneful singing	Same as the preparation/practice lesson plan
Review known songs and concepts	Same as the preparation/practice lesson plan
CORE ACTIVITIES	
Teaching a new song	Same as the preparation/practice lesson plan
Presentation Label the new concept or present the word and/or symbol	Here the T labels the concept, or present the word or symbol for the new concept.
Singing game/ creative movement	Same as the preparation/practice lesson plan
Presentation Word and/or symbol	Here the T labels the concept, or present the word or symbol for the new concept.
SUMMARY ACTIVITIES	
Review the new song Review lesson outcomes Folk song/folk song tales sung by T	Same as in the preparation/practice lesson plan

Discussion Questions

1. What are the three phases of learning a new music element?
2. How are the phases of learning broken into stages?
3. What is the purpose of the kinesthetic stage?
4. What is the purpose of the aural awareness stage?
5. What is the purpose of the visual awareness stage?
6. What are the stages in the associative phase?
7. What is the assimilative phase?
8. Discuss the idea that the model of learning presented in this chapter is too cumbersome for instructors to follow, and that it is much more effective to present information theoretically and then use it to practice the musical skills of reading and writing.

9. Describe the preparation/practice lesson.
10. Describe the presentation lesson

Ongoing Assignment

1. You have been asked to present a talk on the Houlahan/Tacka Learning Theory Model for teaching the music readiness concepts in Kindergarten music. Develop a set of slides for your presentation.

Bibliography

Anderson, William M., and Patricia Shehan Campbell, eds. *Multicultural Perspectives in Music Education*, 2nd ed., Reston, VA: Music Educators National Conference, 1996.

Andress, B. *Music Play Unlimited: Understanding Musical Approaches for Children Ages 2–5*. Brown Mills, NJ: World of Peripole, 1983.

Barbe, Walter B., and Raymond S. Swassing. *Teaching Through Modality Strengths: Concepts and Practices*. Columbus: Zaner-Bloser, 1979.

Barkóczi, Ilona, and Csaba Pléh. Music Makes a Difference: *The Effect of Kodály's Musical Training on the Psychological Development of Elementary School Children*. Kecskemét: Zoltán Kodály Pedagogical Institute, 1982, 138.

Barrett, Margaret. "Children's Aesthetic Decision-Making: An Analysis of Children's Musical Discourse as Composers." *International Journal of Music Education*, 1996, *28*: 37–62.

Barrett, Margaret. "Music Education and the Natural Learning Model." *International Journal of Music Education*, 1992, *20*: 27–34.

Barrett, Margaret. *Graphic Notation in Music Education*. Christchurch, New Zealand: University of Canterbury, 1990.

Begley, S. "How to Build Baby's Brain." *Newsweek*, Spring/Summer 1997, *9*: 28–32.

Bowman, W. "Cognition and the Body." In *Knowing Bodies, Moving Minds* Towards an Embodied Teaching and Learning, L. Bresler, ed., 29–50. Dordrecht, Netherlands: Kluwer, 2004.

Bredekamp, Sue, and Carol Copple, eds. *Developmentally Appropriate: Practice for Early Childhood Programs* (3rd ed.). Washington, DC: National Association for the Education of Young Children, 2009.

Brooks, J. G., and M. G. Brooks. *In Search of Understanding: The Case for Constructivist Classroom*. Alexandria, VA: Association for Supervision and Curriculum Development, 2001.

Bruner, J. *Toward a Theory of Instruction*. Cambridge, MA: Belknap, 1966.

Carson, Shelley. *Your Creative Brain: Seven Steps to Maximize Imagination Productivity and Innovation in Your Life*. San Francisco: Jossey Bass, 2010.

Collins, M., and C. Wilinson, *Music and Circle Time: Using Music, Rhythm, Rhyme and Song*. Thousand Oaks: Sage Books, 2006.

Colwell, Richard, and Carol Richardson, eds. "Section D: Perception and Cognition." In *Handbook of Research on Music Teaching and Learning*. New York: Oxford University Press, 2002.

Crowther, R., and K. Durkin. "Research Overview: Language in Music Education." *Psychology of Music*, 1982, *10*(1): 59–61.

Deakin Crick, R., and K. Wilson, "Being a Learner: A Virtue for the 21st Century." *British Journal of Educational Studies*, 2005, *53*(3): 359–374.

127

Department of Education and Science (now Department for Education, UK). *Curriculum Matters 4: Music from 5 to 16*. London: HM Stationery Office, 1985.

Duffy, Thomas M., and David H. Jonasson. *Constructivism and the Technology of Instruction: A Conversation*. Hillsdale, NJ: Erlbaum, 1992.

Eastlund-Gromko, J. "Student's Invented Notations as Measures of Music Understanding." *Psychology of Music*, 1994, *22*(2): 136–147.

Edwards, L. C. *The Creative Arts: A Process Approach for Teachers and Children* (5th ed.). Upper Saddle River, NJ: Prentice-Hall, 1997.

Eraut, M.. "Non-Formal Learning, Implicit Learning and Tacit Knowledge in Professional Word." In *The Necessity of Informal Learning*, ed. F. Coffield, 12–32. Bristol, UK: Policy Press, 2000.

Feierabend, John. "Integrating Music Learning Theory into the Kodály Curriculum." In *Readings in Music Learning Theory*, ed. Darrell L. Walters and Cynthia Taggart Crump, 286–300. Chicago: G.I.A, 1989.

Flohr, J. S., S. C. Woodward, and L. Suthers. "Rhythm Performance in Early Childhood." Cape Town: International Society for Music Education, 1998.

Folkestad, G.. "Formal and Informal Learning Situations or Practices vs. Formal and Informal Ways of Learning." *British Journal of Music Education*, 2006, *23*(3): 135–145.

Gagne, Robert M. *The Conditions of Learning*. New York: Holt, Rinehart and Winston, 1970.

Gardner, Howard. *Frames of Mind: The Theory of Multiple Intelligences*. New York: Basic Books, 1993.

Goof, C., and C. S. Dweck. "Motivational Orientations That Lead Students to Show Deeper Levels of Reasoning, Greater Responsibility for Their Academic Work, and Greater Resilience in the Face of Academic Difficulty." In *Optimizing Student Success in School with the Other Three Rs: Reasoning, Resilience, and Responsibility*, ed. R. J. Sternberg and R. F. Subotnik, 39–58. Charlotte, NC: Information Age, 2006.

Gordon, Edwin E. *Learning Sequences in Music: Skill, Content, and Patterns*. Chicago: G.I.A., 2003.

Gordon, Edwin E. *The Psychology of Music Teaching*. Englewood Cliffs, NJ: Prentice-Hall, 1971.

Green, L. *How Popular Musicians Learn: A Way Ahead for Music Education*. Aldershot: Ashgate, 2002.

Green, L. *Music, Informal Learning and the School: A New Classroom Pedagogy*. Aldershot: Ashgate, 2008.

Hardwood, Eve, and Kathryn Marsh. *Children's Ways of Learning Inside and Outside the Classroom*. In *The Oxford Handbook of Music Education*, vol. 1, ed. Gary E. McPherson and Graham F. Welch, 322–340. New York: Oxford University Press, 2012.

Hargreaves, David J. *The Developmental Psychology of Music*. Cambridge: Cambridge University, 1986.

Hetland, Lois. "Learning to Make Music Enhances Spatial Reasoning." *Journal of Aesthetic Education*, 2000, *34*(3–4): 179–238.

Jaffurs, S. E.. "The Impact of Informal Music Learning Practices in the Classroom, Or How I Learned How to Teach from a Garage Band." *International Journal of Music Education*, 2004, *22*(3): 189–201.

Johnson, G., and R. Edelsen. "Integrating Music and Mathematics in the Elementary Classroom." *Teaching Children Mathematics*, 2003, *9*: 474–479. Retrieved June 19, 2008, http://www.nctm.org/.

Jorgensen, E. R. *The Art of Teaching Music.* Bloomington: Indiana University Press, 2008.

Katz, S. A., and J. A. Thomas. *Teaching Creatively by Working the World: Language, Music, and Movement.* Englewood Cliffs, NJ: Prentice-Hall, 1992.

Luce, D. W. "Collaborative Learning in Music Education: A Review of the Literature." *Update: Applications of Research in Music Education,* 2001, *19*(2): 20–25.

MacDonald, R. A. R., and D. E. Miell. "Music for Individuals with Special Needs: A Catalyst for Developments in Identity, Communication and Musical Ability." In *Musical Identities,* ed. R. A. R. MacDonald, D. J. Hargreaves, and D. E. Miell, 163–179. Oxford: Oxford University Press, 2002.

McCaleb, S. P. *Building Communities of Learners: A Collaboration Among Teachers, Students, Families, and Community.* Mahwah, NJ: Erlbaum,1997.

McPherson, G. (ed.). *Child as Musician: A Handbook of Musical Development.* New York: Oxford University Press, 2006.

McPherson, G., and S. A. O'Neill. "Student's Motivation to Study Music as Compared to Other School Subjects: A Comparison of Eight Countries." *Research Studies in Music Education,* 2010, *32*(2): 1–37.

Mezirow, J., and Associates. *Learning as Transformation: Critical Perspectives on a Theory in Progress.* San Francisco: Jossey-Bass, 2000.

Mills, J. *Music in the Primary School* (3rd ed.). Oxford: Oxford University Press, 2009.

O'Neill, S. A. "Developing a Young Musician's Growth Mindset: The Role of Motivation, Self-Theories and Resiliency." In *Music and the Mind: Essays in Honor of John Sloboda,* ed. I. Deliège & J. Davidson, 31–46. New York: Oxford University Press, 2011.

O'Neill, S. A., and Y. Shnyshyn. "How Learning Theories Shape Our Understanding of Music Learners." In *MENC Handbook of Research on Music Learning Strategies,* ed. R. Colwell and P. Webster, 3–34. New York: Oxford University Press, 2011.

Peery, J. Craig, Irene Weiss Peery, and Thomas W. Draper, eds. *Music and Child Development.* New York: Springer-Verlag, 1987.

Reimer, Bennett. "Music as Cognitive: A New Horizon for Musical Education." *Kodály Envoy,* Spring 1994, *20*(3): 16–17.

Serafine, Mary Louise. *Music as Cognition The Development of Thought in Sand.* New York: Columbia University, 1988.

Sinor, Jean. "Musical Development of Children and Kodály Pedagogy." *Kodály Envoy,* Spring 1980, *6*(3): 6–10.

Temmerman, N. "An Investigation of the Music Activity Preferences of Pre-School Children." *British Journal of Music Education,* 2000, *17*(1): 51–60.

Vygotsky, Lev. *Mind in Society: The Development of Higher Psychological Process.* Cambridge: Harvard University, 1978.

Whitehead, A. N. "Process and reality." *The Gifford Lectures* 1927–28. Corrected edition, ed. D. R. Griffin and D. W. Sherburne. New York: Free Press, 1978.

129

Chapter **5**

Teaching Music Concepts in Kindergarten

Chapter 4 presented a model of learning and instruction that can be used for teaching music concepts as well as developing music skills in the music classroom. The focus of this chapter is to provide teachers with approaches and strategies for teaching music concepts in the Kindergarten music classroom that are based on the model of learning presented in Chapter 4. The teaching strategies are formulaic in structure; ultimately teachers will infuse them with their own musicianship and creativity to accommodate the changing settings of teaching situations. A significant component of the teaching strategies are the questions associated with the cognitive, associative, and assimilative phases of learning. The questions provide the meta-cognitive scaffolding that allows students to understand both the process and product of teaching. Each component of the model of instruction and learning also fosters many opportunities for developing music skills. The videos accompanying this chapter, which include examples showing how to teach kindergarten music concepts, are posted on the companion website (Web 5B). Videos of Kindergarten music teachers discussing the teaching music concepts are also posted on the companion website (Web 5C).

We all need to remember that children come into our classrooms with varied backgrounds. Some children are not developmentally ready to begin music instruction but should be nurtured by the instruction and their classmates. Generally those who appear to be less engaged often catch up. Keep in mind that children not only perform in groups and individually but also as individuals within a group. The components of our model of instruction and learning take this into account. In this chapter we will explore how to teach the music concepts in the Kindergarten classroom using our model, of learning and instruction as explained in Chapter 4.

The following are components of the teaching strategy and how they relate to lesson planning (Chapter 7):

Strategy for Teaching Music Concepts

Cognitive Phase: Preparation Activities
These activities will be explored in lesson plans that prepare the instruction and
   learning of a new concept.

1. Activities for developing kinesthetic awareness: singing and movement
2. Activities for developing aural awareness: describing what you hear
3. Activities for developing visual awareness: make a picture of what you hear

Associative Phase: Presentation Activities
These activities will be explored in a lesson plan that presents a musical concept.

1. Activities to introduce the "label" for the music concept: describing what you
   hear
2. Activities to present the word and/or symbol for the new concept: record what
   you hear

Assimilative Phase: Practice Activities
These activities will be explored in lesson plans that practice a new musical concept.

1. Aural practice of the new concept with the musical skills
2. Visual practice of the new concept with the musical skills

Strategy for Teaching Music Dynamics: Loud and Soft

During the first few weeks of music lessons, the teacher works to develop tuneful singing, the ability to keep the beat, and expansion of children's knowledge of music repertoire. Children should be able to pat the beat and point to iconic representations of the beat before teaching the concept of loud and soft. For example, when singing "Bounce High, Bounce Low" they should be able to pat the beat as well as point to four balls

131

(iconic representations of the beat for a phrase of music). There are normally four beats per phrase in the songs or rhymes that we use to teach children musical concepts. Once the children know a group of songs, the teacher can begin to work on the first concept in our curriculum, loud and soft. Although children might understand what the words *loud* and *soft* mean, many often confuse the concept with high and low. It is important to note that from a music teacher's perspective, children understand readiness concepts only when they can sing a song, keep a beat, and demonstrate the concept with their singing voice or body motions. This is a real task for some children to do well and requires careful preparation. Children need to be guided to recognize loud and soft and to express these dynamics through singing, speaking, and movement. The children will have already experienced the teacher modeling loud and soft in the performance of lullabies and game songs. Once the children know and can perform five or so songs or rhymes while keeping the beat, the teacher can begin working with the concepts of loud and soft. Table 5.1 is a guide as to what children in different age groups can do with the concept of loud and soft.

Table 5.1

Loud/Soft Skills	Three Year Olds	Four Year Olds	Five Year Olds
Speaking	Learning to hear loud and soft with the speaking voice	Learning to hear and perform loud and soft with the speaking voice	Learning to hear, perform loud and soft with the speaking voice, and use symbols to represent loud and soft
Singing Voice	Learning to hear loud and soft with the singing voice	Learning to hear and perform loud and soft with the singing voice	Learning to hear and perform loud and soft with the singing voice, using symbols to represent loud and soft
Movement	Imitates motions that express loud and soft in a song or rhyme	Imitates motions that express loud and soft in a song or rhyme	Independently demonstrates loud and soft through motions in a song

Symbols to Introduce the Concept of Loud and Soft

What symbols can you use to introduce the concept of loud and soft to young children?

The children in your class are likely already familiar with the concepts of nighttime and daytime voices. The two work well in exploring the concept of loud and soft. You can associate nighttime voice with a picture of the moon and daytime voice with a picture of the sun. We can explain to children that we never scream using our daytime voice, as this could damage our singing and speaking voice. With an understanding of these icons, you can also use your hands to show loud and soft to children: having hands apart to show daytime speaking or singing voice, and then hands close together to show nighttime speaking or singing voice. Children have an understanding of daytime and nighttime voices; other constructs can be explored for loud and soft, such as close and far away. In the rhyme, "Engine, Engine" the train whistle could be heard close or far away in the distance. This might be challenging for children; it may be best to begin use just one construct.

Repertoire Teaching Loud and Soft

We suggest the repertoire shown in Table 5.2 for teaching the concept of loud and soft.

Table 5.2

"Song/Chant"	Movement
"A la Rorro, Niño"	Motions with text
"Engine, Engine"	Motions with text
"Bounce High, Bounce Low"	Stationary circle
"Bye Baby Bunting"	Motions with text
"Charlie over the Ocean"	Stationary circle
"Duerme Pronto"	Motions with text
"Hot Cross Buns"	Motions with text
"Lucy Locket"	Stationary circle

The Cognitive Phase of Instruction and Learning: Preparation of Loud and Soft

Singing and Movement: Kinesthetic Stage of Learning

The kinesthetic demonstration of a loud and soft beat is an unconscious activity for the Early Childhood student. How do you apply a kinesthetic activity to the concept of loud and soft? Guide students to feel and keep a beat while singing with a loud voice (daytime voice) or a soft voice (nighttime voice). Avoid using the terms *loud* and *soft* during the kinesthetic phase of instruction. During the kinesthetic phase, children perform song material while exploring the beat in different ways.

- Children sing songs while imitating the motions of the song and singing in a daytime or nighttime voice. Show a picture of the sun for the daytime voice and a picture of the moon for the nighttime voice. You should move the visual to the beat as you sing.
- Sing songs and pat the beat using a daytime or nighttime voice.
- Play games that are associated with the songs that reinforce the concept of loud or soft.
- Point to an iconic representation of beat while singing in a daytime or nighttime voice.

133

Here are sample rhymes and songs, with accompanying kinesthetic activities.

"Engine, Engine, Number Nine"
Say the rhyme "Engine, engine, number nine" and demonstrate the motion of the wheels turning as the train is moving during the daytime (loud voice) or nighttime (soft voice). Guide the students to imitate this motion. Make sure to give the children the tempo by saying, "Engine, Engine, here we go" in a loud or soft voice. We strongly suggest that you not change the tempo or beat motions when switching from loud to soft.

"Bee, Bee, Bumble Bee"
Say the rhyme "Bee, bee, bumble bee" and demonstrate the motion of flapping as the bee says the rhythm using daytime or nighttime voice. Guide the students to imitate these motions.

"Rain, Rain, Go Away"
Sing "Rain, Rain" and point to rain drops drawn to represent the beat as the children sing using a daytime or nighttime voice. Children should keep the beat by patching. Subsequently the students sing "Rain, Rain" and point to rain drops on the board without your help but decide if they want to sing the song using a daytime or nighttime voice.

Describing What You Hear: Aural Awareness
Once approximately 80 percent of the children can independently perform the kinesthetic activities, move on to the aural awareness stage. During this stage, children listen to and describe whether rhymes or songs are chanted or sung with a daytime or nighttime voice. Here are sample aural awareness activities related to specific songs.

"Bounce High, Bounce Low"
- Sing "Bounce High, Bounce Low" and have the children identify whether you are using a daytime or nighttime voice.
- Have children sing using a daytime or nighttime voice while keeping the beat on an instrument.
- Have one child sing, and have the others recognize if she was singing using a daytime or a nighttime voice.

"Rain, Rain"
- Sing "Rain, Rain" quietly and ask the children to pat the raindrops on their knees (this represents the beat).
- Have children sing using a daytime or nighttime voice while keeping the beat on an instrument.
- Have one child sing, and have the others recognize if she was singing using a daytime or a nighttime voice.

Make a Picture of What You Hear: Visual Awareness
Once the majority of the children can independently perform aural awareness activities, it is time to move to the visual phase. You will sing known and unknown songs and the children will determine if you are using your nighttime voice (they choose a picture of the

moon) or daytime (they choose a picture of the sun) to record how you sang. During the visual awareness stage, it is important for children to:

- Select to an appropriate icon to represent how you or another child was singing (sun or moon).
- Point to an iconic representation of the beat as you or another student sings. A child selects an appropriate icon to place in front of the beat chart to record if it was using a daytime or nighttime voice.

Here is a sample visual awareness activity linked to the song "Rain, Rain."

- As you sing "Rain, Rain," ask the children to aurally identify if you were using a daytime or the nighttime. Once children have identified this, ask them to select the visual that best represents the daytime or nighttime, the sun or moon.
- Place this icon in front of a beat chart (4 or 8 beats).
- Ask children to sing with the voice indicated by the icon as you point to the beat chart.

Associative Phase: Presentation
(Label and Record What You Hear)

In the associative phase, you present name and the spelling of the words for the new concept. In a presentation lesson, preparation steps should be reviewed in a condensed manner. During the associative phase it is important to:

- Review kinesthetic activities.
- Review aural awareness activities.
- Review visual awareness activities.
- Present the names *loud* and *soft* for daytime voice and nighttime voice respectively.
- Ask children to sing songs with a loud or soft voice. Chant with your soft speaking voice; chant a rhyme with your loud voice; etc.
- Present the words for loud and soft.
- Sing known songs while pointing to iconic representations of the beat on the board that have *loud* or *soft* written in front of them.
- Show children that in music we use f for loud and p for soft. We can then use p or f in front of a beat chart for reading or writing. Explain to children that these are called dynamic markings in music.

Here are sample presentation activities using the song "Rain, Rain."

- Sing "Rain, Rain" with a daytime or night voice while keeping the beat.
- Children identify whether you or another child is singing using a daytime or nighttime voice.
- Present the terminology "loud" and "soft" to the children. Tell the children that when we are singing with our daytime voice we are using our loud voice, and when we are singing using our nighttime voice we are using our soft voice.

- Ask the class or individual children to sing "Rain, Rain" with a loud or soft voice.
- Present the spelling of the words *loud* and *soft* in written form, making sure the students can spell and say each word.
- Ask children to sing known songs while pointing to iconic representations of the beat on the board that have either *loud* or *soft* written in front of them.
- Ask children to sing known songs while pointing to iconic representations of the beat on the board that have either *p* or *f* written on the board in front of them.

Assimilative Stage of Learning: Aural and Visual Practice

To reinforce knowledge of loud and soft, the children should practice this concept in combination with musical skills over several lessons. For aural practice ask the children to sing a song using a loud or soft singing voice. For visual practice, children should point to iconic representations of the beat with the word *loud* or *soft* placed in front of the beat and sing following the dynamic direction. Another visual practice for children is to have them respond to the teacher's hands. For example, open hands spaced apart represent loud; open hands closer together represents soft. You will notice that in the lesson plan structure provided in this book the children practice the concepts over three lessons; each focuses on reading, writing, or improvisation. You may do these activities with both known and unknown songs.

Table 5.3 has some general activities for practicing loud and soft.

Table 5.3

Skill Area	General Activities
Reading	1. Sing and point to an icon representation chart chart indicating the beats while singing known songs. The beat chart could use sun or moon icons so that C could sing using a loud or soft voice. 2. Place the word *loud* or *soft* in front of the beat chart. C say a rhyme or sing a song. Begin with four beats and move to eight- and sixteen-beat songs.
Writing	1. C place the word *loud* or *soft* in front of icons representing the beat to record how a student or T sang a melody. 2. C write the word *loud* or *soft* in front of icons representing the beat to record how a student or T sang a melody. 3. C write *p* or *f* in front of icons representing the beat to record how a student or T sang a melody.
Improvisation	1. C improvise a motion that will demonstrate the beat of a known or unknown song using a loud voice or a soft voice. The motion should reinforce the concept of loud or soft. 2. C improvise a new text singing with a loud or soft voice.

(Continued)

Table 5.3   (continued)

Inner hearing	1. C follow the mouth of a puppet. When the mouth is open, they sing out loud; when it is closed, they sing inside their head. 2. Determine whether C should sing with a loud or soft voice. 3. C should be encouraged to sing different motives of the song initially with loud and soft and then using inner hearing. 4. C hum familiar songs with a loud or soft dynamic and with movements. 5. C recognize a familiar a song from rhythmic or melodic motives that are clapped or hummed by the T.
Form	1. C echo-sing a song in a loud or soft voice while keeping the beat. Initially this should be done between the T and C, then between two groups of C, and finally between two C. 2. C can decide how to sing a song on the basis of form. For example, "Rain, Rain" uses the form same-and-different. C decide to use *p* for phrase one and *f* for phrase two.
Memory	Sing known and unknown songs to C using a soft or loud voice and ask them if the song was sung using a loud voice or a soft voice.
Part work	1. Ask the C to pat the beat to known or unknown songs using a loud or soft dynamic. 2. Play recorded examples of music in different meters, 2/4 or 6/8, and ask C to move to the beat, walking, skipping, or tapping the beat. Children may be asked to make sure their movements are suitable for "day time" loud or "night time" soft voice.
Expressive elements	1. C decide how to sing a song using either a loud or a soft dynamic and discuss how it changes the song.
Listening	1. C will listen to a piece of music sung or played by the T, and they will identify the piece of music as either loud or soft. 2. Listening examples for loud and soft can be found in Chapter 6.
Instruments	Ask C to accompany the class or other C on a drum either softly or loudly. Discuss how it takes more energy to make a loud sound but more control to make a soft sound.

137

Connections to Literature

We suggest a number of books for Kindergarten instructors. These books all have distinctive sections or thematic content where the teacher can read using a loud or soft voice. Many have sections where students can give voice to characters or animals using a loud or soft voice.

Loud and Soft

Brown, Margaret Wise. *Goodnight Moon*. New York: Scholastic, 1947.
Calmenson, Stephanie. *Engine, Engine, Number Nine*. New York: Scholastic, 1996.
Cannon, Janell. *Stellaluna*. New York: Scholastic, 1993.

Crews, Donald. *Parade*. New York: Greenwillow Books, 1986.

Fleming, Denise. *In the Small, Small Pond*. New York: Holt, 1993.

Frazee, Marla. *Hush Little Baby*. San Francisco: Chronicle Books, 1997.

Gershator, Phillis. *When It Starts to Snow*. New York: Holt, 1998.

Gershator, Phillis. *Listen, Listen*. Cambridge, MA: Barefoot Books, 2007.

Martin, Bill, Jr. *Polar Bear, Polar Bear, What Do You Hear?* New York: Holt, 1997.

Rius, Maria. *The Five Senses: Hearing*. Hauppauge, NY: Barron's Educational Series, 1985.

Seuss, Dr. *My Many Colored Days*. New York: Knopf Books for Young Readers,1996.

Stickland, Henrietta. *Dinosaur Roar*. New York: Dutton Juvenile, 1997.

Strategy for Teaching Beat

Beat is the primary rhythmic concept. All subsequent rhythmic concepts are contingent on a child's ability to perform the beat while singing and during games. For most children the ability to feel pulsation and subsequently hear and maintain a steady beat develops with time and maturity. Before children begin to work with the formal aspects of developing beat, they should have many experiences freely moving to music. Table 5.4 illustrates the beat movement skill levels by age.

Table 5.4

Beat and Movement Skills	Three Year Olds	Four Year Olds	Five Year Olds
Beat	Learning to keep beat at the kinesthetic stage	Learning to keep beat at the kinesthetic stage	Learning to keep beat at the cognitive, associative, and assimilative phases
Movement	Motions performed with the T and/or individually	Game movements with group	More complicated game movements
Instruments used for keeping the beat	Drum (*note*: the use of simple instruments is an extension of the human body. Instruments should be used only after C have had many kinesthetic experiences and have evidenced the ability to maintain the beat with their own bodies.)	Drum and rhythm sticks	Drum, sand blocks, rhythm sticks, cymbals, and triangle

Symbols to Introduce the Concept of Beat

We suggest that you use iconic representations of the beat that relate to the song or rhyme you're preforming. For example, in "Bounce High, Bounce Low" there are two phrases, each with four beats. We can use four balls to represent the beats in each phrase. Children must develop the skill of singing while pointing to the sequence of four balls for each phrase.

Repertoire For Teaching Beat

The repertoire for teaching beat should include simple duple and triple meters, as well as compound meter. Table 5.5 has examples of songs and motions or formations for class performance.

Table 5.5

Song/Chant	Movement
"A la Ronda, Ronda"	Moving circle with motions
"A la Vibora"	Moving circle
"Apple, Peach, Pear, Plum"	Moving circle with motions
"A Tisket, a Tasket"	Stationary circle
"All Around the Buttercup"	Moving circle
"Billy Billy"	Partner line
"Bobby Shafto"	Motions related to text
"Bounce High, Bounce Low"	Stationary circle
"Brinca la Tablita"	Motions related to text
"Cobbler, Cobbler"	Motions related to text
"Engine, Engine Number Nine"	Counting rhyme
"Frog in the Meadow"	Movement related to text
"I Climbed up the Apple Tree"	Motions with text
"Johnny Works with One Hammer"	Motions related to text
"Johnny's It"	Role playing
"Little Sally Water"	Stationary circle
"Looby Loo"	Stationary/moving circle; motions with text
"Lucy Locket"	Stationary circle
"Oliver Twist"	Stationary circle
"Pease Porridge"	Motions related to text
"Pumpkin, Pumpkin, Round and Fat"	Motions related to text
"Queen, Queen Caroline"	Motions related to text
"Rain, Rain"	Motions related to text
"Ring Around the Rosie"	Motions related to text
"See Saw"	Motions related to text
"Snail, Snail"	Moving circle/line
"Star Light, Star Bright"	Stationary circle
"Teddy Bear"	Motions related to text

(Continued)

Table 5.5   Continued

"The Farmer in the Dell"	Motions related to text
"This Old Man"	Motions related to text
"Zapatitos Blanco"	Motions related to text

The Teaching Process

As previously stated, singing while keeping a beat is integral to developing a sense of beat in young children. Most singing activities in the classroom will be accompanied with beat motions. Initially children should be encouraged to imitate the instructor's beat motions accompanying a song; later, they may sing the song while performing motions that they improvise. The instructor may also ask children for motions that can accompany a song and subsequently use them. For example, children could sing the song "Do Do Pity My Case" and substitute words and actions for the third phrase "My clothes to wash when I get home" could become "My dog to walk when I get home." Have children think of other tasks to perform when they get home, and to think of an accompanying action.

Creative movements that accompany songs should be appropriate to the mood of the song and also help students learn the text. Generally children will begin to keep a beat while sitting or standing in a circle. If a child has a problem keeping the beat, ask the child to put his or her hands on a large beach ball as you keep the beat; this usually helps the child feel the vibrations and the beat and realize that the motions stay the same over and over no matter what words are being sung.

As children become more proficient with beat motions, more complicated motions can be added, such as actions that accompany a game song. Three- and four-year-old children may perform motions while sitting or standing. Some teachers prefer to keep beat motions rather large and perform them on the knees, shoulders, head, etc. They reserve hand clapping for showing how the words go (i.e., rhythm). Older children, ages four to six, can walk in a circle and imitate the beat motions of the teacher. Very young children may perform beat motions with the instructor while sitting or standing. Sometimes children need more time to develop their sense of beat. The instructor should ask students to perform a motion to a song, such as hammering to accompany "Hunt the Slipper." It is best to perform beat motions that are at 60–70 beats per minute for one sound on a beat (generally the quarter note) or 120–140 where each sound represents an eighth note. Listen to a metronome and get a sense of how fast this tempo will be for children. If a song contains a rest, it is important for children to keep showing beat motions, but maybe do something different for the beat that contains the rest. For instance, if the children are singing "Hot Cross Buns" and are using a stirring motion to keep the beat, it might be possible for them to show beat 4 of phrase 1 by performing a motion to show the rest. This way the children are keeping the beat, but we are also preparing the concept of rest.

Once children can imitate motions while singing, they can point to visual representations of the beat. We specify that pointing to a visual representation is a kinesthetic activity; you provide the visual representation for the students. The concept of rhythm is not presented until after the beat has been made conscious. We believe that it is important to avoid clapping the rhythm when preparing beat.

You must also furnish the appropriate tempo for children. When preparing to teach beat, it is easiest to select songs, rhymes, or games that begin with quarter notes. You should always set the tempo. Begin a song or rhyme by setting the tempo as follows: "One, two, here we go." Or for the rhyme "Bee, bee, bumble bee," you could say "Bee, bee, here we go."

Children should learn to feel the even pulsation of songs and rhymes and express the pulsation through patting, walking, and other movements. The ability to keep a beat facilitates the learning of songs. You should lead the singing activity and help children recognize when tempi are slower or faster. Rhythm instruments, such as triangles, hand drums, or finger cymbals, may be used to give an appropriate beat accompaniment to singing. It is important for students to feel the beat and also hear it on a number of percussion instruments.

You may use any songs from the repertoire creatively to help the children understand the concept of beat. We use two types of motions for keeping the beat: creative motions, and the traditional motions that accompany a game song. Tempi and meters may vary according to the repertoire. Initially, use large motions with young children to help feel the beat. These motions should be performed while children are seated or standing. After this has been mastered, students may then begin to perform beat motions while moving.

During the initial phase of learning "beat," we believe it is important to not use the word itself in your instructions. We use other words to describe keeping the beat; this will help them realize that their motions stay the same no matter what words we sing. It is important for children to follow the beat that you set. There may be several children whose internal beat cannot quite match yours. Match your beat to theirs; and work from that point. Eventually they will follow your lead.

Keeping the Beat with Stationary Motions

- Sing and tap (keep the beat) on your legs.
- Sing and tap (keep the beat) on the floor.
- Sing and flap your wings.
- Sing and swing your arms to the beat.
- Sing and twist your body from your waist to the beat.
- Sing and reach upward to keep the beat.
- Sing and shake your hands to the beat.
- Sing and use a rocking motion.
- Sing and push your hands in the air or in front of you as if you're pushing your baby brother on a swing.
- Sing and tap on your head, shoulders, or other parts of your body.
- Sing and perform the beat with sand blocks.
- Children stand in a circle, with one child in the middle. The children sing a song and imitate the motion of the child in the center of the circle.

Once students have developed proficiency mirroring motions with both right and left hand, they can then begin to perform motions that are more complicated, such as tapping or pointing with one hand and moving from left to right to keep a beat. For example, as students sing "Johnny Works with One Hammer," students might be asked to fix a hole in a shoe and tap with a hammer. After they have mastered this skill, we can ask them to fix four shoes (pictures on the board) and tap on each one moving from left to right.

Demonstrating Beat with Instruments

Instead of beat motions, children may keep the beat by playing musical instruments. They should be able to follow the beat you set. However, with some beat motions there might be several children whose internal beat cannot quite match yours. In that case, you might ask a child to keep a beat on an instrument to set the tempo and then use this tempo to sing a song. Try asking the child to use sand blocks to imitate the sound of the engine and perform the rhyme "Engine, Engine, Number Nine" to the tempo set by the children. Ask a child to use wood blocks to imitate the sound of a clock; once the tempo is established the class can chant the rhyme "Hickory, Dickory Dock."

Demonstrating the Moving or Traveling Beat

It is important for children to learn how keep a beat while moving. This can involve students' walking, skipping, or passing an object to the beat.

- Sing and walk the beat.
- Sing and pass the beat along to another student by passing a ball or beanbag. This is a great way for children to see, in a visual way, the moving beat.
- Sing and keep motions to a moving circle game or a line game.

Encourage students to demonstrate the beat throughout the entire rhyme or song. This will focus their attention on the continuous motion of pulsation. Motions may then be combined with simple line or circle formations. These simple movements will serve as a foundation for singing games.

Demonstrating Meter

Although we do not deal with the concept of meter in the Kindergarten classroom music lesson, it is helpful to begin to work with children on this concept unconsciously. When singing songs in duple meter, we can encourage students to perform beat motions that emphasize the strong and weak beats. Combining strong and weak beat motions will allow students to develop a sense of meter. Of course, we are not telling them anything about beats, or strong or weak beats, or beats moving in twos or threes; we just want them to experience the meter. Any combination of motions or actions that use a strong and weak beat motion may be used. For example, imagine you are pushing another child on a swing. This motion will provide a feeling for duple meter. It is also helpful if you musically keep the beat using a rhythm instrument. Never distort the rhythm of a song to emphasize the meter; it should always be done through motions or rhythmic accompaniments. Here are additional motions that could be used to feel a strong beat:

- Stamping
- Bending
- Knocking
- Jumping
- Hopping

For feeling duple meter, children can use one of these motions or alternate one of the motions with clapping. With triple meter melodies, children can stamp followed by two claps.

The Cognitive Phase of Instruction and Learning: Preparation of Beat

Singing and Moving: Kinesthetic Activities

During the kinesthetic stage, children perform songs, rhymes, and games while exploring the beat in different ways. The physical demonstration of beat is an unconscious activity for the Kindergarten child at this point; students do not yet call the pulsation they are keeping a "beat," so we refer to the beat by referencing something in the song. For "All Around the Buttercup" we might say "Tap the buttercups," or for "Pease Porridge Hot" we might say "Tap the porridge bowls." You should guide the movement activities without using the term *beat*. Children tap the beat on parts of the body while singing a song (touching heart, touching heads, patching knees, touching shoulders, walking, hopping, or stomping). Children can play games associated with the songs as well as point to an iconic representation of the beat of a song while singing. You may sing a greeting using the pitches of the first phrase of "Snail, Snail" and have the children reply with the same pattern. Repeat this activity and practice the beat by having the children sing a reply and clap what they sing using a steady beat motion. Here are sample kinesthetic beat activities.

143

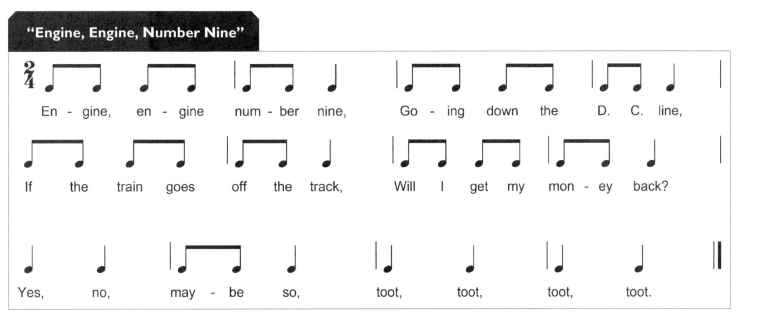

The students will perform wheel motions with their arms as they say the rhyme.

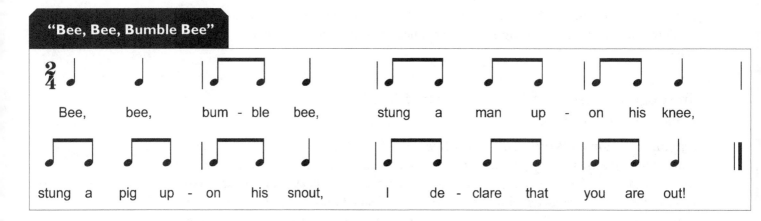

1. The children will perform up and down wing motions while they say the rhyme.
2. The teacher places an iconic representation of the beat of a song on the board, such as eight snails for "Snail, Snail." Sing the song, point to the icons, and then ask individual students to come to the board and sing while pointing to the snails with the beat.

144

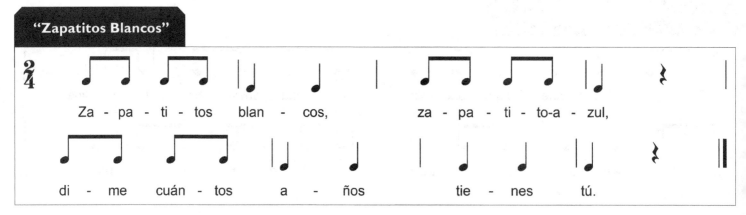

Literal translation: Little white shoes, Little blue shoe, Tell me how old you are.

You might place a visual of four or eight shoes on the board and point to the beat while chanting "Zapatitos Blancos." Individual students can come to the board and point to the beat while chanting.

Helping Children Find the Beat
For students who require some help in keeping the beat, you should sing the song and:

- Take their hands and pat with them

- Tap the beat on their shoulders
- Have the children hold a large beach ball while you tap the beat on the ball

Initially, use songs that begin with one sound on a beat. The following songs all begin with four quarter note beats.

- "Bounce High, Bounce Low"
- "Star Light, Star Bright"
- "Snail, Snail"
- "Two, Four, Six, Eight"

When we use songs that begin with two sounds on the beat, in 2/4 meter that will be represented by two eighth notes, so it is important to establish the sound of the beat. These songs begin with two sounds on the beat:

"Lucy Locket"
"Engine, Engine, Number Nine"
"I Climbed up the Apple Tree"
"Each Peach Pear Plum"
"Doggie, Doggie"
"Little Sally Water"
"Hunt the Slipper"
"Johnny"
"Pumpkin, Pumpkin, Round and Fat"
"Ring Around the Rosy"
"Sol, Solecito"

We should also use songs that contain rests so the children will understand that they must always maintain the beat and that it never stops.

- "All Around the Buttercup"
- "Hot Cross Buns"
- "Pease Porridge Hot"

Describe What You Hear: Aural Awareness Activities

During the aural awareness phase, children answer questions concerning what they hear and feel. First, you should review kinesthetic activities. Guide children to answer the basic question "How many taps did you hear?" or "How many snails did you tap?" Sing a greeting using the pitches of the first phrase of "Snail, Snail." Children reply with the same pattern. Repeat the activity, but this time children must sing and tap, keeping a steady beat motion. Establish that the taps feel the same through the whole song; they don't change the way the words change. Ask children how many taps they heard in greeting or how many taps they heard when they performed "Snail, Snail." Here are sample beat aural awareness activities for the beat.

145

1. Children sing, "Snail, snail, snail, snail," while tapping the snails on their knees (in other words, they are keeping the beat on their knees). Ask, "How many snails did we tap?" or you also ask "How many taps did you hear?" Children sing and tap knees.
2. Sing several songs, known and unknown, for the children; they must identify how many taps they feel and hear in selected phrases of each song. The children sing and tap their knees and count as you sing.

Make a Picture of What You Hear: Visual Awareness Activities

Children figure out how many icons should be drawn on the board to represent the number of taps they heard. These pictures (icons) represent the beat of the music. Pictures of the "heartbeat" will later replace the icons. Here is a sample teaching sequence for an awareness visual activity.

146

1. Children identify the melody of "Rain, Rain" after you hum it. Children then touch imaginary raindrops on their heads while singing "Rain, Rain."
2. During this next activity, you will perform the beat on a hand drum or with rhythm sticks. Children sing the first four beats of "Rain, Rain" while they tap the beat on their knees. Ask, "How many rain drops did you hear? How many rain drops should we put on the board for each phrase?"
3. Choose a child to go to the board, saying, "Sing and place the four raindrops on the board." Consider using magnetic raindrop icons or smartboard icons.
4. Children sing and point to raindrops.

Associative Phase:
Presentation (Label and Record What You Hear)

In the associative phase, you present name and the spelling of the words for the new concept. During the associative phrase it is important to

1. Review the kinesthetic activities
2. Review the aural awareness activities
3. Review the visual awareness activities
4. Present the name beat or heartbeat.
5. Present the word for (heart) beat and the symbol for heartbeat, ♥.

Here is a sample teaching sequence for the presentation of beat.

1. Children identify the melody of "Rain, Rain" after you hum it. They then touch imaginary raindrops on their head while singing "Rain, Rain."
2. During this next activity, you will perform the beat on a hand drum or with rhythm sticks. Children sing the first four beats of "Rain, Rain" while they tap the beat on their knees. Ask, "How many rain drops did you hear? How many rain drops should we put on the board for each phrase?"
3. Choose a child to go to the board, saying, "Sing and place the four raindrops on the board."
4. Children sing and point to raindrops.
5. Remove all visuals and review the number of raindrops they heard.
6. Tell them, "In music we have a special name for the sounds of the raindrops you hear. We call it the *heartbeat* or *beat* in music."
7. Ask children to perform songs and keep the beat.
8. Present the word *heartbeat* on the board and its symbol.
9. Ask children to point to four heartbeats as they sing known repertoire.

Assimilative Phase: Aural and Visual Practice

Once beat has been presented, the children have a name to use for the beat activities they have been performing while singing. Concentrated practice reinforces their new knowledge. The instructor may consider practicing beat in combination with the skills listed in Table 5.6 during several lessons. Practice activities that use familiar as well as unfamiliar repertoire may be selected from these musical skills. Remember to practice the beat both aurally and visually. For aural practice, continue to sing songs and ask the children to keep the beat. Aurally identify the number of beats in each phrase. Improvise new beat motions to a song. For visual practice, ask children to sing and point to heartbeats, or record the number of heartbeats in a phrase of music. Since children already understand the concept of loud and soft, you may also combine the practice of loud and soft with beat.

Table 5.6

Skill Area	General Activities
Reading	C sing and point to a chart indicating the beats while singing known songs. Begin with four beat phrases and expand to eight and sixteen beats.
Writing	C place heartbeat symbols on the board to represent the numbers of beats in a phrase, song, or song greeting.
Improvisation	• C improvise a motion that will demonstrate the beat of a known or unknown song. • C sing a song several times but have to create a different way of showing the beat each time. • C sing a song and change a word with a new accompanying motion. For example, they sing "All 'Round the Brickyard" and improvise a new word instead of step it.
Inner hearing	Direct C to respond to a puppet's mouth. "When the mouth is open, sing out loud; when the mouth is closed, sing inside your head." Perform the beat simultaneously.
Form	Children echo-sing a song while keeping the beat. Initially, this should be done between the T and the class. Once C have enough experience, it may be performed between two groups of C, and finally between two individual C.
Memory	Sing known and unknown songs to C and ask them how many beats they tapped during selected phrases.
Part work	C tap a beat to known or unknown songs and notice that they all look the same when moving together.
Listening	Play recorded examples of music in different meters (2/4, 4/4, or 6/8) and ask students to move to the beat by walking, skipping, or tapping the beat. Listening examples should be no longer than two to three minutes for C. Remember to play a variety of styles of music for C. Listening examples for performing the beat. "March," from *The Nutcracker Suite*, by Peter Ilyich Tchaikovsky "Hornpipe," from *Water Music*, by George Frederick Handel "Spring," from *The Seasons*, by Antonio Vivaldi "The Ball," from *Children's Games*, by George Bizet

Connections to Literature: Beat

We suggest a number of books for use by Early Childhood instructors. The texts have a strong underlying beat, and they all have distinctive sections or thematic content where the teacher can read and the students can accompany, keeping a beat.

Beat
Adams, Pam. *This Old Man.* New York: Child's Play International, 1989.
Calmenson, Stephanie. *Engine, Engine, Number Nine.* New York: Scholastic, 1996.

Crews, Donald. *Freight Train Big Book*. New York: Greenwillow Books, 1993.
Galdone, Paul. *Over in the Meadow*. New York: Aladdin Paperbacks, 1986.
Hoberman, Mary Ann. *Miss Mary Mack*. New York: Little, Brown, 1998.
Piper, Watty. *The Little Engine That Could*. New York: Philomel Books, 2005.
Stutson, Caroline. *By the Light of the Halloween Moon*. New York: Puffin Books, 1994.
Taback, Simms. *This Is the House That Jack Built*. New York: Puffin Books, 2004.
Trapani, Iza. *Row, Row, Row Your Boat*. Watertown, MA: Charlesbridge, 1999.

Strategy for Teaching Tempo: Fast and Slow

Introducing Concept of Fast and Slow

The concept of fast and slow is taught to children after they have an understanding of loud and soft, beat, and high and low related to chant. (The concept of high and low is presented in the next section of this chapter.) Although children may understand the words *fast* and *slow*, it is important that in music fast and slow be demonstrated by singing with a beat motion in songs or rhymes with a fast or slow tempo. Table 5.7 summarizes activities that children should be able to achieve.

Table 5.7

Fast-Slow	Three Year Olds	Four Year Olds	Five Years and Older
Beat	Performs beat	Performs beat at fast and slow tempi	Performs beat at fast and slow tempi. Can identify a fast and slow beat. Can point to beat icons and sing with a fast or slow tempo. Later, C can perform repertoire faster than or slower than . . .
Movement	Imitates fast and slow motions to songs or rhymes with large motions	Imitates fast and slow motions to songs or rhymes with large or small motions	Imitates fast and slow motions to songs or rhymes using large and small motions
Singing	Can sing a song in fast or slow tempi	Can sing a song in fast or slow tempi but with greater BPM (beats per minute) than a three year old	Can sing a song in fast or slow tempi without altering dynamics or other expressive elements

Once the children know approximately five to ten songs or rhymes, and understand the concepts of loud and soft, beat, and high and low related to rhyme, you can begin to work on the cognitive, associative, and assimilative phases of fast and slow.

Using Images to Help Introduce the Concept of Fast and Slow

The children in your class are likely already familiar with the concepts. However, young children are often not able to sing songs at a faster or slower tempo and keep a beat.

Performing songs at different tempi is a skill that requires practice and therefore needs to be developed. It is too abstract to ask children to sing songs using a faster or slower beat. Therefore we use a picture of a hare or rabbit to represent a fast tempo and a snail or tortoise to represent a slow one.

Repertoire for Teaching Fast and Slow

Table 5.8 has repertoire suggestions to give you ideas about songs to work with in class.

Table 5.8

Song/Chant	Movement
"A La Ronda, Ronda"	Moving circle
"Bee, Bee, Bumble Bee"	Stationary circle with motions
"Engine, Engine Number Nine"	Counting rhyme
"Hush Little Minnie"	Motions with text
"Lazy Mary"	Motions with text
"Page's Train"	Moving circle/line
"Apples, Peach, Pear, Plum"	Moving circle with motions
"Bow, Wow, Wow"	Moving circle with motions
"Hush Little Minnie"	Moving with text
"I Climbed up the Apple Tree"	Moving circle with motions
"Sol, Solecito"	Moving in a circle
"Zapatitos Blancos"	Motions with text

The Cognitive Phase of Instruction and Learning: Preparation of Fast and Slow

Singing and Moving: Kinesthetic Activities

Remember, the kinesthetic demonstration of a fast or slow beat is an unconscious activity for the young learner. Working kinesthetically with the concept of fast and slow means that children are physically learning to feel and keep fast and slow tempi. Just because the children are doing the motion or understand the meaning of fast and slow doesn't mean they understand the concept in music. During the beginning stages of teaching fast and slow, children should be encouraged to imitate the motion to accompany a song that you sing; later they can add the singing of the song to their motions.

Sing a song to the children using a fast tempo while showing a picture of a hare, and keep the beat with this icon. Next, sing the song with a slower tempo and show a picture of a snail or tortoise, while keeping the beat with the icon. Then you can ask students to accompany your singing with beat motions that are harelike or turtlelike. It is a good idea to tap a drum so the children can also hear the fast or the slow beat. It is important that you keep the same tempo for the complete song.

Children demonstrate the beat of a greeting or song while "singing like a rabbit" or "singing like a snail." They may sing and point to a visual representation of the beat, and sing and point as if they are singing like a hare or a snail. Place an icon of a hare or snail in front of the beats. Here are kinesthetic activities for fast and slow.

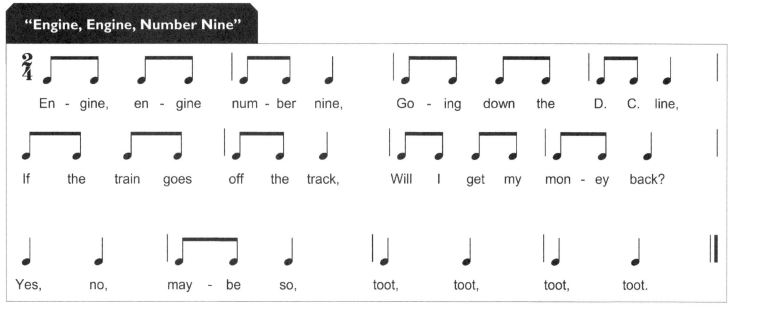

Say the rhyme "Engine, engine, number nine" and demonstrate the motion of the wheels like the hare or the snail. For variety, you might also have the train "going up the mountain" (slow) and "going down the mountain" (fast). Guide the children to imitate this motion as you chant the rhyme. Once the students can perform the motions, they can chant the rhyme as well.

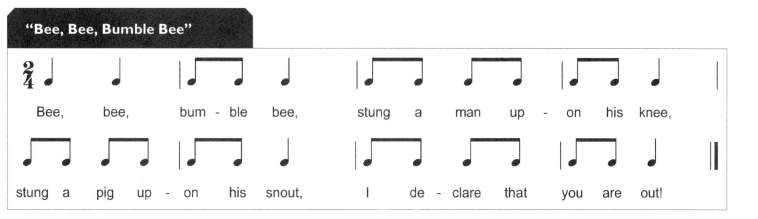

Say the rhyme "Bee, bee, bumble bee" and demonstrate the motion of flapping as the bee is going up the mountain or down the mountain. Guide the children to imitate this motion.

"I Climbed Up the Apple Tree"

Children say the rhyme "I Climbed up the Apple Tree." You can show them a picture of the turtle or the hare, and provide the first four beats of the rhyme on a drum, for children to chant the rhyme and keep the beat. The same procedure may be followed with "Zapatitos Blancos."

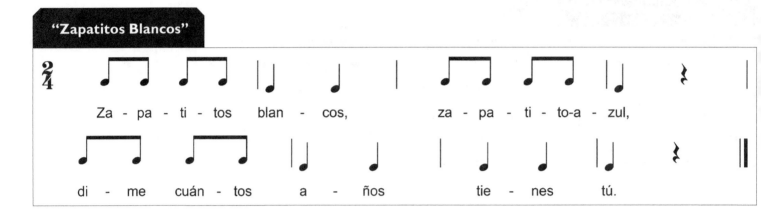

Describe What You Hear: Aural Awareness Stage

During the aural awareness stage children must be able to determine if the singing you perform is like a hare or a snail. Here are sample aural awareness activities that can be used to help the children describe what they're hearing.

Sing familiar songs to the children at different tempi. Children should be able to match motions to indicate the tempo you give them and indicate whether the hare or the turtle performs the song. The children sing familiar songs at different tempi and identify whether they were singing or like a " hare" or " snail." The children hear recorded examples of music and can identify whether the music sounded like "hares" or "snails" performing.

You or another student sings "Bounce High, Bounce Low"; children identify whether the hare or the snail performs the song.

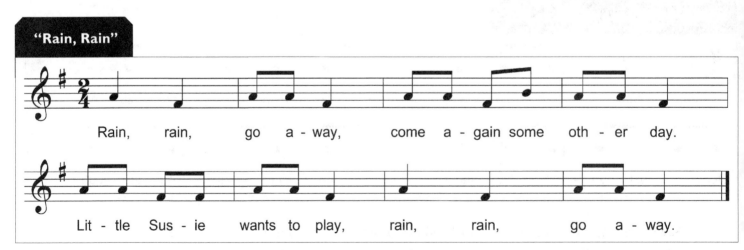

Sing "Rain, Rain" and ask the children to identify if you were singing like a hare or a snail.

Create a Picture: The Visual Awareness Stage

At the visual stage, children represent with icons or pictures what they have heard and experienced. For example, children might figure out if they the heard the song sung like a hare or rabbit,and chose the correct icon. They have to select the hare icon or turtle icon and place it in front of the title of the song or a beat chart for the song. Here is an example of a visual activity using the song "Rain, Rain."

Hum "Rain, Rain" and have the children identify the song. Tap four heartbeats on a drum and ask the children to point to imaginary raindrops (representing the beat) while you sing "Rain, Rain" like a hare. Children identify whether you sang with hare or turtle beats. The children can sing the song again while point to the hare or turtle beat icons. Individual students can also point and sing.

For a more advanced activity, you can ask students to place a hare or snail in front of a beat chart for a song. All the students or else individual students can come to the board and place the rabbit icons on the board and sing "Rain, Rain." Children then sing the song and point to a beat chart.

Associative Phase: Presentation (Label and Record What you Hear)

In the associative phase, you present name and the spelling of the words for the new concept. In a presentation lesson, preparation steps should get a condensed review. We suggest the following procedure.

1. Briefly review the kinesthetic activities.
2. Briefly review the aural awareness activities.
3. Briefly review the visual awareness activities.
4. Present the names "fast tempo" and "slow tempo" for "hare beats" and "turtle beats."

5. Sing the presentation song using the words *fast tempo* or *slow tempo*.
6. Present the words *fast temp* and *slow tempo*.
7. Ask children to sing known songs while pointing to beat icons on the board that have either *fast* or *slow* written in front of them.

Here are sample presentation activities, using the song "Rain, Rain."

1. Sing "Rain, Rain" with hare or snail beat motions.
2. Children identify whether you or another student is singing using a hare or snail beats.
3. Children point to a hare or turtle icon to represent how you or another student was singing.
4. Tell the children that when we are singing with our hare beats we are using a fast beat tempo, and when we are singing using our snail beats we are using our slow beat tempo.
5. Ask the class or individual children to sing "Rain, Rain" with a fast or slow beat.
6. Present the words *fast* and *slow*, making sure the students can spell and say each word.
7. Ask the children to sing known songs while pointing to beat icons on the board that have either "fast" or "slow" written in front of them.

Assimilative Phase: Practice
(Developing Music Performance and Literacy Skills)

Children now have a conscious knowledge of fast and slow. Aural and visual practice activities using known and unknown repertoire to reinforce this knowledge. They should be able to determine if a song is performed at a fast or slow tempo. Practice activities that focus on specific skills are suggested in Table 5.9. Remember to practice fast and slow both aurally and visually. For aural practice, ask the children to sing known repertoire with a fast or a slow beat. Aurally identify the number of beats in each phrase. Improvise new beat motions to a song. For visual practice, ask children to sing with a fast or a slow tempo while pointing to heartbeats, or record the number of heartbeats in a phrase of music. Since children already understand the concepts of loud and soft and beat, you may also combine the practice of loud and soft, beat, and fast and slow.

Table 5.9

Skill Area	General Activities
Reading	C sing and point to a visual chart indicating the beats, while singing known songs using a fast or slow tempo. Begin with four beats and move to eight and sixteen beats. C should place the words "fast tempo" or "slow tempo" in front of the beat charts.
Writing	C place the words "fast tempo" or "slow tempo" to a beat chart for a song performed by the T or other C to record how a melody was sung or chant performed.
Improvisation	C improvise a motion that will demonstrate the beat of a known or unknown song in a fast tempo or slow tempo.

(Continued)

Table 5.9 (continued)

Inner hearing	Ask C to follow the mouth of a puppet. When the mouth is open they sing out loud; when it is closed they sing inside their head but must always keep the beat. Try this activity using a fast and slow tempo.
Form	C echo sing a song while keeping the beat. Initially this should be done between T and child, and then between two groups of C and finally between two individual C. Do this with the same song performed with a slow tempo and then a fast one.
Memory	Sing known and unknown songs to C and determine if it was sung with a fast or slow tempo.
Part work	Divide the class into two groups. Group A improvises a motion when they hear fast music (such as the "Tarantella," from *Pulcinella Suite*, by Igor Stravinsky) and Group B improvises a motion when they hear slow music (such as "Air" from *Suite No. 3*, by Johann Sebastian Bach).
	Play recorded examples of music in different meters, duple or compound, and ask C to move to the beat, walking, skipping, or tapping the beat, whichever is most appropriate according to the tempo.
Expressive elements	C decide how to sing a song with a fast or slow tempo.
Listening	C listen to a piece of music sung or played by the T and identify the piece as either fast or slow.

Connections to Literature: Fast and Slow

We suggest a number of books for Kindergarten instructors. These all have a distinctive beat pattern that you can read in a fast or slow tempo. Reading to the students and having them respond by keeping the beat at different tempi will further help young children understand beat in relation to fast and slow tempi.

Fast and Slow

Ahlberg, Allan. *Each Peach Pear Plum*. New York: Picture Puffin Books, 1986.
Bang, Molly. *When Sophie Gets Angry, Really, Really Angry*. New Rochelle, NY: Spoken Arts, 2000.
Cauley, Lorinda Bryan. *Clap Your Hands*. New York: Puffin Books, 1997.
Crews, Donald. *Freight Train Big Book*. New York: Greenwillow Books, 1993.
Keats, Ezra J. *John Henry: An American Legend*. New York: Dragonfly Books, 1987.
Lester, Helen. *Tacky the Penguin*. London: Sandpiper, 2006.
Lewis, Kevin. *Chugga Chugga Choo Choo*. New York: Hyperion Books, 2001.
Munsch, Robert N. *Mortimer Spanish Edition (Munsch for Kids)* Toronto: Annick Press, 2007.
Seuss, Dr. *My Many Colored Days*. New York: Knopf Books for Young Readers, 1996.

Strategy for Teaching High and Low Voices (Rhymes and Chants)

The concept of high and low is presented to children after they have an understanding of tuneful singing, loud and soft, and beat. A child's understanding of high and low is often mistakenly associated with volume or decibel level rather than vibrations per second. There two steps in working with the concept of high and low:

1. Chanting rhymes using high voice and low voices
2. Singing small-range melodies with a high voice and then a low voice

We will first address the teaching of high and low using chants and rhymes to teach the concept of high and low voice.

Prior to your introducing the concept of high and low, children will have worked on the concepts of tuneful singing, loud and soft, and heartbeat. High and low needs to be addressed in both rhymes and melodies. It is important that children understand that we can say a rhyme with our high or low speaking voice and that we can sing with our high or low singing voice. Subsequently, children must also be taught that melodies are made up of high and low notes. Because this is a complicated process for young children, we have broken up the process for teaching the concept of high and low related to chant and related to melodies. Therefore, once we introduce students to the concept of loud and soft, and beat, then we introduce them to the concept of high and low voices in chants; after we have presented the concept of fast and slow we then introduce them to high and low related to melody. This needs very careful preparation. Table 5.10 lays out performance expectations for young children.

Table 5.10

High and Low Skills	Three Year Olds	Four Year Olds	Five Year Olds
Speaking	Learning to hear and speak with high and low voices	Learning to hear and speak with high and low voices	Learning to hear and speak with high and low voices Using the words *high* and *low* to describe voices
Singing		Learning to sing songs that use the minor third interval	Learning to hear the difference between an octave, a perfect fifth, and a minor third Learning to sing songs that use the minor third interval Learning to sing songs in a higher than normal or lower than normal key to feel the difference

(Continued)

Table 5.10 (continued)

Movement	Some can show a general melodic contour of high and low	Show a melodic contour with hands	Show a melodic contour with hands Independently demonstrate with hands the difference between an octave, a perfect fifth, and a minor third

Once the children know approximately five rhymes and can kinesthetically demonstrate heartbeat, you can begin to work on the cognitive, associative, and assimilative phases for teaching high and low.

Symbols to Introduce the Concept of High and Low Voices

Use of imagery is very important for developing the concept of high and low. Employing such ideas as speaking in "baby" and "grandfather" voices or speaking with a "bird" or "bear" voice is at the heart of introducing the concept of high and low to young children. Try reciting nursery rhymes, silly phrases, or lines from a book that your class is familiar with, in both your "baby" and "grandfather" voices. You may also want to introduce musical instruments that have a high or low sound.

Repertoire to Be Used for Teaching High and Low

Any chant can be spoken in a baby voice, and then repeated in a grandfather voice. Vocal exercises, such as sirens, are also wonderful for helping children explore the extreme high and low ranges of their own voices.

Table 5.11

Song	Movement
"Handy Dandy"	Motions with text
"Engine, Engine Number Nine"	Motions with text
"Bee, Bee Bumble Bee"	Motions with text
"Zapatitos Blancos"	Motions with text

The Cognitive Phase of Instruction and Learning: Preparation of High and Low Voice

Singing and Moving: The Kinesthetic Stage of Learning

Children should continue to feel and perform a beat while singing rhymes and chants with a high voice or a low voice. Even when they accurately perform the motions or understand the meaning of the words high and low, this does not necessarily mean they understand the concept of high or low in music. During the beginning stages of teaching the concept

157

of high and low, children should be encouraged to imitate your voice and motions. You could also use a slide whistle and ask students to move up higher or down lower, depending on what they hear. It is important for children to separate high and low using chants, and then understand that melodies are made up of high and low pitches. Eventually, in first grade children will understand that a song made up of two notes a minor third apart is composed of high and low notes.

When teaching the concept of high and low, you may introduce various tempi and meters while reinforcing the concepts of beat and fast and slow. When children chant a rhyme first with a bird voice and then with a grandfather voice, we keep the beat the same; we can use different beat motions for the bird and the grandfather voice to help the performance of the chant. Here are examples of singing and movement kinesthetic activities.

1. Say the words to a familiar rhyme in either a "bird voice" (high voice) or "grandfather voice" (low voice) while showing pictures of a bird or grandfather. Use smaller motions for the "baby voice" and larger motions for the "grandfather voice." Children imitate your voice as they are shown either the bird or the grandfather icon.
2. Children imitate a motion to the beat while they say the words to a familiar rhyme in either a "bird voice" (high voice) or "grandfather voice" (low voice). You should use smaller motions for the "baby voice" and larger motions for the "grandfather voice."
3. Children perform a motion to the beat while they sing the words to a familiar song in either a "baby voice" or "grandfather" or "bear" voice.

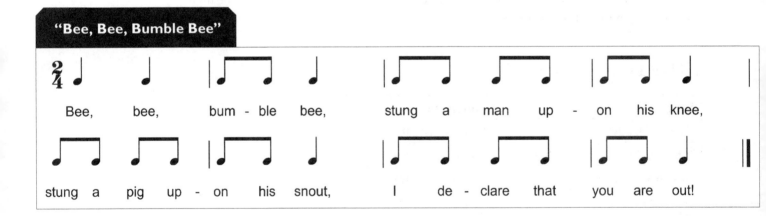

"Bee, Bee, Bumble Bee"

Bee, bee, bum-ble bee, stung a man up-on his knee,

stung a pig up-on his snout, I de-clare that you are out!

Children imitate flapping wings to the beat while they sing or say the words to "Bee, Bee, Bumble Bee" in a "bird voice" (high voice). You should use smaller beat motions for the "bird voice" and larger beat motions for the "grandfather voice." Make sure that the beat is always the same.

Children perform wheel motions to the beat while they chant or say the words to "Engine, Engine Number Nine" in a "bird voice" (high voice). Use smaller motions for the "bird" and larger motions for the "bear voice."

Describe What You Hear: Aural Awareness Stage

Once the majority of the children can perform the kinesthetic activities independently, we move on to aural awareness phase. The children can later do aural awareness activities under your guidance, independently. Here are general activities.

1. Chant familiar rhymes to the children using a "bird voice" or a "grandfather voice." Children should aurally determine if the teacher is chanting using a "grandfather voice" or a "bird voice." Here are sample activities applied to rhymes.
2. Perform "Engine, Engine, Number Nine" and ask the children to say the rhyme back the way you sang it.
3. Say "Engine, engine, number nine" and ask the children if they are singing using a "bird voice" or a "bear voice."
4. You or another student sings the song using a "bird voice" or "bear voice." Children identify if the other students are singing using a "bird voice" or a "bear voice."

Making a Picture of What You Hear: Visual Awareness Stage

Once the majority of the children can perform the activities in the aural awareness phase independently, then it is time to move on to the visual phase. Here are sample visual activities.

1. As you perform "Engine, Engine, Number Nine," ask the children to point to the heartbeat chart and aurally identify if you are using a "bird/baby voice" or "bear/grandfather voice."
2. Ask the children to choose the visual (bird or bear) that best represents how you sang, and place it in front of the beat chart.
3. Ask a student to say "Engine, engine, number nine." Ask another student to repeat the rhyme, but point to the visual that represents how the children sang: "Elizabeth, place the visual in front of the beat icons for 'Engine, Engine,' and chant it the way Andy said the rhyme."

Associative Phase: Presentation (Label and Record What You Hear)

In the associative phase, you present name and the spelling of the words for the new concept. These focus activities outline a process for children to label and record what they hear:

1. Review kinesthetic activities.
2. Review aural awareness activities.
3. Review visual awareness activities.
4. Present the terms *high voice* and *low voice*.
5. Children chant known rhymes using a high voice or a low voice.
6. Present the words *high* and *low*.
7. Children read the instruction, high or low, and chant accordingly.

Here are sample presentation activities using the rhythm "Engine, Engine, Number Nine."

Engine, Engine, Number Nine

1. As you perform "Engine, Engine, Number Nine," ask the children to point to the heartbeat chart and aurally identify if you are using a "bird voice" or "grandfather voice."
2. Ask the children to choose the visual that best represents how you sang, and place it in front of the beat chart.
3. Ask a child to say "Engine, engine, number nine." Ask another child to repeat the rhyme, but point to the visual that represents how the first child sang: "Elizabeth, place the visual in front of the beat icons for 'Engine, Engine,' and chant it the way Andy did."
4. Explain that when we chant a rhyme with a bird voice we are using our high voice. When we chant using a grandfather voice, we are using a low voice.
5. Ask children to chant "Engine, Engine" using a high voice or a low voice.
6. Present the words *high* and *low* to children.
7. Present the word *high* or *low* to the children, and they chant "Engine, Engine" accordingly.
8. Place the word *high* or *low* in front a beat chart for "Engine, Engine," and have the children chant accordingly.

Assimilative Phase: Practice
(Developing Music Performance and Literacy Skills)

Once the concept of high and low is presented, the students have conscious knowledge of it. To reinforce this knowledge, practice is needed. Remember to practice high voice and low voice both aurally and visually. For aural practice, ask the children to chant known rhymes with a high voice or low voice. Aurally identify if a rhyme was chanted with a high or low voice. Improvise a text with a high or low voice. For visual practice, ask children to chant with a high or low voice while pointing to heartbeats, or record the number of heartbeats in a phrase of music. Since children already understand the concepts of loud and soft, beat, and fast and slow, you may also combine the practice of loud and soft, beat, and fast and slow with high and low voice. Practice activities can be chosen from the various ideas suggested by the musical skills seen in Table 5.12.

Table 5.12

Skill Area	General Activities
Reading	1. Ask C to read the word *high* or *low* placed in front of beat icons and to chant the rhyme as per instruction of word.
Writing	1. Ask C to place visuals on the board representing the beat as they are singing using their high voice or low voice. 2. Ask C to record how another child chanted a rhyme by placing the word *high* or *low* in front of a beat chart.
Improvisation	Ask C to improvise a motion that will demonstrate the beat of a known or unknown song using a high voice or a low voice.
Instruments	Ask C to accompany the class or an individual on a drum while chanting in a high or low voice.

(Continued)

Table 5.12   (continued)

Expressive elements	C decide how to chant a rhyme using a high or low voice.
Part work	Ask the C to keep the beat to known or unknown chants using a high or low voice.
Inner hearing	Ask C to chant a rhyme with a bird or bear voice and to follow the mouth of a puppet. When the mouth is open, they sing; when it is closed they sing inside their head.
Listening and memory	Chant known and unknown rhymes to C using a low or high voice and ask them how many beats were in the song.
Listening	C listen to a piece of music sung or played by the T and will identify the piece of music as either high or low.

Strategy for Teaching High and Low Pitches

Once children can switch between high and low speaking voices and singing voices, we can begin to work on the concept of a melody that is composed of high and low pitches. We initially focus on melodies that contain two pitches a minor third apart. For example, the first phrase of the song "Star Light, Star Bright" has a range of two pitches (a minor third). The children should begin to sing simple melodies with a range of a minor third and use hand gestures to indicate the high and low sounds. Once they have mastered this activity, we can include more complicated melodies with a wider range.

Symbols to Introduce the Concept of High and Low Pitches

When we teach the concept of high and low pitches, we focus on the idea that a melody is composed of phrases that contain different pitches. We can use melodic icons to represent the contour of a melody. For example, the first phrase of "Snail, Snail" uses a high pitch followed by a low pitch followed by a high pitch and then a low pitch. We can use pictures of four snails spaced spatially to represent this.

Repertoire to Used for Teaching High and Low Pitches

Table 5.13 lists repertoire that will help teach the concept of high and low pitches. We should choose song material that uses only a minor third interval in the song or in a phrase of a song.

Table 5.13

Song	Movement
"Star Light, Star Bright"	Motions with text
"See Saw"	Motions with text
"Snail, Snail"	Motions moving circle/line
"Sol, Solecito"	Motions with text
"Rain, Rain"	Motions with text

The Cognitive Phase of Instruction and Learning: Preparation of High and Low Pitches

Singing and Moving: The Kinesthetic Stage of Learning

In teaching the concept of high and low, we may introduce various tempi and meters while reinforcing the concepts of loud and soft, beat, fast and slow, and high and low voice. Students imitate gestures while you sing. Here are three high and low activities:

1. The children sing a song and point to a picture that indicates the melodic contour of the melody.
2. They sing a song and point to words written spatially that indicate the melodic contour of the melody.
3. Children use hand gestures that outline the melodic contour of a song independently of the teacher. For example, ask children to close their eyes and point to the words written spatially. At this point we can explain that their songs are composed of phrases and each phrase is made up of different pitches. Pitches create a musical shape or contour.

Here are examples of kinesthetic activities for high and low applied to repertoire.

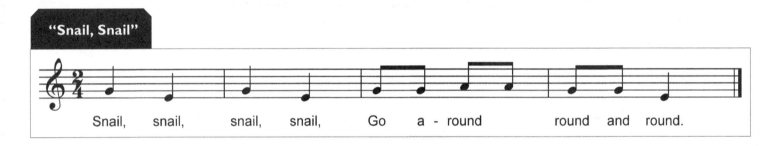

Sing "Snail, Snail" and point to a picture that indicates the melodic contour of the first four beats of the song. Children repeat this activity after you model it.

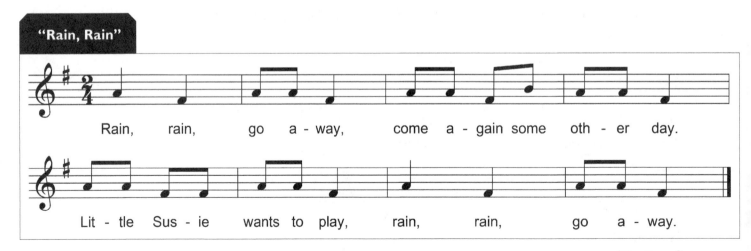

(Continued)

Children may use hand gestures independently that outline the melodic contour of the first four beats of "Rain, Rain."

Remember that these icons represent pitches and not beats. Initially these icons can be pictures related to the song, but eventually they can become more abstract.

    ✱   ✱

        ✱   ✱

The same type of activity may be used with the first four beats of the song "¿Quién Es Esa Gente?" ("Who Are These People?").

"Quien Es Esa Gente."

¿Quién es e - sa gen - te que.an - da por a - hi?
¿Quién es e - sa gen - te que.an - da por a - lla?

¡Ha - ce mu - chao rui - do, no de - ja dor - mir!
¡Ha - ce mu - cha bu - lla, no de - ja so - ñar!

Describe What You Hear: Aural Awareness Stage

Once the majority of the children can perform the kinesthetic activities independently, we move on to aural awareness phase. Here are general activities.

- Children must be able to aurally identify two pitches in a phrase of music composed of a minor third, for example, the first phrase of "Snail, Snail."
- They must aurally identify these notes as being high or low.
- From the time children begin to sing small-range melodies, you should also begin to develop their aural discrimination of high and low pitches, played on the recorder or piano, beginning with the octave, then the perfect fifth and finally, the minor third. For example, play a series of intervals at an octave and have the children indicate the notes with hand gestures. Repeat the activity with notes a fifth apart. You can sing or play simple melodic patterns using just two notes an octave apart, and ask the children to show with their hands the contour of the melody. Sing a song and have the students show high and low sounds by moving their hands to the melodic contour.

As a sample aural awareness activity, sing the first phrase of "Snail, Snail" and have the students keep the beat. Ask these questions:

- Children sing the first phrase of "Snail, Snail" and point to melodic icons representing the melodic contour.
- Children close their eyes, sing the song, and point to the contour of imaginary snails.
- Hum the first two beats of phrase 1 and ask, "How many pitches did you hear? Are the pitches the same or different? Are they in the same place?" We want the children to be able to use the words *high* and *low* to describe pitch.
- Begin by singing the song using the words *high* and *low*, and students can imitate. Once they can imitate with ease, try singing patterns from songs on "loo" and asking students to sing back with high and low as well as show the melodic contour.

You should now move to songs with more complicated rhythm patterns, such as "Rain, Rain," and repeat this process.

Making a Picture of What You Hear. Visual Awareness Stage

Once eighty percent of the children can perform the activities in the aural awareness stage independently, then it is time to move on to visual stage. In this stage the children learn to represent the melodic contour using icons. Here are sample visual activities applied to songs.

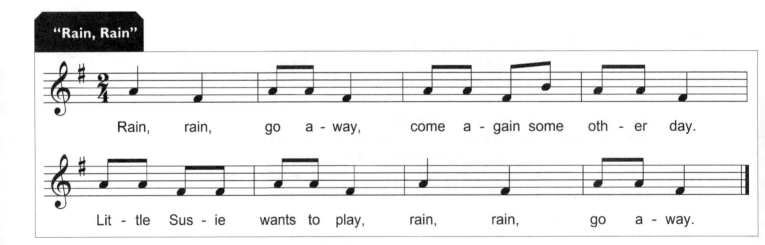

"Rain, Rain"

Rain, rain, go a-way, come a-gain some oth-er day.
Lit-tle Sus-ie wants to play, rain, rain, go a-way.

Here are some visual awareness activities applied to repertoire for "Star Light, Start Bright."

1. Sing the song "Star Light, Star Bright."
2. Ask children to echo back motives from the song and show the melodic contour with their hands.
3. Ask children to echo back the first phrase with high and low.

4. Hum the first phrase, give children star icons or discs, and ask them to arrange the stars to fit the melody.
5. Children sing and point to the icons.

The same activity may be used with the first phrase of "Rain, Rain."

Associative Phase: Presentation (Label and Record What You Hear)

In the associative phase, you present name and the spelling of the words for the new concept. These focus activities outline a process for children to label and record what they hear:

1. Review kinesthetic activities.
2. Review aural awareness activities.
3. Review visual awareness activities.
4. Present the terms high pitch and low pitch and link them to the melodic contour and melody.
5. Show children how to write the words *high pitch* and *low pitch* and *melody* and *contour*. Also show that pitches can be represented by dots placed spatially.
6. Practice applying new terms with new symbols within songs.

Here are sample presentation activities using the song "Star Light, Star Bright."

1. Sing the song "Star Light, Star Bright."
2. Ask children to echo back motives from the song and show the melodic contour with their hands.
3. Ask them to echo back the first phrase with high and low.
4. Hum the first phrase, give children star icons or discs, and ask them to arrange the stars to fit the melody.
5. Children sing and point to the icons.
6. Explain that the first phrase of "Star Light, Star Bright" is made up of high and low pitches. Sing the first phrase with the words *high* and *low* while indicating the contour with hand gestures. Children imitate.
7. Show children how to write the words *high pitch* and *low pitch* and *melody* and *contour*.
8. Children sing the first phrase with the words *high* and *low* while pointing to dots representing the melodic contour.

Assimilative Phase of Learning and Instruction: Aural and Visual Practice

Remember to practice the concept of high and low pitches both aurally and visually using both known and unknown repertoire and music skills. For aural practice, ask children to sing known melodies or phrase from songs composed of a minor third with the words *high* and *low*. For visual practice, ask children to sing phrases with high or low while pointing to dots representing the contour. Since children already understand the concepts of loud and soft, beat, and fast and slow, you may also combine the practice of loud and soft, beat, and fast and slow with high and low pitches.

Practice activities can be chosen from the various ideas suggested by the musical skills in Table 5.14.

Table 5.14

Skill Area	General Activities
Reading	Ask C to place visuals on the board representing the high sounds and low sounds in a piece of music containing two pitches such as "See Saw."
Writing	Ask C to place visuals on the board representing the high sounds and low sounds in a piece of music containing two pitches such as phrase one of "See-Saw."
Improvisation	Ask C to improvise a melody using the high and low pitches using their voices.
Instruments	Ask C to accompany the class or an individual on a pitched instrument using only s-m while singing.
Expressive elements	C decide how to sing a song using different dynamics for high-low section.
Part work	Ask the C to tap to known or unknown songs using a high-pitched or low-pitched instrument to keep the beat.
Inner hearing	Ask C to sing a melody composed of s-m and to follow the mouth of a puppet. When the mouth is open, they sing; when it is closed they sing inside their head.
Listening and memory	Sing known and unknown s-m songs to C and ask how many beats were in the songs.
Listening	C listen to a piece of music sung or played by the T and identify the piece of music as either high or low.

Connections to Literature: High and Low

We suggest these books for Early Childhood instructors to help guide children in their understanding of high and low. Reading to the students using a high or low voice and allowing them to give voice to characters in the books will significantly enliven their understanding of high and low.

Rhythmic Chant in High and Low Voice
Ahlberg, Allan. *Each Peach Pear Plum*. New York: Picture Puffin Books, 1986.
Baker, Keith. *Quack and Count*. New York: Harcourt Brace, 1999.
Brown, Margaret Wise. *Goodnight Moon*. New York: Scholastic, 1947.
Brown, Margaret Wise. *The Train to Timbuctoo*. Racine, WI: Golden Books, 1979.
Carle, Eric. *From Head to Toe*. New York: HarperFestival, 1997.
Ehlert, Lois. *Eating the Alphabet: Fruits and Vegetables from A to Z*. New York: Harcourt Brace, 1989.
Emberley, Ed. *Go Away, Big Green Monster*. New York: Little, Brown, 1992.

Fleming, Denise. *In the Small, Small Pond*. New York: Holt, 1993.

Gollub, Matthew. *The Jazz Fly*, 1st ed. Santa Rosa, CA: Tortuga Press, 2000.

Kalan, Robert. *Jump, Frog, Jump!* Logan, IA: Perfection Learning, 2010.

Keats, Ezra J. *John Henry: An American Legend*. New York: Dragonfly Books, 1987.

Lester, Helen. *Tacky the Penguin*. London: Sandpiper, 2006.

Lucas, Sally. *Dancing Dinos*. New York: Random House, 1933.

Martin, Bill, Jr. *Fire! Fire! Said Mrs. McGuire*. Boston: HMH Books, 2006.

Martin, Bill, Jr. *Panda Bear Panda Bear, What Do You See?* New York: Holt, 2003, 2004.

Pinkney, Brian. *Max Found Two Sticks*. New York: Aladdin Paperbacks, 1994.

Piper, Watty. *The Little Engine That Could*. New York: Philomel Books, 2005.

Portis, Antoinette. *Not a Box*. New York: HarperCollins, 2006.

Williams, Sue. *I Went Walking*. New York: Harcourt Brace, 1989.

Wood, Audrey. *Silly Sally*. New York: Harcourt Brace, 1992.

We suggest these books for Early Childhood instructors to help guide children in their understanding of high and low. They books can be sung to the students using an interval of a minor third (child's chant).

High and Low Melody

Barner, Bob. *Bugs, Bugs, Bugs*. San Francisco: Chronicle Books, 1999.

Calmenson, Stephanie. *Engine, Engine, Number Nine*. New York: Scholastic, 1996.

Carle, Eric. *The Very Busy Spider*. New York: Philomel Books, 1984.

Carle, Eric. *Have You Seen My Cat?* New York: Aladdin Paperbacks, 1997.

Lucas, Sally. *Dancing Dinos*. New York: Random House, 1933.

Martin, Bill, Jr. *Brown Bear, Brown Bear, What Do You See?* New York: Holt, 2004.

Munsch, Robert N. *Mortimer Spanish Edition (Munsch for Kids)*. Toronto: Annick Press, 2007.

Slobodkina, Esphyr. *Caps for Sale*. New York: W. R. Scott, 2004.

Swanson, Susan Marie. *The House in the Night*. New York: Houghton Mifflin, 2008.

Williams, Sue. *I Went Walking*. New York: Harcourt Brace, 1989.

Strategy for Teaching Concept of Rhythm: Patterns of Short and Long Sounds

Rhythm is the final concept that we teach in the Kindergarten classroom. We are capturing only one aspect of rhythm which is duration. We work on this concept after children have an understanding of the concepts of loud and soft, beat, and high and low applied to chants; and fast and slow and high and low applied to melodies. The concept of rhythm can be approached from two orientations depending on the age level and maturity of children. For some it might be sufficient to introduce the concept of rhythm related to clapping the words. Or with older children we can begin to describe rhythm in terms of beats that have one, two, or no sounds. These sounds can also be described as long or short. Table 5.15 represents an overview of rhythmic development for young children.

Table 5.15

Beat and Rhythm Skills	Three Year Olds	Four Year Olds	Five Year Olds
Rhythm	Learning rhythm at the kinesthetic level; clapping the words	Learning rhythm at the kinesthetic level; clapping the words	Learning rhythm at the cognitive, associative, and assimilative phases
Instruments used for keeping the beat	Drum	Drum and rhythm sticks	Drum, rhythm sticks, cymbals, and triangle

Suggested Repertoire for Teaching Rhythm

We have avoided using compound-meter songs for recognizing patterns of short and long sounds.

Table 5.16

"Bate, Bate, Chocolate"	Motions with text
"Bee, Bee, Bumble Bee"	Stationary circle
"Cobbler, Cobbler"	Motions with text
"Con Mi Martillo"	Motions with text
"Doggie, Doggie"	Guessing
"Engine, Engine Number Nine"	Counting rhyme
"Queen, Queen Caroline"	Motions with text
"Rain, Rain"	Motions with text
"See Saw"	Motions with text
"Snail, Snail"	Motions with text
"Sol, Solecito"	Motions with text
"Zapatitos Blancos"	Motions with text

Symbols to Introduce the Concept of Rhythm

When teaching rhythm we focus on two aspects, clapping the way the words go and the concept of long and short sounds. In teaching, we can use a picture of hands clapping to represent the rhythm of words. With more advanced children, we can use pictures to represent the number of sounds on each beat, or pictures to represent the length of sounds using long and short lines to represent long and short sounds.

Cognitive Phase of Learning: Preparation of Rhythm

Sing and Play: The Kinesthetic Stage

Kinesthetic demonstration of rhythm is an unconscious activity for the Kindergarten student. What does it mean to work kinesthetically on the concept of rhythm? It means children are physically learning to feel the number of sounds on a beat, in a phrase, or in a whole song. Just because they can perform rhythmic motions or understand the meaning of the word *rhythm* does not necessarily mean they understand the concept of rhythm in music. Children are quite adept at breaking words up into sounds, but in music class they must be able to clap the rhythm of songs while chanting a rhyme or singing a song of eight to sixteen beats, before we introduce the term *rhythm* to them.

During the beginning stages of teaching rhythm, we encouraged children to clap the rhythm; we describe it as "clapping the way the words go." It is very important that the children feel the difference between rhythm and beat. For this reason, we strongly suggest that the students pat the beat and clap the rhythm. To accomplish this, remind them that the beat does not get faster or slower; it is steady. Then compare the beat with "the way the words go." Three-year-old children should experience feeling the difference between performing beat and rhythm, but they should not be introduced to the word *rhythm*. Children should perform rhythmic activities while the teacher or another student performs the beat. This type of activity reinforces the difference between a steady beat and rhythm.

As teachers, we must make sure that we give the correct tempo to the children. Starting lessons with songs that begin with quarter notes helps with this concern. Later we can progress to songs that begin with eighth-note patterns. It is important that they learn to identify where rests occur in a song. Therefore when clapping the rhythm of a song that contains a rest, be sure to indicate the rest by holding your palms out or putting them on your shoulders. Initially the students will be copying your motion, but later in the aural awareness stage you can ask them about beats that have no sound and begin to introduce them slowly to the concept of the rest. Here are kinesthetic activities applied to rhymes and songs.

It is helpful to set a tempo for a song or rhyme by beginning, "One, two, here we go." Or in the case of a specific song or rhyme, such as "Engine, Engine, Number Nine," the instructor might chant, "Engine, engine, here we go."

The teacher may use any songs from the repertoire creatively to help the children understand the concept of rhythm. Various tempi, dynamics and meters can be used. Use the actions listed here to further aid the children in exploring the concept of rhythm.

1. Children sing and keep the beat while you clap the words. Switch.
2. Divide the class into two groups. Group 1 claps the rhythm while group 2 pats the beat. Then have the groups switch. Once students are secure with the two activities, try this with two children, or one child with you, the teacher.
3. Children sing the song and put the words in their feet. They point to a representation of the rhythm going from left to right.

The following is a sample kinesthetic activity.

"Rain, Rain"

Rain, rain, go a - way, come a - gain some oth - er day.

Lit - tle Sus - ie wants to play, rain, rain, go a - way.

Sing "Rain, Rain" and point to rain drops on the board representing the sounds on the beat; ask students to point to the visual and sing the song. This may be represented using umbrellas for the beat and raindrops for the rhythm.

For students who require some help in performing rhythm, you should sing the song and:

Tap the rhythm on their shoulders.
Take their hands and clap with them.
Tap the rhythm on their desks in front of them.
Play the rhythm on a nonpitched instrument.
Ask the children to place their hands on a beach ball and tap the rhythm of a song as they feel the rhythm on the ball.

The same procedure may be used for "Con Mi Martillo (With My Hammer)."

"Con Mi Martillo (With My Hammer)"

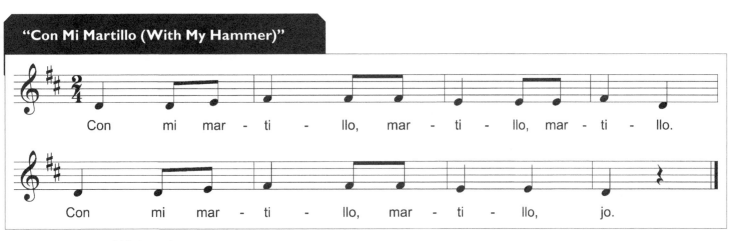

Literal translation: With my hammer, jo.

Describe What You Hear: Aural Awareness Stage

During this stage, children identify whether the teacher or another child sings and taps the beat or claps the way the words go.

If children are more advanced, you might say, "How can we describe these sounds?" or "Now think of the way the words sound. Figure out how you would sing the song using the words *long* and *short*." You may sing a phrase of a familiar song and have the children sing it back using the words *long* and *short*. This is a difficult exercise to conceptualize, and if necessary it can wait until students are in first grade. Here are sample aural awareness activities.

Sing and clap the words of "Bounce High, Bounce Low" or "Con Mi Martillo." Have the children identify whether you clapped the beat or the way the words go.

Here is an example of a more advanced activity.

"Rain, Rain, Go Away"

Sing "Rain, Rain" and ask the children to close their eyes and listen. Tap gently on the board while singing and ask them, "Was I tapping the beat or the way the words go?"

Sing the song and pat the beat.
Sing the song and clap the way the words go.

Sing a phrase of music on "loo" and have the children identify how many beats are in the phrase.

Identify how many sounds are on each beat. For example when children sing the first phrase of "Rain, Rain," they will discover that there is one sound on beats 1, 2, and 4 and two sounds on beat 3.

Children sing the phrase with the words *long* and *short*.

The same procedure may be used with "Bate, Bate, Chocolate." Clearly establish the beat first because this rhyme begins with eighth notes.

"Bate, Bate, Chocolate"

Ba - te, ba - te, cho - co - la - te. Con - ha - ri - na y con - to - ma - te.

Translation: Stir the chocolate with flour and tomatoes.
(making the roux for molé)

172

Creating a Picture: Visual Stage

At the visual preparation stage, children represent the way the words go by choosing an icon that has hands clapping for words or a heart for the beat. Here is a sample strategy to use.

"Rain, Rain"

Rain, rain, go a - way,

1. Sing the first phrase of the song and clap the rhythm. Hide your hands so the students can't see what you're doing.
2. Ask, "Did I tap the beat or clap the way the words go as I sang?" Then ask, "Please choose either the clapping hands or the heartbeat to place in front of the title of the song."

Here is an approach to use with more advanced children.

1. Ask a child to sing the song and point to the raindrops on his or her knees.
2. Ask the children to identify the number of beats per phrase.

3. Hum the first phrase of "Rain, Rain" and ask the children to identify the number of sounds on each beat.
4. Ask them to place the raindrops on the board representing the sounds on each beat.
5. Ask them to clap the way the words go as they sing.
6. For more advanced children, we encourage teachers to use Unifix cubes for a visual awareness activity. Give each student several cubes arranged in groups of four and two, representing long and short, for creating a visual of the rhythm of a song.

Associative Phase: Presentation (Label and Present the Word)

In the associative phase, you present name and the spelling of the words for the new concept. Here is a sample activity for presenting rhythm.

1. Review the kinesthetic activities.
2. Review aural awareness activities.
3. Review visual activities.
4. Present the name *rhythm*. Explain that when we clap the way the words go, we are clapping the rhythm of a rhyme or melody.
5. Sing known repertoire and clap the rhythm.
6. Present the spelling for the word *rhythm* visually.
7. Sing a song while pointing to an iconic representation of rhythm. This may be done with the whole class or individual students.

Assimilative Phase

Once the term *rhythm* is presented both aurally and visually, the children have conscious knowledge of its meaning and to what it refers. Practice the concept of rhythm both aurally and visually using both known and unknown repertoire and music skills. For aural practice, ask children to sing known melodies and clap the rhythm. Aurally determine if you or another child is performing the beat of rhythm of a song. For visual practice, ask children to sing songs while pointing to iconic representations of the rhythm. Since children already understand the concepts of loud and soft, beat, fast and slow, and high and low, you may also combine the practice of loud and soft, beat, fast and slow, and high and low pitches with rhythm.

To reinforce this knowledge, concentrated practice is needed. The students should be able to perform these activities:

1. Switch between performing beat and rhythm at a signal from you.
2. Recognize known songs from hearing a performance of the rhythm only.
3. Echo-clap with you using songs from the repertoire.

You may want to consider practicing rhythm in combination with the musical skills shown in Table 5.17 during several lessons using a Practice Lesson Plan format. Practice activities can be chosen from the various ideas suggested from the musical skills seen in the table.

Table 5.17

Skill Area	General Activities
Reading	1. Have a few song titles written on the board and place the word *rhythm* or *beat* in front of the title. C must sing and either clap the rhythm or keep the beat. 2. Sing and point to a visual that represents the rhythm of a known song and sing using the words *long* and *short*.
Writing	1. Sing a song and clap either the rhythm or the beat. C must place the word *rhythm* or *beat* in front of the song title. 2. C place the text of a song above the beat icons.
Improvisation	C improvise a new word while clapping the rhythm of a song. For example C sing and clap the rhythm for "Here Comes a Bluebird" but must improvise a new color that has only one syllable.
Inner hearing	Ask C to follow the mouth of a puppet. When the mouth is open, they sing out aloud; when it is closed they sing inside their head, but they must continue to clap the rhythm.
Form	1. C clap rhythm patterns from chants and melodies. T sings known songs phrase by phrase and C must sing back and clap the rhythm. 2. C identify which phrases have the same rhythm.
Memory	Sing and clap the rhythm to known and unknown songs.
Part work	1. Sing and keep the beat or rhythm on a rhythm instrument 2. C sing alternative phrases with the T or another child while keeping the rhythm.

Connections to Literature: Rhythm

We suggest these books for Early Childhood instructors. They all have distinctive sections or thematic content that you can read rhythmically. Students can take a repeating refrain in the book and say and clap the way the words go. Books with rhyming words help students develop memory skills and speech fluency.

Ahlberg, Allan. *Each Peach Pear Plum*. New York: Picture Puffin Books, 1986.
Baker, Keith. *Quack and Count*. New York: Harcourt Brace, 1999.
Calmenson, Stephanie. *Engine, Engine, Number Nine*. New York: Scholastic, 1996.
Carle, Eric. *From Head to Toe*. New York: HarperFestival, 1997.
Cauley, Lorinda Bryan. *Clap Your Hands*. New York: Puffin Books, 1997.
Fleming, Denise. *In the Small, Small Pond*. New York: Holt, 1993.
Galdone, Paul. *Over in the Meadow*. New York: Aladdin Paperbacks, 1986.
Gershator, Phillis. *Listen, Listen*. Cambridge, MA: Barefoot Books, 2007.
Hoberman, Mary Ann. *Miss Mary Mack*. New York: Little, Brown, 1998.
Keats, Ezra J. *John Henry: An American Legend*. New York: Dragonfly Books, 1987.
Langstaff, John. *Oh, A-Hunting We Will Go*. New York: Aladdin Paperbacks, 1974.
Lewis, Kevin. *Chugga Chugga Choo Choo*. New York: Hyperion Books, 2001.

Longstaff, John. *Frog Went A-Courtin'*. San Diego: Voyager Books, 1972.

Lucas, Sally. *Dancing Dinos*. New York: Random House, 1933.

Martin, Bill, Jr. *Brown Bear, Brown Bear, What Do You See?* New York: Holt, 2004.

Martin, Bill, Jr. *Panda Bear Panda Bear, What Do You See?* New York: Holt, 2003, 2004.

McNaughton, Colin. *Not Last Night But The Night Before*. Somerville, MA: Candlewick Press, 2009.

Pinkney, Brian. *Max Found Two Sticks*. New York: Aladdin Paperbacks, 1994.

Piper, Watty. *The Little Engine That Could*. New York: Philomel Books, 2005.

Williams, Sue. *I Went Walking*. New York: Harcourt Brace, 1989.

Wood, Audrey. *Silly Sally*. New York: Harcourt, 1992.

Discussion Questions

1. How do we construct a teaching strategy for Kindergarten concepts based on the model of learning presented in Chapter 4?
2. Discuss the role of questioning in developing meta-cognition skills.
3. How does the implementation of the teaching strategy promote independent learning in the classroom?
4. Discuss the notion that some might think the teaching strategies presented in this chapter are too cumbersome for instructors to follow, and it is much more effective to present information theoretically and then use it to practice music skills of reading and writing.

Ongoing Assignment

Develop a teaching strategy for a readiness concept plan based on the model provided in this chapter for your teaching portfolio. Demonstrate how you have infused your teaching strategy with your own creative ideas.

Suggested Reading

Houlahan, Micheál, and Philip Tacka. *Sound Thinking: Developing Musical Literacy*. 2 vols. New York: Boosey & Hawkes, 1995.

Bibliography

Bresler, L. "The Role of Musicianship and Music Education in the Twenty-First Century." In *Musicianship in the 21st Century: Issues, Trends and Possibilities*, ed. S. Leong, pp. 15–27. Sydney: Australian Music Centre, 2003.

Elkind, D. *The Power of Play: How Spontaneous, Imaginative Activities Lead to Happier, Healthier Children*. Cambridge, MA: Da Capo Lifelong Books, 2007.

Hargreaves, D. J. "The Development of Artistic and Musical Competence." In *Musical Beginnings: The Origins and Development of Musical Competence*, ed. I. DeLiege and J. A. Sloboda, pp. 145–170. Oxford: Oxford University Press, 1996.

Hirsh-Pasek, K. and R. M. Golinkoff, with D. Eyer. *Einstein Never Used Flashcards: How Our Children Really Learn and Why They Need to Play More and Memorize Less*. Emmaus, PA: Rodale Press, 2004.

Leong, S., ed., *Musicianship in the 21st Century: Issues, Trends & Possibilities*. Sydney: Australian Music Centre, 2003.

Phillips-Silver, J., and L. J. Thainor. "Feeling the Beat: Movement Influences Infant Rhythm Perception." *Science*, 2005, *308*(1430).

Winkler, I., G. P. Haden, O. Ladinig, I. Sziller, and H. Honing. "Newborn Infants Detect the Beat in Music." *Proceedings of the New York Academy of Sciences*, 2009, *106*: 2468–2471.

Zentner, M., and T. Eerola. "Rhythmic Engagement with Music in Infancy." *Proceedings of the National Academy of Sciences*, 2010, *107*(13): 5768–5773.

Chapter **6**

Cultivating Music Skills and Creativity

In Chapter 5 we applied our model to teaching several music concepts in the Kindergarten classroom. Teaching musical concepts is combined with practicing specific musical skills, referred to as *skill areas*. We are convinced that there is a connection between movement and cognitive skills that should take place while acquiring musical skills. The goal of this chapter is to provide teachers with ideas on practicing concepts in combination with the skill areas that will promote creativity in the classroom. We practice concepts such as loud and soft, beat, high and low, and fast and slow in combination with music skills. Practicing music skills in the music classroom should be (1) appropriate to children's abilities, (2) varied, and (3) motivating. At the end of this chapter, we present sample lessons that bring focused practice to skill areas, though skill areas are practiced throughout the lesson.

Skill Development in the Kindergarten Classroom

The main skills areas to develop in the Kindergarten classroom are

- *Singing.* Children learn to use their singing voices with accurate breathing, posture, range, expression and intonation. They imitate the teacher's vocal model.
- *Movement development.* This is their ability to learn traditional singing games and develop a body of movement skills so they can express space, time, and force through their bodies in relationship to music.
- *Music reading.* This skill requires that children be able to point to icons representing rhythmic and melodic concepts as they sing a song or chant a rhyme. In the

Kindergarten classroom we ask children to read music while pointing to icons that represent the beat, pitches, or sounds on the beat. In addition they should eventually learn to recognize and read words that will be put in front of these icons, such as loud, soft, high, low, fast, and slow, and be able to demonstrate singing or chanting.

- *Writing.* This is their ability to record the effects of a music concept on the performance of repertoire. For example, if children sing "Lucy Locket" with a soft voice, then they should eventually be able to record this by writing or drawing a text that indicates the song and writing the word *soft* beneath the picture. We ask children to record what they hear by using icons that represent the beat, pitches, or sounds on the beat.

- *Improvisation.* Simple improvisations can form part of the practice activities. Making up movements to accompany songs and changing the words to a song should both be used with young children to encourage spontaneity and creativity. The classroom atmosphere for such activities should be free and gamelike so children can make an error without becoming embarrassed. In a gamelike setting, they may be encouraged to have fun while putting their musical skills into practice immediately and instinctively.

- *Part work or ensemble work.* This activity allows children to develop the ability to perform two or more activities simultaneously. Part work may include singing while performing the beat, or singing and clapping the rhythm. At the end of the year, children will develop the ability to walk to the beat and clap the rhythm of the songs. Echo singing or singing songs where one group sings the question and another the answer are components of developing ensemble or two-part singing.

- *Inner hearing.* This is the ability to hear a melody inside one's head without any acoustical stimulation. Inner hearing is also known as audiation.[1] We can promote the development of this skill by practicing singing softly, then by singing silently, mouthing the words, and then by completely inner singing.

- *Form.* This is the phrase structure of a piece of music. Children should be guided to determine and recognize simple forms used in song and listening repertoire both aurally and visually. Determining form begins with the ability to identify same and different phrases, question-and-answer, and call-and-response forms. The ability to identify form significantly affects the development of musical memory and has an impact on the development of movement skills.

- *Memory.* Musical memory is critical to the development of all musical skills. This skill includes learning new songs, and being able to echo-clap or echo-sing patterns from song material, as well as identifying pieces of music and recognizing the sounds of instruments. Teachers need to recognize that nearly all aspects of their teaching help develop both aural and visual memory, especially knowledge of music form.

- *Listening.* This is the ability to aurally and visually understand a piece of music. For children in the Kindergarten classroom, we are developing their ability to listen to music examples for aesthetic reasons as well as to identify music concepts or elements. The best listening activities for children at this age level should begin with a live performance of folksongs and folktales. At this age we want children to recognize when the music is loud or soft, fast or slow, high or low. They should be able to identify a few music instruments. Several types of listening skills are developed in the music class. Both live classroom performances and recorded musical examples are included in this skill area.

- *Instrumental development.* This includes the ability to recognize musical instruments both visually and aurally, as well as to play simple rhythmic and melodic instruments in the elementary classroom.
- *Awareness of Tone Color.* Children need to be able to aurally distinguish several types of sounds. For example, you could show a musical instrument, present its name, play it, and then use the instrument to accompany the singing of a folk song. Present several instruments and use them to accompany singing activities. Once several instruments have been introduced, ask children to close their eyes while you accompany the song with an instrument. Ask them to either name or point to a picture of the instrument used in the accompaniment. As children begin to learn and distinguish each other's voices, they can play voice recognition games. "Doggie, Doggie" is an example of a game song that has vocal recognition built into the game activity.
- *Ear training.* This is the ability to aurally identify basic music concepts and elements. Ear training should be part of the practice activities for all music concepts. It is built into our whole model of learning, most specifically in the Aural Awareness Stage 2 as well as the Assimilative Phase, Stage 1. Ear training is closely aligned with the development of singing. Examples of ear training activities are identifying music sung with a daytime (loud) or nighttime voice (soft), identifying beat or rhythm and the ability to show the contour of a melody with hand motions.
- *Music terminology and music theory.* This is the ability to use standard musical terms and symbols to read and write music.

Developing Reading and Writing Skills in the Kindergarten Classroom

Musical reading and writing are skills that lead to comprehensive musicianship. These two skills may be practiced during each music lesson in a manner that does not detract from the enjoyment of making music. Once you gain the practical experience of working through some of our suggestions, you will undoubtedly begin to develop interesting and varied activities by turning them into inner hearing, memory, and ensemble singing activities.

Sample Beat Reading Activities
- Keep the beat of well-known songs through movement activities while you or another child taps the beat on a percussion instrument.
- Sing a known or unknown phrase of a song with words and have the children sing the phrase back and pat the beat.
- Children point to a chart of either four or eight beat icons and sing known melodies.
- Children point to a chart of either four or eight beat icons with a symbol or word attached and sing known songs. For example, they see a sun or the word *loud* in

front of the beat icons and sing using a loud voice while pointing to beat icons. We also can create beat charts made of icons that refer to a concept being taught, such as four or eight moons or suns, etc.

- Children read the phrase "Sing and Keep the Beat" placed in front of a song, and they must perform the song with the beat.

Sample Rhythm Reading Activities

- Keep the beat of well-known songs through movement activities while you or another child taps the beat on a percussion instrument.
- Sing a known or unknown phrase of a song with words and have the children sing the phrase back and pat the beat.
- Clap the rhythm of well-known songs while you or another child pats the beat.
- Sing a known or unknown phrase of a song with words, and have one child (or all the children) sing the phrase back and clap the way the words go.
- Children point to a chart of either four or eight beat icons; each icon has a representation for one or two sounds on the beat. The children sing known melodies.
- Children point to a chart of either four or eight beat icons; each icon has a representation for one or two sounds on the beat with a symbol or word attached. They sing a known song. For example, they see a moon or the word *soft* in front of the rhythm icons and sing using a soft voice.
- Match song titles to clapped rhythms. List the title or pictures representing two or three songs on the board. Clap the rhythm; children must identify the song.

Sample Melody Reading Activities

- Sing known melodies or phrases while children show the melodic contour.
- The children point to the contour of a known song while you sing. Children guess the title of the song.
- Hum a known song or phrase; have the children identify the song and show the melodic contour on their body as they sing.
- Play a melody on the recorder; children sing the song with words and show the melodic contour.
- Children point to a chart showing the pitches and sing known melodies. It is important to use simple songs such as "Snail, Snail" or "Star Light, Star Bright."
- Children point to a chart showing the pitches with a symbol or word attached, and they sing known songs. For example, they see a sun or the word *loud* in front of the pitches and sing using a loud voice.

Sample Beat Writing Activities

- You or a child sings a song using a loud or soft singing voice; another child must place a picture of the sun or moon in front of a beat chart for the song, recording how it was performed.
- You or a child sings a song using a loud or soft singing voice; another child must place the words *fast tempo* or *slow tempo* in front of a beat chart for the song, recording how it was performed.

- You or a child sings a phrase of a song or a short song either four or eight beats long; another child records how many beats were sung in the song using icons or beat icons.
- Sing a phrase of a song containing *s-m*; have the children use icons or a disc to construct the melodic contour.
- Clap the rhythm of a phrase or song four or eight beats long; have children use icons or Unifix cubes to show the rhythm.

Developing Ear Training Skills in the Kindergarten Classroom

We can develop children's ear-training abilities by using known rhythmic and melodic concepts. Ear-training skills are built into the aural awareness stage of learning as well as the assimilative phase of learning. Here is a sample ear-training activity for each concept.

Sample Ear-Training Activities

- *Loud and soft.* Children listen to a melody that you sing or play on an instrument, or a piece of instrumental music, and decide if the music was played with a daytime or night time voice (cognitive phase) or a loud or soft dynamic (assimilative phase). They may also use their hands to show loud and soft. For example, they can spread their hands apart horizontally for loud and touch their lips with their finger for soft.
- *Beat.* Children listen to a melody that you sing or play on an instrument and determine how many beats were in the music example. Before the beat concept has been introduced to children who are experiencing the cognitive phase of learning about beat, you can sing a song such as "Bounce High, Bounce Low" and have them figure out how many times they heard the ball bounce on the ground (cognitive phase).
- *Fast and slow.* Children listen to a melody that you sing or play on an instrument, or a piece of instrumental music, and decide if they heard snail or hare beats.
- *High and low.* Children listen to you perform a chant and decide if the music was performed with a bird voice or a bear voice (cognitive phase) or high voice or low voice (assimilative phase). They can figure out the high and low pitches of a *s-m* melody by showing the contour with their hands. They should be able to distinguish high and low using two pitches on the piano. Initially begin with notes an octave apart, then a fifth, and finally a minor third, a common interval in children's music. You may progress to more difficult melodies with children that contain pentatonic pitches, and have the children show the melodic contour of the melody while singing back the music motif. Have them echo-sing a four-beat melodic pattern that you sing or play on an instrument (recorder). Lastly, identify nonpitched and pitched instruments. In Kindergarten we want children to aurally recognize the sound of a drum, cymbals, xylophone, and piano.
- *Rhythm.* Perform a song while clapping the rhythm. The children identify whether they hear you clapping the beat or the words to a song (cognitive phase). In the assimilative phase, they can use the word *rhythm*. Children listen to a four-beat melody that you sing or play on an instrument and clap the rhythm motive.

The Development of Inner Hearing

Inner hearing is considered an essential component of the Kindergarten class. Memory plays a critical role in the development of inner hearing.

Sample Inner Hearing Activities

Inner hearing can be practiced in several ways. Here are specific inner hearing activities that can be used in the classroom. We suggest you connect inner hearing to as many activities as possible. The first example is perhaps the most consistently practiced form, used by many music instructors. Be sure to perform the beat in a musical way with each activity.

- Hum a melody; the children must identify the song from the hummed melody. A more challenging activity is for you to sing the second or third phrase or motif of a song (instead of the first) and have children recognize the title of the song.
- Singing phrases/motifs silently. Children sing the motifs of a song using a loud and then a soft voice. Consider using a puppet or symbol or gesture as a signal for them to sing loud or soft. They may sing a song aloud, and at a signal from you they inner-hear a phrase or portion of a phrase. Use a puppet or symbol or gesture as a signal for them to inner-hear or to sing aloud.
- Have the children recognize a song from hearing while you clap its rhythm.

The Development of Music Memory in the Kindergarten Class

- It is important to develop children's ability to sing songs correctly and musically. One way to develop music memory is for them to learn a variety of songs that contain the same form as well as the same rhythmic and melodic building blocks. In this way, the performance of one song will remind them of another.
- Choose songs that have a definite form. They should be short and contain two phrases. Forms can include call-and-response, question-and-answer or two phrases being almost identical.

Sample Music Memory Activities

- Singing songs by means of a call-and-response technique in the classroom is a useful technique in developing aural memory.
- Echo singing or clapping short motives of four or eight beats should be practiced with the class as well as individual children. Echo singing can be done during the introduction of the lesson. Echo clapping of rhythm can be done during the presentation or practice stage of rhythmic development.

Discussion Questions

1. What do we mean when we say that rhythmic and melodic concepts need to be practiced?
2. How can we connect such skill areas as the development of musical memory and inner hearing to the teaching of musical reading and writing? Provide specific examples.

Ongoing Assignment

1. Choose a song and demonstrate how you could develop the skill of reading and writing appropriate for an Kindergarten class.
2. How can you extend such reading and writing activities to develop the music skills of inner hearing and memory?

Form

In Chapter 1 we presented a model of how folksongs may be analyzed. The most important point to be gleaned from the first chapter is that musical motifs are the building blocks of all types and styles of music and are one of the most important musical ideas that the teacher has available to develop a child's knowledge of music. In the Kindergarten classroom, teaching form begins with distinguishing same, different and similar. These simple concepts lead to differentiating binary and ternary forms, a prerequisite for understanding larger sonata and symphonic forms.

Teaching the structure of a song (form) begins early in musical education. As children learn to keep the beat, clap the rhythm of songs, and sing in tune with correct breathing and dynamics, they are already learning significant aspects of musical form such as phrasing and dynamics. It is important for them to grasp the structure of a song so that they can enjoy it from an aesthetic perspective. This information will help with the musical shaping of a performance of the music. Understanding music form will help children develop their music memories. Common music motifs in the music repertoire will act as a source of inspiration for children's own improvisations.

The understanding of musical form is closely linked to the development of musical memory, reading, writing, improvisation, composition, and inner hearing skills.

Activities for Developing a Sense of Musical Form

Any of these activities can be further expanded into composition and improvisation activities.

A. Form and Rhythmic Motifs
1. After singing a song, have children repeat the rhythmic motifs that you clap. Children keep the beat during this activity so they will understand the length of the motif.
2. Children learn to echo-clap song material alternating with you another child. It is important that they understand the length of the motif.
3. Divide the class in half and have children clap the rhythm of the song, alternating groups. For example, group A claps the first phrase and B sings the second phrase.
4. Ask children to echo-clap rhythms with texts, beginning with known motifs and moving to more complex ones. They listen rather than clap while you are

183

performing the rhythmic motif. Use motifs and text that are abstracted from the repertoire the children are singing. Next you can use motifs from songs and create new texts; children must clap the text as well as say it. Relate the text to a book that you are going to read to the children, or maybe a new song you are going to sing for them. Remember that all of these echo claps should follow each other so that children can discern the pulse. It is important to end each rhythmic motif with a quarter note; eighth notes are too difficult for children to clap.

5. Improvise a question rhythm to familiar rhythms with text; children must respond with an answering rhythm.
6. Same and different: children are guided to discover
   a. The number of phrases in a song
   b. The number of beats in each phrase
   c. Which rhythms are the same or different
7. Use apples and bananas to identify same and different phrases in simple songs. For young children, you might call an A phrase "Apple" and a B phrase "Banana."

Consider using rhythm exercises in the music classroom based on motifs from song material and rhymes. Clap a four-beat pattern and ask children to clap an answer that is the same or different. Remember to use one and two sounds on a beat before including beats with no sounds (rests). The same can be done with melodic motifs on a neutral syllable or loo.

B. Form and Melodic Motifs
1. After singing a song, have children repeat the motifs you have sung. Remember to keep the beat throughout the activity.
2. Have the children learn to sing song material alternating with you or another child. It is important that they understand the length of the motif. The idea is for the children to "pass the song around."
3. Divide the class in half and have the children sing the song, in alternating groups. For example, group A sings the first phrase and B sings the second phrase.
4. Ask children to echo-sing, beginning with known motifs and moving to more complex ones. Children listen rather than sing while you are performing the melodic motif. It is important to use motifs that are abstracted from the repertoire children are singing. Begin with known motifs and texts. Later, change the words to the motifs while keeping the same rhythm.
5. Ask the children to echo-sing melodies that contain familiar texts but new melodies that you have composed.
6. Improvise a question melody and have the children respond with an answering melody.
7. Same and different: children are guided to discover
   a. The number of phrases in a song
   b. The number of beats in each phrase
   c. Whether phrases are the same or different
   d. Use apples and bananas to identify same and different phrases in simple songs. For young children, you might call an A phrase "Apple" and a B phrase "Banana."
8. Question-and-answer forms. These forms can be similar (easiest) in A Av (Av means A variant) form, or different in A B form. Explore the concept of form with children.

The easiest form is the question and answer; for example, sing the first two phrases of the song "Doggie Doggie." You can have two pictures of dogs; one is called the Question Dog and the other is the Answer Dog. It is important that the children sing the question-and-answer phrase without any interruption of the beat. Explore question-and-answer form with other known songs. As the children gain confidence in singing questions and answers, it is important that you begin to use motifs that are "open" or " closed"; open motifs require a closing cadence.

Connections to Literature: Form

We suggest these books for Early Childhood instructors to use in developing musical form. The texts have call-and-response sections. These books all have distinctive sections or thematic content where you can read or sing and the students can chant or sing the response.

Antiphonal Singing (Call-and-response) Form

Adams, Pam. *This Old Man*. New York: Child's Play International, 1989.
Boynton, Sandra. *Doggies: A Counting and Barking Book*. New York: Little Simon, 1984.
Boynton, Sandra. *Moo Baa La La La*. New York: Little Simon, 1995.
Carle, Eric. *From Head to Toe*. New York: Harper Festival, 1997.
Carle, Eric. *The Very Busy Spider*. New York: Philomel Books, 1984.
Gollub, M., and J. Love. *Gobble, Quack, Moon*, 1st ed. Santa Rosa, CA: Tortuga Press, 2002.
Martin, Bill, Jr and E. Carle. *Panda Bear, Panda Bear, What Do You See?* New York: Holt, 2003.
Martin, Bill, Jr and E. Carle. *Polar Bear, Polar Bear, What Do You Hear?* New York: Holt, 1997.
Orleans, Ilo and T. Gergely. *Animal Orchestra*. Racine, WI: Little Golden Book, 1958.

Improvisation

Improvisation, the art of composing extemporaneously, is an integral component of the Kindergarten music classroom. Improvisation extends and develops creativity and musicianship and can take many forms. Often, young children invent words and melodies quite naturally. Substituting words in a song and choosing motions to accompany a song are early forms of improvisation.

The instructor should set the parameters for improvisation simply and clearly so everyone can perform the task: "For learners to know how to proceed in their creating, they need to fully understand the parameters within which they will be asked to work. Most often, this kind of groundwork is best laid through a series of performing and listening experiences that precede the creating time."[2]

A basic rule for improvisation games is that the children must keep the beat going. The game should be continuous, without interruption, proceeding until everyone has had a turn. In this way, the instructor can observe and assess which children might need additional help with a particular concept.

Rhythmic and melodic elements as well as form may be practiced through improvisation activities. Instructors should consider the children's age and assess the class's level of understanding to determine appropriate improvisation activities. If possible, some type of improvisation activity should accompany each learned musical concept. The teacher should bear in mind that improvisation is a game for young children; it has merit and value only when it stimulates and enlivens the class.

Once young children know a repertoire of songs, the teacher can begin vocal improvisation in the classroom. Using the same melodic contours and rhythms of known repertoire, the teacher may sing to the children about a character in a story they have read in the class. At a later time, the teacher may encourage the children to sing about what they see in pictures from known stories. Once children have developed the security and confidence of improvisation, then they can be encouraged to sing about such things as their favorite book, toy, animal, food, or movie. When working with question-and-answer forms, it is important for the teacher to understand the difference between using opening motives, such as *smlsm*, or closing motives, such as *mrd*.

Sample Activities for Developing Rhythmic Improvisation

Activities that involve improvising rhythmic elements are usually the first to be incorporated into music lessons. Here are suggested kinesthetic, aural, and visual activities for practicing rhythm and developing improvisation skills. Many of the suggestions used for developing form can be used in developing improvisation.

Kinesthetic Activities for Improvising Rhythms

Begin with simple activities. Movements to accompany songs, changing the words to a song, echo clapping, and echo singing should be used with young children to encourage spontaneity and creativity. The classroom atmosphere for these activities should be informal and gamelike so they can make an error without becoming self-conscious.

- Improvise a motion to a song suggested by the text. In the song "Hunt the Slipper," children can perform motions related to the text of the song, such as performing the tapping motion of hammer to the beat. When singing "Hot Cross Buns," they can perform motions related to baking, such as a stirring or scooping motion.
- Improvise a motion to the beat. In the song "That's a Mighty Pretty Motion," children may select a motion for the class to imitate, such as clapping, jumping, patting, tapping, etc.
- Improvise a motion for the rhythmic form of a folksong. For example, children may sing "Hot Cross Buns" while walking in a circle. They walk clockwise for the A phrases and counterclockwise for the B phrase.
- Improvise a two-beat rhythmic ostinato using body motions such as clapping hands for beat 1 and patting knees for beat 2.
- Toward the very end of the Kindergarten year, children can improvise a rhythmic ostinato using Orff instruments.

Aural Activities for Improvising Rhythms

- Improvising an answer to a four-beat rhythmic question
  1. As the instructor, establish the beat.
  2. Clap a rhythmic motive, and have a child echo the pattern.
  3. Clap a rhythmic motive, but have the children echo with a different one.
- Question and answer
  1. As the instructor, establish the beat.
  2. Clap a four-beat pattern, and have the children respond with a different four-beat pattern.

- Improvising new words in a song
  - Children can improvise a new word or words in a song. For example, in "Here Comes a Blue Bird," they can improvise a new color for the bird.
  - Individual children echo-sing motives from a song. This can be done with text or on a neutral syllable.
  - You can also add hand movements to indicate the direction of the melodic line. Use motives from well-known songs, and songs to be used later on.
  - Make sure the children echo without hesitation.
  - Sing to the children, substituting new text to familiar song material, and have the children echo-sing.
  - Listen to Ella Jenkins' version found on iTunes: "Play Your instruments and make a pretty sound." Jenkins sings a phrase and repeats echo with an instrument so that children can sing the echo.
- Improvising new rhymes
  - Children improvise new words to a familiar rhyme. For example, for "I Climbed up the Apple Tree" children can be encourage to create a new rhyme: "I climbed up the Christmas Tree/All the bells fell on me/Christmas Pudding, Christmas Pie/Did you ever tell a lie?"

Visual Activities for Improvising Rhythms

Improvise a number of ways of performing a song. Children point to a beat chart and sing a song based on a word that they have selected from a group of flashcards (such as loud or soft, fast or slow, high or low) to put in front of their beat chart.

Sample Activities for Developing Melodic Improvisation

Kinesthetic Activities for Improvising Melodies

- Improvising motions
  - Children demonstrate the melodic contour of a melody through improvised motions and words. For the song "Snail, Snail," improvise motions for the snail.
  - Substitute the word *cat* or *squirrel* for *snail*, and improvise appropriate motions.

Aural Activities for Improvising Melodies

- Improvising text
  - Children may improvise words with simple melodies. For example, you may sing a question to the children using the notes of a known *s–m* melody and have the children improvise an answer using the same notes.
  - Individual children sing greetings to the class that are based on melodic patterns from song materials.
- Substitute text
  - Consider the song "Teddy Bear." Ask children to substitute words for "Teddy Bear," such as "Buzzing Bee" or "Kitty Cat."
- Question and answer
  - Establish the beat.
  - Sing a four-beat melody and have the children respond with a different four-beat melody.

- Improvising new words in a song
  - Sing to the children, substituting new text to familiar song material, and have the children echo-sing.
  - Listen to Ella Jenkins' version found on iTunes: "Play Your instruments and make a pretty sound." Jenkins sings a phrase and repeats echo with an instrument so that children can sing the echo.

Visual Activities for Improvising Melodies

- Present the children with a visual representation of the pitch contour for "Snail, Snail."
- Children can manipulate the icons to create another pattern.

Discussion Questions

1. How can you develop children's kinesthetic, aural, and visual improvisation abilities in the Kindergarten classroom?
2. Discuss the idea that children should be allowed to improvise music freely in the classroom using their own ideas and forms of expression; activities based on the suggestions of this chapter are only another form of reading and writing and do not help children's creative skills.
3. How is music improvisation connected to the teaching of performance and repertoire?

Ongoing Assignment

1. Review the goals for form and improvisation/composition in the curriculum for Kindergarten (Chapter 2).
2. Choose a readiness concept that you are going to teach next year. List the steps that you would use to practice this concept through form, improvisation, and composition.
3. How can you extend the improvisation and composition activities given above to develop inner hearing, memory, and ear-training activities?

References for Practicing Form, Improvisation, and Composition

Alperson, Philip A. "On Music Improvisation." *Journal of Aesthetics and Art Criticism*, Fall 1984, *43*(1): 17–29. See also *Improvisation, Dance, and Movement*. St. Louis: Magnamusic-Baton, 1981.

Barrett, Margaret. "Children's Aesthetic Decision Marking: An Analysis of Children's Musical Discourse as Composers." *International Journal of Music Education*, 1996, 28: 37–62.

Bramhall, David. *Composing in the Classroom*. New York: Boosey & Hawkes, 1989.

Brophy, Timothy S. *The Melodic Improvisations of Children Ages Six Through Twelve: A Developmental Perspective. Journal of Research in Music Education* 53(2): 120–133.

Bunting, R. "Composing Music: Case Studies in the Teaching and Learning Process." *British Journal of Music Education*, 1987, 4(1): 25–52.

Bunting, R. "Composing Music: Case Studies in the Teaching and Learning Process." *British Journal of Music Education*, 1988, 5(3): 269–310.

Campbell, L. *Sketching at the Keyboard Harmonization by Ear For Students of All Ages*. London: Stainer and Bell, 1982.

Chatterly, A. *The Music Club Book of Improvisation Projects.* London: Galliard, 1978.

Cropley. A. K. "Fostering Creativity in the Classroom: General Principles." In *Handbook of Creativity Research* vol. 1, ed. M. A. Runco, pp. 83–114. Cresskill, NJ: Hampton Press, 1997.

Csikszentmihalyi, M. "Society, Culture and Person: A System View of Creativity." In *The Nature of Creativity: Contemporary Psychological Perspectives*, ed. R. J. Sternberg. New York: Cambridge University Press, 1988.

Dadson, P., and D. McGlashan. *The From Scratch Rhythm Workbook.* Portsmouth, NH: Heinemann, 1995.

Dowling, J. W. "Tonal Structure and Children's Early Improvisation and Composition Learning of Music." In *Generative Processes of Music: The Psychology of Performance?* John Sloboda. Oxford: Clarendon Press, 1988, 2nd ed. 2001.

Flohr, J. W. "Young Children's Improvisations: Emerging Creative Thought." *Creative Child and Adult Quarterly*, 1985, *10*(2): 79–85.

Hamann, Donald L., ed. *Creativity in the Music Classroom: The Best of MEJ.* Reston, VA: Music Educators National Conference, 1991.

Harris, Ruth, and Elizabeth Hawksley. *Composing in the Classroom.* Cambridge: Cambridge University, 1990.

Herboly-Kocsár, Ildikó. *Teaching of Polyphony, Harmony and Form in Elementary School*, ed. Lilla Gábor, trans. Alexander Farkas. Kecskemét: Zoltán Kodály Pedagogical Institute, 1984.

Houlahan, Micheál, and Philip Tacka. *Sound Thinking: Music for Sight-Singing and Ear Training*, vol. 2. New York: Boosey & Hawkes, 1991, p. 153.

Kratus, J. "The Use of Melodic and Rhythmic Motives in the Original Songs of Children Ages 5 to 13." *Contributions to Music Education*, 1985, *12*: 1–8.

Kratus, J. "Growing with Improvisation." *Music Educators Journal*, 1991, *78*(4): 35–40.

Laczó, Z. "Psychological Investigation of Improvisation Abilities in the Lower and Higher Classes of the Elementary School." *Bulletin of the Council for Research in Music Education*, 1981, *66/67*: 39–45.

McNicol, R. *Sound Inventions: 32 Creative Music Projects for the Junior Classroom.* Oxford: Oxford University Press, 1992.

Mead, Virginia Hoge. *Dalcroze Eurhythmics in Today's Music Classroom.* New York: Schott, 1994. See also *Music Educators Journal*, September 1993, January 1995, November 1996, November 1997, November 1999.

Michael Eric Bitz. "A Description and Investigation of Strategies for Teaching Classroom Music Improvisation." Doctorate, Columbia University Teacher's College, 3386A.

Pressing, Jeff. "Improvisation: Methods and Models." In *Generative Processes in Music: The Psychology of Performance, Improvisation and Composition*, ed. John Sloboda, pp. 129–178. Oxford: Clarendon Press, 1988.

Sexton, L., and Rosa, E. "I Is for Improvisation: A Classroom Primer." *The Kodály Envoy*, 2010, *36*(2): 16–20.

Sloboda, John, ed. *Generative Process of Music: Performance, Improvisation, and Composition.* New York: Oxford University Press, 2001.

Smith, B., and W. Smith. "Uncovering Cognitive Process in Music Composition: Educational and Computational Approaches." In *Music Education: An Artificial Intelligence Approach*, eds. M. Smith, A. Smaill, and G. Wiggins, pp. 56–73. New York: Springer-Verlag, 1994.

Szabó, Helga. *Énekes improvizácio az iskolában* [*Vocal Improvisation in the Elementary School*], vols. I–V. In Hungarian. Budapest: Zeneműkiadó, 1977.

Szabó, Helga. *Vocal Improvisation in the School I: Canon, Imitation and Fugue.* Trans. Judit Pokoly. Kecskemét: Zoltán Kodály Pedagogical Institute, 1984. This volume traces the development of canon, imitation, and fugue. Numerous musical examples, largely drawn from the fifteenth to eighteenth centuries, are included.

Tillman, June, and Keith Swanwick. "Towards a Model of Development of Children's Musical Creativity." *Canadian Music Educator,*1989, *30*(2): 169–174.

Upitis, Rena. "Can I Play You My Song?" *The Compositions and Invented Notations of Children.* Portsmouth, NH: Heinemann, 1992.

Webster, Peter. "Creativity as Creative Thinking." *Music Educators Journal*, 1990, *76*(9): 22–28.

Whitcomb, Rachel. "Step by Step: Using Kodály to Build Vocal Improvisation." *Teaching Music*, 2003, *10*(5): 34–38.

Wiggins, Jackie. "Children's Strategies for Solving Compositional Problems with Peers." *Journal of Research in Music Education*, 1994, *42*(3): 232–252.

Wiggins, Jackie. *Composition in the Classroom: A Tool for Teaching.* Reston, VA: Music Educators National Conference, 1990.

Winner, Ellen, Lyle Davidson, and Larry Scripp. *Arts Propel: A Handbook for Music.* Cambridge: Harvard Project Zero and Educational Testing Service, 1992.

Winters, G., and J. Northfield. *Starter Composing Packet.* Essex: Longman Group, 1992.

Wood, Donna. *Move, Sing, Listen, Play Preparing the Young Child For Music.* Toronto: Gordon V. Thompson, 1982.

Part Work

The strategies in this section will provide a foundation for approaching two-part singing with confidence. All of these activities give the instructor the means to prepare and practice the musical elements at many levels of sophistication and difficulty. By incorporating these activities into the music class, the instructor enlivens the vocal music program while developing in children a precise and critical awareness of musical elements and performance practice. The sequence (intended for performance of each musical activity) permits an ease and order in enabling children to perform part music.

1. Instructor and class.
2. Class and instructor.
3. Divide class into two groups, each performing their own part. Switch parts.
4. Two small ensembles, each performing their own part.
5. Two children, each performing their own part.

Sample Preparatory Activities for Developing Part Work

- Sing a song while marching, skipping, or walking to the beat.
  - In this activity, the children must concentrate on two tasks at the same time.
- Call-and-Response Singing
  - Although children perform only one phrase of music, they must be able to sing both phrases using inner hearing (audiation) if they are going to be able to sing rhythmically and musically. Call-and-response singing may be applied to folksongs (you may also think of call-and-response singing as responsorial singing).

- Perform or point to a visual of the beat of a song while singing.
  - Children sing while patting the beat or performing the beat on a percussion instrument.
  - Children sing while pointing to a visual of a beat.
- Sing a song while performing the rhythm.
  - Children sing while clapping the rhythm, or while performing the rhythm on a percussion instrument.
- Rhythmic and melodic ostinati
  - Children sing the melody while you clap a rhythmic ostinato.
  - You and the children exchange parts.
  - Divide the children into two groups; one group sings and the other performs the ostinato. Switch tasks.
  - Two children perform the work.

Listening

The goal of this section is to provide instructors with examples of music listening activities to use in their own teaching. The idea is to understand the various principles of teaching music literature, and to inspire instructors to collect examples and repertoire for their own teaching situation. The primary goal of listening in the Kindergarten classroom is finding ways that children can connect to live music performances of singing as well as instrumental playing. This will involve developing a child's attention and will take patient practice on the part of the teacher. Although children listen to music on computers, tablets, and smartphones, it is important to note that children are not necessarily paying critical attention to this music. Our task in the music class is engage children in developing their listening skills. There are two types of listening skills developed in the music classroom: one is related to identifying music concepts or elements, and the other is related to children listening to a piece of music for aesthetic reasons. It is important to create the mood for listening for the children. We should never do too much talking about the piece of music being performed; let the children enjoy listening to the music instead. Remember to repeat the song as often as needed. It is important after the listening to give children time to reorient themselves to the classroom. You will know if the listening experience was successful by the way children take time to reengage with the classroom activities. Give the children time to respond to the music with their own observations.

Kodály writes that a primary goal of a music education is "to make the masterpieces of world literature public property, to convey them to people of every kind and rank."[3] Writing elsewhere, he says further: "Individual singing plus listening to music (by means of active and passive well-arranged experiences) develops the ear to such an extent that one understands music one has heard with as much clarity as though one were looking at a score; if necessary—and if time permits—one should be able to reproduce such a score."[4] Accordingly, incorporating fine examples of music literature into music lessons is something all music instructors ought to consider. A primary goal of teaching should be to use singing and music literacy as a means of opening the world of music literature to children. For the Kindergarten student, the repertoire will mainly be concerned with folk music and instrumental music based on folk music. But "the final purpose of all this must be to introduce pupils to the understanding and love of great classics of past, present and future."[5]

191

You should find ways to encourage active music listening in the music classroom, bearing in mind the children's abilities. In Kodály's words: "It is not enough to listen once, fleetingly, to great works; one has to prepare for them and to follow the notes through the pages both before and after hearing them in order to implant them abidingly in one's mind. Personal participation is worth more than anything else.[6]

Advice for Selecting and Performing Music Literature for Listening

Because most music instructors see their students once or twice a week, the selection of music is important. Here are guidelines to be used when selecting music literature for the classroom.

- Initially, it is important to sing only unaccompanied unison songs for children, so they will not be distracted by an accompaniment.
- Texts should be appropriate for the children. Seasonal songs are also appropriate.
- Sing only once or twice (the children must not try to sing at first). Try to begin with short, simple songs, and gradually introduce more complex ones.
- Try to perform songs for children without any visual aid. Gradually you can use visuals to enhance the musical aspects of a song. For example, use two puppets to sing a song, as this helps with understanding of phrasing and form; it also helps them understand a call-and-response form.
- Have a musician play simple pieces. Include songs that the children have sung in the class. (Use song materials they will recognize.)
- Sing using appropriate emotions.
- Establish good eye contact with the children.
- Look for songs that are stories and that have been turned into children's literature. For instance, children can listen to "All the Little Pretty Horses" or "Hush Little Baby" while you use the children's book of the same title to show the illustrations as you sing.
- Find songs that tell a story.
- Allow children to accompany the song with motions, if the gestures are not distracting to other children.
- Select instrumental music of well-known composers.
- Music must be of the highest quality.
- Music must hold musical appeal for the children.
- Examples used for music listening should be correlated with children's knowledge of concepts.
- Music should be selected from different style periods.
- Aim to include a number of genres of music in your music curriculum.
- Consider using examples that highlight various solo instruments, as well as small and large ensembles. Learning the instruments of the orchestra should be built into the music curriculum.
- Perform a simple arrangement of a folksong. For example, play an instrumental version of a folksong, or even play it in canon.
- Play recordings of children's music, for example:
  - "Nursery Rhymes," The Royal Philharmonic Orchestra with full chorus, conducted by Nick Davies (1998)

Cultivating Music Listening Skills

The same care and attention that goes into selecting song repertoire for the classroom must also be used when selecting music listening examples. Once selections for music listening repertoire are made, we need to prepare the children to listen to music with focus and understanding. Here are guidelines that can be used for developing a teaching strategy for listening to a piece of music sung or played by the music teacher.

Preparation Activities for Music Listening
- Choose a piece of music that you and the children will enjoy.
- Analyze the piece of music. Identify:
  - Character of the music
  - Tempo
  - Dynamic changes
  - Form
  - Thematic material
  - rhythmic building blocks
  - melodic building blocks

This enables you to carefully think about how you are going to perform the music for the children. Consider the phrasing, the use of tone colors, and facial and hand gestures, as well as the addition of an instrument or a visual aid.

Presentation Activities for Listening
1. Make certain children are seated in a comfortable position.
2. Make a brief introduction about the song.
3. Give children a chance to respond to the first hearing.
4. Ask them to share their thoughts about the performance.

Decide how many times you are going to sing or play the music example; consider whether or not children will be actively engaged as they listen repeatedly to the piece of music.

There should be a particular focus for each repeated listening. A music instructor can design listening maps for children, as well as worksheets, to help them organize knowledge of the listening example. Sometimes it is also useful to create a simplified score for singing.

From Folk Music to Art Music
Kodály was convinced that folksongs were the ideal vehicle for leading children to an appreciation and understanding of the works of the great composers. He believed that children should be taught folk music and that folk music ought to lead to the introduction of art music and composed music:

> For instance Haydn, the best to begin with, has manifest connection with folksong, but even in many works of Mozart it is easy to recognize the sublimated Austrian folksong. Beethoven's many themes are also folk-song like. And all the national schools originated already in 19th century are based on the foundations of their own folk music.[7]

If you are aware of the possibilities inherent in folksong materials, you can skillfully guide children to an understanding of art music. You should consider the intellectual capacity and interests of your children and determine the many types of music they will enjoy.

193

Ideally, it is best to introduce them to a live performance of a song or instrumental composition at the earliest stages of musical learning. Folk and ethnic instruments may be used to accompany songs for listening, as well as songs for singing and performance. You or older students who perform on instruments may make the initial listening experiences available for children. Later, those who are studying instruments can demonstrate them for the class.

Singing Folksongs to Children

Singing songs or folksong tales to students is an effective way to develop their listening skills. In Chapter 7 we have provided sample folksongs and folksong tales as one of the summary activities in the sample lesson plans. Additionally, here is a sample of books that illustrate folksong tales:

This Old Man
Miss Mary Mack
Row, Row, Row Your Boat
The Very Lonely Firefly: "Firefly Song"
Go Tell Aunt Rhody
Today Is Monday
All Night, All Day: A Child's First Book of African-American Spirituals
All the Pretty Little Horses
The Farmer in the Dell
There's a Hole in My Bucket
I Had a Rooster
Who Is Tapping at My Window?
Teddy Bear Teddy Bear
The Cat Came Back
Goin' to Boston

Singing Folksongs That Are Incorporated in Art Music Examples

Consider using these activities:

- Sing folksongs for children at the close of music lessons. These songs may be taught to them in a subsequent lesson.
- Play known folksongs for children on a musical instrument, such as a recorder or a dulcimer.
- Have the children listen to the actual composition that includes the folksong.

Table 6.1 offers examples of folksongs connected to music.

Table 6.1

Composer	Composition	Related Song for Classroom Performance
Calliet, Lucian (1891–1985)	*Theme and Variations* on "Pop Goes the Weasel"	"Pop Goes the Weasel"

(Continued)

Table 6.1 (continued)

Composer	Composition	Related Song for Classroom Performance
Copland, Aaron (1900–1990)	*Appalachian Spring*	"Simple Gifts"
McDonald, Harl (1899–1955)	*Children's Symphony* Movement One	"London Bridge", "Baa Baa Black Sheep"
McDonald, Harl (1899–1955)	*Children's Symphony* Movement Three	"The Farmer in the Dell", "Jingle Bells"
Wolfgang Mozart (1756–1791)	*Twelve Variations* on "Ah vous dirai je maman"	"Twinkle, Twinkle Little Star"

Playing Listening Examples for Children That Demonstrate Known Concepts
Consider using these activities.

- The instructor sings known folksongs for children at the close of music lessons. These songs may be taught in a subsequent lesson.
- Play known folksongs on a musical instrument, such as a recorder or a dulcimer.
- Sing a known folksong focusing on a musical concept or element such as beat, loud, soft, fast, slow, high, low, or rhythm. Or you might sing "Doggie Doggie" and figure out the form of the songs as question-and-answer. Notice that each phrase uses four beats. Other songs could include "Pumpkin, Pumpkin." Next you might explore songs that have phrases with eight beats such as "I'm on the Kings Land." You could also have a chart with beat icons and phrase marks showing the question phrase (labeled with an apple for A) and an answer phrase (labeled with a banana for B).
- Then play a piece of music for the children and have them identify characteristics of the piece of music. Is it loud, soft, fast, slow?

Table 6.2 is a brief list of suggested listening examples arranged by concept that may be used to augment and enliven the teaching of musical elements and concepts.

Table 6.2

Concept	Composer	Music Composition
Loud and soft		
Loud	Richard Wagner (1813–1883)	"Overture" *The Flying Dutchman*
Soft	Claude Debussy (1862–1918)	"En Bateau"
Soft	Claude Debussy (1862–1918)	*Suite Bergamasque, III.* "Clair de Lune"
Loud	Ralph Vaughn-Williams (1872–1958)	*The Wasps (Aristophanic Suite).* "March Past of the Kitchen Utensils"

(Continued)

Table 6.2   (continued)

Loud/soft	Joseph Haydn (1732–1809)	*Symphony No. 94 G major,* second movement
Beat		
Simple meter	Sir Edward Elgar (1857–1934)	"Pomp and Circumstance" March, no. 1
	John Philip Sousa (1854–1932)	"Stars and Stripes Forever"
Compound meter	Robert Schumann (1810–1856)	*Album for the Young* "The Wild Horseman"
	Felix Mendelssohn (1809–1847)	*Symphony No. 4, 1.* (Allegro vivace) "The Italian"
Fast and slow		
Fast	Nikolai Rimsky-Korsakov (1844–1908)	*The Tale of Tsar Saltan* "Flight of the Bumblebee"
Fast	Camille Saint-Saëns (1835–1921)	*The Carnival of the Animals:* "Hens and Roosters" or "Aviary"
Slow	Anton Dvorak (1841–1904)	*Symphony no 9 in E minor, II, op.95*
Slow	Claude Debussy (1862–1918)	"En Bateau"
Slow	Camille Saint-Saëns (1835–1921)	*The Carnival of the Animals:* "The Swan"
Slow/soft	Beethoven (1770–1827)	*Piano Sonata No. 14 in C Sharp Minor* "Moonlight"
Slow/fast	Arcangelo Corelli (1653–1713)	*Concerto Grosso in F Major Op. 6,* "Introduction" and Movement 1
High/low		
High/Low	Aaron Copland (1900–1990)	*Circus Music,* "The Red Pony"
High/low	Adriano Banchieri (1568–1634)	"Counterpoint to the Animals"
High/low	Camille Saint-Saëns (1835–1921)	*The Carnival of the Animals:* "Kangaroos"
High/low (minor third)	Ottorino Respighi (1879–1936)	*The Birds, Suite for Orchestra,* Movement 5
Rhythm		
(Bobby Shafto has the same rhythm)	Franz Joseph Haydn (1732–1809)	*Symphony no 94 in G Major,* ("The Surprise") II Andante

(Continued)

Table 6.2   (continued)

Rest	Ludwig van Beethoven (1770–1827)	*Symphony no. 7. A Major, op 92.* Allegretto
Meter Natural pulse in duple meter	Scott Joplin (1867–1917)	Rags
Form		
Call and response	Giovanni Gabrielli (1554–1612)	*Brass Choir Compositions*
Dialogue	Johannes Brahms (1833–1897)	*Movement 1 Clarinet and Piano* (just small sections of this piece to let children listen to a dialogue)
Question and answer	Robert Schumann (1810–1856)	*The Wild Horseman*

Movement and Listening

Singing and movement are essential components of all music lessons. Throughout the lesson the teacher will provide opportunities for students to develop their movement skills. We believe that it will be more effective to incorporate movement throughout the lesson than it is to relegate movement to one specific place in the lesson.

In the music classroom we use traditional games as well as improvisatory activities to develop students' movement skills. The singing games can be used for developing movement vocabulary. For example, in playing a game with students, we give them the chance to imitate movements as well as explore their own movement improvisations. When they play the game "Here Comes a Blue Bird," let them create their own "bluebird dance" while singing the song. You can then play a piece or section of art music, such as "The Birds" by Ottorino Respighi (1879–1936), and the children can perform their dance to the new piece of music. This activity can transition into more free-form styles of movement. Students can create a dance on their own, or they can work or interact on their dance with a friend. By linking movement development to your curriculum in a focused manner you will ensure that your students develop the necessary music skills sequentially. Sometimes it is appropriate to transition from a song to a movement-and-listening activity. For instance, after singing "I See the Moon," ask the children to imagine that they are playing with a magic moon. Let the magic moon land on their hands. Lift the moon up high or down low. Caress the moon with your hands. Move the magic moon around the room using various parts of your body. Try using different ways to move around the room: in a circle, or in a square. Imagine you are carrying a heavy or light moon. Ask, "Can you move the moon in a high, or middle, or low space?" During this time you can play a suitable piece of music such as the Adagio sostenuto of the Piano Sonata in C-sharp Minor, Op. 27, No. 2 ("Moonlight") by Ludwig van Beethoven (1770–1827).

Sing the song "Frosty Weather." Imagine that snow has fallen on the children. Ask them to move around in the snow, which has covered the whole music room. They must find ways of moving with their bodies, perhaps moving in a circle or another shape. During the activity, play the Adagio for Strings and Orchestra in G minor by Tomaso Albinoni (1671–1751) for the children.

Music examples can be used for both nonlocomotor and locomotor activities, as well as free-form movement. An example of a piece of music that you can use in the music classroom is the "Bandinerie" by Johann Sebastian Bach (1685–1750). This is an excellent piece to use for both nonlocomotor and locomotor activities. The first time children hear this piece of music they should imitate your motions; on the second hearing they can stand in a circle and do the beat motions. You can find lots of interesting examples for listening and moving on YouTube, or you can consult a number of listening websites or blogs (to take just one example, http://muswrite.blogspot.com/search/label/schubert).

Discussion Questions

1. How is the skill of music literacy connected to the development of listening?
2. Discuss the notion that young children should be able to identify selected musical compositions, memorize facts about the life of the composer, and pick out specific themes and orchestral instruments.

Ongoing Assignment

Choose a piece of classical (art) music to present to your Kindergarten children next year. Analyze the piece; decide what concepts you can teach the children according to their knowledge of music, and find songs from their repertoire list that will prepare elements found in the art music example. Develop a set of listening exposures and worksheets for the art music example.

References for Listening

Choksy, Lois. *The Kodály Method II. Folksong to Masterwork*. Upper Saddle River, NJ: Prentice Hall, 1999.

Espeland, Magne. "Music in Use: Responsive Music Listening in the Primary School." *British Journal of Music Education*, 1987, *4*(3): 283–297.

Haack, P. "The Acquisition of Music Listening Skills." In *Handbook of Research on Music Teaching and Learning*, ed. D. Colwell, chap. 29. New York: Schirmer Books, 1992, p. 451–465.

Heidsiek, Ralph G. "Folk Quotations in the Concert Repertoire." *Music Educators Journal*, September 1969, *56*(1): 51–53.

Herboly-Kocsár, Ildikó. "The Place, Role and Importance of Art Music in School." *Bulletin of the International Kodály Society*, Spring 1993, *18*(1): 41–44.

Kerchner, J. L. "Creative Music Listening." *General Music Today*, Fall 1996, *10*(1): 28–30.

Montgomery, Amanda. "Listening in the Elementary Grades: Current Research from a Canadian Perspective." *Bulletin of the International Kodály Society*, Spring 1993, *18*(1): 54–61.

Rappaport, Jonathan C. *New Pathways to Art Music Listening: A Kodály Approach Appropriate for All Age Levels*. Marlborough: Pro Canto Press, 1983.

Rodriquez, C. X., and P. R. Webster. "Development of Children's Verbal Interpretive Responses to Music Listening." *Bulletin of the Council for Research in Music Education*, Fall 1997, *134*: 9–30.

Shehan-Campbell, Patricia. "Beyond Cultural Boundaries: Listening as Learning Style." *Bulletin of the International Kodály Society*, Spring 1994, *19*(1): 49–60.

Wood, Donna. *Move, Sing, Listen, Play: Preparing the Young Child For Music*. Toronto: Gordon V. Thompson, 1995.

Building a Lesson Plan Framework
That Incorporates Musical Skill Development

Key skill areas include reading, writing, and improvisation. We can use these three skill areas as a means of developing all other musical skills. The unit plans provide a number of ideas related to specific concepts and elements. These skills can become the basic building blocks for other musical skills, such as form, memory, part work, and listening. In the preceding sections, we explained how reading and writing activities might be expanded to include the development of additional musical skills. For example, when children are asked to read a new song or sing the theme from an art music example, these skill areas may be developed in conjunction with reading:

- Children can identify the form of the example.
- They can inner-hear sections of the melody.
- They may listen to a recording of a listening example.

Developing a Lesson Plan
Framework Based on Musical Skill Development

In previous sections of this chapter, we have presented specific information for developing musical skills that may be incorporated into the preparation and practice, presentation, and practice lesson plan formats. The goal of this section is to offer examples of how musical skills may be incorporated into lesson plan formats. The lesson given here is the same one as presented in Chapter 5, but here it is expanded to include musical skill development. This presents an idea as to how the skill areas can be integrated in the lesson plan. It is our intention that these ideas generate additional ideas that will enliven the lesson.

Using Unit and Monthly Plans to Keep
Track of Music Repertoire and Skill Development

Monthly and unit plans are used for keeping track of children's skills development and repertoire taught. An appendix for this chapter includes monthly plans with suggested ideas for skill development; Chapter 7 contains unit plans for teaching each music concept. Monthly and unit plans serve as a guide for accomplishing curriculum goals. These two types of plans are very similar. Monthly plans provide teachers with a list of songs that should be taught each month and include the concepts being prepared, presented, and practiced. All activities listed for skill areas are for the known concept. Some teachers use monthly plans as a checklist and continue to update the list every year. Unit plans are useful for short-term planning. It is important to review your academic calendar for Kindergarten and make a tentative guess as to when you will be teaching each concept. Remember that you must figure out how many music lessons you are teaching in a year; make allowances for the first few weeks of the year for teaching rhymes, songs, and singing games, and determine how much time you need to allot to end-of-year performances. You can assume that it will take about five lessons minimum to teach each musical concept. The curriculum we suggest assumes that:

- Teachers will spend the month of September teaching classroom rules, song materials, rhymes, games, introducing instruments, reading books, and singing to children
- During the month of December, the music teacher will be preparing the Winter Concert
- During the month of May, the music teacher will be preparing the Spring Concept
- Each month the music teacher will be teaching one concept

Here is a sample unit plan guide for preparing fast-slow and practicing high-low. (We have included unit plans for all concepts in Chapter 7.) There are two sections in a unit plan. Section 1 includes all of the songs needed to teach a new concept as well as to practice a known concept, and Section 2 includes a list of activities for developing music skills connected to the new concept being taught. Each row in section 1 of the unit plan corresponds to a music lesson. Columns 1–3 include songs taught in the introductory activities of the lesson; columns 4–7 include songs taught in the core activities section of the lesson.

Section 1 is seen in Table 6.3.

Table 6.3

Repertoire						
Prepare: Fast/Slow **Practice: High/Low (Chant)**						
Known Songs	Songs/ Activities for Developing Tuneful Singing	Songs to Review Known Concepts and Skills	Teach a New Song: Songs to Prepare Next Concepts	Songs to Prepare/ Present Fast and Slow	Singing Games and Creative Movement	Songs to Practice
"Little Sally Water"	Greeting	"Teddy Bear"	"Bow Wow Wow"	"Engine, Engine Number Nine"	"Ring Around the Rosy"	"Bee, Bee, Bumble Bee"
"Here Comes a Bluebird" and "Bow Wow Wow"	Greeting	"Hey, Hey Look at Me"	"London Bridge"	"Frosty Weather"	"Bow Wow Wow"	"Bee, Bee, Bumble Bee"
"Hey, Hey Look at Me"	Voice exploration	"Frosty Weather"	"London Bridge"	"Engine, Engine Number Nine"	"Bow Wow Wow"	"Bee, Bee, Bumble Bee"

(Continued)

Table 6.3   (continued)

"Bow Wow Wow"	"On the Mountain"	"Engine, Engine Number Nine"	"A la Rueda de San Miguel"	"Hey, Hey Look at Me"	"Little Sally Water"	"Oliver Twist"
"Hey, Hey Look at Me"	"On the Mountain"	"Engine, Engine Number Nine"	"Here We Go 'Round the Mulberry Bush" and "A la Rueda de San Miguel"	"Bee, Bee, Bumble Bee"	"Bow Wow Wow"	"Engine, Engine Number Nine"

Section 2 is seen in Table 6.4.

Table 6.4   Musical Skill Development for Fast and Slow

Musical Skill	Activity 1	Activity 2
Reading	C sing and point to a visual chart indicating the beats, while singing known songs using a fast or slow tempo. Begin with four beats and move to eight and sixteen beats. C should place the words "fast tempo" or "slow tempo" in front of the beat charts.	C sing and read a visual beat chart while singing known songs in different combinations of fast and slow, high and low, loud and soft. Be sure to use unusual combinations such as fast and soft, slow and loud, etc.
Writing	C place the words "fast tempo" or "slow tempo" in front of a beat chart for a song performed by the T or a child. Record how a melody was sung or a chant was performed.	C select between high and low and fast and slow to perform a known song. The class reads a beat chart on the board with the individual's selection.
Improvisation and composition	C improvise a motion that will demonstrate the beat of a known or unknown song in a fast tempo or slow tempo.	C choose whether to sing a song with a fast or slow tempo.
Listening	C listen to a piece of music sung or played by the T and identify the piece of music as either fast or slow.	

(Continued)

Table 6.4 (continued)

"In the Hall of the Mountain King," Grieg	C listen to recorded music that combines fast or slow with high or low and loud or soft. C identify the tempo and dynamics of the piece.	
Part work	Divide the class into two groups. Group A improvises a motion when they hear fast music (such as the "Tarantella," from *Pulcinella Suite*, by Stravinsky), and Group B improvises a motion when they hear slow music (such as "Air" from *Suite No. 3*, by J. S. Bach).	Play recorded examples of music in different meters, 2/4 or 6/8, and ask C to move to the beat, walking, skipping, or tapping the beat, whichever is most appropriate according to the tempo.
Memory	Sing known and unknown songs to C and have them determine if it was sung with a fast or slow tempo.	
Inner hearing	C follow the mouth of a puppet. When the mouth is open, C sing aloud, and when it is closed they sing inside their heads; but they must always keep the beat. Perform this activity using a fast and slow tempo.	
Form	C echo-sing a song while keeping the beat. Initially this should be done between T and C and then between two groups of C and finally between two individual C. Do this with the same song performed with a slow and then a fast tempo.	
Instruments	C play a steady beat on unpitched percussion instruments (bells, sticks, shakers, etc.) that matches the tempo of the music sung or played.	

Summary

The instructor guides children to understand how the new musical knowledge relates to previously learned knowledge within the context of familiar and new musical repertoire. When musical skill areas are incorporated into the lessons, the teacher has ample opportunity to evaluate the children's understanding and to assess their needs. Musical examples should be analyzed both aurally and visually, with the ear always leading the eye. Throughout this stage of learning, the newly learned musical concepts are identified while additional musical concepts are prepared. All musical concepts are practiced over an extended period of time in conjunction with curriculum goals and musical skills or enriching activities.

Lesson Planning

We can now modify our generic lesson plan format to incorporate musical skill development (Table 6.5).

Table 6.5

Outcome	Preparation: Practice:
INTRODUCTORY ACTIVITIES	
In this portion of the lesson, we develop beautiful singing through singing known songs, doing warm-up exercises as well as vocal exercises to help with developing tuneful singing. If the C are preparing a rhythmic concept it is important for them to demonstrate all known rhythmic concepts through singing. For example if the T is working on teaching fast-slow, the children should be able to sing songs and keep the beat with large and small motions. During this part of the lesson the T can integrate some reading skills or writing skills.	
Sing known songs	
Develop tuneful singing	
Review known songs and concepts	
CORE ACTIVITIES	
Teach a new song	Instructors present new repertoire to children for a variety of reasons. Sometimes they wish to teach a song to C to develop their singing ability; sometimes a song may be taught because of a need to provide a musical context for teaching future musical concepts. When teaching a new song, link the new song to the activities in the lesson's introduction—by using the same key, same rhythmic or melodic motives, the same meter, the same character, or simply the same tempo. You may ask the C to describe how you sang the song. You might ask C about the form of the song using the words "same" or "different," call and response, or question and answer form.
Preparation: singing game and creative movement or describe what you hear or create a representation	The T prepares a new concept using familiar materials. The T will be working on kinesthetic activities (sing and move), aural activities (describe what you hear), or visual activities (create a picture).

(Continued)

Table 6.5   (continued)

Creative movement	The T will be performing known games and developing movement skills. These are associated with specific games outlined in the music curriculum under the title of Children as Performers. The T develops C's movement skills on the basis of game activities associated with song material.
Practice: reading or writing or improvisation	The T will be practicing known concepts in conjunction with skill areas. When we prepare a concept kinesthetically we work on the skill area of reading, when we prepare a concept aurally we work on the skill area of writing, and when we are preparing a new concept visually we work on the skill area of improvisation.
SUMMARY ACTIVITIES	
Review the new song Review lesson outcomes Folk song tales sung by T	The T reviews the new songs and reviews the primary outcomes of the lesson. The T can also perform a song as a listening example for the C.

Discussion Questions
1. How are the skill areas of reading, writing, and improvisation related to all other skill areas?
2. How can the various musical skills be incorporated into the preparation/practice, presentation, and practice lesson plan formats? Give specific examples.

Ongoing Assignment

1. Design a preparation and practice lesson plan for a rhythmic concept. Discuss how you've incorporated specific musical skills into your lesson plan.
2. Design a preparation and practice lesson plan for a melodic concept. Discuss how you've incorporated specific musical skills into your lesson plan.

Bibliography
Amabile, T. M. *Creativity in Context: Update to The Social Psychology of Creativity.* Boulder, Co: Westview, 1996.
Amabile, T. M.. *The Social Psychology of Creativity.* New York: Springer-Verlag, 1983.
Azzara, C. D. "Audiation, Improvisation, and Music Learning Theory." *The Quarterly,* 1991, *2*(1–2): 106–109.
Azzara, C. D.. "An Aural Approach to Improvisation." *Music Educators Journal,* 1999, 86(3): 21–25.
Barrett, M. "Freedoms and Constraints." In *Why and How to Teach Music Composition,* ed. M. Kickey, pp. 3–27. Reston, VA: MENC, 2003.
Barrett, M. S. "Inventing Songs, Inventing Worlds: The 'Genesis' of Creative Thought and Activity in Young Children's Lives." *International Journal of Early Years Education,* 2006, *14*(3): 201–220.

Barrett, M. S. "Preparing the Mind for Creativity: A Case Study of Early Music Learning and Engagement." In *Musical Creativity: Insights Form Music Education Research*, ed. O. Odena and G. F. Welch, pp. 51–71. Aldershot: Ashgate, 2012.

Berliner, P. F. *Thinking in Jazz: The Infinite Art of Improvisation*. Chicago: University of Chicago Press, 1994.

Boden, M. A. *The Creative Mind: Myths and Mechanisms* (2nd ed.). London, UK: Routledge, 2004.

Brophy, T. S. "The Melodic Improvisations of Children Ages Six Through Twelve: Developmental Perspective." *Dissertation Abstracts International*, 1999, *59*(9), 3386A.

Burnard, P. "How Children Ascribe Meaning to Improvisation and Composition: Rethinking Pedagogy in Music Education." *Music Education Research*, 2000, *2*(1): 7–23.

Custodero, L. A. "Intimacy and Reciprocity in Improvisatory Musical Performance: Pedagogical Lessons from Adult Artists and Young Children." In *Communicative Musicality: Exploring the Basis of Human Companionship*, ed. S. Malloch and C. Trevarthen, pp. 513–530. Oxford: Oxford University Press, 2009.

Custodero, L.A. "Singing Practices in 10 Families with Young Children." *Journal of Research in Music Education*, 2006, *54*(1): 37–56.

Davidson, L. "Preschool Children's Tonal Knowledge: Antecedents of Scale." In *The Young Child and Music*, ed. J. Boswell, pp. 25–40. Reston: MENC, 1985.

Dissanayake, E. "Bodies Swayed to Music: The Temporal Arts as Integral to Ceremonial Ritual." In *Communicative Musicality: Exploring the Basis of Human Companionship*, ed. S. Malloch and C. Trevarthen, pp. 533–544. Oxford: Oxford University Press, 2009.

Espeland, M. "Compositional Process as Discourse and Interaction: A Study of Small Group Music Position Processes in a School Context." Ph.D. diss., Danish University of Education, Copenhagen, 2006. Published by Hogskolen Stord/Haugesund Stord/Haugesund University College, 2007.

Flohr, J. "Young Children's Improvisations: Emerging Creative Thought." *Creative Child and Adult Quarterly*, 1985, *10*(2): 79–85.

Folkestad, G., D. J. Hargreaves, and B. Lindström. "Compositional Strategies in Computer-Based Music-Making." *British Journal of Music Education*, 1998, *15*(1): 83–97.

Frölich, C. "Vitality in Music and Dance as a Basic Existential Experience: Applications in Teaching Music." In *Communicative Musicality: Exploring the Basis of Human Companionship*, ed. S. Malloch and C. Trevarthen, pp. 495–512. Oxford: Oxford University Press, 2009.

Geringer, J. M. "The Relationship of Pitch-Matching and Pitch Discrimination: Abilities of Preschool and Fourth-grade Students." *Journal of Research in Music Education*, 1983, *31*(2): 93–99.

Gilbert, J. P. "Assessment of Motoric Skill Development in Young Children: Test Construction and Evaluation Procedures." *Psychology of Music*, 1979, *7*(2): 21–25.

Glover, J. *Children Composing 4–14*. London: Routledge Falmer, 2000.

Gordon, E. E. *Learning Sequences in Music: Skill, Content, and Patterns*. Chicago: G.I.A., 1988.

Gratier, M., and G. Apter-Danon. "The Improvised Musicality of Belonging: Repetition and Variation in Mother-Infant Vocal Interaction." In *Communicative*

205

Musicality: Exploring the Basis of Human Companionship, ed. S. Malloch and C. Trevarthen, pp. 301–327. New York: Oxford University Press, 2009.

Haack, P. "The Acquisition of Music Listening Skills." In *Handbook of Research on Music Teaching and Learning*, ed. R. Colwell, pp. 451–465. New York: Schirmer, 1992.

Houlahan, Micheál, and Philip Tacka. *Sound Thinking: Music for Sight-Singing and Ear Training*. Vol. I., p. 109; Vol. II, p. 153. New York: Boosey & Hawkes, 1991.

Kaschub, M., and J. P. Smith, "A Principled Approach to Teaching Music Composition to Children." *Research and Issues in Music Education*, 2009, 7(1):3.

Kratus, J. "A Developmental Approach to Teaching Music Improvisation." *International Journal of Music Education*, 1995, *26*: 27–38.

McPherson, G. E. *Creativity and Music Education: Broader Issues—Wider Perspectives.* In *Children Composing*, ed. B. Sundin, G. E. McPherson, and G. Folkestad. Lund: Lunds University (Malmö Academy of Music), 1998, p. 135–158.

Miell, D., and R. MacDonald. "Children's Creative Collaborations: The Importance of Friendship When Working Together on a Musical Composition." *Social Development*, 2000, 9(3): 348–369.

Runco, M. A. "The Development of Children's Creativity." In *Handbook of Research on the Education of Young Children*, 3rd ed., ed. B. Spodek and O. N. Sarcho, pp. 102–107. New York: Routledge, 2012.

Sundin, B. "Musical Creativity in Childhood: A Research Project in Retrospect." *Research Studies in Music Education*, 1997, 9(1): 48–57.

Tafuri, J. "Processes and Teaching Strategies in Musical Improvisation with Children." In *Musical Creativity Multidisciplinary Research in Theory and Practice*, ed. I. Deliège and G Wiggins, pp. 143–157. Hove, UK: Psychology Press, 2006, p. 134–157.

Wiggins, J. "Children's Strategies for Solving Compositional Problems with Peers." *Journal of Research in Music Education*, 1994, 42(3): 232–252.

Wiggins, J. "Compositional Process in Music." In *International Handbook of Research in Arts Education*, ed. L. Bresler, pp. 453–476. Amsterdam: Springer, 2007.

Wiggins, J. "When the Music Is Theirs: Scaffolding Young Songwriters." In *A Cultural Psychology for Music Education*, ed. M. Barrett, pp. 83–113. Oxford: Oxford University Press, 2011.

Wiggins, Jackie, and Magne Espeland. "Creating in Music Learning Contexts." In *The Oxford Handbook of Music Education*, vol. 1, ed. Gary E. McPherson and Graham F. Welch, pp. 341–360. New York: Oxford University Press, 2012.

Chapter 7

Sequencing and Lesson Planning

In the previous chapter, we applied our model of learning and instruction to teaching music skills to the young learner. The goal of this chapter is to provide teachers with a detailed outline of how to prepare, present, and practice concepts as well as music skills throughout their lesson plans. We will address the importance of how to make transitions between the sections of a lesson plan. There is also a discussion on how learning plans can include strategies for drawing all learners into the music lesson. The chapter ends with thirty- five sample lesson plans for teaching readiness concepts in the Kindergarten classroom.

The videos accompanying this chapter include examples showing kindergarten music lessons and are posted on the companion website (Web 7. Lesson Plans: B).

General Considerations for Lesson Planning

Develop Lesson Plans from Curriculum Goals

Goals for each lesson should be an outgrowth of your curriculum. It in turn should reflect state and national standards as well as the Core Curriculum standards for your school. Teaching children to sing in tune needs to be a primary goal of every lesson. As we've stated several times through this book, you should look for the best song material for each class and make sure that you yourself enjoy singing this material. Plan to use three to five songs in a thirty-minute lesson. The songs you present should be memorized. Keep in mind that every new song you teach should be introduced appropriately. Continuously question whether you've selected the best songs for the preparation, presentation, and practice of a particular concept. Throughout this text and in the lesson plans we offer suggestions for specific songs to use for each lesson activity. There should be a focus to each section of the lesson that can be assessed both informally and formally.

Know Your Song Repertoire

Know your song repertoire. Be able to analyze the materials for each lesson from, performance and pedagogical perspectives. Try to find variety in the song repertoire that you choose for the lesson. In your lessons, any one activity should also prepare the next. Choose songs that have differing characters, moods, and tempi, and listen to authentic recordings/

Relaxation and Concentration

Include periods of relaxation and concentration during the lesson. The pace of a lesson for Kindergarten is significant. Periods of concentration and relaxation have a significant impact on children's learning.

Individual Experiences

Give children individual experiences in the classroom. Work from the group to individual activities.

Transitions in Lesson Plans

Transitions in Lesson Plans (Conscious Connections)

Transitions between songs and activities can become interesting activities that tie the lesson together. They often hold the lesson together entirely. Transitions may be thought of as conscious or unconscious: the former are ones where the children are aware that they are moving between songs or activities, and the latter are what the teacher uses to guide students to various activities. Here are examples of the types of transitions in a lesson plan.

Storyline Connections

Because the music lesson is based on teaching and reviewing songs and song games, connections between songs and activities and transitions are important for introducing the conceptual thread that ties these songs together. For example, in a typical music lesson, sometimes the repertoire used isn't thematically related; consider the selection of "Good Morning Boys and Girls," "Walk Daniel," "Built My Lady a Brand New House," "Bluebird," "Bee, Bee, Bumble Bee," "Goodbye Children." However, the addition of a puppet or stuffed animal and an invitation to join him on his journey and meet his new friends creates a framework in which all of these songs suddenly have a clear relationship to one another; they help tell the story of the puppet's adventure.

Using Specific Directions

It's possible to give children clear directions through signals rather than using language. For example, while they sing a known folk song, you may indicate that they form a circle to play a game while continuing to sing a song. At the end of a section of the song, you could sing children directions using the same melody.

Mood Connections

Children enjoy singing songs with diverse moods. It is important for you to sing all the repertoire with the correct mood, dynamics, tempo, and character. Closing a music lesson with "Star Light" and "I See the Moon" uses good examples of songs that represent nighttime. Children can sing these songs with a slow tempo to illustrate that they are tired and need to go to sleep.

Beat Connections

The children can sing several songs that have the same tempo and keep the beat. For example, at the conclusion of a game, they can keep the beat with their feet or walk to the beat in a circle while you introduce the next song. Keeping the beat going simply means that there is no significant break between songs. When you consciously keep the beat moving between songs, children's attention span is developed. The continued pace helps keep students focused and engaged.

Rhythm Connections

Guide children to sing songs that begin with the same rhythm, as with "Rain Rain" and "See Saw." The rhymes "Bee, Bee, Bumble Bee" and "Queen, Queen Caroline" likewise begin with the same rhythmic pattern. Children can be guided to recognize these connections while singing the songs or chanting the rhymes. For example, you can sing a song and then clap a rhythmic motif from it and ask the students if this reminds them of another song.

Melodic Connections

Guide children to sing songs that have melodic connections. The concluding melodic motif for "Bow Wow Wow," as an example, is the beginning melodic motif for "Hot Cross Buns." By simply saying "That reminds me of another song!" you encourage children to think about songs that share melodic motifs.

Transitions in Lesson Plans (Unconscious Connections)

By "unconscious" connections (rhythmic or melodic), we mean subtle connections that exist between the musical characteristics of songs that you as the teacher are aware of, but that will not be readily apparent to students. You could try out these ideas in a music lesson to create smooth transitions between songs and activities.

Sing Several Songs in a Lesson in the Same Tonality

The three songs "Snail, Snail," "Bounce High, Bounce Low," and "A La Ronda, Ronda" have the same tone set and all begin on the same pitch within the tone set. Singing songs in the same key throughout a lessons creates a unifying thread.

Sing Several Songs or Chant Several
Rhymes That Share the Same Time Signature and Tempo

"Engine, Engine, Number Nine," "Zapatitos Blancos," and "Queen, Queen Caroline" may all be chanted at the same tempo to firmly establish a steady and secure beat and tempo.

Sing Several Songs That Have the Same Form

"Seesaw," "Rain, Rain Go Away," and "Snail, Snail" are all eight beats in length. Considering each as having two phrases of four beats, we would say the three songs share the form A B. They are all children's chants. "Seesaw" and "Rain, Rain Go Away" share the same rhythm in each phrase but have a different melody; all three songs are in A B form.

Recognizing structural similarities between songs is significant in aural and visual discrimination for the kindergarten learner.

Sing Several Songs That Have the Same Character or Mood

The songs "Oliver Twist," "Knock the Cymbals," and "Here Comes a Bluebird" are three game songs. Though differing, they share the same character and joyful spirit and may be paired to generate movement and singing during a lesson while simultaneously developing physical coordination.

In this chapter we present lesson models for teaching core Kindergarten music concepts. It is our hope that you will teach these lessons and then figure out ways of adapting them for your own particular classroom. Although we believe that our lessons are well constructed and conceptualized, it is ultimately important that you find a mode of teaching that reflects your own teaching style as well as personality.

Examples of Lesson Plan Structures for the Kindergarten Classroom

There are basically only three types of lesson plan format:

1. Preparation/practice lesson (preparing a new concept and practicing a known concept)
2. Presentation lesson (labeling the newly learned concept)
3. Review lesson

Preparation/Practice Lesson Plan Format

The preparation/practice lesson may be divided into three sections, corresponding to the attention span of a class at this age level. Here we first present ideas in summary form, and then we go into depth with each section.

Introductory activities (5–6 minutes)
Core activities (15–20 minutes)
Summary activities (5–8 minutes)

Introductory Activities
Here are activities that should be included in the introduction of a lesson.

1. Establish the beginning of the music lesson.
2. Sing known songs or chant known rhymes; this helps develop an important dialogue between you and the students.
3. Work on developing the students' singing voices through breathing exercises and vocal warm-up activities that are related to song material.
4. Sing a roll call with children by offering an individual greeting to each child where he or she has to sing back to you. At the beginning of the school year, you might want to do a greeting to all children who are wearing a certain color, in the event there is not enough time to greet each child. We find it helpful to use a child's chant in the greeting. After children gain experience, you may extend

the range of notes to include melodic turns from songs being used in the class. With experience, individual children can take the role of the teacher and sing a greeting to students.

5. Sing known songs and practice known concepts and skills.

Core Activities

1. Present a new song. This activity should take five to six minutes. Select songs that have good texts and demonstrate them several times using gestures or other visual aids that help develop children's imagination, explaining the vocabulary if necessary. Avoid using a music instrument as an accompaniment in teaching a new song. Also, do not bring in a new song and then immediately apply it to teaching a new concept. Doing this will be a difficult or impossible task for the children.
2. Prepare the new concept kinesthetically ("Sing and move"), aurally ("Tell me what you hear"), or visually ("Make a picture of what you hear").
3. Singing games and developing creative movement abilities are an important part of the Kindergarten music class. They should be reviewed often and played enough to be enjoyed. You may also use the game or movement song to practice known concepts.
4. Practice known concepts in combination with skill areas such as reading, writing, improvisation, and inner hearing.

Summary Activities

1. Review the newly learned song or rhyme.
2. Employ a listening experience. For example, sing a folk song that has an interesting storyline. (This song may be sung over several lessons.) You can also sing the next new song for the children as a listening activity.

Explanation of Sections of the Preparation/Practice Lesson

Introductory Activities
Singing Known Songs
This is the section of the lesson that opens up with a known song and game. It should be lively, energetic, and a chance for the children to enjoy beautiful singing. After the first six weeks of teaching, it can also act as an assessment opportunity whereby children can demonstrate confidently what they can perform independently. If establishing a specific time for music, it is important to give the children a very clear signal of when this time begins so that they can transition into music time from other activities. Using the same song or phrase to begin each lesson helps to establish the ritual of music time, and it clearly communicates your expectation that the children will sit attentively in the circle and get ready to sing and move. The repetition of using the same greeting song at the beginning of each music lesson is very important; it will become familiar and comfortable and recognizable for the children.

Developing Tuneful Singing
The lesson continues with breathing exercises and vocal warmups. These are significant for a number of reasons. Just as athletes warm up their bodies by stretching before the run, the voice benefits from a little "stretching" before singing. Theses warmup exercises

211

are part of children's exploration process in which they discover many of the things their voices can do. Before the age of six, children are still learning to distinguish between (and use at will) their speaking, whispering, shouting, and singing voices. It is important to recognize that some children in your class may literally not know how to sing. Singing is a skill that you can help them develop, in part by helping them understand what singing is not—it is not speaking, and it is not shouting. Vocal exercises such as performing sirens and owl sounds (whoooo), help children to find the part of their voice they will use to sing.

After the vocal exercises, you may also perform a group or individual greeting to the children or do a roll call through singing. This often sung at the beginning of music time so the children become familiar with it and are comfortable singing it. The greeting should be based on song material being used in the class. Singing this song at the very beginning of music time helps the children transtion into sitting attentively in the circle and getting ready to sing. In addition, it is a way to introduce a stuffed animal or puppet, a character who may be used to guide the students through the activities in the lesson.

Reviewing Known Songs and Concepts

Next the children should sing known songs and chant known rhymes to review previouly learned concepts. Reviewing songs is related to what's being taught. If working on a melodic concept, review previously learned melodic concepts. If working on a rhythmic concept, review previously learned rhythmic concepts.

Core Activities Section

Teaching a New Song

To set a musical context for future learning, we suggest teaching a new song during every lesson; it may take children several lessons to master some songs. Children need to be competent singing the song material because the songs are used during the kinesthetic, aural, and visual preparation phases of learning a new concept. Link the teaching of the new song to review of known songs, the last activity in the introduction of the lesson. This can be accomplished by using the same key, the same rhythmic or melodic motifs, the same meter, the same character, or simply the same tempo.

When teaching a new song, it is important to create opportunities for children to listen to the song before they actually begin to sing. Remember that when you teach a new song to students you will also be using activities associated with the cognitive phase of learning.

It is not uncommon for a Kindergarten teacher to sing twenty to thirty songs with her children during the course of a year. However, with children at the ages of three, four, and five, it is a developmentally realistic expectation for them to master only fifteen to twenty songs during the school year. Children demonstrate their mastery of song repertoire if they know the words and melody of a song and can sing it accurately on their own with a steady tempo; at some level, they also understand the meaning of the song. Once children have truly mastered a song, they will be able to improvise sections of it, substituting new words and ideas to fit new situations. In this way, every song that a child masters becomes the seed for numerous musical experiences. Songs also serve a number of purposes in the Kindergarten classroom. Not every song is a good one for children to sing; some are great for children just to listen to, as they provide directions, encourage movement, or are the basis for classroom discussion. The idea of teaching children only fifteen to twenty songs for *singing* should not be confused with only using fifteen to twenty songs in the classroom throughout the year. You may introduce other songs to the students as listening activities that form an important part of their musical development.

Preparing the New Concept
The goal of this section of the lesson is to prepare the children to work with the teacher and their peers to learn about a new concept. This is part of the cognitive phase of instruction and learning and is further broken down into three stages that address the various modes of learning:

Internalize music: the kinesthetic stage
Describe what you hear: the aural stage
Create a picture: the visual stage

This phase of learning and instruction cannot be rushed, as time invested here will prevent confusion and errors later. Spend at least one or two lessons on each stage.

Singing Game/Creative Movement
This section of the lesson is a relaxation point but also an opportunity to develop children's movement skills. Song games are wonderful to use in music lessons because they channel young children's natural desire to move into learning opportunities that reinforce singing, beat, motor skill development, and the practice of singing. When introducing a song game to your children, it is important that they already have mastered the song. Mastering the song means they have developed an internal sense of heartbeat for the song and will be able to align movements with the words in the song. The movement of the game in this case becomes an extension of what they already know and ensures greater success (and control) in the execution of the game. (Of course you will want to teach the song and motions to songs and games that are simple when first introducing them to the students.) If children do not know the song when you introduce the song game, the stimulation of the movement may overwhelm them, and the game may spiral out of control. Once children have mastered the game movements, they can begin to improve other motions to the game; or they can use some of the motions learned and apply them to a listening example.

Practice Section
This is where you can review a known concept in combination with music skills. It is also a chance for you to assess individual learning in the classroom as well as to reteach a concept in an accelerated manner. By working specifically with an individual child or small group of children, you gain insight into their skill level and help them make progress in developing a particular skill. Even while you work with a small group of children, other children in the class are learning by watching you work with their classmates. In the model lessons presented at the end of this chapter, we have focused primarily on the skills of reading, writing, and improvisation, but these skills can be expanded to include other skills.

The assessment opportunities possible within a music lesson are almost limitless, but it is very important to keep in mind that you can only assess children's ability to demonstrate skills they have already been introduced to. There are subtleties in what and how you ask children to do things that may make a huge difference in their ability to demonstrate a concept they know and understand. During this part of the lesson you can assess what learning is taking place.

213

Closing Activities

The final choice of activities will depend on the interests and abilities of the students. Here are some suggested activities.

- Review the new song.
- Review new information taught in the lesson.
- End with a listening activity by singing a song that will be taught later as a new song, or end with a listening activity of a folk song that includes a storyline or a song that the children will enjoy hearing you sing. Initially you can sing this song to students without a visual aid, but it can be repeated at a later lesson with visuals.
- Depending on the content of the lesson, this is a good place to connect what the students are doing in music to other disciplines by getting the children to use critical thinking skills. For instance, you can ask about connections from one subject to another, on the basis of what has occurred in music class and what you know is occurring in other subjects.

Listening activities can serve many purposes. You may wish to sing a song for children that they will soon be learning. You may want to use this time to expose them to new and varied kinds of music, instrumental as well as vocal. Or you may choose to ask children to listen critically to a piece of music (performed live or recorded). Children are able to listen and rely on more advanced skills than imitating the singing of a song or keeping a beat in their bodies. Diverse kinds of music can be used as the basis for introducing and discussing steady beat, high and low, loud and quiet, and fast and slow. This also means exposing children to many kinds of music beyond what they (or you) have the ability to sing.

Just as it is important to give the children in your class a clear signal that music time is beginning, it is also important to bring it to an end. Using the same song or phrase to end every lesson clearly communicates that music time is over, and it helps children transition into other classroom activities.

The Presentation Lesson Plan Format

Once a concept has been prepared kinesthetically, aurally, and visually, you may present the name and the word or symbol of the new concept. We refer to this as the associative phrase of instruction and learning. Here is an explanation of the structure of the presentation lesson plan. The lesson may be divided into three sections, corresponding to the attention span of a class at this age level.

1. Introductory activities (5–6 minutes)
2. Core activities (15–20 minutes)
3. Summary activities (5–8 minutes)

Introductory Activities

1. Begin the class by singing known songs.
2. Develop tuneful singing by doing breathing and vocal warmup exercises, or by singing a greeting to the students.
3. Sing known songs or chant known rhymes. This helps develop and establish class rapport.

Core Activities Section

Teaching a new Song

As previously stated, we suggest teaching a new song during every lesson, recognizing that it may take children several lessons to master some songs. The children need to be competent at singing the song material that will be used during the various preparation phases of learning a new concept. As we mentioned in the preparation and practice lessons, try to link the new song to the introduction, whether by using the same key, same rhythmic or melodic motifs, same meter, same character, or same tempo.

Presenting the Label for the New Concept
1. Review the kinesthetic, aural awareness, and visual activities.
2. Present the name of the new concept using the same song from the preparation lessons that focused on kinesthetic, aural, and visual activities

Singing Game/Creative Movement

This constitutes a relaxation point in the lesson, and also an opportunity to develop students' movement skills.

Presenting the Word and Symbol for the New Concept
1. Review kinesthetic, aural awareness, and visual activities.
2. Present the word or symbol of the new concept using the same song from the preparation lessons that focused on kinesthetic, aural, and visual activities.

Summary Activities
1. Review the newly learned song or rhyme.
2. Review concepts taught during the lesson.
3. Create a listening experience. For example, sing the next new song for the children as a listening activity.

Explanation of the Sections of the Presentation Lesson

The Preparation/Practice lesson plan and the presentation lesson are basically the same except for two sections in the core activities of the lesson plan. In the presentation lesson plan, you present the label for the new concept and immediately ask the children to put it into practice. For example, when presenting loud and soft, once you explain that in music we call our daytime voice and nighttime voice "loud" and "soft" you can ask students to sing songs using their loud or soft voices. After the game, introduce students to the words or symbols representing the new concept. For example, in this section of the lesson you would introduce the spelling and words for "loud" and "soft" and might also introduce the music symbols of p (piano) and f (forte).

The Review Lesson Plan Format

Once a concept has been prepared and presented, you may want to spend time reviewing the new concept, reviewing the new concept with other known concepts or practicing the new concept with music skills areas. The lesson may be divided into three sections, corresponding to the attention span of a class at this age level.

215

1. Introductory activities (5–6 minutes)
2. Core activities (15–20 minutes)
3. Summary activities (5–8 minutes)

Introductory Activities
1. Begin the class by singing known songs.
2. Develop tuneful singing by doing breathing and vocal warmup exercises or singing a greeting to the students.
3. Sing known songs or chant known rhymes. This helps develop and establish class rapport.

Core Activities Section
Teaching a New Song
As previously stated, we suggest teaching a new song during every lesson, recognizing that it may take children several lessons to master some songs. The children need to be competent at singing the song material that will be used during the various preparation phases of learning a new concept. As we mentioned in the preparation and practice lessons, try to link the new song to the introduction, whether by using the same key, same rhythmic or melodic motifs, same meter, same character, or just the same tempo.

Reviewing Known Concepts
During this section of the lesson, you can review several concepts and skills areas. The activities will be similar to the practice section of the preparation/practice lesson.

Singing Game/Creative Movement
This is a relaxation point in the lesson and also an opportunity to develop students' movement skills. During a review lesson you may want to spend more time on this section of the lesson, focusing on developing a child's creative movement.

Summary Activities
- Review the newly learned song or rhyme.
- Review concepts taught during the lesson.
- Create a listening experience. For example, sing the next new song for the children as a listening activity.

Developing a Music Literature Lesson Plan

In the opening chapters of this book we stressed not only the importance of developing children's music skills but also the significance of reinforcing numeracy and literacy skills whenever possible in the music classroom. Using children's books in the music classroom offers teachers a wonderful vehicle for giving children another layer of rich musical activities that enhance music learning as well as develop and reinforce literacy and numeracy skills. If your school has a librarian, use him or her as a resource to find quality literature that will enhance the folk music you teach in your classroom.

As a music teacher, you have several options for incorporating books into a music lesson.

1. Use a book to illustrate the text of a folk song. During the close of a lesson, you can sing a song to students while showing pictures of a book. In the appendix to this book, we furnish teachers with a list of folk songs that are available in picture books.

2. Use folk songs to help develop or expand on the plot of book. If you are singing a song that connects to a known book, use the book to help illustrate the song. For example if you are chanting a rhyme such as "Engine, Engine, Number Nine," connect the chant to a book. Check the appendix for connections between songs and books. Every time you sing these songs in a music lesson, look for opportunities to also link the songs to books. A visual from a book may serve as the connection to a particular folk song.

3. Use a book to develop children's musical skills. For example, developing the ability to explore vocal sounds is important for developing tuneful singing. Incorporating this vocal exploration with reading storybooks is beneficial for both singing and reading purposes. Children love to create sounds for animals or characters that the meet in a book. Creating these sounds is an opportunity for developing the necessary vocal flexibility for tuneful singing. Children can improvise a melody to a recurring refrain or text in a book. Likewise they love to improvise the movements of the characters in a book.

4. Use a book to help practice music concepts. In the appendix to this book we have supplied you with a list of books linked to music concepts. You can use books to help develop students' knowledge of such concepts as loud and soft, fast and slow, high and low, and beat and rhythm.

217

Next we provide a sample music literature lesson plan that may be used for any music literature lesson. We will use the book *Brown Bear, Brown Bear* by Bill Martin and Eric Carle for generating sample activities that can be used with any book. The first step in using a book is to try to link the story line and characters of the book to known rhymes and songs. For instance, in *Brown Bear, Brown Bear* we find many opportunities to connect songs that have themes of colors and bears in the book. An obvious link can be to the song "Teddy Bear"; the text of the book also permits connecting with songs that have texts about various animals in the book.

There are many books that can enhance students' musical skill development. We need to examine how we can use music to bring out the structure and the text of the book. The text and structure of some books may be linked to musical concepts. Remember that you can return to the same book to practice a number of concepts or develop music skills.

Brown Bear, Brown Bear is interesting in several respects regarding text and music. The repeated phrases are very helpful for keeping the beat to a text. Children can also keep the beat with the movements made by the various animals in the book, which also promote antiphonal chanting between teacher and student or between two students. Chanting can be varied through the use of singing the call with a loud or soft voice and the response with the opposite voice. You or the students can also improvise a melody to use with the appearance of the call-and-response. We can use the various animals in the story to developing tuneful singing, for example chanting the repeated phrases with high or low voices.

The lesson is divided into three sections corresponding to the attention span of a class at this age level.

1. Introduction (5–6 minutes)
2. Core activities (15–20 minutes)
3. Closing activities (5–8 minutes)

Introduction

Begin the class by singing a greeting based on a motif from known song material. At the start of the school year, the notes of the child's chant may be used as the greeting. A child's chant is a kind of "teasing" singing a child uses with "I'm telling on you." It is composed of the solfège syllables *s, m,* and *l.* Later, you may extend the range of notes to include melodic turns from songs used in the class. Sing the greeting to the children and ask them to pretend to be one of the characters in the book. If practicing loud and soft, sing the greetings with a loud or soft voice. Show the animals in the books to the children and have them sing to the pictures using the appropriate voice.

- Have children sing to the characters of the book.
- The character in the book (sung by you or another student) sings "Good morning, children."
- The children sing "Good morning, Mr./Ms. _____."

Next sing several songs that can be connected to the main character of the book. If, for instance, the children sing "Teddy Bear, Teddy Bear," they can then change this well-known song in to "Brown Bear, Brown Bear."

Core Activities

1. Read the book to the children.
2. Repeat reading, but as you do so, see if they can use some of the musical concepts taught in the music lesson to enhance the text of story of the book. We offer these suggestions.
    i. The children keep a steady beat as you read the text of the book.
    ii. Try to have them repeat the text "Brown bear, brown bear, what did you see?" Use different voices (perhaps loud and soft) for the children and the beat.
    iii. The children may be able to clap the rhythm of the repeating text.
    iv. Have them play the rhythm of the repeating text on a rhythm instrument to practice inner hearing.
    v. Children can improvise the response to the question and sing in a loud or soft voice as they identify other animals they have seen in the forest.
    vi. Individual children respond in a loud or soft voice according to what they think the animal should sound like.
    vii. Children vocalize the sound of the animal (growl like a bear, caw like a bird, etc.) when the page turns to that animal.
    viii. Children move like the animal as you turn the page to that animal.
3. Use additional songs with the book *Brown Bear, Brown Bear, What Do You See?*

"Let Us Chase the Squirrel"

Sing the song showing the beat through motions. Have the students select animals so as to be the characters in the book. Children should improvise loud or soft movements. Play the game listed in the text, having the students move to the beat. They can point to the beats that are represented by animal icons.

"Down Came a Lady"

Sing the song and change the words of the song to animals and colors from the story. Choose students to be the animals and sing the song using a color that the student is wearing.

For example, change text of "Down Came a Lady" to "Down came a brown bear, down came two, down came another bear and she was dressed in blue. . . ."

Closing Activities

Sing a new song for the children that connects with the book. You might sing them another folk song such as the "Bear Went over the Mountain" or "Daddy Shot a Bear."

Evaluating a Lesson

In this section we give some suggestions for evaluating a music lesson. Evaluate your lesson plan to determine what worked with your children and how your teaching can be improved. A good lesson plan and substantial music curriculum will yield clear answers to these questions:

- Was the lesson presented in a musical manner?
- What were the primary and secondary outcomes of the lesson?
- How were the outcomes of the lesson achieved?
- How many songs and games were used in the lesson?
- Were a variety of song materials used in the lesson?
- What activities used in conjunction with the song material led students to an understanding of the outcomes of the lesson?
- Was singing and making music the emphasis of the lesson?
- Were a variety of songs or rhymes used in the lesson?
- Was there a balance between developing music skills and music concepts?
- Was new material prepared and presented in the lesson?
- Was there a logical sequence and pacing in the lesson?
- Was the culmination of the lesson clear?
- What musical skills were developed in the lesson?
- Were the students active collectively and individually during the lesson?
- Did the lesson plan offer a means to assess student progress?
- Was the lesson enjoyable for the students?
- Was there a place in the lesson where a connection between music and another subject area could be made?
- Did children have a chance to listen to the teacher perform?

Evaluation of Teaching a Concept

These questions should help a teacher identify whether he or she used the right approach when teaching a music concept.

- Did I choose the most appropriate repertoire to teach the new music concept?
- Did I choose the correct musical concept to teach in this particular lesson?

219

- Did the children have the prerequisite skills to understand the new music concept?
- Were my teaching outcomes specific for teaching the music concept?
- Did I review what the students already knew, and did I reinforce new information?
- Did I create an opportunity for students to independently demonstrate their new understanding?

Adapting Lesson Plans for the Inclusive Classroom

Differently abled, gifted, and talented children as well as bilingual children have different needs from other learners, which produces a variety of challenges for the music teacher. Our lesson plans and model of learning and instruction can be adapted to help teachers deal with a range of learners in the Kindergarten music classroom. Since our model of learning is based on a constructivist philosophy, we believe that this model generates myriad opportunities for teachers to develop the music curriculum for all learners in the music classroom. It is important to help children with learning disabilities engage in the process of making music as well as learn how to express themselves musically. All activities developed for the special learner should work well in a larger group setting.

Special Needs Students

We offer here some generic guidelines for teaching children with special needs. It is important for to understand each student's specific learning needs and create unique learning strategies for that child.

Evaluate Your Own Philosophy of Teaching Special Needs Students

Try to evaluate your own philosophy concerning the teaching of the special learner. We should view the special learner as someone who can engage in music activities and who can develop knowledge of music concepts and music skills.

You Are Not Alone

Remember that you are not alone in teaching the special learner. Make sure that you interact with the class teacher and other professionals in the school who can provide guidance as to how to teach special learners in the music classroom. It is also important to communicate with parents about their child. Don't forget to speak to children directly about how they are doing in your music class! Most of the special learners that you teach will have individualized education programs (IEP) or 504 plans on file at the school. Take time to read these reports, as they will greatly help you in developing teaching activities for your students.

Advanced Planning

Once you have created your lesson plan, develop strategies to include special learners in the music-making process in your classroom. Consult with the classroom teacher as to what skills you can reinforce during the music classroom. Also, consider the individual learning preferences of the child. For example, a nonverbal or aggressive student may particularly enjoy pointing activities or movement over verbal questioning and response.

Seating Arrangement

Create a seating arrangement for all your music classrooms. Special learners should be paired with children who will have the patience to explain and help them through these activities. It is important that as a music teacher you be able to model for all children in the class while paying particular attention to special learners. Plan a seat for an in-class aide if necessary, particularly if children will be changing the physical arrangement throughout the class period.

Positive Reinforcement

Offer all children positive reinforcement in the music classroom. Take time to explain to students how they will be rewarded if they follow the rules of the music classroom. Remember to try letting special learners pick a performance activity of their own choosing.

Predictability

Our lesson plans and process of teaching are predictable; this is necessary for special learners. The teacher should be able to break down all tasks for the children and know when to skip steps in teaching or add more steps for certain students. This is an important scaffolding device for all children, but in particular for special learners. Try to follow the sequence of instruction for each activity in the lesson plans. After a while, the children will be able to predict or guess what will happen next in the lesson.

Use Songs That Share Stylistic Elements

We recommend that teachers use repertoire that shares common rhythmic and melodic building blocks, throughout their lessons. This is highly important for the special learner, because it will be easier for them to sing this repertoire as it becomes predictable.

Communicate with Clear Directions or Visual Cues

Guide and explain all directions to students clearly. Sometimes using large motor skills or a visual can help clarify the expectation for children in the music classroom. As an example, if you want students to keep a beat, show a picture of a drum; or if you want students to sing, show them a picture of someone singing. In our approach to teaching, we do use icons in the initial stages of learning to help students with reading and writing activities, but you may have to keep using icons for students with special needs. Remember to use easy-to-read colors and large print for your instructions.

Modeling Behavior

Model all expected behavior. Always choose students who will succeed with the activity before you ask a student with special needs to do so. Sometimes you must pair another student with a special needs student to help with music activities during the music lesson.

Use of Instruments

Use instruments as a means of informing students about expectations, as with a slide whistle for telling students when to stand and when to sit. A melodic instrument might tell students to freeze at a particular activity or return to their seats.

Remember to have a cue for children who are being disruptive during your music class. It is important to continue teaching but give that child a visual clue for changing the behavior.

Pacing

It is important to include time for special learners to digest what you are teaching. If you are asking them to perform a certain activity, give them the space to perform the activity.

Puppets

Use puppets to help students repeat an activity, sing correctly, or learn the words of a song. Try to match the movement of the puppet's mouth to your own, so children will make connections about how to sing correctly.

Teaching Performance Skills

Repetition is an important element in dealing with the special learner. When teaching a new song, sing it several times before asking a question. Make sure you introduce the song without an accompaniment, as that can be a distraction for the special learner. When you ask a question and a student gives an answer, always say "Thank you; let's check," and sing the song again to verify the response. When asking children to play a rhythmic instrument to keep a beat, ask the special learner to put his or her hands around a drum or on top of a drum as you play so the child can feel the sensation of the sound.

Use visuals with words to help students memorize songs; choose a key word or phrase to be printed underneath a picture. Leave these song charts in the music corner so children can review them during play time.

Using Peer Helpers

When teaching folk dances or games, always try to assign a child who can grasp and explain instructions, to help a special learner. It is important to make sure that the tempo is modified when necessary and plenty of repetitions are provided. With each repetition, ask a child to explain what is happening in the game. Sometimes you may have to practice the steps of the dance without singing the song. Following the game sequence that we suggest here in the book will help you engage more of the special learners. Remember to give children adequate time to process all the directions for a game. Reward a helper, for example by letting this child choose a favorite song or class activity or game.

Moving from Sound to Symbol

When teaching music literacy concepts, always try to move from a physical activity to a symbolic activity. Children with special needs learn faster by exploring a concept physically before moving to a more abstract presentation. In teaching a concept such as beat, it is important that students experience singing and moving to the beat before you ask them to point to icons that represent the beat. If we want children to understand a concept like fast and slow beats, it is important for the special learner to see a visual attached to the idea. Passing a ball around a circle to the beat is a very tangible way for students to make the connection between tempo and keeping the beat.

Use of Tools and Visual Aids When Teaching

When teaching children rhythm or melodic concepts, it is important to use a variety of tools. Try these ideas for teaching rhythm:

- Echo-sing melodies with a neutral syllable before asking a students to clap a rhythm
- Clap rhythms
- Tap rhythms
- Play rhythms on an instrument
- Use icons such as a clapping hand to indicate that students should clap the rhythm

For teaching melodic concepts, try using these techniques:

- Echo-sing melodies with a neutral syllable before asking students to show or point to a melodic contour
- Use hands to show contours
- Point to icons
- Use pitched instruments

223

Engage as Many of the Senses as Possible

It is important to engage the learning modalities of all children, but most of all the special learner. In our model of learning and instruction, kinesthetic, aural, and visual learning activities are the core of the learning experience in the music classroom. In our model to teaching, we begin with a kinesthetic activity and move to an aural activity, before working with a visual one. This is an important sequence, for its opportunities to work with special needs students. When asking children to perform an aural activity, always try to connect the activity with a kinesthetic one. Likewise, in asking students to perform a visual activity always connect with both a kinesthetic and visual one.

Performing an Activity Yourself or with a Small Group

Ask a special needs child to perform an activity with the teacher or in a small group. In this text we adhere to a handful of strategies for working with children generally, and these are also great techniques in working with special learners:

- Begin with a class activity
- Work with a smaller group of students
- Work with one student

Space to Escape

Sometimes a special needs student can feel overwhelmed with an activity; we should allow the child to go to a safe space in the music classroom to escape until ready to return. Make sure that you encourage this student to participate meaningfully, if need be, even if it is from the safe place.

We offer here some generic guidelines for teaching bilingual children. It is important to understand each student's specific learning needs and create unique learning strategies for that child.

Evaluate Your Own Philosophy of Teaching Bilingual Children

Try to evaluate your own philosophy concerning the teaching of the bilingual learner.

You Are Not Alone

Remember that you are not alone in teaching the bilingual learner. Make sure you interact with the class teacher and other professionals in the school who can provide guidance as to how to teach bilingual learners in the music classroom. It is also important to communicate with parents about their child. Don't forget to speak to children directly about how they are doing in your music class!

Advanced Planning

Once you have created your lesson plan, develop strategies to include bilingual learners in the music-making process in your classroom. Consult with the classroom teacher as to what skills you can reinforce during the music classroom.

Seating Arrangement

Create a seating arrangement for all your music classrooms. Bilingual learners should be paired with children who will have the patience to explain and help them through music activities in both English and Spanish.

Positive Reinforcement

Offer all children positive reinforcement in the music classroom. Take time to explain to students how they will be rewarded if they follow the rules of the music classroom. Remember to try letting special learners pick a performance activity of their own choosing.

Predictability

Our lesson plans and process of teaching are predictable; this is helpful for bilingual learners. Try to follow the sequence of instruction for each activity in the lesson plans. After a while, the children will be able to predict or guess what will happen next in the lesson.

Communicate with Clear Directions

Develop a list of terms that you can use in both Spanish and English. Remember to use easy-to-read colors and large print for your instructions.

Assessment

Modify your rubric assessments for special learners if you are assessing skills that are a challenge to the particular student. The goal is to document the improvements and accomplishments of your children as well as use this information to continue to challenge and engage children meaningfully. In addition to assessing knowledge of concepts and skills, make sure that you include such components as a child's attitude toward peers, teacher, and the music class.

Gifted and Talented Children

Advanced children can be just as demanding to teach as special learners. It is important to have techniques and activities available so that you can continuously challenge these children's abilities.

Know Your Children

Children who are gifted have their own strengths and challenges. Work with the classroom teacher to find out what these strengths and challenges are. There may also be an educator for the gifted and talented in your building or district whom you can consult. Talk with the child to learn of individual interests to capitalize on in the music classroom. Gifted and talented children may or may not have an IEP.

Advance Planning

Once you have created your lesson plan, it is important to plan ahead and figure out strategies for creating more demanding (but not impossible) tasks for the gifted child to perform in your classroom. Consult with the classroom teacher to find out what kinds of challenging activities these students are working on so that you can reinforce these skills in the music classroom.

Performance and Improvisation

Find ways to challenge gifted and talented students during performance and improvisation activities. Gifted and talented children should be encouraged to perform as soloists with simple rhythmic or melodic instruments. Many times these students can improvise their own rhythmic accompaniment to accompany their singing.

Child as Teacher

Give gifted children the opportunity to assume the role of the teacher. For example, they can sing greetings to other students. Use children to demonstrate a particular movement in a game or sing a particular phrase correctly.

Challenging Music Tasks

Ask children to perform songs on their own for other children. Use gifted children to do the rhythmic accompaniment to class singing. In addition to asking students to create a new text to a well-known song, ask them to accompany themselves with a beat on a rhythmic instrument or movement activity. It is important to try to challenge gifted children through accelerated activities.

Mentors

Pair gifted children with other students in the class who need extra help with a task.

Children as Readers

Use gifted children to read the story that is to be used in a lesson.

Music Instruments

Ask children to create rhythmic instruments that can be used in the classroom.

Unit Plans: Teaching Musical Concepts and Skills in the Kindergarten Classroom

This section includes sample unit plans that can be used to teach music concepts in the Kindergarten music classroom. Unit plans are divided into three sections. The first section gives an overview of five lessons associated with teaching a concept. The lessons are listed down the left side of the chart. As you read across the chart, you see the songs as they are presented in each section of the lesson plan. The second section of the unit plans provides the subsequent "music skill development" and indicates activities for reading, writing, improvisation, etc.

The third section of the unit plan includes a series of five sequenced lesson plans that follows sections 1 and 2 of the unit plans. The lessons have been developed to follow the model of learning and instruction introduced in Chapter 4. All lessons have been field-tested by teachers working in public and private schools in a number of areas in the United States and England. Again, we are grateful to these teachers for extending to us their insights and suggestions.

226

Unit 1:   Lesson Plans for Teaching Tuneful Singing

Lesson Number	Song Repertoire		Reviewing Song/Chant Repertoire	Teaching a New Song/Chant	Reviewing Song/Chant Repertoire	Creative Movement	Teaching a New Song/Chant
	Known Songs	Songs/Activities for Developing Tuneful Singing					
Lesson 1	"Here We Go 'Round the Mulberry Bush"	"Hey, Hey, Look at Me"		"Bee, Bee, Bumble Bee"; "Johnny Works with One Hammer"		"Bobby Shafto"	"Hunt the Slipper"
Lesson 2	"Here We Go 'Round the Mulberry Bush"	"Hey, Hey, Look at Me"	"Bee, Bee, Bumble Bee"	"Engine, Engine, Number Nine"	"Johnny Works with One Hammer"; "Hunt the Slipper"	Charlie Brown Christmas	"Bounce High, Bounce Low"
Lesson 3	"Hey, Hey, Look at Me"	"Engine, Engine, Number Nine"	"Hunt the Slipper"	"Snail, Snail"	"Johnny Works with One Hammer" "Bounce High, Bounce Low"	"	"That's a Mighty Pretty Motion"
Lesson 4	"Hey, Hey, Look at Me"	"That's a Mighty Pretty Motion"	"Hunt the Slipper"	"Seesaw"	"Johnny Works with One Hammer"	"Romeo and Juliet"	"We Are Dancing in the Forest"
Lesson 5	"Engine, Engine, Number Nine"; "Hunt the Slipper"	"That's a Mighty Pretty Motion"	"Bobby Shafto"	"On a Mountain"	"Johnny Works with One Hammer"	"Dance of the Knights" Sergei Prokofiev (1891–1953)	"Star Light, Star Bright"

Musical Skill Development Unit 1

Musical Skill	Activity 1	Activity 2	Activity 3	Activity 4
Reading	Children [C] show phrases of a song in the air while singing (tracing a rainbow in the space in front of them with their hand)	C see four images that represent the four voices (megaphone calling, ear whispering, cell phone speaking, microphone singing) and use the one the teacher [T] selects	T selects two icons to represent whispering and speaking voice and places them in front of each phrase of Bee, Bee, Bumble Bee. Phrases 1 and 2 as whispering, phrases 3 and 4 as speaking voice. C perform as written. T changes the order of the icons to change the performance of the song.	
Writing	C select an icon that represents the one of the four voices that identifies how the T performed.	C select an icon that displays the number 1 or the number 2 in order to identify the number of phrases in a song.	Repeat activity 3 from the reading section above but individual C decide how each phrase must be performed. C identify the correct icons to place in front of each phrase.	
Improvisation and composition	C improvise new text for a song. "Bounce the ball to (Houston, Dallas, Mississippi, Charlie)"	C improvise a new motion for keeping the beat while performing a song.	C choose an icon representing one of the four voices to change how they perform a song.	C improvise a new movement to the types of voices and perform with known songs.
Listening	T reads a book to C using two of the four voices for different characters.	T sings a song to the class for enjoyment. Story songs or echo songs work well.	C listen to a masterwork with an obvious steady beat. "Stars and Stripes Forever," by Sousa	

Part work	C sing a song while keeping the beat.	Half of the C pat the beat with hand drums while the other half sing the song.	C sing the song and march to the beat.	T sings one phrase and C sing the next phrase.
Memory	C perform a known song.	C perform a known chant using the four types of voices.		
Inner hearing	C perform a song using a whispering voice while tapping the beat.	C identify a familiar song from rhythmic or melodic motives that are clapped or hummed by the T.	C fill in missing words of a known song or chant.	
Form	C outline the phrase of a song with rainbow or shooting star icons.	C use different movement for different sections of a piece of music.	Sing a song twice (differently each time) and ask if the song was the same both times.	T sings one phrase and C sing the next phrase.
Instruments	C sing a song while playing a steady beat on hand drums.	C categorize four instruments selected by the T into speaking, calling, whispering, and singing voices, and perform chants/songs while tapping the steady beat on the corresponding instrument. Example: drum = calling; sticks = speaking, sand blocks = whispering; barred instruments = singing.		

Kindergarten: Beginning of the Year, Lesson 1	
Outcome	• Develop tuneful singing • Develop beat skills • Learn song repertoire • Develop listening skills
INTRODUCTORY ACTIVITIES	
Introduction	Use a favorite song to sing to C and lead them into the room and to assigned places. You might want to sing the song and then make up words to the melody that remind C of the classroom rules. This approach starts the class musically, establishes the behavior expectations, and focuses their minds on the task at hand. Using a song such as "Here We Go 'Round the Mulberry Bush" so that C know how to follow you into the music room, and eventually lead them into a circle formation. For example, this text may be to "Here We Go 'Round the Mulberry Bush": Follow me into music class, music class, music class, Follow me into music class as I chant with my speaking voice. Make a circle in music class, music class, music class, Make a circle in music class as we will learn how to sing. Follow me into music class, music class, music class, Follow me into music class as I sing with my singing voice. Stand in a circle in music class, music class, music class, Stand in a circle in music class as we will learn how to sing.

Warm-up and develop tuneful singing	"Hey, Hey, Look at Me"
	CSP: A
	
	• T sings the song and C imitate T's motion.
	• T improvises other motions, such as swinging, swaying, bending, nodding. C copy.
	
	Greeting:
	CSP: A
	
	• T sings a greeting using the pitches of the first phrase of "Snail Snail." C reply with the same pattern.
	
	Breathing:
	
	• T leads C through breathing exercises.
	  Show C how to sip through a straw correctly and expand their waist.
	  Show C how to release air using a "sss" or hissing sound.
	
	Vocalize:
	
	• T plays various patterns on a slide whistle, and C mimic with their voices.
	• T buzzes like a bee, moving from head voice to chest and back up. C imitate.
	
	➤ T: "You sound just like a class full of bees! Oh my goodness, that reminds me…."

	CORE ACTIVITIES
Teach a new song	"Bee, Bee, Bumble Bee" (bee puppet in a flower pot) • T: "Look over at the bee (puppet) sitting in the flower pot. Do you know that this bee did some very bad things earlier today? He stung a man on his knee, and then he stung a pig on his snout. What do you (point to one child) think a snout could be? He promised me he wouldn't sting anyone anymore because he doesn't want to go sit in time out. He did want me to show you how to do the bee dance, though." • T shows the bee dance, created by T, with the rhyme. • T chants and C perform bee dance. Connections to books/literacy: • Brennan-Nelson, Denise. *Buzzy the Bumblebee*. Michigan, Sleeping Bear Press, 1999. • Bentley, Dawn. *Buzz-Buzz, Busy Bees*. Simon & Schuster, 2004. • Carter, David A. *In and Out*. Intervisual Books, 1993. • Fleming, Denise. *In the Tall, Tall Grass*. Holt, 1991. • Twinn, M. *Old Macdonald Had a Farm*. Child's Play (International), 1975. ➤ T: "Bee is looking for his hammer . . . do you see it hiding somewhere?"
Teach a new song	"Johnny Works with One Hammer" (toy hammer) CSP: D • T sings C copy motions. • T: "While Johnny was working with his hammer, he met a friend named Bobby." • T sings "Johnny works with Bobby. . . ." ➤ T: "Johnny was so sad when Bobby had to leave, but Bobby was so excited because he got to go on a trip in a big boat on the sea!"
Creative movement	"Bobby Shafto" CSP: A • T sings song with motions. • T sings song with motions and C copy. • T sings song and C keep the beat. • Play Brandenburg Concerto No. 2 F major, First Movement, BWV1047, by Johann Sebastian Bach (1685–1750) http://www.youtube.com/watch?v=UJbkvmwUMkw • C mirror T's movements. • T claps to the beat. • T taps the beat on several parts of his or her body. • T walks to the beat. ➤ T: "While you were walking around, your wore out your shoes and holes started to appear. Take your shoe and pretend to hammer it while I sing about someone who fixes shoes."

231

Teach a new song	"Hunt the Slipper"
	CSP: A
	• T sings the song while C listen.
	• T: "What do we call a person who fixes shoes?"
	• T uses toy hammer and taps to the beat while singing the song.
SUMMARY ACTIVITIES	
Review the new songs Folk song or folk song tales sung by teacher	Review one or two of the new songs with C. "Over in the Meadow" • T sings the song while C listen. You might use some pictures or visuals. Do not show the book to C at this time as you want them to listen to the song.

Kindergarten: Beginning of the Year, Lesson 2	
Outcome	• Develop tuneful singing • Develop beat skills • Learn song repertoire • Develop listening skills
INTRODUCTORY ACTIVITIES	
Introduction	Use a favorite song to sing and lead C into the room and to assigned places. You might want to sing the song and then make up words to the melody that remind C of the classroom rules. This approach starts the class musically, establishes the behavior expectations, and focuses their minds on the task at hand. Using a song such as "Here We Go 'Round the Mulberry Bush" so that C know how to following you into the music room, and eventually lead them into a circle formation. For example, this text may be sung to the melody of "Here We Go 'Round the Mulberry Bush." Follow me into music class, music class, music class, Follow me into music class while I sing with my singing voice. Make a circle in music class, music class, music class, Make a circle in music class while we learn how to sing. T can vary this activity by introducing C to different types of voices, speaking, singing, calling, and whispering, in the chant.

Warm-up and develop tuneful singing	"Hey, Hey, Look at Me" CSP: A • T sings the song and C imitate T's motions. • T improvises other beat motions. • T sings the word "Hey" using a glissando going from head voice into chest voice and back up. C copy and T monitors for vocal quality. Greeting CSP: A • T sings greeting using the pitches of the first phrase of "Snail Snail." C reply with the same pattern. (T demonstrates first with a puppet so C can hear how they should respond.) Vocal exploration • T draws a "path" on the board, C follow the path with their voice, and it turns out to be the path Mr. Bee took on his way to the flower pot. • C follow the "path" with several vocalizations or vowels (i.e., [i], [ɛ], [a], [o], [u], humming, lip trills, etc.) but end with "buzzing" ([z]). ➤ T: "Oh my goodness, you all sound like a classroom full of bees! . . ."
Review known songs and concepts	"Bee, Bee, Bumble Bee" (bee puppet in a flower pot) • T: "Oh Mr. Bee is sitting on the flowerpot! Do you remember what he did last week in music?" (C give answers). "Well, he told me he was very, very sorry and promises never to be a mean bee again. He taught us something last week. Do you remember how to do his dance?" • T shows the bee dance with the rhyme. • T chants and C perform bee dance. • C chant along with T while doing the bee dance. ➤ T: "Mr. Bee has been so good lately, not stinging anyone, that I decided to give him a reward and take him on a train ride to my favorite city! . . ."
CORE ACTIVITIES	
Teach a new song	"Engine, Engine, Number Nine" • T moves arms to the beat like the wheel of an engine. C copy. • T chants the rhyme while C move their arms like the wheels of engine. • T chants "toot toot toot toot" at the end of rhyme with a high voice and C make a pulling motion. • T draws four engines on the board, or uses four engine icons and points to them on the beat while saying the chant. C use their pointer fingers in the air to help point to the engines. ➤ T: "When Mr. Bee and I were on the train, you'll never guess who we met! It was Johnny!"

233

(Continued)

Review song material	"Johnny Works with One Hammer"
	CSP: D
	• T sings with motions and C copy.
	• C sing and copy motions. C can also suggest other places where the hammer lives (head, hands, shoulders, toes, elbows, back, etc.).
	➢ T: "This song really makes me think about a story I heard once. Would you like to hear it too?"
	Connections to books/literacy:
	• Guthrie, Woody. *Bling Blang*. Candlewick Press, 1954.
	• Walsh, Vivian. *Gluey*. Harcourt, Weekly Reader Children's Book Club, 2002.
Creative movement	"Linus and Lucy," from *A Charlie Brown Christmas*, by Vince Guaraldi Trio (1965) (edited for time to approximately 1:30)
	• C mirror T's movements
	• T claps to the beat
	• T taps the beat on several parts of his or her body
	• T walks to the beat
	• C create their own movements
	➢ T: "Hey, did I ever tell you what happened when we got off the train? No?! You'll never believe this, they dropped us off at the wrong place! We ended up in some city called Shiloh and it was so boring! Luckily, Johnny thought of a really fun game we could play. . . ."
Teach a new song	"Bounce High, Bounce Low"
	CSP: A
	• T sings and bounces a large ball to the beat. T sings with motions and C copy.
	• T sings with other beat motions and C copy.
	• T may pass the ball to individual C to copy his or her motions.
	➢ T: "Well, since we had to walk all the way from Shiloh back to Chicago our shoes got all worn out and we needed someone to fix them. What do we call a person that fixes shoes? . . ."
Review song material	"Hunt the Slipper"
	CSP: A
	• T sings uses hammer to tap the beat on a shoe while singing the song.
	• T sings with motions and C copy.
	• T and C sing the song and play the guessing game.
	SUMMARY ACTIVITIES
Review the new songs	Review one or two of the new songs or rhymes with C ("Engine, Engine, Number Nine")
Folk song or folk song tales sung by teacher	• "Over in the Meadow."

Kindergarten: Beginning of the Year Lesson 3	
Outcome	• Develop tuneful singing • Develop beat skills • Learn song repertoire • Develop listening skills
INTRODUCTORY ACTIVITIES	
Introduction	"Hey, Hey Look at Me" CSP: A • T sings the song and C imitate the T motions. • T improvises other beat motions. • C suggest motions for the class to perform. Last verse: "Hey, hey, look at me. I'm a train, can you see?"
Warm-up and develop tuneful singing	"Engine, Engine, Number Nine" • T moves arms like the wheel of an engine. C copy. • T chants the rhyme while C move their arms like the wheels of an engine. • T chants "toot toot toot toot" at the end of rhyme (spelling) with a high voice and ask C to make a pulling motion. • T uses icons such as a train on the board and points to them to develop beat competence. Greeting CSP: A • T sings greeting using the pitches of the first phrase of "Snail Snail." C reply with the same pattern. Breathing • Hissing tire: T tells one C that she was riding her bike and ran over a nail. "Oh no! All the air leaked out of the tire!" C make the sound of a tire hissing and leaking air (breath development). • C "pump" the tire back up and breathe in through the nose. "Oh no! We ran over a nail again!" Vocal exploration • T uses a slide whistle to encourage C to make various sliding and calling sounds with their voices. ➢ T sings the first phrase of "Hunt the Slipper" on a neutral syllable. C echo and identify the song.

235

Review known songs and concepts	"Hunt the Slipper" CSP: A • T sings and uses a toy hammer to tap the beat on a shoe while singing the song. • T sings with motions and C copy. • T sings with other beat motions and C copy. ➤ T and C continue the beat as T sings the next song.
CORE ACTIVITIES	
Teach a new song	"Snail, Snail" CSP: A • T sings the song and moves two fingers in each hand to the beat like a snail. C copy motions. • T can draw icons or place icons on the board; draw a "snail trail" where Mr. Snail has traveled. C follow the trail with their voices. Connections to books/literacy: • Brown, Ruth. *Snail Trail*. Crown, 2000. (This book is excellent in that it provides vocal exploration ideas to involve C while they're being read to.) • Cutler, Jane. *Mr. Carey's Garden*. Illust. Brian Karas. Houghton Mifflin, 1996. ➤ T: "Do you know that there's a second part to the story? In the second part, Mr. Carey wants to build a snail house in his garden, but he needs help to build it. Who do you think he calls?"
Review song material	"Johnny Works with One Hammer" CSP: D • T sings with beat (hammer) motions and C copy. • T and C sing. • T sings with other motions and C sing and copy. • C suggest other places the hammer can be placed. ➤ T continues the beat as he or she plays the music.

Creative movement	"Linus and Lucy," from *A Charlie Brown Christmas*, by Vince Guaraldi Trio (1965) (edited for time to approximately 1:30); or
	
	"Semper Fidelis" by the Columbia River Group
	
	• C mirror T's movements.
	  • T claps to the beat.
	  • T taps the beat on several parts of his or her body.
	  • T walks to the beat.
	• C create their own movements.
	➤ T: "Wow! You all made some mighty pretty motions!"

Teach a new song	"That's a Mighty Pretty Motion"
	CSP: F#
	• T sings "That's a Might Pretty Motion" with motions for C. • T sings "That's a Might Pretty Motion" with motions; C copy motions. • C may suggest motions for the song. ➤ The final motion used in the song should be the first one used in "Bounce High, Bounce Low."
Review song material	"Bounce High, Bounce Low"
	CSP: A
	• T sings and bounces a large ball to the beat. • T sings with motions and C copy. • T sings with other beat motions and C copy. • T may pass the ball to individual C to copy his or her motions.

SUMMARY ACTIVITIES

Review the new songs Folk song or folk song tales sung by T	• Review one or two of the new songs with C • "The Old Woman and the Pig"

Kindergarten: Beginning of the Year, Lesson 4	
Outcome	• Develop tuneful singing • Develop beat skills • Learn song repertoire • Develop listening skills

INTRODUCTORY ACTIVITIES

Introduction	"Hey, Hey Look at Me"
	CSP: A
	• T sings the song and C imitate T's motion. • T improvises other motions such as swinging, swaying, bending, or nodding, and C copy. ➤ T sings: "Hey, hey, look at me----that's a mighty. . . ."

Warm-up and develop tuneful singing	"That's a Mighty Pretty Motion" CSP: F# • T sings with motions for C. • T sings with motions; C copy motions. • T sings "That's a Mighty Pretty sound" and then does a glissando beginning with a low note moving to high note. C imitate this sound. Greeting CSP: A • T sings greeting using the pitches of the first phrase of "Snail Snail." C reply with the same pattern. • Repeat activity but this time C must sing while clapping the way the words go. Vocal exploration • T blows bubbles and C follow the bubbles with their voice. • T tosses a ball in the air while C vocalize according to the height. ➤ "Aww man! I got bubbles all over my shoes! Now, who's gonna fix my shoes?!"
Review known songs and concepts	"Hunt the Slipper" CSP: A • T sings and uses toy hammer to tap the beat on a shoe while singing the song. • T sings with motions and C copy. • T sings with other beat motions and C copy. ➤ "Thank goodness my shoes got fixed, because I really wanted to play on the playground. Do you know what my favorite playground toy is?"

238

CORE ACTIVITIES	
Teach a new song	"Seesaw" CSP: A • T sings song and asks C to move arms like a see saw. • T sings song with other beat motions and asks C to copy the motions. (T puts the beat motions on his or her shoulders, head, moving fingers to the beat. Do not use the word *beat* at this time.) Connections to books/literacy: • Ayres, Katherine. *Up, Down, and Around*. Candlewick Press, 2007. (This book provides opportunities to creatively vocalize into the head voice; movements can also be added by growing up like carrots while vocalizing or twisting like tomato vines while vocalizing, etc.) • Carter, David A. *In and Out*. Intervisual Books, 1993. • Locker, Thomas. *Cloud Dance*. Voyager Books, 2000. T says: "Oh, great! Somebody broke the seesaw! Do we know anyone that could come and fix it for us?"
Review song material	"Johnny Works with One Hammer" CSP: D • T sings with beat (hammer) motions and C copy. • T and C sing. • T sings with other motions and C sing and copy. • C sing and improvise their own motion.
Creative movement	Play any piece of music with a strong beat with a moderate tempo. C mirror T's movements. Sergei Prokofiev (1891–1953) *Romeo and Juliet*, Op. 64, Dance of the Knights • T claps to the beat. • T taps the beat on several parts of his or her body. • T walks to the beat. • Have C hold hands to form a circle and sway to the beat. (Sometimes T can place a picture of the circle on the ground to help C.) • C create movements.

Teaching a new song	"We Are Dancing in the Forest"
	CSP: A
	• T sings song and has C hold hands and sway back and forth while standing in a circle.
	• Repeat and see if C can join in the at the end of the song and say the text "Wolf, are you there?" If Wolf (T) says, "I'm combing my hair," then sing the song again. If the wolf says, "I'm coming to get you," then C must freeze and wolf catches any child that moves. Another way to play is to have C curl up into a ball and have the wolf decide whom to choose.
SUMMARY ACTIVITIES	
Review the new songs Folk song or folk song tales sung by teacher	Review one or two of the new songs with C • "Bandy Rowe."

Kindergarten: Beginning of the Year, Lesson 5	
Outcome	Develop tuneful singing
	Develop beat skills
	Learn song repertoire
	Develop listening skills
INTRODUCTORY ACTIVITIES	
Introduction	"Engine, Engine, Number Nine"
	• T and C chant the rhyme with motions as they enter the room.
	"Hunt the Slipper"
	CSP: A
	• T: "While you were walking around, you wore out your shoes and holes started to appear. Take your shoe and pretend to hammer it while I sing about someone who fixes shoes."
	• T uses toy hammer and taps to the beat while singing the song.
	➤ T and C continue their beat motion as T sings the next song.

Develop tuneful singing	"That's a Mighty Pretty Motion" CSP: F# • T sings "That's a Might Pretty Motion" with motions for C. • T sings with motions; C copy motions. • T sings and C improvise beat motions for the whole song. • T sings "That's a mighty pretty sound" and then does a glissando beginning with a low note moving to high note. C imitate this sound. Greeting CSP: A • T sings greeting using the pitches of the first phrase of "Snail Snail." C reply with the same pattern. Repeat activity, but this time C must sing, clapping the way the words go. Vocal exploration • C pretend to be a bird, or in a plane, etc., and fly with their voices on a journey through the music room. • C pretend to be various animals by making the sounds of the particular animals. • C mimic the T as he or she sighs in a number of vocal registers. T: "Did I ever tell you about my summer vacation?"
Review known songs and concepts	"Bobby Shafto" CSP: A • T sings song with motions. • T sings song with motions and C copy. • T sings song and C keep the beat. • T sings song C keep beat sing the last work of each phrase. • T sings with beat motions for each phrase, and C copy. • T and C sing and "hide" selected phrases. Connections to books/literacy: • Seeger, Pete. *One Grain of Sand*. Little, Brown, 1957. • Freymann, Saxton, and Joost Elffers. *One Lonely Seahorse*. Scholastic Press, 2000. ➤ T: "Once Bobby and I got to Italy, we climbed this high mountain and found some lady, who we didn't know, and she kept asking us for three things: gold, silver, and ice cream cones!"

CORE ACTIVITIES	
Teach a new song	"On a Mountain" CSP: A • T sings with beat motions; C copy. • C play the game while T sings. • C sing B section of the song ("so jump out. . . ." We use the version with s-m-l-s-m). ➤ T: "We finally got away from that silly lady, and you are never going to believe who we bumped into! . . ."
Review song material	"Johnny Works with One Hammer" CSP: D • T sings with beat (hammer) motions, and C copy. • T and C sing. • T sings with other motions, and C sing and copy. • C sing and improvise their own motion. ➤ C continue their beat motion as T plays the music for creative movement.
Creative movement	• Play any piece of music with a strong beat and a moderate tempo. C mirror T's movements. Sergei Prokofiev (1891–1953) *Romeo and Juliet*, Op 64, Dance of the Knights http://www.youtube.com/watch?v=bBsKplb2E6Q • T claps to the beat. • T taps the beat on several parts of his or her body. • T walks to the beat. • C form a circle holding hands and swaying to the beat. • C create their own movements. ➤ T: "Oh boy, all that moving made me a little tired! I could really use a good-night song. . . ."
Teach a new song	"Star Light, Star Bright" CSP: A • T sings and asks C to rock the baby to sleep to the beat. • Teach C the first phrase; T sings the second phrase.
SUMMARY ACTIVITIES	
Review the new songs Folk song or folk song tales sung by T	• Review one or two of the new songs with C • "Bandy Rowe"

Unit 2: Lesson Plans for Teaching Loud and Soft

Unit 2

Prepare: Loud/Soft			Practice: Tuneful Singing				
			Song Repertoire				
Lesson	Known Songs	Songs/Activities for Developing Tuneful Singing	Reviewing Song/Chant Repertoire	Teaching a New Song/Chant	Preparing Loud/Soft	Creative Movement	Practicing Tuneful Singing
Lesson 1	"Hey, Hey, Look at Me"	Greeting	"Bobby Shafto"	"Hop Old Squirrel"	"Bounce High, Bounce Low"	"Snail, Snail"	"Seesaw" "Engine, Engine, Number Nine"
Lesson 2	"Hey, Hey, Look at Me"	"Engine, Engine, Number Nine"	"Johnny Works with One Hammer"	"Lazy Mary"	"Hunt the Slipper"	"That's a Mighty Pretty Motion"	"Snail, Snail"
Lesson 3	"Seesaw"	"Engine, Engine, Number Nine"	"Hey, Hey, Look at Me"	"Teddy Bear"	"Bobby Shafto"	"Lazy Mary"	"Johnny Works with One Hammer"
Lesson	Known Songs	Songs/Activities for Developing Tuneful Singing	Reviewing Song/Chant Repertoire	Teaching a New Song/Chant	Presenting Loud/Soft	Creative Movement	Presenting Loud/Soft
Lesson 4	"Seesaw"	"Engine, Engine, Number Nine"	"Johnny Works with One Hammer"	"Charlie over the Ocean," and/or "Zapatitos Blancos"	"Snail, Snail"	"On a Mountain"	"Seesaw"
Lesson 5	"That's a Mighty Pretty Motion"	"Greeting Song"	"Bounce High, Bounce Low"	"Doggie, Doggie," and/or "Zapatitos Blancos"	"Hunt the Slipper"	"We Are Dancing in the Forest"	"Bobbie Shafto"

Musical Skill Development

Musical Skill	Activity 1	Activity 2	Activity 3	Activity 4
Reading	C sing and point to sun or moon icons (indicating the beats) while singing "Bounce High, Bounce Low" with a loud or soft voice according to the icon.	C sing "Seesaw" from the board while tracing the phrase marks drawn on the board.	C read phrase marks of "Engine, Engine" from the board using the voice indicated by the icons placed at the beginning of the phrase.	C read phrase marks of "Engine, Engine" from the board using the voice indicated by the words *loud* or *soft* placed at the beginning of the phrase.
Writing	Individual C place one of the four voice icons on the board, indicating how the song is to be performed.	C select the words *loud* or *soft* (flashcards) and place them in front of icons representing the beat to record how a child or T sang a melody.	C to select *p* or *f* icons and place in front of icons representing the beat to record how a child or T sang a melody.	Individual C place loud and soft icons in front of each phrase in a four-phrase song ("Bee, Bee" or "Hunt the Slipper"). It can alternate loud and soft between phrases. Class reads and alters voice according to the icon.
Improvisation and composition	T sings "Bobby Shafto" using "day time" or "night time" voice. C indicate which voice they heard by raising either "day time" icon or "night time" icon.	Individual C sing "Johnny Works with One Hammer" and create a different movement for each "hammer" to be performed by class.	C improvise new text while singing with a loud or soft voice.	T plays recorded examples of music in various meters, 2/4 or 6/8, and asks C to move to the beat while walking, skipping, or tapping the beat during the daytime or nighttime parts. C may be asked to make sure their movements are suitable for "day time" or "night time."
Listening	C listen to a piece of music sung or played by T and they identify the piece of music as either loud or soft.	C listen to piece of music and make a big circle with arms when music is loud and a small circle with fingers when music is soft.	C listen to known song while standing in circle holding hands. C make larger circle for loud and smaller circle for soft.	T plays recorded examples of music that contain varying, but obvious, dynamic changes. T asks C to move when it is soft, and freeze when it is loud.

Part work	C perform the beat while singing known song.	T and C echo-sing known song using a loud or soft dynamic.	C echo-sing known song divided into two groups using a loud or soft dynamic.	C sing known song and perform movements to reflect loud or soft singing.
Memory	T sings known song to C using a soft or loud voice and asks C for description of voice.	T sings known song from previous lesson to C and asks questions for recognition.	C recognize a familiar song from rhythmic or melodic motives clapped or hummed by T.	
Inner hearing	C sing a song following mouth of puppet. When mouth is open, they sing out loud; when closed they sing in their head.	C should be encouraged to sing different motives of the song initially with loud and soft and then using inner hearing.	C hum familiar songs using a loud or soft hum with movements. C sing a known song but inner-hear selected phrases while continuing to tap the beat.	
Form	T and C echo-sing a song in a loud or soft voice while keeping the beat.	C in two groups echo-sing a song in a loud or soft voice while keeping the beat.	Two C echo-sing a song individually in a loud or soft voice while keeping the beat.	C sing "Rain, Rain" based on form using p voice for phrase 1 and f voice for phrase 2.
Instruments	C accompany class by playing a steady on a hand drum either softly or loudly.	C play the beat on unpitched percussion. T performs loud and soft rhythmic patterns and C echo T on drum.	T plays loud and soft rhythmic phrases on hand drum and C imitate with loud and soft foot patterns.	T points to p or f and C keep beat at the correct dynamic level on an unpitched instrument, while singing known songs.

Kindergarten Unit 2: Teaching Loud and Soft Lesson 1	
Outcome:	Preparation: Internalizing a loud or soft singing or chanting voice through kinesthetic activities Practice: Tuneful singing and reading
INTRODUCTORY ACTIVITIES	
Sing known songs	"Hey, Hey, Look at Me" CSP: A • Sing song with a loud and soft singing voice to match the text being sung.
Develop tuneful singing	Greeting CSP: A • T sings a greeting (*s-m*) to C using soft or loud voice and C respond and copy. T uses an icon of a sun (loud) or moon (soft) while singing. • Repeat the activity, but C sing and tap the beat as they respond using a soft or loud voice.
Review known songs and concepts	"Bobby Shafto" CSP: A • C sing while doing beat motions for each phrase. Vocal warm-up • T vocalizes to various animals (cow, dog, cat, etc.) and C echo. • C suggest other animals to vocalize. T uses this to transition into the next song, about the squirrel.
CORE ACTIVITIES	
Teach a new song	"Hop Old Squirrel" CSP: A • T sings song for C while they keep beat. • T sings song with motion and invites C to imitate the motion while T sings. • C sing first half of each phrase ("hop old squirrel") and T sings the response ("eidle-dum, eidle-dum"). • C suggest other ways for the squirrel to move. • T may end the song by singing "Bounce old squirrel." This, of course, reminds him or her of a song.

Prepare music literacy concepts Sing and move	"Bounce High, Bounce Low" CSP: A • T shows sun icon, moves icon to the beat, and sings song in "daytime" singing voice. • C imitate and sing in their daytime voice. • T shows moon icon, moves icon to the beat, and sings song with a "nighttime" singing voice. o T: "This would be a great voice to use when you want to put a baby to sleep." • C imitate and sing in their nighttime voice. • C select icon and the class sings accordingly. Connections to books/literacy: Cronin, Doreen. *Bounce*. Atheneum, 2007.
Singing game/creative movement	"Snail, Snail" CSP: A • C sing "Snail, Snail" and T leads C into a spiral. • C sing "Snail, Snail" and T leads C into a circle from the spiral. • T plays music with a slow tempo and C move like snails around the circle or class. • C and T move like a snail to "Largo" from New World Symphony by Dvorak
Practice music performance and literacy skills Reading	Reading "Seesaw" • C sing song and draw the phrases in the air with their hands. • C sing song and trace the phrases on the board. • T places the word "phrase" (flashcard) on the board and C identify how many phrases are in "Seesaw." • C identify from a group of flash cards the words "singing voice." • T places the flash card "singing voice" in front of the phrase marks and C sing. "Engine, Engine, Number Nine" • C speak and move arms to imitate the wheels of train moving to beat. • C speak and pat the beat. • C chant and draw the phrases in the air with their hands. • C chant and T draws the phrases on the board. • T places the word "phrase" on the board and C identify how many phrases are in "Engine, Engine, Number Nine." • C must identify from a group of flash cards (singing voice, speaking voice, silent voice, calling voice) the words "speaking voice." • T places the flash card "speaking voice" in front of the phrase marks and C chant.

247

SUMMARY ACTIVITIES	
Review the new song Review lesson outcomes	* "Hop Old Squirrel"
Folk song or folk song tales sung by T	* "Over in the Meadow" (read the accompanying book while singing the song).

Kindergarten Unit 2: Teaching Loud and Soft Lesson 2	
Outcome:	Preparation: Analysis of repertoire sung with a loud or soft voice Practice: Tuneful singing and writing
INTRODUCTORY ACTIVITIES	
Sing known songs	"Hey, Hey, Look at Me" CSP: A • T and C sing song with a loud and soft singing voice to match the text being sung. • Use the sun and moon flashcards to avoid the temptation to use the words *loud* and *soft*.
Warm-up and develop tuneful singing	"Engine, Engine, Number Nine" • C chant "Engine, Engine, Number Nine" while keeping the beat with arms and hands moving like the wheels of the engine. • C chant with a "daytime" or "nighttime" voice. • T explores the sounds an engine makes using a descending glissando on the word "toot" and C echo-sound. Voice exploration • T uses a magnetic train icon on the board and then draws a train track that the train has to follow (hills that go up and down, etc.). • "To get from one station to the other, our voices follow the train on the high hills and the low valleys." ➢ T: "Hey, it looks like Engine Number Nine dropped us off in Chicago, where our friend Johnny lives!"
Review known songs and concepts	"Johnny Works with One Hammer" CSP: D • T and C sing with motions using a daytime or nighttime singing voice. T may show icons to indicate which voice C should use. ➢ C continue hammering motion to the beat as T sings "Here Comes a Bluebird."

CORE ACTIVITIES	
Teach a new song	"Lazy Mary" CSP: F • T uses puppets to teach the question-and-answer phrases of this song.
Prepare music literacy concepts Tell me what you hear	"Hunt the Slipper" CSP: A • C sing song and keep the beat • T sings song • T asks, "Was I using my nighttime or my daytime voice?" • C answer "Daytime"; T says, "Let's all sing it together in our daytime voices." • Repeat the process. • Repeat process but with one C singing; class must aurally identify if they were singing with a daytime or nighttime voice. • T and C select body motions to imitate the sounds of tapping of the cobbler at night time or day time. • T and C select instruments such as woodblocks or drums to imitate the tapping of the cobbler at nighttime or daytime. C sing song and keep the beat with an instrument while singing. ➤ T: "Mr. Cobbler made some special shoes . . . for a cat!" Connections to books/literacy: Litwin, Eric, and James Dean. *Pete the Cat: I Love My White Shoes*. New York: Harper, 2008.
Singing game/creative movement	"That's a Mighty Pretty Motion" CSP: F# • T sings song and C keep the beat. • T sings song with motions and invites C to imitate the motion. • T sings and C sing phrase 1, 2, and 3. • T and C sing song with motions suggested by T. • T selects individual child to improvise motions, and class sings and imitates motion. ➤ T ends with the steady beat and continues it into "Snail Snail."

Practice music performance and literacy skills Writing	"Snail, Snail" CSP: A • T: "Use with your singing voice and show the phrase." • C sing and show the phrases in the air while T draws phrases on the board. • C sing and trace the phrases that are written on the board. • T selects one child to trace over the phrase marks that are on the board while class sings. • Another child chooses between two flashcards, one with the words " Speaking Voice" and another with the words " Singing Voice' to place in front of the phrases. • C sing "Snail Snail." • T and C play the game.
SUMMARY ACTIVITIES	
Review the new song Review lesson outcomes Folk song or folk song tales sung by T	• "Lazy Mary" • "The Old Woman and the Pig"

Kindergarten Unit 2: Loud and Soft Lesson 3

Outcome:	Preparation: Creating a visual representation of a loud or soft voice Practice: Tuneful singing and improvisation
INTRODUCTORY ACTIVITIES	
Sing known songs	"Seesaw" CSP: A • T sings "Seesaw" and models moving like a seesaw to a steady beat. • T sings while pointing to a picture of a seesaw. • T and C sing song and perform motions to a steady beat. ➤ T and C continue steady beat motions while continuing the next rhyme/chant.
Develop tuneful singing	"Engine, Engine, Number Nine" • C chant "Engine, Engine, Number Nine" • "Today our engine is taking us to the playground! Let's get on the slide with our voices, like this. . . ." • T demonstrates moving voice up and down in pitch; C join. • Class repeats vocalizing with other playground equipment (swings, seesaw, monkey bars, etc.).

Review known songs and concepts	"Hey, Hey, Look at Me" CSP: A - T shows a flash card with a picture and verb such as marching, jumping, hopping; C imitate the action. - C sing song with a loud and soft singing voice to match the text being sung - T uses sun and moon icons to indicate with which voice to sing. - ➤ The final action may be to "turn around," which will lead T to discover the new song.
CORE ACTIVITIES	
Teach a new song	"Teddy Bear" CSP: A - T sings "Teddy Bear" with motions while holding the bear. - T sings "Teddy Bear" and C perform motions. - T sings "Teddy Bear" and one child does the motions while holding the bear. - Class repeats, choosing a new child each time to come up and hold a Teddy Bear. - Connections to books/literacy: - Rosen, Michael. *We're Going on a Bear Hunt*. Little Simon, 1989.
Prepare music literacy concepts Make a picture	"Bobby Shafto" CSP: A - T selects a helper. When T sings loudly child holds up the sun icon, and when T sings softly child holds up the moon icon. - Helper chooses a classmate to show icons while he or she sings using a loud or soft voice. T repeats process with another known song. - T could have four icons of the sun and four icons of the moon displayed horizontally, four in each row on the board. C or T sings melody and C identify how they're singing by pointing to appropriate row of icons using a steady beat. T may keep steady beat for singer and pointer on a classroom percussion instrument. Another way to do this activity is to create a sun and moon icon for each child and have C hold up the appropriate icon while T is singing. ➤ "My little niece Mary, she's about your age, she hates to get up! We call her Lazy Mary because she won't get out of bed. Let's sing with our daytime voice and help her get out of bed."

Singing game/creative movement	"Lazy Mary" CSP: F • T and C play game by acting out "Lazy Mary" and her mother. • Lazy Mary sleeps at the front of the class. Mother points to daytime or nighttime icons to indicate how class should sing the song. When singing softly, Lazy Mary stays asleep, when singing loudly she awakes suddenly. ➤ "I bet if someone were working with a hammer they would wake Lazy Mary up!"
Practice music performance and literacy skills Improvisation	"Johnny Works with One Hammer" CSP: D Class will sing known songs with beat motions: • C sing and sway side to side to the beat. • C sing and walk the beat. • C sing and tap the beat. • T asks C to substitute other names, such as Mary, Tommy, etc., into the song. • T asks individual child to change name in song as well as the number of hammers. • T asks C to sing, but they can choose to say the number of hammers with their speaking voice or singing voice.
SUMMARY ACTIVITIES	
Review the new song Review lesson outcomes Folk song or folk song tales sung by T	*Teddy Bear* "Bandy Rowe" ("Kitty Alone").

Kindergarten Unit 2: Loud and Soft Lesson 4	
Outcome:	Present the label and the words for loud and soft
INTRODUCTORY ACTIVITIES	
Sing known songs	"Seesaw" CSP: A • T sings "Seesaw" and models moving like a seesaw. • T and C sing with motions using a daytime or nighttime singing voice (T may use icons). ➤ C continue motions into the next song.

252

Develop tuneful singing	"Engine, Engine, Number Nine" • C chant "Engine, Engine, Number Nine" while keeping a steady beat. • T shows C how to do glissando with their voice for the toot at the end of the song by following a visual that descends and ascends. ➤ T: "Our engine is broken and I think we need Johnny to fix it!"
Review known songs and concepts	"Johnny Works with One Hammer" CSP: D • T and C sing with motions using a daytime or nighttime singing voice. • C sing and use a motion that demonstrates a daytime or nighttime singing voice. ➤ C sing and march in a circle. ➤ C continue marching as T sings the new song.
CORE ACTIVITIES	
Teach a new song	"Charlie over the Ocean" and/or "Zapatitos Blancos" CSP: F • C stand in a circle and hold hands and swing arms to the beat, while T sings song, singing the response with a softer voice. • T sings song, singing the response with a softer voice. • T sings song; C sing the echo. • T shows C how to play game. • T and C sing and play the game. ➤ T and C sing the song as T leads the circle in a winding motion, as in the game for "Snail Snail."
Present music literacy concept Label what you hear	"Snail, Snail" CSP: A • One child decides whether to show a sun or moon icon. T and C sing and play the game. • T says, "In music, when we use our nighttime singing voice, we call that our soft singing voice. Let's sing the song 'Star Light, Star Bright' in our soft voice." • T says, "In music, when we use our daytime voice, we call that our loud voice. Let's sing the song 'On a Mountain' in our loud voice."

253

Singing game/creative movement	"On a Mountain" CSP: A • C sing and play the game. Connections to books/literacy: • *We Will Go*. Aladdin Paperbacks. • Lach, William. *Can You Hear It?* Abrams Books for Young Readers, 2006. • Portis, Antoinette. *Not a Box*. HarperCollins, 2006. • Brown, Margaret Wise. *The Train to Timbuctoo*. Golden Books, 1979. • Alexander, Cecil Frances, and Bruce Whatley. *All Things Bright and Beautiful*. HarperCollins, 2001.
Present music literacy concept Record what you hear	"Seesaw" CSP: A • C sing and play the game. • T says, "In music, when we use our nighttime singing voice, we call that our soft singing voice." T shows flashcard with picture of moon and the word "soft": "Let's sing the song 'Seesaw' in our soft voice." • T says, "In music, when we use our daytime voice, we call that our loud voice." T shows flashcard with the picture of a sun and the word "loud": "Let's sing the song with our loud voice."
SUMMARY ACTIVITIES	
Review the new song Review lesson outcomes Folk song or folk song tales sung by T	"Charlie over the Ocean" • T reads for the C one of the following: *Hush Little Baby*, by Sylvia Long, or *Goodnight Moon*, by Margaret Wise Brown. • T sings "Goodnight" while C rock an imaginary baby in arms to the beat.

Kindergarten Unit 2: Loud and Soft, Lesson 5	
Outcome:	Practice of loud and soft
INTRODUCTORY ACTIVITIES	
Sing known songs	"That's a Mighty Pretty Motion" CSP: A • C sing song and play game. • C individually create their own movements to perform; the rest of the class copy.

Develop tuneful singing	Greeting CSP: A • T sings a greeting (*s-m*) to C using soft or loud voice, and C must respond to the greeting and copy the dynamic that T used. • Repeat the activity, but C must sing and tap the beat with their response. ➢ T's final "question" to C may be in reference to the ball (e.g., "Where did my ball go?"). ➢ T finds the ball and sings the next song.
Review known songs and concepts	"Bounce High, Bounce Low" CSP: A • T shows sun icon with the word "loud," moves icon to the beat, and sings song in loud singing voice. • C imitate and sing with their loud voice. • T shows moon icon with the word "soft," moves icon to the beat, and sings song with a soft singing voice. • C imitate and sing with their soft voice. • T selects child to pick an icon and the class sings accordingly. ➢ T chooses a child to pick an icon again, and T sings the new song accordingly
CORE ACTIVITIES	
Teach a new song	"Doggie, Doggie" and/or "Zapatitos Blancos" CSP: A • T sings "Doggie, Doggie" while C tap the beat. • C sing the phrase "Who stole my bone?" • T sings the song and C sing the question they've learned. • For phrase 4 T sings very softly into one cupped hand, "I stole your bone." • Repeat song several times; T may sing phrase 4 louder each time. • For the final repeat, T sings with full voice and reveals that she has the bone in her pocket! Connections to books/literacy: • Leslie, Amanda. *Who's That Scratching at My Door?* Handprint Books, 2001. • Powell, Richard. *Guess What I Have!* Barron's Educational Series, 2001. • Wood, Audrey. *A Dog Needs a Bone.* Blue Sky Press, 2007.

255

Practice music performance and literacy skills	"Hunt the Slipper" CSP: A • T sings song with a loud voice. • T asks, "Was I using my loud or my soft voice?" • C answer, "Loud voice." T says, "Let's all sing it together using our loud voices." • Repeat process but with one child singing; class must aurally identify if child was singing with a soft or loud voice. (C point to flash cards with the words *loud* and *soft* in front of them.) • T and C select body motions to imitate the sounds of tapping of the cobbler, using loud or soft sounds. • T and C select instruments such as woodblocks or hand drums to imitate the tapping of the cobbler and keep the beat using loud or soft noises while singing. ➢ T: "Oh that poor cobbler. He was having such a great time dancing and fixing shoes, and then guess who showed up? The wolf!"
Singing game/creative movement	"We Are Dancing in the Forest" CSP: A • T sings song while class is standing in a circle holding hands and swaying back and forth to the beat. • C create their own dance to the song. • T sings song while class moves in a circle. T shows a flash card with the word "loud" or "soft" and C must sing accordingly. • At the end of the song, C say "Wolf, are you there?" If T (who is the wolf) says "I'm combing my hair," then sing the song again. If the wolf says, "I'm coming to get you," C must freeze. The child who moves is the next wolf. Last child is the winner. ➢ T: "There was one little boy who knew he had to get far away from the wolf. He got on a boat went all the way to Italy!"

Practice music performance and literacy skills	"Bobby Shafto" CSP: A • T writes the title of the song on the board and selects a helper. When T sings loudly, child selects the word loud and places it in front of title of song. • When T sings softly, child selects the word *soft* and places it in front of the title of song written on board. Repeat process with several C. • T could have four icons of a ship shown horizontally in a row on the board (or another picture connected to "Bobby Shafto" such as silver buttons, picture of a boy, etc.). C or T sings melody with a loud or soft voice and selects a child to place the appropriate flashcard ("loud" or "soft") in front of the row of icons. Then child could point to icons using a steady beat while class sings. • T should keep steady beat on classroom percussion instrument while C points. • C listen to second movement of Symphony No. 94 in G major by Haydn and discover the soft and loud sounds.
SUMMARY ACTIVITIES	
Review the new song Review lesson outcomes Folk song or folk song tales sung by T	*Doggie Doggie* • T reads for the C either "Hush Little Baby," by Sylvia Long, or "Goodnight Moon," by Margaret Wise Brown. • T sings "Good Night" while C rock an imaginary baby in arms to the beat.

257

Unit 3: Lesson Plans for Teaching Beat

Unit 3

Prepare: Beat

Practice: Loud/Soft

Lesson	Known Songs	Songs/Activities for Developing Tuneful Singing	Reviewing Song/Chant Repertoire	Teaching a New Song/Chant	Preparing Beat	Creative Movement	Practicing Loud/Soft
			Song Repertoire				
Lesson 1	"Charlie over the Ocean"	"Hello, boys and girls" (smssm) Greeting	"Bounce High, Bounce Low"	"Walk Daniel "	Hunt the Slipper" and/or "Zapatitos Blancos"	"Doggie, Doggie"	"Engine, Engine, Number Nine"
Lesson 2	"Lazy Mary"	"Naming Song"	"Doggie, Doggie"	"I Climbed up the Apple Tree"	"Snail, Snail" and/or "Zapatitos Blancos"	"All Around the Buttercup"	"Hunt the Slipper"
Lesson 3	"Sally Go 'Round the Sun"	"Star Light, Star Bright"	"Lazy Mary"	"Queen, Queen Caroline"	"Snail, Snail" and/or "Zapatitos Blancos"	"Little Sally Water"	"On a Mountain"
Lesson	Known Songs	Songs/Activities for Developing Tuneful Singing	Reviewing Song/Chant Repertoire	Teaching a New Song/Chant	Presenting Beat	Creative Movement	Presenting Beat
Lesson 4	"Queen, Queen Caroline"	"Swoop Cards" Vocal Exploration"	"Bounce High, Bounce Low"	"Down Came a Lady"	"Bee, Bee, Bumble Bee"; "Zapatitos Blancos"	"Charlie over the Ocean"	"Seesaw"
Lesson 5	"Queen, Queen Caroline"	"Star Light, Star Bright"	"Sally Go 'Round the Sun"	"Twinkle, Twinkle"	"Bee, Bee, Bumble Bee"; "Zapatitos Blancos"	"Little Sally Water"	"Snail, Snail"

Musical Skill Development

Musical Skill	Activity 1	Activity 2
Reading	C point to the beat icons while singing known songs.	Several C come to the board and point individually while the class points in the general direction while singing.
Writing	C place heartbeat icons on the board to represent the numbers of beats in a phrase or song or song greeting.	
Improvisation and composition	C sing a song and change a word in a phrase. For example, instead of "I climbed up the apple tree" a child might improvise, "I climbed up the walnut tree" while T keeps the beat on drum.	C sing a song several times but have to create a different way of showing the beat each time.
Listening	C identify how many heart beats are in a phrase.	T plays recorded examples of music in various meters duple and compound meter and asks C to move to the beat by walking, skipping, or tapping the beat.
Part work	C perform the beat to known or unknown songs.	C in group 1 perform the beat as the accompaniment to the C singing in group 2.
Memory	T sings known and unknown songs to C and asks them how many beats they tapped during selected phrases.	C sing known songs and T asks the class how many beats they tapped during selected phrases.
Inner hearing	T directs C to respond to a puppet's mouth: "When the mouth is open, sing out loud; when the mouth is closed, sing inside your head." Perform the beat simultaneously.	T directs class to respond to a puppet's mouth: "When the mouth is open, sing out loud; when the mouth is closed, sing inside your head." Perform the beat simultaneously.
Form	C identify numbers of taps while singing selected phrases.	C identify numbers of taps while singing selected phrases.
Instruments	C perform steady beat on barred Orff instruments while singing a song.	C perform steady beat on barred Orff instruments while singing a song.

Kindergarten: Beat, Lesson 1	
Outcome:	Preparation: internalize beat through kinesthetic motions Practice: singing in a loud or soft singing voice while pointing to icons
INTRODUCTORY ACTIVITIES	
Sing known songs	"Charlie over the Ocean" CSP: F • C sing and play game. • C sing with beat motions.
Develop tuneful singing	Greeting CSP: A • T sings "Hello boys and girls" (*smssm*) and C respond "Hello teacher" using the same singing pattern as T. • T sings "How are you today?"(*ssllsm*) and children respond "We are fine today" using the same singing pattern as T. • T can use this as a way to take attendance and keep track of "matching voices" throughout the year, by having a child lead the greeting, or having C in a circle greet each other (pass greeting around circle until all have been greeted).
Review known songs and concepts	"Bounce High, Bounce Low" CSP: A • T displays (may draw or have premade magnetic icons, for example) four to eight balls in one to two phrases on the board with the word "loud" placed in front of icons; C sing song with a loud singing voice. • T repeats with the word "soft" placed in front of icons; C sing song with a soft singing voice. ➤ T: "I will NEVER forget that day Johnny and I bounced the ball all the way to Shiloh! Along the way we also made another friend and his name was Daniel. Daniel could do all sorts of things. . . ."

CORE ACTIVITIES	
Teach a new song	"Walk Daniel" CSP: A • T sings song to C using a few stationary motions (fly, clap, bend, point, etc.). • T sings song and C must copy motions. • T sings song to C using nonstationary motions (walk, hop, skip, march, etc.) and C copy motions. • C may suggest motions to perform while singing. Connections to books/literacy: • Lively, Penelope. *One Two Three Jump!* Puffin Books, 1998. • Suhr, Mandy. *I Can Move.* Wayland Books, 1993, 2009. • Williams, Sue. *I Went Walking.* Red Wagon Books/ Harcourt, 1989. • Hoberman, Mary A. *Skip to My Lou.* Megan Tingley, 2003. T sings the song again, creating two to three additional verses, ending with "tap Daniel. . . ." This "reminds" T of another song.
Prepare music Literacy concept Sing and move	"Hunt the Slipper" and/or "Zapatitos Blancos" CSP: A • T begins the song tapping his or her shoe with a steady beat. • C join in singing and imitate with their shoe (or hand and fist). • T gives individual C a chance to hammer the shoe while C sing. • C sing song and keep beat with different motions (marching, jumping, etc.). • C sing song and point to picture of four to eight hammers on the board while keeping the beat. (Icons should be arranged in rows of four, representing phrases; icons may be drawn, premade magnets, etc.) T may also use toy hammers for this activity. ➢ T: "Finally, at half past four, the cobbler got to go home and see his doggie, who was very upset because she couldn't find her bone. He sang her this song. . . ."

Creative movements	"Doggie, Doggie" CSP: A • C sing "Doggie, Doggie"; T sings the phrase, "Who stole my bone?" • T sings very softly into one cupped hand, "I stole your bone" • T sings the phrase "Who stole my bone?" and has individual C answer with "I stole your bone." • T and C play the game. ➤ T: "The cobbler's doggie wanted to get back at him for stealing her bone, so guess what she did? She stole his train ticket for Engine Number Nine!"
Practice of music performance and literacy skills Reading	"Engine, Engine, Number Nine" • T places the flash card "loud" or "soft" in front of a four-to-eight-beat iconic representation of that song (e.g., train). • C speak the chant while pointing to icons with the steady beat, using the appropriate voice (loud/soft). • T places the flash card "p" or "f" in front of a four-to-eight-beat iconic representation of that song (e.g., train). T explains that in music we use the p for soft ("sing with a soft voice") and f for forte ("sing with a loud but musical voice"). • C speak the chant while pointing to icons with the steady beat, using the appropriate voice indicated by a p of f dynamic. • T may reinforce steady beat by playing on classroom percussion instrument while class speaks the chant. • T uses puppet and C chant the rhyme. When puppet's mouth is closed, C inner-hear the rhyme; when puppet's mouth is open, C speak aloud in appropriate voice (loud or soft).
SUMMARY ACTIVITIES	
Review the new song Review lesson outcomes Folk song or folk song tales sung by T	• "Walk Daniel" • "The Farmer in the Dell"

Kindergarten: Beat, Lesson 2	
Outcome:	Preparation: aural awareness of beat Practice: loud and soft and writing

INTRODUCTORY ACTIVITIES	
Sing known songs	"Lazy Mary" CSP: F • T and C sing the song and play game.
Develop tuneful singing	Naming Song CSP: A • T sings, choosing one child: "Sing me your name" (*s ml s m*). • Child responds "My name is _____" using the same singing pattern as T. • T goes around the room, asking C to sing their name and adding a steady pulse using body percussion. • If a child is shy, T might have a puppet and ask the child to sing the name of the puppet, or even pretend that it is the puppet asking the questions.
Review known songs and concepts	"Doggie, Doggie" CSP: A • C sing "Doggie, Doggie" with a loud voice and soft voice. • C and T decide which phrase should be sung with a loud and soft voice. • T and C play the game.
CORE ACTIVITIES	

Teach a new song	"I Climbed up the Apple Tree"
	• T says the rhyme for C while tapping a steady beat.
	• T says the rhyme and does the motions with a child.
	  • "I climbed up the apple tree" (climbing motion to a steady beat).
	  • "All the apples fell on me" (tapping head with hands to a steady beat).
	  • "Apple pudding, apple pie" (rubbing stomach to a steady beat).
	  • "Did you ever tell a lie?" (pointing finger at partner to a steady beat).
	• Repeat with several C.
	• C speak the rhyme with T.
	
	Connections to books/literacy:
	
	• Ehlert, Lois. *Eating the Alphabet: Fruits & Vegetables from A to Z*. Harcourt Books, 1989.
	• Ayres, Katherine. *Up Down, and Around*. Candlewick Press, 2007.
	• Krauss, Ruth. *The Carrot Seed*. Scholastic, 1945.
	➤ T: "Do you know who else LOVES to eat apples? Snails!"

263

Develop music literacy concepts Tell me what you hear	"Snail, Snail" and/or "Zapatitos Blancos" CSP: A • C sing song and keep beat. • T: "Let's sing the first part of 'Snail, Snail' and put the snails on your knees." T and C tap the snails on their knees. • T: "Let's sing the first part in your head, but keep the snails on your knees." • T: "How many snails did you tap?" (four) Repeat this process with "Star Light." T can then work with chants or songs that have two sounds on beat 3 of a phrase, like "Bee, Bee Bumble Bee."
Singing game/creative movement	"All Around the Buttercup" (new game) CSP: F# • T sings the song while demonstrating the game. • C play the game (important to keep the beat even with the rest). • Game is like "Duck, Duck, Goose." • After several cycles, C should also sing while playing the game.

Practice of music performance and literacy skills
 	
Writing
	"Hunt the Slipper"
	
	CSP: A
	
	• T sings the song with a loud or soft voice.
	• Child chooses the correct flash card ("loud" or "soft" or " p" or 'f") and T places it in front of a four-to-eight-beat iconic representation (hammers).
	• Class sings the song while pointing at the icons to the steady beat, using the appropriate voice (loud/soft).
	  • Repeat process with another known song ("Johnny Works with One Hammer").
	  • "We Are Dancing in the Forest"
	  • "Bobby Shafto"

SUMMARY ACTIVITIES	
Review the new song Review lesson outcomes Folk song or folk song tales sung by T	"I Climbed up the Apple Tree" "Little Johnny Brown"

264

Kindergarten: Beat Lesson 3	
Outcome:	Preparation: creating a visual representation of beat Practice: loud/soft and improvisation
INTRODUCTORY ACTIVITIES	
Sing known songs	"Sally Go 'Round the Sun" CSP: D • T and C play the game.
Develop tuneful singing	"Star Light, Star Bright" CSP: A • C sing song with beat motions (catching stars in their hands, or pointing to stars). • C imagine they are falling stars and vocalize while flying over mountains, valleys, deserts, oceans, and forests. Vocal Exploration • T finds a bean bag in the shape of a star and throws it up in the air at various heights to have C vocalize according to how high or low T threw it. • T has a picture of a star and travels around the room (going over cabinets and under tables, etc.). Connections to books/literacy: Trapani, Iza. *Twinkle Twinkle Little Star.* Charlesbridge, 1994.
Review known songs and concepts	"Lazy Mary" CSP: F • T and C sing the song and play game. • C determine if they will use loud or soft voices for each phrase of the song.
CORE ACTIVITIES	
Teach a new song	"Queen, Queen Caroline" • T chants and keeps steady beat. • T chants and does motions; C copy. • T and C chant and do motions.

Prepare music literacy concepts Draw a picture of what you hear	"Snail, Snail" and/or "Zapatitos Blancos" CSP: A • T and C play game. • T: "Let's sing the first part of 'Snail, Snail' and put the snails on your knees." T plays steady beat on a drum while C sing. • T: "Let's sing the first part in your head but keep the snails on your knees." • T: "How many snails did you tap?" (four) • T and C sing the song; individual child places the correct number of icons on the board to indicate how many "taps" they performed. (Four snails: can be printed out, be laminated, and have an adhesive magnetic strip put on the back.) • T passes out a class set of icons or paper strips, and C create their own representation. • C sing and point to the icons.
Creative movement	"Little Sally Water" CSP: A • T sings the song and demonstrates how to play the game. • T sings the song and C play the game. • T invites C to join the song. • C sing and play alone.
Practice of music performance and literacy skills Improvisation	"On a Mountain" CSP: A • C sing song and create motions to go along with song. They should use different motions if they sing with a loud or soft voice. For example if they sing with a loud voice they should march to the beat. If they sing with a soft voice they can tap the beat softly. • T plays recording of loud or soft music. C respond by moving through space appropriately (stomping = loud music, tiptoeing = soft music). Excerpts from *Carnival of the Animals* are always easy to use for this type of activity. It may be important to find excerpts that aren't always slow/soft and fast/loud. Often C confuse fast/slow for loud/soft. Examples of music to play for students • *Stars and Stripes Forever*, J. P. Sousa (loud) • *Nuages, Nocturnes*, C. Debussy (soft) • *Circus Music, The Red Pony*, A. Copland (loud) • *Berceuse, The Firebird Suite*, I. Stravinsky (soft)

266

SUMMARY ACTIVITIES	
Review the new song Review lesson outcomes Folk song or folk song tales sung by T	• "Queen, Queen Caroline" • "Skin and Bones"

Kindergarten: Beat, Lesson 4	
Outcome:	Presentation: label the beat, introduce the beat icon, and present the word "beat."
INTRODUCTORY ACTIVITIES	
Sing known songs	"Queen, Queen Caroline" • T chants with motions. C copy. • T chants and does motions. C do motions for "Queen, Queen Caroline." • T and C chant and do motions.
Develop tuneful singing	Vocal Exploration • "Swoop" cards, with swirls, patterns, and shapes for the C to mimic through vocalization. • T shows swoop cards, traces patterns with finger, and vocalizes with the C. T can draw various line/shape patterns on a number of posters, with many colors, and laminate each of them. Putting a magnet strip on the back means each time T can line the patterns up a different way on the board, or even turn them upside down!
Review known songs and concepts	"Bounce High, Bounce Low" CSP: A • T and C sing the song and play game. • T and C sing each alternative verse but use loud for T voice and soft for C voice.

267

CORE ACTIVITIES	
Teach a new song	"Down Came a Lady" CSP: F • T sings song three times while C keep beat. • T asks a child, "Do you remember what color Daniel's wife was wearing?" • T sings song and C keep the beat, but this time child sings the word "blue" and T and C sing the song. • T sings and shows C a chart with different colors and their names. • T sings but C sing the color indicated on the chart. Connections to books/literacy: • Otoshi, Kathryn. *One.* KO Kids Books, 2008. • Peek, Merle. *Mary Wore Her Red Dress and Henry Wore His Green Sneakers.* Clarion, 1985. • Rollings, Susan. *New Shoes, Red Shoes.* Orchard Books, 2000. • Lively, Penelope. *One Two Three Jump!* Puffin Books, 1998. • Baker, Keith. *Quack and Count.* Harcourt Brace, 1999.
Present the music concept Label what you hear	"Bee, Bee, Bumble Bee" and/or "Zapatitos Blancos" • C chant "Bee, Bee, Bumble Bee" while keeping a steady beat. • C point to icon of bees; C then put the beat on their knees by pretending to point to the icon on their knees. • T and C chant while tapping the beat. • T chants phrase 1 and asks, "How many bees did we tap?" (four) • C chant and place the correct number of icons on the board to represent what they heard. • Repeat with all four phrases • T: "In music, when we count the bees or tap the snails, we have a special name for it. It's called the beat." • T: "Let's chant 'Bee, Bee, Bumble Bee' again and keep the beat." • T: "Let's chant the first phrase of 'Bee, Bee, Bumble Bee' and figure out how many beats were in the phrase." • T: "Let's speak 'Bee, Bee' again and keep the beat. Where should we keep the beat? On our knees? Head? Should we do it several times in several different ways?"

Singing game/creative movement	"Charlie over the Ocean" CSP: F • T sings "Charlie over the Ocean." • T and C play the game. • C find other ways of moving in the ocean as they sing the song.
Presentation of music concept Record what you hear	"Seesaw" CSP: A • C sing the song and the motions of "Seesaw" with their arms. • C sing the song and keep the beat on their knees, shoulders, etc. • T presents the word beat and the symbol. T shows flash card with the word "beat" and the symbol of a heart. • T: "Let's sing 'Seesaw' and point to the heartbeats for this song. C point to four heartbeats on the board while they sing.
SUMMARY ACTIVITIES	
Review the new song Review lesson outcomes	"Down Came a Lady"
Folk song or folk song tales sung by T	"Old Joe Clark"

Kindergarten: Beat, Lesson 5	
Outcome:	Practice of beat
INTRODUCTORY ACTIVITIES	
Sing known songs	"Queen, Queen Caroline" • C chant with beat motions. • C point to beats on the board as they sing.
Develop tuneful singing	"Star Light, Star Bright" CSP: A • C sing song with beat motions (catching stars in the their hands, or pointing to stars). • C imagine they are falling stars and vocalize while flying over mountains, valleys, deserts, oceans, and forests.

Review known songs and concepts	"Sally Go 'Round the Sun" CSP: D • T and C play the game and walk in a circle with beat motions. • C sing song and point to beat chart. T may keep the beat on a classroom percussion instrument. Connections to books/literacy: • Wood, Audrey. *Silly Sally*. Harcourt, 1992. • Brown, Margaret Wise. *Goodnight Moon*. Scholastic, 1947. • Orie, Sandra De Coteau. *Did You Hear Wind Sing Your Name?* Walker, 1995. • Carle, Eric. *The Very Busy Spider*. Philomel Books, 1984. • Carter, David A. *In and Out*. Intervisual Books, 1993.
CORE ACTIVITIES	
Teach a new song	"Twinkle, Twinkle" CSP: D • T sings and C listen while keeping a steady beat on their knees. • T sings phrase 1 and asks C to repeat. • C sing phrase 1 with beat motions and T sings remainder of song. • C sing the song with beat motions.
Practice of music performance and literacy skills	"Bee, Bee, Bumble Bee" and/or "Zapatitos Blancos" • C chant "Bee, Bee, Bumble Bee." • C chant and keep the beat by pointing to four bee icons (T puts each bee into a heartbeat icon); C then put the beat on their knees by pretending to point to the icon on their knees. • T and C chant while tapping. • T chants each phrase and asks, "How many beats did we tap?" (four) • T chants and C place the correct number of heart icons on the board to represent what they heard. • T repeats with each phrase. • T: "Let's chant 'Bee, Bee' again and point to the beat." • C improvise beat motions with their bodies to keep beat. • T selects unpitched instruments to keep the beat.

Singing games/creative movement	"Little Sally Water" CSP: A • T and C sing the song and play the game. • The It child performs a beat motion during the singing, which the rest of the class imitates during the song.
Practice of music performance and literacy skills	"Snail, Snail" CSP: A • C sing the song and perform motions. • C sing the song and keep the beat. • T shows flash card with four heartbeats. • T: "Let's point to the heart beats while we sing." (Depending on the age of C, T might ask them to point for only one section of the song.) • T plays a piece of music such as Elgar's *Pomp and Circumstance*. C point to beat on beat chart. C can also march to the music in a circle.
SUMMARY ACTIVITIES	
Review the new song Review lesson outcomes Folk song or folk song tales sung by T	"Hop Old Squirrel" "Old Joe Clark"

271

Unit 4: Lesson Plans for Teaching High/Low Voice

Unit 4

| | Prepare: High/Low Voice | | | Practice: Beat | | | |
				Song Repertoire			
Lesson	Known Songs	Songs/Activities for Developing Tuneful Singing	Reviewing Song/Chant Repertoire	Teaching a New Song/Chant	Preparing New Concept: High/Low Voice	Creative Movement	Practicing Known Concept: Beat
Lesson 1	"Hop Old Squirrel"	"Bee, Bee, Bumble Bee"	"Sally Go 'Round the Sun"	"Oliver Twist"	"Bee, Bee, Bumble Bee," "Zapatitos Blancos"	"Charlie over the Ocean"	"Snail, Snail"
Lesson 2	"Oliver Twist"	Musical Greeting	"Hop Old Squirrel"	"Frosty Weather"	"Bee, Bee, Bumble Bee," "Zapatitos Blancos"	"Little Sally Water"	"Snail, Snail"
Lesson 3	"Frosty Weather"	"Bee, Bee, Bumble Bee"	"Little Sally Walker"	"It's Raining"	"I Climbed up the Apple Tree"	"Teddy Bear"	"Snail, Snail"
Lesson	Known Songs	Songs/Activities for Developing Tuneful Singing	Reviewing Song/Chant Repertoire	Teaching a New Song/Chant	Presenting High/Low Voice	Creative Movement	Presenting High/Low Voice
Lesson 4	"It's Raining"	Musical Greeting	"Hop Old Squirrel"	"Little Johnny Brown"	"Bee, Bee, Bumble Bee"; "Zapatitos Blancos"	"Here Comes a Bluebird"	"I Climbed up the Apple Tree"
Lesson 5	"Little Johnny Brown"	"Handy Dandy"	"Little Sally Water"	"Ring Around the Rosie"	"I Climbed up the Apple Tree"	"Frosty Weather"	"Snail, Snail"

Musical Skill Development

Musical Skill	Activity 1	Activity 2
Reading	C look at pictures of a bird or bear that are placed in front of beat icons and chant the rhyme according to which word is displayed.	C read the words "high" or "low" on flash cards placed in front of beat icons and chant the rhyme according to which word is displayed.
Writing	C place visuals on the board representing the beat as they are chanting using their high voice or low voice.	C record how another child chanted a rhyme by placing the words "high" or "low" in front of a beat chart.
Improvisation and composition	C improvise a motion that will demonstrate the beat of a known or unknown song using a high voice or a low voice.	C decide how to chant a song either using a high or low voice. C perform beat high in the air or low by their feet according to the voice used.
Listening	C listen to a piece of music sung or played by the teacher and identify the piece as high or low.	C show high and low with their bodies
Part work	C perform steady beat to known or unknown songs; C perform beat high in the air or low by their feet according to which voice is being used.	T and C echo-chant known rhythms with a high/low voice.
Memory	T chants known and unknown songs to C using a low or high voice and asks them about the number of taps they performed with the chant, and if T was singing using a high voice or a low voice.	T chants known songs to class using a low or high voice and asks the class about the number of taps they performed with the chant, and if they were singing using a high voice or a low voice.
Inner hearing	C chant with a bird or bear voice while following the mouth of a puppet. When the mouth is open, they chant out loud, and when it is closed they chant inside the head.	C chant a known song with high/low voice, but inner-hear a phrase, determined by T, of another child.
Form	T and C echo-chant or rhyme songs in high/low voice.	C in groups echo-chant a known rhyme in high or low voice.
Instruments	C use a drum or a barred Orff instrument to accompany the class or another child while chanting in a high or low voice.	C choose a high or low drum to accompany the class while another child chants in a high or low voice.

Kindergarten: High and Low Voice, Lesson 1	
Outcome:	Preparation: internalize high/low voice through kinesthetic activities
	Practice: beat and music reading
INTRODUCTORY ACTIVITIES	
Sing known songs	"Hop Old Squirrel"
	CSP: A
	• T sings the song while C listen and keep steady beat.
	• T performs beat motions and C copy.
	• T performs other motions such as walking, jumping, skipping, etc.
	• T should end with flying.
	➤ T: "Hey! I know something that flies: a bee! Do we know any rhymes about a bee?"
Develop tuneful singing	"Bee, Bee, Bumble Bee"
	• One child chants "Bee, Bee" and steps to a steady beat as C march.
	• T: "Let's follow the bee with our voices."
	• T uses bee icons/visual for vocal exploration, moving from low to high sounds.
	➤ T: "I really like bees, but I met a girl named Sally who LOVES bees! She likes them so much she would walk all around the sun to find some. And that's exactly what she does every day: Sally goes around the sun, Sally goes around the moon, and Sally goes around the sun again, every afternoon!"
Review known songs and concepts	"Sally Go 'Round the Sun"
	CSP: D
	• T and C play the game and walk in a circle with beat motions using a loud or soft voice.
	➤ T: "The problem with Sally was that she wasn't always very nice to her friends. I had to tell her to stop teasing her friend Oliver Twist because he had a hard time touching his knees, toes, and heels. She would sing this song to tease him. . . ."

CORE ACTIVITIES	
Teach a new song	"Oliver Twist" CSP: A • T sings song with motions and C keep the beat. • T sings and C keep the motions. • C sing and point to beat chart on the board. Connections to books/literacy: • Carle, Eric. *From Head to Toe*. HarperFestival, 1997. • Lucas, Sally. *Dancing Dinos*. Random House, 1933. • Martin, Bill, Jr. *The Maestro Plays*. Voyager Books, 1996. • Hoberman, Mary Ann. *Miss Mary Mack*. Little, Brown, 1998. • Suhr, Mandy. *I Can Move*. Wayland Books, 1993, 2009. • Cronin, Doreen. *Wiggle*. Atheneum Books for Young Readers, 2005.
Prepare music literacy concepts Sing and move	"Bee, Bee, Bumble Bee" • T moves icon (picture of grandfather or bear or bird) to the beat while speaking the rhyme. When T speaks with a low pitch, T shows the grandfather; when T speaks with high inflection, T shows the bird. • C chant the rhyme using appropriate voice (high/low). • C speak and move like grandfather or bear or like the bird. T always models moving to the steady beat. • C point to beat icons with a picture of a grandfather or bird placed in front by T, and C speak with bear/bird voice. T can use a bear for the low pitch if desired. T could use the book *Brown Bear, Brown Bear, What Do You See?* by Bill Martin, Jr., and Eric Carle during this lesson if the bear icon is being used.

275

Singing game/creative movement	"Charlie over the Ocean"
	CSP: F
	• T sings "Charlie over the Ocean."
	• T and C play the game.
	➤ C find other ways of moving in the ocean as they sing the song.
Practice of music performance and literacy skills Reading	"Snail, Snail" CSP: A
	• T places eight to sixteen (depending on the song) heartbeat icons on the board.
	• C sing song and keep the beat while T points to the heartbeats.
	• T repeats and asks a child to come to the board and point while the class sings.
	• T repeats the activity but puts the word "loud" or "soft" or "p" or "f" in front of the beat chart.
	• T passes out four heartbeats to each child and has C make their own heartbeat chart like the one on the board.
	• C sing song or rhyme while pointing to their own heartbeat chart.
	• T asks C to "think the song in your head" during certain phrases while reading the heartbeats on the board. This can be done with puppet. C sing song or rhyme while pointing to their own heartbeat chart.

SUMMARY ACTIVITIES

Review the new song	"Oliver Twist"
Review lesson outcomes	
Folk song or folk song tales sung by T	"I Had a little Rooster"

Kindergarten: High and Low Voice, Lesson 2	
Outcome:	Preparation: aural awareness of repertoire chanted in a high or low voice
	Practice: beat and writing

INTRODUCTORY ACTIVITIES

Sing known songs	"Oliver Twist"
	CSP: A
	• Sing song and play game.

Develop tuneful singing	Music Greeting CSP: A • T sings greeting and C answer and keep the beat. • T and C pretend to yawn, stretch, etc., as vocal exploration.
Review known songs and concepts	"Hop Old Squirrel" CSP: A • T sings the song while C listen and keep the beat on their knees. • T performs the motions and C join. • C make up other motions such as walk, jump, crawl, skip, slide, march, wiggle as they sing the song. • C sing using their loud or soft voices.
CORE ACTIVITIES	
Teach a new song	"Frosty Weather" CSP: C • T sings song and C keep the beat. • T sings song and show C the motions. • C sings "Frosty Weather." • C sing and play game. Connections to books/literacy: • Orie, Sandra De Coteau. *Did You Hear Wind Sing Your Name?* Walker, 1995. • Stojic, Manya. *Rain.* Dragonfly Books, 2000. • Locker, Thomas. *Cloud Dance.* Voyager Books, 2000. • Gershator, Phillis. *When It Starts to Snow.* Henry Holt, 1998.
Prepare music literacy concepts Tell me what you hear	"Bee, Bee, Bumble Bee" • T moves icon (picture of grandfather or bird) to the beat while C chant the rhyme using appropriate voice (high/low). • C chant and move like a bird (flying in the air) or like grandfather (bent over with a cane). • C point to beat icons on the board (grandfather or bird) and speak with appropriate voice (high or low). • T speaks with high voice and asks, "Was I using my grandfather voice or my bird voice?" • After C answer "bird," T says, "Let's all say it with our bird voices." • T repeats process, speaking in a low voice. • Repeat process with another rhyme.

277

Singing game/creative movement	"Little Sally Water"
	CSP: A
	• T sings song with motions and C keep the beat.
	• C sing and play the game.
	• T: "Ever since I saw Sally get stung, I try to stay far away from bees! Mostly I like to stay around things that are slow and don't fly. Like snails!"
Practice of music performance and music literacy concepts Writing	"Snail, Snail"
	CSP: A
	• C sing song while keeping steady beat.
	• C sing song and show phrases; C determine how many phrases are in the song.
	• T writes the phrase marks on the board.
	• T and C figure out how many beats are in each phrase. T: "Let's sing the first phrase and count how many beats we tap." C: "Four."
	• T gives a child a set of heartbeats (predetermined by the length of the song).
	• The child must place the correct number of beats under phrase while the class sings the phrase again.
	• T repeats with the rest of the phrases.
	• T repeats with other songs and individuals.
SUMMARY ACTIVITIES	
Review the new song	• "Frosty Weather"
Review lesson outcomes	• "There Was a Man"
Folk song or folk song tales sung by T	Book connection: *There Was a Cold Lady Who Swallowed Some Snow!* by Lucille Colandro

Kindergarten: High and Low Voice, Lesson 3	
Outcome:	Preparation: create a representation for high and low voices
	Practice: beat and improvisation
INTRODUCTORY ACTIVITIES	
Sing known songs	"Frosty Weather"
	CSP: A
	• C sing and play the game.

Develop tuneful singing	"Bee, Bee, Bumble Bee" • T chants "Bee, Bee" as C march to song. • C chant and perform the motions. • C continue the motions but choose which phrases they will inner-hear. • T and C make the sounds of bees humming. ➢ T: "Uh oh, we'd better get rid of these bees. My friend Sally is coming over and she's been scared of bees ever since she got stung. . . ."
Review known songs and concepts	"Little Sally Water" CSP: A • C sing song and play game. • C sing song and point to beat icons on the board. ➢ T: "Poor Sally . . . first she gets stung by a bee and then her father injured his head last night as he was going to bed, and now he can't get up!"
CORE ACTIVITIES	

Teach a new song	"It's Raining"
	
	CSP: A
	
	• T sings the song and C keep the beat.
	• T asks questions about the text and musical aspects of the song; C must listen to the song for the answer (repeating song as many times as needed):
	   • "How many phrases?"
	   • "Did I sing using loud or soft singing voice?"
	   • "Who bumped their head?"
	
	Connections to books/literacy:
	
	• Stojic, Manya. *Rain*. Dragonfly Books, 2000.
	• Locker, Thomas. *Cloud Dance*. Voyager Books, 2000.
	• Adams, Pam. *This Old Man*. Child's Play International, 1989.
	• Gershator, Phillis. *When It Starts to Snow*. Henry Holt, 1998.

279

Prepare music literacy concepts Draw a picture	"I Climbed up the Apple Tree" • T moves icon (picture of grandfather or bird) to the beat while C chant and move a similar icon (grandfather or bird) with the steady beat. • T speaks with low/high voice and asks, "Was I using my grandfather or bear or bird voice?" • T: "Show me with your body which voice I was using." Or C can place an icon of a grandfather or bird in front of a beat chart and C chant and point. • Repeat process with another known rhyme. Book Connections: *Chicka Chicka 123* by Bill Martin, Jr., and Michael Sampson
Singing game/creative movement	"Teddy Bear" CSP: A • C sing with motions. • C create new beat motions to perform while singing the song.
Practice of music performance and literacy skills Improvisation	"Snail, Snail" CSP: A • T and C sing song while C improvise motion to the beat of the same song. • T invites a child or two to improvise motions for the class that will also indicate whether the song should be sung loud or soft.
SUMMARY ACTIVITIES	
Review the new song Review lesson outcomes Folk song or folk song tales sung by T	• "It's Raining" • "There's a Hole in the Bucket"

Kindergarten: High and Low Voice, Lesson 4	
Outcome:	Presentation: introduce the words and spelling for high and low voice

INTRODUCTORY ACTIVITIES	
Sing known songs	"It's Raining" CSP: A • C create beat motions to perform while singing this song.
Develop tuneful singing	Music Greeting CSP: A • T sings "Hello boys and girls" (*smssm*) and C respond "Hello teacher" using the same singing pattern as T. • T sings "How are you today?"(*ssllsm*) and C respond "We are fine today" using the same singing pattern as T. "I Climbed up the Apple Tree" • C play game. • C choose which phrases they will "say in their head" until they are inner-hearing the entire chant.
Review known songs and concepts	"Hop Old Squirrel" CSP: A • T sings "Hop Old Squirrel" as C act out the song. • T and C perform the song while walking, jumping, hopping, skipping, etc., with a loud and soft voice. Connections to books/literacy: • Ricketts, Ann, and Michael Ricketts. *Rhyme Time.* Brimax Books, 1998. • Twinn, M. *Old Macdonald Had a Farm.* Child's Play (International), 1975.
CORE ACTIVITIES	
Teach a new song	"Little Johnny Brown" CSP: E • T sings and uses a blanket, handkerchief, or bandana to illustrate the song. • T sings and has individual C fold the corners of the "comfort." • Repeat with other C. • C clap while singing the song.

Presentation of music concept Label what you hear	"Bee, Bee, Bumble Bee" • C point to icon (grandfather or bear or bird) while keeping steady beat and chanting with bear/bird voice. • T and C chant with a grandfather or bird voice and T asks, "Were we using our grandfather voice or our bird voice?" • A child places the correct icon in front of beat chart on board. C points and class chants. • T says, "In music, when we use our bird voice, we call that our high voice. Let's chant 'Bee, Bee, Bumble Bee' in our high voice." • T says, "In music, when we use our grandfather voice, we call that our low voice. Let's chant 'Bee, Bee, Bumble Bee' in our low voice." ➢ C continue the beat into the next song.
Singing game/creative movement	"Here Comes a Bluebird" CSP: A • T and C sing and play game. ➢ T: "When I was a kid, I tried to follow a bluebird out into the garden too. I wanted to see its nest, so . . . 'I climbed up the apple tree'. . . ."
Presentation of music concept Record what you hear	"I Climbed up the Apple Tree" • C point to icon (grandfather or bear or bird) while keeping steady beat and chanting with grandfather/bird voice. • T and C chant with a grandfather or bear or bird voice; T asks, "Were we using our grandfather voice or our bird voice?" • A child places the correct icon in front of beat chart on board. C points and class chants. • T says, "In music, when we use our bird voice, we call that our high voice." T shows a flash card with "high" written on it. C chant "I Climbed up the Apple Tree" with their high voice. • T says, "In music, when we use our grandfather or bear voice, we call that our low voice." T shows a flash card with "low" written on it. C chant "I Climbed up the Apple Tree" with their low voice.
SUMMARY ACTIVITIES	
Review the new song Review lesson outcomes Folk song or folk song tales sung by T	• "Little Johnny Brown" • "Rocky Mountain"

Kindergarten: High and Low Voice, Lesson 5	
Outcome:	Practice high and low
INTRODUCTORY ACTIVITIES	
Sing known songs	"Teddy Bear" and "Little Johnny Brown" CSP: E • C sing and play the game.
Develop tuneful singing	"Handy Dandy" (new chant and game) • T and C play game. T places the pitches high and low at least an octave apart and then sees if children can sing. T can try placing the pitches high and low a fifth apart. (When we are working with high/low in a melody we can practice using the interval of a minor third.)
Review known songs and concepts	"Little Sally Water" CSP: A • C sing song and play game. • A child points to the beat chart and class sings. Connections to books/literacy: • Wood, Audrey. *Silly Sally*. Harcourt, 1992.
CORE ACTIVITIES	
Teach a new song	"Ring Around the Rosie" CSP: A • T sings the song and C keep the beat. • T asks questions about the song and C must listen to T sing again for the answer ("What was in my pocket?" "When do we fall down?"). • T sings song and C perform motions. • C sing and play the game.
Practice of music performance and literacy skills	"I Climbed up the Apple Tree" • C play game. • T asks C to use a high voice and play the game. • T asks C to use a low voice and play the game.
Singing game/creative movement	"Frosty Weather" CSP: A • C sing and play game.

Practice of music performance and literacy skills	"Snail, Snail" CSP: A • C sing and play game. • C sing and point to heart beats with the word "high" or "low" placed in front of the beat charts on the board. • C sing and keep the beat while one child points to the beat chart on the board. • T plays "Stars and Stripes Forever" by John Philip Sousa (1854–1932) and keeps the beat and points to the beat chart.
SUMMARY ACTIVITIES	
Review the new song Review lesson outcomes	"Ring Around the Rosie"
Folk song or folk song tales sung by T	"Rocky Mountain"

Unit 5: Lesson Plans for Teaching Fast and Slow

Unit 5

Prepare: Fast/Slow			Practice: High/Low				
			Song Repertoire				
Lesson	Known Songs	Songs/Activities for Developing Tuneful Singing	Reviewing Song/Chant Repertoire	Teaching a New Song/Chant	Preparing New Concept: Fast/Slow	Creative Movement	Practicing Known Concept: High/Low
Lesson 1	"Little Sally Water"	Musical Greeting	"Teddy Bear"	"Bow Wow Wow"	"Engine, Engine, Number Nine"	Ring Around the Rosie"	"Bee, Bee, Bumble Bee"
Lesson 2	"Little Sally Water"	Musical Greeting	"Hey, Hey, Look at Me"	"Here Comes a Blue Bird"	"Frosty Weather"	"Bow Wow Wow"	"Bee, Bee, Bumble Bee"
Lesson 3	"Hey, Hey, Look At Me"	"On the Mountain"	"Frosty Weather"	"London Bridge"	"Engine, Engine, Number Nine"	"Bow Wow Wow"	"Bee, Bee, Bumble Bee"
Lesson	Known Songs	Songs/Activities for Developing Tuneful Singing	Reviewing Song/Chant Repertoire	Teaching a New Song/Chant	Presenting Fast/Slow	Creative Movement	Presenting Fast/Slow
Lesson 4	"Bow Wow Wow"	"On the Mountain"	"Engine, Engine, Number Nine"	"A la Rueda de San Miguel"	"Hey, Hey, Look at Me"	"Little Sally Water"	"Oliver Twist"
Lesson 5	"Hey, Hey, Look at Me"	"On The Mountain"	"Engine, Engine, Number Nine"	"Here We Go 'Round the Mulberry Bush" and "A la Rueda de San Miguel"	"Bee, Bee, Bumble Bee"	"Bow Wow Wow"	"I Climbed up the Apple Tree"

Musical Skill Development

Musical Skill	Activity 1	Activity 2
Reading	C sing and point to a visual chart indicating the beats, while singing known songs using a fast or slow tempo. Begin with four beats and move to eight and sixteen beats. C should place snail icons or the words "fast tempo" or "slow tempo" in front of the beat charts.	C sing and read a visual beat chart while singing known songs in different combinations of fast/slow, high/low, loud/soft. Be sure to use unusual combinations, such as fast/soft, slow/loud, etc.
Writing	C place the words "fast tempo" or "slow tempo" in front of a beat chart for a song performed by the T, or C record how a melody was sung or a chant was performed.	All C select between high/low and fast/slow to perform a known song. The class reads a beat chart on the board with the individual child's selection.
Improvisation and composition	C improvise a motion that will demonstrate the beat of a known or unknown song in a fast tempo or slow tempo.	C choose whether to sing a song with a fast or slow tempo.
Listening	C listen to a piece of music sung or played by the T and identify the piece of music as either fast or slow. *In the Hall of the Mountain King*, Grieg	C listen to recorded music that combines fast/slow with high/low and loud/soft. C identify the tempo and dynamics of the piece.
Part work	Divide the class into two groups. Group A improvises a motion when they hear fast music (such as the "Tarantella" from *Pulcinella Suite*, by Igor Stravinsky) and Group B improvises a motion when they hear slow music (such as "Air" from Suite No. 3, by Johann Sebastian Bach).	T plays recorded examples of music in different meters, 2/4 or 6/8, and asks children to move to the beat, walking, skipping, or tapping the beat, whichever is most appropriate according to the tempo.

Memory	T sing known and unknown songs to C and have them determine if it was sung with a fast or slow tempo.	T sing known songs to the class and has them determine if it was sung with a fast or slow tempo.
Inner hearing	C follow the mouth of a puppet. When the mouth is open they sing out loud; when it is closed they sing inside their head. But they must always keep the beat. Perform this activity using a fast and slow tempo.	C sing a known song with fast or slow, but inner-hear selected phrases.
Form	C echo-sing a song while keeping the beat. Initially this should be done between T and C and then between two groups of C and finally between two individual C. Do this with the same song performed with a slow and then a fast tempo.	
Instruments	C will play a steady beat on unpitched percussion instruments (bells, sticks, shakers, etc.) that matches the tempo of the music sung or played.	C will play a steady beat on an unpitched instrument to accompany a song, but they should decide which instrument are to be used for fast and which for slow.

Kindergarten: Fast and Slow, Lesson 1	
Outcome:	Preparation: internalize fast/slow through kinesthetic activities
	Practice: high/low chant through reading
INTRODUCTORY ACTIVITIES	
Sing known songs	"Little Sally Water" CSP: A • C sing and play game. • C sing song as if Sally is tired and sleepy, or awake.
Develop tuneful singing	Musical Greeting CSP: A • T sings a greeting to C using the pitches of the first phrase of "Snail Snail" (*s-m*) and C respond with an answer. • Repeat the activity but using different tempi.
Review known songs and concepts	"Teddy Bear" CSP: A • T hums the melody and C recognize the song. • C sing the song with motions.
CORE ACTIVITIES	
Teach a new song	"Bow Wow Wow" CSP: D • T sings song and C keep the beat. • T sings the song and does the motions with C. • T and C repeat many times. C sing the song and do the motions without a partner. Sometimes we need to teach a song over several lessons because of the words and game.

Prepare music literacy concepts Sing and move	"Engine, Engine, Number Nine" • C pat the beat and chant "Engine, Engine." • T: "Let's pretend to move like a tortoise." T shows tortoise icon, taps a slow beat, and chants. • T taps/plays (on hand drum) four beats as an intro and C tap a "tortoise" beat while chanting "Engine, Engine, Number Nine." • T: "Let's pretend to move like a hare." T shows hare icon, taps a fast beat, and chants "Engine, Engine Number Nine." • T taps/plays (on hand drum) four beats as an intro and C tap a "hare" beat while chanting "Engine, Engine Number Nine." Connections to books/literacy: • Calmenson, Stephanie. *Engine, Engine, Number Nine*. Scholastic, 1996.
Singing game/creative movement	"Ring Around the Rosie" CSP: A • C sing and play game.
Practice of music performance and literacy concepts Reading	"Bee, Bee, Bumble Bee" • C chant the rhyme. • C figure out how many beats are in each phrase. • C choose one flash card ("high" or "low") and place it in front of eight-beat iconic representation of that song on the board. • Class chants the rhyme while pointing to icons on the steady beat, using the appropriate voice (high/low). • Class repeats process with another known song or rhyme.
SUMMARY ACTIVITIES	
Review the new song Review lesson outcomes Folk song or folk song tales sung by T	"Bow Wow Wow" "Did You Feed My Cow?"

Kindergarten: Fast and Slow, Lesson 2	
Outcome:	Preparation: aural awareness of fast/slow repertoire Practice: high/low chant through writing

INTRODUCTORY ACTIVITIES	
Sing known songs	"Little Sally Water" CSP: A • C sing song and play game.
Develop tuneful singing	Musical Greeting CSP: A • T sings a greeting to C using the pitches of the first phrase of "Bounce High" (*s-l-s-m*) and C respond with an answer. • T repeats the activity but using different tempi.
Review known songs and concepts	"Hey, Hey, Look at Me" CSP: A • T sings the first verse as "Hey, hey, look at me. I am patting can you see?" • T sings song while acting out various motions; invites C to participate. • T and C perform motions and sing like a tortoise or hare. • T performs last verse as "marching." ➤ C continue marching in a circle as T sings the next song.
CORE ACTIVITIES	
Teach a new song	"Here Comes a Bluebird" CSP: A ➤ T sings song while C keep the beat. ➤ T sings and C perform the motions. ➤ T and C sing and play the game. Sometimes we need to teach a new song over several lessons to review the words and steps involved in playing the game. Connections to books/literacy: Deetlefs, Rene. *The Song of Six Birds*. Dutton Children's Books, 1999.

290

Develop music literacy concepts Tell me what you hear	"Frosty Weather" CSP: A • T taps picture of tortoise or hare for four beats while singing the first phrase of the song. This is the cue for the children to sing song. • C sing the song and march the steady beat at the appropriate tempo. • C sing and move slowly like the tortoise (on hands and knees) or quickly like the hare (walking quickly in place). (T will always provide the tempo for C.) • C sing and point to beat icons with a tortoise or hare placed in front of the beat chart. • T moves at a slow tempo while singing a known song or chant and asks, "Was I singing and moving like the tortoise or the hare?" • After C answer "tortoise," T says, "Let's all sing and move like the tortoise." • T repeats process, singing and moving at a fast tempo. • T: "Sing the song back to me, and show me with your body which animal you are." • T taps the beat on an instrument and after four beats C have to start singing. T: "Did I play the beat like a tortoise or hare?"
Singing game/creative movements	"Bow Wow Wow" CSP: D • T sings song and C keep the beat. • T sings the song and does the motions with one child. • Repeat many times with other C. • C inner-hear the song and play the game.

Practice of music performance and literacy skills Writing	"Bee, Bee, Bumble Bee" • C chant. • C figure out how many heartbeats are needed for each phrase and place hearts on board. • C chant and one child chooses a flash card ("high" or "low") and places in front of eight-beat iconic representation of that song to represent the way the song was sung. Class sings song while pointing to icons using a steady beat and the appropriate voice (high/low). • Class repeats process with other known chants.

SUMMARY ACTIVITIES

Review the new song Review lesson outcomes Folk song or folk song tales sung by T	• "Here Comes a Bluebird" • "Miss Mary Mack"

Kindergarten: Fast and Slow, Lesson 3	
Outcome:	Preparation: creating a visual representation for fast/slow Practice: high/low chant practice through improvisation
Introductory Activities	
Sing known songs	"Hey, Hey, Look at Me" CSP: A • T sings song while acting out motions; invites C to participate. • T and C perform motions and sing like a tortoise or hare.
Develop tuneful singing	"On the Mountain" CSP: A Voice Exploration • C sing song and play game. • T draws pictures of mountains and valleys on the board. • C point with fingers and follow the mountains and valleys with voice.

Review known songs and concepts	"Frosty Weather" CSP: A • C sing song and keep the beat. • C sing song and point to a beat chart. • T places "p" or "f" in front of beat chart and C sing song with correct dynamics.
CORE ACTIVITIES	
Teach a new song	"London Bridge" CSP: A • T sings song and C keep the beat motion. • T sings and C show the movements. • T and C sing and play the game. ➢ C continue marching to the beat while T chants the next rhyme.
Prepare knowledge of music literacy concepts Draw a picture	"Engine, Engine, Number Nine" • T gives the tempi and motions by saying, "Engine, engine, here we go" to the beat. C chant the rhyme. • T points to beat icons and taps the beats while C chant "Engine, Engine." • T chants with fast/slow voice and asks, "Was I using my tortoise or hare speed?" • "Show me with your body which animal I was using." • C chant and move like tortoise/hare. • T asks C how to create a picture of what they're hearing. From T's pre-made icons, C discover how many tortoise heartbeats or hare heartbeats they need to point to in order to complete chant. (C can draw heartbeats and draw a tortoise or hare in front of the beat chart.) • C point and chant. • T repeats process (if the "tortoise" tempo was used first, repeats with "hare" tempo). ➢ C continue the beat into the next song.
Singing game/creative movement	"Bow Wow Wow" CSP: D • T sings song and C keep the beat. • T sings the song and does the motions with one child. • C practice the motions, phrase by phrase, with a partner. • T and C sing and play the circle game.

293

Practice of music performance and literacy skills Improvisation	"Bee, Bee, Bumble Bee" • C chant the rhyme. • T asks individual C to decide whether to say the first phrase in a high or low voice. and the other C chant the remaining phrases in a speaking voice. T plays recording of music with contrasting tessitura. C respond by moving through space appropriately (standing on tiptoe = high, crawling on ground = low). • "The Aviary" and "The Elephant" from *Carnival of the Animals* by Camille Saint-Säens Connections to books/literacy: • *Carnival of the Animals*: Classical Music for Kids (Book and CD) by Barrie Carson Turner and Sue Williams, music by Camille Saint-Saëns. Henry Holt, 1999.
SUMMARY ACTIVITIES	
Review the new song Review lesson outcomes Folk song or folk song tales sung by T	• "London Bridge" • "This Old Man"

Kindergarten: Fast and Slow, Lesson 4	
Outcome:	Presentation: label the sound and show the words "fast" and "slow"
INTRODUCTORY ACTIVITIES	
Sing known songs	"Bow Wow Wow" CSP: D • C sing song and play game. • C inner-hear the song and play the game.
Develop tuneful singing	"On the Mountain" CSP: A • T: "Let's go visit our friend on the mountain. Look at how far away those mountains are. Let's climb them with our voices first." • T and C vocalize to pictures of various mountaintops. • C sing and play the game.

Review known songs and concepts	"Engine, Engine, Number Nine" • T gives the tempi and motions by saying "Engine, engine, here we go," and C perform the rhyme, • T points to beat icons and taps the beat while C chant "Engine, Engine, Number Nine." • Repeat process with another known rhyme.
CORE ACTIVITIES	
Teach a new song	"A la Rueda de San Miguel" CSP: D • T sings song while C keep the beat motion. • T sings and shows C the actions of the game. • T sings while C perform the game. • After approximately three cycles, C echo the first phrase of the chant ("a lo maduro, a lo maduro"). They will be "in charge" of this portion. • If it is accessible, after approximately three more cycles, C echo-phrase one of the songs ("a la rueda, rueda de San Miguel"). C will be in charge of this portion as well.
Presentation of music literacy concept Label what you hear	"Hey, Hey, Look at Me" CSP: A • T sings the first verse as "walking." • C sing song and suggest beat motions they may perform. • T: "In music, when we sing or speak like a tortoise we are using a slow tempo. When we sing or speak like a hare we are using a fast tempo." • C sing the song with a fast or slow tempo. ➢ C continue the beat at an appropriate tempo for the next song.
Singing game/creative movement	"Little Sally Water" • C sing and play game. Connections to books/literacy: • Wood, Audrey. *Silly Sally*. Harcourt, 1992.

295

Presentation of music literacy concept Record what you hear	"Oliver Twist" CSP: A • T and C chant and play game. • T: "In music, when we sing or chant like a tortoise we are singing with a slow tempo. Let's sing 'Oliver Twist' with a slow tempo"; C sing "Oliver Twist" with slow tempo. • T: "Instead of using a picture of a tortoise, we use the word 'Slow' in music. It is spelled S-L-O-W." T places the "slow" icon on the board. • T: "When we sing or chant like a hare we are singing with a fast tempo"; C sing "Oliver Twist" with a fast tempo. • T: "Instead of using a picture of a hare, we use the word 'Fast' in music. It is spelled F-A-S-T." T places the "fast" icon on the board.
SUMMARY ACTIVITIES	
Review the new song Review lesson outcomes Folk songs or folk song tales sung by T	• "A la Rueda de San Miguel" • "The Animals Went in Two by Two"

Kindergarten: Fast and Slow, Lesson 5	
Outcome:	Practice of fast and slow
INTRODUCTORY ACTIVITIES	
Sing known songs	"Hey, Hey, Look at Me" CSP: A • T sings song while acting out motions; invites C to participate. • C sing and perform motions with a fast or slow tempo.
Develop tuneful singing	"On the Mountain" CSP: A • "Let's go visit our friend on the mountain. Look at how far away those mountains are. Let's climb them with our voices first." • T and C vocalize to pictures of various mountaintops. • C point with fingers and follow mountains and valleys with voice.

Review known songs and concepts	"Engine, Engine, Number Nine" • T gives the tempi and motions by saying, "Engine, engine, here we go" to a steady beat; C chant. • T points to beat icons and taps four beats; C chant "Engine, Engine." • T chants with fast/slow voice and asks, "Was I using my fast or slow voice?" • C answer appropriately. • T: "Show me with your body which voice I was using." • T repeats process with another known rhyme.
CORE ACTIVITIES	
Teach a new song	"Here We Go 'Round the Mulberry Bush" and/or "A la Rueda de San Miguel" CSP: F • T sings song; C keep the beat motion. • T sings and shows C the motions.
Practice of music performance and literacy skills	"Bee, Bee, Bumble Bee" • T: "In music, when we sing or chant like a tortoise it is called s-l-o-w. Let's chant with a slow tempo." C chant "Bee, Bee" with slow tempo. • T: "Instead of using a picture of a snail, we use the word 'slow' in music. It is spelled S-L-O-W." T places the "slow" icon on the board. • T: "When we sing or chant like a hare it is called singing with f-a-s-t tempo. Let's go fast this time!" C chant "Bee, Bee" with fast tempo. • T: "Instead of using a picture of a hare, we use the word 'fast' in music. It is spelled F-A-S-T." T places the "fast" icon on the board. Connections to books/literacy: • Brennan-Nelson, Denise. *Buzzy the Bumblebee*. Sleeping Bear Press, 1999. • Bentley, Dawn. *Buzz-Buzz, Busy Bees*. Simon & Schuster, 2004.
Creative movement	"Bow Wow Wow" CSP: D • T sings song and C keep the beat. • T sings the songs and does the motions with one child. • Class repeats many times.

297

Practice of music performance and literacy skills	"I Climbed up the Apple Tree" • T gives the tempi and motions by saying, "I Climbed up the Apple Tree, one, two, here we go" to a steady beat; C chant. • T: "How many beats did we tap in each phrase?" C: "Four." • T points to beat icons and taps four beats; C chant "I Climbed up the Apple Tree." • T chants with fast/slow voice and asks, "Was I using my fast or slow voice?" Individual C must decide what word to put in front of beat chart. • T: "Show me with your body which voice I was using." • Child puts the word fast or slow in front of beat chart and C sing and point. • T sings "Pages Train" for C, and they must move with a fast or slow beat depending on the tempo. T changes the tempo after each performance.
SUMMARY ACTIVITIES	
Review the new song Review lesson outcomes Folk songs or folk song tales sung by T	• "Here We Go 'Round the Mulberry Bush" • "Old Roger Is Dead"

Unit 6: Lesson Plans for Teaching High and Low Melody

Unit 6

Prepare: High/Low Involving Melody				Practice: Fast/Slow			
			Song Repertoire				
Lesson	Known Songs	Songs/ Activities for Developing Tuneful Singing	Reviewing Song/Chant Repertoire	Teach a New Song/Chant	Preparing New Concept: High/ Low Involving Melody	Creative Movement	Practicing Known Concept: Fast/Slow
Lesson 1	"Here We Go 'Round the Mulberry Bush"	Vocal Exploration	"I Climbed up the Apple Tree"	"¿Quién Es Esa Gente?"	"Snail, Snail"	"Firefly" (new song and game)	"Hey, Hey, Look at Me"
Lesson 2	"Rain, Rain"	Vocal Exploration	"Seesaw"	"¿Quién Es Esa Gente?"	"Snail, Snail"	"Here Comes a Bluebird"	"Bee, Bee, Bumble Bee"
Lesson 3	"Seesaw" and "¿Quién Es Esa Gente?"	Naming Song	"Hunt the Slipper"	"Oats, Peas, Beans, and Barley Grow"	"Snail, Snail"	""Here Comes a Bluebird"	"On the Mountain"
Lesson	Known Songs	Songs/ Activities for Developing Tuneful Singing	Reviewing Song/Chant Repertoire	Teach a New Song/Chant	Presenting New Concept: High/ Low Involving Melody	Creative Movement	Presenting New Concept: High/ Low Involving Melody
Lesson 4	"Teddy Bear" and "Oats, Peas, Beans, and Barley Grow"	Naming Song	"Queen, Queen Caroline"	"A Sailor Went to Sea"	"Snail, Snail"	"Thread Follows the Needle"	"Rain, Rain"
Lesson 5	"A Sailor Went to Sea" and "Doggie, Doggie"	Naming Song	"Seesaw"	"Touch Your Shoulders"	"Snail, Snail"	"Oats, Peas, Beans, and Barley Grow"	"Rain, Rain"

Musical Skill Development

Musical Skill	Activity 1	Activity 2	Activity 3
Reading	C read the word "high" or "low" in front of beat icons and chant the rhyme following high and low. "Rain, Rain"	C point and touch icons on board representing the high and low sounds in a known song containing two pitches "Seesaw"	C point to the "rainbow" (drawing the phrase in the air) while singing a known song "Rain, Rain"
Writing	C place visuals on board representing the beat as they are singing using their high voice or low voice.	C identify how another child chanted a rhyme by placing the word "high" or "low" in front of a beat chart.	C place visuals on the board representing the high sounds and low sounds in a piece of music containing two pitches. "Seesaw"
Improvisation and composition	C improvise a motion that will demonstrate the beat of a known or unknown song using a high voice or a low voice.	C will improvise a movement showing high and low in a known song with two pitches "Seesaw"	C sing different text to known s-m songs.
Listening	T plays recorded examples of music in various meters, 2/4 or 6/8, and asks C to move to the beat, while walking, skipping, or tapping the beat.	C listen to teacher sing or hum "Ring Around the Rosie" and fall to the ground on the last sound.	T reads a book to C, using different voices such as whispering, calling, singing using only s-m, and speaking. "Brown Bear, Brown Bear"
Part work	One half of class keeps the beat and other half sings a known s-m song "Snail, Snail"	T sings a known song, and class keeps the beat on their lap. "Seesaw"	T sings a phrase of a song, and C sing next phrase. "Queen, Queen Caroline"

Memory	C identify a known song that the T hums or plays on recorder.	C perform a known song or chant.	C identify songs from *s-m* motifs.
Inner Hearing	C sing with a bird or bear voice by following the mouth of two puppets. When mouth is open, they sing in high voice for bird, low for bear. When mouth is closed, they sing inside the head.	C whisper a known song while keeping the beat. "Good Night"	T turns out the lights and C sing in their head, singing out loud when the lights come on for *s-m* songs.
Form	C walk in a circle in one direction for one phrase of a song, and then walk in the opposite direction for next phrase.	C march in place for one section of a song, and then step into the circle for next section.	C perform different movements for *s-m* songs in the repertoire.
Instruments	T accompanies class using a steady beat on a drum or other unpitched instrument while class sings a song with high and low pitches "Rain, Rain"	T plays various high and low pitches on an instrument (piano, recorder, violin, trumpet, etc.), and C identify it as a high pitch or low pitch. C figure out how to play *s-m* songs on the xylophone.	C categorize barred instruments as high (glockenspiels and soprano xylophones) or low (alto and bass xylophones).

Kindergarten: High and Low Melody, Lesson 1	
Outcome:	Preparation: internalizing high and low pitches through kinesthetic activities
	Practice: fast and slow and reading
INTRODUCTORY ACTIVITIES	
Sing known songs	"Here We Go 'Round the Mulberry Bush"
	CSP: F
	• T and C sing the song and play the game.
	• C suggest other beat motions they may perform while singing the song.
Develop tuneful singing	Vocal Exploration
	• T and C vocalize mimicking a slide whistle.
	• T sings "Hello children" using *s-m* and moving a puppet to the melodic contour. T asks C to point to the puppet as the question is sung again.
	• T shows C how to respond pretending their hands are puppets and moving to the contour of the response.
	• T sings "How are you today?" with *s-m* and using puppet.
	• C respond "We are fine today" using the same singing pattern as the teacher and moving their hands as puppets to the contour of the song.
Review known songs and concepts	"I Climbed up the Apple Tree"
	• C chant and play game.
	• T presents flash cards with the words "fast" and "slow."
	• C choose and perform the chant accordingly.
	• T presents flash cards with the words "high" and "low."
	• C choose and perform a combination of fast/slow and high/low.
CORE ACTIVITIES	
Teach a new song	"*¿Quién Es Esa Gente?*"
	CSP: A
	• T sings song and C keep beat.
	• T: "Have you ever tried to go to sleep but it was sooooo noisy in your house that you just COULDN'T do it? Well that's what this song is about!"
	• C pretend to go to sleep while T sings and plays the hand drum to the beat.
	• T chooses C to be "Sleepers" and "Walkers."
	• "Walkers" may choose instruments to play to the beat while the remaining C sleep.
	• "Walkers" switch with "Sleepers"; all C walk to the beat while T sings.

Prepare music literacy concepts Sing and move	"Snail, Snail" CSP: A • T and C play game. • T and C discover the form of the song. T sings each phrase and C discover if the second phrase was the same or different. • T sings and places the contour of the first phrase on her body (shoulders = high; waist = low). • C sing and copy. • T sings song, points to icons representing the melodic contour of the pitches of the first phrase on the board, and then keeps the beat on body while singing second phrase. • T sings and points to melodic contour of first phrase in the air and keeps the beat on body while singing second phrase. • C sing and copy.
Singing game/ creative movement	"Firefly" (new song and game) CSP: A • T sings song and C keep the beat. • C pretend they are fireflies, performing scarf motions while the T sings the song or plays recording. (See Elizabeth Mitchell's recording entitled *Tsuki*.) Connections to books/literacy: • Carle, Eric. *The Very Busy Spider*. Philomel Books, 1984.
Practice of music performance and music literacy skills Reading	"Hey, Hey, Look at Me" CSP: A • C sing song with phrase motions. • C figure out the form of the song—if the phrases are the same or different. • C identify how many beats are in each phrase. • C sing and point to the beat icons. • T places the word "fast" or "slow" in front of the beat icons and C have to sing. • C select an unpitched percussion instrument to keep the beat while singing in a fast or slow tempo. • C create body motions that match the fast or slow tempo.
SUMMARY ACTIVITIES	
Review the new song Review lesson outcomes	• "¿Quién Es Esa Gente?"
Folk song or folk song tales sung by T	• "The Tailor and the Mouse"

Kindergarten: High and Low Melody, Lesson 2	
Outcome:	Preparation: aural analysis of melodies containing high and low pitches Practice: fast and slow and writing
INTRODUCTORY ACTIVITIES	
Sing known songs	"Rain, Rain" CSP: A • T sings while C play game ("Sleepers" and "Walkers"). • All C walk while T sings the song.
Develop tuneful singing	Vocal Exploration • T and C pretend to be an owl, making a high-pitched "hoooo" sound. • C copy T, making their "hoooo" progressively higher each time. • T makes an owl sound, sliding down and up an octave. • T repeats at a perfect fifth and then a minor third (in the key of the next song).
Review known songs and concepts	"Seesaw" CSP: A • T sings song and shows phrases in the air. • C trace the phrases on the board. • C identify whether the phrases are the same or different. • T places an apple icon in front of the first phrase on board and banana icon in front of the second phrase. • C place "fast" and "slow" icons in front of the phrases and perform accordingly. • T may choose a child to perform the song either fast or slow.
CORE ACTIVITIES	
Teach a new song	"¿Quién Es Esa Gente?" CSP: A • T sings song and C keep the beat motion. • T sings song and C perform game movements, made up by T, in a circle. Connections to books/literacy: • Calmenson, Stephanie. *Engine, Engine, Number Nine*. Scholastic, 1996. • Orleans, Ilo. *Animal Orchestra*. A Golden Book, 1958 • Na, Il Sung. *A Book of Sleep*. Knopf, 2007.

Prepare knowledge of music literacy skills Tell me what you hear	"Snail, Snail" CSP: A • C sing and show the phrases in the air. • C determine the form of the song (T: "Are phrase 1 and phrase 2 the same or different?"). • T and C sing and point to shoulders (high) and waist (low) for phrase 1 and perform a beat motion for phrase 2. • T hums the first two pitches of phrase 1 before asking each of these questions: • T: "How many notes did you hear?" (Two) • T: "Can you describe the two notes?" (One is high and one is low) • T sings the first two pitches with the words "high" and "low." • T repeats for the pitches on beats 3 and 4. • T: "Let's sing the first phrase of 'Snail, Snail' using the words 'high' and 'low'." • C place "high" on the shoulders and "low" on the waist and sing phrase 2 using a beat motion. Conceptual Exercise: • T should play notes on the piano (upper and lower) at first separated by an octave, then a fifth, and then a minor third; C must indicate with their arms the high and low notes.
Singing game/ creative movement	"Here Comes a Bluebird" CSP: A • C sing and play game.
Practice music performance and music literacy skills Writing	"Bee, Bee, Bumble Bee" • C chant the rhyme while keeping a steady beat. • C figure out how many heartbeats are needed for each phrase and place hearts on board. • One child points to beat icon chart on the board. • C chant in either slow or fast tempo. • Child chooses one flash card ("fast" or "slow") and places it in front of eight-beat iconic representation of the chant. Class chants while pointing to icons using a steady beat and appropriate tempo.
	SUMMARY ACTIVITIES
Review the new song Review lesson outcomes Folk song or folk song tales sung by T	• "¿Quién Es Esa Gente?" • "Oats, Peas, Beans, and Barley Grow"

305

Kindergarten: High and Low Melody, Lesson 3	
Outcome:	Preparation: creating a representation of high and low in a melody
	Practice: fast and slow and improvisation
INTRODUCTORY ACTIVITIES	
Sing known songs	"¿Quién Es Esa Gente?" and "Seesaw"
	CSP: A
	• T sings while C play game.
	• All C walk the beat while T sings the song.
Develop tuneful singing	Naming Song
	CSP: A
	• T sings "Sing me your name" (*s ml s m*) while rolling a ball to a child.
	• Child who receives the ball responds, "My name is _____" using the same singing pattern as T.
	• Class responds with "Her [His] name is _____."
	• T goes around the room asking C to sing their names.
	• T changes the dynamic of the "call" to loud, multiple times; child responds loudly and class responds loudly.
	• T changes the dynamic of the "call" to soft multiple times; child responds softly and class responds softly.
Review known songs and concepts	"Hunt the Slipper"
	CSP: A
	• C sing with beat motions.
	• C point to phrase 1 on board (where the melodic contour is outlined by T) and keep beat motions for remainder of song.
	• C choose at what tempo the songs should be sung.
	• C may volunteer to sing the song alone at either a fast or slow tempo.
CORE ACTIVITIES	
Teach a new song	"Oats, Peas, Beans, and Barley Grow"
	CSP: F#
	• T sings song and C keep the beat.
	• T sings while C act out the motions of the song.
	Connections to books/literacy:
	• Ehlert, Lois. *Eating the Alphabet: Fruits & Vegetables from A to Z*. Harcourt Books, 1989.

Prepare knowledge of music literacy concepts Draw a picture	"Snail, Snail" CSP: A • C sing the song. • Review kinesthetic and aural awareness activities. • T gives C manipulatives to create a representation of the melodic contour of phrase 1 (T: "Show me what phrase 1 looks like"). • C sing and point to their representation. • One child places snails high and low on board. • C sing and point at the representation on the board and make corrections if necessary.
Singing game/creative movement	"Here Comes a Bluebird" CSP: A • C sing and play game.
Practice of performance and music literacy skills	"On the Mountain" CSP: A • C sing song while keeping a steady beat. • C sing song but create new motions to demonstrate the tempo at which they are singing. (T: "Use your bodies as another way to show fast/slow.") • T plays recordings of music (*Flight of the Bumblebee*, *Trois Gymnopedies*, and "The Swan" from *Carnival of the Animals*) with contrasting tempi. • C respond to the music by moving through space appropriately.
SUMMARY ACTIVITIES	
Review the new song Review lesson outcomes Folk song or folk song tales sung by T	• "Oats, Peas, Beans, and Barley Grow" • "Old Mister Rabbit"

Kindergarten: High and Low Melody, Lesson 4	
Outcome:	Presentation: presenting the concept of high and low and the words "high" and "low."
INTRODUCTORY ACTIVITIES	
Sing known songs	"Oats, Peas, Beans, and Barley Grow" and/or "Teddy Bear" CSP: A • T and C sing the song. • C sing the song and act out the motions.

Develop tuneful singing	Naming Song CSP: A • T uses a puppet and sings "Sing me your name" (*s ml s m*) to a child. • Child responds with "My name is _____" using the same singing pattern as T. • Class responds with "Her [His] name is _____." • T goes around the room asking C to sing their names. • T changes the dynamic of the "call" to loud, multiple times; child responds loudly and class responds loudly. • T changes the dynamic of the "call" to soft multiple times; child responds softly and class responds softly. • C may ask the puppet what her name is, and the puppet replies, "My name is Caroline." ➢ T: "Yes, boys and girls, you guessed right, this is Her Highness, Queen Caroline. . . ."
Review known songs and concepts	"Queen, Queen Caroline" • C perform the chant with the actions. • C performs the chant alone. • C respond appropriately by creating a beat motion in the tempo that T gives. ➢ T: "As it happens with queens sometimes, Caroline got very bored and decided she should like to discover a new land, just like good queens ought to do. So she sent her sailors off to sea to see what they could see. . . ."
CORE ACTIVITIES	
Teach a new song	"A Sailor Went to Sea" CSP: G • T sings and demonstrates the motions while C keep the beat. • T sings verse 1 again and C copy the motions. • T sings the remaining verses and C perform the motions. Connections to books/literacy: • Carle, Eric. *Mister Seahorse*. Philomel Books, 2004.
Presentation Label what you hear	"Snail, Snail" CSP: A • T and C sing and play the game. • Review kinesthetic, aural, and visual awareness activities. • T: "In music, a phrase in a song is made up of notes that we call pitches. Pitches can be high or low, and this creates the shape of a melody or melodic contour. Let's sing the first phrase of 'Snail, Snail' with the words 'high' and 'low'." • T hums the first phrase of "Snail Snail" and C sing back with words high and low. Repeat process for other songs that use the same melodic pattern. • T and C sing and play the game.

Singing game/ creative movement	"Thread Follows the Needle" CSP: A • T and C sing and play the game. • C sing and pat the beat. ➢ C continue the beat while T sings the next song.
Presentation Record what you hear	"Rain, Rain" CSP: A • T and C sing "Rain, Rain." • C sing phrase 1 with high and low hand motions and perform beat motions for phrase 2. • C sing phrase 1 with the words "high" and "low" and keep beat motions for phrase 2. • C arrange discs in the shape of the melodic contour of the song. • T draws this on board and introduces the words "high pitch," "low pitch," and "melodic contour." C identify the high pitches and low pitches. • T and C sing song and point to representations.
SUMMARY ACTIVITIES	
Review the new song Review lesson outcomes Folk song or folk song tales sung by T	"A Sailor Went to Sea" "Mister Frog Went a-Courtin'"

Kindergarten: High and Low Melody, Lesson 5	
Outcome:	Practice of high and low in a melody
INTRODUCTORY ACTIVITIES	
Sing known songs	"A Sailor Went to Sea" and/or "Doggie, Doggie" CSP: A • C sing with movements. • C suggest other body parts that may be substituted in the song.

Develop tuneful singing	Naming Song CSP: A • T sings "Sing me your name" (*s ml s m*) while rolling a ball to a student. • C who receives the ball responds, "My name is _____," using the same singing pattern as T. • Class responds with "Her [His] name is _____." • T goes around the room asking S to sing their names. • In the same tonal pattern, T sings, "What's your favorite playground toy?" to one child. • Child responds with "Mine is the _____." • The class echoes, "Hers [His] is the _____." • C ask T the same question. ➤ T replies "Mine is the seesaw."
Review known songs and concepts	"Seesaw" CSP: A • C sing with beat motions. • C point to phrase 1 on board (where T has incorrectly placed the melodic contour). • T: "Which pitches should be high and which pitches should be low?" • C rearrange the icons on the board accordingly. • C sing the song and keep the beat on their body. ➤ C continue the beat into the next song.
	CORE ACTIVITIES
Teach a new song	"Touch Your Shoulders" CSP: A • T sings song and C keep the beat. • C stand and put out their hands; T sings songs and taps each child's hand with a button. • Class repeats, but T has one child keep the beat on a drum. • T sings while C pass the button to the beat of the drum. Connection to books/literacy: • Powell, Richard. *Guess Who's Hiding!* Baron's Educational Series, 2001.

310

Practice of performance and music literacy skills	"Snail, Snail" CSP: A • C sing and play game. • C sing phrase 1 using the words "high" and "low" and keep beat for phrase 2. • T gives one child four snails; child places snails high and low on board. • T: "Where are the music pitches? Describe the music contour of the song." (high, low, high, low)
Creative movement	"Oats, Peas, Beans, and Barley Grow" CSP: A • T sings song and C keep the beat motion. • T sings song and C perform actions in circle created by T. ➤ C continue the beat into the next song.
Practice of performance and music literacy skills	"Rain, Rain" CSP: A • T and C sing "Rain, Rain". • C determine how many phrases are in the song. • C draw phrases in the air while T draws phrase marks on the board. • C determine if the phrases are the same or different. • C place an apple or banana icon in front of each phrase. • C sing phrase 1 with high and low hand motions and keep beat motions for phrase 2. • T hums phrase 1 and asks C to arrange discs to create the melodic contour of phrase 1. • C identify the pitches and music contour. • C practice spelling the words "high" and "low, melody and contour" • C sing "Rain, Rain."
SUMMARY ACTIVITIES	
Review the new song Review lesson outcomes Folk song or folk song tales sung by T	• "Touch Your Shoulders" • "When I First Came to This Land"

311

Unit 7: Lesson Plans for Teaching Rhythm

Unit 7

Prepare: Rhythm				Practice: High/Low			
				Song Repertoire			
Lesson	Known Songs	Songs/Activities for Developing Tuneful Singing	Reviewing Song/Chant Repertoire	Teach a New Song/Chant	Preparing New Concept: Rhythm	Creative Movement	Practicing Known Concept: High/Low
Lesson 1	"Hey, Hey, Look at Me" and "Touch Your Shoulders"	Greeting Activity using *l s m* pitches	"Bee, Bee, Bumble Bee"	"Two, Four, Six, Eight?"	"Rain, Rain"	"We Are Dancing In the Forest"	"Snail, Snail"
Lesson 2	"Bee, Bee, Bumble Bee" and "Two, Four, Six, Eight"	Greeting Activity using *l s m* pitches	"Hey, Hey, Look at Me"	"Caracol Col Col"	"Rain, Rain"	"Hop Old Squirrel"	"Snail, Snail"
Lesson 3	"Little Sally Water"	"Bee, Bee, Bumble Bee"	"Seesaw"	"Caracol Col Col"	"Rain, Rain"	"All Around the Buttercup"	"Snail, Snail"
Lesson	Known Songs	Songs/Activities for Developing Tuneful Singing	Reviewing Song/Chant Repertoire	Teach a New Song/Chant	Presenting New Concept: Rhythm	Creative Movement	Presenting New Concept: Rhythm
Lesson 4	"Teddy Bear" and "Caracol Col Col"	"Bee, Bee, Bumble Bee"	"We Are Dancing in the Forest"	"Looby Loo"	"Rain, Rain"	"Just from the Kitchen"	"Seesaw"
Lesson 5	"Little Sally Water" and "Looby Loo"	"Bee, Bee, Bumble Bee"	"Teddy Bear"	"Frog in the Meadow"	"Rain, Rain"	"Looby Loo"	"All Around the Buttercup"

Musical Skill Development

Musical Skill	Activity 1	Activity 2	Activity 3	Activity 4
Reading	One child taps iconic representations of the rhythm while others perform the beat with (a) body percussion or (b) unpitched percussion instruments.	C tap iconic representations of the rhythm while singing known songs; (a) T taps on the classroom board or on worksheets, or (b) T has a selected child play the representation on an unpitched percussion instrument while singing.	C identify known songs from rhythmic representations on the board.	
Writing	T sings and performs beat or rhythm. C place the icons or word "beat" or "rhythm" on the board.	T sings or plays a known song on the piano or recorder and individual C write or place the beats on the board while the class is singing.	C write the rhythm of a known eight-beat song or chant with icons.	One child sings or plays a known song and the class writes or places the beats on the board while singing.
Improvisation and composition	C improvise movements to the beat.	One child improvises a steady beat movement on different parts of the body to known and unknown songs; other C imitate.	C take turns improvising four beat rhythm patterns on a drum while the other C keep the beat.	C decide where to place the long and short sounds on their body while performing a known song. For example, the "short" sounds would be clapped, and the "long" sounds would be patted.
Listening	T sings known songs and C clap back the rhythm.	One child sings known songs and the class claps back the rhythm.	C listen to Mvt 2 Symphony No. 7 Op. 92 Ludwig van Beethoven (1770–1827) and/or Symphony No. 94 II Andante Franz Joseph Haydn (1732–1809)	

(Continued)

Part work	T or a child sings known songs while C play the beat on instruments and clap the rhythm; (a) in small groups, or (b) individually.	C sing a known song while patting the heartbeat on different parts of their bodies, changing on the T cue to rhythm.	C march to the beat while singing and clapping the rhythm.	C do responsorial singing.
Memory	C sing or say known songs or chants with "long" and "short" instead of the words.	C identify songs from T's clapping of the rhythmic motif.		
Inner hearing	While T is tapping the rhythm beats on the board or worksheets, C sing the song in their heads, changing on T cue.	T sings songs on loo while C tap the rhythm on their lap or on instruments and identify the song.	C clap the rhythm of known songs while inner-hearing the melody.	
Form	C identify the form of a song and display the form with shapes.	C draw phrases on the board and identity the form as same of different.		
Instruments	C will play the steady beat on claves or other unpitched percussion instrument while T claps the rhythm.	C tap the rhythm or known songs on unpitched percussion instruments.		

Kindergarten: Rhythm, Lesson 1	
Outcome:	Preparation: internalizing rhythm through kinesthetic activities Practice: reading high/low melody
INTRODUCTORY ACTIVITIES	
Sing known songs	"Hey, Hey, Look at Me" and "Touch Your Shoulders" CSP: A • C sing song perform the motions. • C suggest other body parts they may incorporate into the song. • C sing and perform the beat.
Develop tuneful singing	Greeting Activity CSP: A • T sings a greeting to C using the pitches *la, so,* and *mi.* • T sings the greeting while quietly playing the rhythm of the words on a hand drum. • C must sing *and* clap the rhythm of their response to T.
Review known songs and concepts	"Bee, Bee, Bumble Bee" • C chant "Bee, Bee" with beat motions. • T chants phrase 1 and asks, "How many beats did we tap?" (four) • C chant and individuals place the correct number of heart icons on the board to represent what they heard. • Repeat with all phrases. • T: "Let's chant 'Bee, Bee' again and point to the beat." • C improvise beat motions on their body to keep beat. • C use classroom percussion instruments to keep the beat. Connections to books/literacy: • Fleming, Denise. *Beetle Bop.* Harcourt, 2007. • Brennan-Nelson, Denise. *Buzzy the Bumblebee.* Sleeping Bear Press, 2003. • Bentley, Dawn. *Buzz-Buzz, Busy Bees.* Simon & Schuster, 2004. • Carter, David A. *In and Out.* Intervisual Books, 1993. • Fleming, Denise. *In the Tall, Tall Grass.* Henry Holt, 1991. • Twinn, M. *Old MacDonald Had a Farm.* Childs Play (International), 1975. • Kohl, Michael, Daniel Weiner, and Bari Weissman. *There Was an Old Woman Who Swallowed a Fly.* Weekly Reader Books, 1981.

315

CORE ACTIVITIES	
Teach a new song	"Two, Four, Six, Eight" CSP: D • T sings song and C keep the beat. • T sings song and C march to the beat. • C stand and put out their hands; T sings songs and taps each child's hand with a button. • Repeat but have one child keep the beat on a drum. • T sings while C pass the button to the beat of the drum. • C sing and T demonstrates the game.
Prepare knowledge of music literacy concepts Sing and move	"Rain, Rain" CSP: A • C sing and keep the beat. • T sings and claps the rhythm. • C identify what T is doing. • T shows icon of hands clapping. • C sing and "clap the way the words go." Depending on the age of the C, T may choose to simply show an icon for hands clapping or can show icons representing the sounds on the beat. • C sing the song while T points to an iconic representation of the rhythm. • C sing the song and point to the iconic representation of the rhythm. • T selects several C to come to the board and point to the icons of the first phrase while the class is singing "Rain, Rain." • C sing the song while clapping the rhythm in their hands. (T may say, "Put the words of the song in your hands" or "Clap the way the words go.") • T presents a heart icon representing the beat. • When T points at the heart, C perform the beat. If T points at the clapping hands, C perform the rhythm.
Singing game/creative movement	"We Are Dancing in the Forest" CSP: A • T sings songs and C keep the beat. • T selects one child to play the beat on an instrument. • C sing and play the game. Connections to books/literacy: • Martin Jr., Bill. *Panda Bear, Panda Bear, What Do You See?* Henry Holt, 2003. • Williams, Sue. *I Went Walking*. Red Wagon Books/Harcourt, 1989.

316

Practice of music performance and music literacy skills Reading	"Snail, Snail" CSP: A • C sing and play game. • C sing phrase 1 on neutral syllables and identify that there are two pitches. • C label the two pitches as "high" and "low." • C sing phrase 1 using the words "high" and "low" and sing and "clap the way the words go" for phrase 2. • T places melodic contour flash cards of "Snail, Snail" on the board. • C sing the contour with "high" and "low." • T places flash cards with the melodic contour of other known songs on the board. • C sing the contour with "high" and "low" and identify the name of the song. • T asks C to move their bodies to match the shape of the melody (crouch/stand, arms high/low, shoulders/waist, etc.).
SUMMARY ACTIVITIES	
Review the new song Review lesson outcomes	• "Two, Four, Six, Eight"
Folk song or folk song tales sung by T	• "Bingo"

Kindergarten: Rhythm, Lesson 2	
Outcome:	Preparation: aural analysis of sounds on a beat Practice: high/low melody and writing
INTRODUCTORY ACTIVITIES	
Sing known songs	"Two, Four, Six, Eight" and "Bee, Bee, Bumble Bee" • C sing and play the game. • C chant and "clap the way the words go."
Develop tuneful singing	Greeting Activity CSP: A • T sings a greeting to C using the pitches *la, so,* and *mi.* • Repeat the activity but C must sing *and* clap the rhythm of the response. • The class pats the beat while T sings and claps the question to one child (who will sing and clap her or his response).

Review known songs and concepts	"Hey, Hey, Look at Me" CSP: A • C sing song and keep the beat. • T sings song and plays the rhythm on drum. • C sing song and clap the way the words go. • T sings the last verse with "I am jumping can you see. . . ." Connections to books/literacy: • Lively, Penelope. *One, Two, Three, Jump!* Puffin Books, 1998.
CORE ACTIVITIES	
Teach a new song	"Caracol Col Col" CSP: F# • T sings song and C keep the beat. • T: "In America we sing our song 'Snail, Snail'. Well, in Mexico little children also have a song about a snail, and it's called 'Caracol Col Col'." • T sings song and C perform the winding motion. • C sing the first phrase alone ("Caracol col col") and trace the path of the snail on their hand. • C sing phrase 1, T sings the remaining while patting the beat. ➤ C continue the beat into the next song.
Develop knowledge of music literacy concepts Tell me what you hear	"Rain, Rain" CSP: A • C sing song and keep the beat. • C sing song and clap the way the words go. • T sings the song and keeps the beat or taps the words. C must decide if the T kept the beat or the way the words go. Note: This activity should take place using a hand drum. Additionally, C should *not* be able to see if T is tapping. T accomplishes this by having C hide their eyes, or perform the activity hiding his or her hands. T should remember to use the phrase "clap the way the words go" instead of rhythm. More challenging activity: • T: "Let's sing 'Rain, Rain' and put the words in our hands." • C sing the song on a neutral syllable and continuing to clap the words. • T: "Let's sing the first phrase of 'Rain, Rain' again but tap the beat." • T: "How many beats did we tap?" (four) T repeats the phrase singing on a neutral syllable while tapping beat.

318

	• T: "Did all of the beats have the same amount of sounds?" (no)
	• T: "Which beat had the most sounds?" (beat three) (Here T may wish to describe the sounds as long and short; if that's the case, proceed with the next activities.)
	• T: "How could we describe these different sounds?" (Long and short)
	• T: "Let's sing 'Rain, Rain' and put the words in our hands."
	• T: "Let's sing the first phrase of 'Rain, Rain' with the words 'long' and 'short' while we tap the words in our hands."
	➢ C inner-hear the song and clap the rhythm of the words while T sings the next song.
	An alternate suggestion:
	• C sing song and keep the beat.
	• T sings and claps the words, and C echo. (Note: C at this point should not be made conscious that they are clapping the words; try not to allow C to see your hands.)
	• T sings and plays the beat on a hand drum.
	• T: "Was I playing with the beat or not-the-beat?" (Beat)
	• T sings and plays the rhythm on a hand drum.
	• T: "Was I playing with the beat or not-the-beat?" (Not the beat)
	• T sings and plays the rhythm on a hand drum.
	• T: "If I wasn't playing the beat, then what was I playing?" (The words)
	• C sing and clap the words.
	• T introduces icons (heart for beat, clapping hands for rhythm).
	• C sing while performing either the beat or rhythm; they aurally identify which by pointing/tapping the appropriate icon.
Singing game/creative movement	"Hop Old Squirrel"
	CSP: A
	• T sings and C listen while keeping the steady beat.
	• C sing and play the game.
	• C suggest other steady beat motions they could perform while singing (snap, chop, tap, flick, etc.).
	➢ T ends the song with "Walk old squirrel . . ." as he or she winds up the circle in preparation for the next song.

Practice of music performance and music literacy skills Writing	"Snail, Snail" CSP: A • T: "Let's sing 'Snail, Snail' and make the shape of the melody with our bodies." • C sing the song and identify the high and low sounds. • C sing the first phrase with "high" and "low." • T places multiple icons on the board and asks one child to make the icons into the melodic contour of the song. • C sing phrase 1 using the words "high" and "low" while pointing, and sing phrase 2 with text and beat motions. • Repeat with the first phrases of "Teddy Bear," "Rain, Rain," "Hunt the Slipper," and "Doggie, Doggie." • Repeat process but each child has a set of icons to build the phrases.
SUMMARY ACTIVITIES	
Review the new song Review lesson outcomes Folk song or folk song tales sung by T	• "Caracol Col Col" • "Scotland's Burning"

Kindergarten: Rhythm, Lesson 3	
Outcome:	Preparation: creating a visual representation of the rhythm of a melody
	Practice: improvisation of high/low melody
INTRODUCTORY ACTIVITIES	
Sing known songs	"Little Sally Water" CSP: A • C sing song and play the game. • C sing and march to the beat.
Develop tuneful singing	"Bee, Bee, Bumble Bee" • T chants "Bee, Bee" as C march to beat. • T chants a buzzing sound using the rhythm of "Bee, Bee." • C imitate the buzzing sound. • T lip-trills a phrase of "Bee, Bee" and C imitate. • C march to the beat and "buzz" and clap the words.

Review known songs and concepts	"Seesaw" CSP: A • C sing "Seesaw" and "put the words in their hands." • C sing on "loo" and continue to clap the words. • C inner-hear the melody and clap the words. • T: "Let's sing the first phrase of 'Seesaw' again but tap the beat." • T: "How many beats did we tap?" (four) T repeats phrase. • T: "Did all of the beats have the same amount of sounds?" (no) • T: "Which beat had the most sounds?" (beat three) • T: "How could we describe these sounds?" ("Long" and "short") • T: "Let's sing the first phrase of 'Seesaw' with the words 'long' and 'short' while we tap the words in our hands." • C sing the song and pretend be on a seesaw with a partner (moving up and down to the beat).
CORE ACTIVITIES	
Teach a new song	"Caracol Col Col" CSP: F# • T sings song and C continue moving up and down. • C move in a circle while T sings the song. • T reminds C they are "in charge" of singing the first phrase ("Caracol col col"). • T sings phrase 2 and C echo. • C will be in charge of singing phrases 1 and 2. • T and C sing and play the game. ➤ C continue moving in a circle while T sings the next song.
Prepare knowledge of music literacy concepts Draw a picture	"Rain, Rain" CSP: A • C sing and show the phrases. • Review kinesthetic and aural awareness activities. • T gives C long and short strips of paper or Unifix cubes. • T: "Show me what that phrase looks like with your Unifix cubes." • T selects a child to put the correct picture on the board, and C sing and point to the phrase. • C sing the song and clap the words. • T plays in canon on an Orff instrument.

Singing game/ creative movement	"All Around the Buttercup" CSP: F# • C sing the song and move into formation for the game. • T and C sing and play game. Connections to books/literacy: • Baker, Keith. *Quack and Count*. Harcourt Brace, 1999. • Deetlefs, Rene. *The Song of Six Birds*. Dutton Children's Books, 1999.
Practice of music performance and literacy skills Improvisation	"Snail, Snail" CSP: A • C sing "Snail, Snail" and keep the beat. • C sing phrase 1 using the words "high" and "low" and sing phrase 2 using the text while keeping the beat. • T improvises a new insect or animal for first phrase, and C sing second phrase while keeping the beat. (Ex. Bear, bear, bear, bear, go around and round and round, etc.) • C improvise names of other animals. • C improvise names of other animals and create high and low motions for that animal.

SUMMARY ACTIVITIES

Review the new song Review lesson outcomes	• "Caracol Col Col"
Folk song or folk song tales sung by T	• "Liza Jane"

Kindergarten: Rhythm, Lesson 4	
Outcome:	Presentation of the concept of rhythm and the spelling of the word "rhythm"

INTRODUCTORY ACTIVITIES

Sing known songs	"Teddy Bear" and/or "Caracol Col Col" CSP: A • C sing song and perform the motions. • C and T sing "Teddy Bear" using a call-and-response method (T: "Teddy bear, teddy bear." C: "Turn around").

322

Develop tuneful singing	"Bee, Bee, Bumble Bee" • T chants "Bee, Bee" as C march to song. • T chants a buzzing sound to C using the rhythm of the chant; C echo. • T lip-trills a phrase of "Bee, Bee" and C echo. • C march the beat and "buzz" and clap the words. ➢ C continue marching the beat while T claps the next song.
Review known songs and concepts	"We Are Dancing in the Forest" CSP: A • T claps the rhythm of the song and C identify it. • C sing song and keep the beat. • C sing the song and clap the words. • C sing and briefly play the game. ➢ C sing the song and move back to the circle.

CORE ACTIVITIES

Teach a new song	"Looby Loo" CSP: D • T sings song and C swing arms to the beat in a circle. • T sings song and C skip to the beat in a circle. • T sings the remaining verses and C perform the motions being sung. • C sing the refrain and T sings the verses. • C create a new beat motion to perform while singing the song. ➢ C continue their beat motion while T sings the next song.
Presentation Label what you hear	"Rain, Rain" CSP: A • C sing the song. • Review kinesthetic, aural, and visual awareness activities. • T: "When we have long sounds and short sounds that make a pattern in music, we call it the 'rhythm'." • C sing the song and clap the rhythm of the song while T plays the rhythm on an instrument. • C sing the song and clap the rhythm of the song, and T chooses a child to play the rhythm on an instrument. Connections to books/literacy: • Stojic, Manya. *Rain*. Dragonfly Books, 2000. • Locker, Thomas. *Cloud Dance*. Voyager Books, 2000.

323

Singing game/creative movement	"Just from the Kitchen"
	CSP: E
	• T sings song and C keep the beat.
	• C stand in a circle with an empty space.
	• T joins circle and sings song (calls the name of a child to move to the empty space).
	• T sings the song and calls out another child to move to the new empty space.
	• T sings; C bend their knees on beat 1 and stand back up on beat 3.
	➢ C continue the bending and rising motion while T sings the next song.
Presentation Record what you hear	"Seesaw"
	CSP: A
	• T: "Let's sing 'Seesaw' and put the words in our hands."
	• Class repeats by singing on "loo" and continuing to clap the words.
	• Class repeats a third time by inner-hearing the melody and clapping the words.
	• T reviews kinesthetic, aural, and visual awareness activities.
	• T: "When we have long sounds and short sounds that make a pattern in a phrase of music, we call it the 'rhythm'. We write the word rhythm like this. . . ." (T writes *R-H-Y-T-H-M* on the board.)
	• C sing "Seesaw" and clap the rhythm.

SUMMARY ACTIVITIES	
Review the new song	• "Looby Loo"
Review lesson outcomes	
Folk song or folk song tales sung by T	• "Turn the Glasses Over"

Kindergarten: Rhythm, Lesson 5	
Outcome:	Practice of rhythm
INTRODUCTORY ACTIVITIES	
Sing known songs	"Little Sally Water" and/or "Looby Loo"
	CSP: A
	• C sing song and play game.
	• C sing the song and tap the beat.
	Connections to books/literacy:
	• Wood, Audrey. *Silly Sally*. Harcourt, 1992.

Develop tuneful singing	"Bee, Bee, Bumble Bee" • T chants "Bee, Bee" as C march to song. • T chants a buzzing sound to C using the rhythm of the chant. C echo. • T lip-trills a phrase of "Bee, Bee" and students echo. • C march to the beat while "buzzing" and clapping the words.
Review known songs and concepts	"Teddy Bear" CSP: A • C identify the song T has clapped as "Teddy Bear." • C sing the song and perform the motions. • C sing the song, but inner-hear and clap the words "teddy bear." • T places the word "beat," beat icons, and the word "rhythm" on the board. • T points to either "beat" or "rhythm" and selects a child to perform correct motion (tapping beat or clapping rhythm) while class sings song.

CORE ACTIVITIES

Teach a new song	"Frog in the Meadow" CSP: C • T sings song and C swing arms to the beat while standing in a circle. • T sings song and C step to the beat while moving in a circle. • T sings other actions such as "tap," "bend," "nod," etc., and C perform the motions. • C may suggest motions to perform.
Practice of performance and music literacy skills	"Rain, Rain" CSP: A • C assess whether the beat of "Jim Along Josie" is too fast, too slow, or just right. • C adjust the tempo accordingly. • T reviews kinesthetic, aural, and visual awareness activities. • T: "When we have long sounds and short sounds that make a pattern in music, we call it the 'rhythm'." • C sing the song and clap the rhythm of the song while T plays the rhythm on an instrument. • C sing the song and clap the rhythm of the song, and T chooses a child to play the rhythm on an instrument. • T plays an open bordun to the steady beat on D and A, while C play the rhythm of the song on an unpitched instrument.

325

Singing game/ creative movement	"Looby Loo" CSP: D • C sing song and play game while T accompanies on the xylophone. ➢ T continues the accompaniment while singing the next song.
Practice of performance and music literacy skills	"Bobby Shafto" CSP: A • C sing the song and trace the phrases in the air while T draws them on the board. • C sing the song and clap the rhythm of the song while T traces the phrases. • C sing and trace the phrases while T performs the rhythm; C inner-hear the song and clap the rhythm while T traces the phrases. • T: "Which phrases sound the same?" (one, two, and three) • T: "Let's sing the first phrase and tap the beat." • T: "How many beats did we tap?" (four) T repeats phrase while tapping the beat. • T: "Did all of the beats have the same amount of sounds?" (no) • T: "Sing the phrase with the words 'short' and 'long'." • T: "Let's sing the last phrase and tap the beat." • T: "How many beats did we tap?" (four) T repeats phrase while tapping the beat. • T: "Did all of the beats have the same amount of sounds?" (no) • T: "Which beat had one sound?" (beats three and four) • T: "How could we describe this sound?" (long) • T: "How could we describe the other sounds?" (short) • T: "Let's sing the last phrase and sing using the words 'long' and 'short'." • C sing the whole song using "short" and "long." • T gives each child a bag of large and small strips and C must create a picture of the rhythm (they may also use Unifix cubes). • T creates a picture of the rhythm on board. • C sing and point to picture on the board. • C sing and clap rhythm. • C listen to *Symphony No. 94* in G Major, "The Surprise," Andante, by Franz Joseph Haydn (1732–1809). This melody has the same rhythm as "Bobby Shafto."
SUMMARY ACTIVITIES	
Review the new song	"Jim Along Josie"
Review lesson outcomes	
Folk song or folk song tales sung by T	"Sailing over the Ocean"

Discussion Questions

1. How can we use the Houlahan/Tacka model of instruction and learning to develop lesson plans in order to teach children?
2. How are lesson outcomes related to each part of the lesson?
3. How important are music transitions in a lesson plan?
4. Teaching is meant to be fun. Will the lesson plan templates and model lessons provided in the chapter help teachers sleep better at night?
5. Should music in the Kindergarten classroom be taught as a form of play or a means of learning about music concepts?

Ongoing Assignment

1. Choose a concept and develop a sequence of lessons for teaching.
2. Review the lesson plans you have designed. Try to indicate how you will move smoothly from one activity to another.
3. Observe a Kindergarten music lesson. What is the focus of the lesson? How does it compare to the lesson plan structures used in this chapter?

Bibliography

Abeles, H. F., and Custodero, L., eds., *Critical Issues in Music Education: Contemporary Theory and Practice.* New York: Oxford University Press, 2010.

Atterbury, B. W. *Mainstreaming Exceptional Learners in Music.* Englewood Cliffs, NJ: Prentice Hall, 1990.

Banks, J., M. Cochran-Smith, L. Moll, A. Richert, K. Zeichner, and P. LePage. "Teaching Diverse Learners," In *Preparing Teachers for a Changing World What Teachers Should Learn and Be Abel to Do*, ed. L. Darling Hammond and J. Bransford, pp. 232–274. San Francisco: Jossey-Bass, 2005.

Bannan, N., and S. Woodward. "Spontaneity in the Musicality and Music Learning of Children." In *Communicative Musicality: Exploring the Basis of Human Companionship* ed. S. Malloch and C. Trevarthen, pp. 465–494. Oxford: Oxford University Press, 2009.

Batshaw, M. L. *When Your Child Has a Disability.* Baltimore: Brookes, 2001.

Bjrkvold, J. R. *The Muse Within: Creativity and Communication, Song and Play from Childhood Through Maturity.* New York: HarperCollins, 1992.

Boshkoff, Ruth. "Lesson Planning the Kodály Way." *Music Educators Journal*, October 1991, 78(2): 30–34.

Bruey, C. T. *Demystifying Autism Spectrum Disorders A Guide to Diagnosis for Parents and Professionals.* Bethesda, MD: Woodbine House, 2004.

Bruni, M. *Fine Motor Skills in Children with Down Syndrome A Guide for Parents and Professionals.* Bethesda, MD: Woodbine House, 2006.

Bush, J. E. "Importance of Various Professional Development Opportunities and Workshop Topics as Determined by In-Service Music Teachers." *Journal of Music Teacher Education*, 2007, 16(2): 10–18.

Coleman, J. G. *The Early Intervention Dictionary A Multidisciplinary Guide to Terminology.* Bethesda, MD: Woodbine House, 2006.

Colwell, C. M. "Learning Disabilities in the Music Classroom: Implications for the Music Educator." *Update: Applications of Research in Music Education*, 2002, 21(2): 9–16.

Colwell, C. M., and Thompson, L. K. "'Inclusion' of Information on Mainstreaming in Undergraduate Music Education Curricula." *Journal of Music Therapy*, 2000, 37(3): 205–221.

Conroy, M., K. Sutherland, A. Snyder, and S. Marsh. "Classwide Interventions: Effective Instruction Makes a Difference." *Teaching Exceptional Children*, 2008, 40(6): 24–30.

Conway, C. M. "Issues Facing Music Teacher Education in the 21st Century: Developing Leaders in the Field." In *Critical Issues in Music Education: Contemporary Theory and Practice*, ed. H. Abeles and L. Custodero, pp. 259–275. New York: Oxford University Press, 2010.

Culton, C. L. *The Extent to Which Elementary Music Education Textbooks Reflect Teachers' Needs Regarding Instruction of Students with Special Needs: A Content Analysis.* Unpublished doctoral diss., University of Iowa, 1999.

Dalrymple, N. *Competencies for People Teaching Individuals with Autism and Other Pervasive Developmental Disorders* (ERIC Document Reproduction Service No. ED 363 980), 1993.

Davis, W. B., K. E. Gfeller, and M. H. Thaut. *An Introduction to Music Therapy: Theory and Practice.* Boston, MA: McGraw-Hill, 1999.

Drake, Susan M. *Planning the Integrated Curriculum: The Call to Adventure.* Alexandria, VA: Association for Supervision and Curriculum Development, 1993.

Epstein, A. S. *The Intentional Teacher: Choosing the Best Strategies for Young Children's Learning.* Washington, DC: National Association for the Education of Young Children, 2007.

Goffin, S. G. *Curriculum Models and Early Childhood Education: Appraising the Relationship.* New York: Merrill, 1994 2nd ed: S.G. Goffin and C. Wilson. Upper Saddle River, NJ: Prentice Hall, 2001.

Hagedorn, V. S. "Accommodations for Special Needs Students: What We Can Do." *General Music Today*, 2002, 15(3): 20–22.

Hammel, A. M., and R. M. Hourigan. *Teaching Music to Students with Special Needs: A Label-Free Approach.* New York: Oxford University Press, 2011.

Horstmeier, D. *Teaching Math to People with Down Syndrome and Other Hands-On Learners.* Bethesda, MD: Woodbine House, 2004, (2008 published ISBN#: 978-3-8364-7663-8).

Hourigan, R. M. *Teaching Music to Students with Special Needs: A Phenomenological Examination of Participants in a Fieldwork Experience.* Doctoral diss., University of Michigan, 2007.

Hourigan, R. M. "Preservice Music Teachers' Perceptions of Fieldwork Experience in a Special Needs Classroom." *Journal of Research in Music Education*, 2009, 57(3): 152–168.

Kame'enui, E. J. "A New Paradigm: Responsiveness to Intervention." *Teaching Exceptional Children*, 2007, 39(5): 6–7.

Kay, K. *Uniquely Gifted: Identifying and Meeting the Needs of the Twice-Exceptional Student.* Gilsum, NH: Avocus, 2000.

Klein, L. G., and J. Knitzer. "Effective Preschool Curricula and Teaching Strategies." *Pathways to Early School Success*, Issue Brief No. 2. New York: Columbia University, National Center for Children in Poverty, 2006.

Kumin, L. *Early Communication Skills for Children with Down Syndrome: A Guide for Parents and Professionals (3rd ed.).* Bethesda, MD: Woodbine House, 2012.

Lewis, R. B., and Doorlag, D. H. *Teaching Special Students in General Education Classrooms.* Upper Saddle River, NJ: Pearson, 2006, 8th Ed. 2010.

McClannahan, L. E., and P. J. Krantz. *Activity Schedules for Children with Autism Teaching Independent Behavior.* Bethesda, MD: Woodbine House, 2010.

McCord, K. "Moving Beyond 'That's All I Can Do': Encouraging Musical Creativity in Children with Learning Disabilities." *Bulletin of the Council for Research in Music Education,* 2004, 159: 23–32.

Oelwein, P. L. *Teaching Reading to Children with Down Syndrome A Guide for Parents and Teachers.* Bethesda, MD: Woodbine House, 1995.

Regelski, Thomas A. "On 'Methodolatry' and Music Teaching as Critical and Reflective Praxis." *Philosophy of Music Education Review,* Fall 2002, 10(2): 102–123.

Schweinhart, L. J., and D. P. Weikart. *Lasting Differences: The High/Scope Preschool Curriculum Comparison Study Through Age 23.* Monographs of the High/Scope Educational Research Foundation, vol. 12. Ypsilanti, MI: High/Scope Press, 1997.

Sousa, D. A. *How the Gifted Brain Learns.* Thousand Oaks, CA: Sage Corwin, 2003.

Van Dyke, D. C., P. Mattheis, S. S. Eberly, and J. Williams. *Medical and Surgical Care for Children with Down Syndrome: A Guide for Parents.* Bethesda, MD: Woodbine House, 1995.

Van Tassel-Baska, J. *Excellence in Educating Gifted and Talented Learners.* Denver: Love, 1998.

Voss, K. S. *Teaching by Design: Using Your Computer to Create Materials for Students with Learning Differences.* Bethesda, MD: Woodbine House, 2005.

Winders, P. C. *Gross Motor Skills in Children with Down Syndrome: A Guide for Parents and Professionals.* Bethesda, MD: Woodbine House, 2003.

Winebrenner, S. *Teaching Gifted Kids in the Regular Classroom Strategies and Techniques Every Teacher can use to meet the Academic needs of the Gifted and Talented.* Minneapolis: Free Spirit, 2001.

Zirkel, P. "What Does the Law Say? New Section 504 and Student Eligibility Standards." *Teaching Exceptional Children,* 2009, 41(4): 68–71.

Chapter 8

Assessment and Evaluation in Kindergarten

In Chapter 7 we described several lesson plan formats that can be used for teaching music concepts and skills. The purpose of assessment in the classroom is to evaluate the work of both children and teachers in the classroom. This chapter gives an overview of how to assess a child's word and development as well as how to assess the music instructor. Videos of kindergarten music teachers discussing these assessment tools are posted on the companion website (Web 8B).

By assessing a child's skill development and the teacher's classroom teaching, we can develop strategies to improve music learning and music teaching. Properly done, assessment leads to the development of a more effective music program.

Assessment of Child Learning

During a music lesson, the teacher has a chance to assess a child's progress. In assessing child during a lesson, the teacher is generally assessing the performance of the whole class while observing those children who require more attention. This is known as a "formative" assessment. The teaching and learning activities are modified or adjusted during the lesson. For example, during the introduction of a preparation/practice lesson, the teacher can assess children's singing, as well as their knowledge of known concepts. She or he can make a number of opportunities available for individual singing so as to assess performance. If there are time constraints, the music teacher may decide to evaluate only certain areas of the curriculum such as singing, reading, writing, and creativity. Once the assessment becomes part of the regular routines of classroom teaching, it is easier to discern areas of weakness and develop teaching strategies to improve child learning.

Generally there are two occasions for teachers to assess child learning in the classroom. In some cases, they may decide to conduct an assessment during a music lesson, or it may be at another time. Assessment can be done as a group activity, or if the teacher is unsure of a child's skills, it may be done individually.

There are four steps to developing assessment rubrics in the Kindergarten classroom:

Step 1. Determine the components of an assessment profile chart.
Step 2. Determine the activities you will use to assess these areas.
Step 3. Create assessment rubrics for each of these areas.
Step 4. Make a class profile that summarizes the children's scores.

Step One: Determining the components of an Assessment Profile Chart

Developing an assessment profile chart for each child in the class enables the teacher to record information concerning child progress and growth. It is not expected that teachers assess every skill area; only those skills that are important for children and their music program might be selected. The individual assessment profile keeps track of and records a child's understanding. This profile will allow teachers to develop additional teaching strategies to improve child learning.

For example, a child's profile may contain a section for each time a teacher does an assessment of child learning. It is probably best to assess all concepts being taught in the classroom. The teacher might decide to do an assessment for loud and soft, beat, high and low in chant, fast and slow, and high and low in melody and rhythm. That means there will be six sections in a child's profile related to the concepts we are teaching. Sometimes a teacher will have time to do only four assessments and may decide to combine the testing of two concepts.

Singing assessment can happen at various times throughout the music lesson. The assessment of reading, writing, and improvisation may be done as part of the practice activities for a lesson.

Child profiles should contain a space to record comments. A class profile can be developed where the names of the child and the recorded grades for singing, reading, writing, and improvisation are recorded. This information allows the instructor to see where adjustments in teaching or lesson planning need to be made. Assessment allows teachers to plan on the basis of their children's learning and responses.

It is important to include in the assessment general observations relating to how the child participates in the music classroom for example. Here are suggestions for inclusion in the general comments section of the child profile.

Age Three or Four

These considerations for working with children three or four years of age are adopted from Forrai[1]:

Does the child pay attention when someone sings?
Does the child like to play games?
Does she chant or hum during the day?
When does the child sing to himself or herself? (Is it in a group or individually?)
Is the child able to maintain a steady beat when initiated by an adult?
What is the child's participation in informal music experience? (Does the child join in, or go away? Does the child pay attention from a distance?)

Age Five or Six

These considerations apply to working with children five or six years of age[2]:

Does the child gladly take part in a singing game?

Does the child sing or only take part in the game?

Is the child able to adapt movement to the beat and tempo of song repertoire?

Is the child happy if chosen to play a game? How are the child's friendships being made? How has this changed from the beginning of the year?

Does the child accept rules?

How fast did the child understand the comparative concepts (e.g. loud or soft)? Is the child able to use them?

Does he or she have new ideas about games, melodic motives, and rhythms?

In games is the child a leader, or a participant? Or does the child play a passive role?

Sometimes we forget that assessment is not just judgment; it is a call to action on the part of the teacher to plan accordingly in the future. Table 8.1 is a sample of an Individual Assessment Profile chart containing the music skills to be assessed.

Table 8.1 Sample Individual Assessment Profile

Assessment of singing	Comments
Assessment of reading skills	Comments
Assessment of writing skills	Comments
Assessment of creative skills	Comments
General comments	

Step Two: Assessment Activities

For each component of the assessment, the teacher must decide what activities will be assessed. Table 8.2 shows sample assessment activities that teachers can select from.

Table 8.2 Sample Assessment Activities

Assessment of Singing	Comments
Here are sample assessment activities that can be used in the music classroom. • Singing with a loud or soft singing voice • Singing and clapping/tapping the beat • Singing using fast or slow tempos • Singing a melody containing two pitches with the words *high* and *low* • Singing and clapping the rhythm of a melody/chant • Singing while playing games with correct sequence of movements • Singing and playing simple rhythmic instruments	

(Continued)

Table 8.2   Continued

Assessment of reading skills	Comments
Here are sample assessment activities that can be used in the music classroom. • Reading icons/words to identify how to sing a melody with either a loud or soft voice • Reading and pointing to beat icons as a child sings a melody • Chanting a rhyme with a "high" or "low" voice and pointing to beat icons • Reading icons/words to identify how to chant a rhyme with a "high" or "low" voice • Reading icons/words to identify how to sing a melody with a fast or slow tempo • Reading icons/words to identify how to sing a melody with two pitches a minor third apart with the words high and low • Reading icons/words to identify the rhythm of a melody/chant	
Assessment of writing skills	Comments
Here are sample assessment activities that can be used in the music classroom. • Using icons/words to record if a song was sung with a loud or soft voice • Using beat icons to record how many beats were in a song or phrase • Using icons/words to record if a rhyme was chanted with a loud or soft voice • Using icons/words to record if a song was sung with a loud or soft voice • Using icons to write a song containing two pitches a minor third apart. • Using icons/words to record the rhythm of a melody/chant	
Assessment of creative skills	Comments
Here are sample assessment activities that can be used in the music classroom. • Singing a greeting to a T or another child • Singing new words to a familiar song or chant song • Singing about the text of a story • Singing a song with improvised beat motions • Improvising by clapping a four-beat rhythm pattern • Improvising a four-beat rhythm pattern on a music instrument • Improvising a rhythmic ostinato • Improvising beat motions to a piece of art music • Improvising movements to a song or piece of art music	

Once the teacher has decided what skills and activities will be used for assessment, he or she can design a more specific assessment profile. Here is a sample assessment for performance, reading, writing, and improvisations for the concept of loud and soft.

Table 8.3 Assessing Children's Knowledge of a Music Concept

Assessment of singing • Singing with a loud or soft singing voice	Comments
Assessment of reading • Singing and reading icons/words to identify how to sing a melody with either a loud or soft voice	Comments
Assessment of writing • Using icons/words to record whether a song was sung with a loud or soft voice	Comments
Assessment of improvisation skills • Improvising movements that reflect loud or soft dynamics, fast or slow tempo, "high" or "low" pitches to a song or piece of art music	Comments

Step Three: Creating Assessment Rubrics for Singing, Reading, Writing, and Improvisation Skills

Once assessment activities have been determined, we need a scoring rubric to help evaluate the information that has been collected. These are only samples and should be modified to suit the teacher and teaching situation. The next sections discuss examples of assessment rubrics that may be used for performance, music literacy, and improvisation.

Assessment of Performance: Singing

Keep in mind that in the process of learning to sing tunefully, young children often sing the melody reasonably correctly but at a lower tonality, or sometimes, but more rarely, higher. Achievement is a process with young children, very much influenced by their individual developmental stages. Of course, it is part of the joy of teaching young children music to watch and nurture their musical development. As we started in the introduction, the overall goal in Kindergarten education is more one of nurturing the process of development of musical skills than of expecting a certain level of achievement. This is the gigantic difference between Kindergarten music education and what begins in the elementary school.

Assessment of tuneful singing can be done during the class lesson. When we assess tuneful singing we observe what the child is able to demonstrate in singing. The assessment of tuneful singing will change for each concept. For example, in our curriculum the beginning of the year focuses on the concept of loud and soft; the assessment of tuneful singing should reflect this. Later the child will be expected to sing repertoire with a fast and slow tempo, at which time assessment should reflect tempo.

Here is a sample of what can be assessed within the context of tuneful singing. The child will sing known songs with:

Tuneful singing
Dynamics of loud or soft
Correct beat motions
A high or low voice
A fast or slow tempo
Clapping the rhythm

Table 8.4 is an example of an assessment rubric for singing. For some teachers it is crucial to know whether the child actually used a singing voice in tune, or out of tune in the singing voice, or a speaking voice (obviously this would be out of tune or maybe an octave lower). It may be helpful to include this information in the comment section of the rubric. The two sections are important because the teacher can use this information later if talking with a parent. It gives the "grade" but it also offers a little room for the intangibles to be documented in the comments section.

Table 8.4   Sample Assessment Rubric for Singing

Criteria		Comments
4 Advanced	Child sings repertoire tunefully, making no errors.	
3 Proficient	Child sings repertoire tunefully, making a few errors in singing that do not detract from the overall performance.	
2 Basic	Child sings repertoire but make errors that detract from the overall performance.	
1 Emerging	Child does not sing tunefully.	

Sometimes teachers might prefer to use a three-point rubric instead of a four-point scale. All of the rubrics in this chapter can be modified, and the teacher can certainly use a three-point scale. Table 8.5 presents an example.

Table 8.5   Sample Three-Point Assessment Rubric for Singing

Criteria		Comments
3 Advanced	Child sings repertoire tunefully, making no errors.	
2 Proficient	Child sings repertoire tunefully, making a few errors in singing that do not detract from the overall performance.	

(Continued)

335

Table 8.5 (continued)

	Criteria	Comments
1 Developing	Child sings repertoire but make errors that detract from the overall performance.	
0 Not yet evident		

The next four tables are examples of assessment rubrics for singing related to music concepts.

Table 8.6   Sample Assessment for Singing with Loud and Soft Voice

	Criteria	Comments
4 Advanced	Child sings in tune and in a loud or soft voice, making no errors.	
3 Proficient	Child sings in tune in a loud or soft voice, making a few errors that do not detract from the performance.	
2 Basic	Child sings in a loud or soft voice but makes errors that detract from the performance.	
1 Emerging	Child does not sing in tune in a loud or soft voice.	

Table 8.7   Sample Assessment for Singing with High and Low Voice

	Criteria	Comments
4 Advanced	Child sings a song in a "high" or "low" voice, making no errors.	
3 Proficient	Child sings a song in a "high" or "low" voice, making a few errors that do not detract from the performance.	
2 Basic	Child sings a song in a "high" or "low" voice, making errors that detract from the performance.	
1 Emerging	Child does not sing in tune in a "high" or "low" voice.	

Table 8.8 Sample Assessment for Singing with Words "High" and "Low"

	Criteria	Comments
4 Advanced	Child sings a song containing two pitches a minor third apart, using the words "high" and "low," making no errors.	
3 Proficient	Child sings a song containing two pitches a minor third apart, using the words "high" and "low," making a few errors that do not detract from the performance.	
2 Basic	Child sings a song containing two pitches a minor third apart, using the words "high" and "low," making errors that detract from the performance.	
1 Emerging	Child does not sing a song containing two pitches a minor third apart, using the words "high" and "low."	

Table 8.9 Sample Assessment for Singing with Melodic Contour

	Criteria	Comments
4 Advanced	Child sings a song in tune and with musical phrasing, while accurately showing the melodic contour with hand gestures.	
3 Proficient	Child sings a song in tune but makes a few mistakes in musical phrasing, or in showing the melodic contour with hand gestures that do not detract from the overall performance.	
2 Basic	Child sings a song making several melodic or rhythmic errors, while showing the melodic contour with hand gestures that detract from the overall performance.	
1 Emerging	Child does not sing and show melodic contour with hand gestures.	

Assessment of Music Literacy: Reading and Writing Skills

You may want to have examples of several types of assessment for music literacy skills. Assessing the reading and writing abilities of children is important. These assessments will be related to the concepts being explored in the music lesson. It is important to note that music literacy and improvisation skills are always assessed in connection with the child's ability to keep a beat.

Table 8.10   Sample Assessment Rubrics for Reading

	Criteria	Comments
4 Advanced	Child points to beat icons with the word "loud" or "soft" placed in front of the icons and sings using the correct dynamic, making no errors.	
3 Proficient	Child points to beat icons with the word "loud" or "soft" placed in front of the icons and sings using the correct dynamic, making some errors that do not detract from the overall performance.	
2 Basic	Child points to beat icons with the word "loud" or "soft" placed in front of the icons and sings using the correct dynamic, making errors that detract from the performance.	
1 Emerging	Child does not point to the beat icons with the "loud" or "soft" placed in the front of the beat icons and sings.	

Sometimes you might want to relate the assessment to a specific song. Here are samples of assessment rubrics for reading connected to a song.

Table 8.11   Sample Assessment of Pointing to Beat Icons While Following a Written Directive

	Criteria	Comments
4 Advanced	Child points to beat icons with the word "loud" or "soft" placed in front of the icons and sings "Rain, Rain" with the appropriate dynamics, making no errors.	
3 Proficient	Child points to beat icons with the word "loud" or "soft" placed in front of the beat icons and sings "Rain, Rain," making a few errors that do not detract from the performance.	
2 Basic	Child points to beat icons with the word "loud" or "soft" placed in front of the icons and sings "Rain, Rain," making errors that detract from the performance.	
1 Emerging	Child does not point to the beat icons with the word "loud" or "soft" placed in the front of the beat icons and sings "Rain, Rain."	

Table 8.12   Sample Assessment of Pointing to (Heart) Beat

	Criteria	Comments
4 Advanced	Child can sing "Rain, Rain" and point to the (heart) beat, making no errors.	
3 Proficient	Child can sing "Rain, Rain" and point to the (heart) beat, making a few errors that do not detract from the performance.	
2 Basic	Child can sing "Rain, Rain" and point to the (heart) beat, making errors that detract from the performance.	
1 Emerging	Child does not sing "Rain, Rain" or point to the (heart) beat.	

The next table is a sample of a writing assessment. Initially a child may select a card with the word *loud* or *soft* written on it. Later in the year, the child may write the words herself.

Table 8.13   Sample Assessment of Child's Recording of Loud and Soft

	Criteria	Comments
4 Advanced	Child records with words whether a song was sung using a loud or soft dynamic by placing icon before beat icon chart and performing the song with the appropriate dynamic, while pointing to beat icons, making no errors.	
3 Proficient	Child records with words whether a song was sung using a loud or soft dynamic by placing icon before beat icon chart and performing the song with the appropriate dynamic, while pointing to beat icons, making a few errors that do not detract from the performance.	
2 Basic	Child records with words whether a song was sung using a loud or soft dynamic by placing icon before beat icon chart and performing the song with the appropriate dynamic, while pointing to beat icons, making errors that detract from the performance.	
1 Emerging	Child does not report if a song was sung using a loud or soft dynamic.	

And here is a sample-writing assessment connected to a song (Table 8.14).

Table 8.14   Sample Assessment of Recording Loud and Soft Dynamic in "Snail, Snail"

	Criteria		Comments
4 Advanced	Child records with words whether "Snail, Snail" was sung using a loud or soft dynamic by placing icon before beat icon chart and performing the song with the appropriate dynamic, while pointing to beat icons, making no errors.		
3 Proficient	Child records with words whether "Snail, Snail" was sung using a loud or soft dynamic by placing icon before beat icon chart and performing the song with the appropriate dynamic while pointing to beat icons, making a few errors that do not detract from the performance.		
2 Basic	Child records with words whether "Snail, Snail" was sung using a loud or soft dynamic by placing icon before beat icon chart and perform the song with the appropriate dynamic while pointing to beat icons, making errors that detract from the performance.		
1 Emerging	Child does not record if "Snail, Snail" was sung using a loud or soft dynamic.		

Assessment of Creative Skills: Improvisation

You may want examples of several types of assessment for capturing the level of a child's creative skills. These assessments will be related to the concepts being explored in the music lesson. What is assessed in improvisation can be the ability to sing a familiar song with a new text, or the ability to improvise movements that reflect loud or soft dynamics of a song or a piece of art music. Here are samples of assessment rubrics for improvisation.

Table 8.15   Sample Assessment of Improvising New Words to a Song

	Criteria		Comments
4 Advanced	Child sings known repertoire tunefully, improvising a new word or words to the song, making no errors.		
3 Proficient	Child sings known repertoire tunefully, improvising a new word or words to the song, making a few errors in singing that do not detract from the overall performance.		

(Continued)

Table 8.15   (continued)

	Criteria	Comments
2 Basic	Child sings known repertoire tunefully, improvising a new word or words to the song, making errors in singing that detract from the overall performance.	
1 Emerging	Child does not sing known repertoire tunefully, improvising a new word or words to the song.	

Table 8.16   Sample Assessment of Improvising Movement to a Tempo

	Criteria	Comments
4 Advanced	Child improvises movements to a listening example that reflect the tempo of the example, making no errors.	
3 Proficient	Child improvises movements to a listening example that reflect the tempo of the example, making a few errors that do not detract from the overall performance.	
2 Basic	Child improvises movements to a listening example that reflect the tempo of the example, making errors that detract from the overall performance.	
1 Emerging	Child does not improvise movements to a listening example that reflect the tempo of the example.	

And these are samples of assessment rubrics for improvisation related to a music concept.

Table 8.17   Sample Assessment of Improvising New Word with Loud Voice

	Criteria	Comments
4 Advanced	Child sings known repertoire tunefully, with a loud voice, improvising a new word or words to the song, and making no errors.	
3 Proficient	Child sings known repertoire tunefully, with a loud voice, improvising a new word or words to the song, and making a few errors in singing that do not detract from the overall performance.	
2 Basic	Child sings known repertoire tunefully, with a loud voice, improvising a new word or words to the song, and making errors in singing that detract from the overall performance.	
1 Emerging	Child does not sing known repertoire tunefully, with a loud voice, improvising a new word or words to the song.	

Table 8.18   Sample Assessment of Improvising New Beat Motion

	Criteria	Comments
4 Advanced	Child sings known repertoire tunefully, with a loud or soft singing voice, improvising a new beat motion to the song, and making no errors.	
3 Proficient	Child sings known repertoire tunefully, with a loud or soft singing voice, improvising a new beat motion to the song, and making a few errors in singing that do not detract from the overall performance.	
2 Basic	Child sings known repertoire tunefully, with a loud or soft singing voice, improvising a new beat motion to the song, and making errors in singing that detract from the overall performance.	
1 Emerging	Child does not sing known repertoire tunefully, with a loud or soft singing voice, improvising a beat motion to the song.	

Assessment Rubrics for Musical Concepts

This section of the chapter offers sample assessment rubrics for particular concepts.

Table 8.19   Loud and Soft Singing Assessment Rubric

Child can a sing melody using a loud or soft voice			
Child name: _____		Date: _____	Class: _____
Criteria	Levels	Grade Given	Comments
Child sings the melody of "See Saw" tunefully, using a loud or soft singing voice, making no errors.	4 Advanced		
Child sings the melody of "See Saw" tunefully, using a loud or soft singing voice, making only a few errors in singing that occasionally detract from the overall performance.	3 Proficient		
Child sings the melody of "See Saw" tunefully, using a loud or soft singing voice, making some errors in singing that detract from the overall performance.	2 Basic		

(Continued)

Table 8.19 (continued)

Child can a sing melody using a loud or soft voice			
Child name: _____		Date: _____	Class: _____
Criteria	**Levels**	**Grade Given**	**Comments**
Child does not sing the melody of "See Saw" tunefully, using a loud or soft singing voice.	1 Emerging		

Table 8.20   Loud and Soft Reading Assessment Rubric

Child can read the word *loud* or *soft* placed in front of beat icons and sing a melody or chant a rhyme using the required voice			
Child name: _____		Date: _____	Class: _____
Criteria	**Levels**	**Grade Given**	**Comments**
Child reads the word *loud* or *soft* placed in front of beat icons and chants "Engine, Engine Number Nine" using the required voice, making no errors.	4 Advanced		
Child reads the word *loud* or *soft* placed in front of beat icons and chants "Engine, Engine Number Nine" using the required voice, making only a few errors that occasionally detract from the overall performance.	3 Proficient		
Child reads the word *loud* or *soft* placed in front of beat icons and chants "Engine, Engine Number Nine" using the required voice, making some errors that detract from the overall performance.	2 Basic		
Child does not use the required voice when reading the word *loud* or *soft* placed in front of beat icons for "Engine, Engine Number Nine."	1 Emerging		

343

Table 8.21 Loud and Soft Writing Assessment Rubric

Child can place the word *loud* or *soft* in front of beat icons to record how a melody was sung with a loud or soft voice			
Child name: _____	Date: _____	Class: _____	
Criteria	Levels	Grade Given	Comments
Child can place the word *loud* or *soft* in front of beat icons to record how a song was sung, making no errors.	4 Advanced		
Child can place the word *loud* or *soft* in front of beat icons to record how a song was sung, making only a few errors that do not detract from the activity.	3 Proficient		
Child can place the word *loud* or *soft* in front of beat icons to record how a song was sung, making some errors that detract from the writing activity.	2 Basic		
Child does not place the word *loud* or *soft* in front of beat icons to record how a song was sung.	1 Emerging		

Table 8.22 Loud and Soft Improvisation Assessment Rubric

Child can create movements to a song to reflect if the song was sung using a loud or soft dynamic			
Child name: _____	Date: _____	Class: _____	
Criteria	Levels	Grade Given	Comments
Child can improvise beat motions to "On the Mountain" reflecting if it was sung with a loud or soft voice, making no errors.	4 Advanced		

(Continued)

Table 8.22 (continued)

Child can create movements to a song to reflect if the song was sung using a loud or soft dynamic			
Child name: _____	Date: _____	Class: _____	
Child can improvise beat motions to "On the Mountain" reflecting if it was sung with a loud or soft voice, making some errors that do not detract from the performance.	3 Proficient		
Child can improvise beat motions to "On the Mountain" reflecting if it was sung with a loud or soft voice, making errors that detract from the performance.	2 Basic		
Child does not improvise beat motions to "On the Mountain" reflecting if it was sung with a loud or soft voice.	1 Emerging		

Table 8.23   Beat and Singing Assessment Rubric

Child can a sing melody keeping a steady beat			
Child name: _____		Date: _____	Class: _____
Criteria	Levels	Grade Given	Comments
Child sings the melody of "Snail, Snail," keeping a beat with no errors.	4 Advanced		
Child sings the melody of "Snail, Snail," keeping a beat, making only a few errors in singing that occasionally detract from the overall performance.	3 Proficient		
Child sings the melody of "Snail, Snail," keeping a beat with errors that detract from the overall performance.	2 Basic		
Child does not sing the melody of "Snail, Snail" tunefully, and does not keep the beat motions.	1 Emerging		

Table 8.24   Beat and Reading Assessment Rubric

Child can sing or chant a rhyme or melody while pointing to four- or eight-beat icons			
Child Name: _____		Date: _____	Class: _____
Criteria	Levels	Grade Given	Comments
Child can sing "Snail, Snail" while pointing to beat icons, making no errors.	4 Advanced		
Child can sing "Snail, Snail" while pointing to beat icons, making only a few errors that occasionally detract from the overall performance.	3 Proficient		
Child can sing "Snail, Snail" while pointing to beat icons, making errors that detract from the overall performance.	2 Basic		
Child does not sing while pointing to four-beat icons.	1 Emerging		

Table 8.25   Beat and Writing Assessment Rubric

Child can place four- or eight-beat icons on the board or on paper and sing or chant a rhyme or melody while pointing to the beat icons			
Child name: _____		Date: _____	Class: _____
Criteria	Levels	Grade Given	Comments
Child can place four-beat icons on the board and sing "Snail, Snail" while pointing to icons, making no errors.	4 Advanced		
Child can place four-beat icons on the board and sing "Snail, Snail" while pointing to beat icons, making only a few errors that occasionally detract from the overall performance.	3 Proficient		
Child can place four-beat icons on the board and sing "Snail, Snail" while pointing to beat icons, making errors that detract from the overall performance.	2 Basic		

(Continued)

Table 8.25   (continued)

Child can place four- or eight-beat icons on the board or on paper and sing or chant a rhyme or melody while pointing to the beat icons			
Child name: _____		Date: _____	Class: _____
Criteria	Levels	Grade Given	Comments
Child does not place four-beat icons on the board and sing "Snail, Snail" while pointing to beat icons.	1 Emerging		

Table 8.26   Beat and Improvisation Assessment Rubric

Child can create beat movements to a song			
Child name: _____		Date: _____	Class: _____
Criteria	Levels	Grade Given	Comments
Child can improvise beat motions to "Snail, Snail," making no errors.	4 Advanced		
Child can improvise beat motions to "Snail, Snail," making some errors that do not detract from the performance.	3 Proficient		
Child can improvise beat motions to "Snail, Snail," making errors that detract from the performance.	2 Basic		Detractions noted:
Child does not improvise beat motions to "Snail, Snail."	1 Emerging		

Table 8.27   High and Low Assessment Rubric

Child can chant a rhyme using a high or low voice			
Child Name: _____		Date: _____	Class: _____
Criteria	Levels	Grade Given	Comments
Child can chant *Engine, Engine #9* with a high or low voice making no errors.	4 Advanced		

(Continued)

Table 8.27 (continued)

Child can chant a rhyme using a high or low voice			
Child Name: _____		Date: _____	Class: _____
Criteria	Levels	Grade Given	Comments
Child can chant *Engine, Engine #9* with high or low voice making only a few errors that occasionally detract from the overall performance.	3 Proficient		
Child can chant *Engine, Engine #9* with high or low voice making errors that detract from the overall performance.	2 Basic		
Child does not chant *Engine, Engine #9* using a high or low voice.	1 Emerging		

Table 8.28 High and Low Reading Assessment Rubric

Child can read the words *high* and *low* placed in front of beat icons and chant a rhyme or melody using the required voice			
Child name: _____		Date: _____	Class: _____
Criteria	Levels	Grade Given	Comments
Child reads the word *high* or *low* placed in front of beat icons and chants "Engine, Engine Number Nine" using the required voice, making no errors.	4 Advanced		
Child reads the word *high* or *low* placed in front of beat icons and chants "Engine, Engine Number Nine" using the required voice, making only a few errors that occasionally detract from the overall performance.	3 Proficient		
Child reads the word *high* or *low* placed in front of beat icons and chants "Engine, Engine Number Nine" using the required voice, making some errors that detract from the overall performance.	2 Basic		
Child does not read the word *high* or *low* placed in front of beat icons and chants "Engine, Engine Number Nine" using the required voice.	1 Emerging		

Table 8.29 High and Low Writing Assessment Rubric

Child can place the words *high* and *low* in front of beat icons, to record if a chant was sung with a high or low voice, and perform it with the appropriate voice			
Child name: _____	Date: _____	Class: _____	
Criteria	Levels	Grade Given	Comments
Child listens to the chant "Engine, Engine Number Nine" performed in a high or low voice, selects the word to identify how the chant was performed, and then performs it in the appropriate high or low voice while pointing to beat icons, making no errors.	4 Advanced		
Child listens to the chant "Engine, Engine Number Nine" performed in a high or low voice, selects the word to identify how the chant was performed, and then performs it in the appropriate high or low voice while pointing to beat icons, making only a few errors that do not detract from the activity.	3 Proficient		
Child listens to the chant "Engine, Engine Number Nine" performed in a high or low voice, selects the word to identify how the chant was performed, and then performs it in the appropriate high or low voice while pointing to beat icons, making some errors that detract from the writing activity.	2 Basic		

349

(Continued)

Table 8.29   (continued)

Child can place the words *high* and *low* in front of beat icons, to record if a chant was sung with a high or low voice, and perform it with the appropriate voice			
Child name: _____	Date: _____	Class: _____	
Criteria	Levels	Grade Given	Comments
Child does not place the word *high* or *low* in front of beat icons to record how "Engine, Engine Number Nine" was performed.	1 Emerging		

Table 8.30   High and Low Improvisation Assessment Rubric

Child can create movements to a rhyme to reflect if the song was sung using a high or low dynamic			
Child name: _____	Date: _____	Class: _____	
Criteria	Levels	Grade Given	Comments
Child can improvise beat motions to "Engine, Engine Number Nine" that reflect whether it was sung with a high or low voice, making no errors.	4 Advanced		
Child can improvise beat motions to "Engine, Engine Number Nine" that reflect whether it was sung with a high or low voice, making errors that do not detract from the performance.	3 Proficient		
Child can improvise beat motions to "Engine, Engine Number Nine" that reflect whether it was sung with a high or low voice, making errors that detract from the performance.	2 Basic		
Child does not improvise beat motions to "Engine, Engine Number Nine" that reflect whether it was sung with a high or low voice.	1 Emerging		

Table 8.31   Fast and Slow Singing Assessment Rubric

Child can a sing melody using a fast or slow tempo			
Child name: _____		Date: _____	Class: _____
Criteria	Levels	Grade Given	Comments
Child sings the melody of "See Saw" tunefully, using a fast or slow tempo, making no errors.	4 Advanced		
Child sings the melody of "See Saw" tunefully, using a fast or slow tempo, making only a few errors in singing that occasionally detract from the overall performance.	3 Proficient		
Child sings the melody of "See Saw" tunefully, using a fast or slow tempo, making some errors in singing that detract from the overall performance.	2 Basic		
Child does not sing the melody of "See Saw" tunefully, using a fast or slow tempo.	1 Emerging		

351

Table 8.32   Fast and Slow Reading Assessment Rubric

Child can read the words *fast* and *slow* placed in front of beat icons and sing or chant a rhyme or melody using the required voice			
Child name: _____		Date: _____	Class: _____
Criteria	Levels	Grade Given	Comments
Child reads the word *fast* or *slow* placed in front of beat icons and chants "Engine, Engine Number Nine" using the required tempo, making no errors.	4 Advanced		
Child reads the word *fast* or *slow* placed in front of beat icons and chants "Engine, Engine Number Nine" using the required tempo, making only a few errors that occasionally detract from the overall performance.	3 Proficient		

(Continued)

Table 8.32   (continued)

Child can read the words *fast* and *slow* placed in front of beat icons and sing or chant a rhyme or melody using the required voice			
Child name: _____		Date: _____	Class: _____
Criteria	Levels	Grade Given	Comments
Child reads the word *fast* or *slow* placed in front of beat icons and chants "Engine, Engine Number Nine" using the required tempo, making some errors that detract from the overall performance.	2 Basic		
Child does not read the word *fast* or *slow* placed in front of beat icons and chants "Engine, Engine Number Nine" and does not use the required tempo.	1 Emerging		

Table 8.33   Fast and Slow Writing Assessment Rubric

Child can place the words *fast* and *slow* in front of beat icons to record how a melody was sung with a fast or slow voice			
Child name: _____		Date: _____	Class: _____
Criteria	Levels	Grade Given	Comments
Child can listen to a song sung in a fast or slow tempo, select the word to identify how the song was performed, and then perform it in the appropriate fast or slow tempo, making no errors.	4 Advanced		
Child can listen to a song sung in a fast or slow tempo, select the word to identify how the song was performed, and then perform it in the appropriate fast or slow tempo, making only a few errors that do not detract from the activity.	3 Proficient		
Child can listen to a song sung in a fast or slow tempo, select the word to identify how the song was performed, and then perform it in the appropriate fast or slow tempo, making some errors that detract from the writing activity.	2 Basic		

(Continued)

Table 8.33   (continued)

Child can place the words *fast* and *slow* in front of beat icons to record how a melody was sung with a fast or slow voice			
Child name: _____		Date: _____	Class: _____
Criteria	Levels	Grade Given	Comments
Child does not place the word *fast* or *slow* in front of beat icons to record how a song was sung.	1 Emerging		

Table 8.34   Fast and Slow Improvisation Assessment Rubric

Child can create movements to a song to reflect if the song was sung using a fast or slow tempo			
Child Name: _____		Date: _____	Class: _____
Criteria	Levels	Grade Given	Comments
Child can improvise beat motions to "On the Mountain," reflecting a fast or slow tempo, making no errors.	4 Advanced		
Child can improvise beat motions to "On the Mountain," reflecting a fast or slow tempo, making some errors that do not detract from the performance.	3 Proficient		
Child can improvise beat motions to "On the Mountain," reflecting a fast or slow tempo, making errors that detract from the performance.	2 Basic		
Child does not improvise beat motions to "On the Mountain" reflecting a fast or slow tempo.	1 Emerging		

Table 8.35   High and Low (Melodic) Assessment Rubric

High and Low Assessment Rubric Child can sing and *s-m* melody using the words high and low			
Child name: _____		Date: _____	Class: _____
Criteria	Levels	Grade Given	Comments
Child sings the first phrase of "Snail, Snail" using the words *high* and *low*, making no errors.	4 Advanced		

Table 8.35 (continued)

High and Low Assessment Rubric Child can sing and *s-m* melody using the words high and low			
Child name: _____		Date:_____	Class: _____
Criteria	Levels	Grade Given	Comments
Child sings the first phrase of "Snail, Snail" using the words *high* and *low*, making only a few errors that occasionally detract from the overall performance.	3 Proficient		
Child sings the first phrase of "Snail, Snail" using the words *high* and *low*, making errors that detract from the overall performance.	2 Basic		
Child does not sing "Snail, Snail" using the words *high* and *low*.	1 Emerging		

Table 8.36   High and Low Reading Assessment Rubric

Child can read the words *high* and *low* placed in front of beat icons and chant a rhyme or melody using the required voice			
Child name: _____		Date: _____	Class: _____
Criteria	Levels	Grade Given	Comments
Child reads an *s-m* melodic contour of a phrase with the words *high* and *low*, making no errors.	4 Advanced		
Child reads an *s-m* melodic contour of a phrase with the words *high* and *low*, making only a few errors that occasionally detract from the overall performance.	3 Proficient		
Child reads an *s-m* melodic contour of a phrase with the words *high* and *low*, making some errors that detract from the overall performance.	2 Basic		
Child does not read an *s-m* melodic contour of a phrase with the words *high* and *low*.	1 Emerging		

Table 8.37 High and Low Writing Assessment Rubric

Child writes the melodic contour of an *s-m* melody or phrase using discs			
Child name: _____	Date: _____	Class: _____	
Criteria	Levels	Grade Given	Comments
Child writes the melodic contour of the first phrase of "Snail, Snail" using discs, making no errors.	4 Advanced		
Child writes the melodic contour of the first phrase of "Snail, Snail" using discs, making only a few errors that do not detract from the activity.	3 Proficient		
Child writes the melodic contour of the first phrase of "Snail, Snail" using discs, making some errors that detract from the writing activity.	2 Basic		
Child does not write the melodic contour of the first phrase of "Snail, Snail" with discs.	1 Emerging		

Table 8.38 High and Low Improvisation Assessment Rubric

Child can improvise a melody composed of *s-m* to a known chant			
Child name: _____	Date: _____	Class: _____	
Criteria	Levels	Grade Given	Comments
Child can improvise a melody composed of *s-m* for "Engine, Engine Number Nine," making no errors.	4 Advanced		
Child can improvise a melody composed of *s-m* for "Engine, Engine Number Nine," making some errors that do not detract from the performance.	3 Proficient		

(Continued)

Table 8.38   (continued)

Child can improvise a melody composed of *s-m* to a known chant			
Child name: _____		Date: _____	Class: _____
Criteria	Levels	Grade Given	Comments
Child can improvise a melody composed of *s-m* for "Engine, Engine Number Nine," making errors that do detract from the performance.	2 Basic		
Child does not improvise a melody composed of *s-m* for the chant "Engine, Engine Number Nine."	1 Emerging		

Step Four: Developing a Class Profile

During the academic year the teacher will assess child learning three or four times depending on the assessment philosophy of the school. Normally, teachers evaluate child performance four times a year. It is important to capture child achievement on a class profile summary sheet. This will enable the teacher to document levels of success in the classroom as well as develop strategies for improving children's abilities. Every class profile should include:

Grading period
Outcomes for grading period
Assessment activities for grading period
Alphabetized list of children's names with their individual scores for each assessment
   activity

Figure 8.1   Template for Class Profile

Grading Period
Outcomes for Grading Period (List all outcomes for the grading period, reading, writing, singing, etc.)
Assessment activities for the Grading Period (List the outcomes you will test for this specific grading period)
Alphabetized list of Child names and assessment activity scores for the grading period.
Reflection on Child Learning and Implications for Future Teaching

Evaluating Music Teaching

The next set of rubrics are primarily designed for music teachers who teach Kindergarten music. Occasionally, classroom teachers who have some knowledge of music are required to teach Kindergarten music with or without the help of the music teacher. Teachers or supervisors can use these assessment rubrics for evaluating a teacher's performance in the classroom. Some are more appropriate for use before, during, or after the lesson. The rubric below was created to evaluate the teacher's ability to plan and teach. When evaluating a music teacher the supervisor should always include comments; it is important for the evaluator to make comments that are related to research and principles of highly effective teaching.

The supervisor should check to see if the music teacher knows[3]:

The principles on which the goals of music education are based

The work of Zoltán Kodály in the area of music education, his principles as they pertain to preschool education, his writings, and his works written for children.

The characteristics of children's songs from the point of view of tone set, rhythm, and motivic structure.

The main types of children's games so that movement elements in them can be varied in their style.

Children's musical developmental characteristics during the preschool years

The musical development of children before preschool, and the goals necessary to prepare for elementary school.

The professional literature on musical development before Kindergarten.

The curriculum of the music program in the first and second grade of elementary school.

International folk songs and their musical characteristics (particular motives, meters, and rhythms).

The supervisor should observe whether the teacher could demonstrate these abilities[4]:

Clap and walk a steady beat during the performance of a song or rhyme.

Invent simple movements through which to express the steady beat

Express the rhythm of a song or rhyme through movement, clapping, or percussion instruments.

Preform both the steady beat and the rhythm of a song or rhyme at the same time.

Demonstrate the metric accents (duple or compound meter) of a song or rhyme.

Recognize children's songs, folk songs, and rhymes from their rhythm.

Create simple rhythm in motives with text that is appropriate to the rhythm of the language.

Tap simple rhythmic ostinatos while singing a song.

Begin children's songs at a number of pitches as well as give the appropriate starting pitch (approximately D to B).

Correctly start songs that begin with minor or major thirds one after the other.

Maintain an appropriate tempo (quarter note = 60–120) while singing and walking

Sing a song or recite a rhyme softly and loudly without changing the tempo.

Create melodic motives (within the range of a sixth) with text; sing a new text to known motives; sing a new melody to a known text (in both echo and question-and-answer form).

357

Sing an inner or ending motive from any known song.

Speak in a singing manner (spontaneous conversation, story, poem, or doll playing).

Demonstrate high and low pitches in the air; create a variety of playful rhymes to demonstrate pitch and spatial relationships.

Perform both folk and composed songs in a manner appropriate to preschool children and to the characteristics of the song.

Prepare a syllabus for the year's teaching by choosing the appropriate song material to fit with the goals for the year.

Choose appropriate material for music listening for the children.

Create a syllabus for age-grouped and nonage-grouped children.

Evaluation Rubrics for Measuring Teacher Effectiveness

There are three components to this rubric:

1. Assessment of teaching: curriculum planning
2. Assessment of teaching: lesson planning and outcomes
3. Assessment of teaching: teaching a lesson

Assessment of Teaching: Lesson Planning and Outcomes

We have chosen to use a four-point rubric, but a three-point rubric can also be used.

Table 8.39 Assessment of Teaching: Curriculum Planning

Criteria		Comments
4 Highly effective	Curriculum planning fosters appropriate outcomes and active musical behaviors, as evidenced by the teaching portfolio.	
3 Effective	Curriculum planning does not always foster appropriate outcomes and active musical behaviors, but does not detract from planning, as evidenced by the teaching portfolio.	
2 Developing	Curriculum planning does not always foster appropriate outcomes and active musical behaviors, and sometimes detracts from planning, as evidenced by the teaching portfolio.	
1 Ineffective	Curriculum planning does not foster appropriate outcomes and active musical behaviors, and detracts from planning, as evidenced by the teaching portfolio.	

Table 8.40 Assessment of Teaching: Lesson Planning (Three-Point Rubric)

	Criteria	Comments
Highly effective 3	Lesson planning fosters appropriate outcomes and active musical behaviors, as evidenced by the teaching portfolio.	
Effective 2	Lesson planning does not always foster appropriate outcomes and active musical behaviors but does not detract from planning, as evidenced by the teaching portfolio.	
Developing 1	Lesson planning does not always foster appropriate outcomes and active musical behaviors and sometimes detracts from planning, as evidenced by the teaching portfolio.	
Ineffective 0	Lesson planning does not foster appropriate outcomes and active musical behaviors and detracts from planning, as evidenced by the teaching portfolio.	

Assessment of Teaching: Designing a Lesson Plan

The following assessment rubrics evaluate the teacher's ability to create outcomes based on the music curriculum. Evidence of lesson plans built on children's previous knowledge is critical to the design of a well-structured lesson, as well as to the various teaching strategies that will be used throughout the lesson. This evaluation also takes place before the lesson. These rubrics offer teachers a continuing opportunity for self-reflection and teaching improvement.

Table 8.41 Evaluation of Outcomes

	Criteria	Comments
4 Highly effective	Outcomes describe appropriate active musical behaviors within the lesson.	
3 Effective	Outcomes do not always describe appropriate active musical behaviors within the lesson but do not detract from the lesson.	

(Continued)

Table 8.41   (continued)

	Criteria	Comments
2 Developing	Outcomes do not always describe appropriate active musical behaviors within the lesson and sometimes detract from the lesson.	
1 Ineffective	Outcomes do not describe appropriate active musical behaviors within the lesson and consistently detract from the lesson.	

Table 8.42   Evaluation of Selection of Music Material

	Criteria	Comments
4 Highly effective	Selection of music material is always appropriate.	
3 Effective	Selection of music material is not always appropriate but does not detract from the lesson.	
2 Developing	Selection of music material is not always appropriate and sometimes detracts from the lesson.	
1 Ineffective	Selection of music material is not appropriate and consistently detracts from the lesson.	

Table 8.43   Evaluation of Knowledge of Children's Prior Background

	Criteria	Comments
4 Highly effective	There is evidence that outcomes are built on C's prior knowledge.	
3 Effective	It is not always evident that outcomes are built on C's prior knowledge, and this sometimes detracts from the lesson.	
2 Developing	It is not always evident that outcomes are built on C's prior knowledge, and this detracts from the lesson.	
1 Ineffective	Outcomes are not built on C's prior knowledge, and this consistently detracts from the lesson.	

Table 8.44   Evaluation of Sequential Teaching

	Criteria	Comments
4 Highly effective	Sequential teaching is always evident.	
3 Effective	Sequential teaching is not always evident but does not detract from the lesson.	
2 Developing	Sequential teaching is not always evident and sometimes detracts from the lesson.	
1 Ineffective	Sequential teaching is not evident and consistently detracts from the lesson.	

Table 8.45   Evaluation of Musical Transitions Between Teaching Segments

	Criteria	Comments
4 Highly effective	Musical transitions between teaching segments are always evident.	
3 Effective	Musical transitions between teaching segments are not always evident but do not detract from the lesson.	
2 Developing	Musical transitions between teaching segments are not always evident, and this sometimes detracts from the lesson.	
1 Ineffective	Musical transitions between teaching segments are not always evident, and this consistently detracts from the lesson.	

Table 8.46   Evaluation of Alternating Periods of Concentration and Relaxation

	Criteria	Comments
4 Highly effective	There is a balance between periods of concentration and relaxation activities in the lesson.	
3 Effective	There is some imbalance between periods of concentration and relaxation activities in the lesson, but this does not detract from the lesson.	

(Continued)

Table 8.46 (continued)

	Criteria	Comments
2 Developing	There is an imbalance between periods of concentration and relaxation activities in the lesson, and this sometimes detracts from the lesson.	
1 Ineffective	There is an imbalance between periods of concentration and relaxation activities in the lesson, and this detracts from the lesson.	

Assessment of Teaching: Teaching a Lesson

The next assessment rubrics evaluate the teacher's ability to transform a script for a lesson into practice. This evaluation takes place during the teaching of the lesson.

Table 8.47 Evaluation of Teacher's Musicality

	Criteria	Comments
4 Highly effective	The T's musicality is evident.	
3 Effective	The T demonstrates a few musicality errors, but this does not detract from the lesson.	
2 Developing	The T demonstrates musicality errors that sometimes detract from the lesson.	
1 Ineffective	The T's musicality errors consistently detract from the lesson.	

Table 8.48 Evaluation of Teacher's Own In-tune Singing

	Criteria	Comments
4 Highly effective	In-tune singing is evident.	
3 Effective	In-tune singing is not always evident, but this does not detract from the overall lesson.	

(Continued)

Table 8.48   (continued)

	Criteria	Comments
2 Developing	In-tune singing is not always evident, and this sometimes detracts from the lesson.	
1 Ineffective	In-tune singing is not evident, and this consistently detracts from the lesson.	

Table 8.49   Evaluation of Teacher's Functional Keyboard Skills

	Criteria	Comments
4 Highly effective	Functional keyboard skills are evident.	
3 Effective	Errors in functional keyboard skills occur but do not detract from the lesson.	
2 Developing	Errors in functional keyboard skills sometimes detract from the lesson.	
1 Ineffective	Errors in functional keyboard skills consistently detract from the lesson.	

Table 8.50   Evaluation of Teacher's Instrumental Skills

	Criteria	Comments
4 Highly effective	Instrumental skills are evident.	
3 Effective	Errors in instrumental skills occur but do not detract from the lesson.	
2 Developing	Errors in instrumental skills sometimes detract from the lesson.	
1 Ineffective	Errors in instrumental skills consistently detract from the lesson.	

Table 8.51 Evaluation of Appropriateness of Teacher's Starting Pitches for Songs

	Criteria	Comments
4 Highly effective	Appropriate starting pitch of songs is evident.	
3 Effective	Appropriate starting pitch is not always correct but does not detract from the lesson.	
2 Developing	Appropriate starting pitch is not always correct, and this sometimes detracts from the lesson.	
1 Ineffective	Appropriate starting pitch is not correct, and this consistently detracts from the lesson.	

Table 8.52   Evaluation of Appropriateness of Teacher's Tempo for Songs

	Criteria	Comments
4 Highly effective	Appropriate tempo of songs is evident.	
3 Effective	Appropriate tempo of songs is not always logical, but this does not detract from the lesson.	
2 Developing	Appropriate tempo of songs is not always logical, and this sometimes detracts from the lesson.	
1 Ineffective	Appropriate tempo of songs is not logical and consistently detracts from the lesson.	

Table 8.53   Evaluation of Teaching of In-tune Singing

	Criteria	Comments
4 Highly effective	Sequenced teaching strategies for developing in-tune singing are evident.	

(Continued)

Table 8.53 (continued)

	Criteria	Comments
3 Effective	Sequenced teaching strategies for developing in-tune singing are not always evident, but this does not detract from the lesson.	
2 Developing	Sequenced teaching strategies for developing in-tune singing are not always evident, and this sometimes detracts from the lesson.	
1 Ineffective	Sequenced teaching strategies for developing in-tune singing are not evident, and this consistently detracts from the lesson.	

Table 8.54 Evaluation of Teacher's Development of Children's Musical Skills

	Criteria	Comments
4 Highly effective	There is a balance among the musical skills being taught in the lesson.	
3 Effective	There is some imbalance among the musical skills being taught in the lesson, but it does not detract from the lesson.	
2 Developing	There is an imbalance among the musical skills being taught in the lesson that sometimes detracts from the lesson.	
1 Ineffective	There is an imbalance among the musical skills being taught in the lesson, and this constantly detracts from the lesson.	

Table 8.55 Evaluation of Teacher's Flexibility in Adaptation of Lesson Plans

	Criteria	Comments
4 Highly effective	Flexibility and adaptation of lesson plans is always appropriate.	

(Continued)

Table 8.55 (continued)

	Criteria	Comments
3 Effective	Flexibility and adaptation of lesson plans is not always appropriate but does not detract from the lesson.	
2 Developing	Flexibility and adaptation of lesson plans is not always appropriate and sometimes detracts from the lesson.	
1 Ineffective	Flexibility and adaptation of lesson plans is not appropriate and consistently detracts from the lesson.	

Table 8.56 Evaluation of Appropriateness of Teacher's Pacing of Lesson

	Criteria	Comments
4 Highly effective	Appropriate pacing of lesson is evident.	
3 Effective	Appropriate pacing of lesson is not always present, but this does not detract from the lesson.	
2 Developing	Appropriate pacing of lesson is not always present, and this sometimes detracts from the lesson.	
1 Ineffective	Appropriate pacing of lesson is not present, and this consistently detracts from the lesson.	

Table 8.57 Evaluation of Teacher's Questioning Technique

	Criteria	Comments
4 Highly effective	Questioning technique is always effective.	
3 Effective	Questioning technique is not always effective but does not detract from the lesson.	
2 Developing	Questioning technique is not always effective and sometimes detracts from the lesson.	
1 Ineffective	Questioning technique is not effective and consistently detracts from the lesson.	

Table 8.58 Evaluation of Teacher's Error Correction Through Modeling

	Criteria	Comments
4 Highly effective	Error correction is evident.	
3 Effective	Error correction is not always evident, but this does not detract from the lesson.	
2 Developing	Error correction is not always evident, and this sometimes detracts from the lesson.	
1 Ineffective	Error correction is not evident, and this constantly detracts from the lesson.	

Table 8.59 Evaluation of Teacher's Classroom Management and Discipline

	Criteria	Comments
4 Highly effective	Successful classroom management is evident.	
3 Effective	Appropriate classroom management is not always evident but does not detract from the lesson.	
2 Developing	Appropriate classroom management is not always evident and sometimes detracts from the lesson.	
1 Ineffective	Appropriate classroom management is not evident and consistently detracts from the lesson.	

Table 8.60 Evaluation of Learning: Child Participation

	Criteria	Comments
4 Highly effective	75% or more of C are participating successfully in observed activities.	
3 Effective	50% or more of C are participating successfully in observed activities.	

(Continued)

Table 8.60   Continued

	Criteria	Comments
2 Developing	25% or more of C are participating successfully in observed activities.	
1 Ineffective	Fewer than 25% of C are participating successfully in observed activities.	

Table 8.61   Evaluation of Learning: Teacher Assessment of Child

	Criteria	Comments
4 Highly effective	Appropriate child assessment tools are evident.	
3 Effective	Appropriate child assessment tools are not always evident but do not detract from the lesson.	
2 Developing	Appropriate child assessment tools are not always evident and sometimes detract from the lesson.	
1 Ineffective	Appropriate child assessment tools are not evident and consistently detract from the lesson.	

Discussion Questions

1. Discuss the role of assessment in the Kindergarten music class.
2. How do we informally and formally assess children's musical skills and knowledge in the Kindergarten music classroom? Provide examples of each kind of assessment.
3. Discuss the notion that there is inadequate time to assess child learning during a music lesson every week; music is meant to be a fun activity and assessment should not be a required part of a time-constrained music curriculum.

Ongoing Assignment

1. Develop a child profile sheet and formal assessment activities to be used in Kindergarten class, as well as the accompanying rubrics. Include the profile sheets and assessment tools in your teaching portfolio. What kinds of comments will you include in your assessment sheet?
2. Imagine that it is the end of the next year at your new school and you are having a conference with the parents of a child from an Kindergarten class. In preparation for the meeting, develop a detailed profile for the child. Explain to the parents how their child is succeeding in your class and what implications exist for their child's learning across the curriculum.

3. Because of your incredible success in the classroom, you have been asked to become the head of the music department during the second semester of next year in your new school. Your new responsibilities include evaluating Kindergarten teachers' teaching portfolios, teachers' lesson plans, teachers' musicianship skills, and a lesson taught by the teachers in your department. How will you prepare yourself for your new role as department head?

Bibliography

Abbott-Shim, M., and A. Sibley. *Assessment Profile for Early Childhood Programs, Research Version.* Atlanta: Quality Assist, 1992.

Barker, L. B., and C. J. Searchwell. *Writing Meaningful Teacher Evaluations Right Now: The Principal's Quick-Start Reference Guide.* Thousand Oaks, CA: Corwin, 2010.

Bergan, J., and J. Feld. "Developmental Assessments: New Directions." *Young Children,* 1993, *48*(5): 41–47.

Bredekamp, S., and T. Rosegrant, eds. *Reaching Potentials: Appropriate Curriculum and Assessment for Young Children: Vol. 1.* Washington, DC: National Association for the Education of Young Children, 1992.

Brophy, T. S. *Assessing the Developing Child Musician: Guide for General Music Teachers.* Chicago: G.I.A., 2000.

Colwell, R. "The Status of Arts Assessment: Examples from Music." *Arts Education Policy Review,* 2003, *105*: 11–18.

Boyle, David J., and Rudolf E. Radocy. *The Measurement and Evaluation of Musical Experiences.* New York: Schirmer, 1987.

Froseth, J. O., and M. A. Weaver. *Music Teacher Self-Assessment: A Diagnostic Tool for Professional Development.* Chicago: G.I.A., 1996.

Hills, T. "Assessment in Context: Teachers and Children at Work." *Young Children,* 1993, *48*(5): 20–28.

Saracho, O., and B. Spodek, eds. *Issues in Early Childhood Educational Evaluation and Assessment and Evaluation.* New York: Teachers College Press, 1997.

Schweinhart, L., and A. Epstein. "Curriculum and Evaluation in Early Childhood Education." In *Issues in Early Childhood Educational Evaluation and Assessment,* ed. O. Saracho and B. Spodek, pp. 48–59. New York: Teachers College Press, 1997.

Chapter **9**

Organizing Your Teaching Resources for the Kindergarten Classroom

The goal of this chapter is to present and discuss how to organize your teaching resources for teaching Kindergarten music. This chapter will also summarize how you can use this text to access information for your teaching and assessment. We suggest that teachers create a teaching resource folder divided into sections. Video of Kindergarten music teachers talking about the organization of teaching resources is posted on the companion website (Web 9B).

What Are the Components of a Teaching Resource Folder?

A teaching resource folder contains practical information that an instructor will use for teaching music in the Kindergarten classroom. The information contained in each section of this portfolio should be updated throughout the instructor's professional career. It is important that attendance at a professional development workshop entail updating teaching resource folder with practical information. There are two sections in a resource binder; one includes resources for teaching and the other contains information pertaining to assessment. The instructor may choose to develop a hard-copy or an electronic version of the folder.

Section One: Key Components of a Teaching Resource Folder

Statement of teaching philosophy and reflective practice
Songs to be used in teaching
Curriculum goals
Books to be used in the Kindergarten classroom
Techniques for developing the singing voice
Techniques for developing movement skills

Techniques for playing instruments
Techniques for teaching music concepts
Techniques for developing music skills
Lesson plans for the first few weeks of class
Lesson plans
Assessments and rubrics to be used for assessment in teaching
Resource materials, video, iTunes lists, and recordings to be used in teaching

Table 9.1 links the divisions of the resource binder to chapters in this book.

Table 9.1   Contents of a Teaching Resource Binder

Components of a Teaching Portfolio	Related Chapter
1. Statement of teaching philosophy	Chapter 2
2. Songs to be used in teaching	Chapter 1
3. Curriculum goals	Chapter 2 Appendix 1
4. Books to be used in the Kindergarten	Chapter 1 Appendix 2
5. Techniques for developing the singing voice	Chapter 3
6. Techniques for developing movement skills	Chapter 3
7. Techniques for playing instruments	Chapter 3
8. Techniques for teaching music concepts	Chapter 5
9. Techniques for developing form, rhythmic and melodic improvisation, part singing, and listening	Chapter 6
10. Getting started: lesson plans for the first few weeks of class	Chapter 1
11. Lesson plans for teaching Early Childhood concepts and skills	Chapter 7
12. Assessments and rubrics to be used for assessment in teaching	Chapter 8
13. Resource materials, video, iTunes lists, and recordings to be used in teaching	Chapter 9

Statement of Teaching Philosophy and Reflective Practice
The first component of your teaching resource folder is a statement concerning your philosophy of music education that will shape the design of your Kindergarten curriculum. This statement lays out a rationale for the inclusion of music in the curriculum and should be linked to the school's mission, vision, and philosophy statement. The philosophy statement is for the instructor a basis for developing realistic curriculum goals and lesson plans. In Chapter 2, we briefly summarize Zoltán Kodály's philosophy of music education, which may constitute a model for developing a personal philosophy of music education.

Songs and Rhymes for Teaching

In this section of your portfolio, keep a copy of songs for developing singing, movement, and instrumental skills for each grade. In selecting repertoire, you may want to ask yourself these questions:

How many songs should be used for developing singing and movement skills?

How many songs should be multicultural?

How many songs need to be included for specific holidays, seasonal songs, commemoration days, and patriotic celebrations?

Which songs are best used for linking music literacy and reading literacy?

How many songs should you include that will be listening experiences for the children? (Children will not be required to sing these songs.)

What songs will represent diverse musical styles?

In other words, how will you address the songs children listen to outside of school? How do you connect the selection of different types of repertoire to developmentally appropriate musical practices (particularly music literacy)?

Chapter 1 also offers some ideas concerning the selection of repertoire. Procedures and guidelines for analyzing this repertoire from both music theory and pedagogical perspectives are also included in this chapter. Consult Appendix 1 for a list of songs and books.

Curriculum Goals

Curriculum goals give you as the instructor a practical guide for creating a sequenced and well-structured musical education for your children. The curriculum goals, outcomes, and objectives should meet local, state, and national standards as well as reflect current research findings. You may wish to look at the emerging discussions on Core Curriculum Standards and design your curriculum to reflect these standards.

Once you have developed a philosophy statement, it will be easier to determine your curriculum goals. Curriculum goals are broad in nature and should incorporate the same language as your philosophy statement. For example, curriculum goals for teaching music may include:

Repertoire for developing singing, instrumental performance, and movement

Performance goals for developing singing, ensemble singing, movement, and playing instruments

Music literacy goals for teaching music concepts and elements as well as the development of music skills

Creative goals that include the development of improvisation and composition skills

Listening goals

Curricular connections to other disciplines

Reading Books

In this section of your binder, keep a list of books that you might want to use in teaching music in the early childhood classroom. When making a selection for the music classroom, remember to choose books:

That follow a call-and-response structure

That have repeated phrases

Where the text can be accompanied by a beat
Where children can clap the rhythm of the text easily
Where children can say part of a repeated refrain
Where the melodic patterns from other songs may be used to sing a text
That illustrate a song
That have clear pictures that can be used for text or song improvisation
That have characters and animals that can be used with known song materials
That are good for developing a sequence of events

Techniques for Developing the Singing Voice
This section of your teaching portfolio includes strategies for developing singing. Chapter 3 provides sequential steps to follow.

Techniques for Developing Movement Skills
This section of your teaching portfolio includes strategies for developing the children's movement skills. Again, Chapter 3 presents sequential steps to follow.

Techniques for Developing Children's Instrumental Skills
This section of your teaching portfolio includes strategies for developing children's instrument skills. See Chapter 3 for steps to follow.

Techniques for Teaching Music Concepts
This component of your teaching portfolio includes strategies for teaching music concepts in the Kindergarten classroom. Chapter 5 has teaching strategies for specific musical concepts to be introduced in the classroom.

Techniques for Developing Form, Rhythmic and Melodic Improvisation, Part Singing, and Listening
This section of the portfolio lists suitable strategies and activities for developing reading, writing, inner hearing, and improvisation/composition skills appropriate for early childhood. Chapter 6 presents techniques for developing these skills.

Getting Started: Lesson Plans for the First Few Weeks of Class
This section of your resource binder should include samples of lessons that you use during the first few weeks of teaching. There are a number of sample lessons in Chapter 1.

Lesson Plans for Teaching Kindergarten Concepts and Skills
This section of your resource binder should include a copy of lesson plans from which you intend to teach throughout the year. In Chapter 7 we have supplied you with model lessons that you can use for developing your own. We have also included unit plans giving an overview of concepts and skills that are taught for each set of lessons plans.

Assessments and Rubrics
The purpose of assessment is to improve instruction. Assessment is an essential component of teaching and learning. Assessment also allows you as the teacher to continue to reflect on curricular decisions and adjust things on the basis of student understanding and achievement, as well as the individual needs of the children. Assessment tools can be used

to inform parents and administrators about each child's progress in developing musical skills. Additionally, these tools can be used in advocacy efforts. You should determine how to assess musical growth throughout the year and design rubrics to measure children's musical growth and development. Include these assessment activities and scoring rubrics in this section of the portfolio. In Chapter 8 we furnish examples of assessment and scoring rubrics.

Resources

In this section of your resource binder you should include lists of videos, iTunes examples, or YouTube addresses that might be helpful in your teaching. This is good place to have several generic lesson plans that can be used by a substitute teacher.

This component of your teaching portfolio includes items such as internet resources, sources for purchasing instruments and others for books and recordings, as well as videos that reinforce additional areas of the curriculum.

Section Two: Assessment

In this section of your resource folder we suggest you keep all information related to assessment in the classroom. It should include (1) a section for evaluating students (comprising assessments, individual child's profiles, and class profiles). In Chapter 8 we have given you samples of children's assessment that you can use to develop your own assessment rubrics in the classroom. It is important to have a class profile for every child in your class. You might want to also have a "to work on" file such as recordings of singing or videos as part of this assessment. This information is especially important during parent teacher meetings, and for use when you teach these students in a later grade.

There should also be (2) a section for assessment of the teacher (comprising supervisor reports and peer teaching reports). The teacher may wish to include their supervisor and peer teaching reports. It is important to work with your supervisor to develop an assessment rubric that assesses teaching in the classroom. Sometimes the supervisor may want to use only a standard rubric form and may not capture all of the wonderful things going on your classroom.

Discussion Questions and Activities

1. What components should be included in a teaching resource portfolio for Kindergarten music?
2. Review the National or State Standards for Kindergarten Music Education in your state. How do these standards have an impact on a music curriculum?
3. Interview a successful Kindergarten music instructor in your community and find out what the teacher's long-term and short-term plans for music instruction entail.
4. Identify web resources that could be useful for music instructors.

Ongoing Assignment

1. Imagine that you have been hired by a school to teach Kindergarten music. Create a teaching resource portfolio binder, and tab it according to the teaching

portfolio components. This is an ongoing assignment, and you will be adding to this portfolio as you progress through all the chapters in the book.

2. Speak to a Kindergarten music teacher. Find out how she or he keeps track of all of the resources used in the music lessons.

Bibliography

Andress, B., and J. Feierabend. "Creating a Link Between Elementary and Preschool Music." *Teaching Music*, December 1993: 27–28.

Bredekamp, S., ed. *Developmentally Appropriate Practice in Kindergarten Programs Serving Children from Birth Through Age 8*. Washington, DC: National Association for the Education of Young Children, 2009.

Brosterman, N. *Inventing Early Childhood*. New York: Abrams, 1997.

Choksy, L., R. M. Abramson, A. Gillespie, and D. Woods. *Teaching Music in the Twentieth Century*. Upper Sadle River, NJ: Prentice Hall, 2001.

Drake, Susan. M. *Planning the Integrated Curriculum: The Call to Adventure*. Alexandria, VA: Association for Supervision and Curriculum Development, 1993.

Gardner, H. *Frames of Mind The Theory of Multiple Intelligences*. New York: Basic Books, 2011.

Klein, L. G., and J. Knitzer. "Effective Preschool Curricula and Teaching Strategies." *Pathways to Early School Success*, Issue Brief No. 2. New York: Columbia University, National Center for Children in Poverty, 2006.

Moore, T. L. E. C. "Perceptions and Practices of Kindergarten Teachers Regarding the Role of Music in the Early Childhood Curriculum." Doctoral diss., Indiana State University, 1990. Dissertation Abstracts International, 52(2A), 0421.

Music Educators National Conference. 1994. *National Standards for Art Education*. Reston, VA: MENC. Retrieved September 24, 2004.

Schweinhart, L. J., and D. P. Weikart. "Lasting Differences: The High/Scope Preschool Curriculum Comparison Study Through Age 23." *Monographs of the High/Scope Educational Research Foundation*, vol. 12. Ypsilanti, MI: High/Scope Press, 1997.

Starting Points: Meeting the Needs of Our Youngest Children. New York: Carnegie Corporation of New York, 1994.

Turner, M. E. "A Child-Centered Music Room." *Early Childhood Connections*, 2000, 6(2): 30–34.

Appendix 1 Songs and Related Children's Literature for the Kindergarten Classroom

"A la Ronda, Ronda"

MM: ♩ = 120   CSP: A

A   la   ron - da   ron - da,   so - pla - ra   el   zon - da,

en   la   huer - ta   de   Pa - lan   las   ci - rue - las   ca - e - ran

Literal translation:

Round and round, the hot north wind swirls,

In the garden of Palan, the plums will fall.

GAMES:	CONNECTIONS TO BOOKS/ LITERACY:
	Lively, Penelope. *One Two Three Jump!* Puffin Books, 1998.
	Ayres, Katherine. *Up, Down, and Around.* Candlewick Press, 2007.

"A la Rorro, Niño"

MM: ♩ = 120   CSP: F#

A la ro - rro, ni - ño, ya. la ro - rro - rro;

duér - me - te, mi ni - ño, y duér - me - te ya.

Literal translation:

To the rorro boy, and to the rorrorro;

Go to sleep, my boy, go to sleep now.

GAMES:	CONNECTIONS TO BOOKS/LITERACY:
	Na, Il Sung. *A Book of Sleep*. Alfred A. Knopf, 2007.
	Lewison, Wendy Cheyette. *Going to Sleep on the Farm*. Trumpet Club, 1992.
	Bentley, Dawn. *Sleepy Bear*. Intervisual Books, 1999.

"A la Rueda de San Miguel"

MM: ♩ = 120   CSP: C

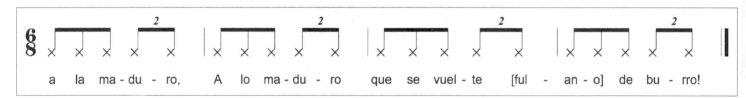

a la ma - du - ro, A lo ma - du - ro que se vuel - te [ful - an - o] de bu - rro!

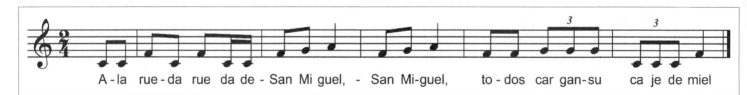

A - la rue - da rue da de - San Mi guel, - San Mi-guel, to - dos car gan-su ca je de miel

Literal translation:

To the wheel, wheel of Saint Michael, Saint Michael,

Everybody carries their box of honey

To the brave, to the brave [perpson's name] turns of the donkey.

"A la Vibora"

MM: ♩ = 100   CSP: C

A la vi-bo-ra, vi-bo-ra de la mar,
por a-qui pue-den pa-sar. Por a-qui yo
pa-se-ré, y?u-na ni-ña de-ja-ré. U-na ni-ña
¿cuál se-rá? ¿la dea-de-lan-teo la de?a-trás?

Translation:

To the snake, the snake,
Of the sea, of the sea.
"All of you can pass through here. Those up front run quickly. Those at back are left behind."
The game is similar to *London Bridge*.

GAMES:	CONNECTIONS TO BOOKS/LITERACY:
1. Children walk in a circle while holding hands and singing.	Carter, David A. *In and Out*. Intervisual Books, 1993.
2. They face toward the center of the circle.	Bentley, Dawn. (2004). *Buzz-Buzz, Busy Bees*. Simon & Schuster, 2004.
3. On the word *fulano* they substitute a child's name.	
4. That child then turns around and faces away from the circle while still holding hands.	
5. The game ends when everybody is facing away from the center of the circle.	

"Al Ánimo"

MM: ♩ = 96   CSP: A

Al á - ni-mo, al á - ni - mo, que se.ha ro - to la fuen - te

Al á - ni-mo, al á - ni-mo, man-dad-la.a com-po - ner.___

Verses:

2. Al á-ni-mo, al á-ni-mo,
no te-ne-mos di-ne-ro
Al á-ni-mo, al á-ni-mo,
no-so-tros lo te-ne-mos.

3. Al á-ni-mo, al á-ni-mo,
¿de que es e-se di-ne-ro?
Al á-ni-mo, al á-ni-mo,
de cas-ca-ras de hue-vo.

4. Al á-ni-mo, al á-ni-mo,
Pa-sen los ca-ba-lle-ros.
Al á-ni-mo, al á-ni-mo,
que ha-bre-mos de pa-sar

Translation:
1. Come on, come on,
The fountain is broken.

To the spirit, to the spirit,
We've got to fix it.

2. Let's go, . . .
We have no money
Come on . . .
We do have it.

3. Come on now, . . .
Where did you get the money?
Come on . . .
From an eggshell.

4. Let's go, . . .
Let the gentlemen pass.
"To the Spirit" . . .
We shall pass by.

GAMES:	CONNECTIONS TO BOOKS/LITERACY:
1. The game is played like London Bridge.	Orie, Sandra De Coteau. *Did You Hear Wind Sing Your Name?* Walker and Company, 1995.
	Walsh, Vivian. *Gluey.* Harcourt; Weekly Reader Children's Book Club, 2002.
	Spier, Peter. *London Bridge Is Falling Down.* Doubleday, 1967.
	Ricketts, Ann, and Michael Ricketts. *Rhyme Time.* Brimax Books, 1988.

"All Around the Buttercup"

MM: ♩ = 88   CSP: A

All a - round the but - ter - cup, one two three,

If you want a nice young friend, just choose me.

GAMES:	CONNECTIONS TO BOOKS/LITERACY:
Game 1: 1. Children stand in a circle, forming windows by raising their hands upwards. 2. Choose one child to weave in and out of the windows. 3. On the last word of the song, the child taps the child in front of him or her, who then becomes the leader of the line. 4. The last child left becomes the "buttercup" in the center of the new circle, and the game begins again. **Game 2:** 1. With one child standing in the middle, have a small group of students holds hands in a circle around the child. 2. The group sings the song as they walk around the circle. 3. On the last word, the child in the middle chooses someone in the circle. 4. The student chosen drops both hands, turns around in place and faces the outside, and then joins hands with the circle again. 5. This continues until all have been chosen and all are facing the outside of the circle. 6. On the last repetition, sing the song slower, and on the last phrase of the song the children walking in the circle kneel on one knee and hold their hands up in the air to represent the flower's "petals" while the person in the middle remains standing and holds his or her arms up in the air to form the "stamen," or "the sweet stuff the bees like."	Deetlefs, Rene. *The Song of Six Birds.* Dutton Children's Books, 1999. Ehlert, Lois. *Eating the Alphabet: Fruits & Vegetables from A to Z.* Harcourt, 1989. Fleming, Denise. *Beetle Bop.* Harcourt, 2007. Hubbell, Patricia. *I Like Cats.* A Cheshire Studio Book, 2003. Lively, Penelope. *One Two Three Jump!* Puffin Books, 1998. Lucas, Sally. *Dancing Dinos.* Random House, 1933. Pinkney, Brian. *Max Found Two Sticks.* Aladdin Paperbacks, 1994. Saport, Linda. *All the Pretty Little Horses.* Clarion Books, 1999.

"Amasee"

MM: ♩ = 126   CSP: A

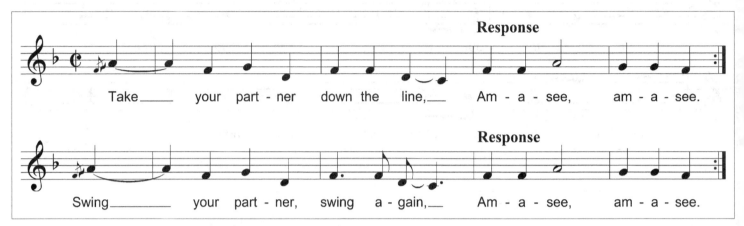

GAMES:	CONNECTIONS TO BOOKS/LITERACY:
1. Children form two lines, partners facing each other.	Lowery, Linda. (2008). *Twist with a Burger, Jitter with a Bug*. MaxBooks.
2. On verse 1, head couple takes hands and struts down the set between the lines.	Cauley, Lorinda Bryan. (1997). *Clap Your Hands*. Puffin.
3. On verse 2, this couple swings right elbows at the bottom of the set.	Lucas, Sally. (1933). *Dancing Dinos*. Random House.
4. Dance begins again with second couple. Set shifts up a little each time, as a new couple reaches the bottom. Go until all couples have completed a turn.	Langstaff, John. (1963). *Ol' Dan Tucker*. Harcourt, Brace & World.
5. A leader may be chosen to sing the lines, with the group coming in on the words "amasee."	Hayes, Sarah. (1988). *Stamp Your Feet: Action Rhymes*. William Morrow.
	Hamanaka, Sheila. (1997). *The Hokey Pokey*. Simon & Schuster Children's.

382

"The Animals Went in Two by Two"

MM: ♩. = 90   CSP: D

The an - i - mals went in two by two Hur - rah!_____ Hur - rah!_____

The an - i - mals went in two by two Hur - rah!_____ Hur - rah!_____

The an - i - mals went in two by two, The el - e - phant and the kan - ga - roo,

And they all went in - to the ark For to get out of the rain._____

Verses:

2. The animals went in three by three,
hurrah! hurrah!
The animals went in three by three,
hurrah! hurrah!
The animals went in three by three,
the wasp, the ant, and the bumble bee
And they all went into the ark,
for to get out of the rain.

3. The animals went in four by four,
hurrah! hurrah!
The animals went in four by four,
hurrah! hurrah!
The animals went in four by four,
the great hippopotamus stuck in the door
And they all went into the ark,
for to get out of the rain.

4. The animals went in five by five,
hurrah! hurrah!
The animals went in five by five,
hurrah! hurrah!
The animals went in five by five,

they warmed each other to keep alive
And they all went into the ark, for to get
out of the rain.

5. The animals went in six by six,
hurrah! hurrah!
The animals went in six by six,
hurrah! hurrah!
The animals went in six by six,
they turned out the monkey because of his
tricks
And they all went into the ark,
for to get out of the rain.

6. The animals went in seven by seven,
hurrah! hurrah!
The animals went in seven by seven,
hurrah! hurrah!
The animals went in seven by seven,
the little pig thought he was going to
heaven
And they all went into the ark, for to get
out of the rain.

GAMES:	CONNECTIONS TO BOOKS/LITERACY:
This is a song story for the teacher to sing to the children. The teacher may show pictures of the animals and sings to help students learn the verses of the songs (and the names of animals).	Twinn, M. (1975). *Old Macdonald Had a Farm*. Child's Play (International). Galdone, Paul. (1986). *Over in the Meadow*. Aladdin Paperbacks. Langstaff, John. (1957, 1985). *Over in the Meadow*. Voyager Books. Baker, Keith. (1999). *Quack and Count*. Harcourt Brace. Adams, Pam. (1989). *This Old Man*. Child's Play (International). Baker, Keith. (1994). *Big Fat Hen*. Voyager Books. Stojic, Manya. (2000). *Rain*. Dragonfly Books.

"Apples, Peaches"

MM: ♩ = 120

Ap - ples, pea - ches, pears and plums, Tell me when your birth - day comes.

GAMES:	CONNECTIONS TO BOOKS/LITERACY:
Children raise their hand when the month of their birthday is chanted during the rhyme.	Ayres, Katherine. *Up, Down, and Around*. Candlewick Press, 2007. Cronin, Doreen. *Bounce*. Atheneum Books for Young Readers, 2007. Ahlberg, Allan. *Each Peach Pear Plum*. Picture Puffin, 1986. Ehlert, Lois. *Eating the Alphabet: Fruits & Vegetables from A to Z*. Harcourt Books, 1989. Krauss, Ruth. *The Carrot Seed*. Scholastic, 1945. Eric, Carle. *Today Is Monday*. PaperStar, 1993. Gelman, Rita Golden. *More Spaghetti I Say*. Turtleback, 1993. Hutchins, Pat. *Don't Forget the Bacon!* Live Oak Media, 1992. Maccarone, Grace. *Oink! Moo! How Do You Do?* Cartwheel Books, 1994. Sierra, Judy. *Counting Crocodiles*. Sandpiper, 2001. Taback, Simms. *This Is the House That Jack Built*. Puffin, 2004.

"Bate, Bate, Chocolate"

MM: ♩ = 80

Ba - te, ba - te, cho - co - la - te. Con - ha - ri - na y con - to - ma - te.

Translation: Stir the chocolate with flour and tomatoes. (Making the roux for mole.)

"Bee, Bee, Bumble Bee"

MM: ♩ = 100

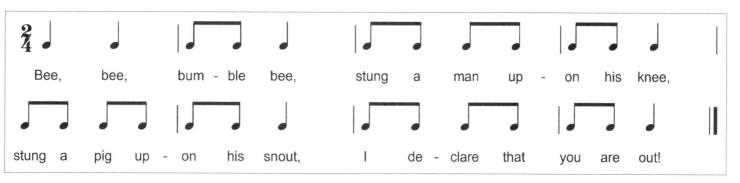

Bee, bee, bum - ble bee, stung a man up - on his knee,

stung a pig up - on his snout, I de - clare that you are out!

GAMES:	CONNECTIONS TO BOOKS/LITERACY:
This is a four-beat, four phrase rhyme. All actions are done to the beat. You or a child may lead the activity.	Brennan-Nelson, Denise. *Buzzy the Bumblebee*. Sleeping Bear Press, 1999.
1. First phrase: children flap arms like a bee.	Bentley, Dawn. *Buzz-Buzz, Busy Bees*. Simon & Schuster, 2004.
2. Second phrase: children point to their knees.	Carter, David A. *In and Out*. Intervisual Books, 1993.
3. Third phrase: children point to their nose.	Fleming, Denise. *In the Tall, Tall Grass*. Henry Holt 1991.
4. Fourth phrase: children point to select someone to lead the rhyme.	Twinn, M. *Old Macdonald Had a Farm*. Child's Play (International), 1975.
	Kohn, Michael, and Daniel Weiner. *There Was an Old Woman Who Swallowed a Fly*, 1981.

"Billy, Billy"

MM: ♩ = 90   CSP: D

Here's the way we Bil - ly, Bil - ly, Bil - ly, Bil - ly, Bil - ly, Bil - ly,

Here's the way we Bil - ly, Bil - ly, all night long.

Verses:

1. Step back Sally, Sally, Sally, Walkin' down the alley, all night long.

2. Here comes the second one, just like the other one, Here comes the second one, all night long.

GAMES:	CONNECTIONS TO BOOKS/LITERACY:
1. Have the children choose a partner. 2. *Verse 1:* a. Taking the partner's hands, twist back and forth on the dotted rhythms. 3. *Verse 2:* a. With the partners facing each other, have the children make two rows. b. On measures 1 and 2, alternate a step-clap motion, stepping backward. c. On measure 3, the end person on the right struts down the "alley" (between the partners). d. He or she will take the place at the end on the opposite side of the alley. 4. *Verse 3:* a. The partner remaining must go down the alley imitating the first partner's motion, and then stand opposite the partner. Play the game twice so everyone has a turn to improvise.	Na, Il Sung. *A Book of Sleep.* Alfred A. Knopf, 2007. Bryan, Ashley. *All Night, All Day: A Child's First Book of African-American Spirituals.* Aladdin Paperbacks, 1991. Guthrie, Woody. *Bling Blang.* Candlewick Press, 1954. Martin Jr., Bill. *Brown Bear, Brown Bear.* Henry Holt, 2004. Orie, Sandra De Coteau. *Did You Hear Wind Sing Your Name?* Walker and Company, 1995. Lionni, Leo. *Frederick.* Trumpet Club, 1967. Lewison, Wendy Cheyette. *Going to Sleep on the Farm.* Trumpet Club, 1992. Wood, Audrey. *Silly Sally.* Harcourt, 1992.

"Blue"

MM: ♩= 96   CSP: B

I had a dog and his name was Blue. I had a dog and his name was Blue.

I had a dog and his name was Blue. Bet you five dol-lars he's a good dog, too.

Verses:

2. Ev-ry night just about good dark, . . .
Blue goes out and begins to bark.

3. Ev'rything just in a rush, . . .
He treed a possum up a white-oak bush.

4. Possum walked out on the end of a limb, . . .
Blue sat down and talked to him.

5. Blue got sic and very sick, . . .
Sent for the doctor to come real quick

6 Doctor came and he came in a run, . . .
Says, "Old Blue, your hunting's done."

7. Blue died and he died so hard, . . .
Scratched little holes all around in the yard.

8. When I get to heaven I think what I'll do, . . .
Take my horn and blow for Blue.

387

"Bobby Shafto"

MM: ♩= 88   CSP: A

Bob - by Shaf - toe's gone to sea, Sil - ver buck - les on his knee,

He'll come back and mar - ry me, Pret - ty Bob - by Shaf - toe.

GAMES:	CONNECTIONS TO BOOKS/LITERACY:
1. Have children do different actions to the beat.	Langstaff, John. *Frog Went A-Courtin.* Harcourt Children's Books, 1955.
2. Once they know the song well enough, have them choose a partner and sit across from each other on the floor.	Seeger, Pete. *One Grain of Sand.* Little, Brown, 1957.
3. Holding hands, they will gently rock back and forth in time to the music.	Harriet, Ziefert. *When I First Came to This Land.* Scholastic, 1998.

"Bought Me a Cat"

MM: ♩ = 160   CSP: D

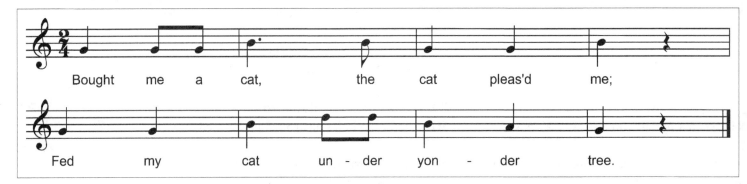

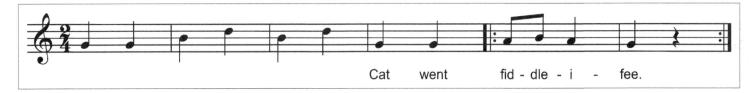

Verses:

2. Bought me a hen and the hen pleased me,
I fed my hen under yonder tree.
Hen goes chimmy-chuck, chimmy-chuck,
Cat goes fiddle-i-fee.

3. Bought me a duck and the duck pleased me,
I fed my duck under yonder tree.
Duck goes quack, quack,
Hen goes chimmy-chuck, chimmy-chuck,
Cat goes fiddle-i-fee.

4. Bought me a goose and the goose pleased me
I fed my goose under yonder tree.
Goose goes hissy, hissy,

Duck goes quack, quack,
Hen goes chimmy-chuck, chimmy-chuck,
Cat goes fiddle-i-fee.

5. Bought me a sheep and the sheep pleased me,
I fed my sheep under yonder tree.
Sheep goes baa, baa,
Goose goes hissy, hissy,
Duck goes quack, quack,
Hen goes chimmy-chuck, chimmy-chuck,
Cat goes fiddle-i-fee.

6. Bought me a pig and the pig pleased me,
I fed my pig under yonder tree.

Pig goes oink, oink,
Sheep goes baa, baa,
Goose goes hissy, hissy,
Duck goes quack, quack,
Hen goes chimmy-chuck, chimmy-chuck,
Cat goes fiddle-i-fee.

7. Bought me a cow and the cow pleased me,
I fed my cow under yonder tree.
Cow goes moo, moo,
Pig goes oink, oink,
Sheep goes baa, baa,
Goose goes hissy, hissy,
Duck goes quack, quack,
Hen goes chimmy-chuck, chimmy-chuck,
Cat goes fiddle-i-fee.

8. Bought me a horse and the horse pleased me,
I fed my horse under yonder tree.

Horse goes neigh, neigh,
Cow goes moo, moo,
Pig goes oink, oink,
Sheep goes baa, baa,
Goose goes hissy, hissy,
Duck goes quack, quack,
Hen goes chimmy-chuck, chimmy-chuck,
Cat goes fiddle-i-fee.

9. Bought me a dog and the dog pleased me,
I fed my dog under yonder tree.
Dog goes bow-wow, bow-wow,
Horse goes neigh, neigh,
Cow goes moo, moo,
Pig goes oink, oink,
Sheep goes baa, baa,
Goose goes hissy, hissy,
Duck goes quack, quack,
Hen goes chimmy-chuck, chimmy-chuck,
Cat goes fiddle-i-fee.

389

GAMES:	CONNECTIONS TO BOOKS/LITERACY:
Use pictures to illustrate the text as you sing through the song for the children. They initially sing "fiddle li fee, fiddle li fee." Later they may sing more of the verses.	Hubbell, Patricia. *I Like Cats*. A Cheshire Studio Book, 2003. Slavin, Bill. *The Cat Came Back*. Albert Whitman, 1992.

"Bounce High, Bounce Low"

MM: ♩ = 88   CSP: A

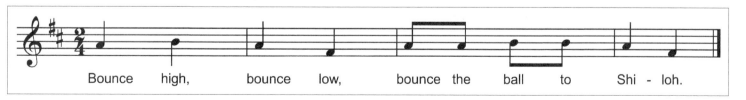

Bounce   high,   bounce   low,   bounce the   ball   to   Shi - loh.

GAMES:	CONNECTIONS TO BOOKS/LITERACY:
1. Form a circle. 2. Pass a ball from child to child in a drop-catch pattern, with the ball hitting the floor on accented beats, picked up, and passed on. 3. Keep this activity in time with the singing.	Carter, David A. *In and Out*. Intervisual Books, 1993. Cronin, Doreen. *Bounce*. Atheneum Books for Young Readers, 2007. Jorgensen, Gail. *Crocodile Beat*. Aladdin Paperbacks, 1998. Carle, Eric. *From Head to Toe*. HarperFestival, 1997. Williams, Sue. *I Went Walking*. Red Wagon Books/Harcourt, 1989.

"Bow, Wow, Wow"

MM: ♩ = 96   CSP: D

Bow, wow, wow,   whose dog art thou?   Lit-tle Tom-my Tuck-er's dog   bow, wow, wow.

GAMES:	CONNECTIONS TO BOOKS/LITERACY:
1. Have the children get into pairs. 2. They stamp three times (right, left, right) on "Bow, wow, wow." 3. One child points finger at partner to the rhythm on "Whose dog art thou?" 4. Partners clasp hands and quickly circle in place on "Little Tommy Tucker's dog." 5. They stamp three times, turning away from partner on "Bow, wow, wow" and facing a new neighbor.	Wood, Audrey. *A Dog Needs a Bone*. The Blue Sky Press, 2007. Saport, Linda. *All the Pretty Little Horses*. Clarion Books, 1999. Hubbell, Patricia. *I Like Cats*. A Cheshire Studio Book, 2003. Twinn, M. *Old Macdonald Had a Farm*. Child's Play (International), 1975. Leslie, Amanda. *Who's That Scratching at My Door*? Handprint Books, 2001.

"Brinca la Tablita"

MM: ♩= 96   CSP: A

Brin - ca la tab - li - ta, ya yo la brin - que,

brin - ca la tua ho - ra qué yo me - can - se.

Translation:

Jump over the board. I jumped it. Jump it again. I am already tired.

"Built My Lady"

MM: ♩= 108   CSP: F#

Built my la - dy a fine brick house,

Built it in the gar - den I

Put her in but she jumped out! So

fair thee well my dar - lin'

GAMES:	CONNECTIONS TO BOOKS/LITERACY:
1. Have two children hold hands and make a house.	Galdone, Paul. *Over in the Meadow.* Aladdin Paperbacks, 1986.
2. Have another child stand in the middle.	Guthrie, Woody. *Bling Blang.* Candlewick Press, 1954.
3. The "houses" should all form a circle so that the person in the middle can duck out of one and into another.	Langstaff, John. *Frog Went A-Courtin.* Harcourt Children's Books. 1955.
4. While singing the song, the house is being built by a gentle movement of the arms going up and down.	Walsh, Vivian. *Gluey.* Harcourt; Weekly Reader Children's Book Club, 2002.
5. At the third line of the song, the child in the middle of the house ducks out and goes to the next one.	Fleming, Denise. *In the Small, Small Pond.* Henry Holt, 1993. Fleming, Denise. *In the Tall, Tall Grass.* Henry Holt, 1991.
6. The game continues; change children.	Portis, Antoinette. *Not a Box.* Harper Collins, 2006.
	Swanson, Susan Marie. *The House in the Night.* Houghton Mifflin, 2008.
	Leslie, Amanda. *Who's That Scratching at My Door?* Handprint Books, 2001.

"Burnie Bee"

MM: ♩ = 88

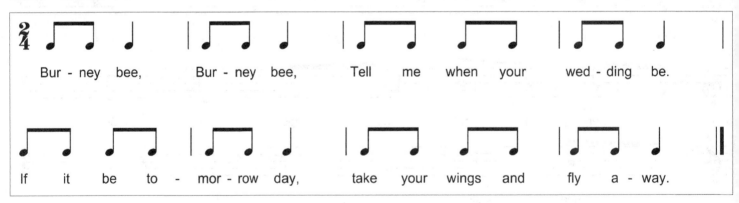

Bur - ney bee, Bur - ney bee, Tell me when your wed - ding be.

If it be to - mor - row day, take your wings and fly a - way.

GAMES:	CONNECTIONS TO BOOKS/LITERACY:
Choosing game. Children sit in a circle but leave an empty space. You or another student points around the circle to another child. At the end of the rhyme the selected child "flies" to the empty place in the circle. The game repeats until several children have changed places in the circle.	Fleming, Denise. *Beetle Bop.* Harcourt, 2007. Brennan-Nelson, Denise. *Buzzy the Bumblebee.* Sleeping Bear Press, 1999. Langstaff, John. *Frog Went A-Courtin.* Harcourt Children's Books, 1955. Cannon, Janell. *Stellaluna.* Scholastic, 1993. Deetlefs, Rene. *The Song of Six Birds.* Dutton Children's Books, 1999.

"El Burrito del Teniente"

MM: ♩ = 96   CSP: G

Translation:

The donkey carries a burden but doesn't care.

"Button You Must Wander"

MM: ♩ = 96   CSP: D

GAMES:	CONNECTIONS TO BOOKS/LITERACY:
Variation 1: 1. Players sit in a circle with legs crossed. 2. Pick a child who is It, and have him or her sit in the middle with eyes closed. 3. While singing the song, the players pass an object around. 4. At the completion of the song, the last child to have the object sings, "I have the button." 5. The child who is It will guess by voice identification. **Variation 2:** 1. Have children form a standing circle. 2. Left hand extended to the left and fingers curled up to conceal any contents in the left hand. 3. The child chosen to be It is in the middle of the circle. 4. A small object, such as a coin or a pebble, is passed to the beat using the right hand to pass. (The left hand always remains in the same place.) 5. The object is to hide the object from the child who is It. 6. At the completion of the song, the child who is It has three guesses to tell who has the object.	Bryan, Ashley. *All Night, All Day: A Child's First Book of African-American Spirituals.* Aladdin Paperbacks, 1991. Segal, Lore. *All the Way Home.* A Sunburst Book, 1973. Lewison, Wendy Cheyette. *Going to Sleep on the Farm.* Trumpet Club, 1992. Brown, Margaret Wise. *Goodnight Moon.* Scholastic, 1947. Powell, Richard. *Guess Who's Hiding!* Barron's Educational Series, 2001. Powell, Richard. *Guess What I Have!* Barron's Educational Series, 2001. Bentley, Dawn. *Sleepy Bear.* Intervisual Books, 1999. Brown, Margaret Wise. *The Train to Timbuctoo.* Golden Books, 1979. Calmenson, Stephanie. *Engine, Engine, Number Nine.* Scholastic, 1996. Ayres, Katherine. *Up, Down, and Around.* Candlewick Press, 2007. Rosen, Michael. *We're Going on a Bear Hunt.* Little Simon, 1989.

394

"Bye, Baby Bunting"

MM: ♩ = 96   CSP: C

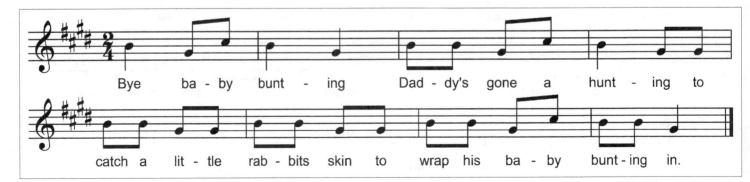

GAMES:	CONNECTIONS TO BOOKS/LITERACY:
Children rock a stuffed animal to the beat.	Rosen, Michael. *We're Going on a Bear Hunt.* Little Simon, 1989.
	Langstaff, John. *Oh, A-Hunting We Will Go.* Aladdin Paperbacks, 1974.
	Langstaff, John. *Over in the Meadow.* Voyager Books, 1957, 1985.
	Rob, Jackie. *Sheep Says Baa!* Bang on the Door Series, 2003.

"Caracol Col Col" (Little snail snail snail)

MM: = 88   CSP: E

Ca - ra - col   col   col   sa-ca tus   cuer - nos por el   sol.

ya____   vie - nen de ma - tar   por la o - ri - lla del____   mar.

Literal translation:
Little snail snail snail, dry your feelers in the sun.
They have just withdrawn by the shore of the sea.

GAMES:	CONNECTIONS TO BOOKS/ LITERACY:
	Walsh, Vivian. *Gluey.* Harcourt; Weekly Reader Children's Book Club, 2002.
	Brown, Ruth. *Snail Trail.* Crown, 2000.

"Charlie over the Ocean"

MM: ♩ = 138   CSP: G

Verses:

1. Leader: Charlie over the ocean,
Ring: Charlie over the ocean,
Leader: Charlie over the sea,
Ring: Charlie over the sea,
Leader: Charlie caught a black fish,
Ring: Charlie caught a black fish,
Leader: Can't catch me.
Ring: Can't catch me.

2. Leader: Charlie over the ocean,
Ring: Charlie over the ocean,
Leader: Charlie over the sea,
Ring: Charlie over the sea,
Leader: Charlie caught a blackbird,
Ring: Charlie caught a blackbird,
Leader: Can't catch me.
Ring: Can't catch me.

GAMES:	CONNECTIONS TO BOOKS/ LITERACY:
Variation 1 a. Have children join hands in a ring and skip to their right. b. Choose someone to be the leader who stand outside the circle, skipping in the opposite direction. c. The leader begins the song, and the circle sings the song back to him or her. d. When the leader says "Charlie caught a blackbird," he or she touches someone in the ring and then begins to run around the circle. e. The child who was touched tries to catch "the leader." f. If the child touched on the shoulder cannot catch the other before the leader reaches the empty space, then the second child is the leader. g. If the child touched on the shoulder catches the leader, then he or she remains on the outside of the circle and continues as the leader.	Aardema, Verna. *Bringing the Rain to Kapiti Plain.* Puffin Books, 1981. Orie, Sandra De Coteau. *Did You Hear Wind Sing Your Name?* Walker and Company, 1995. Fleming, Denise. *In the Small, Small Pond.* Henry Holt, 1993. Baker, Keith. *Quack and Count.* Harcourt Brace, 1999. Deetlefs, Rene. *The Song of Six Birds.* Dutton Children's Books, 1999.

(Continued)

GAMES:	CONNECTIONS TO BOOKS/ LITERACY:
Variation 2 a. Have the children form a circle. b. Choose a child to move around the circle, carrying a handkerchief. c. At the end of the song the child will drop the handkerchief behind another child in the ring and start to run around the ring. d. The child with handkerchief behind him or her starts to run after the first child. e. If the second child catches the first before reaching the empty spot, the first child is It. f. If the child does not catch the other child, the second child is It. **Variation 3** a. Choose a leader to stand in the center of the circle that the children form. b. Blindfold the leader. c. When the line "Charlie caught a blackbird" is sung, the circle squats, moving about from side to side, as the leader tries to find one of the children in the circle.	

397

"Cherry Pie"

MM: ♩ = 80   CSP: A

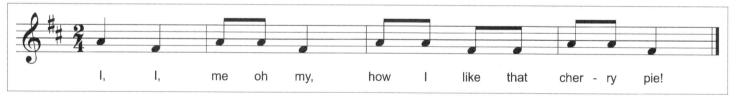

I, I, me oh my, how I like that cher - ry pie!

GAMES:	CONNECTIONS TO BOOKS/ LITERACY:
1. As a starter activity, ask a child to choose a type of pie (e.g., apple). The class then sings a verse about a rhubarb pie, instead of an apple pie. 2. For younger children who are growing in confidence with their singing voices, this song, when performed as a circle game in which each child in turn suggests a pie and sings about it, is a great incentive for children to sing on their own. 3. After all the children have sung individually, the class repeats, so that pitch-matching is experienced.	Ehlert, Lois. *Eating the Alphabet: Fruits & Vegetables from A to Z.* Harcourt Books, 1989. Ayres, Katherine. *Up, Down, and Around.* Candlewick Press, 2007. Eric, Carle. *Today Is Monday.* PaperStar, 1993.

"Chickama Craney Crow"

MM: ♩ = 92   CSP: A

GAMES:	CONNECTIONS TO BOOKS/ LITERACY:
1. Choose one player to be the "witch," and another player to be the "Craney Crow." 2. The witch hides, crouching behind a desk, ad lib. 3. The other players line up behind the Craney Crow, with hands on the shoulders of the one before them, led by Craney Crow. 4. They are the "chickens," who march around in front of the "witch's hiding place," singing the song in a taunting manner.	Deetlefs, Rene. *The Song of Six Birds.* Dutton Children's Books, 1999. Carle, Eric. *From Head to Toe.* HarperFestival, 1997. Suhr, Mandy. *I Can Move.* Wayland Books, 1993, 2009. Baker, Keith. *Quack and Count.* Harcourt Brace, 1999.

(Continued)

GAMES:	CONNECTIONS TO BOOKS/ LITERACY:
5. When the words: "What time, old witch?" is sung, she rushes out from her hiding place and shouts "one" or the number of the victim she seizes. 6. That "chicken" then joins the witch. 7. The line is formed again behind Craney Crow. 8. The game goes until the "witch" has caught half the group. 9. She then draws a magic line and a tug-of-war ensues. 10. The first player pulled over to the witch's side becomes the new witch; or the other side, Craney Crow.	

"Chini, Mini"

MM: ♩ = 80 CSP: G

A nonsense game or verse similar to "Eeny, meeny, miny, mo."

GAMES:	CONNECTIONS TO BOOKS/ LITERACY:
	Deetlefs, Rene. *The Song of Six Birds*. Dutton Children's Books, 1999.

"Clap, Clap"

MM: ♩ = 80   CSP: A

Verse 2:
Stamp, stamp, stamp your feet,
Stamp your feet together.

GAMES:	CONNECTIONS TO BOOKS/ LITERACY:
1. The children form two circles, one within the other.	Cauley, Lorinda Bryan. *Clap Your Hands*. Puffin, 1997.
2. The players face each other, moving together.	Carter, David. *If You're Happy and You Know It Clap Your Hands*. Cartwheel, 1997.
3. At the end of the song, the children standing in the outward circle skip to their right.	Hayes, Sarah. *Stamp Your Feet: Action Rhymes*. William Morrow, 1988.
4. The game is repeated with new partners.	

"Clap Your Hands Together"

MM: ♩ =100   CSP: G - A

GAMES:	CONNECTIONS TO BOOKS/ LITERACY:
1. Have the children form a circle with one child, It, in the middle.	Carle, Eric. *From Head to Toe*. HarperFestival, 1997.
2. While singing the song, the children act out the words.	Ehlert, Lois. *Eating the Alphabet: Fruits & Vegetables from A to Z*. Harcourt Books, 1989.
3. On "Make a happy circle" the players walk around to their left.	Locker, Thomas. *Cloud Dance*. Voyager Books, 2000.
4. On "Then you cut the cake," the child in the middle touches the joined hands of two players in a slicing motion.	Martin Jr., Bill. *The Maestro Plays*. Voyager Books, 1996.
5. Those two players then drop hands and run around the circle in opposite directions.	Carter, David A. *In and Out*. Intervisual Books, 1993.
6. The first one back to place and to tap It's outstretched hand is the winner and gets to be in the middle of the circle for the next repetition.	Rob, Jackie. *Sheep Says Baa!* Bang on the Door Series, 2003.

"Closet Key"

MM: ♩ = 100   CSP: F

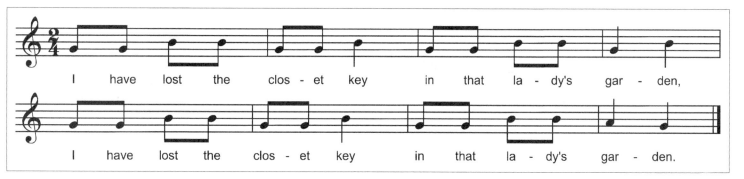

I have lost the clos-et key in that la-dy's gar-den,
I have lost the clos-et key in that la-dy's gar-den.

Help me find the key in that lady's garden,
Help me find the key in that lady's garden.
I've found the closet key in that lady's garden,
I've found the closet key in that lady's garden.

GAMES:	CONNECTIONS TO BOOKS/LITERACY:
1. Have children form a circle, putting their hands behind their back.	Swanson, Susan Marie. *The House in the Night*. Houghton Mifflin, 2008.
2. One child walks around and places a key in another child's hand.	Brennan-Nelson, Denise. *Buzzy the Bumblebee*. Sleeping Bear Press, 1999.
3. The walker now leads the singing of stanzas 1 and 2.	
4. The child who has the key leads the singing in stanza 3.	Westcott, Nadine Bernard. *The Lady with the Alligator Purse*. Little, Brown, 1998.
5. This child is the one who now places a key in someone else's hands.	

"Con Mi Martillo" (With my hammer)

MM: ♩ = 80   CSP: F

Con mi mar-ti-llo, mar-ti-llo, mar-ti-llo.

Con mi mar-ti-llo, mar-ti-llo, jo.

Literal translation: With my hammer, jo.

"Cuckoo"

MM: ♩ = 80   CSP: A

Cuc-koo, what are you? I'm a bird. Do you sing? Yes, I do. Sing, then! Cuc-koo!

GAMES:	CONNECTIONS TO BOOKS/ LITERACY:
Voice identification game.	Cannon, Janell. *Stellaluna*. Scholastic, 1993.
	Aardema, Verna. *Bringing the Rain to Kapiti Plain*. Puffin Books, 1981.
	Deetlefs, Rene. *The Song of Six Birds*. Dutton Children's Books, 1999.

"Dance Josey"

MM: ♩ = 108   CSP: F

Chick-en in the fence post, can't dance Jo-sey, Chick-en in the fence post, can't dance Jo-sey,

Chick-en in the fence post, can't dance Jo-sey, Hel - lo Su - san Brown-y - o.

Lyrics:

Choose your partner and come dance Josey, *(Sing three times)*
Hello Susan Browny-o.
Chew my gum while I dance Josey, *(Sing three times)*
Hello Susan Browny-o.
Shoestring's broke and I can't dance Josey, *(Sing three times)*
Hello Susan Browny-o.
Hold my mule while I dance Josey, *(Sing three times)*
Hello Susan Browny-o.
Crank my fad while I dance Josey, *(Sing three times)*
Hello Susan Browny-o.
Hair in the butter, can't dance Josey, *(Sing three times)*
Hello Susan Browny-o.
Briar in my heels, can't dance Josey, *(Sing three times)*
Hello Susan Browny-o.
Stumped my toe, can't dance Josey, *(Sing three times)*
Hello Susan Browny-o.

GAMES:	CONNECTIONS TO BOOKS/ LITERACY:
This is a more complex circle game for elementary school children. In Kindergarten, children may simply move around in a circle while singing the song.	Twinn, M. *Old Macdonald Had a Farm.* Child's Play (International), 1975. Post, Jim, and Janet Post. *Barnyard Boogie.* Accord, 2002. Greene, Rhonda Gowler. *Barnyard Song.* Atheneum Books for Young Readers, 1997. Orie, Sandra De Coteau. *Did You Hear Wind Sing Your Name?* Walker and Company, 1995. Bemelmans, Ludwig. *Madeline.* Viking Press, 1939.

"Dinah"

MM: ♩ = 108   CSP: F

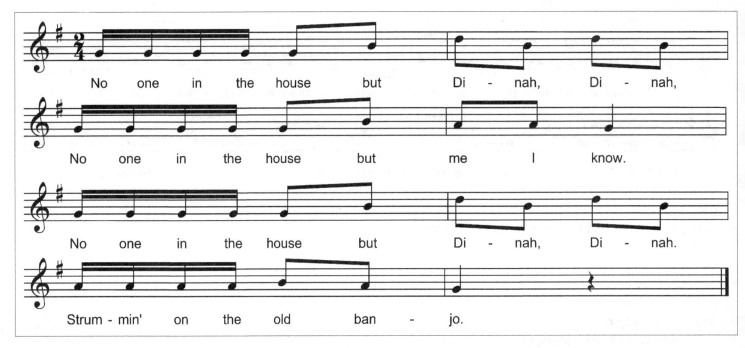

No one in the house but Di - nah, Di - nah,

No one in the house but me I know.

No one in the house but Di - nah, Di - nah.

Strum - min' on the old ban - jo.

Verses:

1. No one in the house when I came in.
(Three times)
Playing on the violin.

2. No one in the house but me alone
(Three times)
Playing on the slide trombone.

3. No one in the house that I have met
(Three times)
Playing on the clarinet.

4. No one in the house when e'er I come
(Three times)
Playing on the big bass drum.

GAMES:	CONNECTIONS TO BOOKS/ LITERACY:
The song ends with the words "old banjo." Have the children choose (improvise) different instruments for the ending of the song and act out playing that instrument.	McPhail, David. *Mole Music*. Henry Holt, 1999.
	Swanson, Susan Marie. *The House in the Night*. Houghton Mifflin, 2008.
	Segal, Lore. *All the Way Home*. A Sunburst Book, 1973.
	Orie, Sandra De Coteau. *Did You Hear Wind Sing Your Name?* Walker and Company, 1995.
	Bemelmans, Ludwig. *Madeline*. Viking Press, 1939.

"Do, Do Pity My Case"

MM: ♩ = 90   CSP: A

Do do pit-y my case, In some la-dy's gar - den.

My clothes to wash when I get home, In some la-dy's gar - den.

GAMES:	CONNECTIONS TO BOOKS/ LITERACY:
1. Step in a circle for the first two phrases.	Brennan-Nelson, Denise. *Buzzy the Bumblebee.*, Sleeping Bear Press, 1999.
2. Perform the actions described in the last two.	Westcott, Nadine Bernard. *The Lady with the Alligator Purse.* Little, Brown, 1998.
3. Add further actions (chores, e.g., "dog to walk" or "room to clean") to create more verses.	Ehlert, Lois. *Eating the Alphabet: Fruits & Vegetables from A to Z.* Harcourt Books, 1989.

405

"Doggie, Doggie"

MM: ♩ = 120   CSP: A

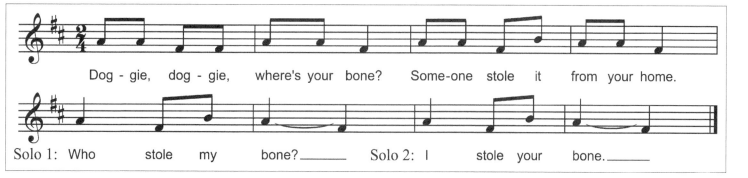

Dog - gie, dog - gie, where's your bone? Some-one stole it from your home.

Solo 1: Who stole my bone?_____ Solo 2: I stole your bone._____

GAMES:	CONNECTIONS TO BOOKS/ LITERACY:
Class sits in circle; OR for a challenge, in scattered formation. 1. Child A is in the middle (or at the front of the class for scattered formation) with blindfold on or eyes closed. 2. Child B has bone. (Teacher can use a rawhide chew bone.) 3. Class sings first two phrases of song. 4. Child A sings phrase 3: "Who has my bone?" 5. Child B sings phrase 4: "I have your bone." 6. Child A has to guess who has the bone. 7. Child B then becomes the dog.	Leslie, Amanda. *Who's That Scratching at My Door?* Handprint Books, 2001. Powell, Richard. *Guess What I Have!* Barron's Educational Series, 2001. Powell, Richard. *Guess Who's Hiding!* Barron's Educational Series, 2001. Wood, Audrey. *A Dog Needs a Bone.* Blue Sky Press, 2007. Hubbell, Patricia. *I Like Cats.* A Cheshire Studio Book, 2003.

"Doña Araña" (Miss Spider)

MM: ♩ = 96   CSP: F

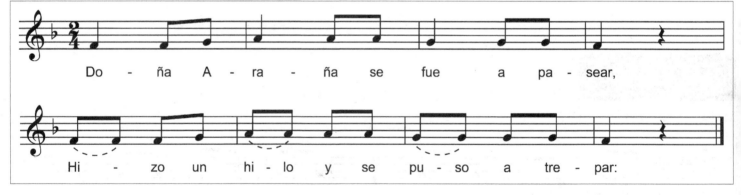

Do - ña A - ra - ña se fue a pa - sear,

Hi - zo un hi - lo y se pu - so a tre - par:

Verse:
Vi-no el vien-to,
la hi-zo bai-lar,
vi-no la tor-men-ta,
la hi-zo ba-jar.

Literal translation:
Miss spider went for a stroll,
She spun a thread and tried to climb up,
Along came a wind that caused her to dance,
Along came a rain storm that made her come down.

GAMES:	CONNECTIONS TO BOOKS/ LITERACY:
	Carle, Eric. *The Very Busy Spider*. Philomel Books, 1984.
	Stojic, Manya. *Rain*. Dragonfly Books, 2000.
	Finn, Isobel. *The Very Lazy Ladybug*. Tiger Tales, 1999.
	Aardema, Verna. *Bringing the Rain to Kapiti Plain*. Puffin Books, 1981.

"Down Came a Lady"

MM: ♩ = 120   CSP: F

Down came a la - dy, down came two.

Down came old Dan - iel's wife and she was dressed in blue.

GAMES:	CONNECTIONS TO BOOKS/ LITERACY:
Choosing. Change the color at the end of the song "... and she was dressed in 'red'."	Otoshi, Kathryn. *One*. KO Kids Books, 2008.
	Peek, Merele. *Mary Wore Her Red Dress and Henry Wore His Green Sneakers*. Clarion, 1985.
	Rollings, Susan. *New Shoes, Red Shoes*. Orchard Books, 2000.
	Lively, Penelope. *One Two Three Jump!* Puffin Books, 1998.
	Baker, Keith. *Quack and Count*. Harcourt Brace, 1999.

"Duerme Pronto" (El Canto De Madre) (Go to sleep now [Mother's song])

MM: ♩ = 80   CSP: D

Duer - me pron - to ni - no lin - do, duer - me pron - to.y sin llo - rar,

que.es - tas en los bra - zos de tu ma - dre que te va.a can - tar.

Literal translation:

Go to sleep soon, dear little child,

Sleep now without crying

You're in the arms of your mother.

GAMES:	CONNECTIONS TO BOOKS/LITERACY:
A lullaby; children rock a stuffed animal to the beat and sing.	Bentley, Dawn. *Sleepy Bear*. Intervisual Books, 1999.
	Lewison, Wendy Cheyette. *Going to Sleep on the Farm*. Trumpet Club, 1992.
	Na, Il Sung. *A Book of Sleep*. Alfred A. Knopf, 2007.
	Finn, Isobel. *The Very Lazy Ladybug*. Tiger Tales, 1999.

"Duermente"

MM: ♩ = 80   CSP: D

Duer - men - te mi niñ - o, duer - men - te mi sol

duer - men - te pe - da___ zo, de mi cor - a zón.

Translation:

Sleep my love (little girl or boy),

sleep my love.

Sleep piece of my heart.

"En un Plato de Ensalada" (On a plate of salad)

MM: ♩ = 96

Literal translation:
On a plate of salad
Everyone eats in reverse
Churumbe, churumbe,
Jack [as in cards], horse, and king.

409

GAMES:	CONNECTIONS TO BOOKS/LITERACY:
	Ayres, Katherine. *Up, Down, and Around*. Candlewick Press, 2007.
	Ehlert, Lois. *Eating the Alphabet: Fruits & Vegetables from A to Z*. Harcourt Books, 1989.
	Westcott, Nadine Bernard. *The Lady with the Alligator Purse*. Little, Brown, 1998.
	Krauss, Ruth. *The Carrot Seed*. Scholastic, 1945.

"Engine, Engine, Number Nine"

MM: ♩ = 90

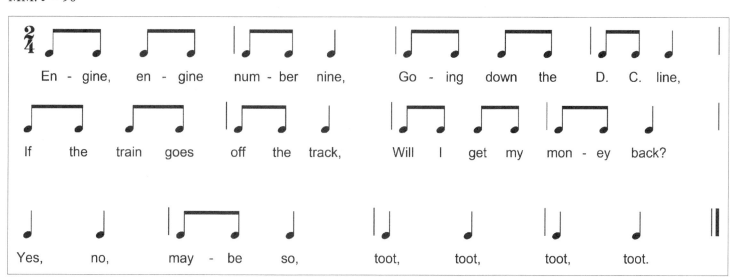

GAMES:	CONNECTIONS TO BOOKS/ LITERACY:
1. Other places can be substituted for "Chicago," for example, "Going down the Washington line. . . ." 2. Children form a line and move their arms in the motion of a turning wheel while chanting the rhyme.	Calmenson, Stephanie. *Engine, Engine, Number Nine.* Scholastic, 1996. Ricketts, Ann, and Michael Ricketts. *Rhyme Time.* Brimax Books, 1988. Alborough, Jez. *Duck in the Truck.* Scholastic, 1999.

"Este Niño Lindo"

MM: ♩ = 80   CSP: F#

Es - te ni - ño lin - do, que na - cio de no - che, quie - re que lo lle - ven a pa - sar en co - che.

Es - te ni - ño lin - do, que na - ció de di - a, quie - re que lo lle - ven a co - mer san - di - a.

Literal translation:
This beautiful boy, that was born during the night,
Wants us to take him for a ride in the car.
This beautiful boy, that was born during the day
Want us to take him to eat watermelon.

GAMES:	CONNECTIONS TO BOOKS/ LITERACY:
A lullaby; gently rock to the beat holding a stuffed animal.	Bryan, Ashley. *All Night, All Day: A Child's First Book of African-American Spirituals.* Aladdin Paperbacks, 1991. Ehlert, Lois. *Eating the Alphabet: Fruits & Vegetables from A to Z.* Harcourt Books, 1989. Carle, Eric. *Mister Seahorse.* Philomel Books, 2004. Finn, Isobel. *The Very Lazy Ladybug.* Tiger Tales, 1999.

"The Farmer in the Dell"

MM: ♩. = 112   CSP: C

The farm - er in the dell, the farm - er in the dell,

Heigh, ho, the Der - ry O, the farm - er in the dell.

Verses:

2. The farmer takes a wife
The farmer takes a wife
Heigh, ho, the derry-o
The farmer takes a wife

3. The wife takes the child
The wife takes the child
Heigh, ho, the derry-o
The wife takes the child

4. The child takes the nurse
The child takes the nurse
Heigh, ho, the derry-o
The child takes the nurse

5. The nurse takes the dog
The nurse takes the dog
Heigh, ho, the derry-o
The nurse takes the dog

6. The dog takes the cat
The dog takes the cat
Heigh, ho, the derry-o
The dog takes the cat

7. The cat takes the rat
The cat takes the rat
Heigh, ho, the derry-o
The cat takes the rat.

8. The rat takes the cheese
The rat takes the cheese
Heigh, ho, the derry-o
The rat takes the cheese

9. The cheese stands alone
The cheese stands alone
Heigh, ho, the derry-o
The cheese stands alone.

411

GAMES:	CONNECTIONS TO BOOKS/LITERACY:
Children stand in a circle holding hands. One is in the middle as the farmer. Children sing song as they walk around circle. Farmer takes a wife, wife takes a child, etc. At the end, the cheese stands alone.	Twinn, M. *Old Macdonald Had a Farm*. Child's Play (International), 1975. Lewison, Wendy Cheyette. *Going to Sleep on the Farm*. Trumpet Club, 1992. Bentley, Dawn. *Buzz-Buzz, Busy Bees*. Simon & Schuster, 2004. Harriet, Ziefert. *When I First Came to this Land*. Scholastic, 1998. Post, Jim and Janet Post. *Barnyard Boogie*. Accord, 2002. Greene, Rhonda Gowler. *Barnyard Song*. Atheneum Books for Young Readers, 1997.

"Firefly, Firefly"

MM: ♩ = 84   CSP: D

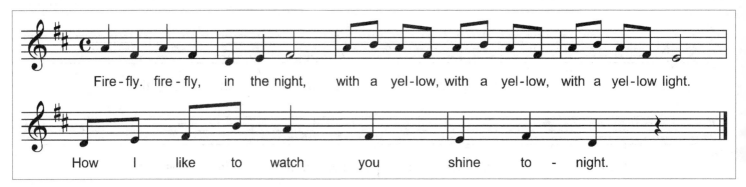

Fire - fly. fire - fly, in the night, with a yel - low, with a yel - low, with a yel - low light.

How I like to watch you shine to - night.

GAMES:	CONNECTIONS TO BOOKS/LITERACY:
Choreograph arm movements to reflect the gentle text of the song.	Fleming, Denise. *Beetle Bop*. Harcourt, 2007.
	Carle, Eric. *The Very Busy Spider*. Philomel Books, 1984.
	Finn, Isobel. *The Very Lazy Ladybug*. Tiger Tales, 1999.
	Carle, Eric. *The Very Lonely Firefly*. Philomel Books, 1995.
	Bentley, Dawn. *Buzz-Buzz, Busy Bees*. Simon & Schuster, 2004.
	Brennan-Nelson, Denise. *Buzzy the Bumblebee*., Sleeping Bear Press, 1999.
	Kohn, Michael, and Daniel Weiner. *There was an Old Woman Who Swallowed a Fly*. Weekly Reader Children's Book Club, 1981.

412

"Five Little Monkeys"

MM: ♩ = 96

Five lit-tle mon-keys jump-ing on the bed. One fell off and bumped their head.

Mom-my called the doc-tor and the doc - tor said, "No more mon-keys jump-ing on the bed."

Verse:

No little monkeys jumping on the bed
None fell off and bumped their heads
Mommy called the doctor, and the doctor said,
"Put those monkeys right to bed!"

GAMES:	CONNECTIONS TO BOOKS/LITERACY:
1. Subtract monkeys one at a time until none are left.	Slobodkina, Esphyr. *Caps for Sale*. Live Oak Media, 2004.
	Christelow, Eileen. *Five Little Monkeys Jumping on the Bed*. Sandpiper, 2006.
	Perkins, Al. *Hand, Hand, Fingers Thumb*. Random House Books for Young, 1998.

413

"Fly, Daniel"

MM: ♩ = 90   CSP: A

Fly, Dan - iel, Fly, Dan - iel,___ Fly Dan - iel, Fly, Dan - iel.___

Verses:

2. Fly way back home, Daniel.   3. On the eagle's wing, Daniel.
Fly way back home, Daniel.   On the eagle's wing, Daniel.

GAMES:	CONNECTIONS TO BOOKS/ LITERACY:
1. Replace "Daniel" with other names, e.g., Peter.	Brennan-Nelson, Denise. (1999). *Buzzy the Bumblebee*. Sleeping Bear Press. Swanson, Susan Marie. (2008). *The House in the Night*. Houghton Mifflin. Orie, Sandra De Coteau. (1995). *Did You Hear Wind Sing Your Name?* Walker and Co. Langstaff, John. (1963). *Ol' Dan Tucker*. Harcourt, Brace & World.

"Frog in the Meadow"

MM: ♩ = 90   CSP: B

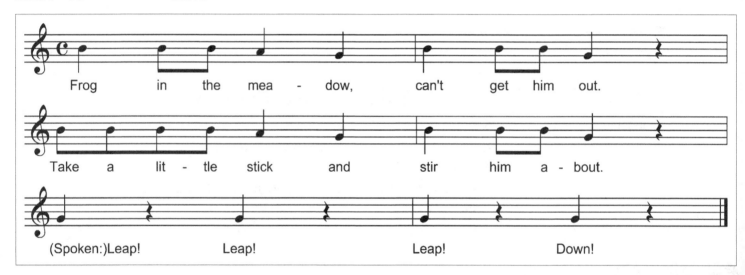

GAMES:	CONNECTIONS TO BOOKS/ LITERACY:
1. Four players are on the floor on their hands and knees, frog fashion, kneeling one in front of the other. 2. During the singing of the song, It or the teacher "stirs," tickles the last frog. 3. During the spoken parts, this frog leaps over the other three, leaning on "down." 4. Repeat the song until all children have had a turn to leap.	Langstaff, John. *Over in the Meadow*. Voyager Books, 1957, 1985. Fleming, Denise. *In the Tall, Tall Grass*. Henry Holt, 1991. Fleming, Denise. *In the Small, Small Pond*. Henry Holt, 1993. Langstaff, John. *Frog Went A-Courtin'*. Harcourt Children's Books, 1955. Lively, Penelope. *One Two Three Jump!* Puffin Books, 1998.

"Frosty Weather"

MM: ♩ = 104   CSP: G-A

Fros-ty weath-er, snow-y weath-er, when the wind blows we all get to-geth-er.

GAMES:	CONNECTIONS TO BOOKS/LITERACY:
1. Children march around the room while singing the song. 2. They improvise other verses, e.g., "Rainy weather, real wet weather, when the rain falls, we all get together."	Alborough, Jez. *Duck in the Truck*. New York, Scholastic, 1999. Orie, Sandra De Coteau. *Did You Hear Wind Sing Your Name?* Walker and Company, 1995. Stojic, Manya. *Rain*. Dragonfly Books, 2000. Lionni, Leo. *Frederick*. Trumpet Club, 1967. Aardema, Verna. *Bringing the Rain to Kapiti Plain*. Puffin Books, 1981. Locker, Thomas. *Cloud Dance*. Voyager Books, 2000. Gershator, Phillis. *When It Starts to Snow*. Henry Holt, 1998.

415

"Goodnight, Sleep Tight"

MM: ♩ = 72   CSP: A

Good - night, sleep tight. Friends will come to - mor - row night.

GAMES:	CONNECTIONS TO BOOKS/LITERACY:
Lullaby; children rock a stuffed animal to the beat of the song while singing.	Brown, Margaret Wise. *Goodnight Moon*. Scholastic, 1947. Bryan, Ashley. *All Night, All Day: A Child's First Book of African-American Spirituals*. Aladdin Paperbacks, 1991. Lewison, Wendy Cheyette. *Going to Sleep on the Farm*. Trumpet Club, 1992. Bemelmans, Ludwig. *Madeline*. Viking Press, 1939. Bentley, Dawn. *Sleepy Bear*. Intervisual Books, 1999.

"Great Big House in New Orleans"

MM: ♩ = 120   CSP: F#

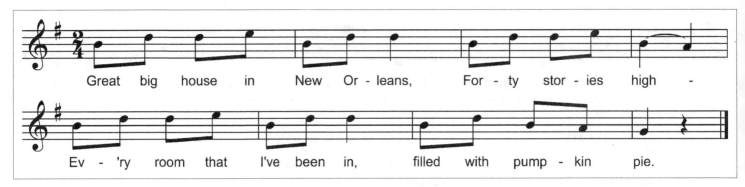

Great big house in New Or - leans, For - ty stor - ies high -

Ev - 'ry room that I've been in, filled with pump - kin pie.

Lyrics:

2. Went down to the old mill stream
To fetch a pail of water
Put one arm around my wife
The other 'round my daughter.

3. Fare thee well, my darling girl
Fare thee well, my daughter,
Fare three well, my darling girl
With the golden slippers on her.

GAMES:	CONNECTIONS TO BOOKS/LITERACY:
This may be too advanced for Kindergarten. The traditional game is outlined here. 1. Have the children form a circle with partners. 2. Have the "ladies" stand on the right side. 3. The circle will sing "Great Big House" and move clockwise. 4. On the lyrics "Went down to the old mill stream," the ladies should take four small steps into the center of the circle and join their hands. 5. On the lyrics "Fetch a pail of water," the "men" should move toward the center and reach both arms across, between two ladies. 6. The men should then join hands at the end of the "Picking up" gesture and swing their arms (on "put one arm") over the heads of the ladies, making a circle behind their backs, at waist level. 7. On "the other round his daughter," the ladies raise their joined hands back over the men's heads and make a circle behind their waists. 8. Everyone sings verse 3 in this position while gently slide-stepping around in a circle, clockwise. On the third "fare thee well" the ladies raise their arms back over the men's heads, freeing the dancers, and on the fourth phrase, "with the golden slippers," the men move along one position to be ready to start the next round with a new partner.	Ehlert, Lois. *Eating the Alphabet: Fruits & Vegetables from A to Z.* Harcourt Books, 1989. Otoshi, Kathryn. *One.* KO Kids Books, 2008. Seeger, Pete. *One Grain of Sand.* Little, Brown, 1957. Swanson, Susan Marie. *The House in the Night.* Houghton Mifflin, 2008. Ayres, Katherine. *Up, Down, and Around.* Candlewick Press, 2007.

416

"Handy, Dandy"

MM. ♩ = 90

Han - dy, dan - dy, rid - dle - dee ro, which hand will you have, high or low?

GAMES:	CONNECTIONS TO BOOKS/ LITERACY:
1. Juggle a small object back and forth between two hands while chanting the rhyme.	Carle, Eric. *From Head to Toe.* HarperFestival, 1997.
2. At the end, hide the object in one closed fist; hold one hand high and one hand low.	Ricketts, Ann, and Michael Ricketts. *Rhyme Time.* Brimax Books, 1988.
3. The children must then guess which hand (high or low) holds the object.	
4. When chanting "high," the voice slides up; when chanting "low," the voice slides down.	
5. The children's answer must be pitched high or low (exaggerated).	

417

"Here Comes a Bluebird"

MM: ♩ = 100   CSP: A

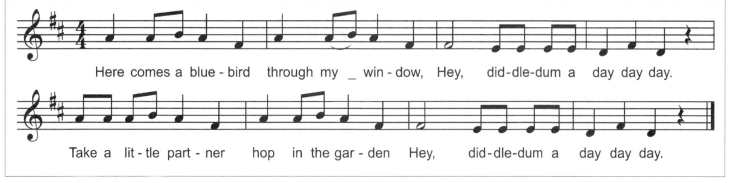

Here comes a blue - bird through my _ win - dow, Hey, did - dle - dum a day day day.

Take a lit - tle part - ner hop in the gar - den Hey, did - dle - dum a day day day.

GAMES:	CONNECTIONS TO BOOKS/ LITERACY:
1. Have children stand in a circle, joining hands together and holding them up (forming windows). 2. Choose one child to walk in and under the arches. 3. On "take a little partner" this child takes a partner, and with two hands joined they face each other, gallop out through the opening where the child was taken from the ring, and back again; or they can dance the same around inside the ring. 4. The first child joins the ring, and the partner becomes the bluebird.	• Deetlefs, Rene. *The Song of Six Birds.* Dutton Children's Books, 1999. • Brennan-Nelson, Denise. *Buzzy the Bumblebee.* Sleeping Bear Press, 1999. • Lively, Penelope. *One Two Three Jump!* Puffin Books, 1998. • Ayres, Katherine. *Up, Down, and Around.* Candlewick Press, 2007. • Ehlert, Lois. *Eating the Alphabet: Fruits & Vegetables from A to Z.* Harcourt Books, 1989.

"Hey, Hey, Look at Me"

MM: ♩= 96   CSP: A

Hey, hey, look at me. I am jump-ing*, can you see?

GAMES:	CONNECTIONS TO BOOKS/ LITERACY:
1. One child thinks of and proposes an action, and they perform it to the pulse during the third and fourth bars. 2. The class repeats the song, copying the action chosen. 3. Actions might include waving, hopping, pointing (fingers), tapping (head or knees), blinking, skipping, bending, etc. 4. All actions should be performed with the pulse (in tempo).	Lively, Penelope. *One Two Three Jump!* Puffin Books, 1998. Cronin, Doreen. *Bounce.* Atheneum Books for Young Readers, 2007. Hoberman, Mary A. *Skip to My Lou.* Megan Tingley, 2003. Quackenbush, Robert M. *Skip to My Lou.* Lippincott Williams & Wilkins, 1975. Westcott, Nadine Bernard. *Skip to My Lou.* Little, Brown, 1989.

"Hickety, Tickety"

MM: ♩ = 90   CSP: A

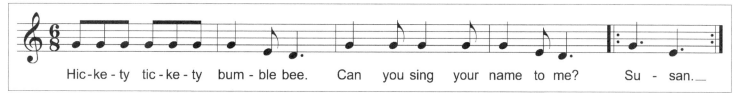

Hic-ke-ty tic-ke-ty bum-ble bee. Can you sing your name to me? Su - san.__

GAMES:	CONNECTIONS TO BOOKS/ LITERACY:
1. The whole class sings the first part of the song, and then you sing somebody's name. 2. The child whose name is chosen gets to sing it back.	Bentley, Dawn. *Buzz Buzz, Busy Bees.* Simon & Schuster, 2004. Orie, Sandra De Coteau. *Did You Hear Wind Sing Your Name?* Walker and Company, 1995. Brennan-Nelson, Denise. *Buzzy the Bumblebee.* Sleeping Bear Press, 1999.

419

"Hunt the Slipper"

MM: ♩ = 100   CSP: A

Cob - bler, Cob - bler mend my shoe, Let it done by half past two.

Half past two is at the door, Let it done by half past four.

GAMES:	CONNECTIONS TO BOOKS/LITERACY:
Children keep the beat on their shoes, pretending to make repairs.	Lively, Penelope. *One Two Three Jump!* Puffin Books, 1998.
	Guthrie, Woody. *Bling Blang.* Candlewick Press, 1954.
	Walsh, Vivian. *Gluey.* Harcourt; Weekly Reader Children's Book Club, 2002.
	Peek, Merele. *Mary Wore Her Red Dress and Henry Wore His Green Sneakers.* Clarion, 1985.
	Otoshi, Kathryn. *One.* KO Kids Books, 2008.
	Swanson, Susan Marie. *The House in the Night.* Houghton Mifflin, 2008.
	Eric, Carle. *Today Is Monday.* PaperStar, 1993.
	Leslie, Amanda. *Who's That Scratching at My Door?* Handprint Books, 2001.

"Hush, Little Minnie"

MM: ♩ = 80   CSP: B

Hush, lit-tle Min-nie and don;t say a word, Pa-pa's going to buy you a mock-ing bird.

It can whis-tle and it can sing, And it can do most an-y-thing.

GAMES:	CONNECTIONS TO BOOKS/LITERACY:
1. Replace words with motions as you keep singing through the song. Replace a word with a motion one at a time.	Na, Il Sung. *A Book of Sleep.* Alfred A. Knopf, 2007.
	Seeger, Pete. *One Grain of Sand.* Little, Brown, 1957.
	Lewison, Wendy Cheyette. *Going to Sleep on the Farm.* Trumpet Club, 1992.
	Brown, Margaret Wise. *Goodnight Moon.* Scholastic, 1947.
	Bentley, Dawn. *Sleepy Bear.* Intervisual Books, 1999.
	Deetlefs, Rene. *The Song of Six Birds.* Dutton Children's Books, 1999.

"I Climbed up the Cherry Tree"

MM: ♩ = 100

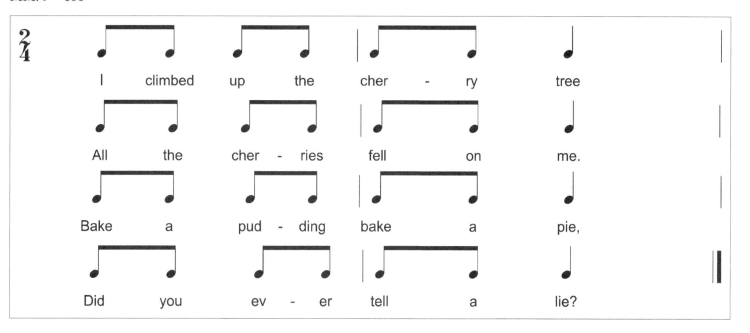

GAMES:	CONNECTIONS TO BOOKS/LITERACY:
1. Replace "cherry" with other fruits.	Ehlert, Lois. *Eating the Alphabet: Fruits & Vegetables from A to Z.* Harcourt Books, 1989.
	Ayres, Katherine. *Up, Down, and Around.* Candlewick Press, 2007.
	Krauss, Ruth. *The Carrot Seed.* Scholastic, 1945.
	Orie, Sandra De Coteau. *Did You Hear Wind Sing Your Name?* Walker and Company, 1995.

"I See the Moon"

MM: ♩ = 90   CSP: A

GAMES:	CONNECTIONS TO BOOKS/ LITERACY:
After learning the song, students may improvise other things that they see. "I see the stars . . .," etc.	Brown, Margaret Wise. (1947). *Goodnight Moon*. Scholastic. Na, Il Sung. (2007). *A Book of Sleep*. Knopf.

"Ida Red"

MM: ♩ = 120   CSP: D

Down the road and a-cross the creek, Can't get a let-ter but once a week.

I - da Red. I - da Blue. I got stuck on I-da too.

GAMES:	CONNECTIONS TO BOOKS/ LITERACY:
Using an "Ida doll," change the colors of the doll's dress and have children recognize the color. This means that the text of last two phrases will have to be changed to rhyme with the color. For example, "Ida Red, Ida Green, prettiest gal I've ever seen."	Otoshi, Kathryn. *One*. KO Kids Books, 2008. Rosen, Michael. *We're Going on a Bear Hunt*. Little Simon, 1989. Langstaff, John. *Oh, A-Hunting We Will Go*. Aladdin Paperbacks, 1974.

"In and Out"

MM: ♩ = 110   CSP: G

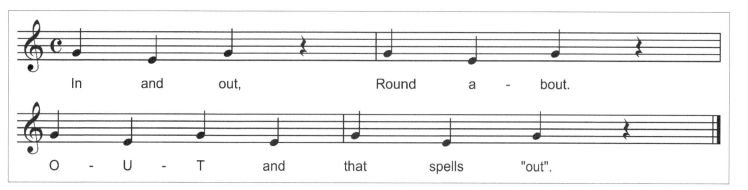

In and out, Round a - bout.

O - U - T and that spells "out".

GAMES:	CONNECTIONS TO BOOKS/ LITERACY:
1. Have the children stand in a circle.	Carter, David A. *In and Out.* Intervisual Books, 1993.
2. Have one child use a beat-pointing motion while pointing to each child in the circle.	Ayres, Katherine. *Up, Down, and Around.* Candlewick Press, 2007.
3. The child who is being pointed to on "out" is the one chosen to begin the game.	Galdone, Paul. *Over in the Meadow.* Aladdin Paperbacks, 1986.
	Langstaff, John. *Over in the Meadow.* Voyager Books, 1957, 1985.
	Ricketts, Ann and Michael Ricketts. *Rhyme Time.* Brimax Books, 1988.

423

"It's Raining, It's Pouring"

MM: ♩ = 104   CSP: G

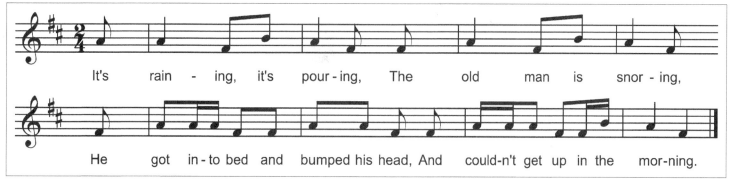

It's rain - ing, it's pour - ing, The old man is snor - ing,

He got in - to bed and bumped his head, And could-n't get up in the mor - ning.

GAMES:	CONNECTIONS TO BOOKS/LITERACY:
	Aardema, Verna. *Bringing the Rain to Kapiti Plain*. Puffin Books, 1981.
	Stojic, Manya. *Rain*. Dragonfly Books, 2000.
	Schubert, Ingrid, and Dieter Schubert. *There's a Hole in My Bucket*. Front Street, 1998.
	Adams, Pam. *This Old Man*. Child's Play International, 1989.

"Jack and Jill"

MM: ♩ = 96   CSP: G

GAMES:	CONNECTIONS TO BOOKS/LITERACY:
	Plume, Ilse. (2004). *The Farmer in the Dell*. David R. Godine.
	Kohn, Michael, and Daniel Weiner. (1981). *There Was an Old Woman Who Swallowed a Fly*.
	Ricketts, Ann and Michael Ricketts. (1988). *Rhyme Time*. Brimax Books.
	Spier, Peter. (1967). *London Bridge Is Falling Down*. Doubleday.

"Jim Along Josie"

MM: ♩ = 84   CSP: B

Hey Jim a - long,___ Jim a-long Jo - sie, Hey Jim a - long,___ Jim a-long Joe.

Hey Jim a - long,___ Jim a-long Jo - sie, Hey Jim a - long,___ Jim a-long Joe.

GAMES:	CONNECTIONS TO BOOKS/ LITERACY:
Children improvise other actions in the song: "Skip, skip along, skip along Josie" or "Hop, hop along, hop along Josie."	Pinkney, Brian. *Max Found Two Sticks.* Aladdin Paperbacks, 1994. Wood, Audrey. *Silly Sally.* Harcourt, 1992. Hoberman, Mary Ann. *Miss Mary Mack.* Little, Brown, 1998.

425

"Johnny Works with One Hammer"

MM: ♩ = 100   CSP: F

John - ny works with one ham - mer one ham - mer one ham - mer

John - ny works with one ham - mer then he works with two.

GAMES:	CONNECTIONS TO BOOKS/ LITERACY:
Children keep a beat on their knee with one hand. Verse 2: Johnny works with two hammers. Children keep a beat with both hands on their knees. Keep adding verses and beat motions with other body parts.	

"Just from the Kitchen"

MM: ♩ = 100   CSP: F

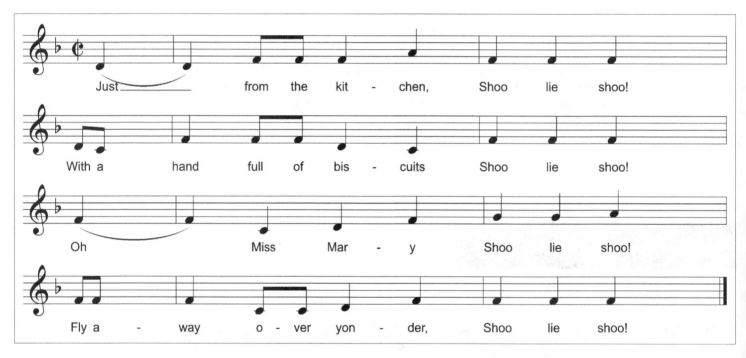

GAMES:	CONNECTIONS TO BOOKS/ LITERACY:
1. All players sit on the floor in a circle, leaving one empty place.	Orie, Sandra De Coteau. (1995). *Did You Hear Wind Sing Your Name?* Walker and Co.
2. On "Oh, Miss _____" named player "flies over" to empty place, etc.	Wood, Audrey. (1992). *Silly Sally*. Harcourt.
3. The game may be played from fixed desks, or in other ways.	Hoberman, Mary Ann. (1998). *Miss Mary Mack*. Little, Brown.

"Knock the Cymbals"

MM: ♩ = 100   CSP: F

Verses:

2. Left hand crossed, do, oh do, etc.   3. Right hand crossed, do, oh do, etc.
Oh-law Susie gal.   Oh-law Susie gal.

427

GAMES:	CONNECTIONS TO BOOKS/ LITERACY:
This may be a bit advanced for Kindergarteners, but initially they can sing and move in a circle.	Brett, Jan. *Berlioz the Bear*. Penguin Young Readers Group, 1991.
Formation is a single circle of players.	McPhail, David. *Mole Music*. Henry Holt, 1999.
Verse 1:	Pinkney, Brian. *Max Found Two Sticks*. Aladdin Paperbacks, 1994.
Measure 1—Walk four small steps to the middle (step, step, step, touch).	Moss, Lloyd. *Zin! Zin! Zin! A Violin*. Aladdin Paperbacks, 1995.
Measure 2—Walk four small steps back (step, step, step, touch).	Martin Jr., Bill. *The Maestro Plays*. Voyager Books, 1996.
Measure 3 and 4—Repeat measures 1 and 2.	Aardema, Verna. *Bringing the Rain to Kapiti Plain*. Puffin Books, 1981.
Verse 2:	Lach, William. *Can You Hear It?* Abrams Books for Young Readers, 2006.
Hold left hand to the middle of the circle and walk around the circle's perimeter.	Friedman, Carol. *Nicky*. Dominick Books, 2003.
Verse 3:	
Repeat verse 2, but with right hand.	
Verse 4:	
Put hands on hips and walk counterclockwise around the circle.	
* It is also possible to promenade with a partner on verse 4, backing up into the circle to repeat the game on the last measure. Or drop hands after promenading and the inside circle moves up one child to have a new partner on the repetition of the game.	

"Let Us Chase the Squirrel"

MM: ♩ = 90   CSP: D

GAMES:	CONNECTIONS TO BOOKS/LITERACY:
1. Variation 1: a. Children form two lines facing each other. b. Each child holds hands up with partner to form a tunnel. c. Two children at the head of the line run through to the opposite end on the word "let." d. You may clap hands each time on "let," or an extra child may play the tambourine each time on "let." e. If time allows, reverse order. **2. Variation 2:** a. Players stand in a circle and number off by ones and twos. b. On verse 1, they circle left. c. Verse 2, first phrase: the ones take four tiny steps in and hold hands. d. Verse 2, second phrase: the twos walk in, putting their hands in between those of the ones and holding hands. e. Verse 2, third phrase: the twos put their arms around the back of the ones and keep holding hands. f. Verse 2, fourth phrase: the ones put their arms around the back of the twos and keep holding hands. g. Verse 3: all players do a "step together" going to their left. h. On the last phrase, they may step back to begin the singing again.	Stojic, Manya. *Rain*. Dragonfly Books, 2000. Twinn, M. *Old Macdonald Had a Farm*. Child's Play (International), 1975.

428

"Let Us Hide the Pumpkin"

MM: ♩ = 100   CSP: A

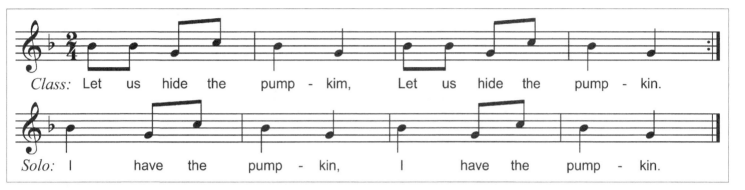

Class: Let us hide the pump - kim, Let us hide the pump - kin.

Solo: I have the pump - kin, I have the pump - kin.

GAMES:	CONNECTIONS TO BOOKS/ LITERACY:
1. Have one child (It) hide his or her eyes.	Leslie, Amanda. *Who's That Scratching at My Door?* Handprint Books, 2001.
2. As the class sings, give "the pumpkin" to another child.	Powell, Richard. *Guess What I Have!* Barron's Educational Series, 2001.
3. The child with the pumpkin sings alone and the one who is It must guess who was singing.	Powell, Richard. *Guess Who's Hiding!* Barron's Educational Series, 2001.
4. The child who sang alone may become the next It.	Williams, Linda. *The Little Old Lady Who Was Not Afraid of Anything.* HarperCollins, 1986.
	Ehlert, Lois. *Eating the Alphabet: Fruits & Vegetables from A to Z.* Harcourt Books, 1989.
	Krauss, Ruth. *The Carrot Seed.* Scholastic, 1945.
	Ayres, Katherine. *Up, Down, and Around.* Candlewick Press, 2007.

"Little Sally Water"

MM: ♩ = 104   CSP: A

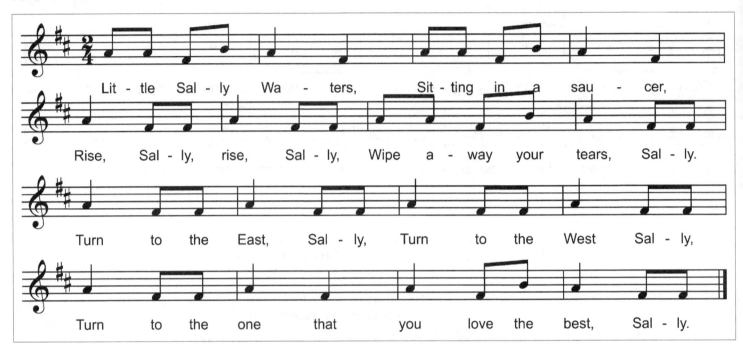

Lit - tle Sal - ly Wa - ters, Sit - ting in a sau - cer,

Rise, Sal - ly, rise, Sal - ly, Wipe a - way your tears, Sal - ly.

Turn to the East, Sal - ly, Turn to the West Sal - ly,

Turn to the one that you love the best, Sal - ly.

GAMES:	CONNECTIONS TO BOOKS/ LITERACY:
1. Have the children join hands in a circle, with one child in the center as "Sally," covering his or her eyes with two hands.	Wood, Audrey. *Silly Sally*. Harcourt, 1992. Cronin, Doreen. *Bounce*. Atheneum Books for Young Readers, 2007. Brennan-Nelson, Denise. *Buzzy the Bumblebee*. Sleeping Bear Press, 1999.
2. The circle moves around as everyone sings the song.	
3. Sally imitates the song all the way through, pointing to another child in the circle at the end of the song while still covering the eyes with one hand, so that the choice is by chance.	
4. The chosen child becomes Sally and goes to the center, and the game starts again.	

"Looby Loo"

MM: ♩ = 120   CSP: F

Here we go loo - by loo,   Here we go loo - by light.

Here we go loo - by loo,   All on a Sat - ur - day night.

You   put   you   left   hand   in,   You   put   your left   hand   out,

You   shake it   a   lit - tle   a   lit - tle a lit - tle and   turn   your-self   a - bout.

Verses:

2. Here we go looby loo
Here we go looby light
Here we go looby loo
All on a Saturday night.
You put your right hand in
You put your right hand out
You shake it a little, a little, a little
And turn yourself about.

3. Here we go looby loo
Here we go looby light
Here we go looby loo
All on a Saturday night.
You put your left leg in
You put your left leg out
You shake it a little, a little, a little
And turn yourself about.

4. Here we go looby loo
Here we go looby light
Here we go looby loo
All on a Saturday night.
You put your right leg in
You put your right leg out
You shake it a little, a little, a little
And turn yourself about.

5. Here we go looby loo
Here we go looby light
Here we go looby loo
All on a Saturday night.
You put your whole self in
You put your whole self out
You shake it a little, a little, a little
And turn yourself about.

GAMES:	CONNECTIONS TO BOOKS/ LITERACY:
1. Children stand in a circle and follow the activities of the verses of the song.	Margolin, H. Ellen. *Goin' to Boston.* Handprint Books, Brooklyn, 2002. Cronin, Doreen. *Bounce.* Atheneum Books for Young Readers, 2007. Eric, Carle. *Today Is Monday.* PaperStar, 1993. London, Jonathan. *Wiggle Waggle.* Scholastic, 1999.

"Lucy Locket"

MM: ♩ = 90   CSP: A

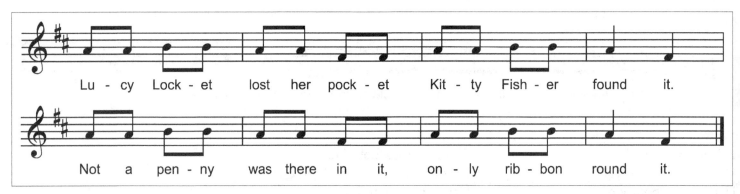

Lu - cy Lock - et lost her pock - et Kit - ty Fish - er found it.

Not a pen - ny was there in it, on - ly rib - bon round it.

GAMES:	CONNECTIONS TO BOOKS/ LITERACY:
1. One child is chosen to leave the room or hide his or her eyes. 2. Another child in the room is given a pocket book or a penny to hide. 3. The child who left the room returns and must guess where the object is hidden. 4. Loud or soft singing from the group is used as a help guide the child to the object.	Pinkney, Brian. *Max Found Two Sticks.* Aladdin Paperbacks, 1994. Hubbell, Patricia. *I Like Cats.* A Cheshire Studio Book, 2003. Wood, Audrey. *Silly Sally.* Harcourt, 1992. Powell, Richard. *Guess What I Have!* Barron's Educational Series, 2001. Powell, Richard. *Guess Who's Hiding!* Barron's Educational Series, 2001. Leslie, Amanda. *Who's That Scratching at My Door?* Handprint Books, 2001.

"Mama, Buy Me a Chiney Doll"

MM: ♩ = 88   CSP: G

Ma - ma buy me a chin - ey doll, Ma - ma buy me a chin - ey doll.

Ma - ma buy me a chin - ey doll, do mam - my do.

GAMES:	CONNECTIONS TO BOOKS/ LITERACY:
Children may improvise other "presents" for their Mama to buy them.	Guthrie, Woody. *My Dolly*. Candlewick Press, 2001. Zemach, Harve. *Mommy, Buy Me a China Doll*. Follett, 1966.

433

Verses:

2. (Well) What would it take to buy it
   with? (Sing three times)
Do, mammy, do.

3. You could take daddy's feather bed
   (Sing three times)
Do, mammy, do.

4. Then where would our daddy sleep?
   (Sing three times)
Do, mammy, do.

5. He could sleep in the puppy's bed
   (Sing three times)
Do, mammy, do.

6. Then where would our puppy sleep?
   (Sing three times)
Do, mammy, do.

7. She could sleep in the horse's bed
   (Sing three times)
Do, mammy, do.

8. Then where could our horsey sleep?
   (Sing three times)
Do, mammy, do.

9. Sleep in the piggy's bed (Sing three
   times)
Do, mammy, do.

10. Then where could our piggy sleep?
    (Sing three times)
Do, mammy, do.

11. She could root out in our front
    lawn (Sing three times)
Do, mammy, do.

12. Then where would our children
    play? (Sing three times)
    Do, mammy, do.

13. Swing on the garden gate (Sing
    three times)
    Do, mammy, do.

14. Yes and get a spanking too. (Sing
    three times)
    Do, mammy, do.

"Naughty Kitty Cat"

MM: ♩ = 90–100   CSP: A–B

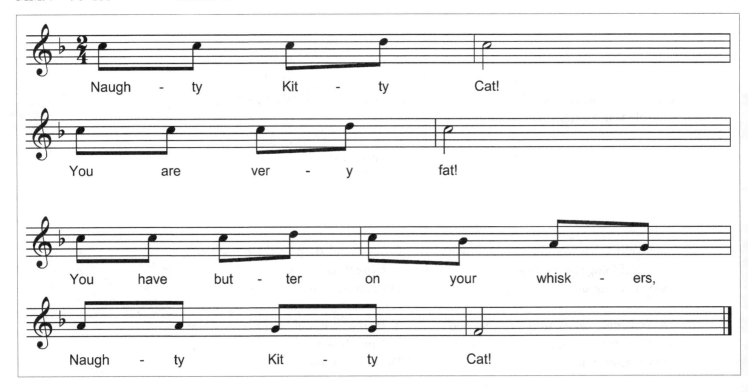

Naugh - ty Kit - ty Cat!

You are ver - y fat!

You have but - ter on your whisk - ers,

Naugh - ty Kit - ty Cat!

GAMES:	CONNECTIONS TO BOOKS/ LITERACY:
1. Have the children form a circle of players. 2. One child is designated "the cat" while another is designated "the mouse." 3. The mouse is inside the circle and the cat is outside the circle. 4. The other children walk around singing the song one time. 5. On the word "SCAT" they "open the windows" (raise their arms) and the cat may chase the mouse. 6. However, you may say "Windows closed" at any time, which means the players must put their arms down. 7. Sometimes the mouse or the cat is caught inside the circle, or maybe *both* are caught inside it. 8. You may set a time limit so that more children get a turn, at which point either the "mouse" wins or the "cat" wins.	Hubbell, Patricia. *I Like Cats*. A Cheshire Studio Book, 2003. Friedman, Carol. *Nicky*. Dominick Books, 2003. Moss, Lloyd. *Zin! Zin! Zin! A Violin*. Aladdin Paperbacks, 1995.

435

"Old Brass Wagon"

MM: ♩= 108   CSP: G

Verses:
Circle to the right, old brass wagon, etc.
Everybody in, old brass wagon, etc.
Everybody out, old brass wagon, etc.
Make up other verses, like "Everybody wave."

GAMES:	CONNECTIONS TO BOOKS/ LITERACY:
Circle formation. Verse 1, children circle left. Verse 2, they circle right. Verse 3, they stand and swing their arms to the beat.	Alborough, Jez. *Duck in the Truck.* Scholastic, 1999. Brett, Jan. *Berlioz the Bear.* Penguin Young Readers Group, 1991. Lively, Penelope. *One Two Three Jump!* Puffin Books, 1998. Ayres, Katherine. *Up, Down, and Around.* Candlewick Press, 2007.

"The Old Woman and the Pig"

MM: ♩ = 92   CSP: D

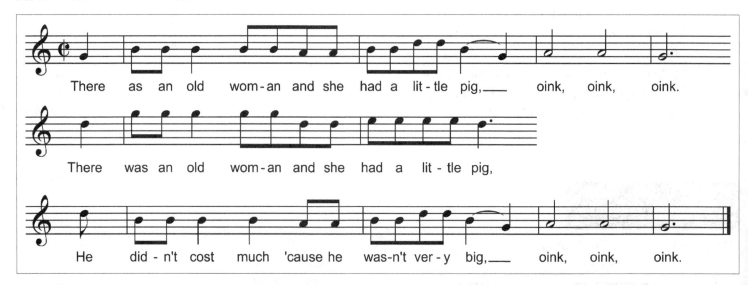

There as an old wom-an and she had a lit-tle pig,— oink, oink, oink.

There was an old wom-an and she had a lit-tle pig,

He did-n't cost much 'cause he was-n't ver-y big,— oink, oink, oink.

Verses:

2. This little old woman kept the pig in a barn,
Oink, oink, oink.
This little old woman kept the pig in a barn,
The prettiest thing she had on the farm,
Oink, oink, oink.

3. But that little pig did a heap of harm,
Oink, oink, oink.

But that little pig did a heap of harm,
He made little tracks all around the barn,
Oink, oink, oink.

4. The little old woman fed the pig on clover,
Oink, oink, oink.
The little old woman fed the pig on clover,
And when he died, he died all over,
Oink, oink, oink.

GAMES:	CONNECTIONS TO BOOKS/ LITERACY:
This is a song that tells a story. The teacher should sing the song to the students. Students may join in singing "oink, oink, oink" as it repeats throughout the verses.	Kohn, Michael, and Daniel Weiner. (1981). *There Was an Old Woman Who Swallowed a Fly*. Taback, Simms. (2007). *There Was an Old Lady*. Child's Play (International). Twinn, M. (1975). *Old Macdonald Had a Farm*. Child's Play (International). Lewison, Wendy Cheyette. (1992). *Going to Sleep on the Farm*. Trumpet Club. Jorgensen, Gail. (1988). *Crocodile Beat*. Aladdin Paperbacks.

"Oliver Twist"

MM: ♩ = 100   CSP: A

Ol - i - ver Twist, you can't do this, so what's the use in try - ing.

Touch you knees, and touch your toes, Clap you hands and a - round you go.

GAMES:	CONNECTIONS TO BOOKS/ LITERACY:
1. Players stand in a circle with one child in the middle. 2. For the first line of the song, the child in the middle makes a motion, which all must follow. 3. On the second line of the song, everyone does what the words say, and on "around you go" the child in the center chooses another player.	Carle, Eric. *From Head to Toe*. HarperFestival, 1997. Lucas, Sally. *Dancing Dinos*. Random House, 1933. Martin Jr., Bill. *The Maestro Plays*. Voyager Books, 1996. Hoberman, Mary Ann. *Miss Mary Mack*. Little, Brown, 1998. Suhr, Mandy. *I Can Move*. Wayland Books, 1993, 2009. Cronin, Doreen. *Wiggle*. Atheneum Books for Young Readers, 2005.

"On a Mountain"

MM: ♩ = 88   CSP: A

1.On a moun-tain stands a la-dy, Who she is I do not know.
2.All she wants is gold and sil-ver, Gold and sil-ver for her beau.

Optional

Now jump in my (name)___ Jump in my (name)___

GAMES:	CONNECTIONS TO BOOKS/ LITERACY:
1. One long rope, two turners.	Seeger, Pete. (1957). *One Grain of Sand.* Little, Brown. Langstaff, John. (1974). *Oh, A-Hunting We Will Go.* Aladdin Paperbacks.
2. Each player takes a turn jumping in and remaining as a jumper in the circle of the rope until a mistake is made.	Lach, William. (2006). *Can You Hear It?* Abrams Books for Young Readers.
3. Each person keeps score of his or her number of jumps.	Portis, Antoinette. (2006). *Not a Box.* HarperCollins.
4. Two may jump at the same time if the rope is long enough.	Brown, Margaret Wise. (1979). *The Train to Timbuctoo.* Golden Books.
	Hoberman, Mary Ann. (1998). *Miss Mary Mack.* Little, Brown.
	Lively, Penelope. (1998). One Two Three Jump! Puffin Books.

"Page's Train"

MM: ♩ = 112   CSP: F#

Pa-ge's train runs so fast Can't see noth-ing but the win-dow glass.

GAMES:	CONNECTIONS TO BOOKS/ LITERACY:
Acting out/windup (line) Initially, the words slow and fast should *not* be used. Instead tell a story that encourages the students to think about how the train is moving "up a hill" or "down a hill" and sing the song keeping the beat at the appropriate tempo.	Calmenson, Stephanie. (1996). *Engine, Engine, Number Nine.* Scholastic. Brown, Margaret Wise. (1979). *The Train to Timbuctoo.* Golden Books. Pinkney, Brian. (1994). *Max Found Two Sticks.* Aladdin Paperbacks.

"Pajarito"

MM: ♩ = 88   CSP: A

Pa - ja - ri - to, tan bo - ni - to, pa - ja - ri - to, ¿Dón - de vas?

¡a la a ce - ra ver - da - der - a pin - pon fue - ra!

Translation:
Beautiful bird beautiful bird,
where are you going?
To the green forest away!

"Pease Porridge Hot"

MM: ♩ = 112   CSP: F#

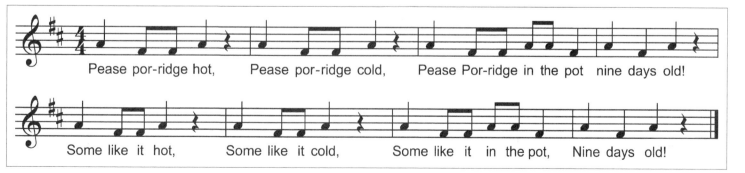

Pease por-ridge hot, Pease por-ridge cold, Pease Por-ridge in the pot nine days old!

Some like it hot, Some like it cold, Some like it in the pot, Nine days old!

GAMES:	CONNECTIONS TO BOOKS/ LITERACY:
This game can be played as a simple "pat clap" to the beat game. Once children can keep the beat themselves, change it into a partner game, where they clap their own hands and then their neighbor's hands to the beat.	Ricketts, Ann, and Michael Ricketts. *Rhyme Time*. Brimax Books, 1988.

"Los Pollitos"

MM: ♩ = 88   CSP: D

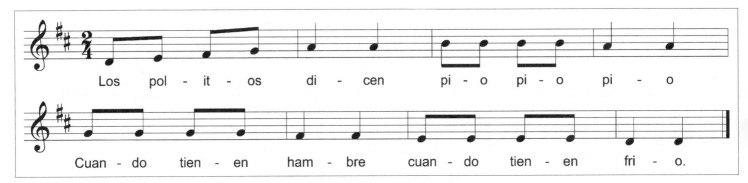

Translation:
The baby chicks say pio, pio, pio
when they are hungry
and when they are cold.

"Queen, Queen, Caroline"

MM: ♩ = 88

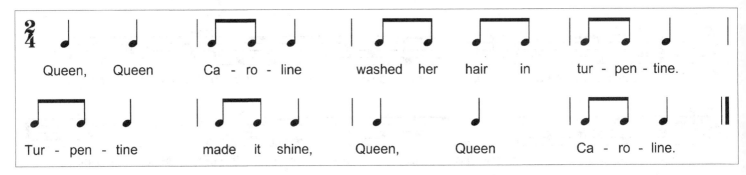

GAMES:	CONNECTIONS TO BOOKS/ LITERACY:
Act out the text of the rhyme with beat motions.	Ricketts, Ann, and Michael Ricketts. *Rhyme Time*. Brimax Books, 1988.
	Hoberman, Mary A. *Skip to My Lou*. Megan Tingley, 2003.
	Quackenbush, Robert M. *Skip to My Lou*. Lippincott Williams & Wilkins, 1975.
	Westcott, Nadine Bernard. *Skip to My Lou*. Little, Brown, 1989.
	Adams, Pam. *This Old Man*. Child's Play International, 1989.

"¿Quién Es Esa Gente?"
"Who Are These People?"

MM: ♩ = 90   CSP: A

Literal translation:

1. Who are all these people making so much noise here?
Making so much noise, they don't let us sleep!

2. Who are all these people walking over there?
Making such a racket, they don't let us dream.

GAMES:	CONNECTIONS TO BOOKS/LITERACY:
	Segal, Lore. *All the Way Home*. A Sunburst Book, 1973.
	Calmenson, Stephanie. *Engine, Engine, Number Nine*. Scholastic, 1996.
	Orleans, Ilo. *Animal Orchestra*. A Golden Book, 1958.
	Na, Il Sung. *A Book of Sleep*. Alfred A. Knopf, 2007.

"Rain, Rain, Go Away"

MM: ♩ = 88   CSP: A

GAMES:	CONNECTIONS TO BOOKS/LITERACY:
	Stojic, Manya. *Rain*. Dragonfly Books, 2000.
	Aardema, Verna. *Bringing the Rain to Kapiti Plain*. Puffin Books, 1981.
	Cronin, Doreen. *Bounce*. Atheneum Books for Young Readers, 2007.
	Seeger, Pete. *One Grain of Sand*. Little, Brown, 1957.
	Locker, Thomas. *Cloud Dance*. Voyager Books, 2000.
	Bemelmans, Ludwig. *Madeline*. Viking Press, 1999.

442

"Ring Around the Rosy"

MM: ♩ = 120   CSP: A

GAMES:	CONNECTIONS TO BOOKS/ LITERACY:
1. Children join hands in a circle and walk around singing the song.	Brennan-Nelson, Denise. *Buzzy the Bumblebee*. Sleeping Bear Press, 1999.
2. At the word "down" they all squat down on their heels and then immediately get up; the game starts again.	Lively, Penelope. *One Two Three Jump!* Puffin Books, 1998.
	Finn, Isobel. *The Very Lazy Ladybug.* Tiger Tales, 1999.
	Ayres, Katherine. *Up, Down, and Around.* Candlewick Press, 2007.
	Spier, Peter. *London Bridge Is Falling Down.* Doubleday, 1967.
	Hoberman, Mary A. *Skip to My Lou.* Megan Tingley, 2003.
	Quackenbush, Robert M. *Skip to My Lou.* Lippincott Williams & Wilkins, 1975.
	Westcott, Nadine Bernard. *Skip to My Lou.* Little, Brown, 1989.

443

"'Round and 'Round"

MM: ♩ = 120   CSP: G

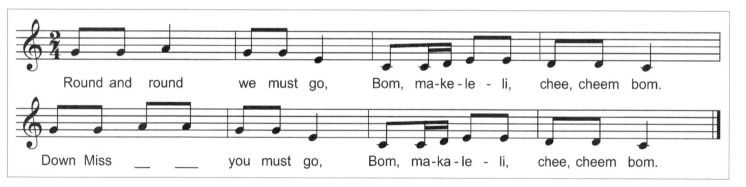

Round and round   we must go,   Bom, ma-ke-le - li,   chee, cheem bom.

Down Miss __ __ you must go,   Bom, ma-ka-le - li,   chee, cheem bom.

GAMES:	CONNECTIONS TO BOOKS/LITERACY:
1. All hold hands in a circle.	Williams, Sarah, and Ian Beck. (1995). *Round and Round the Garden*. Oxford University Press.
2. One player is chosen to be in the middle, and all sing and circle left.	Bullock, Kathleen. (1993). *She'll Be Comin' Round the Mountain*. Simon & Schuster.
3. On the words "Down Miss ____," the center player touches someone in the circle on the head, and that player must crouch down and move on with the rest, but in a crouching position.	Quackenbush, Robert M. (1973). *She'll Be Comin' Round the Mountain*. Lippincott Williams & Wilkins.
	Raffi & Wickstrom, Sylvie. (1990). *The Wheels on the Bus*. Turtleback.
4. The game continues until all are "down."	Zelinsky, Paul. (1990). *The Wheels on the Bus*. Dutton Juvenile.
appropriate tempo.	Ayres, Katherine. (2007). *Up, Down, and Around*. Candlewick Press.

"A Sailor Went to Sea"

MM: ♩ = 108   CSP: E

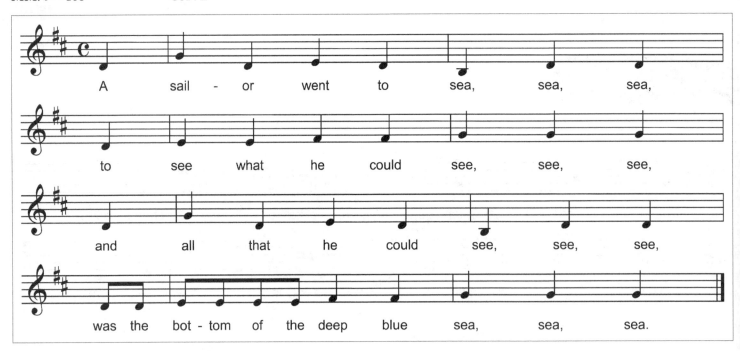

A sail - or went to sea, sea, sea,
to see what he could see, see, see,
and all that he could see, see, see,
was the bot - tom of the deep blue sea, sea, sea.

Verses:

1. A sailor went to knee, knee, knee,
to see what he could knee, knee, knee
but all that he could knee, knee, knee
was the bottom of the deep blue knee, knee, knee

2. A sailor went to toe, toe, toe,
to see what he could toe, toe, toe

but all that he could toe, toe, toe
was the bottom of the deep blue toe, toe, toe

3. A sailor went to sea, knee, toe,
to see what he could sea, knee, toe
but all that he could sea, knee, toe
was the bottom of the deep blue sea, knee, toe.

GAMES:	CONNECTIONS TO BOOKS/ LITERACY:
1. Have students choose a partner. 2. Actions for the song are: A. Verse 1: i. *"A sailor went to . . ."*: nothing on *A*; clap your own hands, partner's right hand, your own hands, partner's hands. ii. Tap your head three times when you sing *"sea, sea, sea."* B. Verse 2: i. "A sailor went to . . .": nothing on *A*; clap your own hands, partner's right hand, your own hands, partner's hands. ii. Pat your knees three times when you sing *"knee, knee, knee."* C. Verse 3: i. *"A sailor went to . . ."*: nothing on *A*; clap your own hands, partner's right hand, your own hands, partner's hands. ii. Touch your toes three times when you sing *"toe, toe, toe."* D. Verse 4: i. *"A sailor went to . . ."*: nothing on *A*; clap your own hands, partner's right hand, your own hands, partner's hands. ii. Touch above the eyes, pat your knees, and touch your toes when you sing *"sea, knee, toe."* 3. Optional: A. After going through the song once or twice, you can tell the children to sing the three words *"sea, knee, toe"* of the last verse in their heads. B. Choose three instruments and assign one instrument to each word; have one child play on the word *"sea,"* another child play on the word *"knee,"* and a third child play on the word *"toe."*	Carle, Eric. *Mister Seahorse*. Philomel Books, 2004.

"Sally Go 'Round the Sun"

MM: ♩ = 112   CSP: D

446

GAMES:	CONNECTIONS TO BOOKS/ LITERACY:
1. Have the children form a circle holding hands and facing to the right, ready to walk in that direction.	Wood, Audrey. *Silly Sally*. Harcourt, 1992. Brown, Margaret Wise. *Goodnight Moon*. Scholastic, 1947.
2. As they are singing, they should walk to the right.	Orie, Sandra De Coteau. *Did You Hear Wind Sing Your Name?* Walker and Company, 1995.
3. When they shout "BOOM!" the children should jump up and change direction.	Carle, Eric. *The Very Busy Spider*. Philomel Books, 1984. Carter, David A. *In and Out*. Intervisual Books, 1993.

"See Saw"

MM: ♩ = 70   CSP: A

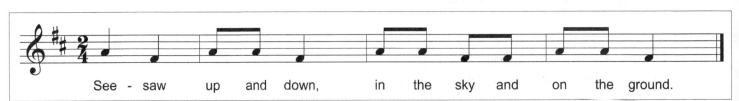

GAMES:	CONNECTIONS TO BOOKS/LITERACY:
	Ayres, Katherine. *Up, Down, and Around.* Candlewick Press, 2007.
	Carter, David A. *In and Out.* Intervisual Books, 1993.
	Locker, Thomas. *Cloud Dance.* Voyager Books, 2000.
	Hoberman, Mary A. *Skip to My Lou.* Megan Tingley, 2003.
	Quackenbush, Robert M. *Skip to My Lou.* Lippincott Williams & Wilkins, 1975.
	Westcott, Nadine Bernard. *Skip to My Lou.* Little, Brown, 1989.

"Skin and Bones"

MM: ♩. = 80   CSP: D

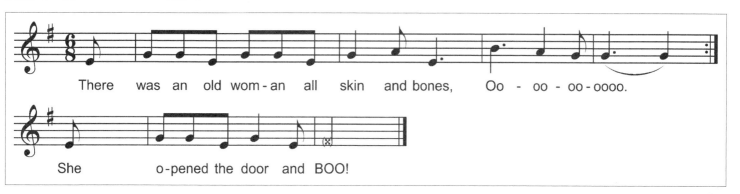

Verses:

1. One night she thought she'd take a walk . . .

2. She walked down by the old graveyard . . .

3. She saw the bones a-lyin' around . . .

4. She went to the closet to get a broom . . .

5. She opened the door . . . BOO!

GAMES:	CONNECTIONS TO BOOKS/LITERACY:
	Suhr, Mandy. *I Can Move.* Wayland Books, 1993, 2009.
	Howard, Arthur. *Hoodwinked.* Voyager Books. Harcourt, 2001.
	Williams, Linda. *The Little Old Lady Who Was Not Afraid of Anything.* HarperCollins, 1986.

"Snail, Snail"

MM: ♩ = 96   CSP: C

GAMES:	CONNECTIONS TO BOOKS/ LITERACY:
Ask questions about the lyrics. 1. "What animal is it about?" (Snails) 2. "Where do they live?" (Shells. Bring in a shell to show.) In Kindergarten, simply play the game by having children hold hands while you lead the line into the formation of a snail shell.	Walsh, Vivian. *Gluey*. Harcourt; Weekly Reader Children's Book Club, 2002. Brown, Ruth. *Snail Trail*. Crown, 2000. Guthrie, Woody. *Bling Blang*. Candlewick Press, 1954.

"Sol, Solecito"

MM: ♩ = 90   CSP: A

Translation:
Sunshine, warm me up a little bit
today and tomorrow
and throughout the week.

"Star Light, Star Bright"

MM. ♩ = 90   CSP: A

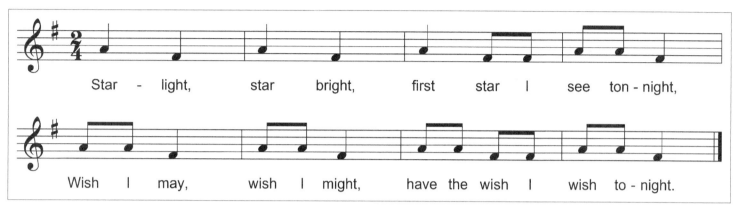

GAMES	CONNECTIONS TO BOOKS/ LITERACY
Children sit in a circle and pass a star shaped beanbag on the beat of the song. The child who has the start on the last beat of the song may make a wish.	Brown, Margaret Wise. *Goodnight Moon*. Scholastic, 1947. Na, Il Sung. *A Book of Sleep*. Alfred A. Knopf, 2007.

449

"The Tailor and the Mouse"

MM: ♩ = 96   CSP: D

Verses:

2. The tailor had a tall silk hat, Hi diddle umkum feedle.
The mouse, he ate it, fancy that! Hi diddle umkum feedle.

3. The tailor thought the mouse was ill, Hi diddle umkum feedle.
He gave him part of a big blue pill, Hi diddle umkum feedle.

4. The tailor thought the mouse would die, Hi diddle umkum feedle.

He baked him in an apple pie, Hi diddle umkum feedle.

5. The pie was cut, the mouse ran out, Hi diddle umkum feedle.
The tailor followed him all about, Hi diddle umkum feedle.

6. The tailor chased him over the lea, Hi diddle umkum feedle.
The last of that mouse he never did see, Hi diddle umkum feedle.

GAMES:	CONNECTIONS TO BOOKS/ LITERACY:
This is a story song that you may sing to the children.	Lionni, Leo. *Frederick*. Trumpet Club, 1967. Walsh, Vivian. *Gluey*. Harcourt; Weekly Reader Children's Book Club, 2002. Langstaff, John. *Frog Went A-Courtin*. Harcourt Children's Books, 1955.

"Teddy Bear"

MM: ♩ = 100   CSP: A

GAME:	CONNECTIONS TO BOOKS/ LITERACY:
Students "act out" the motions of the song.	Rollings, Susan. *New Shoes, Red Shoes*. Orchard Books, 2000.
	Brett, Jan. *Berlioz the Bear*. Penguin Young Readers Group, 1991.
	Martin Jr., Bill. *Brown Bear, Brown Bear*. Henry Holt, 2004.
	Rosen, Michael. *We're Going on a Bear Hunt*. Little Simon, 1989.
	Martin Jr., Bill. *Panda Bear Panda Bear, What Do You See?* Henry Holt, 2003.

"Thread Follows the Needle"

MM: ♩ = 100   CSP: G

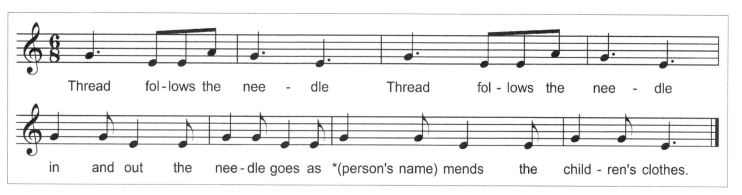

GAMES:	CONNECTIONS TO BOOKS/ LITERACY:
1. Choose a child to be the "needle."	Carter, David A. (1993). *In and Out*. Intervisual Books.
2. The other students form a circle with their arms raised, making arches.	
3. The "needle" goes in and out of the arches and taps people at random as he or she passes.	
4. If someone is tapped, he or she forms a line behind the needle ("the thread"); repeat until no one is left.	

"A Tisket, a Tasket"

MM: ♩= 126 CSP: G

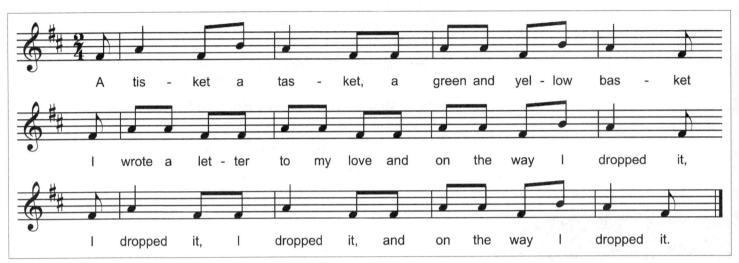

A tis - ket a tas - ket, a green and yel - low bas - ket

I wrote a let - ter to my love and on the way I dropped it,

I dropped it, I dropped it, and on the way I dropped it.

GAMES:	CONNECTIONS TO BOOKS/ LITERACY:
1. Have the children form a circle.	Rollings, Susan. *New Shoes, Red Shoes.* Orchard Books, 2000.
2. Choose a child to walk around the circle, carrying a handkerchief.	Brennan-Nelson, Denise. *Buzzy the Bumblebee.* Sleeping Bear Press, 1999.
3. At the end of the song the child will drop the handkerchief behind another child in the circle and start to run around the circle.	Carter, David A. *In and Out.* Intervisual Books, 1993.
4. The child with handkerchief behind him or her starts to run after the first child.	Baker, Keith. *Quack and Count.* Harcourt Brace, 1999.
5. If the second child catches the first before he or she reaches the empty spot, the first child is It again.	Martin Jr., Bill. *Brown Bear, Brown Bear.* Henry Holt, 2004.
6. If the second child does not catch the other, the second child is It.	Williams, Sue. *I Went Walking.* Red Wagon Books/Harcourt, 1989.
	Peek, Merele. *Mary Wore Her Red Dress and Henry Wore His Green Sneakers.* Clarion, 1985.
	Powell, Richard. *Guess What I Have!* Barron's Educational Series, 2001.

"Touch Your Shoulders"

MM: ♩ = 100   CSP: G

Verse 2:
With your feet go tap, tap, tap.
Now your fingers snap, snap, snap.
Stretch as high as high can be.
While you're there clap one, two, three!

453

GAMES:	CONNECTIONS TO BOOKS/LITERACY:
Act out the text of the song.	Carle, Eric. *From Head to Toe*. HarperFestival, 1997.
	Suhr, Mandy. *I Can Move*. Wayland Books, 1993, 2009.

"Trot, Trot to Boston"

MM: ♩ = 80   CSP: A

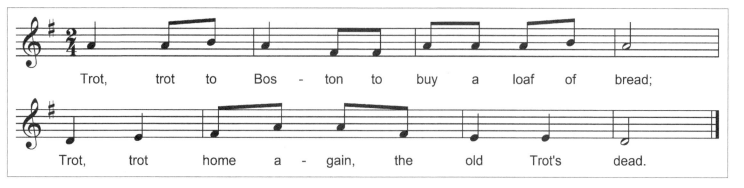

GAMES:	CONNECTIONS TO BOOKS/ LITERACY:
Improvise text. Ask children to change the name of the city "Boston" to other cities in your area.	Margolin, H. Ellen. *Goin' to Boston.* Handprint Books, Brooklyn, 2002. Brandenberg, Aliki. *Go Tell Aunt Rhody.* Macmillan, 1974.

"Two, Four, Six, Eight"

MM: ♩ = 120

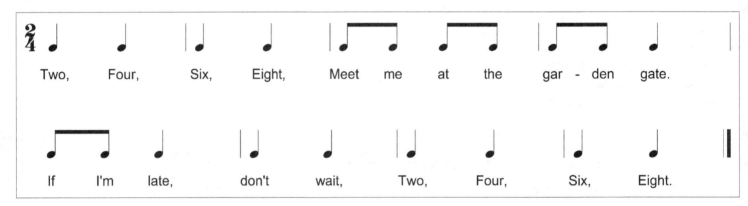

GAMES:	CONNECTIONS TO BOOKS/ LITERACY:
Choosing rhyme.	Lively, Penelope. (1998). *One Two Three Jump!* Puffin Books. Galdone, Paul. (1986). *Over in the Meadow.* Aladdin Paperbacks. Langstaff, John. (1957, 1985). *Over in the Meadow.* Voyager Books. Baker, Keith. (1999). *Quack and Count.* Harcourt Brace. Adams, Pam. (1989). *This Old Man.* Child's Play (International).

"Valentine, Red and Blue"

MM: ♩= 100   CSP: A

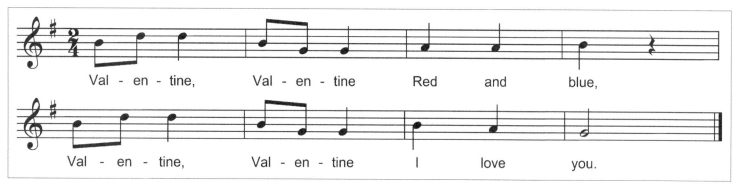

GAMES:	CONNECTIONS TO BOOKS/LITERACY:
Improvise text. Change the colors and make new rhymes.	Otoshi, Kathryn. *One*. KO Kids Books, 2008. Rollings, Susan. *New Shoes, Red Shoes*. Orchard Books, 2000.

455

"We Are Dancing in the Forest"

MM: ♩ = 120   CSP: A

GAMES:	CONNECTIONS TO BOOKS/ LITERACY:
Game 1:	Martin Jr., Bill. *Panda Bear Panda Bear, What Do You See?* Henry Holt, 2003.
1. Children form a circle.	Williams, Sue. *I Went Walking*. Red Wagon Books/Harcourt, 1989.
2. They walk around in a circle singing the song. The "wolf" is in his "den."	
3. At the end of the song, the children ask, "Wolf, are you there?"	
4. If he answers "no—he is brushing his teeth," for example, or doing some other mundane chore, the children repeat the song and ask the question again.	
5. If he answers that he is coming to get them, he runs toward the children, trying to catch one, while they try to reach the safety of the "den."	
6. The child who is caught then becomes a wolf, too, and the game continues until all have been captured.	
Game 2:	
1. Children form circle.	
2. They walk around in a circle singing the song.	
3. They bend at the waist, cover their eyes with their hands, and ask the question, and the wolf can choose to answer "yes" or "no," as in Game 1.	
4. If the wolf answers "yes," the children say "oh, no!" and have to wait in suspense while the wolf prowls around the outside of the circle looking for a victim.	
5. The wolf "bites" (tickles) a child who does not see him coming.	
6. The tickled child is the next wolf, and the game continues.	

"Who's That Tapping at the Window?"

MM: ♩ = 138   CSP: D

Who's that   tap-ping at the win - dow? Who's that   knock-ig at the door?

Mom - my's   tap-ping at the win - dow, Dad - dy's   knock-ing at the door.

GAMES:	CONNECTIONS TO BOOKS/ LITERACY:
1. Have the children sit in a circle.	Leslie, Amanda. *Who's That Scratching at My Door?* Handprint Books, 2001.
2. One child is selected to sit in the middle of the circle such that he or she cannot see who will be singing.	Powell, Richard. *Guess What I Have!* Barron's Educational Series, 2001.
3. Everyone sings the first verse.	Powell, Richard. *Guess Who's Hiding!* Barron's Educational Series, 2001.
4. One child will answer back with, "I am tapping at the window. I am knocking at the door."	
5. The child in the middle now has to guess who was singing.	

457

"Witch, Witch"

MM: ♩ = 100   CSP: G

Witch, witch,   fell in a ditch,   Picked up a pen - ny and   thought she was rich.

"are   you   my   chil - dren?"   "Yes,   we're   you   chil - dren."

Shouted:

"Are   you   my   chil - dren?"   NO-YOU OLD WITCH!

GAMES:	CONNECTIONS TO BOOKS/ LITERACY:
1. A "witch" is chosen and stands facing the group of children.	Howard, Arthur. (2001). *Hoodwinked.* Voyager Books. Harcourt.
2. They move toward her, singing "Witch, witch . . ."	Williams, Linda. (1986). *The Little Old Lady Who Was Not Afraid of Anything.* HarperCollins.
3. The witch responds with, "Are you my children?" to which they reply "Yes" twice.	Sugr, Mandy. (1993, 2009). *I Can Move.* Wayland Books.
4. After the third question, they respond by shouting, "No, you old witch!" and scatter.	
5. The witch must catch someone to replace her, and the next round of the game begins.	

"Zapatitos Blancos"

MM: ♩ = 90

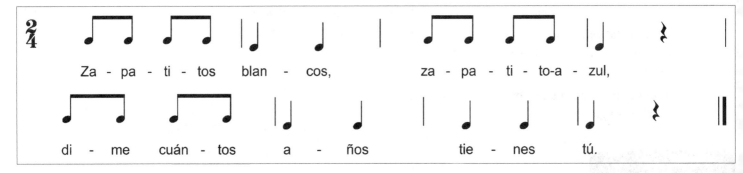

Za - pa - ti - tos blan - cos, za - pa - ti - to-a - zul,

di - me cuán - tos a - ños tie - nes tú.

Literal translation:
Little white shoes,
Little blue shoe,
Tell me how old you are.

GAMES:	CONNECTIONS TO BOOKS/ LITERACY:
Choosing Game. 1. Children sit in circle with legs straight to show shoes. 2. You and children chant the rhyme, pointing to each child's shoes around the circle. 3. When a child is chosen as the rhyme ends, the child says his or her age. You continue, counting the age of the child. 4. The child chosen at the end of the counting pulls his or her legs back and the game continues, until most of the children no longer have their shoes (legs) in the circle.	Rollings, Susan. *New Shoes, Red Shoes.* Orchard Books, 2000. Peek, Merele. *Mary Wore Her Red Dress and Henry Wore His Green Sneakers.* Clarion, 1985. Otoshi, Kathryn. *One.* KO Kids Books, 2008.

459

Appendix 2 Alphabetized List of Children's Literature

Categorizing Children's Books: Musical Themes

Books Related to Singing

Antiphonal Singing (Call and Response)/Form

Adams, Pam. (1989). *This Old Man.* Child's Play International.

Adams, Pam. (1995). *Oh, Soldier, Soldier, Won't You Marry Me?* Child's Play International.

Baer, Gene. (1994). *Thump, Thump, Rat-a-Tat-Tat!* Trumpet Club.

Baker, Keith. (1999). *Quack and Count.* Harcourt Brace.

Boynton, Sandra. (1982). *Moo Baa La La La.* Little Simon.

Boynton, Sandra. (1984). *Doggies.* Little Simon.

Brown, Margaret Wise. (1947). *Goodnight Moon.* Scholastic.

Carle, Eric. (1984). *The Very Busy Spider.* Philomel Books.

Carle, Eric. (1997). *From Head to Toe.* HarperFestival.

Dr. Seuss. (1996). *Mr. Brown Can Moo! Can You?* Random House Books for Young Readers.

Emberley, Ed. (1974). *Klippity Klop.* Little, Brown.

Finn, Isobel. (1999). *The Very Lazy Ladybug.* Tiger Tales.

Gelman, Rita Golden. (1993). *More Spaghetti I Say.* Turtleback.

Gershator, Phillis. (2007). *Listen, Listen.* Barefoot Books.

Gollub, Mathew. (2000). *The Jazz Fly.* Tortuga Press.

Guthrie, Woody. (2000). *Howdi Do.* Candlewick Press.

Hamanaka, Sheila. (1997). *The Hokey Pokey.* Simon & Schuster.

Harriet, Ziefert. (1998). *When I First Came to This Land.* Scholastic.

Hoberman, Mary Ann. (1998). *Miss Mary Mack.* Little, Brown.

Leventhal, Debra. (1999). *What Is Your Language?* Scholastic.

London, Jonathan. (1999). *Wiggle Waggle.* Scholastic.

Martin, Bill., Jr. (1997). *Polar Bear, Polar Bear, What Do You Hear?* Henry Holt.

Martin, Bill., Jr. (2003). *Panda Bear Panda Bear, What Do You See?* Henry Holt.

Martin, Bill., Jr. (2009). *Chicka Chicka Boom Boom.* Paw Prints.

Piper, Watty. (2005). *The Little Engine That Could.* Philomel.

Portis, Antoinette. (2006). *Not a Box.* HarperCollins.

Powell, Richard. (2001). *Guess What I Have!* Barron's Educational Series.

Powell, Richard. (2001). *Guess Who's Hiding!* Barron's Educational Series.

Price, Mathew. (2004). *Peekaboo.* Knopf Books for Young Readers.

Raschka, Chris. (1993). *Yo? Yes!* Scholastic.

Rob, Jackie. (2003). *Sheep Says Baa!* Bang on the Door Series.

Saport, Linda. (1999). *All the Pretty Little Horses.* Clarion Books.

Shannon, George. (1991). *Dance Away!* Greenwillow Books.

Thorne, Donna Sloan, and Marilyn Sloan Felts. (2002). *Buzz and Ollie's High, Low Adventure.* Sloan.

Wellington, Monica. (1994). *The Sheep Follow.* Scholastic.

Williams, Sue. (1989). *I Went Walking.* Red Wagon Books.

Wood, Audrey. (1992). *Silly Sally.* Harcourt.

Singing (Onomatopoeia)/Songs for Vocal Exploration

Adams, Pam. (1995). *Oh, Soldier, Soldier, Won't You Marry Me?* Child's Play International.

Ashman, Linda. (2002). *Can You Make a Piggy Giggle?* Dutton Juvenile.

Baer, Gene. (1994). *Thump, Thump, Rat-a-Tat-Tat!* Trumpet Club.

Baker, Keith. (1999). *Quack and Count.* Harcourt Brace.

Bentley, Dawn. (2004). *Buzz-Buzz, Busy Bees.* Simon & Schuster.

Boynton, Sandra. (1982). *Moo Baa La La La.* Little Simon.

Boynton, Sandra. (1984). *Doggies.* Little Simon.

Brown, Margaret W. (2003). *Two Little Trains.* HarperCollins.

Brown, Margaret Wise. (1979). *The Train to Timbuctoo.* Golden Books.

Calmenson, Stephanie. (1996). *Engine, Engine, Number Nine.* Scholastic.

Cannon, Janell. (1993). *Stellaluna.* Scholastic.

Carle, Eric. (1984). *The Very Busy Spider.* Philomel Books.

Carter, David. (1997). *If You're Happy and You Know It Clap Your Hands.* Cartwheel.

Daniel, Alan, and Lea Daniel. (1994). *Once an Austrian Went Yodeling.* The Wright Group.

Deetlefs, Rene. (1999). *The Song of Six Birds.* Dutton Children's Books.

Dr. Seuss. (1996). *Mr. Brown Can Moo! Can You?* Random House Books for Young Readers.

Emberley, Ed. (1974). *Klippity Klop.* Little, Brown.

Faulkner, Keith. (1996). *The Wide Mouthed Frog.* Dial.

Finn, Isobel. (1999). *The Very Lazy Ladybug.* Tiger Tales.

Fleming, Denise. (1993). *In the Small, Small Pond.* Henry Holt.

Friedman, Carol. (2003). *Nicky.* Dominick Books.

Galdone, Paul. (1986). *Over in the Meadow.* Aladdin Paperbacks.

Gershator, Phillis. (2007). *Listen, Listen.* Barefoot Books.

Gollub, Matthew. (2000). *The Jazz Fly.* Tortuga Press.

Greene, Rhonda Gowler. (1997). *Barnyard Song.* Atheneum Books for Young Readers.

Guthrie, Woody. (1954). *Bling Blang.* Candlewick Press.

Guthrie, Woody. (2000). *Howdi Do.* Candlewick Press.

Jorgensen, Gail. (1988). *Crocodile Beat.* Aladdin Paperbacks.

Lester, Helen. (2006). *Tacky the Penguin.* Sandpiper.

Leventhal, Debra. (1999). *What Is Your Language?* Scholastic.

London, Jonathan. (1999). *Wiggle Waggle.* Scholastic.

Maccarone, Grace. (1994). *Oink! Moo! How Do You Do?* Cartwheel Books.

Martin, Bill., Jr. (1997). *Polar Bear, Polar Bear, What Do You Hear?* Henry Holt.

461

Martin, Bill., Jr. (2009). *Chicka Chicka Boom Boom.* Paw Prints.

Marzollo, Jean. (1997). *Pretend You're a Cat.* Puffin Books.

Moss, Lloyd. (1995). *Zin! Zin! Zin! A Violin.* Aladdin Paperbacks.

Orie, Sandra De Coteau. (1995). *Did You Hear Wind Sing Your Name?* Walker.

Pandell, Karen. (1996). *Animal Action ABC.* Dutton Juvenile.

Pinkney, Brian. (1994). *Max Found Two Sticks.* Aladdin Paperbacks.

Piper, Watty. (2005). *The Little Engine That Could.* Philomel Books.

Post, Jim, and Janet Post. (2002). *Barnyard Boogie.* Accord.

Raffi, and Sylvie Wickstrom. (1990). *The Wheels on the Bus.* Turtleback.

Raschka, Chris. (1993). *Yo? Yes!* Scholastic.

Rob, Jackie. (2003). *Sheep Says Baa!* Bang on the Door Series.

Spier, Peter. (1971). *Gobble Growl Grunt.* Doubleday.

Sykes, Julie. (2007). *Santa's Noisy Night.* Little Tiger Press.

Trapani, Iza. (1999). *Row, Row, Row Your Boat.* Charlesbridge.

Walter, Virginia. (1998). *Hi, Pizza Man!* Orchard Books.

Williams, Linda. (1986). *The Little Old Lady Who Was Not Afraid of Anything.* HarperCollins.

Williams, Sue. (1989). *I Went Walking.* Red Wagon Books.

Yolen, Jane. (1987). *Owl Moon.* Philomel Books.

Zelinsky, Paul. (1990). *The Wheels on the Bus.* Dutton Juvenile.

Books Related to Song Repertoire

American Folk Songs

Bullock, Kathleen. (1993). *She'll Be Comin' Round the Mountain.* Simon & Schuster.

Campbell, Ross. (2008). *The ABRSM Song Book.* ABRSM.

Frazee, Marla. (1997). *Hush Little Baby.* Chronicle Books.

Longstaff, John. (1972). *Frog Went A-Courtin'.* Voyager Books.

Plume, Ilse. (2004). *The Farmer in the Dell.* David R. Godine.

Quackenbush, Robert M. (1973). *She'll Be Comin' Round the Mountain.* Lippincott Williams & Wilkins.

Spier, Peter. (1999). *The Erie Canal.* Corn Hill Waterfront & Navigation.

Lullabies

Brandenberg, Aliki. (1974). *Go Tell Aunt Rhody.* Macmillan.

Brown, Margaret Wise. (1947). *Goodnight Moon.* Scholastic.

Cannon, Janell. (1993). *Stellaluna.* Scholastic.

Frazee, Marla. (1997). *Hush Little Baby.* Chronicle Books.

Na, Il Sung. (2007). *A Book of Sleep.* Alfred A. Knopf.

Saport, Linda. (1999). *All the Pretty Little Horses.* Clarion Books.

Seeger, Pete. (1957). *One Grain of Sand.* Little, Brown.

Related to a Song

Adams, Pam. (1989). *This Old Man.* Child's Play International.

Ayres, Katherine. (2007). *Up, Down, and Around.* Candlewick Press.

Bentley, Dawn. (1999). *Sleepy Bear*. Intervisual Books.

Brennan-Nelson, Denise. (1999). *Buzzy the Bumblebee*. Sleeping Bear Press.

Brett, Jan. (1991). *Berlioz the Bear*. Penguin Young Readers Group.

Brown, Margaret Wise. (1947). *Goodnight Moon*. Scholastic.

Brown, Ruth. (2000). *Snail Trail*. Crown.

Bullock, Kathleen. (1993). *She'll Be Comin' Round the Mountain*. Simon & Schuster.

Carle, Eric. (1995). *The Very Lonely Firefly*. Philomel Books.

Carle, Eric. (2004). *Mister Seahorse*. Philomel Books.

Carter, David. (1997). *If You're Happy and You Know It Clap Your Hands*. Cartwheel.

Cauley, Lorinda Bryan. (1991). *Three Blind Mice*. Putnam Juvenile.

Cauley, Lorinda Bryan. (1997). *Clap Your Hands*. Puffin.

Cronin, Doreen. (2007). *Bounce*. Atheneum Books for Young Readers.

Daniel, Alan, and Lea Daniel. (1993). *I've Been Working on the Railroad*. Wright Group.

Deming, A. G. (1988). *Who Is Tapping at My Window?* Puffin Unicorn.

Ehlert, Lois. (1989). *Eating the Alphabet: Fruits & Vegetables from A to Z*. Harcourt Books.

Flanders, Michael. (1991). *The Hippopotamus Song: A Muddy Love Story*. Joy St Books.

Frazee, Marla. (1997). *Hush Little Baby*. Chronicle Books.

Galdone, Paul. (1986). *Over in the Meadow*. Aladdin Paperbacks.

Hague, Michael. (1993). *Teddy Bear Teddy Bear*. Scholastic.

Hamanaka, Sheila. (1997). *The Hokey Pokey*. Simon & Schuster.

Harriet, Ziefert. (1998). *When I First Came to This Land*. Scholastic.

Hayes, Sarah. (1988). *Stamp Your Feet: Action Rhymes*. William Morrow.

Hoberman, Mary Ann. (1998). *Miss Mary Mack*. Little, Brown.

Hoberman, Mary A. (2003). *Skip to My Lou*. Megan Tingley.

Howard, Arthur. (2001). *Hoodwinked*. Voyager Books.

Hubbell, Patricia. (2003). *I Like Cats*. A Cheshire Studio Book.

Krauss, Ruth. (1945). *The Carrot Seed*. Scholastic.

Langstaff, John. (1972). *Frog Went A-Courtin*. Turtleback.

Langstaff, John. (1974). *Oh, A-Hunting We Will Go*. Aladdin Paperbacks.

Lionni, Leo. (1967). *Frederick*. The Trumpet Club.

Lively, Penelope. (1998). *One Two Three Jump!* Puffin Books.

Locker, Thomas. (2000). *Cloud Dance*. Voyager Books.

Margolin, H. Ellen. (2002). *Goin' to Boston*. Handprint Books.

Martin, Bill., Jr. (2009). *Chicka Chicka Boom Boom*. Paw Prints.

Miranda, Anne. (1997). *To Market, to Market*. Harcourt Children's Books.

Na, Il Sung. (2007). *A Book of Sleep*. Alfred A. Knopf.

Peek, Merele. (1985). *Mary Wore Her Red Dress and Henry Wore His Green Sneakers*. Clarion.

Plume, Ilse. (2004). *The Farmer in the Dell*. David R. Godine.

Powell, Richard. (2001). *Guess Who's Hiding!* Barron's Educational Series.

Quackenbush, Robert M. (1973). *She'll Be Comin' Round the Mountain*. Lippincott Williams & Wilkins.

Quackenbush, Robert M. (1975). *Skip to My Lou*. Lippincott Williams & Wilkins.

Quackenbush, Robert M. (1988). *Pop! Goes the Weasel and Yankee Doodle*. Lippincott Williams & Wilkins.

Raffi, and Sylvie Wickstrom. (1990). *The Wheels on the Bus*. Turtleback.

Rosen, Michael. (1993). *Little Rabbit Foo Foo.* Aladdin Books.

Rounds, Glen. (1973). *Sweet Betsy from Pike Rounds.* Children's Press.

Schubert, Ingrid, and Dieter Schubert. (1998). *There's a Hole in My Bucket.* Front Street.

Seeger, Laura Vaccaro. (2001). *I Had a Rooster.* Viking.

Slavin, Bill. (1992). *The Cat Came Back.* Albert Whitman.

Spier, Peter. (1967). *London Bridge Is Falling Down.* Doubleday.

Sykes, Julie. (2007). *Santa's Noisy Night.* Little Tiger Press.

Taback, Simms. (2007). *There Was an Old Lady.* Childs Play International.

Trapani, Iza. (1999). *Row, Row, Row Your Boat.* Charlesbridge.

Twinn, M. (1975). *Old Macdonald Had a Farm.* Child's Play International.

Westcott, Nadine Bernard. (1998). *The Lady with the Alligator Purse.* Little, Brown.

Wood, Audrey. (1992). *Silly Sally.* Harcourt.

Wood, Audrey. (2007). *A Dog Needs a Bone.* Blue Sky Press.

Zelinsky, Paul. (1990). *The Wheels on the Bus.* Dutton Juvenile.

Song Incorporated into a Book

Adams, Pam. (1989). *This Old Man.* Child's Play International.

Adams, Pam. (1995). *Oh, Soldier, Soldier, Won't You Marry Me?* Child's Play International.

Brandenberg, Aliki. (1974). *Go Tell Aunt Rhody.* Macmillan.

Bryan, Ashley. (1991). *All Night, All Day: A Child's First Book of African-American Spirituals.* Aladdin Paperbacks.

Bullock, Kathleen. (1993). *She'll Be Comin' Round the Mountain.* Simon & Schuster.

Campbell, Ross. (2008). *The ABRSM Song Book.* ABRSM.

Carle, Eric. (1993). *Today Is Monday.* PaperStar.

Carle, Eric. (1995). *The Very Lonely Firefly.* Philomel Books.

Carter, David. (1997). *If You're Happy and You Know It Clap Your Hands.* Cartwheel.

Cauley, Lorinda Bryan. (1991). *Three Blind Mice.* Putnam Juvenile.

Christelow, Eileen. (2006). *Five Little Monkeys Jumping on the Bed.* Sandpiper.

Daniel, Alan, and Lea Daniel. (1993). *I've Been Working on the Railroad.* Wright Group.

Daniel, Alan, and Lea Daniel. (1994). *Once an Austrian Went Yodeling.* Wright Group.

Deming, A. G. (1988). *Who Is Tapping at My Window?* Puffin Unicorn.

Flanders, Michael. (1991). *The Hippopotamus Song: A Muddy Love Story.* Joy St Books.

Frazee, Marla. (1997). *Hush Little Baby.* Chronicle Books.

Guthrie, Woody. (2000). *Howdi Do.* Candlewick Press.

Hague, Michael. (1993). *Teddy Bear Teddy Bear.* Scholastic.

Hamanaka, Sheila. (1997). *The Hokey Pokey.* Simon & Schuster Children's.

Hayes, Sarah. (1988). *Stamp Your Feet: Action Rhymes.* William Morrow.

Hoberman, Mary Ann. (1998). *Miss Mary Mack* Little, Brown.

Margolin, H. Ellen. (2002). *Goin' to Boston.* Handprint Books.

Martin, Bill., Jr. (2009). *Chicka Chicka Boom Boom.* Paw Prints.

Plume, Ilse. (2004). *The Farmer in the Dell.* David R. Godine.

Quackenbush, Robert M. (1973). *She'll Be Comin' Round the Mountain.* Lippincott Williams & Wilkins.

Quackenbush, Robert M. (1975). *Skip to My Lou.* Lippincott Williams & Wilkins.

Quackenbush, Robert M. (1988). *Pop! Goes the Weasel and Yankee Doodle.* Lippincott Williams & Wilkins.

Rosen, Michael. (1993). *Little Rabbit Foo Foo.* Aladdin Books.

Rounds, Glen. (1973). *Sweet Betsy from Pike Rounds.* Children's Press.

Saport, Linda. (1999). *All the Pretty Little Horses.* Clarion Books.

Schubert, Ingrid, and Dieter Schubert. (1998). *There's a Hole in My Bucket.* Front Street.

Seeger, Laura Vaccaro. (2001). *I Had a Rooster.* Viking.

Slavin, Bill. (1992). *The Cat Came Back.* Albert Whitman.

Trapani, Iza. (1999). *Row, Row, Row Your Boat.* Charlesbridge.

Song Related to a Character or a Plot in a Book

Aardema, Verna. (1981). *Bringing the Rain to Kapiti Plain.* Puffin Books.

Adams, Pam. (1989). *This Old Man.* Child's Play International.

Adams, Pam. (1995). *Oh, Soldier, Soldier, Won't You Marry Me?* Child's Play International.

Ashman, Linda. (2002). *Can You Make a Piggy Giggle?* Dutton Juvenile.

Ayres, Katherine. (2007). *Up, Down, and Around.* Candlewick Press.

Bentley, Dawn. (1999). *Sleepy Bear.* Intervisual Books.

Boynton, Sandra. (1982). *Moo Baa La La La.* Little Simon.

Boynton, Sandra. (1984). *Doggies.* Little Simon.

Brennan-Nelson, Denise. (1999). *Buzzy the Bumblebee.* Sleeping Bear Press.

Brown, Margaret Wise. (1979). *The Train to Timbuctoo.* Golden Books.

Brown, Margaret W. (2003). *Two Little Trains.* HarperCollins.

Calmenson, Stephanie. (1996). *Engine, Engine, Number Nine.* Scholastic.

Cannon, Janell. (1993). *Stellaluna.* Scholastic.

Carle, Eric. (1984). *The Very Busy Spider.* Philomel Books.

Carle, Eric. (1988). *Do You Want to Be My Friend?* Philomel Books.

Carle, Eric. (1995). *The Very Lonely Firefly.* Philomel Books.

Carle, Eric. (1997). *Have You Seen My Cat?* Aladdin.

Carle, Eric. (2004). *Mister Seahorse.* Philomel Books.

Cauley, Lorinda Bryan. (1991). *Three Blind Mice.* Putnam Juvenile.

Child, Lauren. (2003). *I Am Too Absolutely Small for School.* Candlewick Press.

Crews, Donald. (1993). *Freight Train Big Book.* Greenwillow Books.

Daniel, Alan, and Lea Daniel. (1994). *Once an Austrian Went Yodeling.* Wright Group.

Faulkner, Keith. (1996). *The Wide Mouthed Frog.* Dial.

Galdone, Paul. (1986). *Over in the Meadow.* Aladdin Paperbacks.

Gelman, Rita Golden. (1993). *More Spaghetti I Say.* Turtleback.

Harriet, Ziefert. (1998). *When I First Came to This Land.* Scholastic.

Harrison, David L. (2001). *When Cows Come Home.* Boyds Mills Press.

Hoberman, Mary Ann. (1998). *Miss Mary Mack.* Little, Brown.

Howard, Arthur. (2001). *Hoodwinked.* Voyager Books.

Kalan, Robert. (2010). *Jump, Frog, Jump!* Perfection Learning.

Krauss, Ruth. (1945). *The Carrot Seed.* Scholastic.

Leslie, Amanda. (2001). *Who's That Scratching at My Door?* Handprint Books.

Lester, Helen. (2006). *Tacky the Penguin.* Sandpiper.

Leuck, Laura. (1999). *Teeny Tiny Mouse.* Sound by Sagebrush.

Lewis, Kevin. (2001). *Chugga Chugga Choo Choo.* Hyperion Book.

465

Locker, Thomas. (2000). *Cloud Dance.* Voyager Books.

Maccarone, Grace. (1994). *Oink! Moo! How Do You Do?* Cartwheel Books.

McBratney, Sam. (2009). *Guess How Much I Love You.* Walker Children's Hardbacks.

Orie, Sandra De Coteau. (1995). *Did You Hear Wind Sing Your Name?* Walker.

Peek, Merele. (1985). *Mary Wore Her Red Dress and Henry Wore His Green Sneakers.* Clarion.

Perkins, Al. (1998). *Hand, Hand, Fingers Thumb.* Random House Books for Young Readers.

Rounds, Glen. (1970). *The Strawberry Roan.* Golden Gate Junior Books.

Sivulich, Sandra Stroner. (1973). *I'm Going on a Bear Hunt.* Dutton Children's Books.

Slavin, Bill. (1992). *The Cat Came Back.* Albert Whitman.

Spier, Peter. (1967). *London Bridge Is Falling Down.* Doubleday.

Sykes, Julie. (2007). *Santa's Noisy Night.* Little Tiger Press.

Taback, Simms. (2007). *There Was an Old Lady.* Childs Play International.

Trapani, Iza. (1999). *Row, Row, Row Your Boat.* Charlesbridge.

Twinn, M. (1975). *Old Macdonald Had a Farm.* Child's Play International.

Williams, Sue. (1989). *I Went Walking.* Red Wagon Books.

Books Related to Music Concepts

Beat

Adams, Pam. (1989). *This Old Man.* Child's Play International.

Adams, Pam. (1995). *Oh, Soldier, Soldier, Won't You Marry Me?* Child's Play International.

Alborough, Jez. (1999). *Duck in the Truck.* Scholastic.

Baer, Gene. (1994). *Thump, Thump, Rat-a-Tat-Tat!* Trumpet Club.

Baker, Keith. (1994). *Big Fat Hen.* Voyager Books.

Baker, Keith. (1999). *Quack and Count.* Harcourt Brace.

Barner, Bob. (1999). *Bugs, Bugs, Bugs.* Chronicle Books.

Boynton, Sandra. (1982). *Moo Baa La La La.* Little Simon.

Brown, Margaret Wise. (1947). *Goodnight Moon.* Scholastic.

Brown, Margaret W. (2003). *Two Little Trains.* HarperCollins.

Brown, Ruth. (2000). *Snail Trail.* Crown.

Calmenson, Stephanie. (1996). *Engine, Engine, Number Nine.* Scholastic.

Carle, Eric. (1997). *From Head to Toe.* HarperFestival.

Carle, Eric. (1997). *Have You Seen My Cat?* Aladdin.

Carter, David A. (1993). *In and Out.* Intervisual Books.

Carter, David. (1997). *If You're Happy and You Know It Clap Your Hands.* Cartwheel.

Cauley, Lorinda Bryan. (1997). *Clap Your Hands.* Puffin.

Crews, Donald. (1993). *Freight Train Big Book.* Greenwillow Books.

Cronin, Doreen. (2005). *Wiggle.* Atheneum Books for Young Readers.

Daniel, Alan, and Lea Daniel. (1993). *I've Been Working on the Railroad.* Wright Group.

Emberley, Ed. (1974). *Klippity Klop.* Little, Brown.

Finn, Isobel. (1999). *The Very Lazy Ladybug.* Tiger Tales.

Fleming, Denise. (1991). *In the Tall, Tall Grass.* Henry Holt.

Fleming, Denise. (1993). *In the Small, Small Pond.* Henry Holt.

Galdone, Paul. (1986). *Over in the Meadow.* Aladdin Paperbacks.

Gershator, Phillis. (2007). *Listen, Listen.* Barefoot Books.

Gollub, Matthew. (2000). *The Jazz Fly.* Tortuga Press.

Guthrie, Woody. (1954). *Bling Blang.* Candlewick Press.

Guthrie, Woody. (2000). *Howdi Do.* Candlewick Press.

Hayes, Sarah. (1988). *Stamp Your Feet: Action Rhymes.* William Morrow.

Hoberman, Mary Ann. (1998). *Miss Mary Mack.* Little, Brown.

Hubbell, Patricia. (2003). *I Like Cats.* A Cheshire Studio Book.

Hutchins, Pat. (1992). *Don't Forget the Bacon!* Live Oak Media.

Jorgensen, Gail. (1988). *Crocodile Beat.* Aladdin Paperbacks.

Kalan, Robert. (2010). *Jump, Frog, Jump!* Perfection Learning.

Keats, Ezra J. (1987). *John Henry: An American Legend.* Dragonfly Books.

Leslie, Amanda. (2001). *Who's That Scratching at My Door?* Handprint Books.

Lewis, Kevin. (2001). *Chugga Chugga Choo Choo.* Hyperion Book.

London, Jonathan. (1999). *Wiggle Waggle.* Scholastic.

Lowery, Linda. (2008). *Twist With a Burger, Jitter With a Bug.* MaxBooks.

Martin, Bill., Jr. (2003). *Panda Bear Panda Bear, What Do You See?* Henry Holt.

Martin, Bill, Jr. (2004). *Brown Bear, Brown Bear.* Henry Holt.

Martin, Bill., Jr. (2006). *Fire! Fire! Said Mrs. McGuire.* HMH Books.

Munsch, Robert N. (2007). *Mortimer Spanish Edition (Munsch for Kids).* Annick Press.

Perkins, Al. (1998). *Hand, Hand, Fingers Thumb.* Random House Books for Young Readers.

Pinkney, Brian. (1994). *Max Found Two Sticks.* Aladdin Paperbacks.

Piper, Watty. (2005). *The Little Engine That Could.* Philomel Books.

Portis, Antoinette. (2006). *Not a Box.* HarperCollins.

Powell, Richard. (2001). *Guess What I Have!* Barron's Educational Series.

Powell, Richard. (2001). Guess Who's Hiding! Barron's Educational Series.

Ricketts, Ann and Michael. (1988). *Rhyme Time.* Brimax Books.

Rollings, Susan. (2000). *New Shoes, Red Shoes.* Orchard Books.

Rosen, Michael. (1993). *Little Rabbit Foo Foo.* Aladdin Books.

Seeger, Pete. (1957). *One Grain of Sand.* Little, Brown.

Shannon, George. (1991). *Dance Away!* Greenwillow Books.

Shaw, Nancy E. (2006). *Sheep in a Jeep.* Sandpiper.

Sivulich, Sandra Stroner. (1973). *I'm Going on a Bear Hunt.* Dutton Children's Books.

Slobodkina, Esphyr. (2004). *Caps for Sale.* Live Oak Media.

Stutson, Caroline. (2009). *By the Light of the Halloween Moon.* Amazon.

Swanson, Susan Marie. (2008). *The House in the Night.* Houghton Mifflin.

Taback, Simms. (2004). *This is the House that Jack Built.* Puffin.

Thorne, Donna Sloan. (2002). *Buzz and Ollie's Steady Beat Adventure.* Sloan.

Trapani, Iza. (1999). *Row, Row, Row Your Boat.* Charlesbridge.

Williams, Rozanne Lanczak. (1995). *Under the Sky.* Creative Teaching Press.

Williams, Sue. (1989). *I Went Walking.* Red Wagon Books.

Fast/Slow

Ahlberg, Allan. (1986). *Each Peach Pear Plum.* Picture Puffin.

Ashman, Linda. (2002). *Can You Make a Piggy Giggle?* Dutton Juvenile.

Baer, Gene. (1994). *Thump, Thump, Rat-a-Tat-Tat!* Trumpet Club.

Bang, Molly. (2000). *When Sophie Gets Angry, Really, Really Angry.* Spoken Arts.

Cauley, Lorinda Bryan. (1997). *Clap Your Hands.* Puffin.

Crews, Donald. (1993). *Freight Train Big Book.* Greenwillow Books.

Daniel, Alan, and Lea Daniel. (1993). *I've Been Working on the Railroad.* Wright Group.

Dr. Seuss. (1996). *My Many Colored Days.* Knopf Books for Young Readers.

Emberley, Ed. (1974). *Klippity Klop.* Little, Brown.

Hoberman, Mary Ann. (2003). *And to Think That We Thought We'd Never Be Friends.* Dragonfly Books.

Keats, Ezra J. (1987). *John Henry: An American Legend.* Dragonfly Books.

Lester, Helen. (2006). *Tacky the Penguin.* Sandpiper.

Lewis, Kevin. (2001). *Chugga Chugga Choo Choo.* Hyperion Book.

Lowery, Linda. (2008). *Twist with a Burger, Jitter with a Bug.* MaxBooks.

Munsch, Robert N. (2007). *Mortimer Spanish Edition (Munsch for Kids).* Annick Press.

Nelson, Lee. (1960). *All the Sounds We Hear.* Steck.

High/Low Chant

Adams, Pam. (1989). *This Old Man.* Child's Play International.

Ahlberg, Allan. (1986). *Each Peach Pear Plum.* Picture Puffin.

Ashman, Linda. (2002). *Can You Make a Piggy Giggle?* Dutton Juvenile.

Baer, Gene. (1994). *Thump, Thump, Rat-a-Tat-Tat!* Trumpet Club.

Baker, Keith. (1994). *Big Fat Hen.* Voyager Books.

Baker, Keith. (1999). *Quack and Count.* Harcourt Brace.

Brown, Margaret Wise. (1947). *Goodnight Moon.* Scholastic.

Brown, Margaret Wise. (1979). *The Train to Timbuctoo.* Golden Books.

Brown, Margaret W. (2003). *Two Little Trains.* HarperCollins.

Brown, Ruth. (2000). *Snail Trail.* Crown.

Calmenson, Stephanie. (1996). *Engine, Engine, Number Nine.* Scholastic.

Carle, Eric. (1988). *Do You Want to Be My Friend?* Philomel Books.

Carle, Eric. (1993). *Today Is Monday.* PaperStar.

Carle, Eric. (1997). *From Head to Toe.* HarperFestival.

Crews, Donald. (1993). *Freight Train Big Book.* Greenwillow Books.

Deetlefs, Rene. (1999). *The Song of Six Birds.* Dutton Children's Books.

Demi. (1998). *The Greatest Treasure.* Scholastic.

Ehlert, Lois. (1989). *Eating the Alphabet: Fruits & Vegetables from A to Z.* Harcourt Books.

Emberley, Ed. (1992). *Go Away, Big Green Monster.* Little, Brown.

Fleming, Denise. (1991). *In the Tall, Tall Grass.* Henry Holt.

Fleming, Denise. (1993). *In the Small, Small Pond.* Henry Holt.

Fleming, Denise. (2007). *Beetle Bop.* Harcourt.

Gershator, Phillis. (1998). *When It Starts to Snow.* Henry Holt.

Gollub, Mathew. (2000). *The Jazz Fly.* Tortuga Press.

Greene, Rhonda Gowler. (1997). *Barnyard Song.* Atheneum Books for Young Readers.

Guthrie, Woody. (2000). *Howdi Do.* Candlewick Press.

Hutchins, Pat. (1992). *Don't Forget the Bacon!* Live Oak Media.

Jorgensen, Gail. (1988). *Crocodile Beat.* Aladdin Paperbacks.

Kalan, Robert. (2010). *Jump, Frog, Jump!* Perfection Learning.

Keats, Ezra J. (1987). *John Henry: An American Legend.* Dragonfly Books.

Leslie, Amanda. (2001). *Who's That Scratching at My Door?* Handprint Books.

Lester, Helen. (2006). *Tacky the Penguin.* Sandpiper.

Lucas, Sally. (1933). *Dancing Dinos.* Random House.

Maccarone, Grace. (1994). *Oink! Moo! How Do You Do?* Cartwheel Books.

Martin, Bill., Jr. (2003). *Panda Bear Panda Bear, What Do You See?* Henry Holt.

Martin, Bill., Jr. (2004). *Brown Bear, Brown Bear.* Henry Holt.

Martin, Bill., Jr. (2006). *Fire! Fire! Said Mrs. McGuire.* HMH Books.

Munsch, Robert N. (2007). *Mortimer Spanish Edition (Munsch for Kids).* Annick Press.

Pinkney, Brian. (1994). *Max Found Two Sticks.* Aladdin Paperbacks.

Piper, Watty. (2005). *The Little Engine That Could.* Philomel Books.

Portis, Antoinette. (2006). *Not a Box.* HarperCollins.

Powell, Richard. (2001). *Guess What I Have!* Barron's Educational Series.

Powell, Richard. (2001). *Guess Who's Hiding!* Barron's Educational Series.

Rollings, Susan. (2000). *New Shoes, Red Shoes.* Orchard Books.

Seeger, Pete. (1957). *One Grain of Sand.* Little, Brown.

Spence, Robert. (2001). *Clickety Clack.* Puffin.

Swanson, Susan Marie. (2008). *The House in the Night.* Houghton Mifflin.

Westcott, Nadine Bernard. (1992). *Peanut Butter and Jelly: A Play Rhyme.* Puffin.

Williams, Sue. (1989). *I Went Walking.* Red Wagon Books.

Wood, Audrey. (1992). *Silly Sally.* Harcourt.

469

High/Low Melody

Adams, Pam. (1989). *This Old Man.* Child's Play International.

Ashman, Linda. (2002). *Can You Make a Piggy Giggle?* Dutton Juvenile.

Barner, Bob. (1999). *Bugs, Bugs, Bugs.* Chronicle Books.

Boynton, Sandra. (1984). *Doggies.* Little Simon.

Brown, Ruth. (2000). *Snail Trail.* Crown.

Calmenson, Stephanie. (1996). *Engine, Engine, Number Nine.* Scholastic.

Carle, Eric. (1984). *The Very Busy Spider.* Philomel Books.

Carle, Eric. (1993). *Today Is Monday.* PaperStar.

Christelow, Eileen. (2006). *Five Little Monkeys Jumping on the Bed.* Sandpiper.

Deetlefs, Rene. (1999). *The Song of Six Birds.* Dutton Children's Books.

Demi. (1998). *The Greatest Treasure.* Scholastic.

Ehlert, Lois. (1989). *Eating the Alphabet: Fruits & Vegetables from A to Z.* Harcourt Books.

Faulkner, Keith. (1996). *The Wide Mouthed Frog.* Dial.

Fleming, Denise. (1991). *In the Tall, Tall Grass.* Henry Holt.

Fleming, Denise. (1993). *In the Small, Small Pond.* Henry Holt.

Fleming, Denise. (2007). *Beetle Bop.* Harcourt.

Gershator, Phillis. (1998). *When It Starts to Snow.* Henry Holt.

Gollub, Mathew. (2000). *The Jazz Fly.* Tortuga Press.

Hubbard, Patricia. (1999). *My Crayons Talk.* Henry Holt.

Jorgensen, Gail. (1988). *Crocodile Beat.* Aladdin Paperbacks.

Leslie, Amanda. (2001). *Who's That Scratching at My Door?* Handprint Books.

Lester, Helen. (2006). *Tacky the Penguin.* Sandpiper.

Lucas, Sally. (1933). *Dancing Dinos.* Random House.

Martin, Bill., Jr. (2003). *Panda Bear Panda Bear, What Do You See?* Henry Holt.

Martin, Bill., Jr. (2004). *Brown Bear, Brown Bear.* Henry Holt.

Munsch, Robert N. (2007). *Mortimer Spanish Edition (Munsch for Kids).* Annick Press.

Portis, Antoinette. (2006). *Not a Box.* HarperCollins.

Powell, Richard. (2001). *Guess What I Have!* Barron's Educational Series.

Powell, Richard. (2001). *Guess Who's Hiding!* Barron's Educational Series.

Slobodkina, Esphyr. (2004). *Caps for Sale.* Live Oak Media.

Swanson, Susan Marie. (2008). *The House in the Night.* Houghton Mifflin.

Williams, Sue. (1989). *I Went Walking.* Red Wagon Books/Harcourt.

Wood, Audrey. (1992). *Silly Sally.* Harcourt.

Loud and Soft

Adams, Pam. (1989). *This Old Man.* Child's Play International.

Adams, Pam. (1995). *Oh, Soldier, Soldier, Won't You Marry Me?* Child's Play International.

Bentley, Dawn. (2004). *Buzz-Buzz, Busy Bees.* Simon & Schuster.

Boynton, Sandra. (1984). *Doggies.* Little Simon.

Brown, Margaret Wise. (1947). *Goodnight Moon.* Scholastic.

Brown, Margaret Wise. (1979). *The Train to Timbuctoo.* Golden Books.

Brown, Margaret W. (2003). *Two Little Trains.* HarperCollins.

Brown, Ruth. (2000). *Snail Trail.* Crown.

Calmenson, Stephanie. (1996). *Engine, Engine, Number Nine.* Scholastic.

Cannon, Janell. (1993). *Stellaluna.* Scholastic.

Carle, Eric. (1984). *The Very Busy Spider.* Philomel Books.

Carle, Eric. (1993). *Today Is Monday.* PaperStar.

Carle, Eric. (1997). *Have You Seen My Cat?* Aladdin.

Cauley, Lorinda Bryan. (1997). *Clap Your Hands.* Puffin.

Crews, Donald. (1986). *Parade.* Greenwillow Books.

Dr. Seuss. (1996). *My Many Colored Days.* Knopf Books for Young Readers.

Ehlert, Lois. (1989). *Eating the Alphabet: Fruits & Vegetables from A to Z.* Harcourt Books.

Fleming, Denise. (1993). *In the Small, Small Pond.* Henry Holt.

Fleming, Denise. (2007). *Beetle Bop.* Harcourt.

Frazee, Marla. (1997). *Hush Little Baby.* Chronicle Books.

Gershator, Phillis. (1998). *When It Starts to Snow.* Henry Holt.

Gershator, Phillis. (2007). *Listen, Listen.* Barefoot Books.

Gollub, Mathew. (2000). *The Jazz Fly.* Tortuga Press.

Guthrie, Woody. (1954). *Bling Blang.* Candlewick Press.

Jorgensen, Gail. (1988). *Crocodile Beat.* Aladdin Paperbacks.

Lester, Helen. (2006). *Tacky the Penguin.* Sandpiper.

Martin, Bill., Jr. (1996). *The Maestro Plays.* Voyager Books.

Martin, Bill., Jr. (1997). *Polar Bear, Polar Bear, What Do You Hear?* Henry Holt.

Martin, Bill., Jr. (2004). *Brown Bear, Brown Bear.* Henry Holt.

Miranda, Anne. (1997). *To Market, to Market.* Harcourt Children's Books.

Nelson, Lee. (1960). *All the Sounds We Hear.* Steck.

Pinkney, Brian. (1994). *Max Found Two Sticks.* Aladdin Paperbacks.

Powell, Richard. (2001). *Guess What I Have!* Barron's Educational Series.

Powell, Richard. (2001). *Guess Who's Hiding!* Barron's Educational Series.

Quackenbush, Robert M. (1988). *Pop! Goes the Weasel and Yankee Doodle.* Lippincott Williams & Wilkins.

Rius, Maria. (1985). *The Five Senses: Hearing.* Barron's Educational Series.

Scotellaro, Robert. (1995). *Daddy Fixed the Vacuum Cleaner.* Willowisp Press.

Seeger, Pete. (1957). *One Grain of Sand.* Little, Brown.

Spence, Robert. (2001). *Clickety Clack.* Puffin.

Spier, Peter. (1971). *Gobble Growl Grunt.* Doubleday.

Stickland, Henrietta. (1997). *Dinosaur Roar.* Dutton Juvenile.

Swanson, Susan Marie. (2008). *The House in the Night.* Houghton Mifflin.

Sykes, Julie. (2007). *Santa's Noisy Night.* Little Tiger Press

Thorne, Donna Sloan. (2002). *Buzz and Ollie's Loud, Soft Adventure.* Sloan.

Thorne, Donna Sloan, and Marilyn Sloan Felts. (2002). *Buzz and Ollie's High, Low Adventure.* Sloan.

Walsh, Vivian. (2002). *Gluey.* Weekly Reader Children's Book Club.

Wellington, Monica. (1997). *Night House Bright House.* Dutton Juvenile

Willems, Mo. (2006). *Don't Let the Pigeon Stay up Late!* Hyperion Press.

Williams, Sue. (1989). *I Went Walking.* Red Wagon Books.

Wood, Audrey. (1992). *Silly Sally.* Harcourt.

Wood, Audrey. (2009). *The Napping House.* Harcourt Children's Books.

Books Related to Music Skills

Music Listening: Listening to Music and Showing the Text

Gollub, Mathew. (2000). *The Jazz Fly.* Tortuga Press.

Guthrie, Woody. (1954). *Bling Blang.* Candlewick Press.

Lach, William. (2006). *Can You Hear It?* Abrams Books for Young Readers.

Musical Instruments (Books with Instruments in Them)

Adams, Pam. (1989). *This Old Man.* Child's Play International.

Baer, Gene. (1994). *Thump, Thump, Rat-a-Tat-Tat!* Trumpet Club.

Brett, Jan. (1991). *Berlioz the Bear.* Penguin Young Readers Group.

Crews, Donald. (1986). *Parade.* Greenwillow Books.

Deetlefs, Rene. (1999). *The Song of Six Birds.* Dutton Children's Books.

Friedman, Carol. (2003). *Nicky.* Dominick Books.

Gollub, Mathew. (2000). *The Jazz Fly.* Tortuga Press.

Lach, William. (2006). *Can You Hear It?* Abrams Books for Young Readers.

Martin, Bill., Jr. (1996). *The Maestro Plays.* Voyager Books.

McPhail, David. (1999). *Mole Music.* Henry Holt.

Moss, Lloyd. (1995). *Zin! Zin! Zin! A Violin.* Aladdin Paperbacks.

Orleans, Ilo. (1958). *Animal Orchestra.* A Golden Book.

Pinkney, Brian. (1994). *Max Found Two Sticks.* Aladdin Paperbacks.

Percussion Instruments

Adams, Pam. (1989). *This Old Man.* Child's Play International.

Baer, Gene. (1994). *Thump, Thump, Rat-a-Tat-Tat!* Trumpet Club.

471

Guthrie, Woody. (1954). *Bling Blang.* Candlewick Press.

Orleans, Ilo. (1958). *Animal Orchestra.* A Golden Book.

Pinkney, Brian. (1994). *Max Found Two Sticks.* Aladdin Paperbacks.

Walsh, Vivian. (2002). *Gluey.* Weekly Reader Children's Book Club.

Williams, Linda. (1986). *The Little Old Lady Who Was Not Afraid of Anything.* HarperCollins.

Books Related to Movement

Adams, Pam. (1989). *This Old Man.* Child's Play International.

Ahlberg, Allan. (1986). *Each Peach Pear Plum.* Picture Puffin.

Ashman, Linda. (2002). *Can You Make a Piggy Giggle?* Dutton Juvenile.

Baer, Gene. (1994). *Thump, Thump, Rat-a-Tat-Tat!* Trumpet Club.

Bang, Molly. (2000). *When Sophie Gets Angry, Really, Really Angry.* Spoken Arts.

Brown, Margaret Wise. (1979). *The Train to Timbuctoo.* Golden Books.

Brown, Margaret W. (2003). *Two Little Trains.* HarperCollins.

Bullock, Kathleen. (1993). *She'll Be Comin' Round the Mountain.* Simon & Schuster.

Calmenson, Stephanie. (1996). *Engine, Engine, Number Nine.* Scholastic.

Carle, Eric. (1997). *From Head to Toe.* HarperFestival.

Carle, Eric. (1997). *Have You Seen My Cat?* Aladdin.

Carter, David. (1997). *If You're Happy and You Know It Clap Your Hands.* Cartwheel.

Cauley, Lorinda Bryan. (1991). *Three Blind Mice.* Putnam Juvenile.

Cauley, Lorinda Bryan. (1997). *Clap Your Hands.* Puffin.

Christelow, Eileen. (2006). Five *Little Monkeys Jumping on the Bed.* Sandpiper.

Crews, Donald. (1986). *Parade.* Greenwillow Books.

Crews, Donald. (1993). *Freight Train Big Book.* Greenwillow Books.

Emberley, Ed. (1974). *Klippity Klop.* Little, Brown.

Flanders, Michael. (1991). *The Hippopotamus Song: A Muddy Love Story.* Joy St Books.

Guthrie, Woody. (2000). *Howdi Do.* Candlewick Press.

Hamanaka, Sheila. (1997). *The Hokey Pokey.* Simon & Schuster.

Harrison, David L. (2001). *When Cows Come Home.* Boyds Mills Press.

Hayes, Sarah. (1988). *Stamp Your Feet: Action Rhymes.* William Morrow.

Hoberman, Mary Ann. (1998). *Miss Mary Mack.* Little, Brown.

Hubbell, Patricia. (2003). *I Like Cats.* A Cheshire Studio Book.

Langstaff, John. (1974). *Oh, A-Hunting We Will Go.* Aladdin Paperbacks.

Lester, Helen. (2006). *Tacky the Penguin.* Sandpiper.

Lewis, Kevin. (2001). *Chugga Chugga Choo Choo.* Hyperion Book.

Lowery, Linda. (2008). *Twist with a Burger, Jitter with a Bug.* MaxBooks.

Marzollo, Jean. (1997). *Pretend You're a Cat.* Puffin Books.

Miranda, Anne. (1999). *Monster Math.* Harcourt Children's Books.

Orie, Sandra De Coteau. (1995). *Did You Hear Wind Sing Your Name?* Walker.

Pandell, Karen. (1996). *Animal Action ABC.* Dutton Juvenile.

Perkins, Al. (1998). *Hand, Hand, Fingers Thumb.* Random House Books for Young Readers.

Price, Mathew. (2004). *Peekaboo.* Knopf Books for Young Readers.

Quackenbush, Robert M. (1973). *She'll Be Comin' Round the Mountain.* Lippincott Williams & Wilkins.

Quackenbush, Robert M. (1988). *Pop! Goes the Weasel and Yankee Doodle.* Lippincott Williams & Wilkins.

Raffi, and Sylvie Wickstrom. (1990). *The Wheels on the Bus.* Turtleback.

Rollings, Susan. (2000). *New Shoes, Red Shoes.* Orchard Books.

Shaw, Nancy E. (2006). *Sheep in a Jeep.* Sandpiper.

Sierra, Judy. (2001). *Counting Crocodiles.* Sandpiper.

Sivulich, Sandra Stroner. (1973). *I'm Going on a Bear Hunt.* Dutton Children's Books.

Suhr, Mandy. (1993, 2009). *I Can Move.* Wayland Books.

Williams, Sarah, and Ian Beck. (1995). *Round and Round the Garden.* Oxford University Press.

Williams, Sue. (1989). *I Went Walking.* Red Wagon Books.

Zelinsky, Paul. (1990). *The Wheels on the Bus.* Dutton Juvenile.

Books Related to Improvisation

Improvising a New Word in the Text

Adams, Pam. (1989). *This Old Man.* Child's Play International.

Ahlberg, Allan. (1986). *Each Peach Pear Plum.* Picture Puffin.

Ashman, Linda. (2002). *Can You Make a Piggy Giggle?* Dutton Juvenile.

Baer, Gene. (1994). *Thump, Thump, Rat-a-Tat-Tat!* Trumpet Club.

Bang, Molly. (2000). *When Sophie Gets Angry, Really, Really Angry.* Spoken Arts.

Bentley, Dawn. (2004). *Buzz-Buzz, Busy Bees.* Simon & Schuster.

Boynton, Sandra. (1982). *Moo Baa La La La.* Little Simon.

Boynton, Sandra. (1984). *Doggies.* Little Simon.

Brown, Margaret Wise. (1947). *Goodnight Moon.* Scholastic.

Brown, Margaret Wise. (1979). *The Train to Timbuctoo.* Golden Books.

Brown, Ruth. (2000). *Snail Trail.* Crown.

Bullock, Kathleen. (1993). *She'll Be Comin' Round the Mountain.* Simon & Schuster.

Calmenson, Stephanie. (1996). *Engine, Engine, Number Nine.* Scholastic.

Carle, Eric. (1993). *Today Is Monday.* PaperStar.

Carle, Eric. (1997). *From Head to Toe.* HarperFestival.

Carle, Eric. (1997). *Have You Seen My Cat?* Aladdin.

Carter, David. (1997). *If You're Happy and You Know It Clap Your Hands.* Cartwheel.

Child, Lauren. (2003). *I Am Too Absolutely Small for School.* Candlewick Press.

Crews, Donald. (1986). *Parade.* Greenwillow Books.

Daniel, Alan, and Lea Daniel. (1993). *I've Been Working on the Railroad.* Wright Group.

Dr. Seuss. (1996). *Mr. Brown Can Moo! Can You?* Random House Books for Young Readers.

Ehlert, Lois. (1989). *Color Zoo.* HarperCollins.

Ehlert, Lois. (1989). *Eating the Alphabet: Fruits & Vegetables from A to Z.* Harcourt Books.

Emberley, Ed. (1974). *Klippity Klop.* Little, Brown.

Emberley, Ed. (1992). *Go Away, Big Green Monster.* Little, Brown.

Fleming, Denise. (1993). *In the Small, Small Pond.* Henry Holt.

Fleming, Denise. (2007). *Beetle Bop.* Harcourt.

Friedman, Carol. (2003). *Nicky.* Dominick Books.

Gollub, Matthew. (2000). *The Jazz Fly.* Tortuga Press.

Guthrie, Woody. (2000). *Howdi Do.* Candlewick Press.

Hamanaka, Sheila. (1997). *The Hokey Pokey.* Simon & Schuster.

Harrison, David L. (2001). *When Cows Come Home.* Boyds Mills Press.

Hoberman, Mary Ann. (1998). *Miss Mary Mack.* Little, Brown.

Hutchins, Pat. (1992). *Don't Forget the Bacon!* Live Oak Media.

Jorgensen, Gail. (1988). *Crocodile Beat.* Aladdin Paperbacks.

Leslie, Amanda. (2001). *Who's That Scratching at My Door?* Handprint Books.

Leuck, Laura. (1999). *Teeny Tiny Mouse.* Sound by Sagebrush.

Leventhal, Debra. (1999). *What Is Your Language?* Scholastic.

Lowery, Linda. (2008). *Twist with a Burger, Jitter with a Bug.* MaxBooks.

Martin, Bill., Jr. (2003). *Panda Bear Panda Bear, What Do You See?* Henry Holt.

Martin, Bill., Jr. (2004). *Brown Bear, Brown Bear.* Henry Holt.

Marzollo, Jean. (1997). *Pretend You're a Cat.* Puffin Books.

Miranda, Anne. (1999). *Monster Math.* Harcourt Children's Books.

Nelson, Lee. (1960). *All the Sounds We Hear.* Steck.

Pandell, Karen. (1996). *Animal Action ABC.* Dutton Juvenile.

Portis, Antoinette. (2006). *Not a Box.* HarperCollins.

Powell, Richard. (2001). *Guess What I Have!* Barron's Educational Series.

Powell, Richard. (2001). *Guess Who's Hiding!* Barron's Educational Series.

Quackenbush, Robert M. (1973). *She'll Be Comin' Round the Mountain.* Lippincott Williams & Wilkins.

Rob, Jackie. (2003). *Sheep Says Baa!* Bang on the Door Series.

Rollings, Susan. (2000). *New Shoes, Red Shoes.* Orchard Books.

Swanson, Susan Marie. (2008). *The House in the Night.* Houghton Mifflin.

Walsh, Vivian. (2002). *Gluey.* Harcourt, Weekly Reader Children's Book Club.

Williams, Linda. (1986). *The Little Old Lady Who Was Not Afraid of Anything.* HarperCollins.

Zemach, Harve. (1966). *Mommy, Buy Me a China Doll.* Follett.

Setting a Refrain in a Text to Music

Adams, Pam. (1989). *This Old Man.* Child's Play International.

Baer, Gene. (1994). *Thump, Thump, Rat-a-Tat-Tat!* Trumpet Club.

Bullock, Kathleen. (1993). *She'll Be Comin' Round the Mountain.* Simon & Schuster.

Calmenson, Stephanie. (1996). *Engine, Engine, Number Nine.* Scholastic.

Carle, Eric. (1984). *The Very Busy Spider.* Philomel Books.

Carle, Eric. (1997). *From Head to Toe.* HarperFestival.

Dr. Seuss. (1996). *Mr. Brown Can Moo! Can You?* Random House Books for Young Readers.

Guthrie, Woody. (1954). *Bling Blang.* Candlewick Press.

Guthrie, Woody. (2000). *Howdi Do.* Candlewick Press.

Hutchins, Pat. (1992). *Don't Forget the Bacon!* Live Oak Media.

Kalan, Robert. (2010). *Jump, Frog, Jump!* Perfection Learning.

Mcdonald, Megan. (1993). *Is This a House for Hermit Crab?* Orchard Books.

Piper, Watty. (2005). *The Little Engine That Could.* Philomel Books.

Quackenbush, Robert M. (1973). *She'll Be Comin' Round the Mountain.* Lippincott Williams & Wilkins.

Serfozo. (1992). *Who Said Red?* Aladdin.

Setting the Text of a Book to a Melody

Bullock, Kathleen. (1993). *She'll Be Comin' Round the Mountain.* Simon & Schuster.

Carle, Eric. (1997). *From Head to Toe.* HarperFestival.

Flanders, Michael. (1991). *The Hippopotamus Song: A Muddy Love Story.* Joy St Books.

Frazee, Marla. (1997). *Hush Little Baby.* Chronicle Books.

Guthrie, Woody. (2000). *Howdi Do.* Candlewick Press.

Hamanaka, Sheila. (1997). *The Hokey Pokey.* Simon & Schuster.

Martin, Bill., Jr. (1996). *The Maestro Plays.* Voyager Books.

Quackenbush, Robert M. (1973). *She'll Be Comin' Round the Mountain.* Lippincott Williams & Wilkins.

Thorne, Donna Sloan, and Marilyn Sloan Felts. (2002). *Buzz and Ollie's High Low Adventure.* Sloan.

Categorizing Children's Books: Nonmusical Themes

Alphabet

Ehlert, Lois. (1989). *Eating the Alphabet: Fruits & Vegetables from A to Z.* Harcourt Books.

Martin, Bill., Jr. (2009). *Chicka Chicka Boom Boom.* Paw Prints.

Pandell, Karen. (1996). *Animal Action ABC.* Dutton Juvenile.

Animals

Aardema, Verna. (1981). *Bringing the Rain to Kapiti Plain.* Puffin Books.

Adams, Pam. (1989). *This Old Man.* Child's Play International.

Alborough, Jez. (1999). *Duck in the Truck.* Scholastic.

Ashman, Linda. (2002). *Can You Make a Piggy Giggle?* Dutton Juvenile.

Ayres, Katherine. (2007). *Up, Down, and Around.* Candlewick Press.

Baker, Keith. (1994). *Big Fat Hen.* Voyager Books.

Baker, Keith. (1999). *Quack and Count.* Harcourt Brace.

Bang, Molly. (2000). *When Sophie Gets Angry, Really, Really Angry.* Spoken Arts.

Barner, Bob. (1999). *Bugs, Bugs, Bugs.* Chronicle Books.

Bentley, Dawn. (1999). *Sleepy Bear.* Intervisual Books.

Bentley, Dawn. (2004). *Buzz Buzz, Busy Bees.* Simon & Schuster.

Boynton, Sandra. (1982). *Moo Baa La La La.* Little Simon.

Boynton, Sandra. (1984). *Doggies.* Little Simon.

Brandenberg, Aliki. (1974). *Go Tell Aunt Rhody.* Macmillan.

Brennan-Nelson, Denise. (1999). *Buzzy the Bumblebee.* Sleeping Bear Press.

Brett, Jan. (1991). *Berlioz the Bear.* Penguin Young Readers Group.

Brown, Ruth. (2000). *Snail Trail.* Crown.

Cannon, Janell. (1993). *Stellaluna.* Scholastic.

Carle, Eric. (1984). *The Very Busy Spider.* Philomel Books.

Carle, Eric. (1988). *Do You Want to Be My Friend?* Philomel Books.

Carle, Eric. (1993). *Today Is Monday.* PaperStar.

Carle, Eric. (1995). *The Very Lonely Firefly.* Philomel Books.

Carle, Eric. (1997). *From Head to Toe*. HarperFestival.

Carle, Eric. (1997). *Have You Seen My Cat?* Aladdin.

Carle, Eric. (2004). *Mister Seahorse*. Philomel Books.

Carter, David A. (1993). *In and Out*. Intervisual Books.

Carter, David. (1997). *If You're Happy and You Know It Clap Your Hands*. Cartwheel.

Cauley, Lorinda Bryan. (1991). *Three Blind Mice*. Putnam Juvenile.

Cauley, Lorinda Bryan. (1997). *Clap Your Hands*. Puffin.

Christelow, Eileen. (2006). *Five Little Monkeys Jumping on the Bed*. Sandpiper.

Cronin, Doreen. (2005). *Wiggle*. Atheneum Books for Young Readers.

Cronin, Doreen. (2007). *Bounce*. Atheneum Books for Young Readers.

Daniel, Alan, and Lea Daniel. (1994). *Once an Austrian Went Yodeling*. Wright Group.

Deetlefs, Rene. (1999). *The Song of Six Birds*. Dutton Children's Books.

Ehlert, Lois. (1989). *Color Zoo*. HarperCollins.

Emberley, Ed. (1974). *Klippity Klop*. Little, Brown.

Faulkner, Keith. (1996). *The Wide Mouthed Frog*. Dial.

Finn, Isobel. (1999). *The Very Lazy Ladybug*. Tiger Tales.

Flanders, Michael. (1991). *The Hippopotamus Song: A Muddy Love Story*. Joy St Books.

Fleming, Denise. (1991). *In the Tall, Tall Grass*. Henry Holt.

Fleming, Denise. (1993). *In the Small, Small Pond*. Henry Holt.

Fleming, Denise. (2007). *Beetle Bop*. Harcourt.

Friedman, Carol. (2003). *Nicky*. Dominick Books.

Galdone, Paul. (1986). *Over in the Meadow*. Aladdin Paperbacks.

Gershator, Phillis. (2007). *Listen, Listen*. Barefoot Books.

Gollub, Matthew. (2000). *The Jazz Fly*. Tortuga Press.

Guthrie, Woody. (1954). *Bling Blang*. Candlewick Press.

Guthrie, Woody. (2001) *My Dolly*. Candlewick Press.

Harriet, Ziefert. (1998). *When I First Came to This Land*. Scholastic.

Henkes, Kevin. (1996). *Chrysanthemum*. Mulberry Books.

Hoberman, Mary Ann. (1998). *Miss Mary Mack*. Little, Brown.

Hoberman, Mary A. (2003). *Skip to My Lou*. Megan Tingley.

Jorgensen, Gail. (1988). *Crocodile Beat*. Aladdin Paperbacks.

Kalan, Robert. (2010). *Jump, Frog, Jump!* Perfection Learning.

Lach, William. (2006). *Can You Hear It?* Abrams Books for Young Readers.

Langstaff, John. (1957, 1985). *Over in the Meadow*. Voyager Books.

Langstaff, John. (1974). *Oh, A-Hunting We Will Go*. Aladdin Paperbacks.

Leslie, Amanda. (2001). *Who's That Scratching at My Door?* Handprint Books.

Lester, Helen. (2006). *Tacky the Penguin*. Sandpiper.

Leuck, Laura. (1999). *Teeny Tiny Mouse*. Sound by Sagebrush.

Lewison, Wendy Cheyette. (1992). *Going to Sleep on the Farm*. Trumpet Club.

Lively, Penelope. (1998). *One Two Three Jump!* Puffin Books.

London, Jonathan. (1999). *Wiggle Waggle*. Scholastic.

Longstaff, John. (1972). *Frog Went A-Courtin'*. Voyager Books.

Lucas, Sally. (1933). *Dancing Dinos*. Random House.

Maccarone, Grace. (1994). *Oink! Moo! How Do You Do?* Cartwheel Books.

Margolin, H. Ellen. (2002). *Goin' to Boston*. Handprint Books.

Martin, Bill., Jr. (1996). *The Maestro Plays*. Voyager Books.

Martin, Bill., Jr. (2003). *Panda Bear Panda Bear, What Do You See?* Henry Holt.

476

Martin, Bill., Jr. (2004). *Brown Bear, Brown Bear.* Henry Holt.

Martin, Bill., Jr. (2006). *Fire! Fire! Said Mrs. McGuire.* HMH Books.

Martin, Bill., Jr. (2009). *Chicka Chicka Boom Boom.* Paw Prints.

Marzollo, Jean. (1997). *Pretend You're a Cat.* Puffin Books.

McBratney, Sam. (2009). *Guess How Much I Love You.* Walker Children's Hardbacks.

Mcdonald, Megan. (1993). *Is This a House for Hermit Crab?* Orchard Books.

McPhail, David. (1999). *Mole Music.* Henry Holt.

Miranda, Anne. (1997). *To Market, to Market.* Harcourt Children's Books.

Na, Il Sung. (2007). *A Book of Sleep.* Alfred A. Knopf.

Nelson, Lee. (1960). *All the Sounds We Hear.* Steck.

Orie, Sandra De Coteau. (1995). *Did You Hear Wind Sing Your Name?* Walker.

Orleans, Ilo. (1958). *Animal Orchestra.* A Golden Book.

Pandell, Karen. (1996). *Animal Action ABC.* Dutton Juvenile.

Perkins, Al. (1998). *Hand, Hand, Fingers Thumb.* Random House Books for Young Readers.

Plume, Ilse. (2004). *The Farmer in the Dell.* David R. Godine.

Portis, Antoinette. (2006). *Not a Box.* HarperCollins.

Post, Jim, and Janet Post. (2002). *Barnyard Boogie.* Accord.

Powell, Richard. (2001). *Guess What I Have!* Barron's Educational Series.

Powell, Richard. (2001). Guess Who's Hiding! Barron's Educational Series.

Ricketts, Ann, and Michael Ricketts. (1988). *Rhyme Time.* Brimax Books.

Rob, Jackie. (2003). *Sheep Says Baa!* Bang on the Door Series.

Rosen, Michael. (1989). *We're Going on a Bear Hunt.* Little Simon.

Rosen, Michael. (1993). *Little Rabbit Foo Foo.* Aladdin Books.

Rounds, Glen. (1970). *The Strawberry Roan.* Golden Gate Junior Books.

Saport, Linda. (1999). *All the Pretty Little Horses.* Clarion Books.

Schubert, Ingrid, and Dieter Schubert. (1998). *There's a Hole in My Bucket.* Front Street.

Seeger, Laura Vaccaro. (2001). *I Had a Rooster.* Viking.

Segal, Lore. (1973). *All the Way Home.* A Sunburst Book.

Shaw, Nancy E. (2006). *Sheep in a Jeep.* Sandpiper.

Sierra, Judy. (2001). *Counting Crocodiles.* Sandpiper.

Sivulich, Sandra Stroner. (1973). *I'm Going on a Bear Hunt.* Dutton Children's Books.

Slavin, Bill. (1992). *The Cat Came Back.* Albert Whitman.

Slobodkina, Esphyr. (2004). *Caps for Sale.* Live Oak Media.

Spence, Robert. (2001). *Clickety Clack.* Puffin.

Spier, Peter. (1971). *Gobble Growl Grunt.* Doubleday.

Stutson, Caroline. (2009). *By the Light of the Halloween Moon.* Amazon.

Taback, Simms. (2004). *This Is the House That Jack Built.* Puffin.

Taback, Simms. (2007). *There Was an Old Lady Who Swallowed a Fly.* Childs Play International.

Thorne, Donna Sloan, and Marilyn Sloan Felts. (2002). *Buzz and Ollie's High, Low Adventure.* Sloan.

Trapani, Iza. (1999). *Row, Row, Row Your Boat.* Charlesbridge.

Twinn, M. (1975). *Old Macdonald Had a Farm.* Child's Play International.

Walsh, Vivian. (2002). *Gluey.* Harcourt.

Wellington, Monica. (1994). *The Sheep Follow.* Scholastic.

Wellington, Monica. (1997). *Night House Bright House.* Dutton Juvenile

Westcott, Nadine Bernard. (1989). *Skip to My Lou.* Little, Brown.

Westcott, Nadine Bernard.(1998). *The Lady with the Alligator Purse.* Little, Brown.
Williams, Sue. (1989). *I Went Walking.* Red Wagon Books.
Wood, Audrey. (1992). *Silly Sally.* Harcourt.
Wood, Audrey. (2007). *A Dog Needs a Bone.* Blue Sky Press.

Body Parts (of Animals and Humans)

Carle, Eric. (1997). *From Head to Toe.* HarperFestival.
Carter, David. (1997). *If You're Happy and You Know It Clap Your Hands.* Cartwheel.
Cauley, Lorinda Bryan. (1997). *Clap Your Hands.* Puffin.
Cronin, Doreen. (2005). *Wiggle.* Atheneum Books for Young Readers.
Cronin, Doreen. (2007). *Bounce.* Atheneum Books for Young Readers.
Faulkner, Keith. (1996). *The Wide Mouthed Frog.* Dial.
Hamanaka, Sheila. (1997). *The Hokey Pokey.* Simon & Schuster.
Hayes, Sarah. (1988). *Stamp Your Feet: Action Rhymes.* William Morrow.
Marzollo, Jean. (1997). *Pretend You're a Cat.* Puffin Books.
Mcdonald, Megan. (1993). *Is This a House for Hermit Crab?* Orchard Books.
Perkins, Al. (1998). *Hand, Hand, Fingers Thumb.* Random House Books for Young Readers.
Rius, Maria. (1985). *The Five Senses: Hearing.* Barron's Educational Series.
Suhr, Mandy. (1993, 2009). *I Can Move.* Wayland Books.

Colors

Adams, Pam. (1989). *This Old Man.* Child's Play International.
Adams, Pam. (1995). *Oh, Soldier, Soldier, Won't You Marry Me?* Child's Play International.
Alborough, Jez. (1999). *Duck in the Truck.* New York, Scholastic.
Baer, Gene. (1994). *Thump, Thump, Rat-a-Tat-Tat!* Trumpet Club.
Baker, Keith. (1994). *Big Fat Hen.* Voyager Books.
Baker, Keith. (1999). *Quack and Count.* Harcourt Brace.
Bang, Molly. (2000). *When Sophie Gets Angry, Really, Really Angry.* Spoken Arts.
Barner, Bob. (1999). *Bugs, Bugs, Bugs.* Chronicle Books.
Bentley, Dawn. (2004). *Buzz Buzz, Busy Bees.* Simon & Schuster.
Boynton, Sandra. (1982). *Moo Baa La La La.* Little Simon.
Boynton, Sandra. (1984). *Doggies.* Little Simon.
Brennan-Nelson, Denise. (1999). *Buzzy the Bumblebee.* Sleeping Bear Press.
Brown, Margaret W. (2003). *Two Little Trains.* HarperCollins.
Bryan, Ashley. (1991). *All Night, All Day: A Child's First Book of African-American Spirituals.* Aladdin Paperbacks.
Carle, Eric. (1988). *Do You Want to Be My Friend?* Philomel Books.
Carle, Eric. (1997). *From Head to Toe.* HarperFestival.
Carle, Eric. (1997). *Have You Seen My Cat?* Aladdin.
Carle, Eric. (2004). *Mister Seahorse.* Philomel Books.
Carter, David A. (1993). *In and Out.* Intervisual Books.
Cauley, Lorinda Bryan. (1997). *Clap Your Hands.* Puffin.
Crews, Donald. (1986). *Parade.* Greenwillow Books.

Crews, Donald. (1993). *Freight Train Big Book.* Greenwillow Books.

Demi. (1998). *The Greatest Treasure.* Scholastic.

Dr. Seuss. (1996). *Mr. Brown Can Moo! Can You?* Random House Books for Young Readers.

Dr. Seuss. (1996). *My Many Colored Days.* Knopf Books for Young Readers.

Ehlert, Lois. (1989). *Color Zoo.* HarperCollins.

Emberley, Ed. (1992). *Go Away, Big Green Monster.* Little, Brown.

Faulkner, Keith. (1996). *The Wide Mouthed Frog.* Dial.

Fleming, Denise. (2007). *Beetle Bop.* Harcourt.

Galdone, Paul. (1986). *Over in the Meadow.* Aladdin Paperbacks.

Guthrie, Woody. (1954). *Bling Blang.* Candlewick Press.

Hubbard, Patricia. (1999). *My Crayons Talk.* Henry Holt.

Jorgensen, Gail. (1988). *Crocodile Beat.* Aladdin Paperbacks.

Langstaff, John. (1957, 1985). *Over in the Meadow.* Voyager Books.

Leslie, Amanda. (2001). *Who's That Scratching at My Door?* Handprint Books.

Leuck, Laura. (1999). *Teeny Tiny Mouse.* Sound by Sagebrush.

Locker, Thomas. (2000). *Cloud Dance.* Voyager Books.

Lowery, Linda. (2008). *Twist with a Burger, Jitter with a Bug.* MaxBooks.

Lucas, Sally. (1933). *Dancing Dinos.* Random House.

Martin, Bill., Jr. (1996). *The Maestro Plays.* Voyager Books.

Martin, Bill., Jr. (2003). *Panda Bear Panda Bear, What Do You See?* Henry Holt.

Martin, Bill., Jr. (2004). *Brown Bear, Brown Bear.* Henry Holt.

Martin, Bill., Jr. (2009). *Chicka Chicka Boom Boom.* Paw Prints.

Orie, Sandra De Coteau. (1995). *Did You Hear Wind Sing Your Name?* Walker.

Otoshi, Kathryn. (2008). *One.* KO Kids Books.

Peek, Merele. (1985). *Mary Wore Her Red Dress and Henry Wore His Green Sneakers.* Clarion Books.

Pinkney, Brian. (1994). *Max Found Two Sticks.* Aladdin Paperbacks.

Powell, Richard. (2001). *Guess What I Have!* Barron's Educational Series.

Powell, Richard. (2001). *Guess Who's Hiding!* Barron's Educational Series.

Rob, Jackie. (2003). *Sheep Says Baa!* Bang on the Door Series.

Rollings, Susan. (2000). *New Shoes, Red Shoes.* New York.

Seeger, Laura Vaccaro. (2001). *I Had a Rooster.* Viking.

Serfozo. (1992). *Who Said Red?* Aladdin.

Thorne, Donna Sloan and Marilyn Sloan. Felts (2002). *Buzz and Ollie's High, Low Adventure.* Sloan.

Westcott, Nadine Bernard. (1998). *The Lady with the Alligator Purse.* Little, Brown.

Williams, Sue. (1989). *I Went Walking.* Red Wagon Books.

Dancing

Ashman, Linda. (2002). *Can You Make a Piggy Giggle?* Dutton Juvenile.

Cauley, Lorinda Bryan. (1997). *Clap Your Hands.* Puffin.

Christelow, Eileen. (2006). *Five Little Monkeys Jumping on the Bed.* Sandpiper.

Hamanaka, Sheila. (1997). *The Hokey Pokey.* Simon & Schuster.

Harrison, David L. (2001). *When Cows Come Home.* Boyds Mills Press.

Langstaff, John. (1963). *Ol' Dan Tucker.* Harcourt, Brace.

Lester, Helen. (2006). *Tacky the Penguin.* Sandpiper.

Lowery, Linda. (2008). *Twist with a Burger, Jitter with a Bug.* MaxBooks.
Lucas, Sally. (1933). *Dancing Dinos.* Random House.
Quackenbush, Robert M. (1975). *Skip to My Lou.* Lippincott Williams & Wilkins.
Shannon, George. (1991). *Dance Away!* Greenwillow Books.
Twinn, M. (1975). *Old Macdonald Had a Farm.* Child's Play International.
Wellington, Monica. (1997). *Night House Bright House.* Dutton Juvenile.

Days of the Week

Carle, Eric. (1993). *Today Is Monday.* PaperStar.
Child, Lauren. (2003). *I Am Too Absolutely Small for School.* Candlewick Press.

Directions/Following Directions

Ayres, Katherine. (2007). *Up, Down, and Around.* Candlewick Press.
Brown, Margaret W. (2003). *Two Little Trains.* HarperCollins.
Carter, David A. (1993). *In and Out.* Intervisual Books.
Cronin, Doreen. (2007). *Bounce.* Atheneum Books for Young Readers.
Hamanaka, Sheila. (1997). *The Hokey Pokey.* Simon & Schuster.
Lewis, Kevin. (2001). *Chugga Chugga Choo Choo.* Hyperion Book.
Maccarone, Grace. (1994). *Oink! Moo! How Do You Do?* Cartwheel Books.
Margolin, H. Ellen. (2002). *Goin' to Boston.* Handprint Books.
Rosen, Michael. (1993). *Little Rabbit Foo Foo.* Aladdin Books.
Shannon, George. (1991). *Dance Away!* Greenwillow Books.
Willems, Mo. (2003). *Don't Let the Pigeon Drive the Bus!* Hyperion Press.

Family

Bang, Molly. (2000). *When Sophie Gets Angry, Really, Really Angry.* Spoken Arts.
Bemelmans, Ludwig. (1939). *Madeline.* Viking Press.
Cannon, Janell. (1993). *Stellaluna.* Scholastic.
Carle, Eric. (2004). *Mister Seahorse.* Philomel Books.
Child, Lauren. (2003). *I Am Too Absolutely Small for School.* Candlewick Press.
Christelow, Eileen. (2006). *Five Little Monkeys Jumping on the Bed.* Sandpiper.
Deetlefs, Rene. (1999). *The Song of Six Birds.* Dutton Children's Books.
Demi. (1998). *The Greatest Treasure.* Scholastic.
Frazee, Marla. (1997). *Hush Little Baby.* Chronicle Books.
Gershator, Phillis. (2007). *Listen, Listen.* Barefoot Books.
Harriet, Ziefert. (1998). *When I First Came to This Land.* Scholastic.
Howard, Arthur. (2001). *Hoodwinked.* Voyager Books.
Hutchins, Pat. (1992). *Don't Forget the Bacon!* Live Oak Media.
Krauss, Ruth. (1945). *The Carrot Seed.* Scholastic.
Langstaff, John. (1957, 1985). *Over in the Meadow.* Voyager Books.
Leuck, Laura. (1999). *Teeny Tiny Mouse.* Sound by Sagebrush.
Martin, Bill., Jr. (2009). *Chicka Chicka Boom Boom.* Paw Prints.
McBratney, Sam. (2009). *Guess How Much I Love You.* Walker Children's Hardbacks.
Miranda, Anne. (1999). *Monster Math.* Harcourt Children's Books.
Pinkney, Brian. (1994). *Max Found Two Sticks.* Aladdin Paperbacks.

Price, Mathew. (2004). *Peekaboo*. Knopf Books for Young Readers.

Rosen, Michael. (1989). *We're Going on a Bear Hunt*. Little Simon.

Saport, Linda. (1999). *All the Pretty Little Horses*. Clarion Books.

Scotellaro, Robert. (1995). *Daddy Fixed the Vacuum Cleaner*. Willowisp Press.

Thorne, Donna Sloan. (2002). *Buzz and Ollie's Loud, Soft Adventure*. Sloan.

Friends

Alborough, Jez. (1999). *Duck in the Truck*. Scholastic.

Bang, Molly. (2000). *When Sophie Gets Angry, Really, Really Angry*. Spoken Arts.

Barner, Bob. (1999). *Bugs, Bugs, Bugs*. Chronicle Books.

Bentley, Dawn. (2004). *Buzz Buzz, Busy Bees*. Simon & Schuster.

Boynton, Sandra. (1982). *Moo Baa La La La*. Little Simon.

Boynton, Sandra. (1984). *Doggies*. Little Simon.

Brown, Margaret W. (2003). *Two Little Trains*. HarperCollins.

Bullock, Kathleen. (1993). *She'll Be Comin' Round the Mountain*. Simon & Schuster.

Cannon, Janell. (1993). *Stellaluna*. Scholastic.

Carle, Eric. (1984). *The Very Busy Spider*. Philomel Books.

Carle, Eric. (1988). *Do You Want to Be My Friend?* Philomel Books.

Carle, Eric. (1997). *Have You Seen My Cat?* Aladdin.

Cauley, Lorinda Bryan. (1997). *Clap Your Hands*. Puffin.

Child, Lauren. (2003). *I Am Too Absolutely Small for School*. Candlewick Press.

Cronin, Doreen. (2007). *Bounce*. Atheneum Books for Young Readers.

Deetlefs, Rene. (1999). *The Song of Six Birds*. Dutton Children's Books.

Dr. Seuss. (1996). *Mr. Brown Can Moo! Can You?* Random House Books for Young Readers.

Emberley, Ed. (1974). *Klippity Klop*. Little, Brown.

Flanders, Michael. (1991). *The Hippopotamus Song: A Muddy Love Story*. Joy St Books.

Gelman, Rita Golden. (1993). *More Spaghetti I Say*. Turtleback.

Gershator, Phillis. (2007). *Listen, Listen*. Barefoot Books.

Gollub, Matthew. (2000). *The Jazz Fly*. Tortuga Press.

Guthrie, Woody. (1954). *Bling Blang*. Candlewick Press.

Guthrie, Woody. (2000). *Howdi Do*. Candlewick Press.

Guthrie, Woody. (2001) *My Dolly*. Candlewick Press.

Hamanaka, Sheila. (1997). *The Hokey Pokey*. Simon & Schuster.

Harrison, David L. (2001). *When Cows Come Home*. Boyds Mills Press.

Hayes, Sarah. (1988). *Stamp Your Feet: Action Rhymes*. William Morrow.

Henkes, Kevin. (1996). *Chrysanthemum*. Mulberry Books.

Hoberman, Mary Ann. (1998). *Miss Mary Mack*. Little, Brown.

Hoberman, Mary Ann. (2003). *And to Think That We Thought We'd Never Be Friends*. Dragonfly Books.

Hoberman, Mary A. (2003). *Skip to My Lou*. Megan Tingley.

Hubbard, Patricia. (1999). *My Crayons Talk*. Henry Holt.

Jorgensen, Gail. (1988). *Crocodile Beat*. Aladdin Paperbacks.

Kalan, Robert. (2010). *Jump, Frog, Jump!* Perfection Learning.

Leslie, Amanda. (2001). *Who's That Scratching at My Door?* Handprint Books.

Leventhal, Debra. (1999). *What Is Your Language?* Scholastic.

Lionni, Leo. (1967). *Frederick.* Trumpet Club.

Lively, Penelope. (1998). *One Two Three Jump!* Puffin Books.

Lucas, Sally. (1933). *Dancing Dinos.* Random House.

Maccarone, Grace. (1994). *Oink! Moo! How Do You Do?* Cartwheel Books.

Marzollo, Jean. (1997). *Pretend You're a Cat.* Puffin Books.

Otoshi, Kathryn. (2008). *One.* KO Kids Books.

Peek, Merele. (1985). *Mary Wore Her Red Dress and Henry Wore His Green Sneakers.* Clarion Books.

Piper, Watty. (2005). *The Little Engine That Could.* Philomel Books.

Post, Jim, and Janet Post. (2002). *Barnyard Boogie.* Accord.

Quackenbush, Robert M. (1973). *She'll Be Comin' Round the Mountain.* Lippincott Williams & Wilkins.

Raschka, Chris. (1993). *Yo? Yes!* Scholastic.

Rosen, Michael. (1993). *Little Rabbit Foo Foo.* Aladdin Books.

Thorne, Donna Sloan, and Marilyn Sloan Felts. (2002). *Buzz and Ollie's High, Low Adventure.* Sloan.

Walsh, Vivian. (2002). *Gluey.* Harcourt.

Fruits/Vegetables/Food

Ahlberg, Allan. (1986). *Each Peach Pear Plum.* Picture Puffin.

Ayres, Katherine. (2007). *Up, Down, and Around.* Candlewick Press.

Carle, Eric. (1993). *Today Is Monday.* PaperStar.

Cronin, Doreen. (2007). *Bounce.* Atheneum Books for Young Readers.

Ehlert, Lois. (1989). *Eating the Alphabet: Fruits & Vegetables from A to Z.* Harcourt Books.

Gelman, Rita Golden. (1993). *More Spaghetti I Say.* Turtleback.

Hutchins, Pat. (1992). *Don't Forget the Bacon!* Live Oak Media.

Krauss, Ruth. (1945). *The Carrot Seed.* Scholastic.

Maccarone, Grace. (1994). *Oink! Moo! How Do You Do?* Cartwheel Books.

Sierra, Judy. (2001). *Counting Crocodiles.* Sandpiper.

Taback, Simms. (2004). *This Is the House That Jack Built.* Puffin.

Walter, Virginia. (1998). *Hi, Pizza Man!* Orchard Books.

Westcott, Nadine Bernard. (1992). *Peanut Butter and Jelly: A Play Rhyme.* Puffin.

Geography

Bullock, Kathleen. (1993). *She'll Be Comin' Round the Mountain.* Simon & Schuster.

Leventhal, Debra. (1999). *What Is Your Language?* Scholastic.

Lewis, Kevin. (2001). *Chugga Chugga Choo Choo.* Hyperion Book.

Quackenbush, Robert M. (1973). *She'll Be Comin' Round the Mountain.* Lippincott Williams & Wilkins.

Spier, Peter. (1999). *The Erie Canal.* Corn Hill Waterfront & Navigation.

Holiday Themed (Halloween, Christmas, Birthday, etc.)

Crews, Donald. (1986). *Parade.* Greenwillow Books.

Howard, Arthur. (2001). *Hoodwinked.* Voyager Books. Harcourt.

Lowery, Linda. (2008). *Twist with a Burger, Jitter with a Bug*. MaxBooks.

Miranda, Anne. (1999). *Monster Math*. Harcourt Children's Books.

Peek, Merele. (1985). *Mary Wore Her Red Dress and Henry Wore His Green Sneakers*. Clarion Books.

Rollings, Susan. (2000). *New Shoes, Red Shoes*. Orchard Books.

Stutson, Caroline. (2009). *By the Light of the Halloween Moon*. Amazon.

Suhr, Mandy. (1993, 2009). *I Can Move*. Wayland Books.

Sykes, Julie. (2007). *Santa's Noisy Night*. Little Tiger Press.

Williams, Linda. (1986). *The Little Old Lady Who Was Not Afraid of Anything*. HarperCollins Children's Books.

Imagination/Adventures

Brown, Margaret W. (2003). *Two Little Trains*. HarperCollins.

Cauley, Lorinda Bryan. (1991). *Three Blind Mice*. Putnam Juvenile.

Cauley, Lorinda Bryan. (1997). *Clap Your Hands*. Puffin Children's Books.

Crews, Donald. (1986). *Parade*. Greenwillow Books.

Daniel, Alan, and Lea Daniel. (1994). *Once an Austrian Went Yodeling*. Wright Group.

Emberley, Ed. (1974). *Klippity Klop*. Little, Brown.

Emberley, Ed. (1992). *Go Away, Big Green Monster*. Little, Brown.

Gershator, Phillis. (2007). *Listen, Listen*. Barefoot Books.

Gollub, Matthew. (2000). *The Jazz Fly*. Tortuga Press.

Harrison, David L. (2001). *When Cows Come Home*. Boyds Mills Press.

Hubbard, Patricia. (1999). *My Crayons Talk*. Henry Holt.

Kohn, Michael, and Daniel Weiner. (1981). *There Was an Old Woman Who Swallowed a Fly*. Weekly Reader Children's Book Club.

Krauss, Ruth. (1945). *The Carrot Seed*. Scholastic.

Lowery, Linda. (2008). *Twist with a Burger, Jitter with a Bug*. MaxBooks.

Martin, Bill., Jr. (1996). *The Maestro Plays*. Voyager Books.

Martin, Bill., Jr. (2009). *Chicka Chicka Boom Boom*. Paw Prints.

Pandell, Karen. (1996). *Animal Action ABC*. Dutton Juvenile.

Piper, Watty. (2005). *The Little Engine That Could*. Philomel Books.

Portis, Antoinette. (2006). *Not a Box*. HarperCollins.

Price, Mathew. (2004). *Peekaboo*. Knopf Books for Young Readers.

Sivulich, Sandra Stroner. (1973). *I'm Going on a Bear Hunt*. Dutton Children's Books.

Swanson, Susan Marie. (2008). *The House in the Night*. Houghton Mifflin.

Thorne, Donna Sloan. (2002). *Buzz and Ollie's Loud, Soft Adventure*. Sloan.

Thorne, Donna Sloan. (2002). *Buzz and Ollie's Steady Beat Adventure*. Sloan.

Thorne, Donna Sloan, and Marilyn Sloan Felts. (2002). *Buzz and Ollie's High, Low Adventure*. Sloan.

Trapani, Iza. (1999). *Row, Row, Row Your Boat*. Charlesbridge.

Westcott, Nadine Bernard. (1998). *The Lady with the Alligator Purse*. Little, Brown.

Williams, Linda. (1986). *The Little Old Lady Who Was Not Afraid of Anything*. HarperCollins.

Williams, Rozanne Lanczak. (1995). *Under the Sky*. Creative Teaching Press.

Nature

Aardema, Verna. (1981). *Bringing the Rain to Kapiti Plain*. Puffin Books.

Brown, Ruth. (2000). *Snail Trail*. Crown.

Cannon, Janell. (1993). *Stellaluna*. Scholastic.

Carle, Eric. (1984). *The Very Busy Spider*. Philomel Books.

Deetlefs, Rene. (1999). *The Song of Six Birds*. Dutton Children's Books.

Fleming, Denise. (1991). *In the Tall, Tall Grass*. Henry Holt.

Fleming, Denise. (1993). *In the Small, Small Pond*. Henry Holt.

Galdone, Paul. (1986). *Over in the Meadow*. Aladdin Paperbacks.

Gershator, Phillis. (2007). *Listen, Listen*. Barefoot Books.

Krauss, Ruth. (1945). *The Carrot Seed*. Scholastic.

Langstaff, John. (1957, 1985). *Over in the Meadow*. Voyager Books.

Langstaff, John. (1974). *Oh, A-Hunting We Will Go*. Aladdin Paperbacks.

Locker, Thomas. (2000). *Cloud Dance*. Voyager Books.

Martin, Bill., Jr. (2009). *Chicka Chicka Boom Boom*. Paw Prints.

Mcdonald, Megan. (1993). *Is This a House for Hermit Crab?* Orchard Books.

Orie, Sandra De Coteau. (1995). *Did You Hear Wind Sing Your Name?* Walker.

Plume, Ilse. (2004). *The Farmer in the Dell*. David R. Godine.

Seeger, Pete. (1957). *One Grain of Sand*. Little, Brown.

Spier, Peter. (1971). *Gobble Growl Grunt*. Doubleday.

Spier, Peter. (1999). *The Erie Canal*. Corn Hill Waterfront & Navigation.

Stojic, Manya. (2000). *Rain*. Dragonfly Books.

Williams, Rozanne Lanczak. (1995). *Under the Sky*. Creative Teaching Press.

Williams, Sarah, and Ian Beck. (1995). *Round and Round the Garden*. Oxford University Press.

Numbers

Adams, Pam. (1989). *This Old Man*. Child's Play International.

Baker, Keith. (1994). *Big Fat Hen*. Voyager Books.

Baker, Keith. (1999). *Quack and Count*. Harcourt Brace.

Galdone, Paul. (1986). *Over in the Meadow*. Aladdin Paperbacks.

Lucas, Sally. (1933). *Dancing Dinos*. Random House.

Miranda, Anne. (1999). *Monster Math*. Harcourt Children's Books.

Moss, Lloyd. (1995). *Zin! Zin! Zin! A Violin*. Aladdin Paperbacks.

Otoshi, Kathryn. (2008). *One*. KO Kids Books.

Problem Solving

Aardema, Verna. (1981). *Bringing the Rain to Kapiti Plain*. Puffin Books.

Ashman, Linda. (2002). *Can You Make a Piggy Giggle?* Dutton Juvenile.

Bemelmans, Ludwig. (1939). *Madeline*. Viking Press.

Bentley, Dawn. (2004). *Buzz Buzz, Busy Bees*. Simon & Schuster.

Boynton, Sandra. (1982). *Moo Baa La La La*. Little Simon.

Brennan-Nelson, Denise. (1999). *Buzzy the Bumblebee*. Sleeping Bear Press.

Brett, Jan. (1991). *Berlioz the Bear*. Penguin Young Readers Group.

Brown, Margaret W. (2003). *Two Little Trains*. HarperCollins.

Cannon, Janell. (1993). *Stellaluna*. Scholastic.

Carle, Eric. (1988). *Do You Want to Be My Friend?* Philomel Books.

Carle, Eric. (1995). *The Very Lonely Firefly*. Philomel Books.

Carle, Eric. (1997). *Have You Seen My Cat?* Aladdin.

Cauley, Lorinda Bryan. (1991). *Three Blind Mice*. Putnam Juvenile.

Christelow, Eileen. (2006). *Five Little Monkeys Jumping on the Bed*. Sandpiper.

Demi. (1998). *The Greatest Treasure*. Scholastic.

Emberley, Ed. (1992). *Go Away, Big Green Monster*. Little, Brown.

Finn, Isobel. (1999). *The Very Lazy Ladybug*. Tiger Tales.

Frazee, Marla. (1997). *Hush Little Baby*. Chronicle Books.

Guthrie, Woody. (1954). *Bling Blang*. Candlewick Press.

Harriet, Ziefert. (1998). *When I First Came to This Land*. Scholastic.

Henkes, Kevin. (1996). *Chrysanthemum*. Mulberry Books.

Keats, Ezra J. (1987). *John Henry: An American Legend*. Dragonfly Books.

Krauss, Ruth. (1945). *The Carrot Seed*. Scholastic.

Lionni, Leo. (1967). *Frederick*. Trumpet Club.

Lucas, Sally. (1933). *Dancing Dinos*. Random House.

Maccarone, Grace. (1994). *Oink! Moo! How Do You Do?* Cartwheel Books.

Martin, Bill., Jr. (2006). *Fire! Fire! Said Mrs. McGuire*. HMH Books.

Mcdonald, Megan. (1993). *Is This a House for Hermit Crab?* Orchard Books.

Piper, Watty. (2005). *The Little Engine That Could*. Philomel Books.

Rosen, Michael. (1993). *Little Rabbit Foo Foo*. Aladdin Books.

Rounds, Glen. (1970). *The Strawberry Roan*. Golden Gate Junior Books.

Schubert, Ingrid, and Dieter Schubert. (1998). *There's a Hole in My Bucket*. Front Street.

Scotellaro, Robert. (1995). *Daddy Fixed the Vacuum Cleaner*. Willowisp Press.

Shannon, George. (1991). *Dance Away!* Greenwillow Books.

Slavin, Bill. (1992). *The Cat Came Back*. Albert Whitman.

Spier, Peter. (1967). *London Bridge Is Falling Down*. Doubleday.

Walsh, Vivian. (2002). *Gluey*. Harcourt.

485

Questions/Guessing

Leslie, Amanda. (2001). *Who's That Scratching at My Door?* Handprint Books.

Martin, Bill., Jr. (1997). *Polar Bear, Polar Bear, What Do You Hear?* Henry Holt.

Martin, Bill., Jr. (2004). *Brown Bear, Brown Bear, What Do You See?* Henry Holt.

Martin, Bill., Jr. (2006). *Fire! Fire! Said Mrs. McGuire*. HMH Books.

Mcdonald, Megan. (1993). *Is This a House for Hermit Crab?* Orchard Books.

Powell, Richard. (2001). *Guess What I Have!* Barron's Educational Series.

Powell, Richard. (2001). *Guess Who's Hiding!* Barron's Educational Series.

Price, Mathew. (2004). *Peekaboo*. Knopf Books for Young Readers.

Rhyming

Ashman, Linda. (2002). *Can You Make a Piggy Giggle?* Dutton Juvenile.

Bentley, Dawn. (2004). *Buzz Buzz, Busy Bees*. Simon & Schuster.

Boynton, Sandra. (1982). *Moo Baa La La La*. Little Simon.

Brennan-Nelson, Denise. (1999). *Buzzy the Bumblebee*. Sleeping Bear Press.

Brown, Margaret Wise. (1947). *Goodnight Moon.* Scholastic.

Calmenson, Stephanie. (1996). *Engine, Engine, Number Nine.* Scholastic.

Cauley, Lorinda Bryan. (1997). *Clap Your Hands.* Puffin.

Daniel, Alan, and Lea Daniel. (1994). *Once an Austrian Went Yodeling.* Wright Group.

Flanders, Michael. (1991). *The Hippopotamus Song: A Muddy Love Story.* Joy St Books.

Fleming, Denise. (1991). *In the Tall, Tall Grass.* Henry Holt.

Fleming, Denise. (1993). *In the Small, Small Pond.* Henry Holt.

Friedman, Carol. (2003). *Nicky.* Dominick Books.

Galdone, Paul. (1986). *Over in the Meadow.* Aladdin Paperbacks.

Gelman, Rita Golden. (1993). *More Spaghetti I Say.* Turtleback.

Gershator, Phillis. (2007). *Listen, Listen.* Barefoot Books.

Gollub, Matthew. (2000). *The Jazz Fly.* Tortuga Press.

Guthrie, Woody. (1954). *Bling Blang.* Candlewick Press.

Hague, Michael. (1993). *Teddy Bear Teddy Bear.* Scholastic.

Hamanaka, Sheila. (1997). *The Hokey Pokey.* Simon & Schuster.

Harriet, Ziefert. (1998). *When I First Came to This Land.* Scholastic.

Harrison, David L. (2001). *When Cows Come Home.* Boyds Mills Press.

Hayes, Sarah. (1988). *Stamp Your Feet: Action Rhymes.* William Morrow.

Henkes, Kevin. (1996). *Chrysanthemum.* Mulberry Books.

Hoberman, Mary A. (2003). *Skip to My Lou.* Megan Tingley.

Hoberman, Mary Ann. (1998). *Miss Mary Mack.* Little, Brown.

Langstaff, John. (1963). *Ol' Dan Tucker.* Harcourt, Brace & World.

Langstaff, John. (1974). *Oh, A-Hunting We Will Go.* Aladdin Paperbacks.

Leuck, Laura. (1999). *Teeny Tiny Mouse.* Sound by Sagebrush.

Lewis, Kevin. (2001). *Chugga Chugga Choo Choo.* Hyperion Book.

Longstaff, John. (1972). *Frog Went A-Courtin'.* Voyager Books.

Lucas, Sally. (1933). *Dancing Dinos.* Random House.

Martin, Bill., Jr. (2004). *Brown Bear, Brown Bear.* Henry Holt.

Martin, Bill., Jr. (2006). *Fire! Fire! Said Mrs. McGuire.* HMH Books.

Martin, Bill., Jr. (2009). *Chicka Chicka Boom Boom.* Paw Prints.

Moss, Lloyd. (1995). *Zin! Zin! Zin! A Violin.* Aladdin Paperbacks.

Plume, Ilse. (2004). *The Farmer in the Dell.* David R. Godine.

Post, Jim, and Janet Post. (2002). *Barnyard Boogie.* Accord.

Powell, Richard. (2001). *Guess What I Have!* Barron's Educational Series.

Raffi, and Sylvie Wickstrom. (1990). *The Wheels on the Bus.* Turtleback.

Ricketts, Ann, and Michael Ricketts. (1988). *Rhyme Time.* Brimax Books.

Rounds, Glen. (1973). *Sweet Betsy from Pike Rounds.* Children's Press.

Saport, Linda. (1999). *All the Pretty Little Horses.* Clarion Books.

Seeger, Laura Vaccaro. (2001). *I Had a Rooster.* Viking.

Shaw, Nancy E. (2006). *Sheep in a Jeep.* Sandpiper.

Slobodkina, Esphyr. (2004). *Caps for Sale.* Live Oak Media.

Spence, Robert. (2001). *Clickety Clack.* Puffin.

Thorne, Donna Sloan, and Marilyn Sloan Felts. (2002). *Buzz and Ollie's High, Low Adventure.* Sloan.

Wellington, Monica. (1997). *Night House Bright House.* Dutton Juvenile.

Westcott, Nadine Bernard. (1989). *Skip to My Lou.* Little, Brown.

Wood, Audrey. (1992). *Silly Sally.* Harcourt.

Wood, Audrey. (2007). *A Dog Needs a Bone*. Blue Sky Press.
Zelinsky, Paul. (1990). *The Wheels on the Bus*. Dutton Juvenile.

School/Work

Child, Lauren. (2003). *I Am Too Absolutely Small for School*. Candlewick Press.
Daniel, Alan, and Lea Daniel. (1993). *I've Been Working on the Railroad*. Wright Group.
Raffi, and Sylvie Wickstrom. (1990). *The Wheels on the Bus*. Turtleback.
Taback, Simms. (2004). *This Is the House That Jack Built*. Puffin.
Zelinsky, Paul. (1990). *The Wheels on the Bus*. Dutton Juvenile.

Shapes

Adams, Pam. (1995). *Oh, Soldier, Soldier, Won't You Marry Me?* Child's Play International.
Carter, David A. (1993). *In and Out*. Intervisual Books.
Crews, Donald. (1986). *Parade*. Greenwillow Books.
Crews, Donald. (1993). *Freight Train Big Book*. Greenwillow Books.
Emberley, Ed. (1992). *Go Away, Big Green Monster*. Little, Brown.
Locker, Thomas. (2000). *Cloud Dance*. Voyager Books.
Martin, Bill., Jr. (1996). *The Maestro Plays*. Voyager Books.
Rob, Jackie. (2003). *Sheep Says Baa!* Bang on the Door Series.
Rollings, Susan. (2000). *New Shoes, Red Shoes*. Orchard Books.
Westcott, Nadine Bernard. (1998). *The Lady with the Alligator Purse*. Little, Brown.

487

Sleeping/Nighttime

Bentley, Dawn. (1999). *Sleepy Bear*. Intervisual Books.
Brown, Margaret Wise. (1947). *Goodnight Moon*. Scholastic.
Christelow, Eileen. (2006). *Five Little Monkeys Jumping on the Bed*. Sandpiper.
Emberley, Ed. (1992). *Go Away, Big Green Monster*. Little, Brown.
Finn, Isobel. (1999). *The Very Lazy Ladybug*. Tiger Tales.
Frazee, Marla. (1997). *Hush Little Baby*. Chronicle Books.
Hague, Michael. (1993). *Teddy Bear Teddy Bear*. Scholastic.
Lewis, Kevin. (2001). *Chugga Chugga Choo Choo*. Hyperion Book.
Lewison, Wendy Cheyette. (1992). *Going to Sleep on the Farm*. Trumpet Club.
Na, Il Sung. (2007). *A Book of Sleep*. Alfred A. Knopf.
Saport, Linda. (1999). *All the Pretty Little Horses*. Clarion Books.
Slobodkina, Esphyr. (2004). *Caps for Sale*. Live Oak Media.
Swanson, Susan Marie. (2008). *The House in the Night*. Houghton Mifflin.
Willems, Mo. (2006). *Don't Let the Pigeon Stay up Late!* Hyperion Press.
Wood, Audrey. (2009). *The Napping House*. Harcourt Children's Books.
Yolen, Jane. (1987). *Owl Moon*. Philomel Books.

Sports

Cronin, Doreen. (2007). *Bounce*. Atheneum Books for Young Readers.
Howard, Arthur. (2001). *Hoodwinked*. Voyager Books.

Rosen, Michael. (1989). *We're Going on a Bear Hunt.* Little Simon.
Trapani, Iza. (1999). *Row, Row, Row Your Boat.* Charlesbridge.

Transportation/Traveling

Alborough, Jez. (1999). *Duck in the Truck.* Scholastic.
Brown, Margaret Wise. (1979). *The Train to Timbuctoo.* Golden Books.
Brown, Margaret W. (2003). *Two Little Trains.* HarperCollins.
Brown, Ruth. (2000). *Snail Trail.* Crown.
Bullock, Kathleen. (1993). *She'll Be Comin' Round the Mountain.* Simon & Schuster.
Calmenson, Stephanie. (1996). *Engine, Engine, Number Nine.* Scholastic.
Carle, Eric. (1997). *Have You Seen My Cat?* Aladdin.
Crews, Donald. (1993). *Freight Train Big Book.* Greenwillow Books.
Daniel, Alan, and Lea Daniel. (1993). *I've Been Working on the Railroad.* Wright Group.
Harriet, Ziefert. (1998). *When I First Came to this Land.* Scholastic.
Lewis, Kevin. (2001). *Chugga Chugga Choo Choo.* Hyperion Book.
Margolin, H. Ellen. (2002). *Goin' to Boston.* Handprint Books.
Nelson, Lee. (1960). *All the Sounds We Hear.* Steck.
Portis, Antoinette. (2006). *Not a Box.* HarperCollins.
Quackenbush, Robert M. (1973). *She'll Be Comin' Round the Mountain.* Lippincott Williams & Wilkins.
Quackenbush, Robert M. (1988). *Pop! Goes the Weasel and Yankee Doodle.* Lippincott Williams & Wilkins.
Raffi, and Sylvie Wickstrom. (1990). *The Wheels on the Bus.* Turtleback.
Rounds, Glen. (1973). *Sweet Betsy from Pike Rounds.* Children's Press.
Shaw, Nancy E. (2006). *Sheep in a Jeep.* Sandpiper.
Spence, Robert. (2001). *Clickety Clack.* Puffin.
Willems, Mo. (2003). *Don't Let the Pigeon Drive the Bus!* Hyperion Press.
Willems, Mo. (2006). *Don't Let the Pigeon Stay up Late!* Hyperion Press.
Williams, Sue. (1989). *I Went Walking.* Red Wagon Books.
Wood, Audrey. (1992). *Silly Sally.* Harcourt.
Zelinsky, Paul. (1990). *The Wheels on the Bus.* Dutton Juvenile.

Weather/Seasons

Aardema, Verna. (1981). *Bringing The Rain to Kapiti Plain.* Puffin Books.
Brown, Margaret W. (2003). *Two Little Trains.* HarperCollins.
Fleming, Denise. (1993). *In the Small, Small Pond.* Henry Holt.
Gershator, Phillis. (2007). *Listen, Listen.* Barefoot Books.
Lionni, Leo. (1967). *Frederick.* Trumpet Club.
Locker, Thomas. (2000). *Cloud Dance.* Voyager Books.
Marzollo, Jean. (1997). *Pretend You're a Cat.* Puffin Books.
Orie, Sandra De Coteau. (1995). *Did You Hear Wind Sing Your Name?* Walker.
Pinkney, Brian. (1994). *Max Found Two Sticks.* Aladdin Paperbacks.
Schubert, Ingrid, and Dieter Schubert. (1998). *There's a Hole in My Bucket.* Front Street.
Stojic, Manya. (2000). *Rain.* Dragonfly Books.
Sykes, Julie. (2007). *Santa's Noisy Night.* Little Tiger Press.

Appendix 3 Children's Literature Related to Music Concepts for the Kindergarten Classroom

Aardema, Verna. (1981). *Bringing the Rain to Kapiti Plain*. Puffin Books.

Adams, Pam. (1995). *Oh, Soldier, Soldier, Won't You Marry Me?* Child's Play International.

Adams, Pam. (1989). *This Old Man*. Child's Play International.

Ahlberg, Allan. (1986). *Each Peach Pear Plum*. Picture Puffin.

Alborough, Jez. (1999). *Duck in the Truck*. Scholastic.

Ashman, Linda. (2002). *Can You Make a Piggy Giggle?* Dutton, Juvenile.

Ayres, Katherine. (2007). *Up Down, and Around*. Candlewick Press.

Baer, Gene. (1994). *Thump, Thump, Rat-a-Tat-Tat!* Trumpet Club.

Baker, Keith. (1994). *Big Fat Hen*. Voyager Books.

Baker, Keith. (1999). *Quack and Count*. Harcourt Brace.

Bang on the Door. (2003). (Series.) Oxford University Press.

Bang, Molly. (2000). *When Sophie Gets Angry, Really, Really Angry*. Spoken Arts.

Barner, Bob. (1999). *Bugs, Bugs, Bugs*. Chronicle Books.

Bemelmans, Ludwig. (1939). *Madeline*. Viking.

Bentley, Dawn. (1999). *Sleepy Bear*. Intervisual Books.

Bentley, Dawn. (2004). *Buzz Buzz, Busy Bees*. Simon & Schuster.

Boynton, Sandra. (1982). *Moo Baa La La La*. Little Simon.

Boynton, Sandra. (1984). *Doggies*. Little Simon.

Brandenberg, Aliki. (1974). *Go Tell Aunt Rhody*. Macmillan.

Brennan-Nelson, Denise. (1999). *Buzzy the Bumblebee*. Sleeping Bear Press.

Brett, Jan. (1991). *Berlioz the Bear*. Penguin Young Readers.

Brown, Margaret Wise. (1947). *Goodnight Moon*. Scholastic.

Brown, Margaret Wise. (1979). *The Train to Timbuctoo*. Golden Books.

Brown, Margaret W. (2003). *Two Little Trains*. HarperCollins.

Brown, Ruth. (2000). *Snail Trail*. Crown.

Bryan, Ashley. (1991). *All Night, All Day: A Child's First Book of African-American Spirituals*. Aladdin Paperbacks.

Bullock, Kathleen. (1993). *She'll Be Comin' 'Round the Mountain*. Simon & Schuster.

Calmenson, Stephanie. (1996). *Engine, Engine, Number Nine*. Scholastic.

Campbell, Ross. (2008). *The ABRSM Song Book*. ABRSM.

Cannon, Janell. (1993). *Stellaluna*. Scholastic.

Carle, Eric. (1984). *The Very Busy Spider*. Philomel Books.

Carle, Eric. (1988). *Do You Want to Be My Friend?* Philomel Books.

Carle, Eric. (1995). *The Very Lonely Firefly*. Philomel Books.

Carle, Eric. (1997). *From Head to Toe*. HarperFestival.

Carle, Eric. (1997). *Have You Seen My Cat?* Aladdin.

Carle, Eric. (2004). *Mister Seahorse*. Philomel Books.

Carter, David A. (1993). *In and Out*. Intervisual Books.

Carter, David A. (1993). *Says Who? A Pop-up Book of Animal Sounds*. Little Simon.

Carter, David. (1997). *If You're Happy and You Know It Clap Your Hands*. Cartwheel.

Cauley, Lorinda Bryan. (1991). *Three Blind Mice*. Putnam Juvenile.

Cauley, Lorinda Bryan. (1997). *Clap Your Hands*. Puffin Books.

Child, Lauren. (2003). *I Am Too Absolutely Small for School*. Candlewick Press, Children's Books.

Christelow, Eileen. (2006). *Five Little Monkeys Jumping on the Bed*. Sandpiper.

Crews, Donald. (1986). *Parade*. Greenwillow Books.

Crews, Donald. (1993). *Freight Train Big Book*. Greenwillow Books.

Cronin, Doreen. (2005). *Wiggle*. Atheneum Books for Young Readers.

Cronin, Doreen. (2007). *Bounce*. Atheneum Books for Young Readers.

Daniel, Alan, and Lea Daniel. (1993). *I've Been Working on the Railroad*. Wright Group.

Daniel, Alan, and Lea Daniel. (1994). *Once an Austrian Went Yodeling*. Wright Group.

Deetlefs, Rene. (1999). *The Song of Six Birds*. Dutton Children's Books.

Demi. (1998). *The Greatest Treasure*. Scholastic.

Deming, A. G. (1988). *Who Is Tapping At My Window?* A Puffin Unicorn.

Dr. Seuss. (1996). *Mr. Brown Can Moo! Can You?* Random House Books for Young Readers.

Ehlert, Lois. (1989). *Color Zoo*. HarperCollins.

Ehlert, Lois. (1989). *Eating the Alphabet: Fruits & Vegetables from A to Z*. Harcourt.

Emberley, Ed. (1974). *Klippity Klop*. Little Brown.

Emberley, Ed. (1992). *Go Away, Big Green Monster*. Little, Brown.

Eric, Carle. (1993). *Today Is Monday*. PaperStar.

Faulkner, Keith. (1996). *The Wide Mouthed Frog*. Dial.

Finn, Isobel. (1999). *The Very Lazy Ladybug*. Tiger Tales.

Flanders, Michael. (1991). *The Hippopotamus Song: A Muddy Love Story*. Joy St Books.

Fleming, Denise. (1991). *In the Tall, Tall Grass*. Holt.

Fleming, Denise. (1993). *In the Small, Small Pond*. Holt.

Fleming, Denise. (2007). *Beetle Bop*. Harcourt.

Frazee, Marla. (1997). *Hush Little Baby*. Chronicle Books.

Friedman, Carol. (2003). *Nicky*. Dominick Books.

Galdone, Paul. (1986). *Over in the Meadow*. Aladdin Paperbacks.

Gelman, Rita Golden. (1993). *More Spaghetti I Say*. Turtleback.

Gershator, Phillis. (1998). *When It Starts to Snow*. Holt.

Gershator, Phillis. (2007). *Listen, Listen*. Barefoot Books.

Gollub, Matthew. (2000). *The Jazz Fly*. 1st ed. Tortuga Press.

Greene, Rhonda Gowler. (1997). *Barnyard Song*. Atheneum Books for Young Readers.

Guthrie, Woody. (1954). *Bling Blang*. Candlewick Press.

Guthrie, Woody. (2000). *Howdi Do*. Candlewick Press.

Guthrie, Woody. (2001). *My Dolly*. Candlewick Press.

Hague, Michael. (1993). *Teddy Bear Teddy Bear*. Scholastic.

490

Hamanaka, Sheila. (1997). *The Hokey Pokey*. Simon & Schuster Children's.

Harrison, David L. (2001). *When Cows Come Home*. Boyds Mills Press.

Hayes, Sarah. (1988). *Stamp Your Feet: Action Rhymes*. Morrow.

Henkes, Kevin. (1996). *Chrysanthemum*. Mulberry Books.

Hoberman, Mary Ann. (1998). *Miss Mary Mack*. Little, Brown.

Hoberman, Mary Ann. (2003). *And to Think That We Thought We'd Never Be Friends*. Dragonfly Books.

Hoberman, Mary A., and Nadine Bernard Westcott. (2003). *Skip to My Lou*. Little, Brown.

Howard, Arthur. (2001). *Hoodwinked*. Voyager Books, Harcourt.

Hubbard, Patricia. (1999). *My Crayons Talk*. Holt.

Hubbell, Patricia. (2003). *I Like Cats*. Cheshire Studio Book.

Hutchins, Pat. (1992). *Don't Forget the Bacon!* Live Oak Media.

Jorgensen, Gail. (1988). *Crocodile Beat*. Aladdin Paperbacks.

Kalan, Robert. (2010). *Jump, Frog, Jump!* Perfection Learning.

Keats, Ezra J. (1987). *John Henry: An American Legend*. Dragonfly Books.

Kohn, Michael, and Daniel Weiner. (1981). *There Was an Old Woman Who Swallowed a Fly*. Weekly Reader Books.

Krauss, Ruth. (1945). *The Carrot Seed*. Scholastic.

Lach, William. (2006). *Can You Hear It?* Abrams Books for Young Readers.

Langstaff, John. (1957, 1985). *Over in the Meadow*. Voyager Books.

Langstaff, John. (1963). *Ol' Dan Tucker*. Harcourt, Brace & World.

Langstaff, John. (1974). *Oh, A-Hunting We Will Go*. Aladdin Paperbacks.

Leslie, Amanda. (2001). *Who's That Scratching at My Door?* Handprint Books.

Lester, Helen. (2006). *Tacky the Penguin*. Sandpiper.

Leuck, Laura. (1999). *Teeny Tiny Mouse*. Sound by Sagebrush.

Leventhal, Debra. (1999). *What Is Your Language?* Scholastic.

Lewis, Kevin. (2001). *Chugga Chugga Choo Choo*. Hyperion.

Lewison, Wendy Cheyette. (1992). *Going to Sleep on the Farm*. Trumpet Club.

Lionni, Leo. (1967). *Frederick*. Trumpet Club.

Lively, Penelope. (1998). *One Two Three Jump!* Puffin Books.

Locker, Thomas. (2000). *Cloud Dance*. Voyager Books.

London, Jonathan. (1999).*Wiggle Waggle*. Scholastic Inc.

Longstaff, John. (1972). *Frog Went A-Courtin'*. Voyager Books.

Lowery, Linda. (2008). *Twist with a Burger, Jitter with a Bug*. MaxBooks.

Lucas, Sally. (1933). *Dancing Dinos*. Random House.

Maccarone, Grace. (1982). *Moo Baa La La La*. Little Simon.

Maccarone, Grace. (1994). *Oink! Moo! How Do You Do?* Cartwheel Books.

Margolin, H. Ellen. (2002). *Goin' to Boston*. Handprint Books.

Martin, Bill., Jr. (1996). *The Maestro Plays*. Voyager Books.

Martin, Bill., Jr. (2003). *Panda Bear Panda Bear, What Do You See?* Holt.

Martin, Bill., Jr. (2004). *Brown Bear, Brown Bear, What Do You See?* Holt.

Martin, Bill., Jr. (2006). *Fire! Fire! Said Mrs. McGuire*. HMH.

Martin, Bill., Jr. (2009). *Chicka Chicka Boom Boom*. Paw Prints.

Marzollo, Jean. (1997). *Pretend You're a Cat*. Puffin Books.

McBratney, Sam. (2009). *Guess How Much I Love You*. Walker Children's Hardbacks.

McDonald, Megan.(1993). *Is This a House for Hermit Crab?* Orchard Books.

McPhail, David. (1999). *Mole Music*. Holt.

Miranda, Anne. (1997). *To Market, to Market*. Harcourt Children's Books.

Miranda, Anne. (1999). *Monster Math*. Harcourt Children's Books.

Moss, Lloyd. (1995). *Zin! Zin! Zin! A Violin*. Aladdin Paperbacks.

Munsch, Robert N. (2007). *Mortimer Spanish Edition (Munsch for Kids)*. Annick Press.

Na, Il Sung. (2007). *A Book of Sleep*. Knopf.

Nelson, Leigh. (1960). *All the Sounds We Hear*. Steck.

Orie, Sandra De Coteau. (1995). *Did You Hear Wind Sing Your Name?* Walker.

Orleans, Ilo. (1958). *Animal Orchestra*. Golden Book.

Otoshi, Kathryn. (2008). *One*. KO Kids Books.

Pandell, Karen. (1996). *Animal Action ABC*. Dutton Juvenile.

Peek, Merele. (1985). *Mary Wore Her Red Dress and Henry Wore His Green Sneakers*. Clarion.

Perkins, Al. (1998). *Hand, Hand Fingers Thumb*. Random House Books for Young Readers.

Pinkney, Brian. (1994). *Max Found Two Sticks*. Aladdin Paperbacks.

Piper, Watty. (2005). *The Little Engine That Could*. Philomel.

Plume, Ilse. (2004). *The Farmer in the Dell*. David R. Godine.

Portis, Antoinette. (2006). *Not a Box*. HarperCollins.

Post, Jim, and Janet Post. (2002). *Barnyard Boogie*. Accord.

Powell, Richard. (2001). *Guess What I Have!* Barron's Educational Series.

Powell, Richard. (2001). *Guess Who's Hiding!* Barron's Educational Series.

Price, Mathew. (2004). *Peekaboo*. Knopf Books for Young Readers.

Quackenbush, Robert M. (1973). *She'll Be Comin' 'Round the Mountain*. Lippincott Williams & Wilkins.

Quackenbush, Robert M. (1975). *Skip to My Lou*. Lippincott Williams & Wilkins.

Quackenbush, Robert M. (1988). *Pop! Goes the Weasel and Yankee Doodle*. Lippincott Williams & Wilkins.

Raffi, and Sylvie Wickstrom. (1990). *The Wheels on the Bus*. Turtleback.

Raschka, Chris. (1993). *Yo? Yes!* Scholastic.

Ricketts, Ann, and Michael Ricketts. (1988). *Rhyme Time*. Brimax Books.

Rius, Maria. (1985). *The Five Senses: Hearing*. Barron's Educational Series.

Rob, Jackie. (2003). *Sheep Says Baa!* Bang on the Door Series. Oxford University Press.

Rollings, Susan. (2000). *New Shoes, Red Shoes*. Orchard Books.

Rosen, Michael. (1989). *We're Going on a Bear Hunt*. Little Simon.

Rosen, Michael. (1993). *Little Rabbit Foo Foo*. Aladdin Books.

Rounds, Glen. (1970). *The Strawberry Roan*. Golden Gate Junior Books.

Rounds, Glen. (1973). *Sweet Betsy from Pike Rounds*. Children's Press.

Saport, Linda. (1999). *All the Pretty Little Horses*. Clarion Books.

Schubert, Ingrid, and Dieter Schubert. (1998). *There's a Hole in My Bucket*. Front Street.

Scotellaro, Robert. (1995). *Daddy Fixed the Vacuum Cleaner*. Willowisp Press.

Seeger, Laura Vaccaro. (2001). *I Had a Rooster*. Viking.

Seeger, Pete. (1957). *One Grain of Sand*. Little, Brown.

Segal, Lore. (1973). *All the Way Home*. Sunburst Book.

Serfozo, Mary. (1992). *Who Said Red?* Aladdin.

Seuss, Dr. (1996). *My Many Colored Days*. Knopf Books for Young Readers.

Shannon, George. (1991). *Dance Away!* Greenwillow Books.

Shaw, Nancy E. (2006). *Sheep in a Jeep*. Sandpiper.

Sierra, Judy. (2001). *Counting Crocodiles*. Sandpiper.

Sivulich, Sandra Stroner. (1973). *I'm Going on a Bear Hunt*. Dutton Children's Books.

Slavin, Bill. (1992). *The Cat Came Back*. Albert Whitman.

Slobodkina, Esphyr. (2004). *Caps for Sale*. Live Oak Media.

Spence, Robert. (2001). *Clickety Clack*. Puffin Books.

Spier, Peter. (1967). *London Bridge Is Falling Down*. Doubleday.

Spier, Peter. (1971). *Gobble Growl Grunt*. Doubleday.

Spier, Peter. (1999). *The Erie Canal*. Corn Hill Waterfront & Navigation.

Stickland, Henrietta. (1997). *Dinosaur Roar*. Dutton Juvenile.

Stojic, Manya. (2000). *Rain*. Dragonfly Books.

Stutson, Caroline. (2009). *By the Light of the Halloween Moon*. Amazon Children's Publishing.

Suhr, Mandy. (1993, 2009). *I Can Move*. Wayland Books.

Swanson, Susan Marie. (2008). *The House in the Night*. Houghton Mifflin.

Sykes, Julie. (2007). *Santa's Noisy Night*. Little Tiger Press.

Taback, Simms. (2004). *This Is the House That Jack Built*. Puffin Books.

Taback, Simms. (2007). *There Was an Old Lady*. Childs Play International.

Thorne, Donna Sloan. (2002). *Buzz and Ollie's Loud, Soft Adventure*. Sloan.

Thorne, Donna Sloan. (2002). *Buzz and Ollie's Steady Beat Adventure*. Sloan.

Thorne, Donna Sloan, and Marilyn Sloan Felts. (2002). *Buzz and Ollie's High Low Adventure*. Sloan.

Trapani, Iza. (1999). *Row, Row, Row Your Boat*. Charlesbridge.

Trapani, Iza. (2002). *Frog Went A-Courtin'*. Charlesbridge.

Twinn, M. (1975). *Old Macdonald Had a Farm*. Child's Play (International).

Walsh, Vivian. (2002). *Gluey*. Harcourt.

Walter, Virginia. (1998). *Hi, Pizza Man!* Orchard Books.

Wellington, Monica. (1994). *The Sheep Follow*. Scholastic.

Wellington, Monica. (1997). *Night House Bright House*. Dutton Juvenile.

Westcott, Nadine Bernard. (1989). *Skip to My Lou*. Little, Brown.

Westcott, Nadine Bernard. (1992). *Peanut Butter and Jelly: A Play Rhyme*. Puffin Books.

Westcott, Nadine Bernard.(1998). *The Lady with the Alligator Purse*. Little, Brown.

Williams, Linda. (1986). *The Little Old Lady Who Was Not Afraid of Anything*. HarperCollins.

Willems, Mo. (2003). *Don't Let the Pigeon Drive the Bus!* Hyperion Press.

Willems, Mo. (2006). *Don't Let the Pigeon Stay up Late!* Hyperion Press.

Williams, Rozanne Lanczak. (1995). *Under the Sky*. Creative Teaching Press.

Williams, Sarah, and Ian Beck. (1995). *Round and Round the Garden*. Oxford University Press.

Williams, Sue. (1989). *I Went Walking*. Red Wagon Books/Harcourt.

Wood, Audrey. (1992). *Silly Sally*. Harcourt.

Wood, Audrey. (2007). *A Dog Needs a Bone*. Blue Sky Press.

Wood, Audrey. (2009). *The Napping House*. Harcourt Children's Books.

Yolen, Jane. (1987). *Owl Moon*. Philomel.

Zelinsky, Paul. (1990). *The Wheels on the Bus*. Dutton Juvenile.

Zemach, Harve. (1966). *Mommy, Buy Me a China Doll*. Follett.

Ziefert, Harriet. (1998). *When I First Came to This Land*. Scholastic.

Appendix 4   Monthly Plans

September

Songs	Concept	Reading	Writing	Improvisation and Composition	Listening	Part Work	Memory	Inner Hearing	Form	Instruments
"Hey, Hey, Look at Me" "Engine, Engine, Number Nine" "That's a Mighty Pretty Motion" "Bee, Bee, Bumble Bee" "Johnny Works with One Hammer" "Hunt the Slipper" "Bobby Shafto" "Bounce High, Bounce, Low"	Tuneful singing	C show phrases of a song in the air while singing (tracing a rainbow in the space in front of them with their hand).	C select an icon that represents one of the four voices to identify how T performed.	C improvise new text for a song. "Bounce the ball to —" (Houston, Dallas, Mississippi, Charlie)	T reads a book to the C using two of the four voices for different characters.	C sing a song while keeping the beat.	C perform a known chant. C perform known songs.	C perform a song using a whispering voice while tapping the beat.	C record the phrase of a song with rainbow or shooting star icons.	C sing a song while playing a steady beat on hand drum.

September

Songs	Concept	Reading	Writing	Improvisation and Composition	Listening	Part Work	Memory	Inner Hearing	Form	Instruments
			C select an icon that displays the number 1 or 2 in order to identity the number of phrases in a song.	C improvise a new motion for keeping the beat while performing a song.	T sings a song to the class for enjoyment; story songs or echo songs work well.	Half the C pat the beat with hand drums while the other half sing the song.			C use different movements for different phrases of a rhyme or song.	
						C sing the song and march to the beat.				
						T sings one phrase and C sing the next phrase.			T sings one phrase and C sing the next phrase.	

(Continued)

October

Songs	Concept	Reading	Writing	Improvisation and Composition	Listening	Part Work	Memory	Inner Hearing	Form	Instruments
"Hey, Hey, Look at Me"; "Engine, Engine, Number Nine"; "That's a Mighty Pretty Motion" "Bee, Bee, Bumble Bee"; "Johnny Works with One Hammer"; "Hunt the Slipper"; "Bobby Shafto"; "Bounce High, Bounce, Low"	Tuneful singing	C show phrases of a song in the air while singing (tracing a rainbow in the space in front of them with their hand).	C select an icon that represents one of the four voices to identify how T performed.	C improvise new text for a song. "Bounce the ball to —" (Houston, Dallas, Mississippi, Charlie)	T reads a book to the C using two of the four voices for different characters.	C sing a song while keeping the beat.	C perform a known song. C perform known songs.	C perform a song using a whispering voice while tapping the beat.	C record the phrase of a song with rainbow or shooting star icons.	C sing a song while playing a steady beat on hand drum.

October

Songs	Concept	Reading	Writing	Improvisation and Composition	Listening	Part Work	Memory	Inner Hearing	Form	Instruments
		C see four images that represent the four voices (megaphone calling, ear whispering, cell phone speaking, microphone singing) and use the one the T selects.	C select an icon that displays the number 1 or the number 2 in order to identity the number of phrases in a song.	C improvise a new motion for keeping the beat while performing a song.	T sings a song to the class for enjoyment. Story songs or echo songs work well.	Half the C pat the beat with hand drums while the other half sing the song.	C perform a known chant using the four types of voices.	C identify a familiar song from rhythmic or melodic motives that are clapped or hummed by T.	C use different movements for different sections of a piece of music.	C categorize four instruments selected by T into speaking, calling, whispering, and singing voices; they perform chants/songs while tapping a steady beat on the corresponding instrument. Example: drum = calling; sticks = speaking; sand blocks = whispering; barred instruments = singing.

(Continued)

October

Songs	Concept	Reading	Writing	Improvisation and Composition	Listening	Part Work	Memory	Inner Hearing	Form	Instruments
		T selects two icons to represent whispering and speaking voice and places them in front of each phrase of "Bee, Bee, Bumble Bee": phrases 1 and 2 as whispering, phrases 3 and 4 as speaking voice. C perform as written; T changes the order of the icons to change the performance of the song.	Repeat activity 3 from the reading section, but C decide individually how each phrase must be performed. T identifies the correct icons to place in front of each phrase.	C choose an icon representing one of the four voices to change how they perform a song.	C listen to a masterwork with an obvious steady beat. *Stars and Stripes Forever*, Sousa	C sing the song and march to the beat.	C perform a known phrase of a song.	C fill in missing words of a known song or chant.	T sings a song twice (differently each time) and asks if the song was the same both times.	
				C improvise a new movement to the types of voices and perform with know songs.		T sings one phrase and C sing the next phrase.			T sings one phrase and C sing the next.	

(Continued)

November

Songs	Concept	Reading	Writing	Improvisation and Composition	Listening	Part Work	Memory	Inner Hearing	Form	Instruments
"Bounce High, Bounce Low"; "Hunt the Slipper"; "Bobby Shafto"; "Snail, Snail"; "Hop Old Squirrel"; "Lazy Mary"; "Teddy Bear"; "Charlie over the Ocean"; "Zapatitos Blancos"; "Doggie, Doggie"	Loud/ soft	C sing and point to sun or moon icons (indicating the beats) while singing "Bounce High, Bounce Low" with a loud or soft voice according to the icon.	Individual C place one of the four voice icons on the board, indicating how the song is to be performed.	T sings "Bobby Shafto" using "daytime" or "nighttime" voice. C indicate which voice they heard by raising either the "daytime" icon or the "nighttime" icon.	C listen to a piece of music sung or played by T and they identify the piece as either loud or soft.	C perform the beat while singing known song.	T sings known song to C using a soft or loud voice and asks C for description of voice.	C sing a song following mouth of puppet. When mouth is open, they sing out loud; when closed they sing in their head.	T and C echo-sing a song in a loud or soft voice while keeping the beat.	One child accompanies class by playing a steady beat on a hand drum either softly or loudly.

November

Songs	Concept	Reading	Writing	Improvisation and Composition	Listening	Part Work	Memory	Inner Hearing	Form	Instruments
		C sing "Seesaw" from the board while tracing the phrase marks drawn on the board.	C select the word *loud* or *soft* (flash card) and place them in front of the icons representing the beat to record how a C or T sang a melody.	Individual C sing "Johnny Works with One Hammer" and create a different movement for each "hammer" to be performed by class.	C listen to piece of music and make a big circle with arms when music is loud and small when music is soft. *Surprise Symphony*, Haydn.	T and C echo-sing known song using loud and soft dynamics.	C recognize a familiar song from rhythmic or melodic motives clapped or hummed by T.	C should be encouraged to sing different motives of the song initially with loud and soft and then using inner hearing.	C in two groups echo-sing a song in a loud or soft voice while keeping the beat.	C play the beat on unpitched percussion. T performs loud and soft rhythmic patterns and C echo T on drum.
		C read phrase marks of "Engine, Engine" from the board using the voice indicated by the icons placed at the beginning of the phrase.	C to select *p* or *f* icons and place in front of icons representing the beat to record how a C or T sang a melody.	C improvise new text while singing with a loud or soft voice.	C listen to known song while standing in circle holding hands. C make larger circle for loud and smaller circle for soft.	C echo-sing known song divided into two groups.		C hum familiar songs using a loud or soft hum with movements. C sing a known song but inner-hear selected phrases while continuing to tap the beat.	Two C echo-sing a song in a loud or soft voice while keeping the beat.	T plays loud and soft rhythmic phrases on hand drum and C imitate with loud and soft foot patterns.

November

Songs	Concept	Reading	Writing	Improvisation and Composition	Listening	Part Work	Memory	Inner Hearing	Form	Instruments
		T places loud and soft icons in front of each phrase in a four-phrase song ("Bee, Bee, Bumble Bee" or "Hunt the Slipper"). It can alternate loud and soft between phrases. C read and alter voice according to the icon.	Individual C place loud and soft icons in front of each phrase in a four-phrase song ("Bee Bee, Bumble Bee" or "Hunt the Slipper"). It can alternate loud and soft between phrases. Class reads and alters voice according to the icon.	T plays recorded examples of music in different meters, 2/4 or 6/8, and asks C to move to the beat while either walking, skipping, or tapping the beat during the daytime or nighttime parts. C may be asked to make sure their movements are suitable for "daytime" or "nighttime."	Play recorded examples of music that contains varying, but obvious, dynamic changes. Ask C to move when it is soft, and freeze when it is loud.	C sing known song and perform movements reflecting loud or soft dynamics.			C sing "Rain, Rain" based on form using *p* voice on phrase 1 and *f* voice for phrase 2.	T points to *p* or *f* and C keep beat at the correct dynamic level on an unpitched percussion instrument while singing known song.

(Continued)

502

January										
Songs	Concept	Reading	Writing	Improvisation and Composition	Listening	Part Work	Memory	Inner Hearing	Form	Instruments
"Hunt the Slipper"; "Zapatitos Blancos"; "Snail, Snail"; "Bee, Bee, Bumble Bee"; "Walk Daniel"; "I Climbed up the Apple Tree"; "Queen, Queen Caroline"; "Down Came a Lady"; "Twinkle, Twinkle"	Beat	C point to the heartbeat icon representation while singing known songs. Several C come to the board and point individually while the class points in the general direction while singing.	C place heartbeat icons on the board to represent the number of beats in a phrase, song, or song greeting.	C change the words in a rhyme. For example, instead of "I climbed up the apple tree" a child might improvise, "I climbed up the walnut tree." All the while, T keeps the beat on a drum.	C identify how many heart beats are in a phrase.	C perform the beat to known or unknown songs.	T sings known an unknown song to C and asks them how many beats they tapped during selected phrases.	T directs C to respond to a puppet's mouth. "When the mouth is open, sing out loud; when the mouth is closed, sing inside your head." Perform the beat simultaneously.	C identify number of heat beats while singing selected phrases.	T performs steady beat on barred Orff instruments while singing a song.
				C sing a song several times but have to create a different way of showing the beat each time.	T plays recorded example of music in different meters (2/4, 4/4, 6/8) and asks C to move to the beat by walking, skipping, or tapping the beat.	C in group 1 perform the beat as accompaniment to the children singing in group 2.	One child sings known and unknown songs to another child and asks how many beats the second child tapped during selected phrases.	One child directs classmates to respond to a puppet's mouth. "When the mouth is open, sing out loud; when the mouth is closed, sing inside your head." T performs the beat simultaneously.		

February

Songs	Concept	Reading	Writing	Improvisation and Composition	Listening	Part Work	Memory	Inner Hearing	Form	Instruments
	High/low voice	C place a picture of a sun or a moon and chant the rhyme according to which word is displayed.	C place visuals on the board representing the beat as they are chanting using their high voice or low voice.	C improvise a motion that demonstrates the beat of a known or unknown song using a high voice or low voice.	C listen to a piece of music sung or played by the teacher and identify the piece as high or low.	C perform steady beat to known or unknown chants; C perform beat high in the air or low by their feet according to which voice is being used.	T chants known and unknown songs to C using a low or high voice and asks them about the number of taps they performed with the song, and whether T was singing using a high voice or a low voice.	C chant with a bird or beat voice while following the mouth of a puppet. When the mouth is open, they chant out loud and when it is closed they chant inside their head.	T and C echo-chant a rhyme in a high or low voice.	C use a drum or a barred Orff instrument to accompany the class or another child while chanting in a high or low voice.
		C read the words *high* or *low* on flash cards placed in front of beat icons and chant the rhyme according to which word is displayed.	C record how another child chanted a rhyme by placing the word *high* or *low* in front of a beat chart.	C decide how to chant a song using a high or low voice.	T plays recorded examples of music in different meters, 2/4 or 6/8, and has C move to the beat, whether walking, skipping, or tapping the beat.	T and C echo-chant known rhymes with a high or low voice.	One child chants known and unknown songs to class using a low or high voice and asks them about the number of taps they performed with the song, and if the child was singing using a high voice or a low voice.	C chant a known chant with high or low voice, but inner-hear a phrase determined by T or another child.	C in groups echo-chant a known rhyme in high or low voice.	One child chooses a high or low drum to accompany the class while another chants in a high or low voice.

(Continued)

March

Songs	Concept	Reading	Writing	Improvisation and Composition	Listening	Part Work	Memory	Inner Hearing	Form	Instruments
"Engine, Engine, Number Nine"; "Frosty Weather"; "Hey, Hey, Look at Me"; "Bee, Bee, Bumble Bee"; "Bow Wow Wow"; "London Bridge"; A la Rueda de San Miguel"; "Here We Go 'Round the Mulberry Bush"	Fast/ slow	C sing and point to a visual chart indicating the beats, while singing known songs using a fast or slow tempo. Begin with four beats and move to eight and sixteen beats; C should place the snail icons or have the words *fast tempo* or *slow tempo* in front of the beat charts.	C place the words *fast tempo* or *slow tempo* in front of a beat chart for a song performed by the T or C and record how a melody was sung or a chant was performed.	C improvise a motion that demonstrates the beat of a known or unknown song in a fast tempo or slow tempo.	C listen to a piece of music sung or played by the T and identify the piece as either fast or slow. *In the Hall of the Mountain King*, Grieg	Divide the class into two groups. Group A improvises a motion when they hear fast music (such as the "Tarantella," from *Pulcinella Suite*, by Igor Stravinsky); Group B improvises a motion when they hear slow music (such as "Air" from *Suite No. 3*, by Johann Sebastian Bach).	T sings known and unknown songs to C and has them determine if it was sung with a fast or slow tempo.	C follow the mouth of a puppet. When the mouth is open they sing out a loud, and when it is closed they sing inside their head; but they must always keep the beat. Perform this activity using a fast and slow tempo.	C echo-sing a song while keeping the beat. Initially this should be done between T and C, and then between two groups of C, and finally between two individual C. Do this with the same song performed with a slow and then a fast tempo.	C play a steady beat on unpitched percussion instruments (bells, sticks, shakers, etc.) that matches the tempo of the music that is being sung or played.

March

Songs	Concept	Reading	Writing	Improvisation and Composition	Listening	Part Work	Memory	Inner Hearing	Form	Instruments
		C sing and read a visual beat chart while singing known songs in different combinations of fast and slow, high and low, loud and soft. T makes sure to use unusual combinations like fast/loud, soft/slow, etc.	One child selects between high/low and fast/slow to perform a known song. The class reads a beat chart on the board with the individual child's selection.	C choose whether to sing a song with a fast or slow tempo.	C listen to recorded music that combines fast/slow with high/low and loud/soft. C identify the tempo and dynamics of the piece.	Play recorded examples of music in different meters, 2/4 or 6/8, and ask C to move to the beat, whether, walking, skipping, or tapping the beat, whichever is most appropriate to the tempo.	One child sings known songs and the class has to determine if it was sung with a fast or slow tempo.	C sing a known song in fast or slow tempo, but inner-hear selected phrases.		C play a steady beat on an unpitched instrument, but decide which instrument should be used for fast and which should be used for slow to accompany the classroom songs.

(Continued)

April

Songs	Concept	Reading	Writing	Improvisation and Composition	Listening	Part Work	Memory	Inner Hearing	Form	Instruments
"Snail, Snail" "¿Quièn Es Esa Gente?"; "Oats, Peas, and Barley Grow"; "A Sailor Went to Sea"; "Touch Your Shoulders"	High/low melody	C read the word *high* or *low* in front of beat icons and chant the rhyme following high and low. "Rain, Rain"	C place visuals on board representing the beat as they are singing using their high voice or low voice.	C improvise a motion that demonstrates the beat of a known or unknown song using a high voice or low voice.	Play recorded examples of music in different meters, 2/4 or 6/8, and ask C to move to the beat, whether, walking, skipping, or tapping the beat.	One half of class keep the beat and other half sing a known *so-mi* song, "Snail, Snail"	C identify a known song that T hums or plays on recorder.	C sing with a bird or beat voice by following the mouth of two puppets. When mouth is open, they sing in high voice for bird, low for beat. When mouth is closed they sing inside their head.	C walk in a circle in one direction for one phrase of a song, and then walk in the opposite direction for next phrase.	One child accompanies class using a steady beat on a drum or other unpitched instrument, while class sings a song with high and low pitches. "Rain, Rain"

(Continued)

April

Songs	Concept	Reading	Writing	Improvisation and Composition	Listening	Part Work	Memory	Inner Hearing	Form	Instruments
		C point and touch icons on the board representing the high and low sounds in a known song containing two pitches. "Seesaw"	C identify how another child chanted a rhyme by placing the word *high* or *low* in front of a beat chart.	C improvise a movement showing high and low in a known song with two pitches. "Seesaw"	C listen to T sing or hum "Ring Around the Rosy" and fall to the ground on the last sound.	T sings a known song, and class keeps the beat on their lap. "Seesaw"	C perform a known song or chant.	C whisper a known song while keeping the beat. "Good Night"	C march in place for one section of a song, and then step onto the circle for next section.	T plays various high and low pitches on an instrument piano, recorder, violin, trumpet, etc.), and C identify it as a high pitch or low pitch. C figure out how to play *s-m* songs on the xylophone.

507

April										
Songs	**Concept**	**Reading**	**Writing**	**Improvisation and Composition**	**Listening**	**Part Work**	**Memory**	**Inner Hearing**	**Form**	**Instruments**
		C point to the "rainbow" (drawing the phrase in the air) while singing a known song. "Rain, Rain"	C place visuals on the board representing the high sounds and low sounds in a piece of music containing two pitches, such as "Seesaw."	C sing different texts to known s-m songs.	T reads a book to C, using different voices such as whispering, calling, singing, and speaking. "Brown Bear, Brow Bear" T sings or chants folk song tales, using four voices: whisper, calling, speaking, and singing. "The Green Grass Grows All Around"	T sings a phrase of a song, and C sing next phrase. "Queen, Queen Caroline"		T turns out the lights and C sing in their head, singing out loud when the lights come on, for s-m songs.	C perform different movements for known s-m songs.	C categorize barred instrument as high (glockenspiels and soprano xylophones) or low (alto and bass xylophones).

June

Songs	Concept	Reading	Writing	Improvisation and Composition	Listening	Part Work	Memory	Inner Hearing	Form	Instruments
"Rain, Rain" "Two, Four, Six, Eight"; "Cara Col Col Col"; "Looby Loo"; "Frog in the Meadow"	Rhythm	C tap iconic representations of the rhythm while others perform the beat with (a) body percussion or (b) unpitched percussion instruments.	T sings and performs beat or rhythm; C place the icons or word *rhythm* on the board.	C improvise movements while T keeps the beat or rhythm for various examples.	T sings known songs and C clap back the rhythm.	T or C sing known songs while C play the beat/rhythm on instruments: (a) in small groups and (b) as individuals.	S sing or say known songs or chants with "long" and "short" instead of the words.	While T taps rhythm on the board or worksheets, C sing the song in their heads, changing with T's cue.	C identify the form of a song and display the form with shapes.	C play steady beat on claves or other unpitched percussion instrument while T taps the rhythm.
		C tap iconic representations of the rhythm while singing known songs: (a) tap on the board or on worksheet, (b) T has a selected child play the representation on an unpitched percussion instrument while singing.	T sings or plays a known song on the piano or recorder and individual C write or place the rhythm on the board while the class is singing.	One child improvises a steady beat movement on different parts of the body to known and unknown songs; other C imitate.		C sing a known song while patting the heartbeat on different parts of the body, changing on T's cue.				C tap the rhythm of known songs on unpitched percussion instruments.

509

(Continued)

C identify known songs from rhythmic representations on the board.	C write the rhythm of a known eight-beat song or chant with icons.	C decide where to place the long and short sounds on their body while performing a known song. For example, the "short" sounds could be tapped and the "long" sounds could be patted.	One child sings known songs and class claps back the rhythm.	C march to the beat while singing and clapping the rhythm.	C identify songs from the T clapping the rhythmic motif.	T sings songs on loo while C tap the rhythm on their lap or on instrument and identify the song.	C draw phrases on board.
	One child sings a known song and individual C write or place the rhythms on the board, while the class is singing.					C clap the rhythm of known songs while inner-hearing the melody.	

Notes

Introduction

1. Houlahan and Tacka, *Kodály Today*, 2008.
2. "Education for Life and Work. Developing Transferable Knowledge and Skills in the 21st Century" (report brief, July 12, 2010 Research Council).
3. The term Early Childhood includes Pre-K and Kindergarten. For a thorough overview of Early Childhood education, see Jordan-Decarbo and Nelson, "Music and Early Childhood Education," 2002.
4. Chen-Hafteck and Mang, "Music and Language," 2012, chap. 2.4, p. 270.
5. Kodály, "Children's Choirs," 1994, p. 120.
6. See Barrett, "Currents of Change," 2007. Green has been a strong proponent of informal learning strategies to be used in music classes. See Green, *Music*, 2008.
7. Trevarthen and Malloch, "Musicality and Musical Culture," 2012, chap. 2.3, p. 254.

About the Companion Website

1. Houlahan, Micheál, and Philip Tacka. *Kodály Today: A Cognitive Approach to Music Education.* New York: Oxford University Press, 2008.

Chapter 1

1. Elliot, *Praxial Music Education*, 2005, p. 258.
2. Barrett, "Commentary," 2012.
3. Chen-Hafteck and Mang, "Music and Language," 2012.
4. Kodály, "Children's Games," 1974, pp. 46–47.
5. Kodály, *Bulletin of the International Kodály Society*, 1985, p. 18.
6. Nettl, "Foreword," 1998.
7. Kodály, "The Role of Authentic Folksongs in Music Education," 1985, p. 18.
8. Ibid.
9. Elliot, *Praxial Music Education*, 2005, p. 258.
10. Jeanneret and Degraffenreid, "Music Education in the Generalist Classroom," 2012, p. 404.
11. Young and Ilari, "Musical Participation from Birth to Three," 2012, p. 281.
12. See Turner, "A Child Centered Music Room," 2000, pp. 30–34; and Bredekamp, *Developmentally Appropriate Practice*, 1987.
13. Kodály, "Children's Choirs," 1974, p. 126.
14. Houlahan and Tacka, *Kodály Today*, 2008.
15. Harwook and Marsh, "Children's Ways of Learning," 2012, pp. 333–334.
16. Chen-Hafteck and Mang, 2012, p. 262.
17. Ibid., p. 261.

18. Armstrong, *The Multiple Intelligences of Reading and Writing*, 2003, pp. 57–58.
19. Strickland, "Music and the Brain in Childhood Development," 2001–02, pp. 100–103.
20. Wolfe, *Brain Matters*, 2001, p. 161.
21. Houlahan and Tacka, *Sound Thinking*, 1996.
22. Another idea to help a child who is having trouble determining the number of syllables in a word is to have the child touch her jaw as she says the word to feel how many times it moved.
23. Neuman, Copple, and Bredekamp, *Learning to Read and Write*, 1987, p. 84.
24. Armbruster, Lehr, and Osborn. *Put Reading First*, 2003, p. 10.

Chapter 2

1. Chen-Hafteck and Mang, "Music and Language," 2012, chap. 2.4, p. 261.
2. Barrett, "Commentary," 2012, chap. 2.1, p. 227.
3. Kodály, "Inauguration," 1985, p. 9.
4. Kodály, "Bartók the Folklorist," 1964, p. 107.
5. Kodály, "Ancient Traditions," 1974, p. 175.
6. Kokas, Joy Through the Magic of Music, 1999.
7. Szönyi, *Musical Reading and Writing 1,* London, Boosey & Hawkes, 1974, p. 11.
8. Dolloff, "Elementary Music Education," 2005, p. 283.
9. *The Teaching Exchange*, January 1999, "Arts Training in Education." See also Gardiner and Fox, "Letter to the Editor," 1996, p. 284.
10. Kodály, "On the Anniversary of Beethoven's Death," 1974, p. 77.
11. Ibid., 122.
12. Kodály, "Music in Kindergarten," 1974, p. 130.
13. Kodály, "Children's Choirs," 1974, p. 121.
14. Kodály, "Fifty-Five Two-Part Exercises," 1974, p. 225.
15. The following are the National Content Standards in Music (from *National Standards for Arts Education*, copyright 1994 by Music Educators National Conference):

    - Singing, alone and with others, a varied repertoire of music
    - Performing on instruments, alone and with others, a varied repertoire of music
    - Improvising melodies, variations, and accompaniments
    - Composing and arranging music within specified guidelines
    - Reading and notating music
    - Listening to, analyzing, and describing music
    - Evaluating music and music performances
    - Understanding relationships between music, the other arts, and disciplines outside the arts
    - Understanding music in relation to history and culture

16. Kodály, "Bicinia Hungarica," 1974, p. 120.
17. Ibid., 145.
18. Seeger, American Folk Songs for Christmas, 1953, p. 21.
19. Kodály, "Role of the Folksong," 1974, p. 36.
20. Ibid., 120.
21. Kodály, "Music in Kindergarten," 1974, p. 141.
22. Kodály, "Children's Choirs," 1974, p. 122.

23. Prior to teaching any rhythmic elements, you must teach the concept of beat in the early childhood classroom and review it in grade one.

Chapter 3

1. Kodály, "Let Us Sing Correctly!" p. 216.
2. Adachi and Trehub, "Musical Lives of Infants," 2012, p. 233.
3. Church, *Learning Through Play*, 1992, p. 6.
4. E. Jensen, *Teaching with the Brain in Mind*, 2005, p. 60.
5. Phyllis Weikart is a leading movement and music educator, and founder of High-Scope's Education Through Movement—Building the Foundation program. She is an Associate Professor Emeritas in the Division of Kinesiology at the University of Michigan; author or coauthor of thirteen books about movement, music, and dance at all levels; and the producer of eight videos and fifteen CDs, including the *Rhythmically Moving* and *Changing Directions* recorded music series. Her wide-ranging experiences have led to the development of a teaching approach that ensures teachers' success with children of all ages. See www.highscope.org.
6. Weikart, *Movement Plus Music*, 1989. See also Carlton and Weikart, *Guide to Rhythmically Moving*, 1997.
7. Langton, "Applying Laban's Movement," 2007, p. 19.
8. Whitcomb, "Step by Step," 2003, pp. 34–38.

Chapter 4

1. Trevarthen and Malloch, "Musicality and Musical Culture," 2012, p. 256.
2. Hargreaves, *The Developmental Psychology of Music*, 1986, p. 215.
3. Perkins, *The Intelligent Eye*, 1998.
4. Choksy, *The Kodály Method*, 1999, pp. 171–173; Houlahan and Tacka, *Sound Thinking*, 1995.
5. Brindle, "Notes from Eva Vendrai's Kodály Course," pp. 6–11.
6. Aiello, "Metacognition Research in Music," 2003, p. 656.
7. For Carson's Taxonomy, see Carson, *Your Creative Brain*, 2010.
8. By "movement activities" we mean singing games as well as gestures and movements that imitate the text of a song or highlight the melodic contour or rhythmic pattern of a phrase.
9. Levi, "Towards an Expanded View," 1989.
10. Cutietta and Booth, "The Influence of Meter," 1996, pp. 222–236.
11. Peretz, *Auditory Agnosia*, 1993, pp. 199–230.
12. According to Jukka Louhivuori, there is an intrinsic link between the stability of melodic formulas and the capacity of short-term memory. Therefore the main role of the instructor should be to solidify melodic and rhythmic formulas and schemes typical for specific music cultures. "Memory Strategies in Writing Melodies," 1999, pp. 81–85.
13. Berk and Winsler, *Scaffolding Children's Learning*, 1995.
14. Bartholomew, "Sounds Before Symbols" 1995, pp. 3–9.
15. Petzold, "The Perception of Music Reading," 1960, pp. 271–319.
16. Hewson, "Music Reading in the Classroom," 1966, pp. 289–302.

17. Gromko and Poorman, "Developmental Trends and Relationships," 1998, pp. 16–23.
18. Perkins, *The Intelligent Eye*, 1998.
19. Bamberger, *The Mind Behind the Musical Ear*, p. 282.
20. Derry, "Cognitive Schema Theory," 1996, pp. 163–174.
21. Davidson and Scripp, " Surveying the Coordinates," 1992, p. 407.
22. Whitehead, "Process and reality," 1978, p. 339.
23. Wiggins and Espeland, "Creating in Music Learning Contexts," 2012, pp. 344–345.
24. O' Neill, "Becoming a Music Learner," 2012, pp. 177–178.
25. Trevarthen and Malloch, "Musicality and Musical Culture," 2012, p. 255.
26. "Education for Life and Work Developing Transferable Knowledge and Skills in the 21st Century" (report brief, July 12, 2012, National Research Council).
27. Carson, *Your Creative Brain,* 2010.
28. Johnson and Edelsen, "Integrating Music and Mathematics in the Elementary Classroom," 2003.
29. Csikszentmihalyi described this state as being in the "flow." See *Creativity*, 1996.
30. Brindle, "Notes from Eva Vendrei's Kodály Course," 2005, pp. 6–11. See also Choksy, *The Kodály Method*, 1999. Both the article and the book present procedures for the teaching of music elements based on the preparation, presentation, and practice model.
31. Choksy, *The Kodály Method,* pp. 171–172. See also Eisen and Robertson, *An American Methodology,* 1997.
32. Eastlund-Gromko, "Student's Invented Notations," 1994, p. 146.
33. See Choksy, *The Kodály Method*, p. 172.

Chapter 6

1. "Audiation" is a term coined by Edwin Gordon. It describes the ability to inner-hear. More information can be found in Gordon's *Learning Sequences*, 1997, pp. 5–6. Note: There is a more current 2012 edition of this book.
2. Wiggins and Espeland, "Creating in Music Learning Contexts," 2012, p. 348.
3. Kodály, "A Hundred Year Plan," p. 160.
4. Kodály, Preface *Musical Reading and Writing*, 1974, p. 204.
5. Kodály. "The Role of Authentic Folk Song," 1985, p. 18. Also found as "Folk Song in Hungarian Music Education."
6. Kodály. "Who Is a Good Musician?" 1974, p. 198.
7. Ibid.

Chapter 8

1. Forrai, *Music in Preschool,* 1995, p. 98.
2. Ibid.
3. Ibid., pp. 95–96.
4. Ibid., pp. 94–95.

Sources

Bacon, Denise. *Let's Sing Together*. New York: Boosey & Hawkes, 1971.

Erdei, Ida, Faith Knowles, and Denise Bacon, eds. *My Singing Bird: 150 Folk Songs from the Anglo-American, African-American, English, Scottish and Irish traditions*. Columbus, OH: Kodály Institute at Capital University, 2002.

Erdei, Peter, and Katalin Komlos. *150 American Folk Songs to Sing, Read and Play*. New York: Boosey & Hawkes, 1974.

Forrai, Katalin. *Music in the Pre-School*. Translated and adapted by Jean Sinor. Rev. ed. Wooloowin, Australia: Clayfield School of Music, 1998.

Houlahan, Micheál, and Philip Tacka. *Sound Thinking: Developing Musical Literacy*. Vols. 1 & 2. New York: Boosey & Hawkes, 1995.

Knowles, Faith, ed. *Vamos a Cantar: 230 Latino and Hispanic Folk Songs to Sing, Read, and Play*. Columbus, OH: Kodály Institute at Capital University, 2008.

Locke, Eleanor. *Sail Away: 155 American Folk Songs to Sing, Read and Play*. New York: Boosey & Hawkes, 2004.

Montoya-Stier, Gabriela. *El Patio de Mi Casa* (Chicago: GIA, 2008.

Credits

Chapter 1

Fig. 1.1. "Little Sally Water." Forrai, *Music in the Pre-School* (tr. Sinor), with permission.

Fig. 1.2. "Pajarito." Houlahan and Tacka, *Developing Musical Literacy I & II*, with permission.

Fig. 1.3. "See Saw." Forrai, *Music in the Pre-School* (tr. Sinor), with permission.

Fig. 1.4. "Sol Solecito." Houlahan and Tacka, *Developing Musical Literacy I & II*, with permission.

Fig. 1.5. "Rain, Rain." Forrai, *Music in the Pre-School* (tr. Sinor), with permission.

Fig. 1.6. "Lucy Locket." Forrai, *Music in the Pre-School* (tr. Sinor), with permission.

Fig. 1.7. "A la Ronda, Ronda." Knowles, *Vamos a cantar*, with permission.

Fig. 1.8. "Chini, Mini." Knowles, *Vamos a cantar*, with permission.

Fig. 1.9. "Hot Cross Buns." Erdei and Komlos, eds., *150 American Folk Songs*, with permission.

Fig. 1.10. "Hop Old Squirrel." Forrai, *Music in the Pre-School* (tr. Sinor), with permission.

Fig. 1.11. "Doña Araña." Knowles, *Vamos a cantar*, with permission.

Fig. 1.12. "Here Comes a Bluebird." Forrai, *Music in the Pre-School* (tr. Sinor), with permission.

Fig. 1.13. "Bow, Wow, Wow." Forrai, *Music in the Pre-School* (tr. Sinor), with permission.

Fig. 1.14. "Caracol Col Col." Knowles, *Vamos a cantar*, with permission.

Fig. 1.15. "Duerme Pronto." Knowles, *Vamos a cantar*, with permission.

Fig. 1.16. "Este Niño Lindo." Montoya-Stier, *El Patio de Mi Casa*, with permission.

Fig. 1.17. "Con mi martillo." Houlahan and Tacka, *Developing Musical Literacy I & II*, with permission.

Fig. 1.18. "Brinca la tablita." Houlahan and Tacka, *Developing Musical Literacy I & II*, with permission.

Fig. 1.19. "Los Pollitos." Houlahan and Tacka, *Developing Musical Literacy I & II*, with permission.

Fig. 1.20. "Who's That Tapping at My Window?" Erdei and Komlos, eds., *150 American Folk Songs*, with permission.

Fig. 1.21. "Who's That Tapping?" Stick notation. Erdei and Komlos, eds., *150 American Folk Songs*, with permission.

Fig. 1.22. "We Are Dancing in the Forest." Forrai, *Music in the Pre-School* (tr. Sinor), with permission.

Fig. 1.23. "Here Comes a Bluebird." Forrai, *Music in the Pre-School* (tr. Sinor), with permission.

Fig. 1.24. "Let Us Chase the Squirrel." Forrai, *Music in the Pre-School* (tr. Sinor), with permission.

Fig. 1.25. "A Tisket, a Tasket." Forrai, *Music in the Pre-School* (tr. Sinor), with permission.

Fig. 1.26. "Snail, Snail." Forrai, *Music in the Pre-School* (tr. Sinor), with permission.

Chapter 3

Fig. 3.1. "Bounce High, Bounce Low." Locke, *Sail Away*, with permission.

Fig. 3.2. "Sol Solecito." Houlahan and Tacka, *Developing Musical Literacy I & II*, with permission.

Fig. 3.3. "Doggie, Doggie." Forrai, *Music in the Pre-School* (tr. Sinor), with permission.

Fig. 3.4. "Lemonade." Houlahan and Tacka, *Developing Musical Literacy I & II*, with permission.

Fig. 3.7. "Doggie, Doggie." Forrai, *Music in the Pre-School* (tr. Sinor), with permission.

Fig. 3.8. "A la Ronda, Ronda." Knowles, *Vamos a cantar*, with permission.

Fig. 3.9. "Star Light, Star Bright." Forrai, *Music in the Pre-School* (tr. Sinor), with permission.

Fig. 3.10. "Bee, Bee, Bumble Bee." Forrai, *Music in the Pre-School* (tr. Sinor), with permission.

Fig. 3.11. "Cobbler, Cobbler." Forrai, *Music in the Pre-School* (tr. Sinor), with permission.

Fig. 3.12. "Zapatitos Blancos." Montoya-Stier, *El Patio de Mi Casa*, with permission.

Fig. 3.13. "Rain, Rain, Go Away." Forrai, *Music in the Pre-School* (tr. Sinor), with permission.

Fig. 3.14. "Hop Old Squirrel." Forrai, *Music in the Pre-School* (tr. Sinor), with permission.

Fig. 3.15. "Hot Cross Buns." Erdei and Komlos, eds., *150 American Folk Songs*, with permission.

Fig. 3. 16. "Here Comes a Bluebird." Forrai, *Music in the Pre-School* (tr. Sinor), with permission.

Fig. 3.17. "Just from the Kitchen." Locke, *Sail Away*, with permission.

Fig. 3.18. "Charlie over the Ocean." Forrai, *Music in the Pre-School* (tr. Sinor), with permission.

Fig. 3.19. "Al Animo." Houlahan and Tacka, *Developing Musical Literacy I & II*, with permission.

Fig. 3.20. "A Tisket, a Tasket." Forrai, *Music in the Pre-School* (tr. Sinor), with permission.

Fig. 3.21. "Lemonade." Houlahan and Tacka, *Developing Musical Literacy I & II*, with permission.

Fig. 3.22. "London Bridge." Public domain. Houlahan and Tacka, *From Sound to Symbol*.

Fig. 3.23. "Snail, Snail." Forrai, *Music in the Pre-School* (tr. Sinor), with permission.

Fig. 3.24. "Sally Go 'Round the Sun." Forrai, *Music in the Pre-School* (tr. Sinor), with permission.

Fig. 3.25. "We Are Dancing in the Forest." Forrai, *Music in the Pre-School* (tr. Sinor), with permission.

Chapter 4

Fig. 4.1. "Engine, Engine Number Nine." Forrai, *Music in the Pre-School* (tr. Sinor), with permission.

Fig. 4.2. "Snail, Snail." Forrai, *Music in the Pre-School* (tr. Sinor), with permission.

Fig. 4.3. "Rain, Rain." Forrai, *Music in the Pre-School* (tr. Sinor), with permission.

Chapter 5

Fig. 5.1. "Engine, Engine Number Nine." Forrai, *Music in the Pre-School* (tr. Sinor), with permission.

Fig. 5.2. "Bee, Bee, Bumble Bee." Forrai, *Music in the Pre-School* (tr. Sinor), with permission.

Fig. 5.3. "Zapatitos Blancos." Montoya-Stier, *El Patio de Mi Casa*, with permission.

Fig. 5.4. "Snail, Snail." Forrai, *Music in the Pre-School* (tr. Sinor), with permission.

Fig. 5.5. "Rain Rain." Forrai, *Music in the Pre-School* (tr. Sinor), with permission.

Fig. 5.6. "Engine, Engine Number Nine." Forrai, *Music in the Pre-School* (tr. Sinor), with permission.

Fig. 5.7. "Bee, Bee Bumble Bee." Forrai, *Music in the Pre-School* (tr. Sinor), with permission.

Fig. 5.8. "Zapatitos Blancos." Montoya-Stier, *El Patio de Mi Casa*, with permission.

Fig. 5.9. "Rain, Rain." Forrai, *Music in the Pre-School* (tr. Sinor), with permission.

Fig. 5.10. "Bee, Bee, Bumble Bee." Forrai, *Music in the Pre-School* (tr. Sinor), with permission.

Fig. 5.11. "Snail, Snail." Forrai, *Music in the Pre-School* (tr. Sinor), with permission.

Fig. 5.12. "Rain, Rain." Forrai, *Music in the Pre-School* (tr. Sinor), with permission.

Fig. 5.13. "Quien Es Esa Gente." Knowles, *Vamos a cantar*, with permission.

Fig. 5.14. "Rain, Rain." Forrai, *Music in the Pre-School* (tr. Sinor), with permission.

Fig. 5.15. "Engine, Engine Number Nine." Forrai, *Music in the Pre-School* (tr. Sinor), with permission.

Fig. 5.16. "Rain, Rain." Forrai, *Music in the Pre-School* (tr. Sinor), with permission.

Fig. 5.17. "Con Mi Martillo." Houlahan and Tacka, *Developing Musical Literacy I & II*, with permission.

Fig. 5.18. "Rain, Rain." Forrai, *Music in the Pre-School* (tr. Sinor), with permission.

Fig. 5.19. "Bate, Bate, Chocolate." Houlahan and Tacka, *Developing Musical Literacy I & II*, with permission.

Fig. 5.20. "Rain, Rain," phrase 1. Forrai, *Music in the Pre-School* (tr. Sinor), with permission.

Appendix 1

Fig. Apx 1.1. "A la Ronda, Ronda." Knowles, *Vamos a cantar*, with permission.

Fig. Apx 1.3. "A la Rorro, Nino." Montoya-Stier, *El Patio de Mi Casa*, with permission.

Fig. Apx 1.5. "A la Rueda de San Miguel." Montoya-Stier, *El Patio de Mi Casa*, with permission.

Fig. Apx 1.7. "A la Vibora." Houlahan and Tacka, *Developing Musical Literacy I & II*, with permission.

Fig. Apx 1.11. "Al Animo." Houlahan and Tacka, *Developing Musical Literacy I & II*, with permission.

Fig. Apx 1.13. "All Around the Buttercup." Forrai, *Music in the Pre-School* (tr. Sinor), with permission.

Fig. Apx 1.17. "Apples, Peaches." Houlahan and Tacka, *Developing Musical Literacy I & II*, with permission.

Fig. Apx 1.21. "Bate, Bate, Chocolate." Houlahan and Tacka, *Developing Musical Literacy I & II*, with permission.

Fig. Apx 1.22. "Bee, Bee, Bumble Bee." Forrai, *Music in the Pre-School* (tr. Sinor), with permission.

Fig. Apx 1.24. "Billy, Billy." Houlahan and Tacka, *Developing Musical Literacy I & II*, with permission.

Fig. Apx 1.26. "Blue." Houlahan and Tacka, *Developing Musical Literacy I & II*, with permission.

Fig. Apx 1.27. "Bobby Shafto." Forrai, *Music in the Pre-School* (tr. Sinor), with permission.

Fig. Apx 1.29. "Bought Me a Cat." Erdei and Komlos, eds., *150 American Folk Songs*, with permission.

Fig. Apx 1.31. "Bounce High, Bounce Low." Locke, *Sail Away*, with permission.

Fig. Apx 1.33. "Bow, Wow, Wow." Forrai, *Music in the Pre-School* (tr. Sinor), with permission.

Fig. Apx 1.35. "Brinca la Tablita." Houlahan and Tacka, *Developing Musical Literacy I & II*, with permission.

Fig. Apx 1.36. "Built My Lady." Forrai, *Music in the Pre-School* (tr. Sinor), with permission.

Fig. Apx 1.38. "Burnie Bee." Forrai, *Music in the Pre-School* (tr. Sinor), with permission.

Fig. Apx 1.82. "El Burrito del Teniente." Houlahan and Tacka, *Developing Musical Literacy I & II*, with permission.

Fig. Apx 1.40. "Button You Must Wander." Houlahan and Tacka, *Developing Musical Literacy I & II*, with permission.

Fig. Apx 1.43. "Bye, Baby Bunting," Forrai, *Music in the Pre-School* (tr. Sinor), with permission.

Fig. Apx 1.44. "Caracol Col Col." Knowles, *Vamos a cantar*, with permission.

Fig. Apx 1.46. "Charlie over the Ocean." Forrai, *Music in the Pre-School* (tr. Sinor), with permission.

Fig. Apx 1.48. "Cherry Pie." Houlahan and Tacka, *Developing Musical Literacy I & II*, with permission.

Fig. Apx 1.50. "Chickama Craney Crow." Forrai, *Music in the Pre-School* (tr. Sinor), with permission.

Fig. Apx 1.52. "Chini, Mini." Knowles, *Vamos a cantar*, with permission.

Fig. Apx 1.58. "Clap, Clap." Houlahan and Tacka, *Developing Musical Literacy I & II*, with permission.

Fig. Apx 1.56. "Clap Your Hands Together." Houlahan and Tacka, *Developing Musical Literacy I & II*, with permission.

Fig. Apx 1.60. "Closet Key." Erdei and Komlos, eds., *150 American Folk Songs*, with permission.

Fig. Apx 1.62. "Cobbler, Cobbler." ["Hunt the Slipper"] Forrai, *Music in the Pre-School* (tr. Sinor), with permission.

Fig. Apx 1.64. "Con Mi Martillo." Houlahan and Tacka, *Developing Musical Literacy I & II*, with permission.

Fig. Apx 1.65. "Cuckoo." Houlahan and Tacka, *Developing Musical Literacy I & II*, with permission.

Fig. Apx 1.67. "Dance Josey." Erdei and Komlos, eds., *150 American Folk Songs*, with permission.

Fig. Apx 1.69. "Dinah." Forrai, *Music in the Pre-School* (tr. Sinor), with permission.

Fig. Apx 1.71. "Do, Do Pity My Case." Forrai, *Music in the Pre-School* (tr. Sinor), with permission.

Fig. Apx 1.73. "Doggie, Doggie." Forrai, *Music in the Pre-School* (tr. Sinor), with permission.

Fig. Apx 1.75. "Dona Arana." Knowles, *Vamos a cantar*, with permission.

Fig. Apx 1.77. "Down Came a Lady." Forrai, *Music in the Pre-School* (tr. Sinor), with permission.

Fig. Apx 1.79. "Duerme Pronto." Knowles, *Vamos a cantar*, with permission.

Fig. Apx 1.81. "Duermente." Houlahan and Tacka, *Developing Musical Literacy I & II*, with permission.

Fig. Apx 1.83. "En un Plato de Ensalada." Montoya-Stier, *El Patio de Mi Casa*, with permission.

Fig. Apx 1.85. "Engine, Engine, Number Nine." Forrai, *Music in the Pre-School* (tr. Sinor), with permission.

Fig. Apx 1.87. "Este Nino Lindo." Montoya-Stier, *El Patio de Mi Casa*, with permission.

Fig. Apx 1.89. "The Farmer in the Dell." Forrai, *Music in the Pre-School* (tr. Sinor), with permission.

Fig. Apx 1.91. "Firefly, Firefly." Houlahan and Tacka, *Developing Musical Literacy I & II*, with permission.

Fig. Apx 1.93. "Five Little Monkeys." Houlahan and Tacka, *Developing Musical Literacy I & II*, with permission.

Fig. Apx 1.97. "Frog in the Meadow." Houlahan and Tacka, *Developing Musical Literacy I & II*, with permission.

Fig. Apx 1.99. "Frosty Weather." Forrai, *Music in the Pre-School* (tr. Sinor), with permission.

Fig. Apx 1.101. "Goodnight, Sleep Tight." Forrai, *Music in the Pre-School* (tr. Sinor), with permission.

Fig. Apx 1.103. "Great Big House in New Orleans." Houlahan and Tacka, *Developing Musical Literacy I & II*, with permission.

Fig. Apx 1.105. "Handy Dandy." Houlahan and Tacka, *Developing Musical Literacy I & II*, with permission.

Fig. Apx 1.107. "Here Comes a Bluebird." Forrai, *Music in the Pre-School* (tr. Sinor), with permission.

Fig. Apx 1.109. "Hey, Hey, Look at Me." Forrai, *Music in the Pre-School* (tr. Sinor), with permission.

Fig. Apx 1.111. "Hickety, Tickety." Houlahan and Tacka, *Developing Musical Literacy I & II*, with permission.

Fig. Apx 1.113. "Hush, Little Minnie." Forrai, *Music in the Pre-School* (tr. Sinor), with permission.

Fig. Apx 1.117. "I Climbed up the Cherry Tree." Houlahan and Tacka, *Developing Musical Literacy I & II*, with permission.

Fig. Apx 1.119. "Ida Red." Forrai, *Music in the Pre-School* (tr. Sinor), with permission.

Fig. Apx 1.121. "In and Out." Houlahan and Tacka, *Developing Musical Literacy I & II*, with permission.

Fig. Apx 1.123. "It's Raining, It's Pouring." Houlahan and Tacka, *Developing Musical Literacy I & II*, with permission.

Fig. Apx 1.127. "Jim Along Josie." Erdei and Komlos, eds., *150 American Folk Songs*, with permission.

Fig. Apx 1.129. "Johnny Works with One Hammer." Forrai, *Music in the Pre-School* (tr. Sinor), with permission.

Fig. Apx 1.133. "Knock the Cymbals." Houlahan and Tacka, *Developing Musical Literacy I & II*, with permission.

Fig. Apx 1.135. "Let Us Chase the Squirrel." Forrai, *Music in the Pre-School* (tr. Sinor), with permission.

Fig. Apx 1.137. "Let Us Hide the Pumpkin." Houlahan and Tacka, *Developing Musical Literacy I & II*, with permission.

Fig. Apx 1.139. "Little Sally Water." Forrai, *Music in the Pre-School* (tr. Sinor), with permission.

Fig. Apx 1.141. "Looby Loo." Houlahan and Tacka, *Developing Musical Literacy I & II*, with permission.

Fig. Apx 1.144. "Lucy Locket." Forrai, *Music in the Pre-School* (tr. Sinor), with permission.

Fig. Apx 1.146. "Mama, Buy Me a Chiney Doll." Erdei and Komlos, eds., *150 American Folk Songs*, with permission.

Fig. Apx 1.148. "Naughty Kitty Cat." Houlahan and Tacka, *Developing Musical Literacy I & II*, with permission.

Fig. Apx 1.54. "Old Brass Wagon." Houlahan and Tacka, *Developing Musical Literacy I & II*, with permission.

Fig. Apx 1.152. "Oliver Twist." Houlahan and Tacka, *Developing Musical Literacy I & II*, with permission.

Fig. Apx 1.158. "Pajarito." Houlahan and Tacka, *Developing Musical Literacy I & II*, with permission.

Fig. Apx 1.159. "Pease Porridge Hot." Forrai, *Music in the Pre-School* (tr. Sinor), with permission.

Fig. Apx 1.143. "Los Pollitos." Houlahan and Tacka, *Developing Musical Literacy I & II*, with permission.

Fig. Apx 1.161. "Queen, Queen, Caroline." Forrai, *Music in the Pre-School* (tr. Sinor), with permission.

Fig. Apx 1.163. "Quien es esa gente?" Knowles, *Vamos a cantar*, with permission.

Fig. Apx 1.165. "Rain, Rain, Go Away." Forrai, *Music in the Pre-School* (tr. Sinor), with permission.

Fig. Apx 1.167. "Ring Around the Rosy." Forrai, *Music in the Pre-School* (tr. Sinor), with permission.

Fig. Apx 1.9. "A Sailor Went to Sea." Houlahan and Tacka, *Developing Musical Literacy I & II*, with permission.

Fig. Apx 1.171. "Sally Go 'Round the Sun." Forrai, *Music in the Pre-School* (tr. Sinor), with permission.

Fig. Apx 1.173. "See Saw." Forrai, *Music in the Pre-School* (tr. Sinor), with permission.

Fig. Apx 1.175. "Skin and Bones." Locke, *Sail Away*, with permission.

Fig. Apx 1.177. "Snail, Snail." Forrai, *Music in the Pre-School* (tr. Sinor), with permission.

Fig. Apx 1.179. "Sol, Solecito." Houlahan and Tacka, *Developing Musical Literacy I & II*, with permission.

Fig. Apx 1.180. "Star Light, Star Bright." Forrai, *Music in the Pre-School* (tr. Sinor), with permission.

Fig. Apx 1.182. "The Tailor and the Mouse." Erdei, Knowles, and Bacon, eds., *My Singing Bird*, with permission.

Fig. Apx 1.184. "Teddy Bear." Forrai, *Music in the Pre-School* (tr. Sinor), with permission.

Fig. Apx 1.190. "Touch Your Shoulders." *Singing Games and Rhymes for Early Years*, Scotland, with permission.

Fig. Apx 1.192. "Trot, Trot to Boston." Houlahan and Tacka, *Developing Musical Literacy I & II*, with permission.

Fig. Apx 1.196. "Valentine, Red and Blue." Houlahan and Tacka, *Developing Musical Literacy I & II*, with permission.

Fig. Apx 1.198. "We Are Dancing in the Forest." Forrai, *Music in the Pre-School* (tr. Sinor), with permission.

Fig. Apx 1.200. "Who's That Tapping at the Window?" Forrai, *Music in the Pre-School* (tr. Sinor), with permission.

Fig. Apx 1.202. "Witch, Witch," Locke, *Sail Away*, with permission.

Fig. Apx 1.204. "Zapatitos Blancos." Montoya-Stier, *El Patio de Mi Casa*, with permission.

Index

535

543